Studies in Economic Ethics and Philosophy

Springer

Berlin
Heidelberg
New York
Barcelona
Budapest
Hong Kong
London
Milan
Paris
Santa Clara
Singapore
Tokyo

Studies in Economic Ethics and Philosophy

P. Koslowski (Ed.)
Ethics in Economics, Business, and Economic Policy
(out of print)
192 pages. 1992

P. Koslowski · Y. Shionoya (Eds.)
The Good and the Economical
Ethical Choices in Economics and Management
(out of print)
212 pages. 1993

H. De Geer (Ed.)
Business Ethics in Progress?
124 pages. 1994

P. Koslowski (Ed.)
The Theory of Ethical Economy in the Historical School
345 pages. 1995

A. Argandoña (Ed.)
The Ethical Dimension of Financial Institutions
and Markets
264 pages. 1995

G. K. Becker (Ed.)
Ethics in Business and Society.
Chinese and Western Perspectives
232 pages. 1996

P. Koslowski
Ethics of Capitalism and Critique of Sociobiology.
Two Essays with a Comment by James M. Buchanan
153 pages. 1996

F. Neil Brady (Ed.)
Ethical Universals in International Business
255 pages. 1996

P. Koslowski and A. Føllesdal (Eds.)
Restructuring the Welfare State
Theory and Reform of Social Policy
410 pages. 1997

G. Erreygers and T. Vandevelde
Is Inheritance Legitimate?
Ethical and Economic Aspects
of Wealth Transfers
236 pages. 1997

P. Koslowski (Ed.)
Business Ethics
in East Central Europe
163 pages. 1997

Peter Koslowski (Ed.)

Methodology of the Social Sciences, Ethics, and Economics in the Newer Historical School

From Max Weber and Rickert
to Sombart and Rothacker

With 2 Figures
and 1 Table

 Springer

Professor Dr. Peter Koslowski
Centre for Ethical Economy and Business Culture
The Hannover Institute of Philosophical Research
Gerberstraße 26
D-30169 Hannover
Germany

Editorial Assistant:
Anna Maria Hauk M.A.

ISBN 3-540-63458-4 Springer-Verlag Berlin Heidelberg New York

Cataloging-in-Publication Data applied for
Die Deutsche Bibliothek - CIP-Einheitsaufnahme

**Methodology of the social sciences, ethics, and economics in the newer
historical school** : from Max Weber and Rickert to Sombart and Rothacker ; with
1 table / Peter Koslowski (ed.). - Berlin ; Heidelberg ; New York ; Barcelona
, Budapest ; Hong Kong ; London ; Milan ; Paris ; Santa Clara ; Singapore ;
Tokyo : Springer, 1997
  (Studies in economic ethics and philosophy)
  ISBN 3-540-63458-4

Hardcover Design: Erich Kirchner, Heidelberg

SPIN 10643509   42/2202-5 4 3 2 1 0 – Printed on acid-free paper

Preface

The volume at hand gives an exposition of the tradition of the Historical School of Economics and of the *Geisteswissenschaften* or human sciences, the latter in their development within the Historical School as well as in Neo-Kantianism and the sociology of knowledge. It continues the discussion started in the year 1994 on the Older Historical School of Economics and the 19th century German contribution to an ethical theory of economics with the Newer Historical School of the 20th century.

Economists, social scientists, and philosophers examine the contribution of this tradition and its impact for present theory. The schools of thought and their approaches to economics as well as to the cultural and social sciences are examined here not as much for their historical interest as for their potential systematic contribution to the contemporary debates on economic ethics, economics, sociology, and philosophy.

The volume at hand contains the proceedings of the Fourth Annual SEEP-Conference on Economic Ethics and Philosophy in 1996, "Economics and Ethics in the Historical School. Part B: Max Weber, Heinrich Rickert, Max Scheler, Werner Sombart, Arthur Spiethoff, John Commons, Alfred Marshall, and Others", held at Marienrode Monastery near Hannover, Germany, on March 27-30th, 1996, together with several additional invited papers.

It followed the SEEP-Conference on Economics and Ethics "Economics and Ethics in the Historical School of Economics. Achievements and Present Relevance. Part A: The Older Historical School, Schmoller, Dilthey, and Others" held in 1994 and published in 1995 under the title *The Theory of Ethical Economy in the Historical School. Wilhelm Roscher, Lorenz von Stein, Gustav Schmoller, Wilhelm Dilthey and Contemporary Theory* as volume 7 in the series at hand.

In the conferences and book publications on the Historical School, a third and final conference will be held in two sections in autumn 1997 on the topic of "Economics and Ethics in the Historical School of Economics. Part C: Economic Ethics and Theory of Capitalism in the German Tradition of Economics - Historism as a Challenge to the Social Sciences", concentrating on

PREFACE

the theory of capitalism and on the challenge that historism presents to today's economic ethics and business ethics.

The focus of the debate has shifted between the first two volumes on the Historical School. The first volume on the Older Historical School concentrates on the ethical and historical theory of economics. With this second volume, the emphasis shifts from "ethical economics" to the theory and methodology of economics and of the cultural and social sciences in the Newer Historical School. The normative question loses importance compared to the 19th century and the methodological problems gain in importance in the development of the Historical School from the 19th to the 20th century. The ethical and cultural dimension is, however, still present.

In the volume at hand, the debate about the German tradition of economics and of the cultural and social sciences is also extended from the Historical School to other approaches in the German tradition, to Neo-Kantianism, the sociology of knowledge in Max Scheler and Karl Mannheim, and to Georg Simmel's approach to the money economy. As in the first volume, the influence of the Historical School on other traditions of thought, in the volume at hand on the Austrian School of Economics and on American, British, Japanese and Russian economic science, is examined in addition to the presentation of the German theorists.

The conference at the basis of this volume and the whole project have been organized by the Centrum für Ethische Ökonomie und Wirtschaftskultur des Forschungsinstituts für Philosophie Hannover - Centre for Ethical Economy and Business Culture, The Hannover Institute of Philosophical Research, Hannover, Germany, with the support of the Fritz Thyssen Stiftung Köln and the Stiftung Forschungsinstitut für Philosophie Hannover.

The editor wishes to thank his co-workers at the Centre for Ethical Economy and Business Culture for their assistance in organizing the conference meetings at Marienrode and Anna Maria Hauk M.A. for her assistance in preparing the manuscript.

A special word of gratitude is due the Fritz Thyssen Stiftung whose financial support made the SEEP-conference in 1996 possible.

Hannover, May 1997   P. K.

Contents

CONTENTS

Part Two

Neo-Kantianism, *Wissenssoziologie* (Sociology of Knowledge), and the Sociological Theory of Money and Exchange

Chapter 3

Chapter 4

Chapter 5

Part Three

Ethics and Economics in Sombart, Spiethoff, Freyer, and in Older German Business Administration

Chapter 6

CONTENTS

Chapter 7

Chapter 8

Chapter 9

Part Four

Austrian Economics and the Historical School

Chapter 10

Chapter 11

CONTENTS

Part Five

The Historical School and American and British Economists: John R. Commons, Frank Knight, Alfred Marshall

Chapter 12

Chapter 13

Chapter 14

Part Six

The Historical School and the Development of Economics in Japan and Russia

Chapter 15

CONTENTS

Chapter 16

Part Seven

The Historical School of Economics and Today's Economics

Chapter 17

Chapter 18

CONTENTS

Part Eight

Theories of History and of Education,
and a Philosophy of the Historical School

Chapter 19

Chapter 20

Conclusion

Chapter 21

Part One

On Max Weber's Contribution

Chapter 1

The Present Relevance of Max Weber's *Wertrationalität* (Value Rationality)

RAYMOND BOUDON

RAYMOND BOUDON

0. Introduction

The concept of "axiological rationality" (my translation of *Wertrationalit-ät*) is possibly one of the most difficult of all the concepts Weber put on the market.

Sometimes, the expression is understood as describing the situations where a social actor acts in conformity with the values he has internalized. Sometimes, it is entirely rejected as meaningless, as a contradiction between the two terms "value" and "rationality". I have conducted no systematic review of the interpretations of the concept. But I would contend that these two attitudes toward the concept are probably the most frequent, namely either the pedestrian interpretation making axiological rationality a synonym of "value conformity" or the skeptical interpretation according to which the expression would not have a clear nor solid meaning.

My own interpretation is that, although Weber has never been entirely clear or analytical on the notion, it is perhaps, once it is properly understood and developed, one of the most fruitful he has ever proposed.

Before I proceed, I would like to make my design as clear as possible. My primary objective is less to reconstruct what Weber "has really meant" when he has conceived and decided to introduce this notion than to stress its "present relevance". The former task would be interesting as such; it would imply collecting the passages where Weber uses or discusses the notion and submitting it to a hermeneutical analysis in the sense of Schleiermacher. But my interest is rather to develop what I perceive as a crucial and extremely fruitful intuition from the part of Weber, to make it perhaps more analytical, and finally to show that it sketches a powerful theory of collective axiological beliefs.

However, when the notion is replaced in the context of Weber's general methodological principles, one gains the feeling that the theory of axiological beliefs I propose here is a plausible interpretation of what Weber had in mind.

4

I. Weber Often Ill Understood

1. Weber as Nietzschean?

What I called the "pedestrian" interpretation of the notion of axiological rationality may be more profound that it may seem at first sight. This first interpretation makes axiological rationality synonym with "value conformity". In other words, endorsing such and such values would in this interpretation not be rational in itself; what would be rational would be the congruence between the values one endorses and one's actions. In other words, this pedestrian interpretation hides possibly a strong thesis: that accepting and endorsing values is not rational; only being congruent with values could be qualified as rational.

This interpretation illustrates a position often represented in economics. Behavior is rational to economists to the extent where it is congruent with preferences. As to preferences themselves, they have to be considered as mere data. They can be rational only in the sense where they should not be contradictory with one another. But economists, with some exceptions, believe that preferences as such cannot be qualified as rational.

Pareto had a similar position. Actions are rational (he would have rather written "logical") to the extent where they aim at some goal with the help of means objectively adequate to the goal.

So, this first pedestrian interpretation implies that Weber would have accepted the idea, considered by Pareto and many economists as trivial, that rationality is a concept which cannot be applied to goals, preferences or values, but only to the capacity of the means used by a subject to reach his goals, to satisfy his preferences or to realize his values. An action would be rational to the extent where it would mobilize means adapted to the goals, preferences or values.

The famous weberian thesis of the "polytheism of values" suggests that, to Weber, values are a matter of personal choice in modern societies. Modern societies would be such that they do not impose prescribed values to social subjects, but propose to them to choose among many sets of values. The positive evaluation of individualism in modern societies would make this choice possible and legitimate. As to the fact that a given individual chooses rather one set of values than another, we can interpret it for instance in a Nietzschean fashion (the values endorsed by an individual are the product of instincts deeply rooted in his personality) or in a Sartrian fashion ("choosing" one's values is a free act, that cannot be inspired by any forces or considerations if it is to be effectively free; in Sartre's words, value choices are "absurd").

Undoubtedly, Weber takes sometimes his inspiration from Nietzsche.[1] His insistence on the point that science would be value-free is wellknown. But it would be hazardous to reverse the statement and to contend that, to him, value would have been science-free, still more, that he would have interpreted value choices in a Nietzschean fashion, or in a Sartrian one.[2]

Is Weber trivial (that would be the case if value rationality would simply mean value conformity)? Is Weber a pragmatist in the sense of Pareto or of the economists (that would be the case if he would have implicitly meant that the notion of rationality is applicable exclusively to the relation means-ends)? Is Weber rather Nietzschean (that would be the case if he would have interpreted values as coming from deep hidden irrational forces)?

2. Weber as Kantian?

Other writers, as Lukes, have rejected these interpretations.[3] The British sociologist criticizes severely the use made by Weber of the notion of "rationality": "The use of the word "rational" and its cognates has caused untold confusion and obscurity, especially in the writings of social theorists", he writes. This remark is explicitly directed against Weber, as a footnote appended to this passage makes clear: "I think Max Weber is largely responsible for this. His use of these terms is irremediably opaque and shifting". From the context, it can be detected that this "opacity" is mainly due to the distinction between "instrumental" and "axiological" rationality. "Instrumental rationality" is allright: it corresponds more or less to what Lukes himself proposes to call "rationality" shortly. But this means that, beside instrumen-

---

1   W. HENNIS: *Max Webers Fragestellung*, Tübingen (J.C.B. Mohr [Paul Siebeck]) 1987.

2   W. J. MOMMSEN: *Max Weber und die deutsche Politik, 1890-1920*, Tübingen (J.C.B. Mohr) 1959 or E. FLEISCHMANN: "De Weber à Nietzsche", *Archives européennes de sociologie*, 5, 2 (1964), pp. 190-238, go to far when they seem to draw from Nietzsche's influence on Weber and from the idea that science should be value free, the idea that to him, values would be irrational.

3   S. LUKES: "Some problems about rationality", *Archives européennes de sociologie*, 8, 2 (1967), pp. 247-264, notably pp. 259-60.

tal rationality, no other type of rationality could be defined. What then can be done with the notion of "axiological rationality"? Is not it a contradiction in the terms? To Lukes, the notion of "axiological rationality" could probably have exclusively one possible meaning: it would indicate that the choice of values can be rational. In other words, he probably reads the expression "axiological rationality" as meaning that, not only the choice of means, but the choice of ends could be rational.

In other words, Lukes probably takes seriously Weber's typology of action as it appears notably in the first pages of *Economy and Society*. Beside the familiar category of "instrumental rationality", Weber introduces in this famous pages another type of rationality, "axiological rationality". So, to Lukes, it is evident that rationality in this expression cannot merely mean "conformity". Now, to the British sociologist, the notion of rationality can only mean one thing: the adequation of means to ends, preferences, values. This is what Weber calls "instrumental rationality". So, to Lukes, the idea that there would be another type of rationality, characterizing, not the adequation of means to ends, but the choice of ends, seems meaningless.

So, in contrast with the interpretations I referred to above, Lukes takes seriously the word "rationality" in the expression "value rationality". He refuses to assimilate value rationality to value conformity. I think he is right. Why would Weber have written rationality where conformity would have been clearer? Why did he ostensibly create two kinds of rationality? But as, to Lukes, rationality can mean only instrumental rationality, he fails to understand what "value rationality" could well mean and rejects the expression as useless.

Lukes' criticism has the advantage of dramatizing the discussion. It is true that it is very hard to accept that Weber would have meant conformity and said rationality. It is on the other hand very clear that value rationality has nothing to do with instrumental rationality, nothing to do in other words with the relation between means and ends.

What does it mean then?

The most immediate interpretation would be that Weber would be Kantian, in other words that "value rationality" should be interpreted as an echo to the Kantian notion of "practical reason". Kant was of course, beside Nietzsche, one of the influential thinkers that molded Weber's thinking. Possibly, Lukes has such an interpretation in mind. As a social scientist, he cannot accept the Kantian idea of a universal practical reason though. Nor can he probably accept the idea that Weber's Kantianism could be literal. Consequently, he fails to see what the notion of axiological rationality really means. This can be easily felt at his tone: a strange, ununderstandable; on the whole, a confuse notion, he suggests.

3. How Can a Coherent Positive Content Be Attributed to "Axiological Rationality"?

My own contention is that, if Weber has taken a part of his inspiration from Nietzsche and from Kant, his notion of axiological rationality cannot be reduced to any of the three plus one interpretations which I have just gathered. To me, as I said, the notion is clear, fruitful, analytical, original and can be reduced neither to Kant nor to Nietzsche. It is moreover crucial to the social sciences.

But before I try to make the meaning of the notion clearer and to make explicit and develop the program it contains, it is necessary to go back to some key points in Weber's sociology and methodology.

II. The Methodological Principles of Weber's Sociology

1. Methodological Individualism Against "Kollektivbegriffe"

In a famous letter to R. Liefmann[4], Weber makes clear that what we now call "methodological individualism" (MI) should be adopted, not only by economists, but by all social scientists. The letter is addressed to an economist, to an economist moreover belonging to the marginalist school. So,

---

4   "(...) Wenn ich nun jetzt einmal Soziologe geworden bin (...), dann wesentlich deshalb, um dem immer noch spukenden Betrieb, der mit Kollektivbegriffen arbeitet, ein Ende zu machen. Mit anderen Worten: auch Soziologie kann nur durch Ausgehen vom Handeln des oder der, weniger oder vieler Einzelnen, strikt 'individualistisch' in der Methode also - betrieben werden", Letter to R. Liefmann, March, 9th, 1920 quoted by W. MOMMSEN: p. 44, in: "Max Weber's Political Sociology and his Philosophy of World History", *International Social Science Journal*, 17, 1 (1965), pp. 23-45.

when Weber writes in this letter "(...) auch Soziologie kann nur (...) strikt 'individualistisch' in der Methode (...) betrieben werden", the "auch" is unambiguous: it means that, as marginalist economics, sociology can and should use an individualistic methodology. The expression "methodological individualism" is almost literally written ("individualistisch in der Methode"). What does Weber mean by so saying? That the ultimate stage of any sociological explanation of a social phenomenon can and should consist in finding out why the actors behaved the way they did to the effect of producing the phenomenon in question. "Methodological individualism" as we know it does not say more. It does not say more under Weber's pen either.

The letter goes as far as to propose what can be read as a "demarcation" in Popper's sense between good scientific sociology and bad sociology. The bad one is a sociology where "Kollektivbegriffe herumspuken". Thanks to the MI postulate, these collective concepts currently in use as far as the explanation of social phenomena is concerned can be avoided. It is difficult to identify what Weber had specifically in mind and even whether he had anything specific in mind by introducing this distinction, but the meaning of the expression is clear. He wanted to exclude from sociology the pseudo-explanations evoking obscure social factors (e.g. "national mentality") and making them the causes of sociological phenomena. He goes even so far as to claim that he became sociologist to eradicate such pseudo-explanations.

2. Meaningful to the Actor

So, to Weber, explaining a social phenomenon is making it the outcome of individual actions, attitudes or beliefs. This is the very definition of MI. But Weber's sociology rests on another principle: the "understanding principle": *explaining* the actions, beliefs, attitudes of an actor means "understanding" them; understanding them means *reconstructing their meaning to the actor*. I would add moreover that reconstructing their meaning to the actor means in most cases reconstructing the reasons he has to endorse them.

It is essential to recall and comment upon these basic principles of Weber's methodology, for they are frequently misunderstood. The notion of "understanding" (in Weber's sense) is notably very often presented and discussed in a caricatural fashion, as Abel's article illustrates.[5]

It should also be stressed that the individuals sociologists deal with in their analyses are, according to Weber, idealtypical individuals rather than actual concrete individuals. Here again, Weber suggests that sociologists follow a principle familiar to economists. Economists too explain the macrophenomena they are interested in by making them the outcomes of understandable actions of idealtypical individuals (e.g. the "consumer", the "producer", etc.).

Other essential remark: "understanding" is not a mysterious activity. It is on a contrary an operation familiar in any scientific discipline: the sociologist introduces conjectures as to the reasons accounting for some action, and checks that these conjectures are compatible with observed data. If I see somebody cutting wood, I introduce the conjecture that he will put the wood in his chimney to get warmer. If he cuts wood on a summer sunny day, I will have to reject the conjecture and to find some other more acceptable one. Of course, any "understanding" operation involves an empathic moment. In the famous example I refer to here, I introduce the statement "he wants to get warmer" because I know myself from my own experience that being cold is unpleasant and that he feels probably like me on this point. For the rest, the conjectures about the reasons have to be checked against data exactly as any conjecture in any scientific discipline.

Another essential point of Weber's methodology is contained in his famous typology of actions contained in the first pages of *Economy and Society*. I already alluded to this typology earlier. Actions can be explained by reasons belonging to the register of instrumental rationality, by reasons belonging to the register of axiological rationality, by the submission of the actor to traditions, or by affective reasons.

Examples.

First type: I wear a coat because the weather is cold and that a coat is an easy way of struggling against cold.

Second type: I do not steal because I believe one should not steal.

Third type: I shake his hand because he is French and because Frenchmen use to shake hands when they meet.

---

5 T. ABEL: "The Operation Called Verstehen", in : H. ALBERT (Ed.): *Theorie und Realität. Ausgewählte Aufsätze zur Wissenschaftslehre der Sozialwissenschaften*, Tübingen (Mohr) 1964, pp. 177-188.

Fourth type: She protected him because she liked him.

Understanding an action means to Weber: locating the action is the proper category in this typology, and, within this category, reconstructing the causes of the action.

Another important principle of Weber's methodology is what Popper was to call later the "zero hypothesis"[6]: try to interpret an action as rational, as grounded on reasons; if this appears impossible, try the explanation by tradition or by affective factors.

The most plausible assumption about the woodcutter is that he cuts wood because he wants to get warm; if not, because he wants to show his neighbour how to cut wood; if not, because he belongs to a sect of woodcutters in which cutting wood is a duty; if not, he may cut wood because in his country everybody cuts wood everyday at that time of the day (traditional action); if not, he may cut wood because he feels a compulsion to cut wood (affective action), etc.

This variation on a familiar Weber's example aims at illustrating the natural character of the "zero hypothesis": sociologists are concerned mostly, as economists, by all these prosaic individual actions which produce, once aggregated, the collective phenomena they are interested in. They are essentially interested by these situations where many people behave in the same way, so that these individual actions produce a collective effect. Now, in the circumstances where these prosaic actions are the same from one individual to the next, this results generally from the fact that they are inspired, not by individual idiosyncrasies, but by simple more or less obvious reasons. Hence the advice given by Weber and Popper to social scientists: try to find the simple reasons behind the individual actions before sketching more complicated conjectures.

---

6   K. POPPER: "La rationalité et le statut du principe de rationalité", in: E. M. CLAASEN (Ed.): *Les fondements philosophiques des systèmes économiques*, Paris (Payot) 1967, pp. 142-150.

III. Why These Principles?

Why these principles? I leave aside their realism. I mean that it is true that social phenomena are very often the aggregate outcome of actions inspired by simple reasons.

Thus, the French landlords of the eighteenth century leave their land and buy a royal office *because* it gives them influence, prestige and power.[7] The farmers whom they put on their land have on their side no capacity of innovation. On the whole, what Tocqueville calls the "administrative centralization" of France has the effect that buying a royal office is more rewarding in France than in England. This circumstance generates a strong landlord absenteeism and hence a stagnation of agriculture. This famous analysis is a good illustration of Weber's principles: methodological individualism, understanding the *meaning* of the decisions taken by the idealtypical landlords and farmers, in other words reconstructing the reasons of the decisions they took.

I considered this example because it makes clear a crucial point, namely that explanations that are able to make a social phenomenon the outcome of understandable individual actions is "final" in the sense that it contains no black boxes. Here, the macrophenomenon represented by the stagnation of French agriculture relatively to the British one is explained as the effect of understandable actions from the part of the idealtypical French landlords. Once such an explanation is produced, it generates no further question. It does not contain any black box.

By contrast, when a Lévy-Bruhl explains magical beliefs by referring to a "Kollektivbegriff" as "primitive mentality", he creates a big black box. The sociologist who learns that some ritual has to be explained by the fact that the members of a far tribe is governed by a "primitive mentality" would perhaps ask the biologist to explain to him why the brain of the so-called primitive is wired in a different fashion from ours. At any rate, explanations using concepts as "primitive mentality", "national spirit", "socialization", etc. are not "final". I am not saying they should be rejected, merely that they suggest

---

7 A. DE TOCQUEVILLE: "L'Ancien Régime et la Révolution", in: TOCQUEVILLE: *De la démocratie en Amérique, Souvenirs, l'Ancien Régime et la Révolution*, introduction et notes de Lamberti J.-C. et Mélonio F., Paris (Laffont) 1986, p. 1036sq.

immediately further questions: what are the mechanisms behind the words "socialization", "primitive mentality", etc.

One of the main appeal of the set of methodological principles advocated by Weber is that it produces "final" explanations without black boxes, beside being realistic.

1. Applications: Two Examples from Weber

a) Mithraïsm

Weber's analyses are often sketchy, though powerful. Why did the Mithra cult penetrate so easily into the Roman Empire?[8] Why was it particularly appealing to the Roman civil servants? Answer: because they had strong reasons to find it appealing. The traditional Roman religion was a religion of peasants: it did not speak to civil servants. Why would they consider the landmarks between the fields as gods? By contrast, Mithra religion gives the stature of a god to a unique figure, half real half unreal; the Mithra-believers are promoted from one rank to the next higher by being submitted to uniformized, well defined, impersonal procedures. They have reasons to feel appealed by this religion: it appears to them as familiar, since its general features can easily be seen as a transposition of the rules and rituals governing the Roman civil service. Roman civil servants are promoted also after having been submitted to standardized examinations. At the top of the hierarchy sits the Emperor, who is both a human figure and the symbolic representation of an entity, the Roman Empire. So, the civil servants have reasons to prefer Mithraïsm to the traditional Roman religion. These reasons are understandable. The theory explains why the Roman civil servants were a powerful vector in the diffusion of Mithra cult. Of course, the reasons are not of the utilitarian or instrumental type; still they are reasons; these reasons are the genuine causes of the individual conversions of the civil servants and, by aggregation, the causes of the macrophenomenon "diffusion of Mithraïsm in the Roman Empire".

b) Magical Beliefs

In a few lines of *Economy and Society*, Weber sketches a powerful theory of magic: "Wie das Quirlen den Funken aus dem Holz, so lockt die "magi-

---

8   M. WEBER: *Wirtschaft und Gesellschaft*, Tübingen (Mohr) 1922.

sche" Mimik des Kundigen den Regen aus dem Himmel. Und der Funken, den der Feurquirl erzeugt, ist genau ebenso ein "magisches" Produkt wie der durch die Manipulationen des Regenmachers erzeugte Regen"[9]. To the magician, "the action of the firemaker is not less magical than the action of the rainmaker", he writes. This means: we, Westerners, make a difference between the fire- and the rainmaker and we consider this difference as obvious. The former believes in a causal relation which is true; the latter in a causal relation which is false. *To us*, the latter belief is magical, the former is not. But why do we make the difference? Because we have strong reasons to do so. As we have been taught the theory of the transformation of energy, we know that kinetic energy can be transformed into thermic energy, so that the firemaker behaves in congruence with a valid causal belief. By contrast, we do not see any grounded causal belief underlying the behaviour of the rainmaker. But what about the primitive themselves, asks Weber? They have no reasons of knowing the theory of the transformation of energy, nor of having an intuitive access to a theory which mankind has taken centuries before discovering it. So, the primitive have no reason to make a distinction between fire- and rainmaking, while we have strong reasons to consider the distinction as obvious. *To them*, the two are equally magical.

These two examples are sufficient to show that Weber applies effectively his methodological principles in his empirical analyses. Moreover and more importantly, they show that these methodological principles are the source of the "final" character of his analyses. Compare the theory of magic sketched by Weber to Lévy-Bruhl's. The latter rests upon a big black box ("primitive mentality") no corporation has been able to open. The former contains no black box at all.

---

9   M. WEBER: *Wirtschaft und Gesellschaft* , *op. cit.*, II, Kap. IV, §1, p. 227.
See R. BOUDON: "European sociology: the identity lost?", in: B. NEDELMANN, P. SZTOMPKA (Eds.): *Sociology in Europe. In search of identity*, New York/ Berlin (de Gruyter) 1993, pp. 27-44.

IV. Moral Feelings

If we keep in mind the basic principles of Weber's methodology, we see easily that, to him, explaining collective beliefs means: reconstructing the meaning to the social actors of these beliefs.

Now, collective beliefs, as individual beliefs, can be positive or normative. I/we can believe that something is true or that something is right, legitimate, good, wrong, illegitimate, bad, etc. Why could not the general principles used in the case of collective descriptive beliefs be applied to the case of prescriptive, normative, axiological beliefs?

I submit in other words that, given the general methodology of Weber, the category of "axiological rationality" expresses the principle that normative and more generally axiological beliefs should be understood as meaningful to social actors, and, moreover, exactly as descriptive beliefs, as meaningful to the actors because they are grounded in their mind on strong reasons. Actions can be meaningful to social actors because they are grounded on instrumental reasons ("instrumental rationality"). But they can also be meaningful to social actors because they are grounded on axiological reasons ("axiological rationality").

This interpretation has possibly two arguments in its favour. First, it excludes the conjecture that, for some obscure reason, Weber would have confused rationality and conformity. Second, it is tightly congruent with Weber's general methodology.

1. Values Rest on Strong Reasons

Accepting the idea that normative, moral and generally axiological feelings and beliefs can be grounded on strong reasons does not evidently lead to endorse the Kantian theory of morals. The notion of "axiological rationality" is in other words "cognitivist" (as Kant's theory of morals) in the sense that, to Weber as to Kant, moral beliefs are caused by reasons. But the similarity between the two authors stops at this point.

The same distinction would be true of many theories of moral feelings and generally of axiological beliefs produced by contemporary social sciences: they are also cognitivist without being Kantian in any way. Moreover, they can be considered as particular versions of the general theory sketched by the notion of "axiological rationality". I will consider some examples of these theories.

a) Functionalism

I will insist on a first theory of moral feelings and generally axiological beliefs that is "cognitivist" in the sense of moral philosophers (it explains moral feelings by the reasons actors have to believe in them). This theory is clearly not Kantian though. And it appears immediately as an illustration of Weber's notion of "axiological rationality".

A very simple example shows that we can explain familiar moral reactions by the strong reasons which inspire them. Piaget, the Swiss psychologist and sociologist, made himself famous notably by his memorable pages on the marbles game.[10] When one of the children playing marbles cheats, he will attract immediately a negative reaction from the others. Why? Not because the children would have internalized cultural norms according to which playing marbles and following the rules of the marbles game would be good, for, without having been told that cheating at the marbles game is bad, any child reacts negatively against cheating. So, the rejection of cheating is not inspired by socialization or tradition. Why this reaction? Because the children find the game interesting, and for this reason play it. Now, cheating destroys the game: it makes it uninteresting.

So, the children have strong reasons to reject cheating and, as many observations show, they are very early aware of these reasons.

The basic assumption of *functionalism* (in the most interesting versions of this theory) is, as this example makes clear, that an attitude, an action, a decision, an institution, etc. are perceived as good, legitimate, acceptable by individuals when they have the effect of making that an interaction system individuals are interested in functions properly, efficiently and smoothly. In the same way, an attitude, an action, etc. will be considered negatively when they have detrimental effects on the interaction systems individuals are interested in. This assumption is illustrated by the case of the marbles game. It can be illustrated by much more complex examples.

First of all, it can be noted that many observations have confirmed Piaget's views. Even very young children can explain that cheating is bad because it generates detrimental effects on a social interaction system they like

---

10 J. PIAGET: *Le jugement moral chez l'enfant*, Paris (Alcan) 1932; Paris (P.U.F.) 6ᵉ ed., 1985.

(the marbles game). In other words, they believe that something is good or bad because they feel they have strong reasons of thinking so, and not because they would have been socialized to the idea. This illustrates, according to my basic contention here, Weber's category of "axiological rationality": they think that cheating is bad because they have strong reasons of thinking so.

Though it is a particular illustration of Weber's "axiological rationality" theory, the functionalist theory is powerful. Simple as its principles are, it explains a host of moral feelings. To wit: why do we consider as legitimate that many organizations select their members? Because, without this institutional disposition, members could eventually be attracted into the organization that would be detrimental to the very objectives of the organization. For this reason, selecting their members is considered as a legitimate right of many organizations. Nobody has ever struggled against the idea that a football club or an academy should be deprived of their right of selecting their members. As cheating in the case of the marbles game, being deprived of this right for a football club would be detrimental to the objectives of the club and threatening to its very existence.

The functionalist theory provides also a convincing explanation of the collective feelings related to social inequalities. Against a current but false view, people accept easily social inequalities provided they can see their functional basis. Thus, people accept easily the idea that those with heavier responsibilities, those exposed to particular risks in their occupational life, those who have gained their competence thanks to a long and difficult training, those who have to deal with more difficult tasks, those who are less easily replaced in their function, etc. are more highly rewarded.

It can be easily observed in this respect that social life produces very normally and very spontaneously such inequalities of rewards with a functional basis. These inequalities not only are not discussed, they are on the contrary positively perceived. Thus, the football player whose talent has made possible the victory of his team will be particularly admired. The composer who expresses with sounds categories of emotions which had not been expressed before and who by so doing makes the language of music more powerful will be admired and celebrated, perhaps not immediately, but in the long run. See the obvious example of Beethoven: before him, one would have considered as crazy the idea that highly complex feelings, as the feeling of freedom, of hope, of optimism, could be expressed in a musical score. By this achievement notably, he gained a unique position in the collective memory. So does the scientist who has produced an important discovery or who has produced a fruitful change in our representation of the world. In the same way, the political man who has brought his country into a peaceful and opulent situation will be admired, even if he is severely criticized as any political man normally is as long as he remains active on the political battlefield. Negative examples could obviously as easily be mentioned.

I evoke these familiar and diverse examples to give an exact impression of the wide scope of the collective moral feelings and generally axiological beliefs that can be effectively explained by the functionalist theory I have considered in this section and more generally by the "cognitivist" theories that make moral and axiological beliefs the effect of strong reasons.

b) Rational Choice Theory

A today very influential theory, the so-called "*rational choice theory*" (RCM) is another example, not entirely unrelated to functionalism, of a theory which is also "cognitivist" in the sense that it explains normative beliefs by the reasons actors have to endorse them.[11] As functionalism, it is also rather inspired by the utilitarian than by the Kantian tradition, and it can moreover, as functionalism again, be considered as a particular illustration of a more general "axiological rationality" theory I am trying to sketch here, following Weber's lead.

Many current decisions in private or public life can effectively be accounted for by this "rational choice model".

Take the example of the judge who studies a case or of the teacher who examines a candidate. They will have after some time the impression that they have spent the *appropriate* time on the task. They will have the feeling that spending less time would have been *unfair* and more time *inadequate*. Why? Because they know that, spending less time, they would have run the risk of being unfair to the candidate or to the case, while spending too much time, since they have a limited amount of time, they would have been unfair to the other candidates or cases.

By the nature of the situation, the problem the teacher or the judge have to face is namely to minimize the sum of two costs. The longer the time

---

11 J. S. COLEMAN: *Foundations of Social Theory*, Cambridge/London (The Belknap Press of Harvard University Press) 1990; A. OBERSCHALL: "Règles, normes, morale: émergence et sanction", *L'Année sociologique*, n° 44: "Argumentation et Sciences Sociales" (1994), pp. 357-384; K. D. OPP: *Die Entstehung sozialer Normen*, Tübingen (J.C.B. Mohr) 1983.

spent on the decision, the more likely the decision to be fair. The longer the time spent on a given case, the smaller the time left to the others and the greater the risk of unfairness to the others. As the informations tend to be redundant over time, the curve relating the two types of costs will be convex. The first type of cost is a monotonic decreasing convex function of time. The risk of being unfair decreases with the time spent but more slowly over time. The other curve is a monotonic convex increasing function of time. The risk of being unfair to others increases more and more quickly with time. The two functions can be represented in a graphical way. If a case is more difficult, or a candidate more difficult to evaluate, the parameters of the curves will move and the minimization points, the points where the curves cross one another, will also move. If the number of cases to be treated is lower, the congestion curve will have obviously another form.

I took this example, because it shows that such prosaic value statements as "I have spent the right time on the case" can be analyzed in a satisfactory fashion with the Rational Choice Model. Moreover, the example shows that the reasons underlying ordinary everyday value statements can be so strong that they can easily be represented in a mathematical fashion.[12]

2. Why Weber Introduces Two Kinds of Rationality

At this point, an important distinction should be introduced: functionalism, as the "rational choice theory" of norms, as well as most theories of norms proposed by modern sociologists are "consequentialist". In other words, for these theories, an action, a decision, an institution, etc. is positively or negatively valued considering its potential positive or negative effects on social systems (in the case of functionalism) or on individuals (in the case of the RCM).

Weber's notion of "axiological rationality", more precisely the theory which can be developed on the basis of this notion, not only contains these theories as elements, but it transcends them in the sense that it does not say that the reasons underlying the normative beliefs are necessarily of the consequential type. This point is very important in any discussion of Weber's two "rationalities". If the ultimate ground of normative beliefs is to be found on the side of the potential consequences or effects on systems or individuals of

---

12 I lean here on my book R. BOUDON: *Le juste et le vrai*, Paris (Fayard) 1995.

actions, decisions, attitudes, institutions, etc., then "axiological rationality", being consequentialist, would not be clearly distinct from "instrumental rationality". "X is good" would be synonymous of "X generates good outcomes", or of "X is a good means to reach the objectives followed by such and such individual or system". In other words, Weber's distinction implies that, to him, "axiological rationality" cannot (or at least cannot *always*) be reduced to "instrumental rationality".

That the reasons underlying axiological beliefs are not always consequential or instrumental is a crucial point in itself, as far as the analysis of axiological beliefs is concerned. It is also essential, if one wants to understand why Weber introduced an autonomous category of "axiological rationality".

The most classical example in discussions about morals, the example of the negative value attached to the act of stealing, shows namely that many moral feelings are not the product of instrumental rationality.

The idea that moral judgments would be basically irrational was probably in modern times expressed in the most provocative fashion by Mandeville. Stealing provokes a negative feeling. But this feeling cannot be rationally justified, suggests Mandeville. Of course, stealing has negative consequences as far as the victim is concerned, but the consequences are good to the thief. Of course, society mobilizes all kinds of threats and penalties against thieves. But if the thief can be deterred from stealing, he cannot be convinced that stealing is bad.

Mandeville's argument was a blessing to Karl Marx, who evokes it and makes it more systematic.[13] The social consequences of stealing are ambiguous, he contends, some being socially bad, some good. It is bad to the rich, but provides jobs to lawyers and locksmiths. We could easily go further than Marx. Thieves are a blessing to insurance companies. And not only to them. See what happens today in poor urban areas: thanks to thieves, poor people can get at lower prices many goods, as electronic goods, they could not afford otherwise. They do not even necessarily know that the low price they pay for them is the effect of the fact that the goods have been stolen. In many cases, they have simply the impression of being offered a bargain. This dual market has the happy consequence of inverting Caplovitz' famous theorem.[14] As,

---

13 K. MARX: Matériaux pour l' "économie", in: *Oeuvres Economie*, tome II, ed. établie par M. Rubel, Paris (Gallimard) 1968, p. 399-401.
14 D. CAPLOVITZ: *The Poor Pay More*, London (Macmillan), New York (Free Press) 1967.

because of their scarce resources, the poor are limited to low quality products, said Caplovitz, it turns out that "the poor pay more" their refrigerators or washing machines. Right. But, thanks to thieves, "the poor pay less" their video- , tape-recorders or Hi-Fi sets. Possibly, this unintended redistribution from the rich to the poor is more efficient than the redistribution generated by fiscal policies. In that case, thieves would achieve what political men are unable to accomplish. Moreover, since it makes the demand broader, stealing has a positive effect on supply. So, stealing is possibly good, not only from a social, but as well from a macroeconomic viewpoint, since it has plausibly the positive effect of reducing unemployment.

Mandeville's and Marx' sarcasms and paradoxes are finally more profound than they seem. They demonstrate by a *demonstratio ad absurdum* that it is impossible to show that stealing is a bad thing, when starting from a consequential viewpoint.

Nobody has proposed to legalize stealing, though. From which source comes then our conviction that stealing is bad? Not from its consequences. From which origin then?

To show that stealing is bad, to explain in other words the normal feeling which expresses itself through the value statement "stealing is bad", one has to reconstruct the non consequential reasons behind it. They are not difficult to find. Social order is based on an adequation between retribution and contribution. With the exception of particular circumstances, when for instance citizens are physically or mentally unable to contribute, a retribution must correspond to a contribution. Now, stealing is a typical violation of these basic principles of social organization, since the thief attributes to himself unilaterally a retribution without offering any contribution as a counterpart. So, any theft violates the basic principles of the social link and as such cannot be accepted.

This case, obvious as it is, shows that reasons, though of the non consequential type, can easily be discovered behind the negative feelings normally aroused by the act of stealing. This example has important consequences: it shows that the basic argument on which the irrational theories of morals are grounded, namely the argument that no reasons can be found behind the negative feelings produced by stealing and other deviant forms of behavior need not be accepted. No consequential argument can prove that stealing is bad. No instrumental reasons can convince that thieves should be prosecuted. But axiological reasons can.

This example suffices to suggest that the weberian notion of axiological rationality, once properly developed, solves very important theoretical problems and many sociological puzzles. It explains why a theft even of very little importance from a utilitarian viewpoint produces such a strong reaction from the part of the victim. Sociological analyses often fail to understand this crucial point: "Why such a strong reaction to a minor theft, while the thief is a poor man, a marginal individual toward whom society is so unfair?" is a question often heard. Yes, but unfairness is not a valid answer to unfairness and what counts in a theft is the fact that it violates the basic principles of any social exchange and thus breaks the social link.

This example has also the advantage of showing that a utilitarian analysis in the style of the rational choice model is irrelevant here. The indignation of the observer of a theft will grow, other things equal, if the thief has robbed a weak human being, an old woman for instance. But it will hardly grow with the amount stolen. The so-called minor delinquency is an important social problem today, not because the amount of the minor violations of the law has increased, but because the small rate of prosecution gives the public the feeling that the political authorities care not enough enforcing the basic principles of the social link. All these puzzles cannot be explained without the category of axiological rationality.

The examples I have just evoked were taken from ordinary life. Other examples can be taken from political life, as the example of the action of the Western powers against *apartheid*. Introducing democracy in South Africa was *ex ante* risky. Hence, from a consequential viewpoint, it was hard to decide whether the action should be taken. But analytical reasons, axiological reasons were lexicographically superordered here to consequential reasons and to axiological principles of lower order. This explains why the political pressures against *apartheid* were generally approved by public opinion in the West.

So, the category of "axiological rationality" invites to developing a theory which would make the functionalist theory, the Rational choice theory, but also the so-called "exchange theory"[15] or the contractualist theory (the two important latter theories will be only mentioned here without further developments) particular cases of this theory.

---

15 A. HEATH: "Review Article: Exchange Theory", *British Journal of Political Science*, I, 1, janv. (1971), pp. 91-119; G. C. HOMANS: "Social Behavior as Exchange", *American Journal of Sociology*, 63, 6 (1958), pp. 597-606.

V. "Gesinnungsethik" and "Verantwortungsethik"

The example of stealing and the other examples I have evoked makes clear that at least some of our moral feelings are not grounded on consequential reasons. It illustrates the category of "axiological rationality". Also, it helps understanding another classical weberian distinction.

These examples show namely that one should not present the choice between *Verantwortungsethik* and *Gesinnungsethik*, the "ethics of responsibility" and the "ethics of conviction", as constituting always an open choice, for in some cases, axiological rationality dominates consequential rationality. Thus, the progress in medicine has reduced infant mortality and this circumstance is generally and rightly acknowledged as being responsible for underdevelopment and hence for all the evils generated by underdevelopment. But who would accept that reducing infant mortality was not a desirable progress? In that case, axiological rationality dominates consequential rationality, and the ethics of conviction dominates the ethics of responsibility.[16]

The "cognitivist" analysis of these sentiments which can be derived from Weber's notion of "axiological rationality" has the advantage of explaining easily why, when I believe that "X is good, legitimate, fair, etc.", I am at the same time normally convinced that the generalized Other[17] should endorse the same statement: my sentiment being grounded on reasons which I see as transsubjectively valid, the other people should have the same sentiment.

16 D. BELL: *La fin de l'idéologie*, Paris (PUF) 1997 shows that the negative accent Weber puts on *Gesinnungsethik* has to be related with G. Lukacs, who was present at the private discussions Weber organized in his home and frightened him by his fanaticism, as he frightened Thomas Mann, since he appears as the jesuit Naphta in *Der Zauberberg* (Lukacs was, it seems, proud of this portrait). The conceptual distinction transcends obviously these circumstances, however.

17 G.-H. MEAD: *Mind, Self and Society. From the Standpoint of a Social Behaviorist*, Chicago (The University of Chicago Press) 1934.

VI. Back to Kant?

So far, I have presented an interpretation of Weber's notion of "axiological rationality". Moreover, I have sketched a general theory of moral feelings which could be inspired by this famous category. In this final part of the paper, I would like to sketch an answer to some objections likely to be opposed to this theory.

The marbles players have strong reasons not to accept cheating. Generalizing from this example, I would contend that, when we believe that X is good or bad, we have *always* strong reasons – though we can be more or less conscious of these reasons – of believing that X is good or bad. This assumption implies, in other words, that moral convictions are not different in essence from positive convictions. I believe that the square root of 2 is irrational in the mathematical sense, that it cannot be expressed as the ratio of two integers p and q, because I have strong reasons of believing so. If we take seriously the notion of axiological rationality as I interpret it, we should also accept the idea that the source of moral convictions lies in strong reasons. To use a somewhat provocative formulation, I would say that moral truths are established in the same way as positive truths.

Strange as the idea may appear at first glance, it is not difficult to illustrate it. I will start from a trivial example. Why is democracy considered a good thing? Because the statement that it is a good thing is grounded on solid reasons.

I need only refer here briefly to classical theories to make this point more concrete. A good government serves rather the interests of the citizens than its own interests. For this reason, the members of the government should be exposed to the risks of reelection. Electing the government does not insure that the best candidates will be elected, but limits the risk that they disregard the interests of the people. Democracy does not and cannot prevent corruption. But it makes it less likely than other types of regimes. A legally elected government can overthrow democracy. But there is no absolute protection against this risk. An independent press and an independent judiciary system are indispensable elements of a democracy, since, by their critical function, they can avoid corruption or political mismanagement. Of course, judges and media can become corrupted. But other judges and media people will plausibly have an interest in denunciating the corruption of their colleagues.

If we examine these arguments, we see easily that they derive from principles, for instance that any government should serve the interests of the people rather than its own. Starting from this principle, the argument then shows that elections, an independent press or judiciary system are appropriate means to reach the goal of making more likely than less that the government serves the interests of the people rather than its own.

My objective is not to defend democracy, nor to be original in matters of political philosophy, but only to suggest that there is no substantial difference between the way positive and normative statements are grounded. We believe that the square root of two is irrational because we have strong reasons of believing so. We believe that democracy is a good thing because we have strong reasons of believing so, the reasons which have been developed by writers as Montesquieu, John Stuart Mill, Tocqueville[18] and others. We would never dream of explaining our belief in physical statements by making them the effect of some obscure instinct or of socialization. Why should we evoke such mysterious mechanisms as far as normative statements are concerned?

The objection will possibly be made at this point that political philosophers develop their theories from principles, and that these principles cannot be demonstrated. Otherwise, they would not be principles. Right. But the objection can be raised against *any* theory, positive as well as normative. Any physical theory for instance rests also on principles. And the principles cannot be demonstrated except by other principles and thus *ad infinitum*. This paradox, christened as "Münchhausen's trilemma", because it evokes this German legendary figure who tried to get out from a pool by drawing his own hairs, has never stopped science. As K. Popper has shown[19], the fact that we need frameworks to think on any subject and principles to develop any theory does not prevent us from criticizing the frameworks and principles. We endorse principles in normative as in positive matters, because they are fruitful. If they are not, we reject them.

Trivial as it may appear, this popperian observation that we need principles before we can derive consequences from them and that we need to see the

---

18 I have left aside here the consequentialist arguments in favor of democracy (as: it makes economic development easier). They have been developed again recently by M. OLSON: "Dictatorship, Democracy and Development", *American Political Science Review*, vol. 87, n°3, sept. (1993), pp. 567-576.

19 K. POPPER: "The myth of the framework", in: E. FREEMAN (Ed.): *The abdication of philosophy*, La Salle, Ill. (Open court) 1976, pp. 23-48.

consequences before we can judge the principles implies that knowledge, against a received idea, is *circular*. This was stressed by some sharpminded thinkers, as Georg Simmel.[20] In the normative as in the positive case, we have to accept the Münchhausen's trilemma and also the fact that, because knowledge is circular, the trilemma is not contradictory with the possibility of reaching truth and objectivity.

This example of democracy suffices to show that a value statement "X is good" can be as objective as any positive statement. If the feeling that "democracy is a good thing" were not objectively grounded, one would not observe a consensus on the subject. One would not understand that against the principles -basic in international relations- which require to respect the sovereignty of foreign states, pressures on foreign governments to the effect of instauring or developing democracy is generally well understood and approved by the public opinion. How could these collective feelings be otherwise explained? Theory and empirical sociology converge here. (Of course, I am not saying that consensus is a proof of truth, but only that when consensus appears, it has to be explained by making it the product of reasons likely to be perceived as objectively strong).

An objection can be made here: namely that democracy was certainly not always considered so. Still before the First World War, universal voting right was criticized. A Pareto for instance saw in this right another of these symptoms of human craziness he liked to collect and prophesied that it would generate social chaos. Does not this show that our belief that democracy is good is a product rather of socialization than of reason and that it has little to do with our beliefs in scientific statements?

The fact that moral truths are historical is far, though, from being a deadly objection against the theory of axiological beliefs which I develop here on the basis of Weber's "value rationality".

Consider scientific beliefs. Aristotelian physicists believed that any physical move is produced by some force or set of forces.[21] This sheet of paper

---

20 G. SIMMEL: *Les problèmes de la philosophie de l'histoire*, Paris (Presses Universitaires de France) 1984, Introduction by R. Boudon. Original: *Die Probleme der Geschichtsphilosophie*, München (Duncker & Humblot) 1892.

21 I follow here P. DUHEM: *Le système du monde*, Paris (Hermann et Cie) 1954, tome 1, pp. 371-372: "Aucun corps inanimé ne peut être en mouvement s'il n'est soumis à l'action d'un moteur qui soit distinct de lui et extérieur à lui; il faut que ce moteur, pendant toute la durée du mouvement, lui soit constamment appliqué, soit sans cesse en contact avec lui".

moves because I apply force to it. If I would not apply force, it would not move. This point seems so trivial that insisting on it can easily appear as bizarre. What I want to say by evoking it is that Aristotelian physicists had strong reasons for believing that any move is the effect of some force. But they drew from this statement conclusions that appeared acceptable to them and are unacceptable to us, for instance that, when a ship keeps on sliding after the wind has suddenly fallen, some force should be responsible for this move. They tried consequently to figure out what this force could be and introduced the assumption that the move of the ship produced a turmoil. This turmoil was for its part supposed to produce force pushing the boat, which was finally held responsible for the fact that it kept moving. But after a while, Buridan came and said: "If the argument were right, the hypothetical turmoil would have the effect that the straw on a strawheap should fly in opposite directions depending as to whether the heap is located at the front or at the back of the deck".[22] As the direction where the straw flies does not actually depend on the location of the straw heap on the deck of a ship, Aristotelian physicists came -slowly- to the conclusion that the principle according to which there would be no move without force producing it was false. And they came to a new principle, which we now consider as evident, namely that a body that moves needs a force to be stopped, exactly as a body not moving needs a force to be brought into move. This is the so-called "principle of inertia". The feeling of obviousness which it produces today in our mind is well the product of history.

The same kind of story could be told on normative as well as positive statements.

As reported by George Trevelyan[23] Voltaire did not conceive that a society could function orderly when writers were allowed to publish what they wanted before he came to England. And, to come back to my earlier example, as long as actual democratic regimes or at least political regimes embodying some of the features of what we call democracy did not exist actually, they were not conceived; nobody could imagine them, nor *a fortiori* give them a positive value. Then, at the occasion notably of civil struggles in England in

---

22 J. BURIDAN: *Questions sur la physique*, develops the so-called "theory of impetus", according to Duhem a first formulation of the principle of inertia as we know it. Question 12 of Book VIII in particular criticizes the principles of Aristotelian physics using this example of the strawheap.

23 G. M. TREVELYAN: *Histoire sociale de l'Angleterre*, Paris (Laffont) 1993.

Cromwell's time (I follow again Trevelyan here), the principle of the separation of the executive and legislative powers appeared and its effects started being evaluated and positively appreciated. Much later, theories of democracy were developed by analysts as Montesquieu, John Stuart Mill and others who presented the principle of the separation of powers as crucial. At this point, it started being perceived as evident, in the same fashion as the principle of inertia appeared as evident after it was understood that it solved many physical puzzles.

But the story does not end at this point and further objections were opposed to other principles of democracy we consider today as obvious. As I said before, still at the time of the First World War, the argument that universal voting right would produce chaotic political effects was currently developed. But this right was introduced in many places and produced no chaotic effects. So, an argument which was strong before became weakened under the attack of experience. Freedom of the press would produce all kinds of undesirable effects, was also an argument frequently heard before it become eroded. Freedom of the press does produce undesirable effects. But restricting it produces still much more undesirable effects. Nobody would doubt about it now. Capital punishment is necessary; without capital punishment, crime will increase, it was argued. Capital punishment was abolished in many places without producing any increase in crime rates. From that moment, it was perceived, not only as barbarian, as contradictory with basic values, but as useless, so that the public evaluation of it changed progressively, exactly as the aristotelian notion of the turmoils responsible for the move of ships and arrows was progressively eroded.

So, the rational (alternatively: the "cognitivist") theory of moral feelings I propose here following Max Weber, not only is *not* contradicted by the fact that moral convictions change over time, but it can explain this change more easily than other types of theories. The fact that science is historical, that a statement that was treated yesterday as false is treated today as true was never held as an argument against the possibility of reaching truth in scientific matters; in the same way, in moral matters, the fact that some institutions were held as bad yesterday and are now considered as good is not an argument against the fact that moral evaluations are grounded on strong reasons in the mind of people. Moreover, normative irreversibilities can, as scientific irreversibilities, hardly be explained if not by a rational history. The principle of inertia is objectively better than the principles it replaced. Because it is objectively better, it created historical irreversibility. In the same fashion, as noted by Tocqueville, we will never see again somebody explaining that he enjoyed being the spectator of a capital execution.

The argument that change in moral values confirms relativism rests finally on a fallacy. Truth, moral or positive, *is not* historical. But the research of truth, positive or normative, *is* historical. The fact that science has a history is not an argument against the possibility of scientific truth. The fact that morals has a history is not an argument in favor of moral relativism. Truth cannot be reached at once. History does not legitimate historicism, contextual variability does not justify sociologism or culturalism.

Of course, I do not contend by so saying that there are no historical contingencies. On the contrary, the role of contingencies should be stressed. If there were no contingencies, there would be no innovations, neither scientific nor moral. On this point, we must definitely stop following Hegel's intuitions. Nobody can foretell that tomorrow totalitarian regimes will not reappear, eventually spread over the planet. But unless men's memory is destroyed, the idea that democracy is better than despotic regimes will remain present in human minds.

I do not contend either that an axiological truth lies hidden ready to be discovered on all subjects. This view is false as far as positive knowledge is concerned. On many questions we do not know the truth. We did not know until the recent years whether bees have a language or not in spite of the fact that von Frisch got the Nobel prize in 1953 for having "proved" it. On many moral questions, we are in the same situation. Life brings continuously to the surface new positive and normative questions. Many of them remain provisionally unsolved, while others are possibly unsolvable.

We are now in a position to answer the question raised by the title of this section: the dynamic side of the moral theory which can be derived from Weber is sufficient to show that the notion of "axiological rationality" takes us far from Kant.

I will conclude with a single sentence: Weber's hints are presently extremely relevant because they propose to overcome the shortcomings of both the Kantian and the utilitarian traditions.[24]

---

24 The ideas I have presented in this conference are developed in a more extensive fashion notably in a recent paper: "La rationalité axiologique", in: S. MESURE (Ed.): *La rationalité des valeurs*, Paris (PUF) 1997.

Discussion Summary

ANNETTE KLEINFELD

Paper discussed:
RAYMOND BOUDON: The Present Relevance of Max Weber's
Wertrationalität (Value Rationality)

In a first part of the discussion the relevance of methodological individualism for the explanation of human behavior was discussed. Weber's statement that all collective concepts are black boxes was considered as a strong statement without sufficient proofs, and the status of methodological individualismus to be an adequate model for explaining human behaviour was doubted (KOSLOWSKI, FURUBOTN).

The second part of the discussion concentrated on Weber's real intentions with regard to his notion of "Wertrationalität". The following objections against the thesis of the paper were raised: Firstly, it has to be differentiated between consequentialist and non-consequentialist, axiological ethical positions. The former is close to, but not identical with an axiological rational position. Secondly, how close or not close is this to Weber's real intentions? Thirdly, two things are missing, usually being mentioned by Weber in the context of his notion of *Wertrationalität*: that he is not interested in a logical consistency of *Wertrationalität*, and that the expressive significance of *Wertrationalität* is - unlike in the concept of a consequentialist ethics (*Verantwortungsethik*) - the value rational *action*. What has to be rational according to Weber is the relationship between value and reflection. The cognitive dimension of an axiological position is universalizable. Only to this respect it is Kantian. Presenting the other cheek when someone strikes one's cheek is the main paradigm for a non-consequentialistic position. The funtionalistic, sociological solution of Weber however, is not immune against the accusation of being consequentialist itself (RINGER).

Against this interpretation of Weber's concept of rationality as being instrumental it has been objected with reference to Boudon's paper, that the concept of value rationality is based on norms that are understood as something given and of general validity. Therefore, it is not justified to insinuate that a functionalism underlies the type of rationality of Weber's conception. Weber does not assume that the norm was chosen with regard to one's own interests. Value rationality can be understood as the German version of social-contract theory which is based on a commonly accepted value or conviction too (YAGI).

It was doubted that Weber has said anything that would allow to interpret him in a consequentialist sense. The examples given in the paper are no proofs for such an interpretation, but rather show that Weber's concept of value rationality in the sense of axiological rationality actually corresponds to Kant's principle of the good will: The modus of justification is logical coherence, the final aim with regard to which someone acts is the axiom of value (*Wertaxiom*) (ACHAM).

The last part of the discussion was dedicated to the question of the present relevance of Weber´s *Wertrationalität*. Three questions were raised:
1. Is it functionally useful?
2. Is it immune to criticism?
3. Is everybody convinced by it?

From an economic standpoint only question 1. and 3. are relevant, while question 2. asks for the moral philosophical status of the Weberian concept of value rationality (CASSON). Being a kind of rationality that is based on functionalistic arguments, and identifying value with the welfare function, i.e. with social utility, the term *Wertrationalität* is only a different name for a kind of ethics which is in effect utilitarian. On the other hand, a social motivation must not necessarily be utilitarian as Weber argues (RINGER).

Regarding the first question, it was objected that the ideal of a truely rational decision can be fulfilled only under perfect conditions requiring a completeness of knowledge which humans, due to their contingency, never have. Real life, however, shows that sometimes one has to strive for the impossible to reach a maximum of the possible (ACHAM, RINGER).

Chapter 2

Max Weber and Ludwig von Mises, and the Methodology of the Social Sciences

RICARDO F. CRESPO

I. Characteristics of the Methodology of the Social Sciences
   According to Max Weber
II. The Methodological Thought of Ludwig von Mises
III. Mises's Criticism of Weber
IV. In Defense of Weber
V. *Neither* Weber *nor* Mises, or Better: Weber *and* von Mises

It is evident that the richness of thinkers like Weber and von Mises cannot be fully captured in a short paper. In 1971 Walter G. Runciman said that the bibliography about Max Weber's methodology consisted of about 600 works[1]. In the early 1970's Wolfang Schluchter and Guenther Roth added that an additional one hundred essays were written every year[2]. Twenty years have gone by since. Thus, the attainment of complete knowledge of Weber's thought is almost unachievable. Besides, in a recently published book, Wilhelm Hennis, who knows Weber's work very well, affirms that "seldom has anyone had such bad fortune in the avoidance of misunderstanding. The libraries written on the 'Weber thesis' would otherwise never ever have been written". And he continues: "Hence Weber has to be read fresh and 'without prejudice'. And that means the *entire* corpus of his work"[3]. Hennis shows us

---

1   Cf. W. G. RUNCIMAN: *A Critique of Max Weber's Philosophy of Social Sciences*, Cambridge (Cambridge University Press) 1972, p. vi.
2   Cf. W. SCHLUCHTER, G. ROTH: *Max Weber's Vision of History. Ethics and Methods*, Berkeley, Los Angeles, London (University of California Press) 1979, p. 1.
3   W. HENNIS: *Max Weber. Essays in Reconstruction*, London (Allen & Unwin) 1988 (transl. by Keith Tribe), pp. 27 and 22.

a new and unsuspected Weber. For him, Weber would not be one of the fathers of the sociology, but rather belongs to the tradition of the classical practical or moral sciences[4], since he is interested in human nature and the kind of life caused by modernity[5]. This interpretation is quite different from the usual one -he realizes[6]-, but his knowledge and his arguments are so convincing that we have to take them into account. Hennis's essays could constitute something of a turning point in the hermeneutics of Weber's work. Nevertheless I shall quote him as one opinion, together with those of the traditional interpretations. Von Mises's work is almost as extensive as the one of Weber. Thus, the following paper will use the original texts and only some of the secondary literature.

I. Characteristics of the Methodology of the Social Sciences According to Max Weber

It is well known that the principal condition of scientificity imposed by Weber on the social sciences is the *Wertfreiheit*[7]. Weber is very clear in sustaining this in his various works, and it is not necessary to spend time quoting him. It is enough to mention his two famous essays "The Meaning of 'Ethical Neutrality' in Sociology and Economics" and "Objectivity in Social Science and Social Policy"[8]. One should also mention his lecture "Science as

---

4 Cf. *ibid.*, pp. 103, 104 where he affirms: "Weber belongs to the late tradition of practical science; and he finds a place in the pre-history of modern social science only if his central questions and concerns are neglected".

5 Cf. *ibid.*, pp. 35, 36, 43, 44, 61, 69, 73, 90, 108. "The 'cultural problems of man' remain the object of his work. And this means: the problems arising form the insertation of man (*Mensch*), a being capable of social action, in social constellations which in turn form these persons, develop their capacities or alternatively deform them up..." (69).

6 Hennis mentions Georg Lukács and Herbert Marcuse, on the one hand, and Leo Strauss and Eric Voegelin, on the other, within those who broke with Weber: *op. cit.*, p. 21.

7 Value-freedom, ethical neutrality or value-neutrality. On the translation to English of this German word, cf. SCHLUCHTER, *op. cit.*, pp. 65-6 (note).

8 Translated and edited by Edward Shils and Henry Finch in: *The Methodology of the Social Sciences*, Glencoe, Illinois (The Free Press) 1949, *passim*. The

Vocation", where he states that we cannot expect from science any answer about the sense of life and the values[9]. This Weberian position aimed at the future direction of the methodological intentionality of the social sciences from then on. However it is also well known that the value-free criterion is not absolutely imposed by Weber, basically for two reasons.

The first one is sustained by many: it seems that when Weber really does social science he is not coherent and does not respect this principle. The Weber of the paramount socio-historical investigations would not be the same as that of the strict *Wertfreiheit*. In his research, the evident intentionality of objectivity and the implicit assumption of some values is mixed. Thus, for example, Wilhelm Hennis says that Max Weber's 'Political writings', above all his Constitutional writings of the war years, ignored this principle[10]. Eric Voegelin refers to this Weberian position as a "positivism with laments". He tries to give an explanation about the reason why Weber did not dare to take the step towards a 'science of order'. Voegelin even says that with Weber's work positivism comes to an end and leaves open the way to the rehabilitation of the classical political science[11]. Leo Strauss also affirms that "the value judgements which are forbidden to enter through the front door of political science, sociology or economics, enter these disciplines through the back

---

Essay on Objectivity -"Die Objektivität sozialwissenschaftlicher und sozialpolitischer Erkenntnis"- was first published in *Archiv für Sozialwissenschaft und Sozialpolitik* in 1904, on the occasion of the joint assumption of its editorialship by Weber, Sombart and Jaffé, and the other Essay -"Der Sinn der *Wertfreiheit* der soziologischen und ökonomischen Wissenschaften"- was prepared in 1914 and published in a revised form in *Logos* in 1917. Both reprinted in: M. WEBER: *Gesammelte Aufsätze zur Wissenschaftslehre*, 2nd. ed. Tübingen 1951.

9 M. WEBER: *Wissenschaft als Beruf*. About its date, cf. ROTH and SCHLUCHTER, *op. cit.*, pp. 112ff.

10 Cf. W. HENNIS: *Política y filosofía práctica*, Buenos Aires (Sur) 1973, p. 143 (*Politik und Praktische Philosophie*, Neuwied, Berlin [Luchterhand] 1963, trans. by Rafael Gutiérez Girardot). The English translation is mine. Also cf. the reference to this matter by RONALD INGLEHART: "Coercion and Consent: ...", in: PETER KOSLOWSKI (Ed.): *Individual Liberty and Democratic Decision-Making*, Tübingen (J.C.B. Mohr) 1987, p. 181.

11 E. VOEGELIN: *The New Science of Politics*, Chicago (University of Chicago Press) 1952, Introduction, nn. 3 and 4, *passim*.

door"[12]. More recently, Lawrence Scaff said that "even Weber's methodological argumentation took on a different cast depending on the specific context"[13]. Mises himself complains about it: "Max Weber, he says in his *Grundprobleme der Nationalökonomie* of 1933, explicitly combatted this confusion [the value judgement that identifies rational action with correct action] although,..., he repeatedly fell into it in other passages of his writings"[14]. I will look into the Misesean criticism in more detail.

The second "relativization" of the *Wertfreiheit* is done by Weber himself, as part of his own theory of the social sciences. This issue has given rise to an extensive literature. On the one hand, values are involved in the making of concepts in the social sciences. That is to say, the same content is determined by values. "The problems of the empirical disciplines are, of course, to be solved 'non-evaluatively'... But the problems of the social sciences are selected by the value-relevance of the phenomena treated"[15]. Weber is careful in distinguishing between value-relevance (*Wertbeziehung*) and value judgement (*Werturteil*). However in the opinion of many authors, this distinction is very problematic, and even though Weber searches objectivity, he eventually ends in a certain relativism. "In the cultural sciences, he affirms, concept-construction depends on the setting of the problem, and the latter varies with the content of culture itself"[16]. In the social field a valorative determination is needed to obtain a scientific problem. We need a selection ruled by values, that are variables. "They [the evaluative ideas] are, says Weber, naturally, historically variable in accordance with the character of the culture and the ideas which rule men's minds"[17]. It does not only depend on the values of the analyzed culture, but also on the values of the researcher. "There is no absolutely

---

12 L. STRAUSS: *What is Political Philosophy? and Other Studies*, Glencoe, Illinois (The Free Press) 1959, p. 21.

13 L. SCAFF: "Historicism in the German Tradition of Social and Economic Thought", in: P. KOSLOWSKI (Ed.): *The Theory of Ethical Economy in the Historical School*, Berlin, Heidelberg, New York, Tokyo (Springer) 1995, p. 320.

14 L. VON MISES: *Epistemological Problems of Economics*, trans. by George Reisman, Princeton, Toronto, London, New York (D. van Nostrand Company, Inc.) 1960, p. 93 (*Grundprobleme der Nationalökonomie*, Jena [Gustav Fischer] 1933).

15 WEBER: *The Methodology*..., loc. cit., p. 21.

16 *Ibid.*, p. 105.

17 *Ibid.*, p. 84.

'objective' analysis of culture, he says, -...- of social phenomena independent of special and 'one-sided' viewpoints according to which -expressly or tacitly, consciously or unconsciously- they are selected, analyzed and organized for expository purposes. The reason for this lies in the character of the cognitive goal of all research in social science which seeks to transcend the purely *formal* treatment of the legal or conventional norms regulating social life". "All knowledge of cultural reality, as may be seen, is always knowledge from *particular points of view*". And, "undoubtedly, all evaluative ideas are 'subjective'"[18].

As Michael Lesnoff says, "at a purely verbal level ... Weber believed that both natural and social science could be and should be value-free [but] at a slightly deeper level ... Weber held that [in] social science ... concepts must inevitably reflect the interests of the social scientists"[19]. Karl-Otto Apel adds, "there is *one* area where Max Weber ... transgresses this border-line between the rational and the irrational or between value-free science and normatively engaged value-judgments. It is not by accident that this area is represented by science and its history"[20]. The so wished objectivity fails in relativism. As Barry Hindess says, "the theorical arbitrariness implicit in the epistemology of ideal types ensures that the evaluation of the usefulness of type concepts cannot be objective... Once values are called in to perform a theoretical task the 'objectivity', 'value-freedom' and the like must go by the board. Weber's conception of scientific objectivity is a logical impossibility; it contradicts the fundamental concepts of his epistemology"[21]. Schluchter also points out these problems: "Weber has been called a nihilist [by Leo Strauss for example[22]], a relativist, and a decisionist. He is all of these things if you believe in the existence and discernability of an objective meaning of the world"[23]. It would be long and senseless here to go through Schluchter's entire interpreta-

---

18 *Ibid.*, pp. 72, 81, 83.

19 MICHAEL LESNOFF: "Technique, Critique and Social Science", in: S. C. BROWN (Ed.): *Philosophical Disputes in the Social Sciences*, Sussex (Harvester Press), New Jersey (Humanities Press) 1979, p. 95.

20 K.-O. APEL: "Toward a Reconstruction of Critical Theory", in: S. C. BROWN, *op. cit.*, p. 136.

21 B. HINDESS: *Philosophy and Methodology in the Social Sciences,* Sussex (Harvester Press) 1977, p. 38. Cf. also pp. 24, 33-9, 48 and 232.

22 Cf. L. STRAUSS: *Natural Right and History*, Chicago & London (The University of Chicago Press) 1953, pp. 42ff.

23 *Op. cit.*, pp. 58-9.

tion. The same applies to Runciman who also warns us about this matter.[24] I close this issue with a quotation from Raymond Aron, whose observations about Weber are still current and insightful: "If every reconstruction has a selective character and if it is ruled by a system of values, there will be so as many historical or sociological perspectives as there are system of values used in the selection"[25].

In conclusion, the *Wertfreiheit* is not and it cannot be observed strictly in the field of the human sciences. This does not mean a failure, but a very realistic feature that has to be incorporated and does not diminish the scientific notes of these disciplines. Hennis surprises us once again in his very thorough and documented studies when he says "that one cannot comprehend the passion with which Weber held to the postulate of value-freedom if it is seen as having primarily a 'logical-methodological' foundation". It is mainly a question of freedom from academic judgements. The value-freedom principle has a primarily pedagogical intention, provided by his fight against the arbitrariness of the German academic policies of his time: "In Germany *'freedom of science' exists within the bounds of political and ecclesiastical acceptability* -and not outside this bounds". 'Value-freedom' is seen as 'impartiality'[26].

Another tendency in Weber's methodology, one that is tighly connected with the former, is the contingent, probable and unfinished character of knowledge in human sciences[27]. This is seen in the almost merely instrumental character of the ideal types. They are not to be confused with reality nor with what ought to be done. They can change with cultures and their evolutions. It also shows in the partiality and probability of the causal relationships[28].

---

24 *Op. cit.*, pp. 37ff., 50, 52, 60.

25 R. ARON: *Les étapes de la pensée sociologique*, Paris (Gallimard) 1965, T. II, p. 235. The English translation is mine. Cf. also his Introduction to *Le savant et le politique*, Paris (Plon) 1959, that gathers Weber's "Politik als Beruf" and "Wissenschaft als Beruf".

26 W. HENNIS: "The pitiless 'sobriety of judgement': Max Weber between Carl Menger and Gustav von Schmoller -the academic politics of value freedom", in: *History of the Human Sciences*, 4/1, 1991, p. 34 and *passim*. Cf. also HENNIS: *Max Weber. Essays...*, p. 161.

27 Cf. ARON, *op. cit.*, pp. 227ff.

28 Cf. WEBER: *The Methodology...*, pp. 43ff., 89ff. Also ARON, *op. cit.*, pp. 244ff. and RUNCIMAN, *op. cit.*, p. 36.

This is the case in economics, among the other social sciences. Weber also says that economics cannot be finished in the causal study, even though it is still a science. "In addition to the formulation of pure-ideal typical formulae and the establishment of such causal economic prepositions -...- *scientific* economics has other problems. These problems include the causal influence of economic events on the whole range of social phenomena (by means of the hypotheses offered by the economic interpretation of history). Likewise included among the problems of economics is the analysis of the various ways in which non-economic social events influence economic events"[29]. It is necessary to do this broader study, like he does in his outstanding *Economy and Society*[30], also a scientific work, that does not disdain economic theory. The following declaration made together with Sombart proves it: "We both attribute the greatest significance to so-called 'theory' in the context of political economy, that is, 'theory' in our sense of the rational formation of concepts, types and systems ... We are only opponents of *bad* theories and the false conceptions of their *meaning* for methodology. Our published works contain sufficient evidence [of our intentions] ... to place research in political economy on a more secure footing. We believe to have shown through this work that it is high time to replace discussion of the alternatives -either 'historical' or 'theoretical'- which has lasted much too long, with a different and deeper knowledge of the various 'directions' in our science (1917, p. 348)"[31]. Economic science is, according to Weber, something more than economics. Yet, it is still a science with its theory. The only remaining problem would be, as Peter Koslowski very well points out, "the weakness of ethics in historicism"[32]. If values enter in science but remain random, we fall into relativism. Therefore, what has to be sustained is that ethics is also a science and for economics to be a science, it must also be ethical. Hennis underlines some statements by Weber, dealing with economics as a political, practical or moral science, following the Historical School, es-

---

29 WEBER: *The Methodology...*, loc. cit., pp. 45-6.
30 WEBER: *Economy and Society*, New York (Bedminster Press) 1968; edition prepared by Guenther Roth and Claus Wittich on the 4th German edition of *Wirtschaft und Gesellschaft*, Tübingen (J.C.B. Mohr [Paul Siebeck]) 1956.
31 W. SOMBART and M. WEBER: "Erklärung", *Archiv für Sozialwissenschaft und Sozialpolitik* (1917), p. 348, quoted by SCAFF, *op. cit.*, pp. 322-3.
32 P. KOSLOWSKI: "Ethical Economy as Synthesis of Economic and Ethical Theory", in: P. KOSLOWSKI (Ed.): *Ethics in Economics, Business, and Economic Policy*, Berlin, Heidelberg, New York (Springer) 1992, p. 35.

pecially that of Karl Knies. "... A science of man, and that is what economics is, inquires above all in to the *quality of men* who are brought up in those economic and social conditions of existence" and "The science of economic policy is a *political* science", Weber affirms in his Freiburg address for the Political Economy (*Nationalökonomie*) Chair in 1894[33]. In von Mises, we will not find ethics, but a perspective that *could* contain it.

II. The Methodological Thought of Ludwig von Mises

I shall start with a few aspects of Misesean Praxeology. Von Mises sustains a clear distinction between two kinds of knowledge: natural sciences, and sciences of human action. Within the latter, he distinguishes sociology and history. The first one -natural- is hypothetical-deductivist. The second one -sociology- does not require empirical data. It arises from *a priori* principles about human action and deduces consequences from them. Mises gathers them in *Grundprobleme* under the name of sociology, and later renames it praxeology[34]. "The purpose of this book, he says in the Preface to the German Edition of 1933, is to establish the logical legitimacy of the science that has for its object the universally valid laws of human action, i.e., laws that claim validity without respect to place, time, race, nationality, or class of the actor ..."[35]. As for history, it refers to past facts, from which we cannot deduce laws for the future and therefore is clearly different from the other two sciences.

I concentrate on praxeology. "The science of human action that strives for universally valid knowledge is the theoretical system whose hitherto best elaborated branch is economics. In all of its branches this science is a priori, not empirical. Like logic and mathematics, it is not derived from experience; it is prior to experience. It is, as it were, the logic of action and deed. ... Our science ..., disregarding the accidental, considers only the essential. Its goal is the comprehension of the universal, and its procedure is formal and axiomat-

---

33 WEBER: "National State", pp. 436-7, quoted by HENNIS, *Max Weber. Essays* ..., p. 117. Cf., for his continuity with Knies, HENNIS, pp. 129ff.

34 In: L. VON MISES: *Human Action. A Treatise on Economics*, 3rd revised ed., San Francisco (Fox & Wilkes) 1966.

35 MISES: *Epistemological Problems*, loc. cit., pp. xiii-xiv.

ic. It views action and the conditions under which action takes place not in their concrete form, as we encounter them in everyday life, nor in their actual setting, as we view them in each of the sciences of nature and of history, but as formal constructions that enable us to grasp the patterns of human action in their purity"[36]. That is to say, it is possible to achieve a scientific knowledge about the basic principles of human action by another method different from the classical positivist one.

Nevertheless it is necessary, as some other commentators on Mises have already done, to criticize some aspects of his theory. First, the way in which, according to Mises, the basic principles are known, i.e., their aprioristic character. "What we know about the fundamental categories of action -action, economizing, preferring, the relationship of means and ends, and everything else that, together with these, constitutes the system of human action- is not derived from experience. We conceive all this from within, just as we conceive logical and mathematical truths, a priori, without reference to any experience". He continues: "... No kind of experience can ever force us to discard or modify a priori theorems. They are not derived from experience; they are logically prior to it and cannot be either proved by corroborative experience or disproved by experience on the contrary"[37]. The principles of human action are a kind of first principles. "As an a priori category the principle of action is on a par with the principle of causality ... 'In the begining was the deed'"[38]. Where is the clue to the necessary disconnection between the first Misesean principles and the experience? In their a priori origin. For classical philosophy, the principles are grasped by an act of intuition. This is proper of the habit called *nous* by Aristotle for the theoretical principles, and *synderesis* (Greek) - in the Middle Ages following the Stoic tradition - in the case of the practical principles. These intuitions do not come from any concrete experience, but we cannot have them without previous experience. Therefore they can never be opposed to experience. I think that Murray Rothbard is right when he says: "Ludwig von Mises, as an adherent of Kantian epistemology, asserted that the concept of action is a priori to all experience ... Without delving too deeply into the murky waters of epistemology, I would deny, as an Aristotelean and neo-Thomist, any such alleged 'laws of logical structure'. Instead I would call such laws 'laws of reality', which the

---

36 *Ibid.*, pp. 12-3.
37 *Ibid.*, pp. 13-4 and 27.
38 *Ibid.*, p. 14.

mind apprehends from investigating and collating the facts of the real world. My view is that the fundamental axiom and subsidiary axioms are derived from the experience of reality and are therefore in the broadest sense empirical"[39].

One must also criticize the extent of these principles. It seems that there is no place for mistakes in Mises's theory. As Don Lavoie pointed out: "Many of the subjectivist followers of Ludwig von Mises, including Professor Lachmann and most of Mises's methodological critics, have expressed a certain dissatisfaction with the language in which Mises casts his method for a general science of action. Mises sometimes presents his apriori science as what Imre Lakatos called a Euclidean system, a privileged category of knowledge, uniquely certain and immune to all criticism. It was built from a set of self-evident axioms from which strictly deductive arguments can be cranked out mechanically"[40]. They find it too formalistic. And they think that Mises's "view of market process as at least potentially terminating in a state of long-run general equilibrium ... appears to require revision"[41]. In practical matters, certainty is limited to very few principles only.

In conclusion to this, another criticism is pertinent: von Mises's defense of *Wertfreiheit*. This is an issue on which he agrees with Weber. Indeed, as mentioned above, von Mises criticizes Weber for his ambiguity on this question. "It is no part of the task of science, Mises says, to examine ultimate questions or to prescribe values and determine their order of rank"[42]. This led

39 M. ROTHBARD: "Praxeology: The Methodology of Austrian Economics", in: EDWIN G. DOLAN (Ed.): *The Foundations of Modern Austrian Economics*, Kansas City (Sheed & Ward, Inc.) 1976, p. 24. I would like to point out the excellent essay of Gabriel Zanotti, who postulates and proves that it is possible to deduce the Misesean praxeology principles from philosophical postulates: cf. "Fundamentos Filosóficos y Epistemológicos de la Praxeología", *Libertas*, 13 (Buenos Aires 1990), pp. 75-185.

40 D. LAVOIE: "Euclideanism versus Hermeneutics: A Reinterpretation of Misesean Apriorism", in: ISRAEL M. KIRZNER (Ed.): *Subjectivism, Intelligibility and Economic Understanding*, New York (New York University Press) 1986, p. 195-6.

41 D. LAVOIE: "From Mises to Shackle: An Essay on Austrian Economics and the Kaleidic Society", *Journal of Economic Literature*, 14 (1986), p. 60. However, I think that Lachmann's thesis on the approximation of Weber and Mises is not right (cf. p. 56).

42 MISES: *Epistemological Problems...*, p. 49. Cf. also MISES: *Human Action*, loc. cit., Chapter XXXIX,3.

him to identify the intentionality of action with its rationality. "The assertion that there is irrational action is always rooted in an evaluation of a scale of values different from our own" ... "Action is, by definition, always rational. One is unwarranted in calling goals of action irrational simply because they are not worth striving for from the point of view of one's own valuations"[43]. The rationality of all actions drives into formalism. "The universally valid theory of economic action, he says, is necessarily formal"[44]. So all the problems are connected and begin with the value-free attempt. There seems to be something implicit in this criticism, i.e., that since value-free science is impossible, values ought to be introduced into science, but not arbitrary values -in this I agree with von Mises- but scientific ones.

III. Mises's Criticism of Weber

Mises himself stated: "My essay [*Grundprobleme*] was directed especially against Max Weber's epistemology"[45]. I have already said that von Mises's criticism begins in the very Preface to the German edition of the *Grundprobleme*, and is clearly a direct consequence of their different epistemologies. Von Mises acknowledges that "it is to the investigations of Windelband, Rickert and Max Weber that we owe the clarification of the logical problems of the historical sciences. [But] to be sure, the very possibility of a universally valid science of human action escaped these thinkers"... "In Max Weber's view also, continues Mises, economics and sociology completely merge into history. Like the latter, they are moral or cultural sciences and make use of the same logical method. Their most important conceptual tool is the ideal type, which possesses the same logical structure in history and in what Max Weber regarded as economics and sociology"[46]. He often praises

---

43 MISES: *Epistemological Problems...*, pp. 33-4.
44 *Ibid.*, p. 160.
45 MISES: *Notes and Recollections*, South Holland, Ill. (Libertarian Press) 1978, trans. by Hans F. Sennholz, p. 123.
46 MISES: *Epistemological Problems...*, pp. x, xi; cf. also pp. xiii, xiv, 12. Raimondo Cubeddu has recently emphasized that Weber distinguishes between *Naturwissenschaften* and *Geisteswissenschaften* and that human sciences belong to the latter. Weber does not consider the possibility of a theoretical

Weber and his efforts to set the methodological principles of sociology, but Weber's work was not enough. "Weber was one of the most brilliant figures of German science of the twentieth century"[47], he fought against the mainstream of the Historical School, the German pseudo-historicism, all his life[48]. He also says that "the life of Max Weber was an uninterrupted inner struggle against the doctrines of the Socialism of the Chair ... To be sure, his name is praised, but the true substance of his work is not recognized"[49]. But, "Max Weber, it is true, was not sufficiently familiar with economics and was too much under the sway of historicism to get a correct insight into fundamentals of economic thought"[50]. "Economics was alien to him. He was appointed professor of economics without having dealt with this science before"[51]. This affirmation seems to be a little bit hard on the author of *Economy and Society*. In fact, it all depends on the concept of economics; here is the key. The problem, according to von Mises, is Weber's historicist tendency. "Windelband, Rickert and Max Weber knew only the natural science and history; they were strangers to the existence of sociology as a nomothetic science ... In his views economics and sociology were historical sciences ... Weber places 'historian and sociologist' in the same category: the task of both is 'cognition of cultural reality'"[52]. "The difference between sociology and history is considered as only one of degree ... According to him, social science is logically conceivable only as a special, qualified kind of historical

---

study of human action. Cubeddu thinks that, according to Mises, the reason of Weber's misunderstanding of human action and social sciences is his insufficient understanding of the subjectivist economy. Cf. "La critica a Weber nel *Privatseminar* di Mises", in: *Tra Scuola Austriaca e Popper. Sulla Fillosofia delle Scienze Sociali*, Napoli (Edizioni Scientifiche Italiane) 1996, 1.4.

47 MISES: *Epistemological Problems...*, p. 74.

48 Cf. MISES: *Notes and Recollections*, p. 9. Cf. also MISES: *Theory and History*, London (Jonatan Cape) 1958, pp. 308-9. Cf. about the intermediate position of Weber in the *Methodenstreit*, between Menger and the Historical School, RUNCIMAN, *op. cit.*, pp. 12, 24, 69 and 79, and WILHEM HENNIS: "The pitiless", *op. cit.*, pp. 27-59.

49 MISES: *A Critique of Interventionism*, New Rochelle, New York (Arlington House Publishers) 1977, p. 104 (*Kritik des Interventionismus*, Gustav Fischer Verlag, 1929, trans. by Margit von Mises).

50 MISES: *Human Action*, loc. cit., p. 126.

51 MISES: *A Critique...*, loc. cit., p. 103.

52 MISES: *Epistemological Problems...*, pp. 74-5.

investigation"[53]. "The investigations collected in Weber's posthumously published major work, *Wirtschaft und Gesellschaft*, belong to the best that German scientific literature of the last decades has produced. Yet in their most important parts they are not sociological theory in our sense"[54]. If we delve deeply into this subject, we can realize that this historical view of the sciences of culture depends, as Raymond Aron accurately underlines, on the Weberian concept of understanding (*verstehen*), "an intrinsic intelligibility of human phenomena", in its individuality[55]. In consequence, von Mises says, the Weberian rational types are part of history, rather than of theory: "They are obtained in *each* of the individual phenomena taken into consideration"[56]. Von Mises gives more relevance to conceptualizing, that refers to universals, than to „understanding" that is about the individual[57].

A direct consequence of the latter is the criticism to the Weberian classification of social meaningful action. In brief, Weber distinguishes two kinds of action: "Social action, like all action, may be oriented in four ways. It may be: (1) *instrumentally rational (zweckrational)*, that is, determined by expectations as to the behavior of objects in the environment and of other human beings; these expectations are used as 'conditions' or 'means' for the attainment of the actor's own rationally pursued and calculated ends; (2) *value-rational (wertrational)*[58], that is, determined by a conscious belief in the value for its own sake of some ethical, aesthetic, religious, or other form of behavior...; (3) *affectual* (especially emotional), that is, determined by the actor's specific affects and feeling states; (4) *traditional*, that is, determined by ingrained habituation"[59]. Although for Weber there are no pure actions, the economic ones are predominantly of the first kind (*zweckrational*). Von Mises thoroughly examines this classification and demonstrates that all four types of behavior can be reduced to the first one. The opposite supposition ignores, according to Mises, the universality of the sociological laws and the freedom

---

53 *Ibid.*, p. 77.
54 *Ibid.*, pp. 105-6.
55 Aron, *op. cit.*, p. 231.
56 Mises: *Epistemological Problems...*, p. 78 and cf. ff.
57 *Ibid.*, pp. 132-4. Also cf. Mises: *Human Action*, loc. cit., Chapter 2, nn. 7-10.
58 Mises translated 'purposive-rational' and 'valuational' respectively, *ibid.*, p. 82.
59 Weber: *Economy and Society*, pp. 24-5.

from value-judgements[60]. For Mises, Weber was not alone in this mistake. First there were the classical economists[61]. Indeed, "Menger and Böhm-Bawerk are the ones responsible for this misunderstanding of the theory"[62]. "Max Weber's attempt to separate rational action from other action on the basis of such distinctions was the last of its kind"[63]. The common error is to reduce economic action to rational calculation, which supposes a material content, and therefore a misunderstanding of the marginalist theory[64].

Let us now turn from Mises's criticism of Weber and from the connection to their diverse epistemologies to Weber again.

IV. In Defense of Weber

It is necessary to recover Weber as an economist. He was more than an economist, but he also was one. The differences in the point of view between him and von Mises do not mean that we should not think of Weber as an economist. Weber begins his lecture "Science as Vocation", by saying, "we the economists". Indeed, he had studied economics during his studies of law -1882 to 1883-. He also, as I have already said, took over the Chair of Political Economy at Freiburg University in 1894, and in 1896 he replaces Knies in Heidelberg. I have already mentioned his wide concept of the task of economics. Therefore, he also suggests a broad object of economics, including the 'economic' events, the 'economically relevant' phenomena and the 'economically conditioned phenomena'[65]. His definition of what is specifically economic is highly modern, because, for him, it is a kind of human action

---

60 Cf. MISES: *Epistemological Problems...*, pp. 82-5, 89 and 93.

61 Cf. *ibid.*, pp. 146ff.

62 *Ibid.*, p. 167. This is not the place to analyze Mises's criticism of his own antecessors. We think that what he states against Menger's distinction between real and imaginary wants (pp. 171-4) is especially interesting. Cf. MENGER's *Principles of Economics*, Glencoe, Ill. (The Free Press) 1950, p. 53 (*Grundsätze der Volkswirtschaftslehre*, Vienna 1871, 2nd. ed. 1923, pp. 4ff., transl. by J. Dingwall and B. Hoselitz).

63 MISES: *Epistemological Problems...*, p. 148.

64 Cf. *ibid.*, pp. 93, 146-8, 157.

65 Cf. WEBER: *The Methodology...*, *loc. cit.*, pp. 63ff.

that includes immaterial needs. "Specifically economic motives, he says, -...-operate wherever the satisfaction of even the most inmaterial need or desire is bound up with the application of *scarce* material means"[66]. He also distinguishes technique from economics and includes services within the economic goods [67]. His perceptions show that he was a mature economist.

Concerning von Mises's criticism, it is not possible to outline a straight answer by Weber, because although he knew him, and had a high opinion of his[68], von Mises wrote the *Grundprobleme* more than ten years after Weber's death. Although directed to another authors[69], the following statement of Weber could very well apply to von Mises, with all its nuances: "The 'abstract'-theoretical method even today shows unmediated and ostensibly irreconciliable cleavage from empirical-historical research. The proponents of this method recognize in a thoroughly correct way the methodological impossibility of supplanting the historical knowledge of reality by the formulation of laws or, vice versa, of constructing 'laws' in the rigorous sense through the mere juxtaposition of historical observations. Now in order to arrive at these laws -for they are certain that science should be directed towards these as its highest goal- they take it to be a fact that we always have a direct awareness of the structure of human actions in all their reality. Hence -so they think-science can make human behavior directly intelligible with axiomatic evidentness and accordingly reveal its laws. The only exact form of knowledge -the formulation of immediately and intuitively *evident* [a priori for Mises] laws- is however at the same time the only one which offers access to events which have not been directly observed. Hence, at least as regards the fundamental phenomena of economic life, the construction of a system of abstract and therefore purely formal propositions analogous to those of the exact natural sciences, is [for them] the only means of analyzing and intellectually mastering the complexity of social life."[70]

This affirmation characterizes von Mises's position very well, although Weber did not direct it to Mises. For Weber the system of axioms and deductions takes part in the task of establishing ideal types and causal relationships, with all the limitations of ambiguity, contingence and dependence on the values that they possess. We certainly know that he was referring to

---

66 *Ibid.*, p. 65; also cf. WEBER: *Economy and Society*, Part I, Chapter 2.
67 In: WEBER: *Economy and Society*, Part I, Chapter 2.
68 Cf. HENNIS: "The Pitiless...", *op. cit.*, p. 49.
69 Hennis says that he is thinking of Menger: *Max Weber. Essays...*, p. 143.
70 *Ibid.*, p. 87.

Menger from similar statements in another essay: "K. Menger's work is not methodologically complete, but it introduces extremely well-formed thoughts" ... "The principles that constitute economic *theory* as such not only, as everyone knows ... *fail* to represent 'the totality' of our science, they are moreover only one means for the analysis of the causal relationships of empirical reality, albeit a means that is often underrated. As soon as we seek to grasp and explain causally this reality itself as a complex of cultural significations [...], then economic theory stands revealed as a summation of 'ideal-typical' concepts. That means that its principles represent a series of *intellectually* constructed processes that rarely, if ever, appear in an 'ideal purity' in historical reality;..."[71]. That is to say, Weber appreciates the Austrian theory, but only as a part of a wider science. I suggest that this hypothetical answer by Weber to Mises might have some coincidence with the criticism of later Austrian -or better, radical subjectivist- followers of von Mises himself, as we have seen in part two of this paper.

Mises's criticism arises from his own narrow point of view. If the science of human action can only be deductive from *a priori* principles, any other theory falls outside it, and therefore is historical. But this does not mean that he is right. From the point of view of other authors the Weberian ideal types are not only historical instruments but also sociological ones.

V. *Neither* Weber *nor* Mises, or Better: Weber *and* Mises

By taking elements from both von Mises and Weber, I propose an alternative position that comes closer to what I consider as the other criterion of scientificity: realism and the applicability of theory.

This supposes the negative task of isolating the inadequate elements of the theories of Weber and Mises, and the adoption of those judged as proper. To begin with Weber, one must put aside *Wertfreiheit*, as he finally does. But if we have to insert values, we also have to do away with his arbitrari-

---

71 M. WEBER: "Marginal utility and the 'psychopathological basic law'", in: M. WEBER: *Gesammelte Aufsätze zur Wissenschaftslehre*, 5th ed., Tübingen (J.C.B. Mohr [Paul Siebeck]) 1982, pp. 396-7, quoted by HENNIS: "The Pitiless...", *op. cit.*, p. 30.

ness. Otherwise we would end in an unsustainable cultural relativism. If the scientific insertion of values into science can be done, one could agree with the Weberian view of economics as a science. Social or humane sciences without values are impossible. A human science that involves values is attainable. This affirmation may shock some social scientists, especially economists, since it renders the framework of economics to be insufficient.[72]

One of the failures provoked by the modernity is manifested in the theory of the social sciences. The gap between the Is- and Ought-Propositions leads to a theoretical and neutral treatment of practical questions, to a lack of presence of ends in an environment in which these are essential. They were separated from science, as irrational elements that can only be taken as outside data. Ends were -and commonly are- a matter of a decision that exceeds the scientific realm. Jürgen Habermas attributes to Weber a very important role in this dissolution when he says: "Since Max Weber clarified the so called dispute about the values-judgements (...), the social sciences have come completely apart from the normative elements, from the already forgotten heritage of classical politics -they sense it in this way at least, as a theorical-scientific evidence"[73]. And Peter Koslowski says: "There is a certain irrational passion for dispassionate rationality ... which bans any kind of moral motivation or thinking in terms of values from social science"[74].

The disconnection between the science and the ends automatically drives to another disconnection: that of the social sciences among themselves. The social sciences become transformed into an assembly of private knowledge that brings them together but without subordinating them to politics which would give them unity. They lack the common orientation that could give them a secure course[75]. The reaction to this position has arisen from the political philosophers, who have themselves demonstrated the possibility of a valorative human science -and the impossibility of the contrary. Some antecestors as Leo Strauss, Eric Voegelin, Hannah Arendt and many more, fore-

---

72 See also for a criticism of the current state of economics DAVID COLANDER and
    ARJO KLAMER: *The Making of an Economist*, Boulder (Westview Press) 1990,
    and DAVID COLANDER: "The Lost Art of Economics", *Journal of Economic
    Perspectives*, 6 (1992), 3, p. 196.
73 *Teoría y praxis*, Buenos Aires (Sur) 1966, p. 10 (*Theorie und Praxis*, Neuwied,
    Berlin [Luchterhand] 1963, transl. D. J. Vogelmann -to English, mine).
74 P. KOSLOWSKI: *Ethics of Capitalism and Critique of Sociobiology*, Berlin,
    Heidelberg, New York, Tokyo (Springer) 1996, p. 40.
75 Cf. W. HENNIS: *Política y...*, *op. cit.*, pp. 54, 147 and *passim*.

told the emergence of what is now the movement of "the rehabilitation of practical science or practical philosophy". In this current, we can name thinkers of diverse origins and philosophical tendencies: Manfred Riedel[76], Wilhelm Hennis, Helmut Kuhn, Hans Georg Gadamer, Robert Spaemann and others. The social sciences are very slowly in the application of this new paradigm. The strengh of the preceding tendency is so great that it would probably take a long time to induce a change, specially in economics. That would suppose a strong turn of the research mentality towards a way of thinking alien to most economists. But it would probably be worth trying to follow the reasoning of these thinkers. In this field, we can take advantage of Weber's above mentioned contributions, i.e., his wide view of economics, specially if Hennis's theses are correct.

Let us turn to Mises now. His affirmations about the possibility of stating some general principles of human action, and his insistence on intentionality -i. e., the teleological character of actions are correct. On the other hand, the aprioristic origin of the general principles that drives him into the thesis of their infallibility and lack of link with experience as well as into their excessive formalism must be discarded. This holds also true for Mises's ethical neutrality. The fundamental characteristic of human action is to be ethical, precisely since it is teleological. Human action always receives an ethical qualification. Even though ethics and economics are diverse sciences, according to the Aristotelian view, economic action must be ethical to be a science; and the economic sciences, being a kind of human action, ought to be practical, i.e., moral, both at the individual and political level[77].

Weber sustains the need for a wide scientific knowledge about the economy and von Mises the possibility to obtain some fundamental principles from that knowledge. These two contributions, with the previous reservations, are the basis of a new proposal: a science of the economy with a main core of basic and theoretical elements, but simultaneously including cultural and ethical knowledge, valorative knowledge about the economy, with a subordinate formal instrument, i.e., current economics. According to Hennis this proposal would agree with Weber's thought, and would form an evolution of

76 Editor of a basic book on the matter: M. RIEDEL (Ed.): *Rehabilitierung der praktischen Philosophie*, Freiburg (Rombach) 1972-3.
77 ARISTOTLE: *Politics*, I, 8, 9. We developed a thoroughly study about Aristotle's fruitful notion of *oikonomiké* in: R. CRESPO: "La concepción aristotélica de la economía", *Philosophia* (Mendoza 1993), and R. CRESPO: "La acción económica en Aristóteles", *Analogia* (Méjico 1996).

the ideas of the Historical School, but with more emphasis on the theorical elements.

There are many economists -although not the majority- that have suggested the introduction of valorative elements in their science. Thus, this science will become more of the practical type in the classic sense. John Neville Keynes says: "It is universally agreed that in economics the positive investigation of the facts is not an end in itself, but is to be used as the basis of practical *enquiry*, in which ethical considerations are allowed their due weight"[78]. We can also mention Roy Harrod[79], Lindley M. Fraser[80], Colin Clark[81], Albert Hirschman[82] and others without dealing with the difficult questions about welfare economics[83]. Lionel Robbins has realized that it is necessary to develop a valorative knowledge about the economy, and suggests calling it with the old name of "Political Economy"[84]. Peter Koslowski has proposed an "Ethical Economy" program[85]. Finally, Kenneth Boulding

---

78 J. N. KEYNES: *The Scope and Method of Political Economy* (1890), 4th. ed. New York (A. M. Kelley & Millman) 1963, p. 47.

79 R. HARROD: "Scope and Method of Economics", *The Economic Journal* (1938), p. 396.

80 L. M. FRASER: "How Do We Want Economists to Behave?", *The Economic Journal* (1932), p. 562.

81 In, e.g., C. CLARK: *The Conditions of Economic Progress*, 3rd. ed. London (Mac Millan) 1967, pp. 30ff.

82 In, e.g., A. HIRSCHMAN: *L' économie comme science morale et politique*, Paris (Ed. Gallimard-du Seuil) 1984, *passim*.

83 I think that this is not a proper way, because it is simply an extension of the Neoclassical model.

84 Cf., e.g., L. ROBBINS: *Political Economy: Past and Present*, London (Mac Millan) 1976, p. 3; L. ROBBINS: *Autobiography of an Economist*, London (Mac Millan) 1971, p. 150. For a more comprehensive study of Robbins's thought, see R. CRESPO: "La noción de economía y el método de su ciencia en Lionel Robbins", *Philosophica*, 18 (Valparaíso 1996).

85 Cf. P. KOSLOWSKI: *Prinzipien der Ethischen Ökonomie. Grundlegung der Wirtschaftsethik und der auf die Ökonomie bezogenen Ethik*, Tübingen (J.C.B. Mohr) 1988; P. KOSLOWSKI: "Ethical Economy as Synthesis of Economic and Ethical Theory", in P. KOSLOWSKI: (Ed.): *Ethics in Economics, Business, and Economic Policy*, Berlin, Heidelberg, New York, Tokyo (Springer) 1992, pp. 15-56; and JEAN-PIERRE WILS: "Economy Bounded. Reflections About Peter Koslowski's Program of Ethical Economy", in: P. KOS-

should be mentioned who said that "the concept of a value-free science is absurd", and has pleaded: "Let us return then to economics as a moral science"[86]. This is the issue that can and should be retrieved from the work of Max Weber and Ludwig von Mises.

LOWSKI, Y. SHIONOYA (Eds.): *The Good and the Economical*, Berlin, Heidelberg, New York, Tokyo (Springer) 1993, pp. 89-108.

86 K. BOULDING: "Economics as a Moral Science", *American Economic Review*, LIX (1969), p. 4.

Discussion Summary

BETTINA LÖHNERT

Paper discussed:
RICARDO CRESPO: Max Weber and Ludwig von Mises, and the
                    Methodology of the Social Sciences

Oral presentation discussed:
FRITZ RINGER: Max Weber on Causal Analysis and Interpretation

I. Max Weber and Ludwig von Mises

The first part of the discussion concentrated on the problem of integrating ethics and economics within a scientific framework.

The speaker claimed that economics as a science must also be ethical. Here he refered to Aristotle who said that all human action intends to be ethical and therefore also economics has to be an ethical science (CRESPO).

To this statement the objection was uttered that if one is fighting value-free science as absurd one substitutes scientific correctness with political correctness (ACHAM). The Weberian claim to ethical pluralism and moral individualism could only be defeated by a successfully revived scientific ethic, which does not exist (RINGER).

The next part of the discussion centered around Weber's conception of value-free science. If you start from the proposition that the interests of the investigators affect the choices of ideal types and the choices of the topics for study, it does not necessarily follow, and probably also Weber would think so, that you end up with a relativism with respect to the objectivity of the results of the enquiry. Weber said, even though we might ask some questions, e.g. about Western capitalism, a Chinese might not understand, the causal claims derived from these questions should be as demonstratable for the Chinese as they are to me. Weber therefore tries to separate the impact of the changeable interests of investigators upon the choice of the explanandum, but does not in any way question the validity of the causal claims, that arise in the process of study.

Also the questions asked by natural scientists are by no means merely theory-driven but often also dictated by contemporary interests. This becomes very visible e.g. when natural scientists react to certain cultural concerns with some particular disease or some particular desaster. Supposedly the study of different kinds of diseases in cows will now increase rapidly in England.

The fact that the interests of the investigators do affect the questions, in Weber's mind did not prove that the findings were in themselves relative in the sense that they were only true for some people (RINGER).

Questions about the relationship between mainstream economics and ethics as well as problems of terminology dominated the last part of the discussion.

Attempts to involve ethical consideration in economics through the instruments of mainstream economic theory, e.g. the consideration and integration of externalities, were estimated as a controversial strategy in the search for a synthesis of ethics and economics. Oftentimes mainstream economics are a too mechanistic system to achieve this task (AVTONOMOV, CRESPO).

It was critizied that in the refereed conception of Lionel Robbins' political economy the ethical dimension of the economy to a large extent is insured through the economic dimension. This leaves a large role for conventional economics in terms of the technical implementation of policy. But if the policy makers have this ethical dimension, what is the attitude of the economic agents who make up the economy? Are not they ethical actors, too? Or do they have a different ethical system than the political agents? What could then be the ethics of the political elite who control the other ethical agents? In Lionel Robbins theory of economic policy the ethics is in the mind of the people that design the policy and he does not avoid perpetuating the idea that people in the economy are fundamentally selfish and egotistical in their motivation. Ethics comes in through the policy maker but the people in the economy are still seen as driven by materialistic interest (CASSON).

As Robbins distinguishes between economics and economic policy some clearifications in the terminology of the notions of economics, political economy, economic policy seemed to be necessary. Especially the term political economy is very equivocal. James Buchanan distinguishes between pure economics and political economy. You can use the instrument of pure economics as an analytical tool in different spheres, e.g. an economic theory of politics, which is also called political economy or the new political economy.

One has to be very clear about the definition of political economy. Is it just a synonym for economics in the older Smithian sense or is it used as a discription of an application of economic theory to politics? The newer use of political economy is better because it distinguishes between the core of economic theory as pure economic and the application of this theory to different spheres, like e.g. of economics to politics. In analogy to this use of the term "political economy" Koslowski named his approach of the application of economics on ethical and cultural questions "Ethical Economy". That is also Schumpeters methodological approach. He puts all questions of ethical, political and cultural economy under the term economic sociology (*Wirtschaftssoziologie*). This, of course, can be critical because in the end all interesting questions are moved out of economics and into the disciplines at the edge of economics and would leave only the very formal microeconomic theory at the center of pure economics. Mises restricts economics to this core in the Schumpeterian sense of pure economics. Everything else for him is history, as he calls it (KOSLOWSKI).

II. Max Weber on Causal Analysis and Interpretation

The discussion concentrated around the definition and function of Weber's concepts of causal explanation and the ideal type.

It was discussed what problem Weber tried to solve with his concept of causalism (YAGI).

In general Weber wanted to clarify the relation between particularity and generality. He wanted to explain and interprete this relation and thereby bring two divergent strands in the social sciences together (RINGER).

The suggestion was made to compare the concept of the ideal type and causal explanation with the ideas of Le Play, who was interested in the archetypical ideal type of various professions. Furthermore the ideas of the statistician Quételet could be of relevance for the understanding of Weber's concept of ideal types. Quételet was a great magician of large numbers and was not interested in the ideal type but in the mean, the average. He drew his conception of social sciences only from mean values. According to his conception of the social sciences the positivists can derive values only from mean values. Therefore the relation of Le Play to Quételet can be compared to the relation between the ideal type and causality. Quételet has shown that the discovery of the average has to do with our own shaping of normal expectations. Insofar also his conception is a causal one.

Furthermore it seems to be evident that Weber is a disciple of Mill's concept of similarity and significance. Causality as motivation is the very idea that Weber has implemented into Mill's system of logic (ACHAM).

The speaker disagreed with this interpretation and definition of Weber's concept of the ideal type. He pointed out that the ideal type as a device would not make sense, except in the context of the dyadic causal model, whether applied to the interpretation of action or other processes and their outcomes. But if we do not define the ideal type as a hypothesis, we, of course, have to deal with the question, what it actually is. If it were merely the mean, we should put it in the field and look for deviation in reality. That would be an insane tactic unless we already know exactly what kind of deviation we are looking for.

Neither does the ideal type want to construct the avarage like Quételet does. That would make the ideal type itself an empirical, inductive construct, and thus a positive construct.

Mill's methode of differences and similarities, on the other hand, is entirely static whereas Weber is looking for a dynamic approach. The aim of the speaker's work is to show both the dynamic and the structural character of some aspects of Weber's work.

It was suspected that Weber was silent on Dilthey, because he could only draw on Dilthey's works published before *Der Aufbau der geschichtlichen Welt in den Geisteswissenschaften* (The structure of the historical world in the humanities). Weber only knew Dilthey's previous book *Einleitung in die Geisteswissenschaften. Versuch einer Grundlegung für das Studium der Gesellschaft und der Geschichte* (Introduction into humanities), which he suspected of subjetivism (RINGER).

Weber has in some respect misunderstood Dilthey. Weber's sense of "Sinnadäquatheit" (adequacy to the meaning, rational adequacy) and "Kausaladäquatheit" (causal adequacy) are in some sense found in Dilthey's first book. Weber accuses Dilthey to argue only from an empathetic point of view. But Dilthey is showing that the phenomena of the moral sciences (*Geisteswissenschaften*) are connected to the idea of rules. He stresses the point that rules are not laws and is in this respect similar to Weber and to Wittgenstein (ACHAM).

Part Two

Neo-Kantianism, *Wissenssoziologie* (Sociology of Knowledge), and the Sociological Theory of Money and Exchange

Chapter 3

Value Theory and the Foundations of the Cultural Sciences. Remarks on Rickert

GUY OAKES

I. Rickert and the *Methodenstreit*

In the early 1880s, a series of disputes arose in German academia over the aims, subject matter, and methods of the social sciences. Although the *Methodenstreit* -- the controversy over methods -- began as a debate between historicists in German economics and marginal utility theorists in Vienna, by the eve of World War I, these disputes embraced philosophy, historiography, and sociology. The result was a crisis in the social sciences. Because of the privileged status enjoyed by the partisans in the debate, German university professors who were regarded as the stewards of the fundamental values of western civilization, it was translated into a crisis of modern culture.

Several interlocking issues were at stake. There was a debate over the aims of the social sciences. Here the issue was formed as a choice between an abstract theory of society, perhaps grounded in general laws of historical development, and an exposition of the singular features of social formations and cultural traditions. There was a debate over method. Is there a sense in which every legitimate scientific investigation must follow the same logic?

Or are there methods distinctive to the social sciences? These two debates were tied to a third controversy over the subject matter of the social sciences. Are human history, society, and culture indistinguishable in principle from nature and open to the same sorts of explanations and methods used in the natural sciences? Or does the fact that human beings ascribe meaning and value to their conduct require modes of interpretation for which there are no models in the natural sciences?

Finally, there was a debate about the relation between social science and social policy. This controversy was anchored in opposing views concerning science and politics, theoretical and practical reason, and the interests on which theory and practice are based. Can solutions to the practical problems of social life be derived from social science? Can social science achieve the status of an impartial judge, qualified to settle conflicts among political, economic, and ethical values because it stands above the struggles of history? Or is it an illusion to ascribe a special axiological status to science. Is science merely one value sphere among others? Are there scientific values and interests that deprive science of the authority to validate value judgments and resolve conflicts between them?

Some 100 years after they were originally posed, these issues continue to dominate the conversation about the character of the social sciences. The aims, methods, subject matter, and interests of these disciplines remain contested territory. Moreover, the German debate at the turn of the century still sets the terms, defines the problems, and frames the limits of this discussion.

If these claims seem extravagant, consider a few of the main issues in the current debate: positivism versus historicism; the primacy of explanatory theories and theoretical research programs versus the primacy of interpretation and hermeneutics; foundationalism versus perspectivism; theory construction versus its deconstruction; structural analyses versus post-structural genealogies; logic versus rhetoric; the role of narrativity and the competing claims of master and local narratives; the status of alternative conceptual schemes and the problem of adjudicating their competing claims to validity; the question of the status of scientific rationality and the problem of whether there is a plurality of incommensurable but equally legitimate criteria for rationality, each appropriate to its own sphere; the interplay between theoretical and extra-theoretical interests and the question of the interpenetration of knowledge and power.

These were also the main issues of the *Methodenstreit*. Although academic parlance and philosophical styles have changed several times over the last century, the persistence of the chief problems of the *Methodenstreit* in subsequent debates over the social sciences exhibits a striking continuity of controversy.

One important contribution to the *Methodenstreit* was Heinrich Rickert's attempt to construct the foundations of a historical science that would interpret the meaning of human conduct and its artifacts. His most influential book -- a magnum opus monstratum of more than 700 pages with the ungainly title *Die Grenzen der naturwissenschaftlichen Begriffsbildung*: "The Limits of Concept Formation in Natural Science" -- is, indeed, "the classical book" of neo-Kantian philosophy of history" (Gadamer 1967, p. 2). In *Die Grenzen*, Rickert pursues an ambitious strategy. In a critique of the logic of natural science, he argues that a historical science of culture based on positivist premises is impossible. In a critique of the limits of history, he attempts to prove that a science of history requires premises that are independent of history, thereby undertaking to refute the "absolute relativism of the sophists and modern empiricists," the enemies of reason who were intent on reducing philosophy to a melange of contingent world-views that varied with historical context and circumstance (Rickert 1986, p. 222). Finally, he proposes to achieve all this by means of arguments that are purely "formal," or, as we would say today, epistemological. In its intentions, Rickert's philosophy of history is anti-metaphysical. He repudiates the constructions of the total process, scope, and meaning of history produced by the tradition of German idealism and reconceptualizes the philosophy of history as a theory of historical knowledge. Because he understood the domain of history as culture, Rickert's theory of historical knowledge was a methodology of the cultural sciences. In the Rickertian philosophical lexicon, methodology should not be understood in its contemporary sense, as an ensemble of research techniques, but rather as a theory of concept formation. The methodology of the cultural sciences is an analysis of the concepts essential to the constitution of these sciences.

Die Grenzen[1] resembles one of those massive bourgeois villas built in the neo-classical style favored during the *Kaiserreich*. Instead of conducting

---

1   *Die Grenzen* was originally published in two parts. The first three chapters, which comprise Rickert's critique of positivism, appeared in 1896. Rickert completed chapters 4 and 5, which develop his own theory of historical knowledge, in 1901, and published the entire first edition in 1902. A second edition followed in 1913, a third and a fourth in 1921, and a fifth in 1929. The most significant addition of new material in subsequent editions is the

the reader on a tour around the exterior of this house, its ample grounds, and the surrounding neighborhood, I will restrict myself to an inspection of its foundations and interior layout. Perhaps it is just as well that space does not allow a leisurely survey of this interior. Like the great houses of the Wilhelmian period, *Die Grenzen* tends to fatigue and overwhelm with the tedium of excessive detail. The reader will be spared an exposé of the elaborate furnishings, decoration, and ornamentation of this stately structure. In short, I will confine myself to fundamentals: the analysis Rickert employs to construct the bases for a historical science of culture; the main premises of this analysis, which he borrows from his teacher Wilhelm Windelband; and some of its more important implications.

II. Windelband: Positivism, Value Theory, and History

Die Grenzen, Rickert notes, had an important precursor: the 1894 lecture of his *Doktorvater* Wilhelm Windelband: "History and Natural Science." He even suggests that a careful reading of Windelband might create the impression that his own book was, at least in some respects, a derivative and redundant enterprise whose its main ideas had been anticipated by his teacher.[2]

---

long ninth section of chapter 4 ("Nonreal Meaning Configurations and Historical Understanding"), which first appeared in the edition of 1921. It represents Rickert's most systematic response to Wilhelm Dilthey's alternative to a positivist philosophy of history. Wherever possible, I will cite the 1986 abridged translation of the fifth edition. All emphases in quotations are in the original. This essay draws liberally on OAKES (1988, 1990).

2 RICKERT (1902), p. 302n. 2, a footnote that Rickert struck from subsequent editions. In his writings, Rickert attempts to maintain an uneasy balance between ritual deference to Windelband and declarations of intellectual independence. The cultivation of his reputation dictated that he stress the latter stance over the former, a position with which he became more comfortable after Windelband's death in 1915 (RICKERT [1915a], pp. 173-75, 419-21, 446; [1915b], 24-30; [1921], 26-28, 124-25, 136-37; [1929], 55-56, 269-70, 368). Emil Lask, who studied with both Windelband and Rickert, also makes a case for the originality of *Die Grenzen* (LASK [1913]). Troeltsch

VALUE THEORY AND FOUNDATIONS OF CULTURAL SCIENCES

Two theses of "History and Natural Science" became important premises in *Die Grenzen*: the doctrine of the individuality of values and the distinction between nomothetic and idiographic knowledge. Equally important, Rickert adopts the conception of philosophy and the method of philosophical argument that Windelband advocates in his essays of the 1880s and 1890s.

In the summer of 1882, on the eve of his appointment at Strasbourg, Windelband observed that he would be expected to use his professorship to oppose positivism, which threatened to impose "the stamp of radicalism" on the university (Köhnke 1995, pp. 65-66 n. 33]. "*Die Bekämpfung des Positivismus*" -- "combatting positivism": This is an apt description of the programmatic philosophical essays Windelband published during his Strasbourg period.[3] These studies were formed by two objectives: to attack current trends in German thought that threatened to destroy philosophy by reducing it to history or psychology and to defend an autonomous conception of philosophy that would establish its academic legitimacy and independence from the empirical sciences, thereby securing institutional space for a philosophy curriculum with its own professorships, seminars, and budgets in the German university system.

In his reconstruction of the course of German philosophy following the death of Hegel, Windelband traces the disintegration of idealism and the ascendancy of philosophical positivism. Positivism translated philosophical questions into problems that could be solved by the empirical sciences. Epistemology, ethics, and aesthetics, the territory of Kant's three critiques, were annexed by history and psychology. Philosophy as an independent mode of

---

takes roughly the same view (TROELTSCH [1922], pp. 559-65). In the decade before World War I, Windelband, Rickert, and Lask were the leading figures in the Southwest German School of neo-Kantianism. There is no satisfactory study of the Southwest German School, and the literature in English is especially thin. However, see WILLEY (1978). On the relations between the philosophical positions of Windelband and Rickert, see SCHNÄDELBACH ([1974], pp. 137-59; [1983], pp. 129-34, 180-85). Windelband is a major figure in Köhnke's historical sociology of neo-Kantianism (KÖHNKE [1986]).

3 Windelband's principal essays of this period are collected in *Präludien: Aufsätze und Reden zur Philosophie und ihrer Geschichte*, published in five editions in his lifetime between 1883 and 1914. See especially: "Immanuel Kant" (1881), "Was ist Philosophie?" (1882), "Normen und Naturgesetze" (1882), "Kritische oder genetische Methode?" (1883), and "Geschichte und Naturwissenschaft" (1894) (WINDELBAND [1924]).

investigation disappeared, along with the concepts of philosophical truth and validity. The only truths were empirical, and the only arguments that could claim validity were based on the methods of the empirical sciences. There were no timeless or absolute truths or standards of truth, but only historically variable and psychologically contingent claims to truth that varied from age to age and person to person. (Windelband 1909).

Windelband's response to philosophical positivism is to attack its foundations. Positivism confused causal questions about the historical genesis of knowledge with conceptual questions about its truth and validity. Issues concerning the conditions for the logical possibility of knowledge were misconstrued as problems of fact concerning its psychological determinants. Because it conflated empirical causes and logical grounds, questions of explanation and questions of justification, and the concepts of existence and value, positivism was unable to provide a satisfactory account of either philosophy or the empirical sciences. After reality had been parceled out among the various empirical sciences, the question of their epistemic bases -- their claim to validity -- remained open and unexamined. This question was the legitimate and necessary task of philosophy.

Because validity can be ascribed only to values, Windelband conceives philosophy as a general theory of value, or axiology: the science that explores the grounds of values that are unconditionally necessary and universally valid. If values constitute the subject matter of philosophy, "critique," the inquiry into the validity of values, is its method. This view of philosophy entailed the rejection of epistemological realism and all versions of a representational theory of knowledge. The truth of a claim is not determined by a correspondence between a proposition and some objective state of affairs independent of consciousness. On the contrary, truth is a value that can be ascribed to propositions only if they satisfy absolute standards or norms of thought. All thought is subject to these absolute standards. The main task of philosophy is to elucidate the universally and necessarily valid values that define the norms of thought. These values constitute the "*Normalbewußtsein*": the "normal consciousness" or, more appropriately, the "normative consciousness." It follows that epistemology is situated within the theory of value. Just as there are ethical rules that have the force of moral absolutes and principles of perception that qualify as aesthetic absolutes, so there are absolute values on which thought itself is grounded. Because truth is a value, logic itself is subordinated to the theory of value.

64

VALUE THEORY AND FOUNDATIONS OF CULTURAL SCIENCES

In "History and Natural Science," Windelband argues that the object of any value is unique. An event that occurs more than once, an item of which there is more than one instance, or a case that falls under some more general category is of no axiological significance. To employ a concept that Windelband would have found useful, every value concept is a rigid designator requiring a unique object (Kripke 1980; Wagner 1987). Because only unique entities are possible objects of values, there is a one-to-one relationship between value concepts and their objects. Windelband traces the individualistic conception of values to the historiography of Christian theology, in which history is reduced to the story of God and his works. Everything of significance is embraced by a single narrative, the events and characters of which are unique: the creation, the fall of humanity, the chronicle of the chosen people, the incarnation, crucifixion, and resurrection of Christ, the characters of the Bible, the stories of the church fathers -- indeed, the soul and fate of every person -- are all unique and nonrepeatable. This doctrine is the basis of the interest in knowledge of what is individual: We have a theoretical interest in unique entities and events because they are the only things to which we ascribe values.

This cognitive interest in knowledge of individual phenomena cannot be satisfied by any natural science, regardless of its precision and completeness. This is because natural science brackets the distinctive qualities of things in order to disclose their common properties. Natural science represents the unique event as a case that exemplifies a type or an instance that falls under a general concept. This is the meaning of the claim that natural science is grounded in a nomothetic interest: Its objective is to develop a system of abstract laws from which the nature of things, their generic properties, can be derived. For natural science, "the colorful world of the senses" and the "earthy aura of perceptual qualities," which are essential to the individual identity of things, are cognitively irrelevant detritus (Windelband 1980, p. 179). Because natural science distinguishes reality from what really happened, it has no interest in events for their own sake and is "utterly indifferent to the past." In Windelband's metaphor, the natural sciences "drop anchor in the sea of being that is eternally the same. They are not concerned with change as such, but rather with the invariable form of change" (Windelband 1980, p. 179).

The cognitive interest of historical science, on the other hand, is idiographic. Its objective is to cover the territory that natural science leaves unexplored: the individual qualities of entities and events. History is concerned with the singular and unique aspects of things that cannot be reduced to abstract concepts or derived from general laws. Accordingly, history reconstructs "the true shape of the past" and produces "images of men and human life in the total wealth and profusion of their uniquely peculiar forms and with their full and vital individuality preserved intact" (Windelband 1980, p. 179).

The idiographic cannot be reduced to the nomothetic: "All subsumption under general laws is useless in the analysis of the ultimate causes or grounds of the single, temporally given phenomenon" (Windelband 1980, p. 184). Because the law and the event, the nomothetic and the idiographic, constitute the "ultimate, incommensurable entities of our world view", concrete reality cannot be derived from nomological regularities, (Windelband 1980, p. 185). It follows that our cognitive interest in individual phenomena that are defined by values can be satisfied only by historical science.[4]

III. Rickert: The Theory of Historical Knowledge as the Methodology of the Cultural Sciences

Die Grenzen begins where Windelband's lecture ends. The objective of historical science is knowledge of individual entities. However, in the concluding remarks of "History and Natural Science," the individual datum of history is characterized as a "residuum of incomprehensible brute fact" and an "inexpressible and indefinable phenomenon" (Windelband 1980, p. 184). Where does this conclusion leave the question of the possibility of historical knowledge?

---

4   Without mentioning Dilthey, Windelband emphasizes that the nomothetic/ idiographic dichotomy should not be confused with the distinction between the natural sciences and the *"Geisteswissenschaften"* – literally "sciences of the mind," or "human sciences" (DILTHEY [1973]). He insists that his dichotomy is based on purely formal and logical considerations. It marks a "methodological" rather than a "substantive" difference and distinguishes not two spheres of things, but two types of knowledge. The dichotomy is not ontologically grounded in differences between two kinds of entities, but axiologically defined by differences between two types of interests. It follows that nature and history are not two modes of being, but the logical objects of two different modes of investigation (WINDELBAND [1980], pp. 173-75).

In Rickert's epistemology, an item becomes a possible object of knowledge only when concepts are formed that represent it. This means that the problem of historical knowledge posed at the end of Windelband's lecture is the problem of forming concepts that represent the distinctive properties of concrete reality. Although these properties mark the beginning point of concept formation and the basis from which all conceptualization proceeds, Windelband's conclusion entails that they are not possible objects of concepts. Because concrete reality cannot be known, it marks the limits of all concept formation. Because reality cannot be conceptualized, it remains "irrational": irreducible to concepts. The result is a "*hiatus irrationalis*" between concept and reality.[5] We can know only what we can conceptualize. Since reality lies outside the limits of conceptualization, it is not a possible object of knowledge. In view of the dualism of concept and reality, how is historical knowledge possible? Is there any sense in which, the *hiatus irrationalis* notwithstanding, the individual can become an object of knowledge?

Rickert addresses these questions by developing a theory of individual or historical concept formation. The individual is defined as an object of historical knowledge by reference to what Rickert calls "value relevance" or a "value relation" (*Wertbeziehung*). Distinctive aspects of reality can be conceptualized only by defining them in terms of their relevance to values. The relation between historical individuals and values is a consequence of the consideration that the historical individual is the object of a position taken on some value. As a result of this value position, meaning is ascribed to the historical individual. Although history as a science does not take value positions, it investigates the meanings of entities that instantiate, exhibit, or express these positions. In his analysis of this theory, Rickert states four requirements that must be satisfied by the values that define value relevancies.

Historical centers. The values that define value relevancies must be drawn from the "centers" of historical interest, the primary subject matter of history. Historical centers are the persons whose value positions are responsible for the significance that is ascribed to all other historical phenomena. It follows that this first requirement is satisfied only if the historical actors whose conduct is the ultimate object of concept formation in history have made a commitment on the values that define value relevancies. This means that the

---

5   The concept is due to Emil Lask, who borrowed it from Fichte. See his doctoral dissertation *Fichtes Idealismus und die Geschichte*, completed under Rickert's direction in 1901 (LASK [1923]).

values that constitute the basis of concept formation in history are "derived from the historical *material itself*." They articulate positions on which "the beings or centers themselves -- the object of the representation -- act in a valuative fashion" (Rickert 1986, p. 127).

The value/valuation dichotomy. The historical sciences relate values to historical individuals in a purely theoretical fashion. They do not use values as standards of valuation to pass judgments on historical individuals. Although the historical individual is defined in terms of values, it is not judged on their basis. Thus the doctrine of value relevance is based on a distinction between valuations (*Wertungen*) or value judgments (*Werturteile*) and value relevancies (*Wertbeziehungen*). Rickert regards this distinction as the key to his solution to the problem of concept formation in history: "Insofar as the value perspective is decisive for history, this concept of the 'value relation' -- in opposition to 'valuation' -- is actually *the* essential criterion for history as a pure science" (Rickert 1986, p. 91).

The value/valuation dichotomy is crucial to Rickert's project in *Die Grenzen* because of his view of the irrationality of valuations. Value judgments, positive or negative valuations of meaning, are irrational in the sense that there are no principles for adjudicating conflicts between them. If all values were value judgments, the doctrine of value relevance would transpose the irrationality of value judgments onto the conceptual apparatus of the historical sciences. As a result, the claim of these disciplines to qualify as sciences would be defeated. The axiological basis of the historical sciences, which is essential to a solution of the problem of individual concept formation, would nullify their validity as sciences. Rickert's strategy for escaping this consequence is an obvious one: He argues that value relevancies are independent of practical value judgments.

> If the connection of values to objects is essential to historical science without compromising its objectivity, that is because there is a mode of value connection that does not coincide with a practical commitment and a valuation. In other words, it is because objects can be related to values in a purely *theoretical* fashion without thereby valuating these objects as deserving of praise or blame (Rickert 1924, p. 60).

Rickert's defense of the independence of value relevancies and value judgments rests on three arguments. Conflicting value judgments are possible only on the basis of a common frame of reference defined by value relevancies; thus the latter must be independent of the former. In addition, value relevancies and value judgments must be independent because of the differing interests that define them. Finally, although conflicting value judgments are ultimately incommensurable, there are principles for resolving conflicts between value relevancies, which again shows that the former are independent of the latter. In light of these considerations, Rickert concludes that it is possible to "rigorously distinguish" the theoretical domain of value relevance from the practical domain of valuation (Rickert 1986, pp. 94-95).

Although the value/valuation dichotomy remained the linchpin of Rickert's philosophy of history, his commitment to this thesis wavered as he grew old and Germany became young again. After the Nazi *Machtergreifung* of 1933, Rickert quickly discovered that conflicts between inconsistent value positions were not irresolvable after all. On the contrary, a principle for their resolution suddenly appeared quite obvious. The very existence of German culture was in the balance. "Therefore, no German who wants to have an *impact* on culture in Germany today should resist the predominance of national-political cultural goals." But suppose that a German of Rickert's time found that his own values did not conform to the political exigencies of the moment. Suppose there were a conflict between his conception of what German culture ought to be and the cultural values of the state. In view of the irrationality of value positions, how can such a conflict be decided? The solution is surprisingly simple: "He is obliged to accommodate his views on the meaning of contemporary life to the historical situation" (Rickert 1934, p. 233).

In sum, when the existence of a culture -- which Rickert identifies as the political culture of the nation -- is at stake, all cultural values must be subordinated to the values of the national state. Conditions of national emergency create a system of cultural values in which all goods are subsumed under the political values represented by the state. Here the aging advocate of timeless validities, universal principles, and absolute values begins to speak the new language of political decisionism. At this point, the distance between Rickert and Carl Schmitt is very difficult to gauge. The irrationality of value judgments is eliminated by a new meta-axiological principle: All values are compromised to the interests of national political necessity. The National Socialist slogan of the existential demands of the moment is elevated to the status of an objective value. The irrational is rationalized. Indeed, the real political demands of the day become rational because they are transposed into ultimate axioms in Rickert's hierarchy of values.

Cultural values. The values that define value relevancies do not express merely personal or subjective preferences. They articulate general norms, recognition of which is required of all members of a community. Rickert calls these norms "cultural values." Culture, the universe of cultural values, is the logically required subject matter of the historical sciences, which Rickert christens as the cultural sciences: the disciplines that investigate the meaning of reality insofar as it is constituted as historical individuals defined by reference to cultural values (Rickert 1986, pp. 82-83).

Objective validity. Finally, the cultural values that define value relevancies must be "objectively valid," binding upon everyone, regardless of historical variations in world-views, ideologies, and conceptual schemes. The appreciation of these variations and the understanding of their potentially relativistic consequences are not recent developments and did not depend upon the appearance of the jargon of postmodernism. The reception of the writings of Nietzsche and Dilthey, the crisis of historicism, the inception of *Lebensphilosophie*, and the furious responses to these developments on the part of the German philosophical establishment demonstrate that current debates over relativism are largely a reprise of a controversy that began roughly a century ago, with concepts, doctrines, and arguments repackaged and simplified for the contemporary mass retail market in intellectual goods.[6]

Following the logic of Kant's metaethics, Rickert argues that values qualify as objective only if they are unconditionally valid. Objective values should not be confused with values that everyone accepts, even if this de facto commitment is historically and culturally universal. Nor should they be conflated with values that are entailed by norms that everyone acknowledges. The validity of objective values is based on a categorical requirement that is independent of both the empirical maxims expressed in de facto commitments and the hypothetical imperatives expressed by norms.

> We must not only assume that certain values are in fact acknowledged by all the members of certain communities; we must also assume that the acknowledgment of values in general can be required as indispens-

---

6 In his *Die Philosophie des Lebens*, Rickert flays Nietzsche, Simmel, Bergson, and Scheler as the advocates of a new, fashionable, destructive, and ultimately nihilistic relativism. For Windelband and Rickert, Nietzsche was the new Mephistopheles of German thought, a seductive and dangerous poet-philosopher. On Rickert's response to this development in German philosophy, see GIUGLIANO [1987, 1996].

able for every scientist, and thus that the relation of unique and individual reality to *some* values that have a general validity that is more than empirical is *necessary*. Scientific necessity can be ascribed to a historical representation only under this condition (Rickert 1986, pp. 105-106).

Because cultural values express "purely human value positions" -- de facto value commitments, the subjective validity of which is not diminished by the consideration that they may be the product of a universal consensus -- the cultural sciences depend upon a transcendental presupposition: namely, the requirement that "*some* values are *unconditionally* valid and that all human value positions stand in a more or less proximate *relation* to them that is defined as more than capricious. If this were not so, purely scientific history with a value-relevant, individualizing concept formation could never be written" (Rickert 1986, p. 205).

Rickert emphasizes that this presupposition is purely formal. It does not entail the objective validity of any given cultural value, regardless of its universality or the strength of the consensus on its validity. However, he also insists that such a formal requirement is sufficient to solve the problem of the possibility of historical knowledge. Suppose that "*some* values or other are absolutely valid," even though the question of which values satisfy this condition remains open. And suppose also that the cultural values that define value relevancies approximate these objective values more or less closely. In that case, the problem of the axiological bases of the cultural sciences -- the elimination of subjectivity and contingency from value relevancies -- is solved. Rickert summarizes his case in the following terms.

> For suppose that at least *some* values or other are absolutely valid. And suppose that, in consequence, substantively embodied and normatively general human values objectively approximate them more or less closely. Then human cultural development also has a necessary relation to unconditionally valid values. As a result, the attempt to establish knowledge of the unique process of history with reference to normatively general values can no longer be regarded as a product of mere caprice (Rickert 1986, p. 205).[7]

---

7 Notwithstanding Rickert's usual caveats concerning the exclusively formal import of his statements on the objective validity of values, it seems that there are certain privileged cultural values that he elevates to this sublime status. See, for example, his judgment on the indubitable cultural significance of

IV. From the Critique of Metaphysics to Scholasticism

Although Rickert's main foil in *Die Grenzen* is positivism, he also rejects metaphysics as a basis for the historical sciences. In Rickert's view, the definitive feature of metaphysics is the premise of ontological dualism: the postulate of two worlds, an authentic or absolute reality that transcends consciousness and an ontologically inferior world of phenomena that are objects of consciousness. Although the two worlds are connected by a process of representation, emanation, or reflection, the phenomenal world is an imperfect realization of the world of true being (Rickert 1915a, pp. 117-19; 1986, p. 208).

For Rickert and his contemporaries, German idealism as developed by Wilhelm von Humboldt, J. G. Droysen, and, above all, Hegel was the paradigmatic expression of a metaphysical conception of history. In Rickert's interpretation of this tradition, history is a series of stages in which a comprehensive plan is progressively realized in accordance with an inevitable logic of development. Historical events are manifestations of the ideas or concepts from which they are derived. This process of derivation is both logical and ontological. Because the concepts of absolute reality are epistemic grounds of historical phenomena or conditions for the possibility of historical knowledge, knowledge of history is a deduction of historical events from concepts. Because concepts are ontological grounds of historical events or conditions for the possibility of historical existence, they are also the ultimate causes of historical phenomena. Thus historical causation is both a conceptual and a real connection. History is an ontological and logical emanation in which

---

Martin Luther: "It can never occur to a historian to claim that Luther's personality is historically *unimportant*" (RICKERT [1986], p. 93). Rickert considers the possibility that a historian "completely alien to German and Christian social life" might regard Luther as historically insignificant. However, he disposes of this possibility by arguing that if the alien historian understood the concept of religious values, he would have the conceptual apparatus necessary to understand Luther on the basis of the values that define "German and Christian" historiography. Thus even for the alien historian, there is a sense in which the cultural value of Luther's personality would retain its objective validity (RICKERT [1986], p. 200).

historical events are produced and entailed by a single, unified conceptual process.

Rickert argues that history as a science is impossible on these assumptions. A metaphysics of history rules out a solution to the basic problem of concept formation in history. This is the problem of identifying a principle of selection: Given the infinite complexity of reality, how can historically significant entities be differentiated from historically irrelevant and axiologically indifferent phenomena? On the premises of a metaphysics of history, this question has no answer. If the empirical world is the emanation of absolute reality, every empirical phenomenon is equally necessary for the realization of true being. In that case, every historical event has the same meaning. If all historical events are merely stages in the realization of the absolute, then every historical individual has the same significance. This means that no historical individual has any significance. Since historical entities are defined by reference to their differential meaning, historical individuals would no longer be possible. Historical concepts that distinguish historical individuals both from one another and from the historically indifferent manifold of reality could no longer be formed. As a result, Rickert concludes, "history no longer exists" (Rickert 1986, p. 213). It follows that history is possible only on the basis of nonmetaphysical premises. For Jakob Burckhardt, a metaphysics of universal history that reconstructs a total process, ultimately leading to the realization of some final end or purpose, was laughable. For Rickert, it was a logical impossibility.

Although Rickert rejects the old metaphysics of Hegel and German idealism, his own strategy for solving the problem of historical knowledge by positing a domain of objective values revives an even older metaphysics. In basing historical knowledge on ahistorical values to which he ascribes a super-validity that is not of this world, Rickert goes beyond Hegel and further back --not back to Kant, but to scholasticism: Reality is anchored in a timeless and transcendent teleology of objective values (Wagner 1987).

In the Rickertian scheme of things, the world cannot be reduced to reality. In addition to realities, subjects and objects that exist, there are values that do not exist. In Rickert's world, only real things exist: subjects or persons who take positions on values and the objects to which values are ascribed. But if values do not exist, it what sense can it be said that there "are" values? What does it mean to say that a value is something that is "not nothing" even though it does not exist (Rickert 1921, p. 12)? Rickert's answer to these questions is not easy to follow. The domain of values is not existence, but validity. Put another way, if, contrary to an important tradition in 20th century philosophy, existence and validity are understood as predicates, then only existence can be predicated of realities and only validity can be predicated of values. Because it can be said that values are valid or invalid, but not that they exist, the question of their existence is absurd. Values form "an autonomous sphere that lies *beyond subject and object*" (Rickert 1910, p. 12). Objective values obtain independent of all actors and acts of valuation. They are axiological objects (*Wertobjekte*) that hold validly even if their validity is acknowledged by no one. This is the sense in which "nonreal values obtain as an autonomous domain in opposition to all real objects, which also form an autonomous domain" (Rickert 1921, p. 114).[8]

Rickert's repudiation of metaphysics is based on an elaborate metaphysical conceit. The unconditionally valid values that provide the foundation for the cultural sciences are distinguished from the cultural values on which historical actors take a position only by postulating a realm of timeless and transcendent objective values. Thus Rickert rejects the old metaphysics of Hegel and reintroduces an even older metaphysics of scholasticism under a new name: the project of constructing a system of values. The definitive feature of the old metaphysics remains: the dualism of an empirical world and a hidden, privileged, and more authentic world. In Rickert's thought, the higher world is axiologically rather than ontologically privileged. His metaphysics postulates transcendent values rather than transcendent beings.

V. From the Critique of Historicism to Decisionism

The historical turn that embraced the various historical schools in 19th century German thought -- from theology and philosophy to jurisprudence, economics, linguistics, folklore, and musicology -- has aptly been character-

---

8 Because reality and values jointly constitute the world, there must be some sense in which there are values, even if this sense does not entail existence. This reasoning leads Rickert, the champion of "scientific philosophy," to indulge in quasi-oracular utterances, such as the claim that "there are objects that exist and objects that do not exist" (RICKERT [1921], p. 116). On the problems posed by Rickert's conception of values, see SEIDEL (1968) and OBERER (1987).

ized as a "historization of history": the repudiation of ahistorical and metaphysically grounded models of the historical process and the rejection of the premise that history is a function of timeless laws of change that transcend history itself. The mind transposed all of existence into history and finally translated itself into a historical artifact. This result defined a new historical consciousness in two senses: a consciousness of existence as historical and a reflexive consciousness of reason itself as a product of history. In the final analysis, historical consciousness was the knowledge of its own limits and contingency: the self-knowledge of reason as circumscribed by history (Schnädelbach 1983).

In opposition to historicism, which holds that history defines the limits of reason, Rickert argues that history as a science is possible only if reason defines the limits of history. By historicizing all values, historicism denies the premise on which the possibility of historical science depends: the transcendental assumption that there are values the validity of which is independent of the contingencies of history. Rickert did not vacate the temple of German idealism in order to rebuild on its site a "glass house of relativism" (Rickert 1986, p. 222). In the introduction to *Die Grenzen*, he contends that a consistent historicism would "end in relativism, even in nihilism" (Rickert 1986, p. 18). Historicism is relativistic because it entails that the validity of all values is subject to the caprice of history. As a result, no value can be more or less valid than any other. It is nihilistic because the historical contingency of all values negates the presupposition on which the objective validity of any value can be established: the possibility of values the validity of which transcends history. A historical science of culture is grounded in value relevancies that are ultimately defined by objective values. This means that historical science is possible only by determining the limits of history. The boundaries of history can be defined only by premises that are independent of the process of historization, and thus lie outside history.

In the same way that the Enlightenment required a critique of theoretical reason that established the limits of concept formation in natural science, the historicist enlightenment required a critique of historical reason that would establish the limits of concept formation in historical science. However, that critique could not be produced by employing the logic of the historicist enlightenment itself: namely, by combatting historicism with its own weapons. A critique in the older, Kantian sense was necessary: an inquiry into the metahistorical premises on which the possibility of historical knowledge depends. This meant that it was necessary to fortify a domain of reason that is located beyond history. Thought is not exhausted by the historical consciousness. On the contrary, historical consciousness is possible only on the basis of a transcendental consciousness that defines the limits of history.

In order to escape the consequences of historicism, Rickert introduces an absolute distinction between values and reality and posits a realm of ahistorical objective values. However, he also maintains that there are different types of value that form distinctive value spheres and structure reality on the basis of quite different principles. These value spheres constitute different "worlds." The pragmatic world of everyday life is not "*the* world, but rather merely one of the possible worlds, in addition to which others are equally possible" (Rickert 1921, p. 8). Pragmatics, science, ethics, aesthetics, and religion form distinctive orders of value. On their basis, human beings construct different worlds by drawing the distinction between what is significant and what is not in different ways.

Rickert argues that there is no final principle, independent of these various spheres of value, by means of which choices among them can be made. Choices among value positions taken in different axiological spheres and decisions about the relative validity of value claims made on the basis of different orders of value cannot be justified by universal principles of value, because there are no such principles. These issues are decided by subjective value judgments. Rickert leaves the choice among ultimate values and value spheres to the personal dispositions of the individual. If such a choice has any basis at all, it is grounded in the individual's own "personal and extrascientific or suprascientific character" (Rickert 1921, p. 407).

All of which is to say that Rickert's system of objective values entails a decisionistic conception of value choices. In the metaphorical language made famous by Max Weber, each of the value spheres of modern culture is ruled by its own gods or demons, the divine or diabolical powers that hold sway over the various axiological orders of life. Because of the polytheism of values and the war of the gods of culture, there is an "irreconcilable conflict" and an "eternal struggle" among the various spheres of value. This is why the individual must choose among ultimate values and decide, not infer or deduce, "which is God for him and which is the devil." As a personal decision, this choice is binding only on the individual, and only because it expresses his "ultimate standpoint" (Weber 1946, p. 148).

"Two paths are open," Weber observed: "Hegel or -- *our* way of handling things" (Schluchter 1996, p. 227 n. 9). Hegel's way was the metaphysics of history, which Rickert rejected. Weber's way was to accept historicism and the war of the gods. Rickert attempted to find a third way: to steer a course between the dead sea of metaphysics and the shifting shoals of historicism on which all navigators were doomed to destruction. Rickert's third course proved to be an illusion. His system of values led in two directions. The theory of objective values ends in metaphysics. The theory of autonomous value spheres ends in decisionism. Thus did Rickert unwittingly embrace the mutually inconsistent positions of his enemies.

References

DILTHEY, WILHELM: *Einleitung in die Geisteswissenschaften, Gesammelte Schriften*, vol. I, Stuttgart (Teubner) 1973.

GADAMER, HANS-GEORG: "Das Problem der Geschichte in der neueren deutschen Philosophie", in: H.-G. GADAMER: *Kleine Schriften*, vol. I, Tübingen (Mohr) 1967, pp. 1-10.

GIUGLIANO, ANTONELLO: "H. Rickert tra Philosophie des Lebens e Lebensphilosophie", *Atti dell'Accademia di Scienze Morali e Politiche*, XCVIII (1987), pp. 277-95.

GIUGLIANO, ANTONELLO: "Note sulla critica filosofica di Rickert e Heidegger alla psicologia delle 'visioni-del-mondo' di Jaspers", *Atti dell'Accademia di Scienze Morali e Politiche*, CVI (1996), pp. 165-222.

KÖHNKE, KLAUS-CHRISTIAN: *The Rise of Neo-Kantianism*, tr. R.J. Hollingdale, New York (Cambridge University Press) 1991.

KÖHNKE, KLAUS-CHRISTIAN: "Sinn für Institutionen. Mitteilungen aus Wilhelm Windelbands Heidelberger Zeit (1903-1915)", in: HUBERT TREIBER and KAROL SAUERLAND (Eds.): *Heidelberg im Schnittpunkt intellektueller Kreise*, Opladen (Westdeutscher Verlag) 1995, pp. 32-69.

KRIPKE, SAUL: *Naming and Necessity*, Cambridge (Harvard University Press) 1980.

LASK, EMIL: "Rez. der 2. Aufl. von Rickerts *Grenzen der Naturwissenschaftlichen Begriffsbildung*", *Logos*, 4 (1913), pp. 246-48.

LASK, EMIL: *Gesammelte Schriften*, vol. I, Tübingen (Mohr) 1923.

OAKES, GUY: *Weber and Rickert*, Cambridge (MIT Press) 1988.

OAKES, GUY: *Die Grenzen der kulturwissenschaftlichen Begriffsbildung*, Frankfurt (Suhrkamp) 1990.

OBERER, HARIOLF: "Transzendentalsphäre und konkrete Subjektivität", in H.L. Ollig (Ed): *Materialien zur Neukantianismus-Diskussion*, Darmstadt (Wissenschaftliche Buchgesellschaft) 1987.

RICKERT, HEINRICH: *Die Grenzen der naturwissenschaftlichen Begriffsbildung*, Tübingen (Mohr) 1902, ^{2}1913, ^{3,4}1921, ^{5}1929.

RICKERT, HEINRICH: "Vom Begriff der Philosophie", *Logos*, I (1910-11), pp. 1-34.

RICKERT, HEINRICH (1915a): *Der Gegenstand der Erkenntnis*, Tübingen (Mohr) 1915.

RICKERT, HEINRICH (1915b): *Wilhelm Windelband*, Tübingen (Mohr) 1915.

RICKERT, HEINRICH: *Die Philosophie des Lebens*, Tübingen (Mohr) 1920.

RICKERT, HEINRICH: *System der Philosophie*, Tübingen (Mohr) 1921.

RICKERT, HEINRICH: *Die Probleme der Geschichtsphilosophie*, Tübingen (Mohr) 1924.

RICKERT, HEINRICH: *Grundprobleme der Philosophie. Methodologie, Ontologie, Anthropologie*, Tübingen (Mohr) 1934.

RICKERT, HEINRICH: *The Limits of Concept Formation in Natural Science*, tr. Guy Oakes, New York (Cambridge University Press) 1986.

SCHLUCHTER, WOLFGANG: *Unversöhnte Moderne*, Frankfurt (Suhrkamp) 1996.

SCHNÄDELBACH, HERBERT: *Geschichtsphilosophie nach Hegel*, Frankfurt (Suhrkamp) 1974.

SCHNÄDELBACH, HERBERT: *Philosophy in Germany, 1831-1933*, tr. Eric Matthews, New York (Cambridge University Press) 1983.

SEIDEL, HERMANN: *Wert und Wirklichkeit in der Philosophie Heinrich Rickerts*, Bonn (Bouvier) 1968.

TROELTSCH, ERNST: *Der Historismus und seine Probleme*, Tübingen (Mohr) 1922.

WAGNER, GERHARD: *Geltung und normativer Zwang. Eine Untersuchung zu den neukantianischen Grundlagen der Wissenschaftslehre Max Webers*, Freiburg (Alber) 1987.

WEBER, MAX: *From Max Weber: Essays in Sociology*, tr. H.H. Gerth and C. Wright Mills, New York (Oxford University Press) 1946.

WILLEY, T. E.: *Back to Kant*, Detroit (Wayne State University Press) 1978.

WINDELBAND, WILHELM: *Die Philosophie im deutschen Geistesleben des XIX. Jahrhunderts*, Tübingen (Mohr) 1909.

WINDELBAND, WILHELM: *Präludien: Reden und Aufsätze zur Philosophie und ihrer Geschichte*, Tübingen (Mohr) 1924.

WINDELBAND, WILHELM: "History and Natural Science", *History and Theory*, XIX (1980), pp. 166-85.

Chapter 4

The Sociology of Knowledge and Diagnosis of Time with Max Scheler and Karl Mannheim

KARL ACHAM

I. Introduction

When Earle Edward Eubank visited European sociologists in the summer of 1934, he held conversations with Hans Freyer, Franz Oppenheimer, Werner Sombart, Ferdinand Tönnies, Alfred Vierkandt, Alfred Weber and Leopold von Wiese in Germany and with Othmar Spann and Erich Voegelin in Austria. They were asked to appraise and define their attitude to a number of German speaking sociologists and also, primarily, to name those authors who, for them, were the most significant. Including the nine taking part in the conversations with Eubank, the talk turned to some 36 sociologists from German-speaking countries. From today's point of view, one of the remarkable outcomes of this lay in the fact that Max Scheler and Karl Mannheim were each mentioned only once during the talks: Max Scheler by Alfred Vierkandt, who gave Scheler's work and influence a positive rating, and Karl Mannheim by Leopold von Wiese, who assessed him very affirmatively.[1]

What Scheler and Mannheim have in common is, of course, not limited to these circumstances. The relationship established between them in the title of this article is in no way an artificial one, and this is particularly demonstrated by the fact that Mannheim's first article that distinctively dealt with sociology of knowledge, *"Das Problem einer Soziologie des Wissens"* (1925) [*"The Problem of a Sociology of Knowledge"*], reads like a detailed critique of Scheler's treatise *"Probleme einer Soziologie des Wissens"* [*"Problems of a Sociology of Knowledge"*][2], which had just appeared for the first time in 1924. Moreover, in the *Prager Presse* in 1937, Mannheim characterised Scheler's book *Die Wissensformen und die Gesellschaft [Forms of Knowledge and Society]* from the year 1926 - along with some others - as a work of "revolutionary significance".[3] There were still, however, definite characteristics common to both authors, of which only two are to be especially highlighted here: a certain disquiet and striving after a compensation for and reconciliation of the heterogene.

Although, initially, Scheler stood under the influence of his neo-idealistic mentor Rudolf Eucken, after his meeting with Edmund Husserl (1901) he subscribed to the phenomenological method, which, however, he soon arbitrarily refashioned and, in doing so, he held himself open all the time to the influences of the life-philosophy of Wilhelm Dilthey and Henri Bergson. Again, Mannheim at the start stood close to Georg Lukács and the Budapest Marxists coming over from Idealism, without, indeed, later sharing their Bolshevistic leanings; rather was he to show himself, in his thinking, increasingly associated with the sociology of Max Weber as well as with pragmatic American philosophy. If, as with his scandal-enshrouded liaisons with women and love affairs, Scheler experienced a series of transformations and "turn-

---

1   Cf. DIRK KÄSLER: *Soziologische Abenteuer*, pp. 35f., 72 and 162.

2   This treatise appeared first as an introductory part of the collected work *Versuche zu einer Soziologie des Wissens [Essays on a Sociology of Science]* (München 1924) commissioned by the Cologne Research Institute for Social Sciences. It was then incorporated by Scheler in the first edition of the book *Forms of Knowledge and Society* in 1926.

3   Cf. KURT H. WOLFF: "Karl Mannheim", pp. 342f.

ings" in his basic religious bearings, in consequence of which he arrived at a pantheistic metaphysic, so too is Mannheim's thinking stamped, above all, by changes in attitude connected with emigration from Hungary to Germany and later from Germany to Great Britain. He moved ever more from being the contemplative analyst of philosophies of life to being the apologist for what was characterised by him as a "planned State" and this was on the basis of the experimental style of pragmatic philosophy as well as of having regard for Europe's social-political traditions.[4] After 1933, the consequence was, for Mannheim, a fundamental transformation of the questions to be posed. If he was asking, in his German period, how one can be fair to the Mind in its unpredictability and inexhaustibility even when showing most ruthlessly its relativity throughout Society, so, for him, in his English phase, the question was to a large extent how Society itself is to be saved, from which, ultimately, even the possibilities of an intellectual conduct of life are inseparable.

If gradually a balance between the intellectual and the social came to pass with Mannheim, so, with Max Scheler, towards the end of his life, the wish was expressed for a reconciliation of the heterogeneous tendencies, within the intellectual and the social spheres also. In the essay "Der Mensch im Weltalter des Ausgleichs" [*"Mankind in the Age of Adjustment"*] in 1927, Scheler summarised his discussions of basic historical-philosophical ascendancy and descendancy theories as follows: "If I had to inscribe *one* name on the door of the age that is approaching, which should reflect the comprehensive tendency of this era, then it seems to me that there is only one suitable one - it is called 'Adjustment'."[5] This adjustment, according to Scheler affected natural as well as intellectual differences: racial tensions, mentalities, male and female casts of mind, capitalism and socialism, upper and lower classes, civilised and primitive peoples, technical science and education in the humanities, economic and intellectual interests as well as the various one-sided ideas about Man or the images of Man.[6] According to Scheler this tendency to-

---

4 Mannheim worked at the London School of Economics. This University School was a creation of the Fabian Society and, in accordance with the wishes of its founders, it was supposed to be demonstrated here that science can give directive rules to policy. After the Second World War, a new State and a new Society was supposed to be built. Salvation was to be expected from planning and Mannheim, too, probably tried to conform to this expectation.

5 MAX SCHELER: *Späte Schriften*, p. 151.

6 Cf. *ibid.*, p. 152.

wards adjustment is Mankind's inescapable destiny. It is nevertheless the task of the Mind and the Will to direct this adjustment, so that it is commensurate with a development of the values of the specific individual and social type.[7] Scheler's endeavours are very similar to the efforts of Ernst Troeltsch for a "cultural synthesis" and it was not for nothing that he was consequently also described as the "Philosopher of the Synthesis" or of the "third way".[8] Mannheim's attempt, yet again, consisted in substantiating evidence of a compatibility of epistemological and of sociology of knowledge questioning, and thus to show how the repute of the question of truth is not brought into doubt by so doing, that the cultural significance or "validity" of assertions are perceived in their dependency on social data. In his English period, moreover, Mannheim strove for a compromise or - expressed more circumspectly - for a proof of the complementary nature of two other orientations: the principles of democracy and of planning. Thus, he concluded in his book *Mensch und Gesellschaft im Zeitalter des Umbaus* [*Man and Society in an Age of Reconstruction*]: "We can perhaps say that it [...] is indeed impossible to come to a compromise between the old principle of 'laisser-faire' liberalism and planning but, that notwithstanding, planning and democracy are not only compatible with one another but mutually complementary".[9]

The efforts of Scheler and Mannheim, which are traceable in their books, for a synthesisation of one-sided or seemingly one-sided positions represents a reflection upon wholly determinist contemporary ways of thinking. The advocates of the historic humanities as a body were, up to the end of the first World War and then yet again until 1933, tied to general conceptions of State and Society, which subsequently seemed to be overtaken by a reality of a completely different kind. Hence, Scheler's and Mannheim's "syntheses" are likewise not simply eidetic imaginative conceptual collages but rather combinations or resultants of alternative maxims for action. Sociology, which after the first World War had risen to an intellectual height that had to be reckoned with, had made great efforts to look for answers to the questions of the day, which were exercising the minds of the general public. So it turned to that science from which one expected that it would make possible the clarification and orientation, which had previously been sought in the humanities.

---

7   Cf. *ibid.*
8   Cf. with this WALTER L. BÜHL: "Max Scheler", p. 190.
9   KARL MANNHEIM: *Mensch und Gesellschaft im Zeitalter des Umbaus*, p. 423; cf. original, p. 364.

Even the sociological works of Scheler and Mannheim were seen as a contribution to the theory of social practice, which should make it possible to transform the world of ideas by act of will and, therefore, if need be, to understand syntheses of images of the world as syntheses of behaviour and to carry them over into new forms of integrated activities.

II. Sociology of Knowledge

After 1918, Sociology was the place in Germany where the humanities, which had fallen into a crisis with their unsolved problems were raised into consciousness. On the one hand, its interest was applicable to modern society, while the historic cultural sciences were looking at the past and, on the other, it made the boundaries of the humanities themselves visible to a certain degree. It was precisely for the reason that it seized on current social and cultural questions, which the humanities did not even pose, that it gained self-confidence and a certain reputation in society. The sociology of knowledge is an excellent example of that. If conventional philosophy was committed to positivism, formal apriorism, material apriorism and historicism, in connection with which a real absence of relationships was presupposed, between the systematic orientation of the philosophy and the historic view of social events, between therefore, in the narrower sense, the theoretical and the historico-empirical domains, then the modern sociology of knowledge orientation seemed to be able to leap this boundary. Hence, the decisive argument between material apriorism, that is Max Scheler's doctrine of values, on the one side, and the historism, as it was represented, after Dilthey, in a simply exemplary manner by Karl Mannheim, did not end up in a basic clash of alternative viewpoints but in debates about under what historico-social operating conditions invariant human needs and the value orientations, corresponding to them can adopt quite differing forms of being realised or of themselves being transformed in their essence. The problem, inherent in this debate, of the relationship between socio-cultural stratification and experience of reality, between a place in society and a perspective view of things as they are, became both for Scheler and for Mannheim the object of the demonstration analysis of the sociology of knowledge. Mannheim furnished it with the name of "Relationism" and tried in this manner to demarcate it from a gnoseological relativism.

1. Scheler

It is not easy to isolate Scheler's sociology of knowledge from his teachings on the philosophy of life. A critique as to the limited meaning of the
concept of science underlies it, as it is presupposed in Comte's three-phase
model of the history of the mind's development in mankind. What the latter
had endeavoured to prove as a sequence of styles of thinking in the course of
history, - religion, metaphysics, positive science - is seen by Scheler as a
simultaneously provable expression of "forms of knowledge"; and as far as it
touches on the specific leading sector of social development, the factors of
blood, power and economy are predominant in the course of human history,
according to Scheler. Concerning this, though, there will be still something
further to say below.

Regarding the co-existing forms of knowledge, to judge the development
of knowledge of the whole of humanity according to a minor stretch of curve
in the development of modern western countries appears to Scheler to be a
presumptuous and untenable positivist idea. Thus Scheler shows that he is
impressed by Wilhelm Dilthey too, when the latter points out in his typology of philosophies that, - like the case of Kant's three faculties of the soul,
understanding, reason and discernment - three diverse forms of rationality correspond to the philosophical orientations of "Naturalism", of the "Idealism of
Liberty" and of "objective Idealism".[10] Like Dilthey, Scheler too is of the
opinion that what is called "cognition theory" pays heed to only *one* kind of
cognition, namely that of *positive science*. For that reason an analysis of different forms of knowing or thinking is needed, in which, though, "*the unity
of the idea of knowledge* must not be lost on account of the new discoveries
of the kinds and forms of knowing and perceiving".[11] Thus, according to
Scheler, knowledge has to be defined without a particular kind of this knowledge being used in the definition. For knowledge is, for Scheler

> a *circumstance of being* - and one, at that, which presupposes the
> forms of being of the whole and the part. It is the condition of the par-
> ticipation of an existent being with the being *per se* as it is of another
> existent being, by which no kind of alteration of any description is
> sown within this being as it is. The "known" becomes "part" of that

---

[10] Cf. with this WILHELM DILTHEY: *Weltanschauungslehre*, pp. 19-22 and pp.
100-118.

[11] MAX SCHELER: *Die Wissensformen und die Gesellschaft*, p. 201.

which "knows", without, though, moving from its position in any respect while doing so or becoming otherwise changed at all.[12]

With these definitions of knowledge Scheler constituted his doctrine of the Perspectivism or Aspectual Character of "forms of knowledge".

In a certain way analogous to Dilthey, Scheler outlined his own three-membered typology of knowledge, which one may, with good reasons, call a typology of cognition interests. In diverse dissertations he drew a distinction between the awareness of salvation or redemption, awareness of having been cultured and awareness of accomplishment and power.[13] There are, according to Scheler, three wholly differing *motives* (to wit, self-affirmation by surrender to a Higher Power - wonder, - an aspiration for power and ambition to command), three different *origins* and *methods of acquiring knowledge* (the charismatic leader's divine contact - thinking ideas out - inductive and deductive conclusions), three different *leadership model types* (homo religiosus - mentor - researcher and technician), on which these three orientations of knowledge are based.[14] Scheler, moreover, is at pains also to point out specific forms of these three forms of knowledge's developmental movement and of the disciplines appropriate to them and, further, the different *basic social forms*, in which the acquisition of knowledge and its preservation are presented, their different *functions* in human society as well as, finally, their diverse *social origin,* arising from classes, occupations and social groups.[15]

According to Scheler, each of the major spheres of culture has developed in their history up to now one of the three sorts of knowledge in a specifically concentrated manner: in India it has been the lore of redemption and the vital psychic technique of Man's winning power over himself, in China and Greece the knowledge of education and in Western lands, since the beginning of the 12th Century the knowledge of the working of the constructive technical sciences.[16] In a manner typical of him and reminiscent of Ernst

---

12 *Idem*, p. 203.
13 Cf. MAX SCHELER: *idem*, pp. 65-67 and p. 205 as well as *Späte Schriften*, pp. 75-84.
14 Cf. MAX SCHELER: *Die Wissensformen und die Gesellschaft*, pp. 68f.
15 Cf. *idem*, pp. 69-123, and MAX SCHELER: "Die positivistische Geschichts-philosophie des Wissens und die Aufgaben einer Soziologie der Erkenntnis", pp. 61-66.
16 Cf. MAX SCHELER: *Die Wissensformen und die Gesellschaft*, p. 125 and p. 210.

Troeltsch's "cultural synthesis", Scheler pointed out that, at that juncture, mankind's entire potentiality for cognition, and thus integral knowledge, would only be revealed with the union of the European and the Asiatic cultures of knowledge.[17]

Scheler enlarges the *co-existence* of types of knowledge systems by the proof of a *sequence* of the primacy of active factors in the course of the historical development which was established by using the resources of historical sociology. Thereby the moot question concerns a three-phase model of the universal history, which endeavours, on the one hand, to integrate the conceptions of the main representatives of the three major trends and, on the other, to historicise them: the conceptions of the "racial nativism", of the "politism" and the "economism". Gumplowicz and Gobineau here, the Rankeans and their successors there, and, then, Karl Marx and the socialist social theoreticians - all, according to Scheler, representing a biased orientation of universal history. With them, for the most part, there an effective assumption that the active factor of the historical development, seen by each as independent variables, always has the same causal significance for the entire process of history. Against that, Scheler established:

> In the course of history, there are *no constant* independent variables among the three highest main group of real factors - Blood, Power and Economy - but there are, notwithstanding, *laws on the ranking of the specific primacy* of their inhibiting and dis-inhibiting effectiveness in the history of the intellect, i.e. there is for each a *differing* law on ranking for specified *phases* of the course of a culture's history.[18]

Scheler sees - like Gumplowicz, Weber and Marx - the connection between demographic-ethnic, political and economic conditions, on the one hand, and cultural evaluations and intellectual formation on the other. He does not want, however, to be satisfied with the proof of correlations between the two classes of events but wants rather to know how to comprehend this framework of "realistic factors" and "idealistic factors" as conditions of effective agency, under which the values, conceived by him as absolute, develop in their concrete and very multifarious form.

Alongside the proof of the real factors it is the *ethos* in particular that supplies, for Scheler, the point of approach for his historical-sociological as well as for his anthropological analysis. This idea encompasses those biolog-

---

17 Cf. *idem*, pp. 135-158 and pp. 210f.
18 *Idem*, p. 44.

ical-behavioral components, which are being examined today by ethology and which - as Walter L. Bühl has remarked - was labelled by Scheler with the term "drive", which has given cause for constant misunderstandings; the idea encompasses, as well, the cultural components in the sense of a value-orientated behaviour.[19] As far as the culture is concerned, we stand, according to Scheler, within the framework of fixed environmental structures and collectives, inasmuch as our behavioural patterns for generations have been widely handed down to us and in this manner have become second nature. It is equally as valid to connect these empirical ideal factors and the empirical real factors now to the world of the values already assumed from time to time to be invariable as well as to the logical and axiological principles. Scheler, therefore, is no gnoseological relativist in the sociology of knowledge but - entirely within the meaning of the designation later formulated by Karl Mannheim - a gnoseological "relationist" and he is, in the doctrine of values, a representative not of the axiological relativism, but doubtless for all that of occasional relativism.

Scheler's view that, behind every transformation of the images of the world, such a thing as proof of the conditions for their creation and of the cultural significance of each of them is feasible can be admitted to only if it presupposes the binding force of invariable logical principles and rules. He, who even in his later work developed a typology of five basic anthropological ideas[20], already gave early voice to its science-friendly relationism as a sociology of knowledge:

> The *images* of the world may revolve ceaselessly along in the stream of the times but the design laws for the begetting of these images stand firm. The notion of an image of the world common to the historical humanity has gone to the grave along with Grecian knowledge.[21]

According to Scheler, the actualising factors of the natural world, but also of the historico-social world, in respect of the logical-noological principles and laws assumed as pre-existent for each and every cognisance of matters of fact or values, - these factors possess only a relevance of facticity; a relevance of truth is not part of these factors. Thus in the scientific world, the manifold empirical conditions determine solely the 'to be' or 'not to be' of images of

---

19 Cf. WALTER L. BÜHL: "Max Scheler", p. 202 f.
20 Cf. MAX SCHELER: *Späte Schriften,* pp. 124-144.
21 Cf. MAX SCHELER: *Frühe Schriften,* p. 361.

the world, of society and of mankind, and this is true both for their
descriptive and for their normative content.

In the analyses of the sociology of knowledge, which he devoted to the
normative conceptions or to the "currently established philosophies of ways
of looking at the world"[22] as he called them, it ought not in his view be a
matter of tearing sociology apart into two sections, a " sociology of the actual" and a "sociology of the culture". Scheler wanted much more to comprehend ideas, in the way Max Weber did, as "switchmen" of the interests,[23]
and, as a consequence, the task of the sociology of knowledge can consist in
the following in regard to its normative content: in the -

> Examination of the entity and action, valuation and behaviour of Man,
> which are, *in the main, intellectually* conditioned and directed at intel-
> lectual i.e. *'ideal'* ends - and [in the] examination of the mainly in-
> stinct-driven actions, valuations and behaviours (the drive to propa-
> gate, the drive to feed and the drive for power) and, at the same time,
> at the action, valuation and behaviour intentionally aimed at *actual* al-
> teration of realities according to their social determination.[24]

Scheler holds, however, that, by a 'sociology of knowledge-based' reconstruction of actions and valuations, it is a matter not only of reference to subjective value attitudes, collective traditions and patterns of behaviour, but
rather a matter of these themselves , in their turn, being equally in reference
to an intellectual world of transhistorical values as the empirical forms of
knowledge and images of the world are to a transhistorical logical-noological
world. This specifically intellectual world now determining it for the attribution of qualitative value, has, however, no creative power whatsoever its nature. In connection with this, Scheler introduces the image of the "lock",
which for quite definite empirical active factors - natural or cultural - reads:

> The *'fatalité modifiable'* of the actual history, therefore, in no way
> determines the positive *content of meaning* of the works of the intel-
> lect, but it probably obstructs, disinhibits, retards or accelerates the ac-
> tion and *actualisation* of their meaningful content. To employ an im-

---

22 Cf. for example MAX SCHELER: *Schriften zur Soziologie und Weltanschauungslehre*, p. 23.

23 Cf. MAX WEBER: *Gesammelte Aufsätze zur Religionssoziologie*, Bd. 1, Tübingen (J.C.B. Mohr [P. Siebeck]) 1920, pp. 252f.

24 MAX SCHELER: *Die Wissensformen und die Gesellschaft*, p. 18.

age: - it opens and closes in a fixed manner and order the *lock-gates* of the intellectual current.[25]

As has still to be indicated later, the assumption in question by Scheler of an ideal world of values and norms is of outstanding significance for the specific character of his analyses of time diagnostics.

It has not been the complete rejection by Scheler also, in union with Dilthey, of a monistic conception of reality, and thus an epistemological "philosophy of absoluteness", which, as a consequence, brings about a depreciation of our standards of cognition. It is not Dilthey's differentiating out of three basic types of philosophy and Scheler's of three fundamental forms of knowledge that has undermined the criteria to be found in our knowledge of the world and of our selves and led to an attitude of gnoseological relativism. It was only in the course of further discussion regarding German sociology of knowledge, with a social cast of all forms and content of thought coming under the review, that the problem of historical and cultural relativism within the framework of the doctrine of cognition was allowed to become virulent. This second degree historicism, that had also endeavoured to identify as "entity-dependent" those noological assumptions, which allow the relativity of results of cognition and their contingent validity to be determined, ought to be brought, first of all, into close connection with the sociology of knowledge of Karl Mannheim, - though this is also probably contrary to the actual intention of its author.

2. Mannheim

Karl Mannheim's work is a paraphrase of the historism theme and simultaneously a disputation with its central substance. Already in his article on *"Historism"* in 1924, the problem of of the whole and the parts, as well as of Relativity and Relativism move into the foreground of the studies under the titles "Situation-dependency" and "Perspectivism". The subject of the historian, according to Mannheim, is only accessible at all from different viewpoints and can organise itself for a human consciousness only in terms of perspectivism. Nevertheless, it does not resolve itself into the different images that are possible for it, since one perspective, insofar as it is correct, is verifiable also from the other perspectives. Mannheim took up these ideas

---

25 *Idem*, p. 40.

again in the treatise *"Das Problem einer Soziologie des Wissens"* [*"The Problem of a Sociology of Knowledge"*] (1925) in which he reveals that he is unable to share that fear, which the contemporary thinking was expressing towards Relativism:

> For us a 'Relativism', which makes the matter difficult, in that it thrashes out all those factors, which argue for the partiality, entity-bound nature of a from time to time attainable assertion, is preferable to that 'Absolutism' which, to be sure, proclaims on principle the absoluteness of its own standpoint or of the 'Truth *per se*', but is *de facto* at least just as partial as any of its opponents, and what is worse, in its theory of cognition, does not even know how to begin with the problems of the time- and entity-bound nature of the concrete thinking in question and does not see how this entity-bound nature projects into the structure and forms of movement of knowledge.[26]

In the passage just mentioned, just as in the article "The Sociology of Knowledge", which, from the third edition on of *Ideologie und Utopie* forms the fifth chapter of this book, Mannheim is concerned above all to set the so-called structural aspect i.e. "the way one views a thing, what one comprehends by it and how one construes for oneself the content of a matter in thought",[27] in a relationship with the currently dominant "philosophical system", with the historical political data, but also particularly with the position of the onlooker within the social structure. Mannheim called this methodical reference to a historical-social and cultural situation "Relationalising", while he called the proof of the limited validity of statements by reference to a definite situation of such a type "Particularisation". These are the basic concepts of the sociology of knowledge, which in his lecture on "The Present Tasks of Sociology: its Teaching Content" at a conference of university lecturers in sociology in February 1932, Mannheim characterises as a program of research, "which looks into those propositions, which are particularist views of definite standpoints despite their absolutised form of statement"; by it, he also means that it can "lead to an extremely fruitful revision of our knowledge of the humanities and of social science."[28] As a special discipline, the sociology of knowledge has two areas of research: the teaching of ideologies and the sociology of knowledge in the narrower sense of the word. While the

---

26 KARL MANNHEIM: *Wissenssoziologie*, p. 311.
27 KARL MANNHEIM: *Ideologie und Utopie*, p. 234.
28 KARL MANNHEIM: *Die Gegenwartsaufgaben der Soziologie*, p. 18.

teaching of ideologies "[has] to reveal all of the conscious and unconscious lies and faulty interpretations, with which everyday popular sociology and the political and non-political groups bemuse themselves and each other"[29], *the sociology of knowledge* wants "to work out, far beyond the conscious and half-conscious lies of everyday life and of the party groupings, that missing constitutive approach to thinking, which is found in the sciences themselves and for which the scientist, in the main, is not to be called on to account in person."[30]

Mannheim's program should not result in an erosion of our standards of knowledge, that not having been its intention, much though conjectures of that kind were fostered by certain contemporaries, Ernst Robert Curtius[31] being in the van among them all. A good three years before the afore-mentioned lecture, that is in 1929, Mannheim had written in *Ideologie und Utopie* [*Ideology and Utopia*]:

> there would be [...] nothing more frivolous and more wrong than to argue somewhat as follows: Since, demonstrably, all historical-political thought is based to a certain degree on a metatheoretical option, so one cannot have any confidence at all in thinking *per se;* therefore it is also immaterial, how one argues in theory from case to case. So everyone ought to rely on his instinct, on his most personal intuition or on his own interests, and decide in favour of just how it suits him. In doing so, it could be that each one feels comfortable in his partiality and, moreover, still have a good conscience as well. Such a propagandistic exploitation of our analyses should be countered by the reply that there is a radical difference between a mindless commitment to party and an irrationalism, confining itself out of mental laziness to pure decision of the will and propaganda and a radically disturbing research on objectivity, which [...] still discovers a remnant of the partial and the vital in the thought structure itself.[32]

Like Dilthey, Mannheim too is anxious to achieve objective knowledge in the historical transformation of phenomena, but also in the transformation of the views of the world to be assumed for their representation and analysis, by referring to the contingent conditions, with which their existence is inter-

---

29 *Idem.*
30 *Idem*, p. 20.
31 ERNST ROBERT CURTIUS: *Deutscher Geist in Gefahr*, Stuttgart, Berlin (Deutsche Verlagsanstalt) 1932.
32 KARL MANNHEIM: *Ideologie und Utopie*, pp. 87f.

locked. He sought to achieve this aim through an analysis of the "entity-bound nature" of our knowledge of the world and of one's self, something which of late is supposed to permit a "re-setting of the perspectives." Mannheim holds that the "Relationism"[33], thus pursued, ought to make it possible to cope with the dire consequences of historic relativism. It cannot escape notice that he has occasionally fallen short of the claims formulated by himself in the putting of his program into practice.[34]

Ideologie und Utopie is the only book that Mannheim wrote in Germany. With the "Relationism" developed in it, the author referred to the mutable historico-social conditions of our images of humanity, society and the world. All forms of knowledge are to be seen and interpreted in relation to defined forms of social life. Everything spiritual is to be understood either as concerning *Ideology* or as *Utopian*. According to Mannheim, Ideology and Utopia are "entity-transcendent", deriving from a consciousness, "that does not coincide with the order of life in which it finds itself placed."[35] To give Utopia an orientation towards elements for acting on, which do not contain at the same time an actualised "being", so with ideologies it is then a matter of being paralysed at any possible time in an outmoded state of consciousness, and thus a matter of the harmful non-contemporaneity of those left behind. The definition "ideology" is now applied by Mannheim in a *particularist* manner, in that when specified ideas of the opposing group are demonstrably inadequate as to their "being", it is applied *totally*, if the opponent's whole world of thought falls under this judgement:

> While the particularist definition of ideology wants to address as ideologies only *part of the opponent's assertions* - and these only with regard to their *substance* - the total definition of ideology puts into question the whole philosophy of the opponent (including the apparatus of categories) and wants also to understand the categories of the collective subject.[36]

Moreover, there is according to Mannheim yet a further specification of the significance of the definition of ideology which is of importance: the application of the definition of ideology is *special*, when a particular opponent

---

33 Cf. KARL MANNHEIM: *Ideologie und Utopie*, pp. 71f. and pp. 242-244.
34 Cf. to this KARL ACHAM: "Rationalitätsansprüche im Lichte von Wissenssoziologie und Weltanschauungslehre", pp. 94-104.
35 Cf. KARL MANNHEIM: *Ideologie und Utopie,* pp. 169-173.
36 *Idem*, p. 54; cf. also pp. 228f.

is supposed to be made uncertain in his opinions, but *general* , if one has the courage, to see not only the opposing standpoints "as ideological but, in principle, everything, *even one's own standpoint too.*"[37] Mannheim differed from the Marxists in that he turns the "entity-bound nature" of ideological thinking into the characteristic of *all* social thinking and logically demands also of the Marxists that they admit the relativity of their own thinking, including even its ideological character. In this, he remains thus far associated with Marxism, when he attributes a particular significance to the Utopia, to the striving ideal of classes climbing up over the contemporary order of life. For Mannheim, of course, this Utopian hope is not the creation of only *one* wholly specific class, so that there are different forms of Utopian thinking. It is not seldom that this has the consequence of reciprocally paralysing these Utopias, and nonetheless Mannheim holds that it demands a passion for thought, to preclude that ideological numbing of a biased perspectivism in the sociology of thought: "In the sociology of knowledge, nothing really happens other than that we [...] let ourselves face as well our way of thought, which has now become critical, in the form of a situation report and the associations of one intention, aimed at the totality, win through."[38]

The research intention, voiced by Mannheim here, is not a matter of glossing over and excusing the perspectivity, but of asking how cognition and objectivity are possible under the assumption of such a perspectivity.

> With the visual image of a space object, it is indeed just as little a source of error, that the space object may have been *only* measurable as an entity in terms of perspectivity, and the problem does not consist in how it might be possible to bring it to a state of a non-perspectivist image, but rather how, by comparing the various views, one gets to see what is perpectivist, as such, and, thereby, what objectivity of a new kind might be achievable.[39]

The stimulus for research in the sociology of knowledge might then be conveyed thus,

> that it does not lead to the absolutising of an entity-*dependent* nature, but that precisely in the discovery of this in existing intuitive visions is to be seen the first step towards the dissolution of its entity-*restricted* nature. By the very fact that I add the register of views to a

---

37 *Idem*, p. 70.

38 *Idem*, p. 93.

39 *Idem*, p. 255.

view that takes itself to be absolute, in a certain sense I am already neutralising the particularist nature of the view.[40]

Mannheim clarified, with emphasis, his basic hypotheses regarding theories of cognition, but also the intention, pursued by him with the sociology of knowledge, when he says: -

> It is not a matter here of asserting that there is no objectivity and that the appeal to the current perception brings no fulfilment and response, but that these responses, in terms of an entity, are possible only in certain aspect-dependent cases. [...] In the case of entity-dependent thought, objectivity will mean only something that is a new and other thing: [...] that, if one [...] stands in various aspect-structures, 'objectivity' is only to be established circuitously, in that it is namely here that it aims at being understood correctly but in both of its aspect-structures, but different things seen arise from the structural difference between the two modes of seeing and objectivity strives for a formula for the mutual convertibility and transferability of these two varying perspectivistic views.[41]

Just as, according to knowledge of the laws of geometrical perspective an image may be carried over into another perspective - although even this too is always an image in a defined perspective - and as one may, through the multiplicity of the perspectives, always achieve greater perceptive capacity, a greater "fecundity in the face of the empirical material"[42], so one attains wider and deeper knowledge in the course of corresponding social science researches.

With this conception Mannheim draws an analogy to that old view of the sciences of religion and culture, which is perhaps expressed in Lessing's ring parable: Just like every religion, so every social class but also every society sees a part of the truth; and just as, according to Max Scheler, it is not possible for *one* nation and culture to unite all particularist views in itself, but it is only for all cultures, including those in the future, to do so in common effort, so Mannheim too rejects any sort of metaphysical bias. The synthesis of the different particularist aspects can, for all that, according to him, be effected only by such a group of men, which is capable of the disclosure of - as Max Scheler called them - the implicit assumptions contained in the various

---

40 *Idem*, p. 259.
41 *Idem*, p. 258.
42 *Idem*, p. 259

"relatively natural philosophies".[43] Mannheim sees this social grouping, standing above the particularism of the aspects, in the "unattached social intelligence", designated previously thus by Alfred Weber. The not completely harmless underestimation of the social dependency of the intellectual class has been pointed out in a series of critiques of Mannheim's sociology of knowledge, - from Max Horkheimer, via Joseph A. Schumpeter and Karl R. Popper up to Theodor Geiger. Mannheim's representation of the intellectuals expresses less a descriptive result of the examination than, much more, a normative expectancy. He maintains that the intellectuals form a class between the classes, but not above them, and he does not consider them qualified to confront the problems of the day from several perspectives and not from one single perspective only. Anyone who looks thus at *Ideologie und Utopie* [*Ideology and Utopia*], will be able to see in the book, first and foremost, a defence and justification of a certain type of the non-party intellectual in the moment before he vanished.

III. A Diagnosis of the Present Day

The potential for time diagnostics lies, for Scheler, in the tension between the intellectual world of the noological and axiological principles, on the one side, and the historico-social world on the other. For Mannheim, for whom the problem of historical relativism was likewise fundamental, the diagnosis of the present occurs before the background of the historical-philosophical basic assumption, that the various contents and forms of the consciousness lag behind or precede the concrete historical order of life. According to him, liberal humanism, which has to be developed between a competitive economy and state socialism and between anarchy and dogmatism, is also confronted by such tensions.

---

43 Cf. MAX SCHELER: *Die Wissensformen und die Gesellschaft*, p. 61-63.

1. Scheler

As with Max Weber before him, where "ideas" of whatever kind *unite* with interests or "tendencies", as he called the collective impulse, so for Scheler too these ideas acquire, only then at that point of union, *indirect* power and efficacy. Thus, it is written at a significant place in his book *Die Wissensformen und die Gesellschaft* [*The Forms of Knowledge and Society*]:

> The spirit, in the subjective and the objective sense [...] determines for *cultural* contents, which can arise there, solely and exclusively their character of a *being as it is*. The spirit as such, however, has *originally* of itself and from its very start *no trace* of 'power' or 'efficacy' to set these its contents too into *a state of being*. It is probably a *'determining factor'* of the potential cultural genesis but not an *'actualisation factor'*. *Negative* actualisation factors or actual *selection* factors from the objective range of the, through understandable intellectual motivation, respectively *feasible*, are at all times rather the *actual compulsively contingent living conditions*, i.e. the particular combination of the actual factors: of the power relationships, of the economical production factors and of the qualitative and quantitative relationships of the population and, additionally to these, the geographical and geopolitical factors, which each of them present. The 'purer' the spirit, the more powerless it is, in the sense of dynamic activity, in society and history.[44]

Doubtless the last sentence would be wrongly interpreted, if it were taken only as evidence for the "powerlessness thesis of the spirit", were it not to mean also, that it is the "spirit" that is the determinant.

Scheler's diagnosis of the present is accompanied by the acceptance of a "world-hour" of the present, which has come out of the "eternal" and by the endeavour to make the eternal accessible once more to homeless humanity in this historical situation. A passage from Scheler's article *"Vorbilder und Führer"* [*"Models and Leaders"*] is instructive as to the intention of his teaching of values:

> I have traced back the fundamental values, which Aristoteles laid down as *to hedú, to chrésimon, to kalón*, to the following five basic sorts: the sphere of value of the *pleasing* or the values of luxury; of the *useful* or the values of civilisation; of the *noble* [...] or the vital values;

---

44 MAX SCHELER: *Die Wissensformen und die Gesellschaft*, p. 21.

of the *intellectual values* or the cultural values; and of the *holy* or the *religious* values. And I have maintained that that person is 'good', who is mentally ready to prefer in each of the cases above the fundamental value which comes second to that which comes before. These fundamental values are unchanging in all historical development; they and their ranking order are mankind's guiding star. [...] It is precisely these basic values that correspond to the five named exemplary models: the model of the *life-artist*, of the *leading spirit of civilisation*, of the *hero*, of the *genius* and of the *saint*.[45]

Out of this over-historical account by Scheler, which also has the stamp of Platonic style, arises a philosophy of history, which one can scarcely find in those of his books, that were tumbling over each other up to 1916, on account of the pure war theology, - worth mentioning here, first and foremost, would be *Der Genius des Krieges und der Deutsche Krieg, Krieg und Aufbau* and *Die Ursache des Deutschenhasses [The Genie of War and the German War, War and Construction, and The Cause of the Hate for Germans]* - which philosophy, however, came plainly to light suddenly towards the end of the first World War and particularly in the fined down diagnoses of the time of his last years of life. In the meaning of this orientation, in 1917 he turned, on the one hand, against every "all-German" trend toward isolation and self-centeredness, which he described as "nonsensical and even un-German"[46], while, on the other, he criticised with equal intensity the "dreary, boring idea of a uniform, single so-called *world culture* as the freemason farce of a *world republic*".[47] The synthesising or even reconciliatory spirit, that is in Scheler at work, expresses itself clearly in his observation:

Cosmopolitanism and national cultural thinking are *not* therefore *contradictions* in regard to the higher culture of the mind, indeed they are not even two different truths but only *sides of one single truth*, and this one truth stands in double opposition to internationalism *and* to cultural 'nationalism'.[48]

Scheler, who had changed from the monarchist and war-enthusiast of the *Genius des Krieges* to a rational republican and pacifist, succumbed initially to the temptation, to identify the basic values established by him with par-

---

45 MAX SCHELER: *Schriften aus dem Nachlaß*, Bd.1, pp. 268f.
46 Cf. MAX SCHELER: *Vom Ewigen im Menschen*, pp. 431f.
47 *Idem*, p. 387.
48 *Idem*, p. 420.

ticular epochs of history and indeed nations. He did not renounce his earlier accounts in their entirety, although he drew back from the initial interpretation of the first World War as a defensive struggle of the Germans to the "vital values" orientated culture against the existing primacy in western civilisation of pure "utility values"; for he transformed this criticism into a general criticism of Utilitarianism and unbridled capitalism. Already before the war, but in particular for some time after it, his criticism of capitalism and the way of life of the bourgeoisie was founded in the antagonistic values already mentioned. Thus, he castigates the "false belief in the natural harmony of mere impulses", which "expects the best distribution of goods from an *absolutely free competition* of the subjects of the economy and from unlimited free trade [...]."[49] Should, later, - for Mannheim - the unbridled capitalism in the sense of the Marxist political economy, to which he felt an affinity, be criticised, then - for Scheler - this is arraigned in a manner reminiscent of Aristoteles of the demon of "pleonexy". There is a sharp distinction to be made between a "free economy" and the false "unsettled system of *rivalry*":

> The spirit and the unlimited drive of the rivalry, of the sheer lust to possess more and to be more, of all against all, *this spirit* is the false one, *not* freedom of the economy as an objective legitimate institution; and this spirit of boundless pleonexy, this specifically unrefined spirit, outraging every genuine feeling of self-worth, this 'common' spirit, in the most cutting sense of the word, can possess a *State* and its economic officials, in principle, quite exactly as well, as it does *not* have to possess individuals, in an economy appreciably more free.[50]

Such a spirit, therefore, in no way necessarily vanishes by introducing a new system of State Socialism, for even this can lead exactly to the one-sided enrichment of the leading officials in the economy as the capitalist competitive system.[51] Additionally to this might come possibilities of the limitation

---

49 *Idem*, p. 393.
50 *Idem*, p. 396.
51 Scheler sketches out an interesting connection between Capitalism and State Socialism, both of which he views as related at the innermost core on the ground of identical setting of targets: "The fact [...] that the medicines of growing State Socialism, hostile to freedom, have become the only possible one, which have the power still to encourage the maximum of popular welfare, is itself one of the most evil *consequences* of the *domination of the capitalist spirit*. The growing preponderance of the spirit of citizens demanding

of personal liberty. Altogether, therefore, Scheler makes himself into an attorney for a morally tamed capitalism, whereby he shows himself to be a moralising advocate of the economic ethic, but only unsatisfactorily, though, as an advocate of ethical institutionalism.

In one of his last publications, the treatise "*Philosophische Weltanschauung*", which appeared in 1928, Scheler projected a very pessimistic picture of the immediate present. The whole picture of the epoch, as he pointed out, bore deeply disturbing features. Of the contemporary movements, that were detrimental to genuine philosophy and science, he stated,

> firstly, the false elevation of the class ideology of the proletariat to a supposedly particular 'science', the 'proletarian science', which is set out in contrast to the 'bourgeois' kind, as if science (differentiating it from 'ideology') could ever be a function of a 'class'; secondly, the false forms of a gnostic new romanticism [...] ; thirdly, the church scholastics advancing ever more strongly into philosophy and science [...]; fourthly, the 'anthroposophical' form and the anti-philosophical and anti-scientific form of a major part of the occultist movements; fifthly, the murky ideologies of the popular ethnic mass movements, which, ignorant of the European reality and intoxicated with imagined racial superiority, [...] do not grasp the new solidarity of the peoples' clamant situation in the world; sixthly, the pretensions of egocentric, ridiculously conceited world medicine-men of every kind [...].

Scheler closed these remarks with the observation: "All of that is ruin and decay", and added to it a challenge, which is accompanied by a sombre fear: "to win back *the freedom to cultivate the mind*, which - should things go further - threatens to be lost to us."[52]

In that work too, which appeared posthumously, *Die Idee des Friedens und der Pazifismus* [*The Idea of Peace and Pacifism*], Scheler was driven by

---

'protection' over the components of the active spirit of enterprise [...] is indeed the *prerequisite*, under which the social policy has only those consequences of welfare. [...] The duration of the dominance of this 'spirit', though, is itself extended and secured by these measures, rather than reduced and abolished. It is surely only these same *basic motives* of the maximum safeguarding of the economic basis of life, which are astir for the want of such legislation [...]. Only the outcome of these motives varies according to the interests of the respective classes." (MAX SCHELER: *Vom Umsturz der Werte*, pp. 383f.)

52 MAX SCHELER: *Späte Schriften*, pp. 88f.

worry about the solidarity and freedom of the peoples of Europe. With great decisiveness, he condemned the revanchist thought being spread around among the youth of Germany, which was contemptuous of the challenge of the day, to "keep Europe away from a new war", which would mean "the total destruction of European culture, its 'Twilight of the Gods'." He condemned in like manner, though, the "often almost servile pacifism, that wickedly abandoned its own people and its whole spiritual tradition", which is similarly widely spread among the young generation.[53] Scheler, who was apparently striving even here for a "levelling-up" or a synthesis, finally repudiated all forms of instrumental pacifism, likewise the mental attitudes of militarism and embraced, as Ernst Nolte has formulated it, "the mental attitude of pacifism and the instrumental militarism, i.e. a state of national armed preparedness, while the positively strengthening all the points of approach to world peace that were still really weak."[54] Scheler died just short of five years before Hitler seized power.

2. Mannheim

The year 1933 and its consequences was of extraordinary importance also for Mannheim's diagnostics of time. Not that he would have avoided the actual problems of the day, prior to 1933,[55] but the German and the English phases in his work are nevertheless clearly to be differentiated one from the other. Mannheim had evolved from being one, who invoked and pointed the way to future "Utopias" to being a theoretician of the "planned State", - prob-

---

53 MAX SCHELER: *Die Idee des Friedens und der Pazifismus*, p. 62.
54 ERNST NOLTE: *Geschichtsdenken im 20. Jahrhundert*, p. 255.
55 Thus Mannheim pointed out in his 1932 lecture on the current task of sociology: "The clearer the need for a *political sociology* appears, the more vigorously must one strive to present precisely the content of this teaching to the student in a value-free non-agitatorial manner. For it would be the death of sociology, if it should have to become merely an instrument for agitation in the hands of one or more parties. It would be just as ruinous for it, if it, deliberately with greater agonising, for reasons of timidity at having possibly to offend, were to want to avoid the political and social themes of life and of our present existence and were to retreat out of pure prudence into abstract elevations [...]." (KARL MANNHEIM: *Die Gegenwartsaufgaben der Soziologie. Ihre Lehrgestalt*, p. 39)

ably also in view of a now virulent counter-Utopia to Marxist as well as to liberal thinking. He is convinced to a most profound degree, "that the self-same causes, which are bringing about the cultural disintegration of the liberal society, are also preparing the way for the dictatorial forms."[56]

In *Ideologie und Utopie* Mannheim lamented that one was getting ever closer to a stage, where the Utopian is destroying itself completely - in the area of politics at any rate. As a result of the many forms they took, the Utopias - wholly in the fashion of rival accounts of research in the area of science - were being ever less effective in parliamentary practice "as contesting confessions of faith, but ever more as mere rival parties, as merely potential research hypotheses".[57] Mannheim's worries recall what already at the beginning of the century Max Weber towards the end of his celebrated work *Die protestantische Ethik und der Geist des Kapitalismus* [*The Protestant Ethic and the Spirit of Capitalism*] charged with being a melancholy possibility: a "mechanised petrifaction with a sort of spasmodic taking-oneself-seriously" that is put on show by "experts without soul and voluptuaries without heart".[58] The same spirit speaks out from the closing sentences of Mannheim's comments on Utopian consciousness in the fourth chapter of *Ideologie und Utopie:*

> While the collapse of the Utopian presents a crisis only to specific classes and means self-elucidation for the general public by objectivity arising from the uncovering of ideologies, the total disappearance of the Utopian would transform the shape of the whole state of becoming a human being. The disappearance of Utopia brings about a static detachment, in which Man himself becomes a thing. The greatest paradox that is imaginable would come to pass, namely that Man, with the most rational mastery over things, becomes the man of impulses, that Man loses, with the emergence of the different forms of Utopia, the will for history and thereby the insight into history, - Man, who has achieved the highest stage of awareness of self after such a long

---

56 KARL MANNHEIM: *Mensch und Gesellschaft im Zeitalter des Umbaus*, p. 92; cf. original, p. 80.

57 KARL MANNHEIM: *Ideologie und Utopie*, p. 216.

58 Cf. MAX WEBER: *Die protestantische Ethik und der Geist des Kapitalismus* [appeared first 1904-05], 6th edition, Tübingen (J.C.B. Mohr [P. Siebeck]) 1972 (= Gesammelte Aufsätze zur Religionssoziologie, Bd. I), p. 204.

sacrificial and heroic development, in which history already becomes not blind fate but its own creation.[59]

According to Mannheim, this means that the world is being benumbed in a non-perspectivist image, in something that is without power to project, and consequently free of any impetus to discover in the present time something that is new in the light of expectation of something of the future time. Mannheim, therefore, anticipates here the ideas of the "de-ideologising" and the "loss of Utopia" in the matter, and as a consequence a completely rationalised world, where the irrational and decision could no longer exist at all.[60]

Already in his first piece of work after Hitler's seizure of power, in the article *"German Sociology (1918-1933)"* published in 1934 in the first volume of the journal *Politica*, Mannheim pointed out unambiguously that from then on his efforts were to be directed neither at an abstract classification system nor at methodical reflections on the essence of sociology, but at a concrete analysis of past and current events. In this he was endeavouring to join the tradition of Max Weber and Werner Sombart, whose analyses, according to Mannheim, helped to formulate a "diagnosis of the present situation."[61] It is made clear in the book *Mensch und Gesellschaft im Zeitalter des Umbaus*, published originally in Leiden in 1935 and appearing in an English version in 1940, as well as in the volume of essays *Diagnosis of Our Time: Wartime Essays of a Sociologist*, published in London in 1943, that the diagnosis of the present, is conveyed smoothly over into a strategy of exercising a systematic influence over the population. The first step, which the democracies must undertake, in contrast to their former *laissez-faire* policy, as Mannheim pointed out, will consist in giving up their completely neutral stance in the area of values.[62] Democratic tolerance can no longer consist in tolerating the intolerable.[63] Furthermore the renunciation of the attitudinal ethic and a turning towards the concrete ethic of responsibility, and, indeed, with the renunciation of a purely formal rationality and a turning towards a "rationality of substance".[64] Mannheim perceives the alternative to the fascist or communist

---

59 KARL MANNHEIM: *Ideologie und Utopie*, p. 225.

60 Cf. *idem*, p. 166.

61 Cf. KARL MANNHEIM: "German Sociology (1918-1933)", p. 218.

62 Cf. KARL MANNHEIM: *Diagnose unserer Zeit*, p. 43; cf. original, p. 26.

63 Cf. *idem*, p. 74; cf. original, p. 49.

64 Cf. KARL MANNHEIM: *Mensch und Gesellschaft im Zeitalter des Umbaus*, pp. 61-70; cf. original, pp. 51-57.

systems in the "third way", which he was propagating, namely "a type of planning, which is not totalitarian, but is controlled by the community, which has preserved for itself the most essential forms of freedom".[65] According to Mannheim, therefore, there exists "absolutely no choice any longer between planning and 'laisser-faire', but only between good and bad planning".[66] There are two fundamental prerequisites, though, for the "planned State" contemplated by Mannheim: the bringing about of a consensus regarding values, in the sense of a fundamental perceptual integration and then also, after that, the basic agreement of those interested in the political happenings, "to carry out research by testing and experimenting with the new potentials of mankind."[67] According to Mannheim, propaganda in a modern "planned democracy" ought to have the aim " of earmarking the disintegrated groups or persons, in order consistently [...] to reintegrate them as quickly as possible."[68]

All in all, in Mannheim's view, a stage of planning ought to be arrived at in community control, which achieves the same degree of rationality and morality as does the technical control of the environment. What, however, the principles of this morality and the content of the rationality of substance are in detail, which Mannheim says are to be distinguished from a pure formalism of values, he divulges to us in very inadequate hints.

IV. Open Questions

Georges Gurvitch once remarked, that the difference between Max Scheler and Karl Mannheim is not sociological but philosophical: Mannheim replaces Scheler's Plato and Augustine by a combination of Hegel and pragmatism.[69] In the following it cannot be a matter of making the delicate meta-

---

65 KARL MANNHEIM: *Diagnose unserer Zeit*, p. 102; cf. original, p. 71.
66 KARL MANNHEIM: *Mensch und Gesellschaft im Zeitalter des Umbaus*, p. 8; cf. original, p. 6.
67 *Idem*, p. 279; cf. original, p. 239.
68 *Idem*, p. 418; cf. original, p. 359.
69 Cf. GEORGES GURVITCH: "Problèmes de la sociologie de la connaissance", in: G. GURVITCH (Ed.): *Traité de sociologie*, Paris (Presses Universitaires de France) 1960, Vol II, pp. 103-136, here p. 117.

physical questions of the relationships of being and time, of immutable orders of knowledge and values and philosophies of history (with Scheler) or actual history and historically mutable consciousness (with Mannheim) into a subject of critical analysis. To present the differing forms of desired, - but also undesired - congruence between the eternal and the temporal, for example between Utopia and Reality, and to examine their implications in respect of cognition theory and value theory, would be to go too far. Only a number of cognition theory questions in respect of the sociology of knowledge as well as a couple of questions of moral philosophy with regard to the proceedings and results of the diagnosis of the present ought to be formulated. These questions will refer above all to the work of Karl Mannheim, since Mannheim still appears to many social scientists today to be a figure of significance in research, whereas Scheler increasingly disappears from their consciousness.

1. On Cognition Theory

Shortly after the appearance of *Ideologie und Utopie*, the question was posed, with particular pointedness by Ernst Grünwald, about the logical status of the total definition of ideology in Mannheim. This concept is either absurd, insofar as Mannheim himself links a theoretical claim for validity to his tenets, for the assertion contradicts the idea that the evidence also for Mannheim's theories determining entity-dependency is irrelevant as to the validity of the statements they contain; or, perhaps, that the conjecture as to ideology is valid for Mannheim's ideas and statements, including his criticism of the assertion concerning the "irrelevance of the validity" of the genesis of the ideas and the assertions.[70]

Mannheim would probably be pointing out, that he is making a distinction between the conceptions of validity and truth, indeed he would perhaps even say, that the proof for the respective relative validity - rather after the style of the changing "cultural meaning" in Max Weber's sense - is only possible on the basis of a definite theory about truth; and, even so, he does not make it easy for one to defend him against a range of critics - from Ernst

---

70 Cf. ERNST GRÜNWALD: *Das Problem der Soziologie des Wissens. Versuch einer kritischen Darstellung der wissenssoziologischen Theorien*, Wien, Leipzig (Braumüller) 1934, pp. 205f.

Grünwald through Alexander von Schelting on to Theodor Geiger - since, with him, clarity in ideas and argumentation is not always expressed as strongly as is the richness of his ideas. As Mannheim himself so unequivocally declared, the total definition of ideology puts the cognitive sphere of the consciousness as a whole into question. That means nothing other than

> that one formerly made revelations only at the psychological level, since one exhibited there socially-associated sources of deception that one drew even the noological-logical levels into the area of attack and also destroyed the noological level of the hostile statements in their validity by social functionalisation.[71]

This marks exactly the transition from the problem of ideology to a way of thinking about sociology of knowledge, a stop-at-nothing kind of thinking - not even giving pause before one's own kind of thinking. Similarly, above all, to Lucien Lévy-Bruhl at the same period, Karl Mannheim too asserts sometimes a determination by social conditions that enters the domain of the logical. In distinction to the views of Max Scheler, he proclaims the necessity of regarding the supertemporal validity of ideas as a derivative of a metaphysical idealism that is untenable as far as measuring cognition goes. Where, however, there is no world of ideas, then talk of 'eternal truth' is also obsolete.

With the "energising" pursued by him of the mental structure for ideological thinking, Mannheim provided a vindication - without, however, wholly wanting to - but did not have the power to convince the advocates of a logical-empirical doctrine of cognition and science. Only in one instance, as Theodor Geiger established, might the direct projection of collective factors into the noological level hold good for certain: if our system of categories were to change simultaneously with social change.[72] It is, of course, not so

---

71 KARL MANNHEIM: *Ideologie und Utopie*, p. 64.
72 Cf. THEODOR GEIGER: "Befreiung aus dem Ideologiebann" [*"Liberation from the sway of ideology"*] [from the literary estate], in TH. GEIGER: *Arbeiten zur Soziologie. Methode - Moderne Gesellschaft - Rechtssoziologie - Ideologie-kritik*, Neuwied a. Rh., Berlin (Luchterhand) 1962 (= Soziologische Texte, Bd. 7), pp. 431-459, here p. 446. - Cf. in connection with this the criticism of the uncertainties of every sort in the sociology of knowledge, associated with the draft of a research program on the sociology of knowledge by RO-BERT K. MERTON: "A paradigm for the study of the Sociology of Knowledge", in: PAUL F. LAZARSFELD, MORRIS ROSENBERG (Eds.): *The Language of Social*

easy to offer evidence that the fundamental logical cognition-related character-istics of happenings of the descriptive, systematising, deductive and elucidat-ing cerebral activity should really have altered in dependence on social-struc-tural, economic or political data.

Perhaps it is altogether better not to burden the expression "sociology of knowledge" itself too much, especially as it is questionable, whether there is such a thing as a sociology of knowledge at all, and not rather a sociology of error as well as of self-deception and of extraneously caused delusion; and whether the judgement is subject to the law of entity-dependency, or not just the actual judgements alone.

2. On Moral Philosophy

Critics have variously remarked, that Mannheim's sociology of knowl-edge suffers from an absence of sociological analysis of the institutions, in which intellectual activity is carried out, but also that the influences of sci-ence and technical science on the social structure had not been examined suf-ficiently. Apart from this undeniable deficiency, there is still another aggra-vating one that presents itself in the area of its practical philosophy. It has to do with the unexplained connection between planning and a previously achieved establishment of a consensus regarding values. To it, the following brief statements apply.

"Planning", so argued Mannheim, "is an act of reconstructing a society with a past in history and coming down to us in an ever more consummate unity, regulated by persons in central positions."[73] He establishes a close connection between the need for planning and the creation of consensus in times of uncertainty and crisis. Like Durkheim, he too was plagued by the feeling of social disorder and both regarded it as their life's mission to look for a solution of the unmanageable problem of social consensus. Mannheim meant by this, that disintegrating groups of society were to be integrated again as quickly as possible - if only at a completely superficial level of feel-ing.[74] Only if we were to have a clear idea of which ethical goals are suitable

---

Research: A Reader in the Methodology of Social Research, New York, Lon-don (Free Press) 1955, pp. 498-510.

73 KARL MANNHEIM: *Mensch und Gesellschaft im Zeitalter des Umbaus*, p. 228; cf. original, p. 193.

74 Cf. *idem*, p. 418; cf. original, p. 359.

to a society and under which social conditions a spirit of community develops, could we consciously plan vital social experiments in modern society.[75] It is precisely the ethical goals, though, which remain extraordinarily vague in Mannheim's discussion. There is neither a definition of the content of individual and social morals nor a clear definition of the planning goal for society as a whole. Mannheim invokes the common welfare[76], the social requirements for "security" and "justice"[77] - but it stays at the level of these clichés with the aid of other invocations, which, likewise, are no more closely defined.

Fundamental to Mannheim's attitude, perfectly characterised as planning euphoria, is the possibility of intersubjective comparison of utility, apparently imputed by him to be completely unproblematical, on the basis of arrangements, in principle, of preferential value that are homogenous or made to be homogenous. This silent assumption of supposed conviction leaves the reader too completely in the dark regarding the range and depth of the planning activities. The statements and aims, delivered in a tone of complete innocence suggest only the suspicion that Mannheim's specific position in the debate is that of the exile, who is endeavouring to transform an alleged chaos of liberalism for the purpose of resisting an aggressive political philosophy in a structured order, in order to be able to protect it from the reproach of rashness and superficiality. Away from their context, many of his recommendations reveal a disagreeable tendency but also within the context mentioned they acquire an odd character. Thus he speaks highly of the intention in the attempts of the more recent pedagogics no longer to breed an "ideal man but that man, who will in all probability be wanted at the next stage of social development."[78] By whom, though? And for what purpose? Although no clarity emerges about the objectives, for Mannheim it is as though it were settled, i.e. "to form the best possible types of mankind according to plan by shaping the different spheres of society with a conscious end in view."[79] In the "creation of the new man", as Mannheim assures us, it is first and foremost a matter of re-shaping his ways of thinking and acting[80], to which end,

---

75 Cf. *idem*, p. 286; cf. original, p. 245.
76 Cf. *idem*, p. 311; cf. original, p. 267, where Mannheim refers to "the good of the whole".
77 Cf. *idem*, p. 404 and p. 416; cf. original, p. 347 and p. 358.
78 *Idem*, p. 241; cf. original, p. 203.
79 *Idem*, p. 261; cf. original, p. 222.
80 Cf. *idem*, p. 175; cf. original, p. 147.

apparently, schools would be in a position to make an important contribution by doing away with marks and certificates, in order, to be precise, "not to rear all too ambitious men and those who delight in competition". In doing this, "one puts an end to a certain type, that is represented all too often in the upper classes of society and which finds its satisfaction only in competing successfully with others."[81]

These upper classes of society, of whom Mannheim is speaking, are, seemingly, identical to a large extent with capitalist entrepreneurs. To them, but also to the consumers, he directs the message: "One will learn that there is nothing sacred about free choice for the consumer, and the entrepreneur will discover that he can run his business better, when he can let himself be guided in his investing by a central plan."[82] One of the reasons for the collapse of the free industrial economy was, according to Mannheim, "the unlimited choice of goods presented to the consumer, whereby production and consumption were difficult to co-ordinate."[83] Referring yet again to the capitalist entrepreneurs, whose anarchical production he is trying to channel through the structures of a planned economy, he recommends to the "progressive groups", that they might "perhaps [sic!] attempt to attract the technical and organisational elites over to them, instead of getting rid of them, as the Russian revolutionaries had done."[84]

Alongside reasons for his assumption of largely identical preferred orders of value among the different individuals, in Mannheim's later writings, one misses above all the feeling for the diversity and complexity of social orders. A metaphor of Friedrich August von Hayek is, in this connection, still ever expressive, which illustrates the awkward character of outline planning, even within capitalist economies, by the simile of a natural phenomenon, which, precisely in order not to spoil the intended effect, may be ventured only as far as a certain "depth of intention":

> We can never construct a crystal by a conscious arrangement of the individual molecules, but we can create the preconditions in which the crystal will form itself. For this purpose, we make use of forces that are known to us, but we cannot determine in advance the position of

---

81 *Idem*, p. 241; cf. original, p. 203.
82 *Idem*, p. 405; cf. original, p. 347.
83 *Idem*, p. 367; cf. original, pp. 314f.
84 Cf. *idem*, pp. 408f.; cf. original, p. 351, where this consideration may be felt to be less provocative.

an individual molecule in the crystal or even the size and position of different crystals. Likewise, we can create the conditions, in which a biological organism will grow and flourish, but for the growth we can create only conditions that favour it. We can determine the size and structure that results, only within narrow limits. Exactly the same is true of spontaneous order within the social domain.[85]

One looks in vain for deliberations of this kind with Mannheim - he leaves everything, at best, irresolute and full of forebodings.

V. Closing Comment

Mannheim seemed to be filled with a simply holy zeal for sociology, which often had naive and, at the same time, seemingly weird consequences. An etiologically half-baked diagnosis was thereby substituted, so to speak, by a quick-acting prophylaxis. With all decisions, one has to start from the principle,

> of evaluating ethical rules according to their contribution to the maintenance of the social order. [...] We may not forget here that the fundamental virtues are in general a matter of habit and quite seldom include careful deliberation and decision by individual people.[86]

Mannheim maintains that habits, like virtues, are so variegated, that the impression that forces itself on the reader is one of their inexhaustible historical plasticity. In such viewpoints, the difference from Max Scheler's interpretations finds clear expression, the endeavour of which has been, of late, an exhibitory analysis of invariant durations in and behind all transformations of our cognition and evaluation.

The relativisation of certain cognitive and normative contents, as it supplies the philosophical analysis in more classificatory style and the sociology of knowledge in a more historicising style, can be interpreted in a manner that varies; firstly as an attempt to make up for the lack of a sense of history, then, perhaps, also as preparation for a fresh claim to absoluteness in the way

---

85 FRIEDRICH A. VON HAYEK: *Freiburger Studien*, p. 35.
86 KARL MANNHEIM: *Mensch und Gesellschaft im Zeitalter des Umbaus*, p. 413; cf. original, p. 355.

that the consequences of a sceptical irritation are used to justify the need for faith. In this respect, Mannheim's work is of a very ambivalent kind, and yet it is true also for him that a historicising insight into the conditionality of knowledge can ultimately only ever happen, when there is an assumption of the unconditionality of the idea of truth on grounds of logical reconstruction. Contrary to Mannheim's interpretations[87], one does not already have to be an advocate of metaphysical idealism, if one considers the point to be, not to overlook the constants in our theoretical and practical attitude to the world.

References

ACHAM, KARL: "Rationalitätsansprüche im Lichte von Wissenssoziologie und Weltanschauungslehre", in: ERNST WOLFGANG ORTH (Hrsg.): *Vernunft und Kontingenz*, Freiburg-München (K. Alber) 1986 (= Phänomenologische Forschungen, Bd. 19), pp. 75-120.

BOCK, MICHAEL: "Die Entwicklung der Soziologie und die Krise der Geisteswissenschaften in den 20er Jahren", in: KNUT WOLFGANG NÖRR, BERTRAM SCHEFOLD, FRIEDRICH TENBRUCK (Hrsg.): *Geisteswissenschaften zwischen Kaiserreich und Republik*, pp. 159-185.

BÜHL, WALTER L.: "Max Scheler", in: DIRK KÄSLER (Hrsg.): *Klassiker des soziologischen Denkens. Zweiter Band: Von Weber bis Mannheim*, München (C.H. Beck) 1978, pp. 178-225.

DILTHEY, WILHELM: *Weltanschauungslehre. Abhandlungen zur Philosophie der Philosophie*, 5. Aufl., Stuttgart-Göttingen (B.G. Teubner-Vandenhoeck & Ruprecht) 1977 (= Gesammelte Schriften, Bd. 8).

HAYEK, FRIEDRICH A. VON: *Freiburger Studien. Gesammelte Aufsätze*, Tübingen (J.C.B. Mohr [P. Siebeck]) 1969.

KÄSLER, DIRK (Hrsg.) : *Klassiker des soziologischen Denkens. Zweiter Band: Von Weber bis Mannheim*. München (C.H. Beck) 1978.

KÄSLER, DIRK: *Soziologische Abenteuer. Earle Edward Eubank besucht europäische Soziologen im Sommer 1934*, Opladen (Westdeutscher Verlag) 1985.

---

87 Cf. KARL MANNHEIM: *Ideologie und Utopie*, p. 255.

KRUSE, VOLKER: "Historisch-soziologische Zeitdiagnostik der 20er Jahre", in: KNUT WOLFGANG NÖRR, BERTRAM SCHEFOLD, FRIEDRICH TENBRUCK (Hrsg.): *Geisteswissenschaften zwischen Kaiserreich und Republik*, pp. 375-401.

MANNHEIM, KARL: *Die Gegenwartsaufgaben der Soziologie. Ihre Lehrgestalt*, Tübingen (J.C.B. Mohr [P. Siebeck]) 1932.

MANNHEIM, KARL: *Diagnose unserer Zeit. Gedanken eines Soziologen*, Zürich-Wien-Konstanz (Europa Verlag) 1951. Original: *Diagnosis of Our Time*, London (Kegan Paul, Trench, Trubner & Co.) 1943.

MANNHEIM, KARL: *Wissenssoziologie. Auswahl aus dem Werk*, eingel. u. hrsgg. v. K. H. WOLFF, Berlin-Neuwied (Luchterhand) 1964.

MANNHEIM, KARL: *Mensch und Gesellschaft im Zeitalter des Umbaus*, 2. Aufl., Bad Homburg v.d.H., Berlin, Zürich (Gehlen) 1967. [The 1st edition of this work appeared in 1935. All subsequent English and German editions are revised and enlarged versions of this book which has been published in Leiden.] Original: *Man and Society in an Age of Reconstruction*, London (F. Routledge & Kegan) 1940.

MANNHEIM, KARL: *Ideologie und Utopie*, 5. Aufl., Frankfurt a. M. (G. Schulte-Bulmke) 1969 [The 5th edition of this book, which appeared for the first time in the list of the F. Cohen publishing house in Bonn in 1929, is an unchanged reprint of the 4th edition of 1965; this latter edition contains the text of the 3rd edition of 1952 and was enlarged by a list of Karl Mannheim's writings and a bibliograhy during the years from 1952 to 1965.]

MANNHEIM, KARL: *Freiheit und geplante Demokratie*, Köln, Opladen (Westdeutscher Verlag) 1970. *Freedom, Power and Democratic Planning*, Oxford (Oxford University Press).

NEUSÜSS, ARNHELM: *Utopisches Bewußtsein und freischwebende Intelligenz. Zur Wissenssoziologie Karl Mannheims*, Neuwied, Berlin (Luchterhand) 1968.

NOLTE, ERNST: *Geschichtsdenken im 20. Jahrhundert. Von Max Weber bis Hans Jonas*, Berlin, Frankfurt a.M. (Propyläen) 1991.

NÖRR, KNUT WOLFGANG, SCHEFOLD, BERTRAM, TENBRUCK, FRIEDRICH (Hrsg.): *Geisteswissenschaften zwischen Kaiserreich und Republik. Zur Entwicklung von Nationalökonomie, Rechtswissenschaft und Sozialwissenschaft im 20. Jahrhundert*, Stuttgart (F. Steiner) 1994.

PLÉ, BERNHARD: "Anknüpfungen der Wissenssoziologie Mannheims an die Verstehensproblematik bei Dilthey: zur Rolle der 'Weltanschauungen' als kulturelles und wissenschaftliches Problem", in: *Annali di Sociologia/Soziologisches Jahrbuch* 8 (1992-I), pp. 173-192.

REMMLING, GUNTER W.: *The Sociology of Karl Mannheim; With a Bibliographical Guide to the Sociology of Knowledge, Ideological Analysis and Social Planning*, New York (Humanities Press) 1975.

SCHELER, MAX: *Die Idee des Friedens und der Pazifismus*, Berlin (Der Neue Geist Verlag) 1931.

SCHELER, MAX: Schriften aus dem Nachlaß, Bd. 1, 2. Aufl., Bern, München (Francke) 1957 (= Gesammelte Werke, Bd. 10).

SCHELER, MAX: *Die Wissensformen und die Gesellschaft*, 2. durchgesehene Aufl. [*2nd revised edition*] (mit Zusätzen [*with addenda*] hrsgg. v. MARIA SCHELER), Bern, München (Francke) 1960 (= Gesammelte Werke. Bd. 8). [The 1st edition of this work appeared in 1926].

SCHELER, MAX: *Schriften zur Soziologie und Weltanschauungslehre*, 2., durchges. Aufl. [*2nd revised edition*] (with addenda and minor publications from the time of the "Schriften", published with a supplement by MARIA SCHELER), Bern, München (Francke) 1963 (= Gesammelte Werke, Bd. 6).

SCHELER, MAX: *Vom Ewigen im Menschen*, 5. Aufl., Bern, München (Francke) 1968 (= Gesammelte Werke, Bd. 5). [This 5th edition of the work, which first appeared in 1921 is without change when compared with the 4th edition from 1954, which was published by MARIA SCHELER.].

SCHELER, MAX: *Frühe Schriften* (with a supplement published by MARIA SCHELER and MANFRED S. FRINGS), Bern, München (Francke) 1971 (= Gesammelte Werke, Bd. 1).

SCHELER, MAX: *Vom Umsturz der Werte. Abhandlungen und Aufsätze*, 5. Aufl., Bern-München (Francke) 1972 (= Gesammelte Werke, Bd. 3). [The 5th edition of this work, which first appeared in 1915 is the unchanged reprint of the 4th edition of 1955].

SCHELER, MAX: *Späte Schriften* (with a supplement) (hrsgg. v. MANFRED S. FRINGS), Bern, München (Francke) 1976 (= Gesammelte Werke, Bd. 9).

SCHELER, MAX: "Die positivistische Geschichtsphilosophie des Wissens und die Aufgaben einer Soziologie der Erkenntnis", in: VOLKER MEJA, NICO STEHR (Hrsg.): *Der Streit um die Wissenssoziologie*, 2 Bde., Frankfurt a.M. 1982, Bd. 1, pp. 57-67. [First appeared in: *Kölner Vierteljahreshefte für Sozialwissenschaften* 1(1921), pp. 22-31].

TENBRUCK, FRIEDRICH: "Wie kann man die Geschichte der Sozialwissenschaft in den 20er Jahren schreiben?", in: KNUT WOLFGANG NÖRR, BERTRAM SCHEFOLD, FRIEDRICH TENBRUCK (Hrsg.): *Geisteswissenschaften zwischen Kaiserreich und Republik*, p. 23-46.

WOLFF, KURT H.: "Karl Mannheim", in: DIRK KÄSLER (Hrsg.): *Klassiker des soziologischen Denkens. Zweiter Band: Von Weber bis Mannheim*, München (C.H. Beck) 1978, pp. 286-387.

Discussion Summary

ANNETTE KLEINFELD

Paper discussed:
KARL ACHAM: The Sociology of Knowledge and Diagnosis of
Time with Max Scheler und Karl Mannheim

The first part of the discussion concentrated on the differences between Scheler and Mannheim. According to Mannheim, Scheler is one of the outstanding pioneers of a "sociologie of knowledge" (*Wissenssoziologie*). However, there is a major difference between Mannheim and Scheler: While Scheler is in favor of absolute values, Mannheim is convinced that the logical, noological sphere is influenced by cultural, societal factors (SHIONOYA, ACHAM).

With regard to historism and the diagnosis of the "Zeitgeist", Mannheim is confronted with the problem of constantly changing societies. In them, a certain paradox arises for the liberal: Why should he be tolerant towards intolerant societies and structures? According to Mannheim we are inhibited to have free research concerning these questions. Besides, there is a contradiction within Mannheim's view about the state. On the one hand, he tries to resist to the idea of a "Zentralstaat" (centralized state) like the one Stalin has realized. On the other hand, he is in favor of a well planned central state. His ideas - ressembling the Platonic concept of the state - about a moral elite which should take the planning of all affairs, are not too far away from Stalin's ideas developed in *Plan und Staat* in 1917 (ACHAM).

A second part of the discussion, starting with Mannheim's retreat from liberalism in the 1930ies (LENGER), dealt with the relationship between intellectuals and liberalism respectively with the role of intellectuals for the state. According to Mannheim's own reflections, intellectuals were more important during the 1920ies than before. He was convinced that there should be a free floating of knowledge and a freely floating intelligentia (*freischwebende Intelligenz*), and that within the topographical situation the conversion in a mathematical sense of different perspectives was possible (ACHAM). Against this, it was raised that during the 1920ies - and even before the first world war (LENGER) - the smallest part of the intellectuals believed in liberalism, since it did not work at this time. Drawing a line between the position of intellectuals and liberalism is justified only from our perspective today where liberalism is working. So, for instance, Hermann Hillen and Ernst Franklin amongst others were convinced that liberalism should be abolished. Also in the work of Ernst Jünger of this time, especially in *Der Arbeiter*, tendencies towards a sort of National-Bolschewism in a global perspective can be noticed (KOSLOWSKI).

Besides, Mannheim's notion of a free-floating knowledge and of a freely floating intelligentia which was supposed to ban relativism is considered to be a misunderstanding, taking a logical problem for a sociological one. The naivity to believe into a managerial elite comes close to madness here (RIN-GER).

Chapter 5

Georg Simmel's Contribution to a Theory of the Money Economy[1]

RAIMUND DIETZ

I. Introduction: The Instrumental and the Systemic View

I should like to start by asking two questions:
(1) What is Georg Simmel's[2] contribution to *economics*?

---

1   Earlier work on Simmel and systems theory was supported by the Fritz Thys-
    sen Foundation (Cologne, Germany). I have benefitted greatly from discus-
    sions with my colleage Vladimir Gligorov (WIIW), Vienna. Translation into
    English by Silvia Plaza.
2   Georg Simmel was a German Philosopher and one of the founders of modern
    (formal) sociology. His main works: 1908: *Soziologie: Untersuchungen über
    die Formen der Vergesellschaftung*; 1900: *Philosophie des Geldes*; 1910:
    Hauptprobleme der Philosophie. Short summaries on his life and work, and
    bibliographical information to be found, e. g., in: TRIER-MAYNTZ (1990);

(2) What is his contribution to our theoretical conception and general understanding of the economy?

With respect to the first question we recall that Simmel opens his main work, "The Philosophy of Money",[3] with the explanation that "not a single line of these investigations is meant to be as statement about economics" (*ibid*, p. 54).[4] He himself lays no claim on his thoughts forming part of political economy. However, attempting to answer question two, we realise that Simmel offers valuable insights into the rise and dynamics of the modern economy. In a certain sense his work constitutes an outline of a theory of the modern age. What interests the economist in Simmel's thinking is that his theory of the modern age evolves around the concept of money. A third question follows from the two initial ones: how is it possible that the answers to the first two questions, i.e. Simmel's contribution to economic science and to our conception of the economy, can differ so strongly? I shall try to give an answer in the form of a simile:

Economic science can be compared to an observer sitting in a boat that is moving downstream in a river. The observer is watching a swimmer trying to catch some floating object. Swimming towards the object the swimmer need not know the velocity of the current, particularly if the river is flowing quietly. Neither need he know where the source or the mouth of that river is located. Another observer may be standing at the bank of the river, or even at some distance from it. He is not only interested in the motives and movements of the swimmer, but also in the "structure" of the medium in which the swimmer moves, because the swimmer's pattern of movement are determined by it. The second observer may even want to know how this "matter", i.e. water, is constituted, whether its structure is stable or subject to decay, or whether it could be substituted by another medium (functional contingency).

The techniques and methods of modern economic science largely correspond to the intention of the first observer to watch and understand the swimmer moving in his medium. The observer assumes that the swimmer is familiar with the medium and that the medium is stable. Social science theo-

---

SCHNABEL, P.-E. (1985); more extensive analysis in: JUNG, W. (1990); and in FRISBY, D. (introduction into Simmel 1990).

3   First edition 1900, second slightlys revised edition 1907. The English version I refer to was edited by D. Frisby, translated by Tom Bottomore and David Frisby, New York (Routledge) 1990.

4   "That is to say, the phenomena ... which economics views from *one* standpoint, are here viewed from another" (*Ibid.*).

reticians like Marx, Simmel, Durkheim, Weber, Habermas or Luhmann cannot afford this kind of "blind" pragmatism regarding the environment in which man acts which generally characterises the economic sciences. They usually keep environments in which agents operate constant or assume them to be exogenously given. The efforts of the social science theoretician must therefore branch out in three different directions:

(a) to study the movements of the swimmer, however operating not only with the hypothesis of purposeful action common in the economic sciences, but also with other motivations such as playfulness;

(b) to explain the movement of the swimmer through the structure of the medium, i.e. to understand the social (systemic, institutional) conditionality of human action; and

(c) to pursue a question that may seem absurd to the image of the swimmer in a river but which is important and topical in social science discourse, i.e. to trace how on the one hand society (in the sense of social system or ensemble of institutions) is explainable as resulting from human action while, on the other hand, individual action is made possible and conditioned by social (collective) institutions. With respect to the image introduced above, to "derive" water from swimmers' movements and simultaneously to explain the swimmers' movements through the quality of the medium water. (This seemingly nonsensical simile may, by the way, explain a fundamental difference between the natural and the social sciences: nature and its laws are pre-established with respect to man, while institutions arise out of action contexts and enable human actions. We are confronted, here, with an evolutionary circle).

If Simmel's position in the economic sciences is not very prominent in spite of his major contribution to a theory of money economy this must be mainly attributed to the different methodological approaches prevalent in economics and the social sciences. There is widespread consensus that the specialised discipline of economics is characterised by the principle of instrumental rationality, i.e. by the attempt to understand reality in the light of purposeful action. Economics is defined as allocation of scarce resources to infinite ends. That, in a way, is its unifying principle. This principle is responsible for the strong position of economics today, exemplified by the dominance of economics among the social sciences: its methods are exported to other disciplines, but not very much is imported into it.[5]

---

5 Its success as a discipline is probably not just based on the "relentless application" of its set of tools in approaching reality (HIRSHLEIFER [1985]), but

However, at the same time, the reduction of analysis to the instrumental aspect of action also constitutes its weakness: for if one is to apply the principle of instrumental rationality rigorously, one would need to keep the social environment in which human beings act constant. This, however, is impossible. In order to take social realities into account, economics must deviate from its own methodological principle. The principle responsible for the success of economics as a discipline thus falls back on it in a negative way. Disregard for the systemic dimension takes a curious form of revenge on economics. In the terminology of psychoanalysis one could call this "somatisation". If a problem is suppressed - in economics the social environment - it finds some specific "somatic" expression. To list just a few examples: "Orthodox" neoclassical economics presupposes a costless allocation of resources - the discovery of this deficiency leads to the theory of transaction costs and institutions (Coase 1988). Traditional economics is static - Schumpeter (1912) makes the entrepreneur the driving force of the economy - and the entrepreneur turns into a deus ex machina in a world still conceived in Walrasian terms (Streit 1993). Traditonal economics assumes perfect information. Hayek denies this and re-interprets the economic problem of allocation under perfect information turning it into a problem of competition as a discovery procedure (Hayek 1945). Most games are modelled as games played against nature, i.e. against given environments. In the Prisoner's Dilemma two players have to decide whether to cooperate or to defect. Defection is rational in the instrumental sense, while joint cooperation is better for both than joint defection. The paradox which arises is the following: In order to act more rationally agents must learn to become irrational (in instrumental sense). Lastly: consider the fictitious communism of the neoclassical tradition (Myrdal 1953). The fact that many economists, even Schumpeter, considered socialism the economic system of the future is more than just an indication that neoclassical economic theory only pretends to be a theory of the market (Lavoie 1985; Stiglitz 1994; Dietz 1995). In fact, for traditional neoclassical economics the market is an economic order that could be replaced by any other one, for example by a government (Buchanan 1979).

The limitations of neoclassical theory become apparent from the fact that the core of orthodox thought does not contain a theory of institutions. One could perhaps say in summary that the suppression of socio-systemic reality

---

mainly due to the increasing dominance of economy over other social subsystems since the end of the Middle Ages.

in neo-classical orthodox thinking leads to attempts to reconstruct it at the neoclassical periphery - but, because social reality is being suppressed, in a distorted way. The suppressed problems are somatised, they *do not form a consistent whole*. Economic thought branches out in different directions, distancing itself from its methodological core, which, however, is less and less able to keep the various branches together.

The most prominent example showing the epistemological limitations of neoclassical theory most clearly is the *theory of money*. According to Hahn (1982) the greatest challenge to orthodox economic thought lies in the fact that it has not yet been possible to find a place for money "in the best developed model of economics". The difficulties in formulating a theory of money encountered by neoclassical economics are quite clearly related to the principle of instrumental rationality. For application of a rational calculus requires stable environments. However, money eludes this requirement on principle because it is the medium of economic action. It simultaneously results from and directs this action. In money we encounter a category which obviously cannot be deciphered solely by instrumental logic.

In my view, Simmel suggests a construction which adequately describes the creative circle from which money emanates and which it accelerates. In section 2 below I shall attempt to summarise Simmel's propositions as succinctly as possible. In section 3 I juxtapose the different construction principles of the neoclassical and Simmel's "models" of the economy.

II. Major Morphological Elements Generated by Exchange
– Simmel as a Theoretician of Self-organisation –

> "Exchange ... is the source of economic values, because exchange is the representative of the distance between subject and object which transforms subjective feelings into objective valuation."
> (Simmel 1990, p. 90).

The essence of Simmel's approach may perhaps be best captured by viewing him as a theoretician of the self-organisation of society and the economy.

Neither traditional neoclassical economics nor the theory of institutions are theories of self-organisation. Neoclassical economics assumes preferences, endowments and maximisation behaviour to be given exogenously. Institutional economics, in turn, introduces institutions from outside and endogenises, at least to a certain extent, preferences , endowments and the behaviour of agents (e.g. profit seeking). In contrast, Simmel endogenises institutions in a meaningful way. Economic institutions arise out of individuals' actions, i.e. mostly out of exchange as communication acts. However, by endogenising even institutions Simmel avoids ending up in a morass of concepts, magnitutes, or processes where everything would depend on everything. Rather, through exchange as *the* constituent element, Simmel traces the emergence and development of the *morphological structure (Gestalt)* of bourgeois society, i.e. the structure of modern capitalist money economy, and he demonstrates that money (not as a quantity but as a quality) is its very essence.

Simmel juxtaposes the autonomy of the money economy's "objective culture" and individual life processes. However, in contrast to Marx he not only regrets the alienation prevalent in this objective sphere of culture, which according to Marx would have to be eliminated by some future society (communism), but he also speaks of the "tragedy of culture"[6] since human beings pay for greater freedom by dependence on things, whereby greater freedom is defined by a change in the type of dependence (for this see below). The morphological structure of the economy, i.e. the revalorisation process of capital which is quite independent of individuals' lives, just makes use of indiduals' needs, motivations, of changing fashions, as its content. Thus, for Simmel in contrast to Walrasian economics, the economy is essentially not driven by needs, but rather determined systemically. In the shape of money, the exchange relation has "crystallised into an autonomous formation". If the ex-

---

6   Simmel's attitude towards modern culture is ambivalent. He also observes very clearly what modern human beings gain through it. At the end of his "Philosophy of Money" he writes: "... the material contents of life become increasingly objective and impersonal, so that the remainder that cannot be reified becomes all the more personal, all the more the indisputable property of the self (SIMMEL [1990], p. 469). Simmel has nothing but ridicule for a shallow cultural criticism which expects miraculous cultural achievements from the condemnation of money. This would only produce "miracles of banality". Cf. also RAMMSTEDT (1994), pp. 30f.

change function crystallises into money as an autonomous formation[7] money replaces the interaction of exchange and thereby enables the existence of modern society.[8]

This closes the autopoietic circle. Freedom of the individual (linked with individual personality) and socialisation are not contradictory but mutually constitute each other. It is the supra-personal entities of "objective culture" which determine the accelerating speed of our lives, or production cycles, or the further differentiation of products and institutions, or the division of labour and consequently also economic growth. What we are trying to find out about are the elements employed in Simmel's theory of the self-organisation of money economy and the morphological structure resulting from them. In pursuing this, we need not confine ourselves to Simmel but may also look at the implications of his approach for a theory of the institutions of modern society.

As stated above, the basic element from which Simmel proceeds is exchange. From this the major structural elements of capitalist society are derived. We distinguish among the following morphological levels or lines of argument:

(1) Exchange, money, capital; credit and interest
(2) Firms and markets
(3) The state and the central bank
(4) Transformation of the "world"; transformation of society; transformation of the individual.

1. Exchange, Money, Capital; Credit and Interest

Exchange is an act of communication characterised by double contingency (Luhmann 1984). People meet as black boxes and learn something

---

7   "If the economic value of objects is constituted by their mutual relationship of exchangeability, then money is the autonomous expression of this relationship. Money is the representative of abstract value. From the economic relationship, i.e. the exchangeability of objects, the fact of this relationship is extracted and acquires, in contrast to those objects, a conceptual existence bound to a visible symbol" (SIMMEL [1990], p. 120).

8   LUHMANN (1984) would call this the substitution of interactions by communication.

about each other, as well as about their own wishes. If they arrive at an agreement, their interaction can be described as a *do-ut-des*-operation.[9]

Money: The most important structural element emerging from exchange is money. It emerges from exchange because every good that is given up to obtain another one fulfils the function of money, in so far as it serves as means of buying something.[10] Simmel wrote: "Money has acquired the value it possesses as a means of exchange; if there is nothing to exchange, money has no value" (Simmel 1990, p. 156). If a commodity is reduced to this function only - to attract goods through exchange - then we call it money.[11] Hence we define money by its liquidity; i.e. by its superior ability to attract goods by way of exchange.

According to Simmel, money is the embodiment of the exchange relation. While emanating from exchange, money is the institution enabling exchange. This is not a logical but a creative circle.

From the exchange function all other functions of money can be derived. Money is a means of storing wealth, or a means of speculation: "... its significance as a means of storing and transporting values is not of the same importance, but is a derivative of the function of money as means of exchange; without the latter, the other functions could not be exercised, whereas its function as means of exchange is independent of them" (Simmel 1990, p. 156).[12] If money enters the picture, exchange ceases to be a simple relationship between two individuals because "realization [of its value] depends upon the economic community as a whole or upon the governments as its representative" (*ibid*, p. 177).

---

9 Or, more generally, I offer you something for which I believe you are able to offer me something that I might need. The products and services which will eventually be exchanged depend on the knowledge the partners have when entering into the process of exchange, and which they acquire during the exchange process. It also depends on the cost and risks of monitoring contracts, etc.

10 The relative value form is the precursor of money. On this, see MARX, *The Capital*, vol. I, chapter 1.

11 The historical emergence of money moves from commodity money to pure (paper) money. Commodity money can still be used for purposes other than buying, while pure money (or money proper) functions only as a means of exchange.

12 This does not imply that all functions are always performed by the one kind of money.

Money as capital: Money as a general medium necessarily becomes the end of economic activity (Simmel 1990, pp. 228ff). Since the simple exchange motive turns into pofit seeking money becomes capital. The function of money therefore is not just to allocate goods needed to satisfy needs (as in the Aristotelian world of oikonomia); it has become an "autonomous supra-individual formation" (Simmel) governed by its own law, or "language", i.e. the "revalorisation" of invested values (chrematistes). Money transforms goods into its "raw material" and creates needs in order to ensure the continuity of the revalorisation process. In short, money is the medium of exchange. Capital results from exchange operations based on the medium of money. One could say that self-reflexive money is capital.[13]

Money and the interest rate: Interest is the price of (for) money. The underlying exchange relation (credit) is money today for money tomorrow. The difference in the quality of the two traded "goods" is just time (if an entrepreneur invests his money into his own firm, the agent involved may be the same). The credit operation is a typical example of a reflexive operation: exchange refers to the medium of exchange.

Everything revolves around money - money is the medium and aim of economic activity - and markets are hierarchically related to each other; one may say that this hierarchy is defined by the respective distance or closeness of goods and markets to money, i.e. by the degree of liquidity of the assets, or, in other words, by the marketability of products. While according to the neoclassical norm of equality of marginal utilities all goods are brought to the same level and all markets are of the same rank, the concept of liquidity implies some hierarchy among markets and a preponderance of money owners over owners of goods (Simmel 1990, p. 217). From this follows that the interest rate is the most important price in the economy. This supports the Keynesian proposition that the interest rate conditions the profit rate, and not the latter the former one, as stipulated by neoclassical theory.

2. Subject and Object – Firms and Markets

Neoclassical axioms assume individuals endowed with perfect information and exposed to parametric prices. This approach seems to be meaningless

---

13 The reader will realise that this is a "morphological" definition of capital which has little to do with the "material or economic" one which is the subject of efforts made by the theory of capital (on this see GAREGNANI [1990]).

from the perspective of selforganisation in which subjects and objects (or individuals and their environments) "mutually define each other's conditions of origination". One is impossible without the other, each one can only originate through the other one. This "mutual definition of the other's conditions of origination" is an evolutionary pattern typical of all self-generating systems. This pattern can be characterised as a creative circle which one may illustrate through an etching by Escher: in this etching we observe that both hands draw each other. This means, they mutually define each other's conditions of origination. They extract themselves by their own means from the etching and form an entity of their own. Their activity (the mutual drawing of each other) defines the conditions on the basis of which they can be distinguished from one another, and which sets them off against the background.

Figure 1: The Pattern of Evolution According to Escher

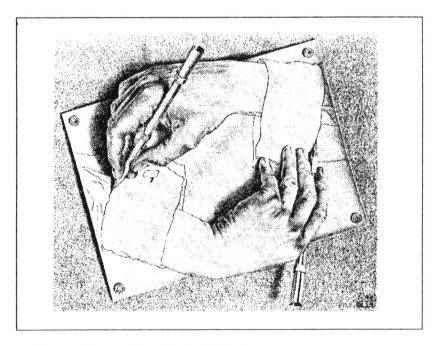

Source: "Drawing hands" by M. C. Escher

This evolutionary pattern is exactly the scheme used by Simmel in his theory of modern (capitalist) society: The white paper on which Escher's hands draw each other corresponds to an image of "society" as a mere conglomeration of unrelated individuals, i.e. an unstructured, chaotic number or individuals, out of which the "order" of a money economy can emerge only after passing through several stages of development. The act of drawing in Escher's etching corresponds to exchange in the economy. Exchange gives autonomy to economic subjects while simultaneously generating markets which form their environment. Exchange generates the paradox of civilisation: (increasing) autonomy of the individual combined with its simultaneously growing socialisation and dependence; the freedom of the subject combined with the simultaneous *objectivisation* of the world. One is impossible without the other, each tendency is linked with the opposing other one (Simmel 1900).

Figure 2: The Pattern of Evolution in Economics

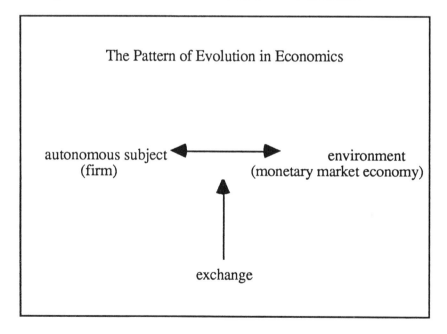

Firms and markets: The fruitfulness of this system-theoretical approach is clearly visible in the case of the relationship between joint stock companies and their monetised environments. The two relate to each other like subjects (agents) to their environment, both generated by exchange. For joint stock companies (subjects) are nothing but bundles of capital (= the expected net value of future exchanges), and markets are the environment which has assumed the nature of an object through exchange communication. (This evolutionary process is illustrated by figure 2, above).

The quasi-parametric nature of markets derives from nothing but exchange communication. Sociologically speaking, the character of markets becomes the more "objective" the more extensively and exclusively communication takes place through exchange, and, economically speaking, markets function the better, the more finely-meshed the network of actual transactions is. Prices acquire social objectivity not because of their "rightness", as being, say, in accordance with a (fictitious) equilibrium or with other criteria that might be applied by an outside observer (e.g. V. Pareto), but through societal exchange communication. According to Simmel, values can be expressed only through exchange. Only through exchange do values obtain a statable amount. Another kind of objectivity in the economy, Simmel (1900, pp. 81f) points out, we cannot attain.

That it is nothing but exchange which gives identity to economic subjects becomes overwhelmingly clear in the case of the incorporated firm, the prototype of a modern enterprise.[14] An incorporated firm has a unique identity, although all its constituents or representatives are exchangeable: the workers and employees, machines, owners, managers - all of them are exchangeable, but the identity of the enterprise remains. The enterprise may merge with others or split up into various others in the way organic cells do; new identities can be built up; etc. In spite of being devoid of substance, the enterprise may refer to itself as an "I", as a legal and economic entity. This quality of incorporated firms, i.e. to be devoid of substance and yet a subject, is solely due to exchange.

This is so because we may define an incorporated firm as an organisational unit whose function it is to communicate successfully in the market,

---

14 Although other subjects besides enterprises (households, the state) also participate in exchange communication and thus contribute to the building of money-economy environments, enterprises are the only *systemic* elements, since their existence derives exclusively from exchange communication, the basic operation of the economy.

126

i.e. it must provide the numerous acts of exchange occurring at different points of time with an addressee that is clearly visible to outsiders - the company name - and it must secondly accommodate technical and financial overheads (fixed costs, overhead costs, risks) by providing a consolidated financial budget. Large enterprises and the modern market economy derive their vitality from this uncanny flexibility.[15]

3. The State and the Central Bank

The state

In this systems-theoretical context the role of the state can be defined as the function of creating institutions that help to sustain exchange communication, and to intervene by fiscal and monetary instruments in order to stabilize that process. Collective action is imperative particularly for complex transactions (e.g. long-distance trade or exchange with a long time-horizon; see North 1991). In addition, the market is neither a just nor a stable mechanism. We know very well today that the formation of expectations is influenced by this process itself. Therefore, a policy that stabilizes expectations may contribute to greater welfare.

The Central Bank

The only exception to the principle of *do-ut-des* in the strict sense of the expression is the injection of fresh money by the central bank. By extending a credit the central bank does not give anything; yet it obtains something, i.e. claims on interest. This exception is the privilege of the "sovereign", in money economies occupied by the central bank. The central bank as an institution derives logically from the de-substantialisation of money (the historical development of commodity to paper money) (Simmel 1990, p. 168). Since the intrinsic value of money is zero (it can be produced at negligible cost) there must be an institution which keeps money tight to put the economy under a macroeconomic budget constraint (Riese 1983).

---

15 In contrast to incorporated firms, partnerships or one-man businesses have an identity because their business assets can be clearly related to a natural person, or group of persons, endowed with their own natural, i.e. psychological or social identity.

4. Transformation of the "World", of Society and of the Individual

"World"

A commodity space can only be imagined as a limited world. Such a world is ruled by the compensation principle: for every profit there is some loss. This view is stylised in the Pareto optimum: one can enhance one's wealth only at the cost of somebody. However, as Simmel stresses, the world is not "given away" (Simmel 1990, p. 292) and it is exchange and even more so money which open up the world. For in the course of exchange the actors learn from each other (bilateral contingency as a basic element of any socialisation process).[16] Secondly, people only conclude agreements if both sides draw some advantage from it. Thirdly, exchange leads to the division of labour, the differentiation of products and to the perfection of technologies (*ibid*, p. 290). Through their application, substances may be separated into an increasing number of components, so that an increasing amount of value can be derived from every material. Simmel thus formulates the principle of uncoupling the exploitation of the environment and economic growth. He calls this the "substantial progress" of culture (*ibid*, p. 290). Lastly, apart from the three effects listed above, the very institution of exchange is welfare-enhancing. According to Simmel, this last, in economical terms external, effect of the institution of exchange represents "the functional progress" of culture. "The concern here is with finding the appropriate forms that make it advantageous for both parties to exchange ownership of specific objects" (*ibid*, p. 290).[17] The advantage of exchange, if compared with robbery, theft, or even gifts, cannot be overestimated according to Simmel. Transition to exchange indeed sets free unimaginable forces. Exchange, he believes (1990, p. 291), reduces the human tragedy of competition. The fight of human beings against each other is diverted and becomes a fight of man against nature. The economy is not a zero-sum game, but a positive-sum one. The market clearly is not a system of arbitrage leading to an optimum

---

16 This thought was developed by PARSON and SHILS (1951) and LUHMANN (1984).

17 Neoclassical economics adresses only the substantial progress brought about by exchange, i.e. the exhaustion of welfare gains within the given economic space. The functional progress of exchange is the (unmeasurable) gain which is to be attributed to exchange as an institution that changes the space in which agents act.

within a predetermined commodity space; rather, it is a discovery procedure as Hayek (1945) has pointed out.

If exchange breaks open the stationary space, money does so even more. For in order to exchange goods against other goods they must have been produced before. Not so in the case of token money. The possibility of injecting fresh money[18] implies that the space of economic goods may be enhanced *ex nihilo*.[19] From this follows the Keynesian proposition that it is not savings which cause investment, but credit-financed investment which causes savings.

Society

Money also transforms society. It brings about individualisation and socialisation; individualisation because it transforms relationships of dependence in such a way that persons need no longer discharge their obligations by personal service but through money. "Money has made it possible for people to join a group without having to give up any personal freedom and reserve" (Simmel 1990, p. 344). On the other hand money socialises, because it increases the frequency of communicative linkages and ensures their proliferation. Money economy does not impose any limit on the magnitude of a particular society. "Big capital", in particular, has no geographical limitation. Hence, social differentiation and quantitative expansion of groups are closely interrelated.

Human beings: simultaneously greedy profit-maximising machines and highly individuated personalities.

Money turns man into something attributed to him or her by neo-classical theory: a self-centred, ruthlessly acting, profit-maximising individual.[20] Money makes it possible for human beings to compare aims and means us-

---

18 This quality, by the way, was anticipated by the minting of coins through which a coin was given a higher than its intrinsic material value (see also MENGER [1909]).

19 However, this Faustian trick (on advice by Mephisto Faust suggests to the emperor the creation of token money; not yet exploited natural resources are to be the collateral, i.e. a mere promise - cf. also H.C. BINSWANGER [1985]). The result is that only with rising investment and therefore rising growth the economy remains stable (BINSWANGER [1994]).

20 Thus, neoclassical economics owes its success to a principle which it fails to to explain.

ing a commensurable, globally recognised measure. This materialistic, money-guided rationality of modern man and the coldness of human relationships that goes with it is often deplored. In part, justly so. However, it is often overlooked that the anonymity of relationships under money economy at the same time also enables highly individual relationships. Thus, love marriages only arose under money economy. The reification of relationships among things and the individuation of persons and their relationships with each other exist side by side.

So far, a number of morphological elements have been described. Simmel's central thesis is that all of them are in one way or another rooted in exchange, and that the vitality of systemic processes is based on both the individual and systemic advantages that money as a "supra-individual formation" (economists call it public good) provides. Since money widens the space of individual decision-making exponentially (individual gain), it enables development (systemic gain). And since it not only is a means of exchange, but has long been the aim of economic activity, it enforces development, in whatever direction it may move. To Simmel, money is the most productive social "invention" of mankind (Simmel 1907, p. 210). It is a prerequisite for fashioning, out of a more primitive society, the order of modern society.

III. Simmel and Economic Science

I hope to have shown that Simmel has indeed provided us with interesting and profound insights about the money economy. It remains to find out what economists could learn from him. I think they would profit most by acknowledging and understanding where his approach is different and why. Since all economics in some way is Walrasian (Blaug 1985), it is perhaps best to juxtapose *Simmel's approach* with that of *neo-classical orthodoxy* (Walrasian economics). I would like to restrict myself to this confrontation in order to highlight the fundamental differences of the two approaches which will be even more interesting since at first sight (but only then) they both appear to be theories based on the concept of exchange. Once the fundamental differences between them have been clarified I shall elaborate on the mediative function which Simmel's approach could assume among different economic schools.

However, in this confrontation with Walrasian economics I shall concentrate on one issue which I consider crucial: *the differing conception of exchange*. In contrast to Simmel the neo-classical theory of value is based on a very rudimentary conception of exchange: instead of on exchange it bases its arguments on the rate of substitution (RoS) and presents this as the rate of exchange (on this see Schumpeter 1908, pp. 49, 135). Exchange as a social action is thus reduced to a *"technical"* fact. Economy as a social nexus is thus represented by a technical construction. Schumpeter, an ardent admirer of Walrasian economics, considers this trick the greatest achievement of economic science and speaks of the "logic of economic things" (*ibid*, p. 260). In Simmel's theory, in contrast, exchange is a social event to which the sociological logic of double contingency applies. These two completely different conceptionalisations of exchange have far reaching consequences regarding the conceptions of *objectivity, value, society*, and with respect to the treatment of *time*, etc.

The substitution rate (rate of substitution, ROS) is the basic element of Walrasian economics. For, if all substitution rates and endowments were known, one could, given the necessary computing capacity (computopia!), calculate the Pareto-optimal allocation point. Since this point is derived from "technical" substitution rates assumed to be objectively given, we may also speak of a *commodity paradigm*, i.e. a commodity space defined by *physical* properties, such as preference and production functions.

Exchange, on the other hand, represents the basic analytical element of a systems-theoretical paradigm. Exchange is viewed as the element on the basis of which (capitalist) economies are organized.

Exchange and the substitution rate are, in other words, the *partes pro toto* of these two paradigms. Whereas Walrasian economics tries to establish the preconditions for *equilibrium* from objectively given data, the systems-theoretical paradigm raises the question of the market economy's *morphological structures* which emerge from exchange. The market is not viewed as an arbitrage mechanism matching given preferences and resources; rather, it is viewed as a system which co-generates realities and puts them in some kind of hierarchical order.

In the following I shall attempt to characterise the *formal* properties of the two different conceptions of "exchange" in the elaboration of the two theories.

NEO-CLASSICAL ORTHODOXY	SIMMEL

Definitions

The rate of substitution (RoS) defines states of indifference for consumers (preferences) and producers (production function).

Exchange (EXC) is a real action between two partners.

Consequences of these definitions with respect to the following criteria:

- Choice versus action

Formally, RoS is a technical ratio $y = y(x)$, derived from the function of $U = U(x,y)$ for any given U, where U denotes utility (or, in the case of a production function, the quantity of a product), and x, y are consumer goods (or production factors, respectively).

In contrast, EXC denotes an action. 'A' exchanges x for y, and 'B' exchanges y for x. However, while RoS implies transitivity and reflexivity, exchanges are never reversible and hence are not transitive.

- Time

RoS has no time dimension. Time is unessential, or symmetric. Hence, in Walrasian theory the decision space is uniform: due to the assumption of rational expectations and complete markets, agents

EXC is an event which disappears at the same moment of time as it happens. Time has only one direction, i.e. time space is asymmetrical. The economic space is made up by the economic agents' expecta-

decide today for all future points of time.

tions, that is it rests on trust: for the economic agents the future exists only if they can expect given events to be followed by successive events. Money, for example, is only accepted because the agents believe that money will buy things tomorrow, i.e. that the system will continue to function.

- (Technical) objectivity versus (social) objectivisation

RoS considers reality as being objectively given. Preferences and production functions are assumed to be given prior to the process of exchange (for a critique see Morgenstern 1972; Buchanan 1979). The ontological epistemology of neo-classical economics requires equilibrium to be defined independently of the activities of agents - to Frank Hahn (1981, p. 79) the "canker at the heart of economics".

EXC produces economic reality. *Ante* exchange, there is only physical but not economic reality. Equilibria however defined are path-dependent.

- Individual and society

Though pretending that the individual is the basic building bloc of neo-classical theory, substitution rate economics reduces the individual to a carrier of preferences only. Traditional value theory does not even allow individuals to reflect on their preferences (Statements as: "I hate my desire to smoke", are not admitted (Ötsch 1991).

The Simmelian approach applies a neo-Kantian (as opposed to a mere utilitarian-instrumental) perspective of the individual. To ask whether an action is rational, we must not ask (as in the utilitarian approach) how it connects the (psychologically) given desires of the actor; we must instead examine the coherence of the autonomous individual's principles' reasoning which determine the action. Reason may override desires (Sudgen 1991).

The place of *society* is taken by the state, or an almighty auctioneer, or simple by an aggregation of representative individuals.

Simmel rejects the view that *society* is a substance, an organism, or an irreducible real entity. On the contrary, society is created by exchange. It is nothing but the sum total of the interactions and interdependencies (the German term *Wechselwirkung* implies both) between individuals - whose unity in turn is constituted only by their mutual interactions and communications.

GEORG SIMMEL'S CONTRIBUTION

- Money

The disaster of neo-classical money theory derives from its value theory. The neo-classical value theory occupies the place which should be reserved to money: "Mainstream monetary theory can be considered as an attempt to introduce a coordination device, money, into a framework which already contains a coordinating device, the Walrasian auctioneer, as an ideal type. In such a framework money cannot be anything else than unessential" (Ees/Garretsen 1992, p. 4).

In the case of Simmel money is the medium of socialisation. Hence money is anything but neutral. Without money a number of groupings exist, but there is no society in the economic sense. Simmel compares money not only with the nervous system but also with human blood circulation. Money is the medium of communication and at the same time the motive force behind economic development. Hence money is anything but neutral.

- Scarcity versus the language of scarcity

In line with these different epistemological approaches we arrive at different definitions of what economics is about.

Traditional theory defines economics as the theory of the optimal allocation of scarce resources to infinite needs. Hence scarcity is defined ontologically: theory pretends that scarcity can be derived from an objective set of data.

What constitutes economics is not a given set of data but the "economic language" in which scarcity is conveyed and communicated among individuals. What Simmel implicitly suggests is the definition of economics as a theory of the language in which scarcity is conveyed / communicated to individuals (see above).

- What or how? Allocation vs. institutions

Substitution-rate economics allows economic subjects to determine the allocation of resources, i.e. to show *what* the result of an allocation process would be if individuals
a) were maximizing their utilities in well defined environments, and
b) were reaching a Pareto-optimum.

Economics based on "real" exchange is theory of the morphology of the system. It deals with the very process of institution-building and its consequences for individual actions.

- Plan vs. market

Equilibrium models of neoclassical theory are auctioneer models. Price formation and the transactions mechanism must be conducted by an auctioneer. No centrally planned economy has ever been as centralized as required by the Walrasian model. Although the Walrasian model is interpreted as being a model of a decentralized economy, with precisely the modest information requirements that are considered its typical advantage, it actually presupposes omniscience. Morgenstern (1972), Arrow (1987), and others point out this contradiction. *Arrow* draws attention to the fact that in a state of disequi-

In a systems-theoretical view the market should be conceived as a "device" which creates economic reality. Simmel does not start from the maket as a mechanism leading to a pre-defined state which we could deduce if all necessary information about substitution rates were known, but from a "social" (communicative) exchange process which produces reality. He does not speak of uncertainty in the sense of not knowing, or not yet knowing, nor about mere correct of false expectations of reality that pre-exist outside or independent of the process of exchange; rather, he says that this reality is and can be

librium the information necessary to return to the Edgeworthian contract curve would represent nothing less than the information needed by a central planner. If one were to accept the Walrasian model as a model of a market economy, one would have to deny the claims to systemic superiority of the market economy (Stiglitz 1994).

generated and is objectivised only through the process of exchange. Viewed in this way, exchange is an indispensable (non-contingent) element of the economy: it is *the unit act of the economy.* It generates knowledge about scarcity, i.e. about what is obtainable, under which conditions, where and from whom.

It is evident that the substitution rate and exchange are similar elements at first sight only. At closer scrutiny one realises that completely different theoretical "buildings" can be erected if one takes these two concepts as foundation stones. And yet both of them, neo-classical economics and Simmel, operate with the same basic elements: individuals and scarcities. However, they group these elements in a completely different manner which results from the differing concept of exchange. "Substitution economics" leads to a theory which proceeds "from top to bottom". Space is finite, static, given. Only at equilibrium are relative prices and allocative proportions defined. In this space we therefore encounter maggots rather than fully-fledged individuals; the place of society is taken up by the omniscient auctioneer. With Simmel, this space receives structure through acts of exchange, and space structures this action. This space is opened up by substantive and functional progress - the world is not "given away", but has a morphological structure. Freedom and socialisation mutually constitute each other. Human beings can only be free because they are disciplined by supra-personal entities - in economic life by money.

Unfortunately, Simmel's work has hardly been taken note of by economists.[21] In spite of his metaphorical language for which he is often criti-

---

21 On the reception of *Simmel* in economics, see mainly the dissertation by FLOTOW (1992) as well as the book review by LAIDLER/ROWE (1980), which appeared on the occasion of the translation of *Die Philosophie des Geldes* into English.

cised, the conception of his "Philosophy of Money", interweaving economic, sociological, cultural, religious and epistemological thinking, is strictly logical, consistent and fruitful. However, it is not the multitude and variety of theoretical links in his work, nor his use of metaphors usually frowned upon in the exact sciences, which may disconcert or even irritate the representatives of those disciplines. The fact that Simmel has at least been rediscovered by modern sociology, mainly in the US, and that he is today celebrated as one of its greatest representatives (Habermas 1983; Schnabel 1985), while in economics, despite declarations to the contrary (Frankel 1977; Frisby 1990; Backhaus 1996), he has barely been noticed, and if noticed he was subsequently forgotten, cannot be attributed just to matters of style; in my view this is due to the differing position of the observer: Simmel is the explorer of systems "standing at the bank of the river", while economists are instrumentalists "sitting in the boat". Why should a modern economist, who has been trained to be led, above all, by the methodical *a priori* of instrumental rationality and who knows that the success of his discipline within the social sciences is based on this self-limitation - why should this economist change direction and allow himself to be drawn into the complexities which the systemic point of view entails?[22]

Nevertheless one should recall that certainly not all economists have allowed themselves to be tied to the procrustean bed of instrumental rationality, be it due to the original vitality of their idea of economy, or because they did not want to swollow the unacceptable consequences of that principle. In order to pay tribute to Simmel not only because of his valuable contribution to the theory of money economy, but also to find out what would be his significance for modern economics, one should confront "The Philosophy of Money", particularly its methodological core, with the approaches of those thinkers and schools of thought which have tried to distance themselves from the respective "orthodoxies" of their time. Here I am particularly thinking of Marx, Menger, Hayek, Keynes and Sraffa.

In a confrontation between the approaches of Simmel and Marx we would, for example, hit upon an interesting similarity between Simmel's theory of exchange and Marx's analysis of the "value form" (exchange value).

---

22 Indeed, even within their profession in the narrow sense, economists hardly show any readiness to learn something new. Coase, who introduces the institutional aspect via transaction costs, laughs about what others have made out of him (COASE [1988]).

Both of them indeed are starting points for a morphology of capitalism. However, one would also note the difference: Simmel rejected Marx's theory of labour value for epistemological reasons. This immediately makes Simmel a liberal. For Marx, exchange and thus bourgeois society are contingent, and to be followed by communism. To Simmel exchange and money are non-contingent elements of a civil world though fragile as it may be (for more details see Dietz 1996).

In a comparison with *Menger* one would perhaps notice that both Menger and Simmel base their theories of money on exchange. Menger's money theory, however, is merely attached to his theory of value which is of a Walrasian type, and turns out to be inconsistent with his value theory. In contrast to the widespread view held by both foes and enemies of general equilibrium theory[23], exchange and Walrasian economics are incompatible (for this see, e.g., Hellwig 1994).

In a comparison with *Hayek* one finds strong similarities in their theoretical positions regarding socio-economic order, but with different evaluations of them. Simmel stresses the deep dilemma of modern culture, while Hayek's position is more affirmative. What unites the two is their evolutionary approach.[24] Therefore, they both rank the cultural dimension, i.e. economic and social institutions, above any rational calculus of the individual. Rationality is thus rather considered a consequence than a precondition of culture and welfare. Thus, both Simmel and Hayek reject rationalism of the cartesian type for the analysis of "systems". In contrast to neo-classical rationalism, which views everything from an ends-means-perspective, Simmel and Hayek derive institutions not from deficits in rationality (uncertainty, asymmetrical information, transaction costs, etc.), but view them as results of development processes that could not be created by design. For both Hayek and Simmel institutions can only form out of human beings living together, or, in other words, be the result of the (historical) process of socialisation. Both share the view that although the totality of institutions *cannot be created* they can be *shaped*. In so far as both of them try to show that "productivity" or social welfare are mainly based on rules, these two evolutionists and proponents of systems theory are in basic agreement with each other. Beyond that both of

---

23 BARANZINI/SKAZZIERI (1986) (Eds.) hold that the Walrasian economics is "exchange economics" while the economics of Ricardo, Keynes, and Sraffa is "production-economics". I think this distinction is very inappropriate for coping with differences in these paradigms.

24 As far as Hayek is concerned, see VANBERG (1994).

them believe that the rationality and vitality of the "whole", which defies explanation, only holds if this "whole" forms a unity which emanate from market- and contractual relations. In this respect *Simmel* and *Hayek* are liberals.

However, although Simmel is older and not an economist, he goes further than Hayek in that he bases the process of constituting the "whole" on exchange and on money as "embodiment" of the exchange relation, while Hayek is content with the generality of a less clearly formulated "order of action" (Handlungsordnung). Simmel differs from Hayek and is thus closer to classical economists like Smith, Marx, and Keynes, although or just because he bases his theory on exchange, in his conception of money as an institution and in his view of money economy as a system. I believe that Simmel thus surpasses evolutionary neo-classical economics and particularly also Hayek. For Hayek stops at the concept of *market economy* and has not much to say about the concept of *capitalism*.[25] This is regrettable since market economies are always capitalist economies.

So I see Simmel as the *builder of a bridge* spanning the Austrian school, on to Keynes, and reaching as far as the neo-Ricardians. The "Austrian" pillar is the individual and its process of exploration and learning; the Keynesian pillar is knowledge about the significance of money for the economy; and the neo-Ricardian models contains notions of morphological structure similar to that found in Simmel. The bridge constructed by Simmel moves from individual exchange acts, on to money and the morphology of capitalism, and back. He transcends the subjectivism of the Austrian school through the objectivity resulting from the morphology of capitalism. But he also transcends the objectivism of the neo-Ricardians since he traces this objectivism back to the communication acts among individuals, i.e. to individual processes. (Freedom of individuals appears as a precondition for the formation of culture). Looking back on his work and his motivations, Simmel writes in his "Anfang einer unvollendeten Selbstdarstellung" (beginning of an incomplete autobiographical description): "I derived the central concepts of truth, value, objectivity, etc., from interdependences and interactions that formed part of a relativity which no longer amounted to a sceptical loosening of all firmness

---

25 This can be proved by looking at Hayek's theory of money. His point of reference in his money-theoretical arguments is the model of an ideal money economy in which money is neutral GIJSEL/HASLINGER [1993]).

but, on the contrary, gave protection against it through a new conception of firmness."[26]

Simmel stresses that not a single line of his philosophy of money is meant to be a statement about economics. He believes it to be his task to pose questions and attempt answers lying outside the traditional scope of the specialised discipline of economics, which ought to be resolved before any economic investigation could even start, or which lie beyond its results. The economist should keep to his or her profession. It is nonsense to try negating a century of professional specialisation. However, the economist should be aware that the object of his or her analysis is a *social* "entitity". He or she will not be able to model man, not to speak of his or her ability to give good advice on how to regulate the (money) economy if he or she has no knowledge of its structure (Gestalt) and the vital forces driving its evolution. For very practical reasons we may sometimes need to know from where the river stems, in which direction it flows and what it is that is flowing.

References

ARROW, K.J. (1959): "Toward a Theory of Price Adjustment", in: M. ABRAMOVITZ ET AL. (Eds.): *The Allocation of Economic Resources*, Stanford, California (Stanford University Press).

BACKHAUS, J. (1996): "Korreferat zu Raimund Dietz", see R. DIETZ (1996).

BARANZINI, M., SCAZZIERI, R. (Eds.) (1986): *Foundations of Economics, Structures of Inquiry and Economic Theory*, Oxford (Basil Blackwell).

BINSWANGER, H.C. (1985): *Geld und Magie - Deutung und Kritik der modernen Wirtschaft*, Stuttgart (Thienemann).

BINSWANGER, H.C. (1994): "Geld und Wachstumszwang" in: H. C. BINSWANGER, P. v. FLOTOW (1994) (Eds.): *Geld und Wachstum*, Stuttgart (Weitbrecht), pp. 81-124.

---

26 Simmel, G., in the sketch "Anfang einer unvollendeten Selbstdarstellung", quoted in: K. GASSEN / M. LANDMANN: *Buch des Dankes an Georg Simmel*; quoted in: W. JUNG: *Georg Simmel zur Einführung*, Berlin (Junius) 1990, p. 9.

RAIMUND DIETZ

BLAUG, B. (1985): *Economic Theory in Retrospect*, Cambridge (Cambridge University Press), fourth Edition.

BUCHANAN, J.M. (1979): *What Should Economists Do?*, Indianapolis (Liberty Press).

COASE, R.H. (1988): *The Firm, the Market and the Law*; Chicago, London (The University of Chicago Press).

COSER, L. (Ed.) (1965): *Georg Simmel*, Englewood Cliffs, New Jersey (Prentice-hall).

DIETZ, R. (1995): *Tausch, Geld und ökonomische Rationalität - Ein von Georg Simmel angeregter Beitrag zur Theorie der Wirtschaft*, Manuskript, Vienna.

DIETZ, R. (1996): "Tausch und Geld - Zur Entstehung der Geldwirtschaft als Ordnung", in: D. CASSEL (Ed.): *Entstehung und Wettbewerb von Systemen*, Berlin (Duncker & Humblot).

EES, H.V., GARRETSEN, H. (1992): *Institutional and Conventional Aspects of a Monetary Economy (and the Usefulness of Game Theory)*, mimeo, Univ. of Groningen.

FLOTOW, P.V. (1992): *Georg Simmels "Philosophie des Geldes" als ökonomisches Werk*, Dissertation Hochschule St. Gallen, Nr. 1327.

FRANKEL, H.S. (1977): *Money: The Conflict of Truth and Authority*, Oxford (Blackwell).

GAREGNANI, P. (1990): "Quantity of Capital", in: EATWELL e.al. (Eds.): *The New Palgrave*, New York-London (W.W. Norton), pp. 1-78.

GIJSEL, P. DE, HASLINGER F. (1993): "Quantitative versus qualitative (Nicht-)Neutralität des Geldes: Anmerkungen zu einer nicht überwundenen Dichotomie", in: STADERMANN/STEIGER (1993) (Eds.), pp. 109-120.

HAHN, F. (1982): *Money and Inflation*, Oxford (Basil Blackwell).

HAYEK, F. A. (1945): „The Use of Knowledge in Society", AER, Vol. 35/4. German: HAYEK (1952), pp. 103-121.

HAYEK, F. A. (1952): *Individualismus und wirtschaftliche Ordnung*, Erlenbach-Zürich (Eugen Rentsch Verlag).

HELLWIG, M. F. (1984): „The Challenge of Monetary Theory", *European Economic Review*, 37, pp. 215-242.

HIRSHLEIFER, J. (1985): "The Expanding Domain of Economics", *AER* (1985/2), December, pp. 53-68.

JUNG, W. (1990): *Georg Simmel zur Einführung*, Berlin (Junius) 1990.

LAIDLER, D., ROWE, N. (1980): "Simmel's Philosophy of Money: A Review Article for Economists", *Journal of Economic Literature*, 18 (March 1980), pp. 97-105.

LAVOIE, D. (1985): *Rivalry and Central Planning. The Socialist Calculation Debate Reconsidered*, Cambridge (Cambridge University Press).

LEVINE D.N. (Ed.) (1971): *Georg Simmel - On Individuality and Social Forms*, Chicago/London.

MARX, K. (1968): *Das Kapital*, Band 1, MEW Band 23, Berlin (Ost).

MENGER, C. (1871): *Grundsätze der Volkswirthschaftslehre*, in: F. A. HAYEK (Hg.): *The Collected Works of Carl Menger*, Vol. I, London (University of London) 1934.

MENGER, C. (1909): *Schriften über Geld und Währungspolitik*, in: F. A. HAYEK (Hg.): *Carl Menger Gesammelte Werke*, Bd. IV, Tübingen (J.C.B. Mohr [Paul Siebeck]) 1970.

MORGENSTERN, O. (1972): "Thirteen Critical Points in Contemporary Economic Theory: An Interpretation", *Journal of Economic Literature*, 10/4, pp. 1163-1189.

MYRDAL, G. (1953), *The Political Element in the Development of Economic Theory*, London (Routledge & Kegan).

NORTH, D. C. (1991): "Institutions", *Journal of Economic Perspectives*, 5/5, pp. 97-112.

OSTROY, J. M., STARR, R. M. (1990): "The Transactions Role of Money", in: KENNETH J. ARROW (Ed.): *Issues in Contemporary Economics*, Vol 1: *Markets and Welfare*, Houndmills (Macmillan), pp. 3-59.

ÖTSCH, W. (1991): "Gibt es eine Grundlagenkrise der neoklassischen Theorie?", *Jahrbücher für Nationalökonomie und Statistik*, 208/6, pp. 642-656.

PARSON, T., SHILS, E. (1951): *Toward a General Theory of Action*, Cambridge, Mass.

PATINKIN, D. (1965): *Money, Interest and Prices*, 2nd ed., New York (Harper & Row).

RAMMSTEDT, O. (1994): Geld und Gesellschaft in der "Philosophie des Geldes', in: H.C. BINSWANGER und P. V. FLOTOW (Eds.): *Geld und Wachstum*, Stuttgart (Weitbrecht).

RIESE, H. (1983): "Geldökonomie, Keynes und die Anderen, Kritik der monetären Grundlagen der Orthodoxie", *Ökonomie und Gesellschaft, Jahrbuch 1*, pp. 103-160.

SCHNABEL, P.-E. (1985): "Georg Simmel", in: A. KUPER, J. KUPER (Eds): *The Social Science Encyclopedia*, London, Boston (Routledge & Kegan Paul), pp. 750-751.

SCHUMPETER, J.A. (1943): *Capitalism, Socialism and Democracy*, Fifth Edition, London (George Allen & Unwin) 1976.

SIMMEL, G. (1900/1907): *Die Philosophie des Geldes*, 6. Auflage, Berlin (Duncker & Humblot), 1958. English: *The Philosophy of Money*, edited by D. Frisby, translated by Tom Bottomore and David Frisby, New York (Routledge) 1990.

STIGLITZ, J., (1990): *Wither Socialism? Perspectives from Economics of Information*, Wicksell Lectures, Stockholm, May 1990.

STREIT, M., WEGNER, G. (1993): "Information, Transactions, and Catallaxy: Reflections on Some Key Concepts of Evolutionary Market Theory", *mimeo*, Jena 1993.

SUDGEN, R. (1991): "Rational Choice: A Survey of Contributions from Economics and Philosophy", *The Economic Journal*, 101, pp. 751-785.

TRIER-MAYNTZ, R. (1990): "Georg Simmel", in: D. L. SILL (Ed.): *International Encyclopedia of the Social Sciences*, London, pp. 251-257.

VANBERG, V. (1994): "Cultural Evolution, Collective Learning, and Constitutional Design", in: D. REISMANN (Ed.): *Economic Thought and Political Theory*, Boston (Kluwer Academic Publisher), pp. 171-204.

Part Three

Ethics and Economics in Sombart, Spiethoff, Freyer, and in Older German Business Administration

Chapter 6

Ethics and Economics in the Work of Werner Sombart

FRIEDRICH LENGER

I. Schmoller's Student
II. Admirer of Marx
III. Weber's Companion
IV. Sombart's Economic Systems:
Changing Perspectives 1902-1934

The work of Werner Sombart (1863-1941) presents an especially interesting case for any attempt to take stock of the contribution of the historical school to the relationship between economics and ethics. One the one hand Sombart started out as a student of Schmoller following many characteristic paths of the historical school. On the other hand he used his reading of Marx to press for a more theoretical historism and sided with Weber in his attempt to separate carefully between scientific propositions and value judgements.[1] When Sombart published the first edition of his opus magnum *Modern Capitalism* in 1902 it was directed above all against "the foggy veils of 'ethical sentiments'" that to him seemed characteristic of the work of the ethical and historical school of economics so dominant in turn of the century Germany.[2] Since he is usually treated as a representative of the last generation of the historical school his critical stance is in need of explanation. It is due to the nature of Sombart's work that such an explanation has to proceed historically

---

1 I use *historism* for *Historismus* since the more common historicism is too closely linked to Popper's critique of it to allow an adequate understanding of this important tradition.
2 WERNER SOMBART: *Der moderne Kapitalismus*, Leipzig (Duncker & Humblot) 1902 (first edition), vol. 1, p. 211; all translations in this text are my own unless otherwise indicated.

itself.[3] It is well known that Sombart changed his political positions considerably over the course of his long life: from the socialism of the chair to fascism, as an East German author stated in the early 1960s, or from state socialism to romantic anticapitalism, as could be argued more accurately.[4] These changes were often accompanied by methodological reorientations and were clearly mirrored in his scholarly work as well. Thus the chronological approach being used in this article is not only the consequence of a déformation professionelle of the historian but also the reflection of Sombart's work itself. This work, however, will only be discussed as far as it touches upon the relationship between ethical values and economic and social science on the one hand, the role of ethical motivation in economic history and in economics more generally on the other.[5]

I. Schmoller's Student

When Werner Sombart studied law and economics (*Staatswissenschaften*) at the university of Berlin his most important teachers were August Meitzen, the historian of agrarian settlement structures to whom Max Weber dedicated his Roman agrarian history, the famous state socialist Adolph Wagner, and last but not least Gustav Schmoller. And it was Schmoller who supervised Sombart's dissertation on the agrarian conditions in the Roman Campagna. Agrarian questions were much discussed in the late 1880s and early 1890s as

---

3   The following analysis is largely based on FRIEDRICH LENGER: *Werner Sombart 1863-1941. Eine Biographie*, Munich (C.H. Beck) 1994. Since the notes are restricted to primary sources and to the most important and most recent secondary literature cf. *ibid.* for further documentation.

4   Cf. WERNER KRAUSE: *Werner Sombarts Weg vom Kathedersozialismus zum Faschismus*, Berlin (Rütten & Loening) 1962; F. LENGER: *Werner Sombart* (as note 3) and for an overview in English ARTHUR MITZMAN: *Sociology and Estrangement. Three Sociologists of Imperial Germany*, New York (Alfred A. Knopf) 1973, pp. 133-264 or more recently BERNHARD VOM BROCKE: "Werner Sombart (1863-1941). Capitalism - Socialism - His Life, Works and Influence Since Fifty Years", *Jahrbuch für Wirtschaftsgeschichte*, 1992/1, pp. 113-182.

5   For a more complete treatment cf. F. LENGER: *Werner Sombart* (as note 3).

is witnessed e.g. by Weber's investigations on rural labour in East Elbian Germany. Two years before Sombart's dissertation appeared the famous association of social policy had discussed settlement questions at its meeting in Frankfurt. Sombart's father, who was a wealthy agrarian entrepreneur and in addition had practical experience with the splitting up of larger estates among settlers, had given the main paper which was then commented upon by Schmoller.[6] Thus the comment of Karl Oldenburg, another student of Schmoller, that Werner Sombart had grown up "in an atmosphere filled with agrarian politics" was well taken.[7]

And there are no indications whatsoever in Sombart's early work that he might have denied his teacher's claim that economics could not be reduced to market relationships but had invariably to do with custom and culture, ethics and morality. This closeness to Schmoller can be seen most clearly in Sombart's attitude towards the peasantry and his opposition against "the Moloch of liberalistic doctrinarianism"[8]. His critique of the agrarian structures in the Roman campagna does not argue with economic efficiency but judges these structures by their social and cultural consequences. The most dangerous of these consequences was the expulsion of tenants and farmers in the interest of the landed aristocracy. "Private property thus loses (...) the best (and the only!) claim to economic justification", Sombart approvingly quoted Adolph Wagner[9]. This agreement with Wagner - and implicitly with Rodbertus - comprised the general subordination of private economic interests to the interests of the state. In the late 1880s this position did not yet bring Sombart into direct opposition to Schmoller. As his teacher in the German case Sombart favoured peasant settlements as the solution to the agrarian problems of the campagna and of Italy more generally. In the 1888 issue of Schmoller's yearbook both authors published articles. While Schmoller showed himself

---

6 Cf. *Verhandlungen der am 24. und 25. September 1886 in Frankfurt a.M. abgehaltenen Generalversammlung des Vereins für Socialpolitik*, Leipzig (Duncker & Humblot) 1887 (= Schriften des Vereins für Socialpolitik, vol. 32) and F. LENGER, *Werner Sombart* (as note 3), pp.41-47.

7 KARL OLDENBERG: "Besprechung von: Werner Sombart, Die römische Campagna", *Schmollers Jahrbuch*, 13 (1889), pp. 693-696.

8 WERNER SOMBART: "Besprechung von: Alberto Cencelli-Perti, La proprietà collettiva", *Schmollers Jahrbuch*, 14 (1890), pp. 1328.

9 W. SOMBART: *Die römische Campagna. Eine sozialökonomische Studie*, Leipzig (Duncker & Humblot) 1888 (= Staats- und sozialwissenschaftliche Studien, ed. by Gustav Schmoller, (vol. VIII:3), p. 116.

consoled by the fact, "that there have been centuries, in which the situation of the peasant has been improved", his student analysed the "family problem in Italy"[10.] In doing so he started out from Schmoller's equation of domesticity and morality and determined family life as "the anchorground of a true cultural existence". If Italy in his view lacked "a well ordered family organization" - which had to include "the natural destination of women as housewives and mothers" - the main reason was "that an economically viable peasantry still exists in only very few regions of Italy"[11].

When he passed his doctoral examinations, one can conclude, Sombart shared with Schmoller the basic outlines of a conservative social policy directed towards the peasantry and based on the morality of the bourgeois family. Included in this agreement was the selfevident understanding of economics as a historical discipline concerned with ethical issues and preparing the ground for social reform. Within this broad consensus the young Sombart showed strong sympathies for Wagner's state socialism, and this sympathy played a role when in 1889 he developed a first understanding of a new school of social science to which he wanted to belong. The three characteristics of this new school, among whose adherents he saw Heinrich Herkner, Alphons Thun or Karl Lamprecht, were a historical approach, a realistic conception and finally "state-socialist or socioeconomic (anti-individualist) thinking (in the direction of Rodbertus-Lassalle)"[12]. The realism Sombart advocated was the realism of Zola, and thus it is not surprising that after leaving the university and working for the Bremen chamber of commerce Sombart's work concentrated on the description of contemporary social ills for a while. The issues he adressed ranged from Italian problems to those of household production in local cigar making and in the Silesian textile industry. In these studies he developed an increasingly critical view of domestic industry, a sphere defended by Schmoller and other social reformers of the older generation because it presumably presented an ideal opportunity for combining industrial labour, family obligations and a partial agrarian self-sufficiency. But when

---

10 GUSTAV SCHMOLLER: "Die soziale Entwicklung Deutschlands und Englands hauptsächlich auf dem platten Land des Mittelalters", *Schmollers Jahrbuch*, 12 (1888), pp. 203-218 and W. SOMBART: "Das Familienproblem in Italien", *ibid.*, pp. 284-298.

11 *Ibid.*, pp. 288, 295, 292p.

12 Werner Sombart to Otto Lang, January 6th, 1889, International Institute for Social History, Amsterdam, Otto Lang collection I, Correspondence Sombart, p. 5.

Sombart took up an extraordinary professorship at Breslau in 1890 his disagreements with Schmoller still were concentrated mainly on questions of social policy and his reputation as a "demagogue in scholarly disguise" stemmed solely from his critical stance towards the labouring conditions in the weaving, iron and mining industries of Silesia.[13]

II. Admirer of Marx

All this was to change rather rapidly. It was Heinrich Braun, a revisionist social democrat and editor of the famous *Archiv für soziale Gesetzgebung und Statistik* (the later *Archiv für Sozialwissenschaft und Sozialpolitik*) to which Sombart frequently contributed, who pressed for a serious study of Marx. And Sombart seems to have read quite a few of Marx' works in 1892 and 1893. Late in 1891 he commented upon the Erfurt program of the German Social Democratic Party. He presented it as the "final victory of Marxist views, whose core is the materialist conception of history". Since at this point he still equated the first part of the program written by Kautsky with Marx' conception of history his reading does not seem to have progressed very quickly. More important, however, is Sombart's evolutionist understanding of a "mechanistic conception of history" according to which "one could watch the development with his arms crossed and wait..."[14]. This was politically quieting but it was also closely linked to Sombart's conviction that "in the whole of marxism (...) there is not a grain of ethic". Sombart developed this position in his critique of Julius Wolf and when he did so in 1892 he now was familiar with the most important writings of Marx and Engels. He insisted upon the "purely theoretical character of marxism" and even offered a

---

13 Cf. F. LENGER: *Werner Sombart* (as note 3), pp. 49-53 for a more complete analysis.

14 Quoted from the report of his paper in: *Neunundsechzigster Jahres-Bericht der Schlesischen Gesellschaft für Vaterländische Cultur* III, pp. 25ff.

class on Marx' writings in the winter term 1892/93.[15] But although - or because - the national press took notice only four or five students attended.[16]

There is no need to sketch Sombart's encounter with Marx in any detail
here. A sympathetic review of the third volume of *Capital* was followed by a
warm obituary for Engels upon his death in 1895 and the famous lectures on
Socialism and the Social Movement a year later.[17] Why was a student of
Schmoller attracted by Marx? There were above all two aspects of the materialist conception of history that the young Sombart found irresistibly attractive although at the same time there were quite a few aspects in Marx' writings - like Hegelian dialectics - that appeared to him hopelessly outdated. The
first of these two aspects attractive to Sombart was the promise of theory, a
promise that was most welcome because he considered the historical school
to be atheoretical. "For a positive development of economic theory", Sombart wrote towards the end of his lengthy review of the third volume of *Capital*, "besides the Austrian school chiefly 'scientific socialism' comes into
question"[18]. This should not be read as an equal estimation of the Austrian
school and of marxism. The latter was by far the more attractive source of
theoretical inspiration because its theory remained a historical one. What
Sombart found in the works of Marx and Engels was a *theoretical historism*
"that aims at a consequently theoretical-abstract treatment of economic phenomena while fully respecting their historical relativity."[19] Thus Sombart
clung to the historism taught by his teacher Schmoller although he wanted to
reconcile this historism with theory.

The second aspect Sombart considered to be absolutely convincing in
Marx was what he called his realism. He shared Marx' scepticism against "all

---

15 W. SOMBART: "Besprechung von: Julius Wolf, Sozialismus und Kapitalisti-
    sche Gesellschaftsordnung", *Archiv für soziale Gesetzgebung und Statistik*, 5
    (1892), pp. 487-498, esp. pp. 489f.
16 Cf. F. LENGER: *Werner Sombart* (as note 3), pp. 78f for a more complete ana-
    lysis and further documentation.
17 For a brief overview in English cf. F. LENGER: "Marx, the crafts and the first
    edition *of Modern Capitalism*", in: JÜRGEN BACKHAUS (Ed.): *Werner Sombart-
    Social Scientist*, Marburg (Metropolis) 1996, vol. 2, pp. 251-273.
18 W. SOMBART: "Zur Kritik des ökonomischen Systems von Karl Marx", *Archiv
    für soziale Gesetzgebung und Statistik*, 7 (1894), pp. 555-594, p. 588
    (quote).
19 W. SOMBART: *Friedrich Engels (1820-1895). Ein Blatt in der Entwicklungs-
    geschichte des Sozialismus*, Berlin (O. Häring) 1895, p. 39.

amiable explanations of history" that "underestimate the role of interests, i.e. in economic life mainly material interests, as moving forces", explanations which "therefore believed in miracles in the social world"[20]. While his admiration for the theoretical historism of Marx still could be interpreted as a certain closeness to the historical school his acceptance of Marx' materialist realism brought him into direct opposition to the ethical component of the tenets of the historical school. This acceptance of the materialist realism of Marx has too be qualified but when in 1896 Sombart applauded Marx for reformulating the most urgent problem in contemporary social science, namely the relationship between ideas and reality, he obviously felt that the problem had not been dealt with adequately by Schmoller and the historical school. The same holds true when the praise is considered he gave to Marx and Engels for freeing the area of social policy from mere phrases.[21] Social policy and its relationship to social science is thus one aspect we will have to consider more closely before coming back to the question how the marxist inspiration contributed to a conception of economic history and economics more generally different from and partly opposed to that of the older historical school.

III. Weber's Companion

Even in the 1890s Sombart was neither a marxist in any meaningful sense of the word nor was he a socialist. Still his views on social policy had changed considerably from his student days when he had accepted Schmoller's standards of morality as the reference point from which to judge economic and social phenomena and when he had shared Schmoller's sympathy for the peasantry and his view of the family as the core of social relationships. As we have already indicated it were in part Sombart's studies on the domestic industries of his time that provoked a new orientation. The labouring conditions here were worse than anywhere else and this had its reason in the almost unlimited dependency of the producers. The putting-out merchants,

---

20 W. SOMBART: *Sozialismus und soziale Bewegung im 19. Jahrhundert*, Jena (Gustav Fischer) 1896, pp. 39ff.
21 Cf. *ibid.*, p. 79.

Sombart noted, did not have to face an organized labour movement nor state regulations on labouring conditions. Furthermore labour in the domestic industries was far cheaper than factory labour, a fact that hindered the development towards the most modern forms of production. Domestic industries were technologically inferior, economically unnecessary, but socially harmful. "The verdict", Sombart concluded one of his articles on domestic industry, "has to be guilty."[22] The basis for this verdict was a vision of German social policy that should aim simultaneously at the rapid development and modernization of industrial capitalism and at the integration of labour and the labour movement into an increasingly democratic political system. This vision Sombart shared with quite a few of his colleagues - like Alfred and Max Weber or Gerhart von Schulze-Gävernitz - who have come to be known as the young generation of the association for social policy and who differed from Sombart mainly in their much stronger emphasis on an imperialist foreign policy as the ultimate goal of modernity, integration and development.[23]

This conception of social policy, that Sombart pursued in quite a few organizations of the social reform movement, was not limited to the area of domestic industry. When Sombart turned to artisans and small traders as his favourite objects of investigation during the second half of the 1890s the main perspective remained the same. He summarized it succinctly in a debate of the association for social policy on the future of the retail trade: "But to want to be moral at the cost of economic progress is the beginning of the end of the entire development of culture"[24]. Sombart's stand provoked harsh criticisms from older members of the association for social policy who usually favoured some measures of protection for those threatened by large capitalist enterprises. It was Sombart who linked this debate over the content of social policy to more general reflections on the role of political ideals in social policy and their relationship to scientific propositions. "The areas out of which

---

22 W. SOMBART: "Die Hausindustrie in Deutschland", *Archiv für soziale Gesetzgebung und Statistik*, 4 (1891), pp. 103-156.

23 Cf. F. LENGER: *Werner Sombart* (as note 3), pp. 93-110 and DIETER LINDENLAUB: *Richtungskämpfe im Verein für Socialpolitik im Kaiserreich vornehmlich vom Beginn des 'Neuen Kurses' bis zum Ausbruch des Ersten Weltkrieges (1890-1914)*, Wiesbaden (Steiner) 1967, vol. 2 (= Vierteljahrschrift für Sozial- und Wirtschaftsgeschichte, Beihefte, vol. 53).

24 *Verhandlungen der am 25., 26. und 27. September 1899 in Breslau abgehaltenen Generalversammlung des Vereins für Socialpolitik*, Leipzig (Duncker & Humblot) 1900 (= Schriften des Vereins für Socialpolitik, vol. 88), p. 253.

the ideals of social policy are usually being taken, are ethics and religion; more recently they have been joined by racial hygiene and nationalism". In this article of 1897 he proceeded not by discussing the relative political merits of these options but analysed the relationship between values and science within these different approaches. His scorn was especially directed against the ethical school of economics. Their representatives, he argued, took their standard by which they intended to measure economic life from economic life itself. Thus accepting the historicity of their standard they were in Sombart's view doomed to take a reactionary stand. To put it differently: Schmoller and his fellow economists of the ethical and historical school were always defending the past against the present or the present against the future. This was unacceptable politically as well as methodologically and Sombart expressed his general sympathy for those positions who used absolute standards to determine the ideals for social policy, i.e. the nationalist orientation so strongly expressed two years earlier by his colleague Max Weber and that of racial hygiene which was to play a role in Sombart's later work - not the least in his books on the role of Jews in economic life.[25]

The substance of the political positions discussed by Sombart need not interest us here. His own position shaded between a general advocacy of productivity and a more specifically described cultural progress. More important in the context of a discussion of the relationship between ethics and economics are his methodological arguments. They went clearly in the direction of advocating a science free of or at least clearly separate from value judgements. This becomes clear from Sombart's discussion of the possible usefulness of an analysis of the ideals governing social policy. A scientific approach, he explained, could only do two things: It could explain *genetically* the emergence of certain ideals or it could treat them *critically*. Such a critique would not yield, however, a ranking of ideals, but could only bring errors and inner contradictions to the fore or analyse the relationship of one ideal to the other. - The message was clear and it was diametrically opposed to the convictions of Schmoller: Under no circumstances whatsoever could the choice between different ideals be based on scientific work.[26]

---

25 Cf. W. SOMBART: "Ideale der Sozialpolitik", *Archiv für soziale Gesetzgebung und Statistik,* 10 (1897), pp. 1-48.

26 Cf. *ibid.* and RITA ALDENHOFF: "Nationalökonomie, Nationalstaat und Werturteile. Wissenschaftskritik in Max Webers Freiburger Antrittsrede im Kontext der Wissenschaftsdebatten in den 1890er Jahren", in: GERHARD SPRENGER (Ed.): Deutsche Rechts- und Sozialphilosophie um 1900, Stuttgart (Stei-

The similarity to Max Weber's position first indicated in 1894/95 is obvious and it is underlined by a comparison with the famous *Geleitwort* to the *Archiv für Sozialwissenschaft und Sozialpolitik* of 1904. Edgar Jaffé had bought the *Archiv für soziale Gesetzgebung und Statistik* in July 1903 and now edited the journal under the new name together with Max Weber and Werner Sombart. The *Geleitwort* had a threefold function: It ought to stress the continuity with the predecessor of the new *Archiv*, it had to explain the position of the new editors (including their views on social policy) and in addition it almost served as an introduction to Weber's famous article on objectivity included in the first volume of the new series. For all three purposes Sombart was a suitable author, and he wrote the first version of the *Geleitwort* with quite a few borrowings from an earlier article he had written on the *Archiv* in 1897.[27] Around the turn of the century both Weber and Sombart stood for a modernist social policy in clear opposition to the ideals of Schmoller and others and they both advocated - in even clearer opposition to the tenets of the ethical school of economics - a clear separation betweeen the sphere of values and that of science. Although Weber expressed the latter point far more convincingly in the years to come the closeness to the young Sombart should be noted. And it was Sombart who was Weber's most important supporter in the debates on value judgements that were to take place at the meetings of the association for social policy or the German society for sociology.

---

ner) 1991 (= Archiv für Rechts- und Sozialphilosophie, Beiheft 43), pp. 79-90.

27 Cf. with detailed references - including a letter of Sombart claiming the authorship of the *Geleitwort* - F. LENGER: *Werner Sombart* (as note 3), p. 143. WILHELM HENNIS: "Die 'Protestantische Ethik' - ein 'überdeterminierter' Text?", *Sociologia Internationalis*, 33 (1995), pp. 1-17, esp. 16 explicitly refutes my claim that Sombart wrote the famous *Geleitwort*, but unfortunately does not confront the evidence for it.

IV. Sombart's Economic Systems: Changing Perspectives 1902-1934

The first edition of *Modern Capitalism* which appeared in 1902 showed clearly where Sombart had departed from Schmoller's example: It pleaded for more theory, it continued the fight against "the foggy veils of ethical sentiments" and it contained - at least implicitly - a justification for the kind of social policy advocated by the so-called younger generation in the association for social policy. This implicit justification originated in an analysis of the artisanal fate in 19th century Germany, that made up about half of the book's almost 1350 pages. The analysis proceeded both historically and theoretically. Sombart's historical investigation carefully described that the artisanal crafts did experience a decline since 1850. His theoretical analysis, however, intended to prove that this decline was inevitable, that the artisanal crafts had to decline vis à vis the competition of industrial capitalism. Sombart's theory of industrial competition that developed this "proof" was heavily influenced by Marx and repeatedly referred to "capitalist interest, which means the same as capital's striving for profit" as "the moving force[s] of modern economic development"[28]. It need not interest us here in any detail. Sombart was quite conscious of the fact that this theoretical claim marked a fundamental difference to Schmoller: "What separates" us, he wrote in the prefatory note to his book "is the constructive in the organization of the material, the radical postulate of uniform explanation from last causes, the building of a social system from all historical phenomena, to put it briefly: it is what I call the specifically theoretical. I might as well say: it is Karl Marx."[29]

Sombart's confession to theory was not meant as a farewell to historism nor as the acceptance of the deductive reasoning of the Austrian school: "To search for economic motivations without reference to the social milieu in which they operate, i.e. as if it were in a vacuum, is nonsense, is simply logically wrong thinking."[30] This comment on the Austrian school makes clear enough that Sombart wanted to reconcile theory and history, that he continued to strive for a *theoretical historism*. Measured against this claim the first edition of *Modern Capitalism* was only a limited success. On the

---

28 W. SOMBART, *Der moderne Kapitalismus* (as note 2), vol. 2, p. 7.
29 *Ibid.*, vol. 1, XXIX.
30 *Ibid.*, XXVIIp.

one hand Sombart did not offer a sufficiently clear exposition of the relationship between his theoretical concepts and the empirical material. In 1903 at the meeting of German historians in Heidelberg he did not succeed in explaining to his colleagues, why his theoretical definitions should not depend upon the accuracy of his historical descriptions. Sombart had already spoken of theoretical concepts as mere "tools of thinking" in his review of the third volume of *Capital* but *Modern Capitalism* did not yet develop this idea in the direction of idealtypical constructions that Weber was to pursue soon. On the other hand - and even more importantly - the genesis of capitalism (title of volume 1) and the theory of capitalist development (title of volume 2) were not sufficiently integrated. The *theory* of capitalist development had its main reference point in the fate of German artisans in the late 19th century, a fate that Sombart showed to be governed by the laws of industrial competition. The *genesis* of capitalism, however, was relegated to late medieval Italy and was presented as a highly contingent historical process. The rather long transition period between the birth and the maturity of the capitalist economic system, the transition from an artisanal phase to a capitalist one, remained very much neglected, a fact that is somewhat surprising given the strong interest Sombart had demonstrated rather early in a "developmental history"[31].

The reconciliation between history and theory was to remain a lifelong preoccupation of Sombart but it is not the only important feature of the first edition of *Modern Capitalism*. Although he had followed Marx repeatedly in his theory of industrial competition Sombart's approach diverged from the tenets of historical materialism in some fundamental respects. This can already be seen in his definition of the artisan: "He aims at a livelihood in accordance with his status, no less but above all no more."[32] The definition of the artisan reflected his general conviction that "the substance of a specific economic form is thus characterized by the final end of economic activity". Or as he expressed "the basic idea of this book" more succinctly: "One will have to get used to form the categories of economics according to the spirit prevalent in economic phenomena"[33]. Following his own program Sombart

---

31 Cf. GÜNTHER ROTH: "Rationalization in Max Weber's developmental history", in: SCOTT LASH, SAM WHIMSTER (Eds.): *Max Weber. Rationality and Modernity*, London 1987, pp. 75-91 on the much discussed developmental history of the 1890s and early 1900s.
32 W. SOMBART, *Der moderne Kapitalismus* (as note 2), vol. 1, p. 86.
33 *Ibid.*, pp. 5 and 202.

found the emergence of a capitalist spirit far more important than the mere accumulation of money since what was needed "to transform the accumulated amounts of money into capital is the capitalist spirit of its owner", namely "all those sentiments of the mind, that we have encountered as peculiar to the capitalist entrepreneur: the striving for profit, the calculating sense, the economic rationalism."[34]

There is no need to summarize Sombart's much discussed account here. Suffice it to note that for him the genesis of capitalism was above all a "psychogenesis", an approach hardly compatible with his alleged marxism.[35] It was already in the prefatory note that Sombart had written: "The first, that to me seems worth stressing, is this: that we should never let us mislead to explain social reality from other last causes than the motivation of living humans."[36] - This should not be read as a refutation of the materialist realism of Marx but rather as a completion. As early as 1896 Sombart had noted the lack of psychological explanation in Marx and proposed to replace the outdated dialectics by such psychological explanations.[37] With this aim he did not stand alone. Simmel wrote his famous *Philosophy of Money* a few years later with the explicit intention "to erect a ground floor to historical materialism in such a way, that the inclusion of economic life among the causes of spiritual culture maintains its explanatory value, while those economic forms themselves are recognized as the result of deeper judgements and tendencies, of psychological, well metaphysical preconditions."[38] Simmel too did not want to refute Marx but to complete his work as a possible base for modern social science.

The relationship between ideas and reality, one can conclude, was among the basic problems Sombart wanted to solve in his *Modern Capitalism*. Sombart's solution gave considerable weight to the independent role of ideas as can be seen in his genealogy of the acquisitive spirit. Whatever one may think of his solution it remains Sombart's merit to have posed the problem of mediating structural processes and ideal factors quite clearly. Contemporaries like Alfred Vierkandt recognized this general importance of Sombart's book, an importance that would not be diminished "if the experts, the

---

34 *Ibid.*, p. 207.
35 *Ibid.*, p. 391.
36 *Ibid.*, p. XVIII.
37 Cf. e.g. W. SOMBART: *Sozialismus und soziale Bewegung*, (as note 20), p. 72.
38 GEORG SIMMEL: *Philosophie des Geldes*, Frankfurt a.M. (Suhrkamp) 1989, 13, (=Georg Simmel-Gesamtausgabe, vol. 6) first published in 1900.

economists and historians, will bring forward all sorts of critical objections against its content."[39] Towards the end of the 20th century one might prefer to judge Sombart's achievement in comparison to Weber. Such a comparative evaluation cannot be offered here but it seems obvious how similar Weber's problematic in his essays on *The Protestant Ethic and the Spirit of Capitalism* is to Sombart's.[40]

The closer investigation of the normative background - be it ethical or religious - of the acquisitive spirit and of economic rationalism became one of the main occupations of Sombart during the last decade before World War I and the books devoted to this question earned Sombart quite a few harsh criticisms from Weber.[41] There is no need to follow these debates or Sombart's attempts to isolate single factors like luxury and war or the allegedly specific qualification of Jews for capitalism here.[42]

Sombart increasingly linked the question of the origins of the capitalist spirit to his more and more critical evaluation of capitalist culture. Already the first edition of *Modern Capitalism* had contained quite a few observations on the nature of capitalism that remind the reader of both Simmel's remarks on the reversal of ends and means as a typical feature of capitalism and of Weber's comment that capitalism once established no longer needed any capitalist spirit for its existence.[43] "With capital having become a person", Sombart had observed, "the person slowly became a thing, a will-less wheel in the giant work of modern business. So it comes that even after the sense for the possession of money has died the entrepreneur locked within the mechanisms of business life still keeps on restlessly acquiring, until he fi-

---

39 ALFRED VIERKANDT: "Jahresbericht über die Literatur zur Kultur- und Gesellschaftslehre aus dem Jahre 1903", *Archiv für die gesamte Psychologie*, 4 (1905), pp. 8-14.

40 For two excellent comparative evaluations of Weber and Sombart cf. PERTTI TÖTTÖ: *Werner Sombart ja kiista kapitalismin hengestä*, Tampere (Vastapaino) 1991 and FREDDY RAPHAEL: *Judaisme et capitalisme. Essai sur le controverse entre Max Weber et Werner Sombart*, Paris (Presses Universitaires de France) 1982.; cf. also F. LENGER: *Werner Sombart* (as note 3), pp. 128-135.

41 Cf. *ibid*, pp. 197-207 and 239.

42 Cf. *ibid.*, pp. 187-232.

43 Cf. LAWRENCE A. SCAFF: *Fleeing the Iron Cage. Culture, Politics, and Modernity in the Thought of Max Weber*, Berkeley, Ca. (University of California Press) 1989 and for an interpretation of Sombart as the analyst of rationalization and alienation FRANCO RIZZO: *Werner Sombart*, Naples (Liguori) 1974.

nally regards acquiring as the real end of all activity and being."[44] But for reasons not to be discussed here what may be read as an analysis of reification and alienation increasingly turned into an expression of Sombart's irritation over the developments of a modern mass society during the years to come.[45]

His critique of capitalist culture gained a new quality when in 1913 he published *Der Bourgeois* a book whose English title *The Quintessence of Capitalism* is a rather imprecise translation but one that captures the content of the book quite well. This summary of both his studies on the origins of the capitalist spirit and of his criticisms of modern mass culture introduced two new aspects. Both were taken from the work of Sombart's friend Max Scheler who had applied the Nietzschean theory of resentment to the bourgeois spirit. For Scheler as well as for Sombart the utilitarian spirit of the bourgeoisie expressed little more than the resentment against the seigneurial mode of life critized by bourgeois authors like Alberti only because it was out of reach for themselves. The merits of this theory of resentment need not interest us here. For Sombart it was closely linked to a second aspect: the acceptance of Scheler's value tables with its clear priority of the values of life and culture over those of utility and comfort[46]. Scheler's material ethic of values did not change Sombart's view of capitalist culture but it provided a seemingly secure basis for his critique of culture. From this basis he attacked the English merchants during World War I as well as the socialist tradition which in the early 1920s he now subsumed under his theory of resentment.[47]

---

44 W. SOMBART, *Der moderne Kapitalismus* (as note 2), vol. 1, p. 397.

45 Cf. F. LENGER: "Die Abkehr der Gebildeten von der Politik. Werner Sombart und der 'Morgen'", in: GANGOLF HÜBINGER, WOLFGANG J. MOMMSEN (Eds.): Intellektuelle im Deutschen Kaiserreich, Frankfurt a.M. (Fischer) 1993, pp. 62-77, 215-218 and F. LENGER: *Werner Sombart* (as note 3), pp. 136-176.

46 Cf. W. SOMBART: *Der Bourgeois. Zur Geistesgeschichte des modernen Wirtschaftsmenschen*, Munich (Duncker & Humblot) 1913; MAX SCHELER: "Das Ressentiment im Aufbau der Moralen", in: MAX SCHELER: *Vom Umsturz der Werte. Abhandlungen und Aufsätze*, Bern (Francke) [5]1972 (= Gesammelte Werke, vol. 3), pp. 33-147 (first published in 1912) and F. LENGER: *Werner Sombart* (as note 3), pp. 232-237.

47 Cf. on the two most repulsive works of Sombart F. LENGER: "Werner Sombart als Propagandist eines deutschen Krieges", in: W. J. MOMMSEN (Ed.): *Kultur und Krieg. Die Rolle der Intellektuellen, Künstler und Schriftsteller im Ersten Weltkrieg*, Munich (Oldenbourg) 1996 (= Schriften des Historischen Kollegs, Kolloquien, vol. 34), pp. 65-76 and F. LENGER: *Werner Sombart* (as note 3), pp. 282-305.

Implicitly his acceptance of Scheler's value tables also questioned the principle of a value-free science, a principle that later regained its prominence in Sombart's writings when attacked by the Nazi dictatorship.[48]

As Rolf Peter Sieferle has noted recently Sombart's neoidealist turn to Scheler's philosophy of values brought him into a difficult position. On the one hand he postulated that values governed reality and that men's will was capable to shape reality according to these values but on the other hand his studies of capitalism continued to reveal the force of structural constraints.[49] This can be seen most clearly in the third volume of *Modern Capitalism* that appeared in 1927, ten years after the appearance of the second edition of *Modern Capitalism*, a completely revised book that had changed from a historical social theory to a constructive economic history.[50] The third volume now carried the story to the present and contained an interesting change of perspective. While the book still displayed many of the virtues of the first edition and while its author correctly noted - "And everything that maybe good in my work it owes to the spirit of Marx." - its main interest was now concentrated on processes of rationalization, objectivation, spiritualization and depersonalization.[51] Since these were the principles of both capitalism and socialism his portrayal of these processes resembled more and more the Weberian iron cage. Still for Sombart there had to be a way out: "The economy is not our fate", he told his readers in 1932, reversing the famous saying of Walther Rathenau. And he continued: "thus the future organization of the economy is not a problem of knowledge but of will."[52] According to Sombart this will should be directed towards an authoritarian state, towards eco-

---

48 Cf. *ibid.*, pp. 377-385.
49 Cf. ROLF PETER SIEFERLE: *Die Konservative Revolution. Fünf biographische Skizzen*, Frankfurt a.M. (S. Fischer) 1995, pp. 74-105.
50 Cf. for a discussion of the changes from the first to the second edition F. LENGER: *Werner Sombart* (as note 3), pp. 219-246; cf. also MICHAEL APPEL: *Werner Sombart - Theoretiker und Historiker des modernen Kapitalismus*, Marburg (Metropolis) 1992.
51 W. SOMBART: *Der moderne Kapitalismus. Historisch-systematische Darstellung des gesamteuropäischen Wirtschaftslebens von seinen Anfängen bis zur Gegenwart*, vol. 3: *Das Wirtschaftsleben im Zeitalter des Hochkapitalismus*, Munich (Duncker & Humblot) 1927, part 1, p. XIX; cf. F. LENGER: *Werner Sombart* (as note 3), pp. 332-345.
52 W. SOMBART: Die Zukunft des Kapitalismus, Berlin (Buchholz & Weißwange) 1932, p. 5.

nomic autarky and it should favour artisans and peasants because only these precapitalist groups were immune to the processes characteristic of both capitalism and socialism. That these ideas forming the basis of his book *German Socialism* in 1934 offered no solution to the problems of the early 1930s is obvious.[53] But it seems ironic that with these ideas Sombart not only returned to his earlier esteem of the peasantry but also repeated what he had identified as the systematic fault of the ethical and historical school in 1897, i.e. to use the standards of the past to cure the problems of the present.

---

53 Cf. W. SOMBART: *Deutscher Sozialismus*, Berlin (Buchholz & Weißwange) 1934 and F. LENGER: *Werner Sombart* (as note 3), pp. 366-377.

Discussion Summary

BETTINA LÖHNERT

Paper discussed:
FRIEDRICH LENGER: Ethics and Economics in the Work of
Werner Sombart

The first part of the discussion centered around the comparison of Sombart's, Weber's, and Schumpeter's conception of the entrepreneur.

Quite obviously Sombart was connected to the theory of Weber's charismatic leader and Schumpeter's entrepreneur. The exchange of ideas on the theory of the entrepreneur could be interpreted as the early version of the theory of the firm (ACHAM).

In his theory of the entrepreneur Sombart went through many changes. He starts out by labeling merchants and Jewish entrepreneurs with a negative image while putting the real entrepreneur on the positive side. In *Der Bourgeois* this had already changed and that may well have been under the influence of Schumpeter. Here he describes the binary opposition between the positive image of the Schumpeterian entrepreneur or charismatic leader in Weber's sense and the negative image of the bourgeois spirit resulting in an utilitarian and hedonistic attitude. Two years later, in *Merchants and Heros* the picture of the merchants changed to the negative again. Because of these many changes there are certainly influences from Schumpeter, maybe indirectly also from Weber, but they never lasted and because of this volatility in position we cannot take Sombart's model of the entrepreneur at the same level as the Schumpeterian model (LENGER).

Schumpeter and Sombart both emphasize the profoundly unethical essence of the entrepreneural spirit. Therefore it is no accident that they both counted pirates as typical entrepreneurs. Here we can find a more general problem of how to integrate the role of the entrepreneur as someone who is breaking the rules into the system of ethics adopted in society (AVTONOMOV).

DISCUSSION SUMMARY

In comparing Sombart's thoughts on bureaucracy to Weber it seems that elements of cultural criticism in Weber were more dominant. Weber's comments on rationality and the difficulties on maintaining a personality under modern circumstances is more frightening and deeper (RINGER).

The second major part of the discussion concerned the different influences on and the importance of Schmoller and Marx in Sombart's work.

It was remarked that Müller-Armack, one of the fathers of the German system of the social market economy (*Soziale Marktwirtschaft*), once noted, that he was most influenced by the Post-Marxist theory of capitalism by Sombart and others. Consequently, we have to take this Marxist strand in Sombart and its influence on the theory of the social market economy more seriously (KOSLOWSKI).

The speaker agreed that this line of tradition is often overlooked. But as surprising this Marxist-Post-Marxist influences might seem at first sight, they have to be explained with Sombart's specific conception of capitalism and socialism, which are only indicated by labeling it an evolutionist reading of Marx. In Sombart's very particular reading of Marx there are no deviding lines between capitalism and socialism. There are just socialist and capitalist elements that continiuously rebalance their weights (LENGER).

Sombart seems to be more impressed with Marx's special conception of ethics than with Schmoller's treatment of ethics (YAGI).

What was attractive for Sombart in Marx is that in his theory, ethics are not important. But Sombart did not keep this position all of his life. For some time the Marxist conception of ethics proved to be useful to argue against Schmoller, but later in life Sombart accepted the value template of Schmoller (LENGER).

In his earlier work Sombart praised the conservative and moralistic approach of Schmoller and then changed his mind completely: First he had seen domestic industries as a stronghold of cultural life, then he all of a sudden condemmed them as socially harmful, economically unnecessary and technologically inferior. The question was raised what his theoretical or psychological motives for this radical change were (CHMIELEWSKI).

In general we can indicate three major sources of influence for these changes in Sombart. Firstly, the change of his professional situation between being a student and working for the chamber of commerce moved him from theory to the reality of economic life. As a student Sombart enjoyed the generous hospitality of some Italian aristocrats, who told him about agrarian life in Italy. This theoretical distance probably caused his more romantic positions during his youth. He actually wanted to own one of his fathers estates and to be a patriarchic squire. But from 1888 on he gets in contact with economic reality.

Secondly, there is the change between a preference for agrarian problems and those of domestic industry. It may well be that the shocking labour conditions in domestic industries in Silesia in 1890 made him change his mind.

Thirdly, Sombart's reading of Marx fostered such a change and made him think of Schmoller as naive and romantic (LENGER).

Obviously Sombart was unsatisfied with Schmoller's theory of economics. But what was Sombart looking for in Marxist theory that he did not find in Schmoller? It is not true that Schmoller did not have a theory. After all the *Grundlagen der Volkswirtschaftslehre* is a sound textbook of economics and is not at all just telling stories. Maybe Sombart was in fact looking for the absolut knowledge in the Hegelian-Marxist sense. This is a common phenomenon of modernity: the periode between 1900-1945 was drunk of histor*icism*, which is quite a different concept than the older histor*ism*, which was more empirical and inductive. We find this general turn towards a Marxist form of historism also in Sombart. Although this line of thinking is not identical with Dialectic Materialism it is still within the same frame of mind. Therefore we have to ask whether Sombart's critique on Schmoller can be described in the dichotomy of theory vs. history. They rather are different concepts of theory and history in Marx and Schmoller. In Marx, the economic theory as the key to social progress entitles the economic reformer to political and intellectual power. This is a very problematic position (KOSLOWSKI).

The speaker responded to this remarkes that Sombart and Schmoller's other students were still waiting for Schmoller's textbook of the *Grundlagen der Nationalökonomie*. During that time, all they had were their lecture scripts of Schmoller which were not very helpful for teaching economics. Maybe this was one reason for Sombart's dissatisfaction with Schmoller's theory.

What Sombart also missed in Schmoller was the discussion of developmental history. Here Marx certainly was not the only inspiration to Sombart. Most prominently Darwin has to be mentioned here. That may explain why Sombart considers Schmoller to be insufficient in theory. It is doubtful whether Sombart really took this turn towards the Marxist grand theory. Although his book *Modern Capitalism* tries to include other inspirations, it essentially remains within the traditional historistic conception of the individual (LENGER).

The polemic against Schmoller should not be taken too serious since it was just a reaction against his great achievements and his fame. The marxist-historist theory of capitalism on the other hand does overrate the generality of a grand theory. The idea of a modern capitalism is misleading, because there are so many forms of capitalisms. Trying to find an overall explanation of the totality of history was the temptation of this period in philosophy and economics, a line of thought that goes back to Hegel's idea of absolute knowledge. Looking on this notion from outside Europe, will seem to be very strange to Non-Europeans today (KOSLOWSKI).

It makes a difference whether we consider Marxist theory under the category of being true or of being fruitful. It might not be true. Nevertheless, Marx's inspiration in the 1890ies was fruitful for Sombart (LENGER).

Chapter 7

Historical Changes and Economics in Arthur Spiethoff's Theory of *Wirtschaftsstil* (Style of an Economic System)

VITANTONIO GIOIA

I. Introduction

The analysis of historical changes represented certainly a pivotal element in the work of representatives of the German historical school. However at the beginning of the 1900s the resultes achieved in reference to this theme after half a century of intense scientific production seemed quite unsatisfactory. The German historical school had yielded interesting historical analysis, new fields of research and original methodological contributions but the effects on the theoretical constructs within historical economics were quite scarce. The sense of frustration and confusion was further increased by the conclusion of *Methodenstreit* and by the awareness of the capability of the Neo-classical approach to produce a rising stratification of new theoretical constructs and new scientific categories. So, while the hiatus between history and theory did not seem to have any negative effects on the scientific productivity of the Neo-classical approach, within the German historical school, instead, the attempt to produce a stronger connection between the theoretical and empirical dimension seemed arid and unfruitful.[1]

A. Spiethoff's work arises in this cultural climate. As a business cycle theoretician he intended to give a contribution also in relation to the methodological field in order to overcome the "sterile contra positions" of *Methodenstreit* and to build a historical economics which was able to create not only statements valid "from an empirical point of view" but also "asserts" of general validity; in short: theories. So, within the coordinates of the *"anschauliche Theorie"*, he constructed two analytical devices, the *Wirtschaftsstil* and the "real type", which could in his opinion represent the answer to the many unsettled questions posed by the German historical school. In this paper we will try to understand the epistemological significance of Spiethoff's attempt.

But it is also useful to remember that Spiethoff represents an interesting case for other reasons.

He is certainly a well known author, but he is known especially for his business cycle theory, while his methodological contribution is completely ignored or only episodically recalled.[2]

Now, if we consider Spiethoff's work we have to observe not only that these two aspects (business cycle theory and epistemological reflection) are closely connected, but also that Spiethoff himself insists on the fact that it is impossible to understand the former without the latter. In this paper we cannot see the strong internal relations between the two sides of Spiethoff's work systematically, but we invert the traditional evaluation of it: we primarily consider Spiethoff's methodological and epistemological reflection and use the references to his business cycle theory only episodically and in order to illustrate particular methodological aspects. Admittedly, this is not the correct approach to Spiethoff's work as a whole. The advantage of such a choice is twofold: we can fix our attention on previously neglected or underevaluated aspects of Spiethoff's reflection; we do this deliberately in order to limit our evaluations exclusively to his epistemological reflection.

---

1   On the evolution, conclusions and theoretical consequences of the *Methodenstreit* cf. HERKNER (1924), SOMBART (1930), HAUSER (1989), GIOIA (1991).

2   On this aspect see the interesting considerations made by CLAUSING (1958) and KAMP (1958).

II. G. Schmoller and A. Spiethoff

As we said, Spiethoff's starting point was given by the sense of dissatis-faction of the representatives of the German historical school at the begin-ning of the 20th century. The first step of his analysis is also necessarily de-termined by the evaluation of Gustav Schmoller's work. Spiethoff is con-vinced that the "Schmoller programme" (Backhaus 1994) did not give the de-sired results not only because of external factors (advances in economics, the success of the Neo-classical school, the results of *Methodenstreit*, etc), but also due to the intrinsic limitations in Schmoller's theory.[3]

In fact, referring to the famous passage from the second volume of the *Grundriß* where Schmoller underlines that the task he has set himself is not that of establishing a new theory, but that of freeing political economy from "false abstractions", Spiethoff sees the function of Schmoller's work as that of eliminating the tautological "self-referentiality" of pure economics. He stresses that on the methodological plane, Schmoller found a different theo-retical vision, but at the same time, he did not develop a paradigm for its sys-tematic exploration. On the evidence of this passage Spiethoff interprets Schmoller's work as an attempt to graft onto the old theories procedures ca-pable of demonstrating their explicative powers.

Spiethoff writes, "The starting points remain the old ones, and they are discussed in detail" from the point of view of their "generality" and from that of the distance separating them from reality by means of the "simplification" that the theories must undergo (Spiethoff 1938, p. 28), but they are not "re-placed by others". In this way it is shown "how much empirical material is lost, if the mental construct derives exclusively, as a logical deduction, from given premises" (Spiethoff 1938, p. 28), but at the same time no single the-oretical hypothesis emerges capable of integrating this empirical material into a new conceptual construct: "the empirical enquiry does not cohere into a new theory" and ends up serving only for "the discussion of the old theories."

It follows that Schmoller's main contribution lies in his criticism of the old theories and in the criticism of the methodological approach of pure eco-nomics, which is incapable of integrating observed reality into theoretical

---

3   References to Schmoller are, of course, present in the entire work of Spiet-hoff, but a systematic analysis of Schmollers contribution to the economics is included in two essays. Cf. SPIETHOFF (1918) and SPIETHOFF (1938).

circuits. Spiethoff states that Schmoller strips "the ideal-typical theory of its linearity and its rigidity", but does not replace it with a theory that can compete with it. Even in Schmoller's pivotal theory of prices and value

> there is no ... use of empirical materials for an autonomous conceptual construct, - laden with empirics - to place alongside the ideal-typical construct, there is no conclusive conceptual scheme demonstrated from the empirical material, to place as a representation of reality alongside the ideal-typical one of pure theory (ideal and real representation) (Spiethoff 1938, p. 29).

From this point of view in Schmoller the attempt to construct a "concrete" theory (*anschauliche*), capable of relating the stages of development of analytical structures to the changes that have meanwhile taken place in the object of enquiry, remains an unfulfilled aspiration. The defect in Schmoller's attempt, which he himself admitted, was probably the fact that he tried to solve this problem with too general an approach, which brought him up against two circumstances that could not converge and complete each other in a single, easily readable theoretical context. In fact, on the theoretical plane, it tended to pose a series of interesting questions-begging; on the empirical plane, the attempt to master an enormous amount of overlapping material in compositions, though meaningful, lacks a unifying theoretical interpretative key. In both cases Schmoller's work could be read as a plea for scientific prudence and as a collection of correct observations, but not as a cohesive explicative theory.

The image that throws most light on Spiethoff's final evaluation of Schmoller's work emerges when he writes of Schmoller creating only a theoretical context where "theory and empirically examined reality are left to fight it out", causing theoretical "bewilderment", since he is not able to tie economics to new certainties. (Spiethoff 1925, p. 29)

The critics, including the most recent, have confirmed the correctness of Spiethoff's interpretation.[4]

---

4 Cf. esp. SCHUMPETER (1926), p. 19; HUTCHISON (1969), pp. 380-3; LANE, RIE-MERSMA (1953), pp. 435-6; VEBLEN (1901), pp. 92-3; MITCHELL (1969), p. 559; FAUCCI (1988), p. 137; SCHEFOLD (1989), ZAGARI (1993), GIOIA (1990, 1991).

VITANTONIO GIOIA

III. *Anschauliche* and Pure Theory

After Schmoller, "far more important than the execution of the king is the question of whether the procedure for the succession has been, or can be, made ready" (Luhmann 1985, p. 8). The attempt to answer this question constitutes the horizon within which Spiethoff moves and within which we can see not only his insistence on the concept of *"anschauliche Theorie"* and the creation of the concept of *Wirtschaftsstil*, but also the analysis of the business cycle, as the basic testing ground for a theoretical approach capable of becoming a candidate for the succession.

In fact, the actual definition of such an approach involves serious problems both for intrinsic reasons regarding its range of theoretical references, and because of the need to overcome the initial obstacle of the strength of the theory which, rather inappropriately, is considered its rival. In the *Preface to the English Edition* of *Krisen* Spiethoff points out:

> Unfortunately there is no generally accepted name for this method. Some call it "empirical-realistic", others "concrete", yet others "observational" (anschaulich). Among English names which have been proposed are "essential-intrinsic theory" (E. Salin), "theory of economic Gestalt" (Redlich), "all-round sociological theory" (H. W. Singer), "realistic theory" (Hero Möiler) (Spiethoff 1953, p. 75).

To arrive at a definition of this method it is useful to start from the term *"anschauliche"* in order to illustrate the essential features of A. Spiethoff's work. This term was first brought into scientific debate by E. Salin in the context of his study of W. Sombart's *Der moderne Kapitalismus* (Salin 1927, p. 314), but it is certainly with Spiethoff himself that it assumes a specific epistemological density both as the distinguishing trait of Schmoller's work and as the key concept of his own analytical approach. [5]

The meaning of this term is difficult to convey outside the German context because of its semantic wealth (and also ambiguity). It comes as no surprise that Fritz Redlich, translator into English of some of Spiethoff's methodological texts, renders it with a paraphrase: "economic Gestalt theory". By using this paraphrase, Redlich explicitly recovers the "Gestalt" category which, taken from psychology, referred to the capacity of the single

---

5 In order to have a general vision in reference to this theme see SPIETHOFF (1932, 1938) and SALIN (1944), cf. especially pp. 208-220.

phenomenon to embrace elements whose interpretative key was to be found in the total psychical life of the person under analysis. (Lane and Riemersma 1953, p. 442)

I prefer to use an expression like "historical-concrete theory" or "historical-concrete economics", to allow for a more direct understanding of the meaning of the term. Moreover, such an expression is suggested by Spiethoff himself when he talks about *"geschichtlich-anschauliche Theorie"*, stressing a procedure of scientific abstraction capable of gathering the constellations of phenomena analysed within contexts that are clearly defined historically.

The "historical-concrete theory", therefore, constitutes an attempt to forge an epistemic link with real events, in order to foreshadow the opening of theory towards the world. In other words, it is an attempt to create theoretical devices, which, when placed alongside the "historically indeterminate economic theories" *(unbedingten und zeitlosen)*, defined mainly within static parameters, enable us to identify the historical causes of the phenomena under analysis and, consequently, the causes of economic changes.

Both theories of pure economics and those of historical-concrete economics are constructed - on a purely formal plane - in a similar way. They presuppose selective criteria and the use of logical and logical-mathematical instruments available to economists. They differ, however, in their presuppositions and in their aims. The axiomatic, arbitrary assumptions of pure economics are replaced by "realistic" starting points in *"anschauliche Theorie"*. As Spiethoff points out:

> Both types of theory separate and isolate but each does so in its own peculiar way. (Spiethoff 1955, p. 12)

And shortly afterwards he continues:

> A distinction has been made between the two types of theory according to the level of abstraction, but no toning down of the level of abstraction, however marked it may be, transforms pure theory into historical-concrete theory, no accentuating of the abstraction, however marked it may be, transforms historical-concrete theory into pure theory. (Spiethoff 1955, p. 12)

It should be clear, then, that both theories are constructed according to criteria of rational acceptability which are typical of science, but they are part of such different referential contexts that they are mutually untranslatable. In fact, if the difference between them were due solely to procedural diversity, the distance between the two types of theory would be easy to eliminate, but this distance is destined to remain precisely because it is rooted in a contrasting approach to the subject under study: it is this difference of approach, and not the different logical procedures, that determines the difference in explicative content.

IV. *Wirtschaftsstil* and Real Type

The concept of "economic style" is among the co-ordinates of historical-concrete or realistic economics. *Wirtschaftsstil* is the intellectual device designed for use within the confines of "historical-concrete" economics and is the fruit of the attempt to simultaneously create assumptions, selection criteria and contexts for the evaluation of scientific statements in a historical perspective.[6]

> The keystone, the essence of the historical-concrete theory lies in the fact that the working hypothesis is controlled on the basis of the observation of reality. This allows for the simultaneous evaluation of initial queries, working hypotheses and empirical research. One of the greatest difficulties in working with the historical-concrete theory is that of really letting empirical research fight it out with theoretical reasoning. (Spiethoff 1948, p. 602)

The concept of *Wirtschaftsstil* has illustrious predecessors in the theory of stages formulated from various theoretical angles by the historical school (among others), but its originality derives from the theoretical aims that Spiethoff attributes to it. The concept was honed - as we will see - through stringent confrontations with the studies conducted by M. Weber (ideal type), W. Sombart (*Wirtschaftssystem*) on the one hand and on the other with Cassel and Schumpeter's attempts to interpret economic phenomena in dynamic terms.

We can start with Spiethoff's definitions: *Wirtschaftsstil* "is not simply derived from experience, but is predicated as on intimate knowledge of economic reality. Its aim is to mirror economic life as a specific set of economic institutions, economic life in its concreteness" (Spiethoff 1953a, p. 452).

---

6   For a careful and vast reflection on the concept of *Wirtschaftsstil*, its genesis and its theoretical evolution cf. WEIPPERT (1943), RITSCHL (1943), SCHACHT-SCHABEL (1943).

ARTHUR SPIETHOFF'S THEORY OF WIRTSCHAFTSSTIL

The *Wirtschaftstil* represents an attempt to build a historical type of an economic system clearly foreshadowing all the features that distinguish it from the other economic systems and all essential causal factors of it. Spiethoff's aim is to construct scientific models characterised by a "unity of form" (*ibid.*) and a "completeness of causal elements" (*ibid.*), in order to deal "in theoretical terms with the typical variations in economic life" (Clausing 1968, p. 133).

These causal elements "are not arbitrarily selected in advance" or "selected to suit a preconceived theoretical system", but they are the result of an empirical research guided by an "explicative idea" (*Erklärungseinfall*). For reasons which will be clearer later, I prefer to translate *Erklärungseinfall* with "explicative idea" and not with "intuitive hypothesis" as Fritz Redlich translates this terms in 1953. And so the style focuses not only on the logical unity of the model, but also on the peculiar features of the system under analysis. Müller-Armack, who used this concept more broadly, shares this definition when he writes:

> Style is a unit of expressions and behaviours which appears in a given period and in all of the different fields of the society (Müller-Armack, 1944, p. 21).

Before discussing the epistemological problems implicit in such a conception it is useful to show the reason of Spiethoff's insistence on the relevance of the historical types for his analysis. Spiethoff starts, as is well known, from the presupposition of the necessity to construct, in economics, historical theory alongside pure theory. Spiethoff believes that such a construct can be realized only on condition of the creation of historical and analytical models, which enable different economic systems and, within the systems themselves, different phenomena or different constellations of phenomena to be judged comparatively. Without scientific models, in Spiethoff's opinion, we do not have the possibility of theoretical reasonings because of the lack of a network of reference and consequently our reflection cannot escape the mere descriptivism which characterized many representatives of the historical school. Schmoller's failure was fundamentally determined by his inability to follow this pathway.

Spiethoff was aware not only of the difficulties of this attempt, but also of the fact that with it he introduced a radical hiatus compared with the usual methodology of the German historical school of economics. But he argues that if we want to explain economic life and its historical changes, we do not have any other alternatives. We must necessarily create theoretical models which give us the possibilities to draw out asserts which are valid not "only from an empirical point of view", but also from a "general" point of view. And we can obtain that only if we build models" valid for all analysed objects included in the field of some given premises" (Spiethoff 1932, p. 51-2).

Such an idea, underlines Spiethoff:

> ... was rarely expressed with such a radicality, but a similar purpose was always present, even if often confusedly (in the German historical school). The starting point was always given very clearly by the rebellion against those absolute solutions equally valid for all economic conditions and to which only a historical theory can be contraposed (Spiethoff 1932, p. 54).

If so, the problem is as follows: why did the German historical school avoid this pathway and why does Spiethoff speak of a radical hiatus introduced by his reflection?

The answer to this problem is connected with the complex relations between the representatives of the German historical school and K. Marx. In fact, Marx certainly follows this pathway and many representatives of the historical school accepted some results of Marx's analysis, but they radically refused his general approach to the study of capitalism and the conclusions of his work. This attitude was probably due to the fact that the idea of accepting the central methodological indication of Marx was seen as a danger or as too important a concession to the theoretician of socialism.

This aspect of the question is clearly set out by Sombart. Sombart, as is well known, criticised both the Marxian conclusion and the ideological content of his analysis, but at the same time he underlines the fact that Schmoller's failure in the creation of a historical theory and his descriptivism were determined by his incapacity to use the methodological lesson of K. Marx adequately. Whoever intends to make historical theories and not mere descriptivism, must proceed "like the mathematician who puts out parenthesis and extracts the recurring constants in each value, so that instead of ab + ac + ad he says a (b+c+d)" (Sombart 1978, or. ed. 1916, p. 92).

In the same way, it is necessary to isolate the "Gestalt" of economic and social systems and on this ground to create the conditions of the construction of historical theories. By doing so, we can obtain - he adds - the "constructive element in the organisation of the empirical material" and "the radical postulate of a unifying explanation" (Sombart 1902, p. XXIX). This is what is missing in G. Schmoller and precisely what is, on the contrary, present in K.

Marx. For this reason he characterised his approach as the attempt at an "intimate connection within a social system of all of the historical expressions, in short, it is the specifically theoretical element. I could also say: it is Karl Marx" (Sombart 1902, p. XXIX).

In my opinion, Spiethoff was equally aware of the theoretical implications of his methodological approach. This awareness arises when he defines his conceptual construct as realtype and underlines the interpretative limits of the Weberian ideal-type.

A realtypical model stresses similarities and uniformities not as they appear by logical deduction from given axiomatic principles, but as a construction based on a relation between theory and investigated reality. This, in fact, allows the isolation of its "regular and essential features" (Spiethoff 1953b, p. 76).[7] If "the real type represents the recurrent regularities of a historical object, stripped of its historical uniqueness" (Spiethoff 1953b, p. 74) we can at same time know its historical peculiarity, the general conditions of its reproduction and the reason for its internal transformations in relation to the actual development mechanisms. And we can obtain theoretical indications, in relation to this second aspect, only if we manage models permanently open to comparison with the changing reality. It is necessary to start - writes Spiethoff - "from a meaningful conception which embodies the preliminary impressions of the pertinent phenomena, their causal relations and the essentials determining the Gestalt of the total situation" (Spiethoff 1953a, p. 459). The scientific task is to aim at "a minimum of distinguishing traits", but he adds:

> In my method the presentation of the characteristic features of a "style" is always open to improvement. On the basis of new observations the number of characteristic features may be increased; but it may also be decreased through improved analysis (Spiethoff 1953a, p. 459).

This aim of the representation of a concrete "real context" and "the completeness of the causal elements" constitutes the trait that distinguishes Spiethoff's methodological approach from the Weberian approach. It reveals, in Spiethoff's opinion, his scientific productivity just when we try to explain the changing reality of an economic system. If it is true - notes Spiethoff - that "the social scientist builds ideal types in order to obtain fixed points of reference in the perpetual flow of history" (Spiethoff 1953a, p. 455), it is

---

7   For a careful reflection on this aspect of Spiethoff's work cf. also WEIPPERT (1943), esp. pp. 79-89.

also true that " a 'real type' would do much better service" in reference to this aspect.

In fact, the ideal type is constructed by putting together elements drawn out of reality through an abstraction process which has in mind particular gnoseological purposes. "This involves a one-sided exaggeration of certain aspect of reality, but is not to be found in it" (*ibid.*, p. 453). The ideal type is strongly determined by his premises and the selection of the analysed phenomena is conditioned by the logical purposes for which an ideal type is built. For this reason the social scientist who works with ideal type legitimately "may have to exaggerate rare phenomena, because, from his point of view, they are essential for his construct" (*ibid.*, p. 456).

On the contrary the scientist who works with real type cannot consider rare phenomena or exaggerate the importance of recurrent phenomena, he has to try a theoretical reproduction of totality under study because a 'real type' originates in the mental process of separating recurring social phenomena from their unique particulars or, if you prefer, of cleansing those phenomena of their unique features" (*ibid.*, p. 455).

In Spiethoff's opinion the real type in defining "a specific pattern of economic life and ... its essential properties" makes possible an adequate comparison between different moments of the same reality or different phenomena within it: all that creates the conditions for the understanding of the historical changes in a given economic reality.

> Reality must be apprehended as a totality and all reasoning on the connection of phenomena and on causal explanation must take place in the network of this real context. (Spiethoff 1932, p. 80)

V. Real Type and Economic Analysis: Some Epistemological Problems

Of course the making of real type implies a peculiar relation between subject and reality which cannot be ignored and Spiethoff, especially in *Synopsis*, develops a careful reflection about it, focusing on the role of the subject in the knowledge process.

In this perspective the "real context" cannot mean a mere reference to empirical material, but refers instead to the capacity to reproduce theoretically the essential links which make a phenomenal whole into a unique reality able to provide interpretative keys of a historically determined uniformity for any observer attempting an interpretation using his own interpretative tools.

The objectivity of such a context does not refer, therefore, to a factual world which forces itself on individuals regardless of their interpretative tools. Thus, subjectivity is not diametrically opposed to this common empiricistic simplification of objectivity. On the scientific plane, subjectivity for Spiethoff implies the attempt to construct general explanatory systems on the basis of a point of view. In this sense, on the procedural side, it is subject to all the checks that make it plausible as a basic element in scientific discourse. In short, a single explanation of a given set of phenomena will make use of a double-sided interpretative key, defined by Weippert (Weippert 1943, p. 82) as *"ontologisch und kulturtheoretisch"*. While on the one hand this stresses the ever-present subjective dimension implicit in every scientific activity (*"kulturtheoretisch"*), on the other it indicates the tendency towards the extra-mental dimension of observed phenomena (*"ontologisch"*).

From this point of view, the interest in the concept of "economic style" seems to derive from the fact that it can make a significant contribution to a debate growing out of the many *Methodenstreit* that have crossed the social sciences scene and that, as Rothacker pointed out, not without reason seem to have fizzled out. Basically, in contrast with what is suggested by the conclusions of many methodological debates, "the most serious clashes between social scientists do not take place between those who want to observe without thinking and those who want to think without observing" (Wright Mills 1962, p. 43). Rather, these differences of opinion are related to "the way of thinking and the way of observing" and above all, "the links between thinking and observing" (Wright Mills 1962, p. 43).

In actual fact, as long as methodological debates continue to be tied to possible divergences in the structure of the explanatory model, it will be difficult to find a solution. The isolation of this point and the subsequent fossilization of the hypothetical-deductive model, regarded as the only acceptable model for scientific explanation, "has created a series of concepts that tend to eliminate every argument in other fields of knowledge (genetics, psychology, stylistics, aesthetics)." (M. Ceruti 1986, p. 23)

However, current epistemological debate has revealed that "many hierarchies" constructed following this model are too "simplistic and many of the eliminations are too heavy-handed" (M. Ceruti 1986, p. 23).

179

Spiethoff's scientific approach can be considered an attempt to break with these "simplifications" and to avoid these "heavy-handed" eliminations by means of an analytical model capable of bringing into question that particular kind of "self-referentiality" typical of scientific discourse, based on what we can call the "Cartesian fallacy". In other words, it is based on the idea that a "worldless individual" (in Elias' words) faces reality in terms of its dehistoricised criteria of rationality. In the cognitive universe of Descartes we have two significant points of departure: the first one insists on the irrelevance of the external world and, consequently, on the truthlessness of the sensorial perception of it; the second one focuses on the certainty that reality is unchanging in its essential features. If we add to that the Cartesian assumption that our mind can only know what it itself produces, we will be able to understand apriorism, atomism and reductionism as the main pathways to build models in which internal consistency is gained through the sacrifice of the external world. (S.C. Dow 1985, pp. 12-7; P.V. Mini 1974, p. 22) Now, it is certainly true that we can work exclusively with our ideas as products of our mind, but we must admit that only from a general point of view we can consider the external world as a product of our mental world.[8]

But if it is so, we have to conclude that the sole theoretical possibility that there isn't full accordance between the internal and external world poses the problem of a careful analysis of the external world in order to find its rules and the reasons for its peculiar dynamics. This recognition does not reduce in Spietoff's opinion the role of the subject in the cognitive process (without a knowing subject, the problem simply does not exist), neither does it reduce the role of models built with the procedures of pure theory.

If we consider this second aspect on the basis of Spiethoff's reflection, we find a clear acceptance of methodological pluralism: cognitive devices, procedures and methods are consequences of our scientific purposes. Spiethoff insists, in particular, on the role of pure economics. It represents an indispensable *Hilfsmittel* for the economic analysis, since it provides a "tool-box" (to use J. Robinson's expression) for all types of economic enquiry. As Spiethoff writes: pure theory is

> an indispensable heuristic device at the bottom of every economic phenomenon. Without it there can be no instruments for the casual explanation of economic life (Spiethoff 1932, p. 55).

---

8   On the complexity of the relation between subject and social and institutional environment cf. SAMUELS (1972) and LAWSON (1994).

ARTHUR SPIETHOFF'S THEORY OF WIRTSCHAFTSSTIL

But pure theory can do that precisely for the reason that it deals with the relations present in all economic systems. It doesn't represent a historical state of the world (Spiethoff 1932, pp. 55-56). That is, in fact, the peculiar task of a "historical theory".

In order to illustrate this aspect Spiethoff's criticism of Schumpeter is particularly significant. Schumpeter in *Das Wesen und der Hauptinhalt der theoretischen Nationalökonomie* tried to reconcile pure theory and realistic enquiry. Regarding the legitimacy of pure economics, he wrote:

> On the one hand we have the arbitrariness of the presuppositions in our theory, on which his system rests, and on the other hand the fact that our theory adapts to phenomena and is influenced by them, which alone gives the theory its content and its value. (Schumpeter 1982 ed. or 1902, pp. 428-9)

According to Spiethoff, the two requirements stated by Schumpeter (arbitrariness of the assumptions and capacity to refer to real phenomena) are valid, but they can in no way be fulfilled in the context of pure theory. In fact, considering the theoretical constructs of pure theory, it is impossible to hypothesize the "extensive coinciding with reality" mentioned by Schumpeter for the simple reason that in this way pure theory "would be deprived of its very nature" (Spiethoff 1932, p. 56) and, in order to verify its assertions, we would have introduced extraneous (realistic) elements, incompatible with the theory's presuppositions and with its need for consistency.

Spiethoff's conclusion is clear, if we aim at a historical representation, we have to consider from the beginning the empirical phenomena and the historical traits of the object under study. Otherwise we risk using the theoretical framework in relation to scientific ends which are different from those for which it was conceived.

And at this point we can deal with the role of the subject in the cognitive process. The fundamental element in Spiethoff's theoretical approach is precisely the fact of knowing that the epistemic self is at once the subject and the object of history. Consequently knowledge can be characterized as the development and the accumulation of styles of thought and analytic models which change as the subjects change and as the world changes. The concepts of economic style and real type therefore refer not to absolute models of knowledge, but rather to explicative structures which are capable of measuring up to the development of history both because of their inner logical need and because of the peculiar type of relationship they have with external changes.

As writes Spiethoff:

> It is our task to find in the ever-changing and varying stream of economic life specific form and specific uniformities, and the concept of economic style is the tool for that end (Spiethoff 1953 a, p. 453).

This means regarding knowledge as a circular process within which the subject is certainly a *conditio sine qua non*, but is at the same time a historically determined condition, since not only the ideational world but also the perceptional world of the subject is determined by criteria, visions, values and evaluation systems which undergo a change in time. In short, it is a question of understanding that man's sociality does not modify the superficial extemporary cultural models of the subject but rather "the physiology of the senses, our perception of the physical world, the colours we distinguish, the smells we are aware of, the sounds we hear" (W. Mills 1962, p. 171).

From this point of view it seems clear that subjectivity is not to be evaluated solely in terms of *a priori* elements, nor therefore in terms of dehistoricized rational behaviour deduced from these *a priori* elements. Subjectivity has its roots in the "cultural patrimony, channelled into traditions, institutions and customs" and "in the aims and beliefs that these involve and inspire" (Dewey 1943, p. 82) and that determine historical models of rationality. It is these historical models of rationality that are capable of explaining the "range of reasons" (W. Mills 1962, p. 171) which predominate in a society in a particular historical phase and that in their turn provide the interpretative key to the historical development of rationality itself. Only on this basis will it be possible to outline new analytic strategies able to go beyond "the individualistic theories of knowledge and behaviour" (M. Douglas-B. Isherwood 1984, p. 69) and to draw up more complex gnoseological models triggered by the recognition that the "single individual", stripped of his historical features, "is a totally useless conceptual principle" (M. Douglas-B. Isherwood 1984, pp. 70-71) for the understanding of economic and social phenomena.

A theory that is scientifically open to historical reality naturally cannot ignore this, even though it still seems difficult to encase all this in an "explicative idea" or to formalize it into an economic model.

The *Erklärungseinfall* is another important category to understand Spiethoff's methodological approach. Spiethoff starts from the presupposition that the explanation of reality is a function of our gnoseological interests and these depend on our points of view.

ARTHUR SPIETHOFF'S THEORY OF WIRTSCHAFTSSTIL

> The material in itself is mute (*stumm*) and it becomes eloquent only when it is compared with (*adequate*) questions to which it could give answers (Spiethoff 1948, p. 662).

The "explicative idea" represents not a hypothesis for the search for a unique causal factor which would determine and would explain the clusters of fact under study, but it is a way to build a model able to embody a "real context" in which there also exist recurrent perturbations as its relevant component. While the single hypothesis can, following a procedure of the idealtypical analysis, exclude those perturbing factors and isolate rightly the main causal relation, the "explicative idea" has to consider all the concrete framework of phenomenal concatenation in order to find its unity of form: the distinctive character of an economic system. And only on this basis it is possible to make an attempt to have an explanation of single phenomena or particular causal relations.

I have also tried - points out Spiethoff - to find in my business cycle theory the unique cause, the crucial causal factor, but that represents an error for the realtypical analysis. (Spiethoff 1948, p. 628)

> The pretension of a unifying cause is in the historical-concrete theory unacceptable (*abwegig*), it uses the reduction to the stylistic characters (*die Zurückführung auf Stilmerkmale*) (ibid).

Consequently, "the explicative idea is not a 'fact' and it will not stand the 'empirical test'", as the crucial test. If anything it is an interpretative network whose confirmation comes from the necessity of its capacity to allow hypotheses, clusters of facts and theoretical statements to be compared in a scientifically fruitful way.

> The historical-concrete theory enables us to cope with this requirement (*of an all-embracing explanation of the phenomena investigated, V.G.*), harmonizing the multiplicity of causes and conditions and bringing them together in an overall view. This type of treatment leads to style traits (*Stilmerkmalen*), which prove to be the most general causes and conditions. This reduction and unification clearly sets up new relations and thus offers supplementary judgements; it does not, however, replace the causes and conditions found previously but the unification sublimates the multiplicity of causes and eliminates the more subtle causal limits (Spiethoff 1948).

It can therefore be concluded that the concept of "economic style" does not contain any element to suggest the idea of truth as the correspondence between assertions and reality or, to use older terminology, as a "mirroring", according to the approach of the "naive" realist.

> Phenomena are selected on the strength of a clearly defined vision of the whole (*des Ganzen*)...The scholar decides which phenomena make up the essence of reality according to a rational evaluation drawn by him from the interplay of phenomena and from the usability of the single phenomena for the explanation of reality (Spiethoff 1932, p. 13).

Consequently, Spiethoff insists:

> The image of reality is not a photograph, but a painting, presupposing the point of view of the observer (Spiethoff 1948, p. 638).

In this sense, Spiethoff seems to adopt a surprisingly modern scientific realism, which like H. Putnam we could consider typical of an "internal realist", or he who believes that asking oneself about the possible states of the world is feasible only within the confines of a theory or a vision of the world (Putnam 1985). Once the real type has been defined, it is a theoretical construct and must be subject to all the measures and procedures of control used for any other theory. In this sense, the relation with reality seems to be a presupposition or a problem to be brought up again later, but not something that can hinder the task of checking the formal correctness of the assertions used. In fact, once the explicative model has been constructed, evaluation of the scientific explanations cannot consist of an endless game of Chinese boxes, stuck on the continuous (and interminable) search for the final bases of our explanations (even when they refer to empirical reality); instead, it must allow the theories constructed to include a summary of the scientific activity that produced them along with internal evaluation processes which permit overall judgements regarding the conditions in which the scientific explanations can be considered correct.

> These economic styles are theoretical constructs, regardless of the point of view that gives rise to them. (Spiethoff 1932, p. 56)

Things being such, the *Wirtschaftsstil* seems to me to present an undeniable advantage on the epistemological plane since it defines a sort of "mental experiment" aimed at determining, for every explanation, a context of reference which explicitly fixes the selection criteria that stake out the area of validity of the explanation and at the same time establishes the network of semantic terms for its control.

VI. Conclusion: Some Critical Remarks

There are some aspects in Spiethoff's work which aren't completely convincing and which I have neglected in order to focus on the main purpose of his methodological reflection: the demonstration of the legitimacy of historical theory. In conclusion of this paper I want to briefly mention two of these aspects: the relation between pure theory and historical theory and secondly the analysis of the role of institutions in economic dynamics.

Spiethoff tried, as we have seen, to indicate the conditions for a fruitful cooperation between pure theory and historical theory and insisted on the possibility for the historical theory to use the results of pure theory. Spiethoff's intention was probably determined by his will to overcome the radical contra-positions of the *Methodenstreit*,[9] but I personally find such a cooperation difficult as long as the two approaches are characterized by different ends and different methodologies. A fruitful cooperation could, in my opinion, have a real chance of success provided common ends for scientific research are established. But this, if we carefully reflect about it, considering the evolution of economics, means that one theoretical approach should accept the ends, methods and analytical procedures of the other, because in the gnoseological field a middle way can only bring confusion and misunderstanding.

Now, Spiethoff insists in all his methodological work on the legitimacy of pure theory and he tries to show the legitimacy of historical theory. He consequently suggests necessity of methodological pluralism within the social sciences. But his proposal to create the conditions of a strong cooperation between pure economics and historical economics seems to me to be a more subtle way to deny or at least to reduce this pluralism. In fact, if we establish the scientific priority of the ends of historical economics, we will show at the same time the theoretical subordination of pure economics to it, for the simple reason that the purposes of its work and the judgements about its scientific productivity derive not from motivations internal to the pure theory, but from the possibility that historical theory (with different ends, different methods and different relations with the cognitive object) can use its

---

9   In *Synopsis* Spiethoff insists on the necessity "of reconciliation in methodological field" in order to achieve "useful working devices" (SPIETHOFF 1948, p. 537).

results profitably. It is significant that Spiethoff ends the discussion concerning the possibility of cooperation between pure and historical theory by saying that such an end could be realised only if pure theory keeps in mind from the beginning the purpuses of the historical theory.[10]

In reference to this, it is also interesting to note that such a problem was posed in a similar way from the early 1970s after the rising of a strong criticism towards the methodological approach of economics and towards its axiomatic-deductive procedures. This criticism was focused on the fact that economists have devoted excessive attention to the strongest links in their chains of reasoning, but too little attention to the relation between economic theories and real world. But when the problem was posed of a stronger link between theory and reality, this aroused awareness that methodological and analytical changes are not as easy as economists would imagine. In particular a closer reflection on this theme revealed the fact that it is impossible to solve the problem of the theories-reality relation by a simple adaptation of the old theories (build with axiomatic-deductive procedures) to the real world. And this for the simple reason that, as noted R. Backhouse, "we do not know which theories, if any, are relevant to the real world". (R. Backhouse 1994, p. 15)

Other problems are, besides, linked to the evaluation of the entire work of Spiethoff: both his methodological conception and his business cycle theory. Certainly, there is a strong ideal link between Spiethoff's methodological approach and his business cycle analysis and Spiethoff himself rightly recalls the exigencies of a unifying interpretation of his work. But if we examine the relations between the two sides of Spiethoff's work more closely, interesting problems arise both about the business cycle theory and about Spiethoff's methodological approach.

At this moment we are neglecting the economic discussion about causal factors which determine the cyclical course of events in the capitalistic economy, because we want to highlight only the relation between the methodological and economic aspect of Spiethoff's work and a singular lacuna which arises in a crucial aspect of his system of explanations: the role of institutions in business cycles.

When Spiethoff defines economic style, he writes: "It mirrors a system of elements held together by interaction, and at the same time reflects a specific

---

10 For some interesting and general reflections on this aspect cf. MAYER (1993), pp. 24-34.

set of economic institutions which are at the root of that system of interacting elements" (Spiethoff 1953a, pp. 450-1).

In his *Business Cycles* Spiethoff insists on this aspect and underlines the fact that economic life after 1919 was still dominated by the influence of business cycles and that "the very strong political influences and interventions were unable to dethrone the business cycles" (Spiethoff 1953, p. 77).

Further, exposing the "highly important" findings of the old theory in relation to the analysis of business cycles, he comes back to these aspects focusing on the connection between every cycle and:

"i. a certain kind of environment;

ii. a certain kind of spiritual disposition" (*ibid.*)

As is well known these topics were widely dealt with by the representatives of the historical school of economics and they were in general examined in reference to the role of institutions. Spiethoff, instead, neither develops the analysis on this theme, nor makes clear his points of reference: G. Schmoller, M. Weber, W. Sombart? All this makes it particularly difficult to fill in this lacuna on the basis of his work and determines a void in his explicative system.

Things being such, we can conclude that Spiethoff elaborates interesting categories and instruments (economic style and real type) of great potentiality for the realisation of historical analysis, but we must also say that his cognitive strategy lacks important explications. Consequently, we can share the opinion about a relevant outcome of his analysis when he writes:

> The point I wish to make is that observational theory claims its rightful place as a genuine form of theory which has an independent existence side by side with pure theory (Spiethoff 1953, p. 76).

But, we must at the same time say that the indicated incompleteness (and some methodological naivety) reduce the effectiveness of his epistemological and methodological ideas. In fact, in Spiethoff's work we can quite clearly see the general relations between theories and historical reality, the way to modify the theories both by means of changes in our vision of the world and by means of changes in the states of the world. But if we do not have a sense of the relations between institutions and economic changes we will find those real changes, which are the object of a historical theory, difficult to analyse.

References

BACKHAUS, J. C.: "Gustav Schmoller and the Problem of Today", *History of Economic Ideas*, n.3/1, 1994.

BACKHOUSE, R. E.: *New Directions in Economic Methodology*, London, New York (Routledge) 1994.

CERUTI, M.: *Il vincolo e la possibilità*, Milano 1986.

CLAUSING, G: Arthur Spiethoff wissenschaftliche Lebenswerk, *Schmollers Jahrbuch*, LXXVIII, 1958.

CLAUSING, G.: Arthur Spiethoff, International Encyclopedia, New York (The Mcmillan Company and The Free Press) 1968.

DEWEY, J.: *Logica, teoria dell'indagine*, Torino 1949.

DOUGLAS, M., ISHERWOOD, B.: *Il mondo delle cose*, Bologna 1984.

DOW, S. C.: *Macroeconomic Thought. A Methodological Approach*, New York 1985.

FAUCCI, R.: "Gustav Schmoller e la scuola storica in Italia", *Quaderni di Storia dell'Economia Politica*, n.2, 1988.

GIOIA, V.: *Gustav Schmoller: la scienza economica e la storia*, Galatina (Lecce) 1990.

GIOIA, V.: "Teorie economiche e storia nel 'Methodenstreit'." Alcune riflessioni, *Economia Politica* 1991.

HAUSER, P.: Historical School and 'Methodenstreit', in: P. SCHIERA, F. TENBRUCK (Eds): *G. Schmoller e il suo tempo: la nascita delle scienze sociali in Germania e Italia*, Bologna-Berlino (Il Mulino-Duncker &Humblot) 1989.

HAUTREY, R. G.: *Der Stand und die nächste Zukunft der Konjunkturforschung*, München 1933.

HERKNER, H.: Zur Stellung Gustav Schmollers in der Geschichte der Nationalökonomie, *Schmollers Jahrbuck*, XLVIII, 1924.

HUTCHISON, T. W.: *A Review of Economic Doctrines 1970-1929*, Oxford 1962, II.

KAMP, M. E.: *Gedenkrede auf Arthur Spiethoff*, Bonn (Peter Hanstein Verlag) 1958.

LANE, F. C., RIEMERSMA, J. C.: "Introduction to Arthur Spiethoff", in: id., *Enterprise and Secular Change*, London 1953.

LAWSON, T.: *A Realist Theory for Economics*, in: R. E. BACKHOUSE, op. cit. 1994.

LOEWE, A.: "Vorwort" to A. SCHWEITZER: *Spiethoffs Konjunkturlehre*, Basel 1938.

LUHMANN, N.: *Come è possibile l'ordine sociale?*, Bari 1985.

MAYER, TH.: *Truth versus Precision in Economics*, Cambridge (E. Elgar) 1993.

MILLS, W. C.: *L'immaginazione sociologica*, Milano 1962.

MINI, P. V.: *Philosophy and Economics*, Gainsville (The University Presses of Florida) 1974.

MITCHELL, W. C.: *Types of Economic Theory. From Mercantilism to Institutionalism*, New York 1969.

MÜLLER-ARMACK, A.: *Genealogie der Wirtschaftsstile* , Stuttgart 1944.

PUTNAM, H.: *Ragione, verità e storia*, Milano 1985.

RITSCHL, H.: Wandlungen im Objekt und in den Methoden der Volkswirtschaftslehre, *Schmollers Jahrbuck*, LXVII. 1943.

SAMUELS, W. J.: *The Scope of Economics Historically Considered*, in: id, *Essays in the History of Heterodox Political Economy*, London (Macmillan) 1972.

SALIN, E.: "Hochkapitalismus", *Weltwirtschaftliches Archiv* 1927.

SALIN, E.: *Geschichte der Volkswirtschaftslehre*, Bern 1944.

SCHACHTSCHABEL, H. G.: Zur Genealogie des Wirtschaftsstils, *Schmollers Jahrbuch*, 67, 1943.

SCHEFOLD, B.,: "Schmoller als Theoretiker?", in: *Gustav Schmollers Lebenswerk. Eine Kritische Analyse aus moderner Sicht*, Düsseldorf 1989.

SCHMOLLER, G.: *Grundriß der Allgmeinen Volkswirtschaftslehre*, II v., Berlin 1978, VII.

SCHUMPETER, J. A.: *L'essenza e i principi dell'economia teorica*, Bari 1982.

SCHUMPETER, J. A.: "Gustav von Schmoller und die Probleme von heute", *Schmollers Jahrbuch* 1926.

SCHUMPETER, J. A.: "Vorwort" to *Der Stand und die nächste Zukunft der Konjunkturforschung*, op. cit. 1933.

SOMBART, W.: *Il capitalismo moderno*, Torino 1978 (ed. or. 1902).

SOMBART, W.: Nationalökonomie, in: *Wertwirtschaftliches Archiv* 1929.

SOMBART, W.: *Die drei Nationalökonomien*, Leipzig 1930.

SPIETHOFF, A.: "Krisen", *Handwörterbuch der Staatswissenschaften*, VI Band, Jena 1925.

SPIETHOFF, A.: "Die Allgmeine Volkswirtschatslehre als geschichtliche Theorie. Die Wirtschaftsstile", *Schmollers Jahrbuch* 1932.

SPIETHOFF, A.: Gustav von Schmoller und die anschauliche Theorie der Volkswirtschaft, *Schmollers Jahrbuch* 1938.

SPIETHOFF, A.: "Anschauliche und reine volkswirtschaftlich Theorie und ihr Verhältnis zueinander, in: *Synopsis*, Heidelberg 1948.

SPIETHOFF, A.: "Business Cycle", *International Economic Papers*, New York 1953.

SPIETHOFF, A.: *Wirtschaftliche Wechsellagen*, Tübingen 1955.

VEBLEN, T.: "Gustav Schmoller's Economics", *Quarterly Journal of Economic* 1901.

WEIPPERT, G.: "Zum Begriff des Wirtschaftsstils", *Schmollers Jahrbuch* 1943.

VITANTONIO GIOIA

ZAGARI, E., SCHEFOLD, B., GIOIA V.: *Gustav Schmoller: metodi e analisi nelle scienza economica*, Galatina (Lecce) 1993.

Discussion Summary

NORBERT F. TOFALL

Paper discussed:
VITANTONIO GIOIA: Historical Changes and Economics in Arthur Spiethoff's Theory of *Wirtschaftsstil* (Style of an Economic System)

It is not possible to understand changes of human behaviour and changes of structures in the economy by arguing with the pure economic theory. Consequently we have to compare situations at different points of time regarding the peculiarities of the structures in the economy. The theoretical component seems to be useful for analysing different elements, which we can compare by going from period to period (FURUBOTN).

For Spiethoff there is an absolute knowledge in the social sciences. By his method of isolation, he analyses different aspects and elements of human behaviour which are crucial for the development of the society. In contrast to the Historical School we need theoretical instruments like the economic theory for analysing changes of these different elements. In this sense Spiethoff's theory is an answer to the relation between Sombart and Schmoller. The key of understanding is the isolation of elements (GIOIA).

Schumpeter speaks about the economic blue print of an economic system. In his book *Capitalism, Socialism, and Democracy* he takes the view that the economic blue print is the economic *Grundplan* (main structure) of socialism or of capitalism. These two economic systems or economic blue prints are working according to special mechanisms for coordinating the economic and political activities. Could one speak of ideal types of socialism or capitalism in Schumpeter? Is there any ideal type of capitalism in Spiethoff or are there sequences of real types of capitalism, existent of capitalism *1*, capitalism *2* up to capitalism *n*? So, if the latter is the case, - it means a sequence of real types (*Wirtschaftsstile*) in Spiethoff -, that would imply that there is some empirical content within such a real type whereas the ideal type of capitalism in general has the function of the species and the real types have the logical status of generic singular cases. Capitalism as an ideal type would mean that a pure theory is possible whereas on the level of Spiethoff's real types we only have the possibility to deal with specific historical generic peculiarities which are the extension of capitalism in the general sense - like Darwin's species and the generic unity: the ideal type of capitalism and the real types of capitalisms. Is this correct and what kind of rationality is used by Spiethoff? (ACHAM).

Schumpeter criticizes the conception of Weber, especially Weber's theory of economic development. Spiethoff wants to connect the pure theory and the theory of reality to get a stronger connection to reality. When Schumpeter speaks about capitalism he differentiates different forms of capitalism - perfect market, monopoly, oligopoly - and he analyses dynamic elements like the dynamic entrepreneur and the dynamic business cycle. Schumpeter's theory is not an equilibrium theory whereas Spiethoff takes up the theories of Marx and Weber for his goals (GIOIA).

The value of a blancmange is eating the blancmange. What value of explanation or what cognitive value has Spiethoff's theory? (MLCOCH).

The capitalism includes different business cycles which have to be understood. But the economy changes in history and because of that the explanations of business cycles have to change. If we can not explain the change of the economy, we will not explain the business cycles (GIOIA).

But that is also abstraction and there is also pure theory (ACHAM).

Yes, but no isolated pure theory. Spiethoff's theory is able to include historical elements (GIOIA).

Firstly, it is not clear to NOPPENEY, why Gioia prefers the term explicative idea for translating the term *Erklärungseinfall* (idea for an explanation). Secondly, reading the term *Erklärungseinfall* NOPPENEY thinks about Schumpeter's introduction in his famous book "History of Economic Analyses". Gioia is asked if he could make clear the difference of the term *Erklärungseinfall* and of Schumpeter's thoughts? (NOPPENEY).

In an empirically research, it is necessary to isolate important elements for analysing. Afterwards we want to weave or spin a network from this elements. The way of weaving this network is the explicative idea. Intuition is a kind of imagination which does not correspond to reality. Spiethoff's work is an empirical research. Schumpeter only constructs theoretical models (GIOIA).

To the differences between Schumpeter and Spiethoff: Spiethoff criticizes Schumpeter's business-cycle-theory. Spiethoff thinks that Schumpeter's theory implies an a-priori-equilibrium which he uses as reference system although there has never been something like that kind of equilibrium in reality. So the starting point of Schumpeter is unrealistic and therefore a connection with reality is not possible. On the other hand, Spiethoff takes an empirical and historical starting point, namely he starts with facts. From this, one can see that Spiethoff criticizes Schumpeter's methodology. Spiethoff accepts from Schumpeter the theory of the dynamic entrepreneur, but Spiethoff's theory is not deductive (HARADA).

Both, Spiethoff and Schumpeter, have formulated a general theory of disequilibrium, but there are differences in the method and in the view of crisises. Schumpeter rejects the general crisis theory of Marx (GIOIA).

Chapter 8

Hans Freyer's Economic Philosophy After World War II

VOLKER KRUSE

I. Biography of Hans Freyer
II. Progress as a "Cataract" – Freyer's Theory of History
III. The Economy of the Industrial Society
IV. The Human Being in Industrial Society
V. Ethics and the Development of the Industrial Society

The work of the sociologist Hans Freyer is not well known, not only in today's English-speaking community of the Social Sciences, but also among the younger German sociologists. Many regard Freyer's biography as having been on the wrong path, because he supported the National Socialist movement at times. His work appears to be an illegitimate deviation from the mainstream of a nomological social science, a "Historical and Social Philosophy" or a "critique of culture". But especially his later works from the 50s and 60s (on which we will concentrate here) include some remarkably modern and relevant aspects.[1]

After giving an overview of Freyer's biography, this paper introduces his theory of history which differs very much from the common idea of history as a process of progress and modernization, although it shows some semantic parallels. The third section describes how the economy of the industrial society works from Freyer's point of view. In the fourth section, I will ask how

---

1 Up to now, the literature on the history of economics and the social sciences has not paid much attention to Freyer's later works from the 50s and 60s. Concerning Freyers's scholary work from the 20s and 30s see MULLER (1987), ÜNER (1992), SIEFERLE (1995). Concerning Freyer's later work see KRUSE (1994).

the structures and functions of the modern economy and society have an effect on the social character of the human being. The final section deals with the possibilities and ways in which the economy and society can be organized from an ethical standpoint. Freyer saw Sociology as a comprehensive Social Science, integrating economic, historical and philosophical-ethical elements.

I. Biography of Hans Freyer[2]

Hans Freyer was born in 1887 in Burgstadt, a small town in Saxony, and grew up in a pious, Protestant family. He first studied Theology in Greifswald and later went to Leipzig to study Literature and Political Economics. In 1911 he received a Ph.D. ("Promotion") and went on to complete his second dissertation in Philosophy, the qualification as a postdoctoral lecturer ("Habilitation"), in 1920. In 1922 he became Professor of Philosophy in Kiel and was named to the first professorship in Germany exclusively devoted to sociology in Leipzig in 1925.

Freyer was a member of a generation that was very much influenced by the "Jugendbewegung" ("Youth Movement"), a specifically German phenomenon which spread rapidly at the turn of the century. It saw itself as a protest movement against industrial civilization and romanticized nature and life in the countryside. Freyer's philosophical-poetic writings emerged in the context of the "Youth Movement": "Antäus - Grundlegung einer Ethik des bewußten Lebens", ("Anteus - Principles of an Ethic of Conscious Life"), Jena 1918 and "Prometheus - Ideen zu einer Philosophie der Kultur" ("Prometheus - Ideas on a Philosophy of Culture"), Jena 1923. In the tradition of Wilhelm Dilthey, Freyer then wrote about the logical priniciples of the Humanities: "Theorie des objektiven Geistes ("Theory of the Objective Mind"), Leipzig 1923. In the late 20s, Freyer became increasingly political. His use of concepts such as "Volk" ("people"), "Volksgemeinschaft" (people's communitity"), "Volkswerdung" ("the development of a people") and "Führer" ("leader") show him to be representative of the right wing of the spectrum of those years. He interpreted the National Socialist movement as a power that

---

2   Concerning Freyer's biography see the outstanding work of JERRY Z. MULLER 1987; in addition, for the early phases of Freyer's life see MANHEIM 1948.

would overcome the particularist interests of class society in favor of a "people's community" (see "Revolution von Rechts"; "Revolution from the Right", Leipzig 1931).

Freyer accordingly welcomed the Third Reich as the surmounting of class society in favor of a united "Volksgemeinschaft" led by the "Führer". Nevertheless, he never became a member of the Nazi party. In 1933 he became the director of the "Institut für Kultur- und Universalgeschichte" ("Institute of Culture- and Universal History"), founded in 1909 by the famous historian Karl Lamprecht, and was named "Führer" of the "Deutsche Gesellschaft für Soziologie" ("German Society of Sociology") which, however, he closed down in 1934. Freyer's political and personal expectations of the Nazi-regime were not fulfilled. The Nazi media either criticized or rejected his work because of its lack of ideological orthodoxy (see Muller 1987, pp. 259f., 297). The Security Service intercepted and read his mail. Beginning in 1935 Freyer's writings carefully handled the topic of the misuse of power and distinguished between legitimate and illegitimate rule. In 1938 he moved to Hungary where he became a visiting professor in German cultural history at the University of Budapest.

In 1944 Freyer fled from the advancing Soviet Army to Leipzig. After the end of World War II, he was able to take up again his teaching activities under the authority of the Soviets, but he was dismissed in 1948 for political reasons. He then worked as an editor at a publisher in Wiesbaden. Afterwards he taught as an emeritus professor at the University of Münster from 1953 to 1963. During this time his interests focused on the structural tendencies of industrial society and on the effects of these structures on the range of freedom and the social character of the human being. His later works (especially "Theorie des gegenwärtigen Zeitalters"; "Theory of the Present Age") attracted a remarkable amount of public interest, but the social sciences never paid much attention to his works. Hans Freyer died in 1969.

II. Progress as a "Cataract" - Freyer's Theory of History

Famous philosophers and sociologists in the 18th- and 19th century saw history as a progressive, universal and teleological process. Even more than that, history was seen as a "history of salvation" (Karl Löwith) in a secularized sense. This comprised the development of freedom and reason (Georg Friedrich Wilhelm Hegel), the self-liberation and emancipation of mankind in communism (Karl Marx), the progress of the human mind toward a social-scienific steering of society (Auguste Comte) or the progress toward a functional differentiated and peaceful human society (Herbert Spencer). Around 1930 Freyer himself understood history as a dialectical, salvation-oriented process leading from "Gemeinschaft" ("community") (thesis) via "Gesellschaft" (antithesis) to the "Volk" ("people") (synthesis).[3]

In the 50s and early 60s Freyer created a very different theory of history based on the concepts of "Schwelle" ("threshold") and "Fortschritt" (as "progrès réel"). According to this approach, history is characterized not by constant progress, but rather by a shift between long-lasting states of relative calmness and by relatively short "Schwellen"-phases. These "Schwellen" revolutionize the conditions of human existence. Freyer defines a "Schwelle" as a qualitative leap in the history of mankind that brings its existence to a new level. In this sense Freyer distinguishes between the following "Schwellen": the settling down of humankind (since 10,000 B.C.), the emergence of advanced civilizations (since 4,000 B.C.), the emergence of transcendent religions (since 1,300 B.C.) and industrial society (see Freyer 1987a; Freyer 1965; Kruse 1990, pp. 147-149). The present society is living in the last-named "Schwelle" in which Freyer situated the concept of progress.

History as a whole is not - as mentioned above - a process of progress. Progress is rather a mode of historical movement that is specific in space and time and that emerged in European culture under specific historical circumstances.[4]

How did Freyer determine the concept of "progress"? First of all, Freyer distinguished between "illusions du progrès" and "progrès réel". "Illusion du progrès" stands for a projection of wishes of a socially and technically perfect world, be it in a Marxist or liberal sense. Seperated from this is the "progrès réel", which is the actual and empirical process that determines the existence of mankind. Freyer's concept of progress thus has nothing to do with values or similar concepts, but rather describes a real, progressive form of historical

---

3 See Freyer (1931).
4 "The combination of science, technology and the capitalist companies and factories is a unique occurrence. In this unit, every single element is determined by the two others but also drives them forward. The industrial culture is based on this occurrence" (Freyer [1965], p. 186).

movement which appeared in European culture during the industrial revolution - fist signs can be found in the period between the 14th and 18th centuries.

This process of progress is marked by a unique structure. It is made up of many sub-processes. As examples Freyer mentioned the "construction of a mechanical production-apparatus", the "progress of industrial technology", "the urbanisation of housing and living conditions", "the increasing dependence of needs on the market", "the rationalization of all interpersonal relationships in and outside the work place", "the bureaucratization of all acts of administration and of all associations" (Freyer 1965, p. 295).

These sub-processes do not go on independently. They influence and drive each other forward. Technological progress accelerates the growth of production which results in new economic resources that in turn push technical progress. In this way, the process of progress in the whole society gains more and more momentum. As Freyer put it: Progress becomes a "Katarakt" ("cataract"), a kind of raging river or a waterfall, but a waterfall that "falls" up and not down. The philosophy of the Enlightenment saw progress as something ethical and made by a mature and responsible human endowed with reason. Freyer's "cataract" concept finally transformed progress into an autonomous, momentous objective process.

What follows from this characterization of progress as a cataract? First of all, it follows that progress is no longer - or perhaps only marginally - steerable, either by the state or by science. It also cannot be controlled under ethical maxims. The situation is rather the other way around. The structural process of progress forces its values onto the acting human being according to the law of the "normative power of the factuality" (see Freyer 1965, p. 300).

The consequences are actually more far-reaching. If progress has gathered a momentum that is largely uncontrollable, then progress could lead to a catastrophe (see Freyer 1965, p. 287). Here Freyer is mainly thinking about large-scale technologies and genetic engineering, but also about ecological dangers.

The progress can lead to a catastrophe, but it does not have to necessarily. It could also possibly lead to a new state of relative calmness. But this of course is not foreseeable at this time. Even if such a state would occur it would not mean the final state of history. "History never ends up in finality" (Freyer 1965, p. 325).[5]

---

5   In the final section we will see the ethical consequences that Freyer drew from this diagnosis.

Freyer's theory of progress conveys two basic insights that do not come from the common theory of social change. Progress (as "progrès réel") is not an universal process and not even a teleological process. It is a time-specific mode of historical movement. The structural signature of the process of progress lies in sub-processes that drive each other forward and thus accerlerate the momentum of the whole process.

III. The Economy of the Industrial Society

We now change the perspective on Freyer's diagnosis from a longitudinal to a cross-sectional perspective and focus on the structure of industrial society. The central area of industrial society is the economy which Freyer describes using four terms: production, consumption, serial production and adaption.

In pre-industrial society production typically took place in distinct and often autarkical units. In industrial society a differentiated economic system emerged.

The Economy in industrial society is a dynamic process that includes four components: the perfection of the means of production, the increase of the efficiency of human work, the multiplication of needs and the tendency of accumulation of capital (see Freyer 1965, p. 229). The common feature of these components is that they run in the mode of progress, but not necessarily continuously: "Technology in the industrial age never" developed "in continuous and small steps, but in waves, pushes and shoves" (Freyer 1957a, p. 6).[6]

The driving force of production is technological progress which in turn is kept in motion by the sciences. Freyer talked about the "Triple-alliance of science, technology and factory-production (Freyer 1966a, p. 161). With this, the character of scientific research changed. In the 19th century, single inventions and discoveries revolutionized the technology of production. But now in the 20th century, progress in research has become an institutionalized and ob-

---

6   The "long wave"-approach, developed by Nikolai Kondratieff in the 20s and rediscovered in the 70s, was already (or still) known by Freyer in the 50s.

jective process that keeps itself in motion through international cooperation and competition (see Freyer 1966, pp. 22f).

However, the production apparatus, science, and technology alone do not guarantee at all the functioning of industrial society. The products also have to be bought and consumed. With this, we come to the second basic category of Freyer's structural analysis of the economy in industrial society: consumption.

The manner of consumption changes fundamentally in industrial society compared to previous eras:

> Consumption as such is the most natural thing in the world. The human being has needs just like any living creature has and must satisfy them in order to live. He/She satisfies these needs by consuming. The industrial system has caused a fundamental change in this basic idea of life. It does not produce because of and towards a natural and given demand, but it produces the products and the needs for the products at the same time. It creates the needs - or at least it stimulates them - and it standardizes them at the same time, so that the needs appear as needs of the masses. Only in this way needs become interesting for the production sector ... Consumption is separated from its natural basis and becomes a question of feasibility and planning. Consumption also becomes a sphere of activity of the applied sciences and of specific technologies, like the natural processes that are transformed in industrial processes of production (Freyer 1965, pp. 240f).

Production and (private) consumption is mainly kept in balance by the "serial character" of each, whereby "serial" means "the negation and overcoming of the individual" (Freyer 1965, p. 248). The mass-production of industrial society is standardized. The consumers' needs have to be standardized and freed of all individual traits as well, in order to keep the sales running. How does this work? Freyer describes the following mechanisms:

- Above all, standardized industrial products are relatively cheap, moreover they are tested and in stock. On the other hand, "every special and individual product is relatively expensive" (Freyer 1965, p. 251).

- Advertising works with clever psychological techniques which appeal to the subconscious and to the need for admiration (Freyer 1965, pp. 247, 251).[7]

---

7 Freyer refers to DAVID RIESMAN's "The Lonely Crowd" (1950) and to VANCE PACKARD's "The Hidden Persuaders" (1959).

- Especially the pressure of conformism is standardizing. This pressure starts with the neighbors - "especially the partly or totally anonymous ones": "Needs which we all have become norms overnight, as well as the products with which we satisfy the needs". Thus, "the normal consumer" is created as a "subjective counterpole to the serial-production" (Freyer 1965, p. 252).

- The principle of standardization is connected to the principle of differentiation. Through this, the single levels of the middle classes can be served in the best way. At the same time, the differentiation of the product palette satisfies the social need to be different from others (Freyer 1965, p. 253).

A further precondition for the functioning of industrial society is "adaption" as the most important pattern of behavior (see the following section IV.).

IV. The Human Being in Industrial Society

What happens to the range of freedom and the social character of the human being in modern industrial society? This question comprises the actual center of Freyer's theory. At this point, ethical aspects are brought up, namely as "value references" ("Wertbeziehungen", Max Weber).

The life in "secondary systems" is constitutive for developing the personality in industrial society. What is meant by this?

Among Freyer's concrete examples of secondary systems are big-city traffic, the modern insurance business, the large company or centralized administration (see Freyer [1955], p. 79).[8] They are characterized by the following features:

- They have not grown in a historical sense, but rather are constructed.

---

8 As counterexamples to secondary system Freyer mentions "marriage, love, friendship, the personal relationship based on faith, and the association based on comradeship". For all of them it is true "that their emergence cannot be intended and that their course cannot be planned. They have to develop and fulfill themselves; they mature, go through their changes, and withstand crises. Regarding all this, they feed themselves on the entire humanity of their human members by constantly appealing to other characteristics" (FREYER [1955], p. 84).

- They are constructed by the system, not by the human being. They are "constructions of function".
- They concern the human being in a certain respect. They do not relate to the whole person.
- They have separated themselves from historical heritage as well as from natural principles. Thus they are "a kind of a second nature" (Freyer 1955, p. 110).
- The mode of action suitable to secondary systems is adaption (Freyer 1955, p. 110).

The working world is paradigmatic for the secondary systems. This area is characterized by "high technology" and "advancing rationalization" (Freyer 1960, p. 307). Typically, production is organized as a system in the sense of factory work. The single operations of work are determined by plan. Thus, work is not a free and independent action but rather an exact execution of functions that were planned in advance and by other people (there are exceptional occupational groups such as medical doctors, educators, artists, etc.). Industrial work is therefore characterized by specialization, heteronomy, subordination to the company's rules and the dwindling of autonomy and personal responsibility (see Freyer 1957, p. 56). Even full automation which eliminated the extreme specialization of Taylor did not change the heteronomy of work, despite the fact that this kind of work demands much higher intellectual and ethical requirements than unskilled labor (see Freyer 1957a, p. 7).

In many regards, life in the working world is paradigmatic for the life in other institutions of industrial society. Its social system "is very consistently constructed in such a way that the human being is always only affected in one respect - sometimes in this respect, somtimes in another one. He/She is never addressed as a whole personality, but as the bearer of a reasonable work (as determined by objective criteria) or as a bearer of an interest that can be schematized and organized" (Freyer 1957, p. 58).

The institutions of industrial society function by bringing "finished situational schemes and behavioral patterns to the human being" (Freyer 1957, p. 58). The better the individuals adapt to these imaginary patterns, the more perfectly the institutions function in industrial society.

Vice versa, it can be said that individual behavior is less problematic and more succussful, the more it adapts to the system's norms - the more it follows the "traffic regulations", so to speak. But if he/she (the human being, V.K.) acts improperly, he/she will never make it over an intersection or will be run over" (see Freyer 1957, p. 58). From this relation between institutions of industrial society and the modern human being results a "transformation of behavior into a Self-Behavior" ("Transformation des Handelns in ein Sich-Verhalten"; see Freyer 1965, pp. 265-373). "The normal behavior of the human being in his/her environment becomes independent of the actual person" (Freyer 1960, p. 308). Motives are not set by the qualities and the character of a person, but by the institutions and situations in which the person is located. In this respect it can be said that the "modern life-structures" - also those of the western world - show "totalitarian traits" (see Freyer 1957, p. 59).

By these means a social character emerges that Freyer describes as a "Man Without Qualities", referring to the novel by Robert Musil:

> The social system standardizes his characteristics and his motivations in advance, just as the factory plans standardize his performance. They also run on rails and follow the switches according to how they are set. Along with the behaviors the apparatus also always objectifies the corresponding opinions, feelings and fundamental attitudes - or at least it threatens to do so. The result is characteristics sans man, statements sans man, and even convictions sans man. (308).

This process of the personality's erosion does not proceed as a social drama, but rather imperceptibly, even voluntarily. The process is sweetened by the advantages of conformed behavior and by the conveniences and pleasures of industrial society.

Freyer's overall assessment of "secondary systems" as typical social forms of highly-developed industrial society is rather ambivalent in the end. On the one hand, "secondary systems" as funcionally differentiated systems raise the standard of living and facilitate social security (systems of social security are secondary systems as well). On the other hand, secondary systems restrict the range of freedom of the individual human being and demand a social character marked by conformity and the willingness to adapt. The secondary systems move the human being further and further from the ideals of the philosophy of the Enlightenment which called for a free, mature and ethically responsible human being.

The secondary systems also fundamentally change the relation between mankind and nature. In pre-industrial society, the human being lived in relative harmony with and was embedded in the natural environment whose fruits he/she used without fundamentally changing the natural conditions. In industrial society, nature becomes a mere resource or the ground for buildings.

Humanity creates a second, artificial nature (that does not dissolve into the first one). It disrupts and destroys ecological cycles. Freyer most clearly describes the risks of the industrial society by means of a metaphor: the human being is "the carcinoma" of the earth and the secondary systems are "secondary growths" (Metastasen) (see Freyer 1955, pp. 246f).

V. Ethics and the Development of the Industrial Society

How can the economy and society of the industrial age be formed from an ethical point of view? In order to answer this question, it has to be clarified how the social sciences have to deal with ethical questions from Freyer's point of view.

In his later years Freyer took a methodological position similar to Max Weber's. Empirical science cannot decide the validity of values ("Werturteilsfreiheit"; "the freedom from value judgments"). But values are necessary to constitute an object of scientific knowledge ("Wertbeziehung"; "value reference"). The social scientist can also judge, whether certain given socio-economic structures are favorable for the realization of certain values. The last-mentioned aspect is of considerable importance in Freyer's later works.

Which ethical position did Freyer take? Since the mid-thirties, Freyer turned away from National Socialism and came to a conservative position which postulated the values of freedom and humanity. These values especially influenced his questions about the range of freedom and the social character of the human being in the industrial age. In this respect, his diagnosis was rather pessimistic. The secondary systems leave the human little room for freedom and for structuring one's life. They foster a mentality of adaption and the social character of a "Man Without Characteristic". Which opportunities did Freyer see to counteract these tendencies? Which chances did he see at all to shape modern economic and societal processes from an ethical standpoint?

In its mode of operation, the industrial society is a "cataract". In its social form, it is an ensemble of secondary systems. According to Freyer, both restrict the ability to ethically organize the economy and society.

From Freyer's point of view, a return to a pre-industrial society is absolutely impossible. "It is an irreversible development that the majority of humankind - after it was cut off from the original, natural sources of food and from the possibility of an autarkical lifestyle - is dependent on the functioning market and on the functioning social apparatus, just as they are dependent on working information technologies. It would be hare-brained to want to change this and therefore it would make no sense to complain about this" (Freyer 1960, p. 309).

Programmatic considerations about an ethical structuring can thus only take place within the boundaries of the existing industrial society. Freyer's most important concern is: How can humankind develop in an industrial society - a humankind that lies not too far from the humanistic ideal of an universal and freely-developing personality?

The secondary systems relate to the individuals only partially and in certain respects and functions (see section IV.). Thus, the structures of industrial society do not create "room in which to live" in which the human being as a whole and as an individual personality can develop itself. Consequently, the fist aim has to be creating and preserving spaces in which the human being can develop as a well-rounded personality.

In the first place, Freyer pleaded for strengthening traditional forms of community, such as the family, the neighborhood, communities in the workplace or communities of people who share certain fundamental attitudes as a counterbalance to industrial society. Freyer believed in the special significance of the family. Although he knew about the loss of function of the family in industrial society, it made him feel optimistic that the family had withstood the difficult circumstances and turmoil of the Second World War and post-war period and that the family could hold its ground in the industrial-societal process of "creative destruction" (Joseph A. Schumpeter).

As a second, Freyer recommended the decentralization of economical and societal organizations, especially of companies and administrations. According to Freyer, the currently predominant principle of organization is characterized by the fact that "the responsibility is concentrated in one and only one point, finds expression in an overall plan and devides many partial tasks which mesh with each other like gear wheels" (Freyer 1957, p. 57): the single worker then only functions as a mere executor of a predetermined plan. Freyer's alternative was "that the common plans are split up into many compartments of responsibility and that the single employee is placed in such a compartment; it is his/her responsibility to work on all the tasks in that compartment" (Freyer 1957, p. 57). Freyer called for an organization of working life that leaves the highest possible amount of responsibility and discretionary powers to the employee.

Finally, Freyer also appealed to the individual human being, "everyone can only look after his/her own human existence" (Freyer 1957a, p. 8). "There are enough opportunities under all circumstances to preserve the personality as such: in the creation of one's own sphere of life, in the maintenance of one's own style, in the maintenance of human relationships" (Freyer 1956, p. 27). Everyone is called upon to try to keep or to win back the autonomy of one's lifestyle. This means in the fist place to resist giving in to every temptation of consumer society; and secondly to avoid becoming simply a cog in the machine through adaption to one's work. Instead, one should try to involve oneself personally.

Therefore, the secondary systems leave little room for ethically shaping society. Even more than that, the dynamic of progress in industrial society cannot be steered ethically. This "progrès réel" has become an entity that is independent of attitudes and decisions. Therefore, progress cannot be shaped according to ethical principles as the Enlightenment had promised, instead it sets the norms of human behavior itself.

How should the human being act in this cataract? The most obvious thing would be a fatalistic attitude, especially since the process of progress could lead to a technical or ecological catastrophe. But history is open in principle. It is possible that the dynamic of industrial society will slow down at some point and a new relative state of calmness will emerge. There are no signs of this, but it is not to be ruled out. Historical development can come to a point where the human being's capacity to shape society once again increases.

In this respect, in the cataract it is not fatalism that is called for but rather an attitude that Freyer describes as "Erwarten" ("expecting"): "Erwarten" not as a "passive attitude", not as "merely standing by and letting things happen, not even merely being prepared for something, but rather being ready, even actively preparing for the expected" (Freyer 1965, p. 326). But there will never be a society that is shaped purely by ethical aspects. Rather, ethical values can always only "be asserted as a counterbalance to the objective structures with which they only can be kept under mutual tension" (Freyer 1965, p. 331).

HANS FREYER'S ECONOMIC PHILOSOPHY

References

FREYER, HANS : *Antäus. Grundlegung einer Ethik des bewußten Lebens*, Jena (Eugen Diederich) 1918.

FREYER, HANS : *Prometheus. Ideen zu einer Philosophie der Kultur*, Jena (Eugen Diederich) 1923.

FREYER, HANS (1923 a): *Theorie des objektiven Geistes*, Leipzig (Teubner) 1923.

FREYER, HANS :*Revolution von Rechts*, Jena (Eugen Diederich) 1931.

FREYER, HANS : *Theorie des gegenwärtigen Zeitalters*, Stuttgart (Deutsche Verlags-Anstalt) 1955.

FREYER, HANS : "Die Dynamik der technischen Entwicklung und die geistige Situation des Menschen", in: *Die 8. Niederrheinische Universitätswoche* (Schriftenreihe der Duisburger Universitäts-Gesellschaft), Duisburg 1956, pp. 20-30.

FREYER, HANS : "Die Persönlichkeit unter den Bedingungen der gegenwärtigen Gesellschaft", in: *Jahresring 1957/58*, pp. 55-68.

FREYER, HANS (1957 a): "Automation - historisch und soziologisch gesehen", *Fördern und Heben*, 7 (Sonderheft), pp. 6-8, 1957.

FREYER, HANS: "Soziologische Aspekte zur Situation der Menschen in der Gegenwart", *Die Therapiewoche*, 10 (1960), pp. 306-311.

FREYER, HANS: *Schwelle der Zeiten*, Stuttgart (Deutsche Verlags-Anstalt) 1965.

FREYER, HANS: "Entwicklungstendenzen und Probleme der modernen Industriegesellschaft", in: *Die Industriegesellschaft in Ost und West. Konvergenzen und Divergenzen*, ed. Hans Freyer, Jindrich Filipec, Lothar Bossle, Mainz (Institut für staatsbürgerliche Bildung) 1966, pp. 9-32.

FREYER, HANS (1966a): "Strukturwandlungen der industriellen Gesellschaft im 20. Jahrhundert", *Recht der Arbeit*, pp. 161-163.

KRUSE, VOLKER: *Historisch-soziologische Zeitdiagnosen in Westdeutschland nach 1945. Eduard Heimann, Alfred von Martin, Hans Freyer*, Frankfurt am Main (Suhrkamp) 1994.

LÖWITH, KARL: *Weltgeschichte und Heilsgeschehen. Die theologischen Voraussetzungen der Geschichtsphilosophie (1949)*, Stuttgart, Berlin, Köln (Kohlhammer) 1990.

MANHEIM, ERNEST: "The Sociological Theories of Hans Freyer. Sociology as a Nationalistic Program of Social Action", in: *An Introduction to the History of Sociology*, ed. H. E. Barnes, Chicago (University Press) 1948, pp. 362-373.

MULLER, JERRY Z.: *The Other God That Failed. Hans Freyer and the Deradicalization of German Conservatism*, Princeton, New Jersey (Princeton University Press) 1987.

VOLKER KRUSE

PACKARD, VANCE: *The Hidden Persuaders*, New York (van Rees Press) 1957.

RIESMAN, DAVID: *The Lonely Crowd*, New Haven (Yale University Press) 1950.

SIEFERLE, ROLF PETER: *Die konservative Revolution. Fünf biographische Skizzen*, Frankfurt am Main (S. Fischer) 1995.

ÜNER, ELFRIEDE: *Soziologie als "geistige Bewegung". Hans Freyers System der Soziologie und die "Leipziger Schule"*, Weinheim (VCH, Acta Humaniora) 1992.

Chapter 9

Business Ethics in Older German Business Administration: Heinrich Nicklisch, Wilhelm Kalveram, August Marx

UDO NEUGEBAUER

I. Introduction

When leaving the traditional rules of salesmanship and accounting as well as commercial and trading sciences ("old" business administration) out of consideration, the "new" business administration is a quite young discipline.

Its origin in Germany can be traced back to the beginning of this century and the foundation of such academies.[1] Within the industrial development and entrepreneurial activities, the question of organizing and leading a business in an appropriate, successful and scientifically sound way has become more meaningful and urgent. This is how "Private enterprise economics" (in German: *Privatwirtschaftslehre*) or "Individual economics" (*Einzelwirtschaftslehre*) have become a scientific discipline like the already established subject of economics.

In German-speaking countries business administration was determined strongly by single direction-finders like Eugen Schmalenbach (for a practical science with emphasis on skilfulness; in German: *Kunstlehre*), Johann Friedrich Schärr and Heinrich Nicklisch (representing the ethic-normative approach), and Wilhelm Rieger for the theoretical approach to business administration.[2] In the second half of the 20th century, business administration was developing towards a pluralistic direction, represented by names like Erich Gutenberg, Edmund Heinen and Hans Ulrich.[3] The Anglo-American view of business administration began to gain an ever stronger and more constant influence on German business administration.[4]

During the development of business administration the subject of ethics was repeatedly considered.[5] Within the framework of this essay, the main characteristics of some famous scholars of the ethically oriented German-speaking business administration - such as Heinrich Nicklisch, Wilhelm Kalveram and August Marx - will be considered more closely. Hereby the approach shall be to compare the main characteristics of these scholars' teachings.

The reason why these representatives and their economic approaches are considered "ethical" is not easily recognized and therefore needs a profound analysis. When regarding this subject superficially it is at least striking that these approaches show very different points of view about ethics, culture and morals. If we regard this matter more closely, it becomes clear that they have tried to put the economical processes and the economically active human be-

---

1   Comp. KLEIN-BLENKERS, REISS (1993), cls. 1417.
2   Comp. KLEIN-BLENKERS, REISS (1993), cls. 1423.
3   Comp. KLEIN-BLENKERS, REISS (1993), col. 1426.
4   Comp. KLEIN-BLENKERS, REISS (1993), col. 1428.
5   Comp. NEUGEBAUER (1994).

ing into a higher context with regard to the motives of human activities and the design of living within society.

In order to clarify the core of Nicklisch's, Kalveram's and Marx's understanding of business administration, we have to focus the image and imagination about the world and the human being, the understanding of economics and business as well as science and practice.[6] Taking the historian's point of view, our emphasis lies on the twenties (Heinrich Nicklisch's ethical-normative point of view) and in the fifties (Christian point of view, represented by Wilhelm Kalveram and August Marx). A more detailed consideration of these approaches shall not only increase understanding but also help the reader understand their meaning for today's society.

II. Heinrich Nicklisch: Ethical-Normative Business Administration

1. Idealistic World-Picture

For the German-speaking business administration, which was consolidating as a science in the beginning of this century, the subject of consideration - the company (*Betrieb*), was an institution with great influence on society and a right to exist only for this reason. Economic practice was therefore an activity with a certain purpose, which was not so much submit to economic laws but to the purpose of serving the whole society. For Nicklisch, the philosophic movements like idealism, materialism and romanticism play a major role[7] for understanding and explaining economic ongoings thoroughly.

The idea of freedom, duty and community was born out of the German idealistic movement. The possibility to decide and act freely in economic matters means to act morally within an economic framework, being responsible and obliged to the community. Similar to Fichte, Nicklisch highly appreciates community and conscience. Feeling and sense as well as harmony with the community play an important role in German romanticism. The imagination of unity and the individual being a part of it is an imprinting way of thinking for that time. Only the community enables human being to

---

6   Comp. NEUGEBAUER (1994), p. 4 ff.
7   Comp. SCHÖNPFLUG (1954), p. 193 ff.

live and grow in personality. However it is also the community which determines the purposes of acting and developing in an economic way.[8]

Materialism is a quite important subject in the works of Nicklisch as well. Man as a spiritual and physical (in German: *Geist- und Körperwesen*) being uses the world's resources being physical to serve him in his existence. His ability to think sensibly enables him to transform nature according to his purposes and needs. Substance is changed by power. Power works physically (power of existence; *Seinskraft*), following the laws of nature and creating changes. Yet at the same time it originates from a human-spiritual power (will-power; *Willenskraft*) which, according to the moral law, influences the design of existence and improves the quality of life. The spiritual and physical possibilities of man to design matter and nature according to his purposes and needs, also deploys him with the responsibility and duties in all his deeds. The company is the chosen place where these transformations take place and responsibility is assumed. This knowledge of legitimacy and the spiritual and physical connections and their summing in the "rules of the organization" (*Organisationsgesetze; organisches Gestalten*) plays a major role in the works and view of Heinrich Nicklisch.[9]

2. Economy and Society

As a physical being, man handles his difficult circumstances, which are determined by need and demand in consent with the laws and rules given by society, but as a cultural being he handles them also according to his inner authority, his conscience. However, he cannot do this in isolation, as an individual, but only as a part of a community, in an appropriate organization built solely for one purpose: the company. If regarded from this perspective, economizing is a common act, a cultural area within our society with the individual business playing a major rule. Thus Nicklisch regards society and economy, ≤individual≤ economy (*Einzelwirtschaft*) and national economy (*Gesamtwirtschaft, Volkswirtschaft*) from an organic-integrating point of view. At the same time he opposes individualized economic selfishness. It is not the interest of the individual but of the community, that must receive priority. Imaginations referring to the fulfillment of sensual needs of happi-

---

8   Comp. SCHÖNPFLUG (1954), p. 204 ff; NEUGEBAUER (1994), p. 15.
9   Comp. NICKLISCH (1932), p. 16 ff, and NEUGEBAUER (1994), p. 16 ff.

ness or self-centered fulfillment are strongly opposed[10]. These imaginations take away man's personal dignity and morals by regarding him only as a means, a purpose, totally alienated: "A competition comes into being, which puts material things into the front and causes mankind to argue and fight for life's basic needs and thus support envy, hatred and bitterness to develop, pushing back the idea of togetherness, isolating one man against the other, just for the sake of the will to survive."[11]

3. The Employee and the Company

Man is the target of economization and plays the role of the mediator in order to reach the target. It is himself, just himself as a spiritual and physical being, who assigns economic objectives and tries to reach them with and through the business community. The working man himself is a value, not an operating resource, nor solely the focus of anybody's interest. He is a part of the corporate community and thus carries responsibility.[12]

The company is an instrument for functional economic transformation and supplying activities. It is involved in society "organically" and is a part of the economic circle of nominal goods and real goods. Its orientation has a social-economic character. The target of corporate economization is the economic principle of economical, purpose-oriented, justified investment of resources (*Wirtschaftlichkeit*). Return on investment is not a main topic.

Nicklisch describes the sequence of operations as "operating process" (in German: *Betriebsprozess*) and "process of profit distribution" (in German: *Ertragsverteilungsprozess*). The operating process describes the inner circle of the business (procurement, production and marketing) and includes profit-making. The distribution of profit hereby plays a major role, because it is only in the national economic circle that it gives way to the consumption of goods and services.[13] The obtained profit is used for covering the internal and labor costs. Each business process has to follow economic rules. The profit distribution process has to meet the ethically-based demand for justice (*Verteilungsgerechtigkeit*).

---

10 Comp. NEUGEBAUER (1994), p. 20 ff.
11 NICKLISCH quoted in NEUGEBAUER (1994), p. 23.
12 Comp. NEUGEBAUER (1994), p. 26 f.
13 Comp. NEUGEBAUER (1994), p. 28 ff.

Nicklisch ascribes a great importance to the human being as employee, especially in considering him not as a cost factor but as advance profit. Manpower is not bought with money but it is regarded as labor input necessary for the business process, as a human factor for profit-making, which through profit distribution gets involved in the economic process. According to Nicklisch, the individual company is a means for real goods procurement (business process) and nominal goods procurement at the same time (profit distribution process). Economy and justice thus are the ethical-normative preconditions for economizing economically, sufficiently, socially and according to one's financial needs.[14]

4. Normative Approach to Science

Since human and economic decisions and activities follow binding social values and cultural rules, scientific research also has to take regard of values as well as of the connection between things. This is why Nicklisch pleads for a "normative science" which does not invent values but takes into account existing values and regulations. The object of this science is not only empirical research on existing business processes, but it especially wants to point out those cultural values and social norms which ought to form the foundation for private business activities. Ethical-normative business science has to submit its object of research, which is business and business process, to this given social system of values. Being occupied with an existing business reality only helps to show the difference between the current business situation and the possible and desirable normative condition. The current social regulations and specific cultural pattern of values cannot be recognized by empirical research but by "thinking sensibly", recognizing and understanding.[15]

A science of individual economic units (*Einzelwirtschaftslehre*) is required, which presents the internal business processes and rules on the one hand and, on the other hand, also makes clear the conditions which the business context and the social, cultural environment are submit to. According to Nicklisch, this is not a capital- or personal interest-oriented entrepreneurial science, nor is it a market-related science of private industry, nor a technocratic management science. Its objective is the individual economic unit (pri-

---

14 Comp. NEUGEBAUER (1994), p. 31 ff.
15 Comp. SCHÖNPFLUG (1954), p. 73 ff.

vate/public business, organization or household). As a science it is supposed to educate the next entrepreneurial generation in a professional and responsible way while still referring to practical requirements.[16]

From a methodological point of view, Nicklisch differentiates between "natural" and "spiritual" contexts as well as between realizing and applying. Natural contexts and relations (= natural laws; *Naturgesetze*) can be found through induction and be deductively applied to the concrete individual case within the "business machinery". However, the spiritual context (= laws of development; *Entwicklungsgesetze*) can only be understood intuitively (and through reinforcement) and has to be integrated in the business by means of education.[17]

5. Critical Review

Heinrich Nicklisch has presented us with a closed concept of business science, where the principles of economy and justice are put in the front, and the economizing human being is put in the center. Business science activities are placed in the economic and social context. Their objectives and their success are not mainly economically determined, but also by social, cultural, community-oriented values and targets. Business science, taking into account these conditions, thus is a normative science based on human economic responsibility. Its aim is to support human identity, sense and harmony beyond professional purposes.

Yet there are critical voices:

· A science should not support a certain value and not be a "like-minded teaching" (*Gesinnungslehre*) or "educating science" (*Erziehungslehre*).

· A strong emphasis of togetherness and community transfigures contradictions and harmonizes conflicts superficially. Moreover, it is old-fashioned and discredited by National Socialism.

· From the scientific point of view the idea of profit distribution and practical applicability must be criticized.[18]

However, there are reasons to acknowledge Nicklisch, especially because of the unity of his approach as well as the human-social aspect. Categorizing

---

16 Comp. NEUGEBAUER (1994), p. 35 ff.
17 Comp. NICKLISCH (1932), p. 22 ff.
18 Comp. NEUGEBAUER (1994), p. 40 ff.

the business purpose into the national economic requirements as well as the human-oriented view of business are judged positively. It is still important today to understand business as a social pattern and at the same time emphasize economic efficiency and justice. In and beyond his time, Nicklisch has influenced German business science and contributed to its acknowledgment as a science.[19]

III. The Christian Understanding of the Economy: Wilhelm Kalveram and August Marx

1. Christian World View

The philosophical basis for Kalveram and Marx is the teaching of Christian faith. As God's ambassador on earth, created in his image, man has to utilize the goods of the earth. The economic treatment of rare goods and the thus necessary working activities are task and service for the kingdom of God and for the use of man as an act of charity. Aims and activities of man are submit to temptations and are not perfect. Activities out of the sense of Christian responsibility happen within a framework of moral order and Christian morals within a cultural community of believers. In this sense, an economy which delights in its own possibilities and successes or in material or immaterial self-enjoyment, is not desirable.

The divine world order is good and sensible. The moral order deriving from that shows the way to man's development and perfection. It builds the basic cultural pattern for a harmonic economic business practice, which is understood as a service of man in harmony with nature. Vice versa the way of economizing is an expression of culture: "A people's culture is determined by many things, not only by the art of building, of law, political life etc., but also very strongly by economic processes as far as they are consciously designed implementations of free will decisions."[20]

Kalveram follows the value-ethical imagination which differentiates between "last values" (*Letztwerten*) and "service values" (*Dienstwerten*). Carrying out economic activities means to produce service values for the sake of

---

19 Comp. NEUGEBAUER (1994), p. 42 ff.
20 MARX (1954), p. 598.

man and society. The economy receives its sense, power and legitimization from its contribution and its harmony with trans-economical cultural values and the Christian faith of living for the neighbor. The way of working and economizing for value-addition is an expression of this business culture and it encourages the respective cultural community. For the individual it means to become responsible and to give orientation to his activities.[21]

2. Economy and Society

Economy and economizing as useful, culture-adding functions of satisfying a society's demands, as a possibility for man to develop in an appropriate and useful way, and as a way to realize a Christian culture: this is the understanding of Kalveram and Marx. "Economy is just a function of the thinking human being and only fulfills its purpose and sense in serving others."[22] Marx rejects every other foundation of the economic purpose. This is especially true for Economic Liberalism with free competition and undisguised ambition. It is also true for the socialist state control with its collective restrictions and monopolized state economy.[23] Economizing is an integral part and expression of a social objective or purpose and does not work automatically or by compulsion. It opens opportunities to design, act freely and creatively on new areas which have to be worked on professionally and responsibly. Moral and sensible decisions and actions are possible, necessary and are required. Thus, for Kalveram, the ethical and economic imperative is "Act in the economy economically! (in German: *wirtschafte wirtschaftsgemäß)*", "Act in the economy in a way appropriate to the purpose of the economic system", e.g. in an economical, efficient, responsible way which follows the sense and purpose of the economy.[24]

3. Man and Business

Man forms and uses the economy. He offers his manpower - and his belief - to the company, yet he needs in return a strengthening leadership - di-

---

21 Comp. Neugebauer (1994), p. 53 f.
22 Marx (1954), p. 595.
23 Comp. Neugebauer (1994), p. 55 f.
24 Comp. Kalveram (1951), p. 18; Neugebauer (1994), p. 56 f.

rective - towards economic, national economic and social objectives and purposes. Economic action only for the purpose of personal development and satisfaction is not what Kalveram and Marx mean. Much more it is economic action according to one's conscience and responsibility as well as necessary competence, which has to be its focus.

From the Christian point of view, the working individual as a person is at the center of all business activities. Yet business does not lose its purposes and laws, but the substantial and personal aims are connected. This means that business has to serve the development of man as a part of his area of living and responsibility. Reversely, the individual has to contribute to the aims and development of the company he works for. The ideal is a synthesis of personal development, successful work for the company, and social prosperity. The employee's development and prosperity, the successful development and safeguarding of the company are two aspects of the same thing.[25]

According to Marx, business is characterized by purpose:
· obligation to pay maintenance and covering personal needs;
· way of action: continuous action according to plan;
· the leading principle: principle of economic rationality;
· organizational form: unity;
· development: continuous change in shape;
· production technique: the value-adding process.[26]

By his skill and his useful behavior, man contributes to the corporate productivity and determines it sensibly and carefully: "This behavior according to a plan, finding its expression in a sensible man's economical activities and, thus, conscious act of charity makes the difference between human work and the action of unconscious, insensible creatures."[27]

The interaction of man and the company, which is characterized mainly by the developing element, becomes evident in education, socialization and individual development. Business as an educational factor influences the one who works and, in return, receives its specific character from him. Both business and man are determined by society's culture. "Since the economy is a function of the thinking man, it only finds its purpose, sense and objective

25 Comp. NEUGEBAUER (1994), p. 58 ff.
26 MARX (1961), p. 3 f.
27 MARX (1961), p. 5.

in serving him. So every company forms one of many partial functions which finally form the overall culture of our society. There is no activity people can do which does not give witness about the attitude of their souls and at the same time forms a part of their cultural actions. Thus every business serves culture and has to take care of its continuity ensured by a corporate education."[28]

From the view of business administration the point is not just to ensure business and prosperity, but also to safeguard jobs and to design work in a humane way. The variables relevant for business administration have to take into account technical, economic, but also social ethical and cultural circumstances and requirements. Within the framework of economic rationality, we have to go for productivity, profitability and economic efficiency at the same time and to the same degree.[29] The same point actually is to clarify the relationship between man and the company: "Man is not made for business, but business is also made for man's development."[30]

4. Business Administration as a Science

Business administration as a science has the following objectives and functions: "Business science has to do research on the means and ways of fulfilling the company's and the economic individual's tasks, and on the forces designing the interaction of economic performances."[31]

Research in this field does not only concentrate on the functional side but also includes the cultural side. Business science as a research discipline not only views the regularity of economic actions. Moreover, the extra-economic determination of objectives and purposes and its fulfillment through private enterprise, rational and profitable work plays a major role. Thus, it also refers to the moral objectives as well as to the substantial, economic actions required. Hereby it receives an ethical and integral characterization.[32]

Business science as a subject taught at universities has a three-fold meaning:

---

28 MARX (1961), p. 10.
29 Comp. NEUGEBAUER (1994), p. 62 ff.
30 KALVERAM (1951), p. 22.
31 KALVERAM (1949), p. 10.
32 Comp. NEUGEBAUER (1994), p. 65 f.

(1) doing research on subjects concerning business administration;

(2) handing on this knowledge in educating future managers;

(3) it also means management: "business politics and -techniques".

Research is the basis of business science. Research background is an integral imagination of the economy, focusing on value-addition in the economic as well as the extra-economic (i.e. social and cultural) sense. The qualification of young professionals is a second core which includes teaching professional knowledge as well as cultivation of personality (ethos). Being conscious that business and economics have to serve man and also the development of a better, more humane society is regarded essential for successfully fulfilling the economic tasks.[33]

According to Kalveram, the objectives of economic research have both a theoretical and a practical side: Theoretically, the business processes, their causes and effects and their regularities are explored objectively. It is also important to put the causal connections into a final general view and imagination of society and how it should develop. Economic action as a form of human activity is not just determined logically and legally but also ethically, since it serves human society and culture. Practically this means to establish methods that make it possible to act in the economy properly, humanely and responsibly, e.g. to conduct economic action "economically" in the sense of "appropriately to the purpose of the economic system", i.e. in the integral (humane, social, cultural) sense of the word described above.[34]

The inductive way to decoding causal connections in business is regarded as a methodologically sensible way of research. Yet knowing causal connections is not sufficient for designing the economic process. Social, ethical and cultural elements are essential for this process and are to be integrated deductively. [35]

5. Business Administration as a Management Philosophy

For Wilhelm Kalveram and August Marx business science is not solely an instrumental, resource- and situation-optimizing management teaching of how to safeguard marketing opportunities and market leadership. Moreover,

---

33 Comp. NEUGEBAUER (1994), p.66 f.

34 Comp. NEUGEBAUER (1994), p. 67 f.

35 Comp. NEUGEBAUER (1994), p. 69.

Christian, humane and cultural attitudes become involved in business administration. Management thus becomes a continuous synthesis of purpose-rational (purpose-oriented, in German: *zweckrational*), design in the sense of construction, and adaptation, and value-rational (value-oriented, in German: *wertrational*), humane design reflection. This is being practically implemented in salary, pricing, employees' participation in the processes, and social care.[36]

Personal development is continued in professional practice, if the company itself (as a place of working and learning) socializes and educates. This takes place at three stages[37]:

· economic stage: the work the employee is required to do;
· social stage: integration in the working community;
· cultural stage: "contributing to life fulfillment of the individual".

Kalveram describes his imagination of business science very impressively using the lighthouse metaphor: "A sailor approaching the coast with his ship, stays in the lightbeam, yet he will operate as a professional navigator in order to avoid cliffs and sandbars ... the entrepreneur has to be led by the idea of economizing rationally, by the perspective to receive a proper profit. The pursuit of profit is not immoral, and an inventory spirit of initiative and readiness to become active is not suspicious to business ethics. We just have to stay in the lightbeam, e.g. all economic actions have to be in accordance with the eternal, natural and moral laws, which form the final borderline and objective for every commercial thought and action."[38]

6. Critical Review

Christian philosophy and the idea of "Conduct economic action economically, humanely and responsibly!" (in German: *Wirtschafte wirtschaftsgemäß!*) which is derived from that, may meet objections. Thus, the empirical side may question the justifiability and legitimacy of an ethical and normative idea of the economy. On the other hand, the practical, practice-oriented approach considers every moral view sceptically and just regards purpose and rationality as legitimate.

---

36 Comp. KALVERAM (1951), p. 21; NEUGEBAUER (1994), p. 69 ff.
37 Comp. MARX (1961), p. 7 ff.
38 KALVERAM (1951), p. 20.

The relation between economic and non-economic objectives is considered contradictory and unharmonic. Finally, some critics believe that "blind" price mechanism and demand-orientation can give better results than continuous, responsible efforts on the economic stage.[39]

The demand and necessity of economizing in a responsible way normally is not denied. Yet it is ascribed either to business practice and corporate policy or to economic and vocational education, (in German: *Wirtschaftspädagogik*) and their personal business ethos - but never to the scientific side.

Oswald von Nell-Breuning defends the claim for conducting economic action economically: the maxim *wirtschafte wirtschaftsgemäß* is not only appropriate from the economic point of view, but also logically true and - last but not least - moral. Ethically right and proper economizing supplement each other.[40]

IV. A Summary of Typology

In the following, the ethically sound approaches analyzed by Heinrich Nicklisch, Wilhelm Kalveram and August Marx are to be summarized according to their characteristics in a synthesis.[41]

(1) Philosophical Model of Business Science
The business is a part of economy and society formed within the framework of cultural development. The idea of society and economy formed in the German-speaking countries is strongly influenced by the traditions of idealism, humanism and Christianity. The economic value-addition is integrated in this extra-economic pattern of thinking and values. Primarily, it does not serve its own aims, self-assertion or self-preservation, but it helps covering human needs and designing a life-style in accordance with the valid cultural values and society's objectives.

---

39 Comp. NEUGEBAUER (1994), p. 72 ff.
40 Comp. NEUGEBAUER (1994), p. 75 ff.
41 Comp. NEUGEBAUER (1994), p. 173 ff.

(2) The Responsibly Acting Person

The individual is considered a part of a society and of a (philosophical-Christian) cultural tradition, which gives him or her security and orientation. The individual is free and able to design his own life-style and to cover his needs and demands. Only the gift of reason makes man an economizing species. However, he is not bound to act, decide and judge responsibly and just. Since his own decisions can be wrong and his results unwelcome, and since he can be selfish, emotional or hungry for power, he is conferred the responsibility for his deeds. As an individual involved in human society, he has to serve society, and not just himself.

(3) Harmonic View of Society

Man is a part of the society, and he has to contribute to its development. This requires the acknowledgment of (Christian-humanistic) cultural values as well as social laws (justice and morality). Not only the way, but also the objectives and purposes of economizing shape and are shaped by culture. So economic processes always are required to offer a social, humanity-serving and culture-sustaining value-addition.

(4) Holistic Understanding of Science

The economist and his science (which is business science in this context) have to be conscious of the higher purposes, cultural values and social rules according to which business or economic action happens. Research and knowledge thus have not just to serve the objective to enlighten causal contexts and the connection of things in a company, but also have to take regard of the social framework of rules and values and to represent it in a practical way. This is how the foundation for a practical, reasonable and responsible economic action is laid. In the framework of teaching and application, the causal know-how of how to do things (in German: *Verfügungswissen*) and the final knowledge of why to do things (in German: *Orientierungswissen*) must be provided, and the development of personality (ethos) must be encouraged.

(5) The Legitimate Way of Economizing

The objective of practically doing business in a company - beside proper, legal and competitive decisions and actions - is also to take regard of reason and values. The aim always has to be to conduct business in a humane, legal, legitimate and responsible way. An economic understanding and personality according to these principles is inevitable.

(6) Employee-Oriented Style of Leadership

In a company, the employees fulfill an economic as well as social culture-sustaining function. They are economic subjects, not just objects in an autonomous mechanism. Thus, within the company, they have to be treated as personalities with rights and duties. Professional work as self-enjoyment or self-exploitation is to be rejected. Man submits himself to work because of an economic necessity and a higher insight and service for the sake of himself and society. To work in order to make one's living in the face of short supply and difficult situations is not the highest call of life. It is just the way to greater challenges of cultural development and an upright living conscious of the life hereafter. Management has to treat the employees responsibly and carefully with all their virtues and vices. This includes the democratic idea as well as social security.

(7) Social-Humane Objectives of a Company

Companies do not primarily serve their own survival, but the real and nominal supply of the economy with goods. Comprehensive business knowledge includes knowing economic aims and extra-economic values and rules. An economically successful management will not just include legitimate but also moral actions, not just success-oriented but also humane actions. The dignity and expectation of an employee must not be narrow-mindedly submitted to profit and profitability.

(8) Business Personality

The ethical models of business administration we have discussed so far are not made for practical application in a "scientific management". Their purpose is to help finding an orientation and knowledge about things, functions and reason in the business context, which helps to conduct business responsibly, socially and humanely. Moreover, they form the theoretical basis of teaching and practice, and they encourage competent and responsible business personalities to develop in favor of a successful business policy.

V. Relevance to Present Times

The ethically-founded, economical ideas developed by Nicklisch, Kalveram and Marx basically were established during the first half of this century. To ensure a better understanding we want to classify and interpret their ideas historically and culturally and afterwards show their relevance for today.

Ethically oriented economists still remember the industrialization and modernization in the eras of war, post-war and reconstruction. So they were aware of the development of the German economy at its different stages, of the freely developing market with its economic success and social collapses, the times of need and short supply in terms of business. They had gathered theoretical and practical knowledge as well as economic and extra-economic experiences, and they were familiar with the idealistic, humanistic, Christian and social-ethical, and traditional way of thinking. The Anglo-American economic pragmatism was not new to them but not convincing either.

German society in those days was a basically "closed" one. Due to many defeats it had to rely on itself, suffering many material and immaterial shortcomings as well as a brain drain. The individual company played an essential role in the economy and society. As a supplier, it was responsible for its objectives, for the way the employees were treated, or the resources were used, for market conduct and conduct towards the demanders as well as for social and material prosperity.

The limits and weaknesses of a self-relying, independent market behavior were evident as well.[42] They affect society and its social and moral structure. Consequently, due to the competitive environment, there is a decline in moral standards, values and customs. Briefs calls this "borderline morals" (in German: *Grenzmoral*), a business morale the standards of which are gradually brought to a threatening decline.

It has been and is the essential aim of the earlier and present German discussions around ethical matters in business science to oppose this tendency:[43] Again and again these discussions reveal the Janus-headed attitude towards success and responsibility, legality and morality.

The answer given by the "elder economists" was to define the idea of "conducting economic actions responsibly and economically" according to the

---

42 Comp. NEUGEBAUER (1994), p. 188 ff.
43 Comp. NEUGEBAUER (1994), p. 191 ff.

wishes, needs and interests of those who conduct economic actions, but to see this idea within its greater social context including its economic consequences and to integrate it into the economic objectives. Thus, corporate economizing was put into an economic context and greater framework of orientation. The company for them was an appropriate social-economic instrument. People working in this surroundings were required an appropriate economic attitude and readiness to take responsibility. An economic personality or culture shaped and carved by such an attitude ("business ethos") includes responsibility finally on all economic sectors and stages.[44]

The relevance of these approaches for today can be found in the following points:[45]

> (1) In the German concept of the Social Market Economy the social-political framework gives certain rules (top-down), which have to be sustained by the economy and the personnel (bottom-up) in a responsible way. The market economy from the point of view of business ethics cannot just be stabilized through supplementing regulations but has to be supported by ethically oriented actions at all relevant stages.

> (2) On the level of the company itself, a dual ethical approach may be successful: On the level of business structures and processes a discourse ethics makes sense to be introduced. On the level of staff and management, an ethics of responsibility is absolutely necessary. In concrete situations or in a single team, the readiness for taking responsibility is essential - just in a situation of ever keener global competition.

References

KALVERAM, W.: "Grundfragen der Betriebswirtschaftslehre", *Betriebswirtschaftliche Forschung und Praxis*, 1 (1949), pp. 10-45.

---

44 Comp. NEUGEBAUER (1994), p. 184 f.
45 Comp. NEUGEBAUER (1994) p. 192 ff

BUSINESS ETHICS IN GERMAN BUSINESS ADMINISTRATION

KALVERAM, W.: "Ethik und Ethos in Wirtschaftspraxis und Wirtschaftstheorie", *Zeitschrift für Betriebswirtschaft*, 21 (1951), pp. 15-22.

KLEIN-BLENKERS, F., REISS, M.: "Geschichte der Betriebswirtschaftslehre", in: W. WITTMANN et al. (Eds.): *Handwörterbuch der Betriebswirtschaft*, vol. 1, 5th ed., Stuttgart (Schäffer-Poeschel) 1993, columns 1417-1433.

MARX, A.: "Die Wirtschaft als Kulturfunktion", *Zeitschrift für Betriebswirtschaft*, 24 (1954) 11, pp. 593- 604.

MARX, A.: "Der Betrieb - ein Erziehungsfaktor?", in: *Beiträge zur Begegnung von Kirche und Welt*, Nr. 61, Rottenburg (Akademie der Diözese Rottenburg) 1961.

NEUGEBAUER, U.: *Unternehmensethik in der Betriebswirtschaftslehre - Vergleichende Analyse ethischer Ansätze in der deutschsprachigen Betriebswirtschaftslehre*, Ludwigsburg, Berlin (Wissenschaft und Praxis) 1994.

NICKLISCH, H.: *Die Betriebswirtschaft*, 7th ed., Stuttgart (C. E. Poeschel) 1932.

SCHÖNPFLUG, F.: *Betriebswirtschaftslehre, Methoden und Hauptströmungen*, 2nd ed., Stuttgart (C. E. Poeschel) 1954.

Part Four

Austrian Economics and the Historical School

Chapter 10

Carl Menger and the Historicism in Economics*

KIICHIRO YAGI

I. Carl Menger as a German Economist
II. The *Grundsätze* and its Reviewers
III. Themes of the Menger-Schmoller Duel of 1883/84
IV. Max Weber's Reception of Menger

I. Carl Menger as a German Economist

A quarter century ago historians of economics celebrated the centenary of the "Marginal Revolution in Economics." Among the three main figures of this revolution, Menger was more fortunate than other two, Jevons and Walras, that he could have a special conference dedicated to him personally in Vienna besides the Bellagio Conference where all the three were honored equally.[1] It was around this year that many historians of economics became aware

---

* To quote from German text I used published English translations as far as they were available to me. In case such did not exist I had to translate the text by myself, adding the original in the footnote. However, to every citation I added the page numbers of the original German text.

1 Papers of two conferences were published in: (Bellagio Conference) BLACK, R. D. C., COATS, A. W., GOODWINN, C. D. W. (Eds.): *The Marginal Revolution in Economics*, Durham, NC. (Duke University Press) 1973; (Vienna Conference) J. R. HICKS AND W. WEBER (Eds.): *Carl Menger and the Austrian School of Economics*, Oxford (Oxford University Press) 1973.

of Menger's peculiar position to the later development of standard marginalist analysis.

Since then, partly owing to the resurgence of the Austrian school of economics, growing numbers of researchers have published their view on this difficult scholar.[2] Some of them have tried to bring Menger back to the intellectual environment of German economists then. E. Streissler, who has been in the front of this direction since then, titled his 1990 paper precisely, "Carl Menger, the German Economist".[3] Meanwhile, personal papers of Menger has been donated to the Duke University and thus become open to the access of researchers. The Hitotsubashi University, the owner of the Carl Menger Library has just recently completed its project of providing microfilms of the total collection of this grand library. Further, there are several lecture notes which have their origins in Menger's lectures at the Vienna University as well as in the study room of the Crown Prince Rudolf.[4] Despite some progress made in these years, it is safe to say that the work to bring Menger into his own milieu is still on the process.

One of the most natural questions arising from the German context of Menger's works is that of his relation to the Historical School. This is the topic I have to deal with. To fulfill this task, I first (section 2) explain the context in which German Historicism became the main enemy to Menger. This is described as Menger's reaction to the reviews to his *Grundsätze*. Then (section 3) I enter into the hot dispute between Menger and Schmoller. Not only Menger's defense of the "abstract theory" but his offensive against the German Historicism is discussed. In the last section (section 4) I interpret Max Weber's attitude to economics around the turn of the century as the outcome of the dispute between two schools. Max Weber showed hot sympathy

---

2   To mention some, MARGARETE BOOS with her *Die Wissenschaftstheorie Carl Mengers*, Wien (Böhlau) 1986, KARL MILFORD with *Zu Lösungsversuchen des Induktionsproblems und des Abgrenzungsproblems bei Carl Menger*, Wien (Verlag der österreichischen Akademie der Wissenschaften) 1988, MAX ALTER: with *Carl Menger and the Origins of Austrian Economics*, Boulder, Col. (Westview Press) 1990, and RAIMONDO CUBEDDU: *Il Liberalismo della Scoula Menger, Mises, Hayek*, Napoli-Milano (Morano) 1992.

3   ERICH STREISSLER: "Carl Menger, der deutsche Nationalökonom", in: B. SCHEFOLD (Ed.): *Studien zur Entwicklung der ökonomischen Theorie*, X (Schriften des Vereins für Socialpolitik, Bd. 115/X), Berlin (Duncker & Humblot) 1990.

4   ERICH STREISSLER, MONIKA STREISSLER (Eds.): *Carl Menger's Lectures to Crown Prince Rudolf of Austria*, Alderschot (Elgar) 1994.

to Menger in his criticism to Historicism, but still remained loyal to the idea of the "social economics" as historical science.

In 1871 Menger published his *Grundsätze der Volkswirtschaftslehre* and dedicated it to Wilhelm Roscher. As Streissler argued already, this fact surely suffices to indicate Menger's sympathy to German economists then, but it is not appropriate to extend this sympathy to Roscher's position as the founder of the German historical school[5]. For Roscher had another face in German economics as a prominent textbook writer. Menger's study of Roscher's textbook during the gestation period of the *Grundsätze*[6] left its signs in the frequent citations from Roscher's *Grundlagen* in the *Grundsätze*. As a theoretical economist Roscher belonged to a peculiar German tradition[7] that dealt with value in exchange under the basic conception of the relation between goods and human needs that should be satisfied by the former. It was to this face of Roscher that Menger confessed his obligation.

> It was a special pleasure to me that the field here treated, comprising the most general principles of our science, is in no small degree so truly the product of recent development in German political economy, and that the reform of the most important principles of our science here attempted is therefore built upon a foundation laid by previous work that was produced almost entirely by the industry of German scholars. Let this work be regarded, therefore, as a friendly greeting from a collaborator in Austria, and as a faint echo of the scientific

---

5   STREISSLER: *ibid*. See also his "The influence of German economics on the work of Menger and Marshall", in: B. J. CALDWELL (Ed.): *Carl Menger and his Legacy in Economics*, Annual Supplement to volume 22, *History of Political Economy*, Durham, NC. (Duke University Press) 1990.

6   See YUKIHIKO IKEDA: "Carl Menger in the 1860s: Menger on Roscher's Grundlagen", in: GERRIT MEIJER (Ed.): *New Perspectives on Austrian Economics*, London (Routledge) 1995. See also YAGI: "Carl Menger's *Grundsätze* in the Making", *History of Political Economy*, 25 (4), Durham, NC. (Winter) 1993.

7   Keith Tribe (*Governing Economy - The Reformation of German Economic Discourse 1750-1840*, Cambridge (Cambridge University Press) 1988, chap. 8 and 9) investigated into the emergence of this type of thought in German economics and saw "a new orthodoxy" in the textbook of K. H. RAU (*Lehrbuch der politischen Ökonomie*, 1826). To refer KARL BRANDT (*Geschichte der deutschen Volkswirtschaftslehre*, Bd. 1.: Von der Scholastik bis zur klassischen Nationalökonomie Freiburg i. Br. [Haufe] 1992) used "the school of use value" (Gebrauchswertschule), which came from O. Spann's naming.

suggestions so abundantly lavished on us Austrians by Germany through the many outstanding scholars she has sent us and through her excellent publications.[8]

As it could be assumed from this writing, Roscher was chosen only as a representative of German economists as a whole. Other Germans in particular F. B. W. Hermann and K. H. Rau[9] might have been chosen by Menger with the equal right to Roscher, if both had been alive in the publication year of the *Grundsätze*. E. Friedländer, H. F. Storch, K. G. Knies[10], A. Schäffle, and H. Rösler were also important to Menger because they made "attempts to determine the factors common to all forms of the value of goods, and thus to formulate the general concept of 'value'". Menger followed their effort "to distinguish the use value of goods from mere utility"[11] and reached to his own subjective concept of value: "Value is therefore nothing inherent in goods, no property of them, but merely the importance that we first attribute to the satisfaction of our needs, that is, to our lives and well-being, and in

8 CARL MENGER: *Principles of Economics*, trans. by J. Dingwall and B. Hoselitz, Glencoe, Ill. (The Free Press) 1950 (hereafter D/H), p. 49. (Carl Menger: *Grundsätze der Volkswirtschaftslehre*, 1871, Wien, in: CARL MENGER: *Gesammelte Werke*, edited by F. A. Hayek, Bd. I, Tübingen [Mohr] ²1968 (hereafter *GWI*), p. X).

9 In the Carl Menger Library, Hitotsubashi University, preserves Rau's textbook in which Menger wrote massive notes in 1867/68. See, *Carl Menger's erster Entwurf zu seinem Hauptwerk "Grundsätze", geschrieben als Anmerkungen zu den "Grundsätzen der Volkswirtschaftslehre" von Karl Heinrich Rau*, Bibliothek der Hitotsubashi Universität, 1963. My investigations into the Carl Menger Papers, Duke University, also confirmed Rau's influence on Menger. (YAGI: "Carl Menger as Editor - Significance of Journalistic Experience for his Economics and for his later Life", *Revue europeenne des sciences sociales*, 30 (1), 1992, ditto, "Carl Menger's *Grundsätze* in the Making", *History of Political Economy*, 25 (4), 1993. However, Rau had died just before Menger published his *Grundsätze*.

10 Knies's concept of "Gebrauchswert in genere" might have stimulated Menger in his reflection in value theory. In my "Carl Knies und die Wertformanalyse von Marx" (to be published 1996 in the Kommentarband to the reprint edition of CARL KNIES: *Das Geld*, 1873, Düsseldorf [Verlag Wirtschaft und Finanzen]) I discussed this concept and Knies' attempt to explain the foundation of money.

11 D/H, p. 292. (*GWI*, p. 78n)

consequence carry over to economic goods as the exclusive causes of the satisfaction of our needs."[12]

At the time of his publishing the *Grundsätze*, Menger seemed to have no anticipation that he should later become the target of the criticism from the Historical School. According to his grand plan Menger considered the *Grundsätze* as "The first General Part" and prepared to write the following part. However, facing the mixed reaction of misunderstanding and maliciousness of reviewers, Menger realized his unprotectedness in the methodological questions that was apparent in his Preface. This made him deviate from the original research plan to the investigation into methodological questions.

II. The *Grundsätze* and its Reviewers

Menger's *Grundsätze* appeared in the period when German economists were divided between free traders and historical economists whose general attitude favored protectionism and social policy. Out of the four reviews that the *Grundsätze* received on German periodicals, one came from the camp of free traders, and two from that of Historical School. The last one appeared on a neutral journal.

The first[13], though praising Menger's work, commented that terms such as "goods of lower order", "goods of higher order" might lead to the "unsound trade policy in the way of F. List". This overreaction of a free trader should be enough to make Menger's disapproval to this stream stronger. He wrote in an author copy of the *Grundsätze* (the Hitotsubashi copy[14]) with his protest against the political subordination over economics: "That political economy

---

12 D/H, p. 116. (*GWI*, S. 78)

13 *Vierteljahrschrift für Volkswirtschaft und Kulturgeschichte*, Jg. 9 (3), pp. 194-205, anonym.

14 Menger arranged three special author copies to prepare for the revised edition of the Grundsätze. The one is in the Carl Menger Library of the Hitotsubashi University, Tokyo and other two are in the Carl Menger Papers, Perkins Library, Duke University, Durham, NC. Menger's notes in the Hitotsubashi copy were transcribed by E. Kauder and published by the Library of Hitotsubashi University (*Carl Menger's Zusätze zu "Grundsätze der Volkswirtschaftslehre"*, Bibliothek der Hitotsubashu Universität, 1961).

a totally neutral science and is neither of the socialists in lecture halls, of free traders, nor of communists."[15]

On the other side, the two reviews[16] from the Historical School were not policy-oriented, but very admonitory. They introduced the *Grundsätze* ironically as a debut of a school boy by the publication of a textbook and advised that young scholars should show their ability by working out monographs first. The contents were very similar as if both reviewers had been in accord. One of the two reviews had the reviewer's initial, G. Sch., no doubt that of Gustav Schmoller. In addition, Roscher's comment on the *Grundsätze* in his *Geschichte der Nationalöonomik in Deutschland* was unexpectedly short and indifferent -- "very abstract" though "original"[17] --. Such treatment that Menger received from German Historical School must have hurt his pride.

The review under the initial of G. Sch. criticized Menger as following:

> Does not the so-called psychological ground of the economic life by each nations and by each ages? Is not the author repeating the wrong and obsolete fiction of the British economistswho wished to deduce the economic life exactly from the assumption of elementary propositions of the abstract and average man as constant and evident entities? Scientists have made their exactresearch by using scales and microscopes. The corresponding direction in economics is that of historical and statistical research."[18]

---

15 "Das politische Econ. eine ganz neutrale Wissenschaft ist, weder katheder-socialistisch noch freihändler, noch communistisch." (*Zusätze*, p. 7).

16 *Jahrbuch für Nationalökonomie und Statistik*, Bd. XVIII, pp. 342-45, annonym. *Literarisches Centralblatt für Deutschland*, 1. Feb. 1873, pp. 142-43, G. Sch.

17 Exactly: "Endlich der Österreicher Carl Menger, mit seiner sehr abstrakten, meist auf gründliche Dogmengeschichte gestützten, immer selbständigen und recht fruchtbaren Begriffanalyse, die z. B. die Preisbildung zuerst beim isolierten Tausche, dann beim Monopolhandel und erst schließlich unter dem Einflusse beiderseitiger Concurrenz erörtert." Wilhelm Roscher: *Geschichte der National-Ökonomik in Deutschland*, München 1874, p. 1040.

18 "Ist nicht die psychologische Grundlage des Wirtschaftlebens eine nach Volk und Zeit wechselnde? Stellt der Verf. nicht damit die alte schiefe Fiktion der Engländer auf, aus einem absolut als feste klare Größe angesehenen Grundtrieb eines abstrakten mittleren Menschen könne das wirtschaftliche Leben richtig abgeleitet werden. Werden ihm damit nicht alle volkswirtschaftlichen Probleme zu rein privat-wirtschaftlichen Fragen? Die Naturwissenschaften

"The wrong and obsolete fiction of the British economists" is nothing other than the "dogma of self-love" since Adam Smith against which economists of the Historical School opposed.[19] Apparently the reviewer changed the meaning of the "exact science" that Menger had used in the Preface. To Schmoller the exactness, if he meant by it the detailed description of a unique historical process, lay in the accurate dealing of statistical data. But to Menger the exactness was guaranteed solely by the procedure of abstraction and reconstruction as he had accomplished in his book. In the preface of the *Grundsätze* Menger presented this procedure as follows:

> I have endeavored to reduce the complex phenomena of human economicactivity to the simplest elements that can still be subjected to accurate observation, to apply to these elements the measure corresponding to their nature, and constantly adhering to this measure, to investigate the manner in which the more complex economic phenomena evolve from their elements according to definite principles.[20]

From today's eyes, the clash might be interpreted as no more than the difference of the research direction between the reviewer and Menger. But, in dealing with the abstract concepts of the theory, the reviewer assumed an ultra-empiricist position that considered "simplest elements" as "psychological" dispositions that reflect in the "average" of the statistics. However, to Menger the "scale" was not always objective, though indeed logical, as was in his value analysis. Precisely, the explanation of the subjective logical relations between goods and the satisfaction of needs gave birth to Menger's concept of value.

However, the problem remains about the relevance of the abstraction. In the preface Menger rejected the reference of "human free will" to "question the existence of the law of economic behavior"[21]. This is the view that Carl Knies, the most consequent methodologist of the Historical School, had taken in his *Politische Ökonomie vom Standpunkte der geschichtlichen Me-*

---

haben exact untersucht mit Waage und Mikroscop; die Richtungen, welche in der Nationalökonomie ihnen entsprechen, sind die historische, statistische etc." (Review with the initial, G. Sch.: *Literarisches Centralblatt*, 1873, No. 5, 1. Feb., p. 143).

19 In the Hitotsubashi copy Menger made the remark on the "dogma of egoism" ("'Dogma' vom Privategoismus") mentioning Knies. (*Zusätze*, p. 2).

20 D/H, p. 46f. (*GWI*, p. VII)

21 D/H, p. 48. (*GWI*, p. VIII)

thode (1853). If Menger would take the subjective side of economic behavior in theory, he must distinguish himself from this destructive position. So, Menger found himself between Scylla and Charybdis of empiricist and ir-rationalist positions both coming from the German Historicism.

It was the fourth review[22] that demanded a reconsideration of the method-ological self-understanding of Menger. The reviewer of the name Hack quoted Menger's methodological statement and argued:

> For example, we do not think that the so-called causal relation be-tween needs and goods is of the nature of cause and result, but of the nature of ends and means. Also, we do not think that the well-known dispute whether the laws of economic behaviors are compatible with the free will is solved by the remark that economic theory is con-cerned, not with practical rules for economic activity, but with the conditions under which men engage in provident activity directed to the satisfaction of their needs.[23]

Both of Hack's disagreements were not directed toward the theoretical core of the *Grundsätze*, but toward the easy understanding in methodological ques-tions that Menger at the stage of 1871 had shown. In the author copy of the *Grundsätze* in the Carl Menger Library (the Hitotsubashi Copy) Menger clearly approved both points raised by Hack. As for the first, the title of the second article of the first chapter was changed from "Über den Causal-Zusam-menhang der Güter" to "Über den teleologischen Zusammenhang der Güter", and in the text the following sentence was added: "Ein Zusammenhang kann ein doppelter sein. Ein mechanischer und ein teleologischer. Ersterer muß let-zterem zu Grunde liegen."[24] This change has the same direction as the revi-sion in the third section of the second chapter, "Über den Zusammenhang der

---

22 *Zeitschrift für die gesamte Staatswissenschaft*, Bd.XXVIII, pp. 183-84, Hack.
23 "Wir meinen z. B., daß der sogenannte Causalzusammenhang zwischen Be-dürfnissen und Dingen nicht als Verhältnis von Ursache und Wirkung, son-dern als das Zweck und Mittel aufzufassen sei; auch dürfte wohl die bekannte Streitfrage, wie sich Gesetze des wirtschaftlichen Handelns mit der Willens-freiheit vereinigen lassen, nicht durch die Bemerkung zu lösen sein, daß die theoretische Volkswirtschaftslehre sich mit praktischen Vorschlägen für das wirtschaftliche Handeln, sondern mit den Bedingungen, unter welchen die Menschen die auf die Befriedigung ihrer Bedürfnisse gerichtete vorsorgliche Tätigkeit entfalten, beschäftige." (HACK; p. 184, Hack quoted from *GWI*, p. IX, D/H p. 48).
24 *Zusätze*, p. 45.

Güter in dem Zweckbewußtsein der Menschen" of the posthumous edition. As for the second disagreement, it was exactly that part of the preface of the *Grundsätze* Hack had quoted which was erased in the Hitotsubashi copy without any alternative.[25]

As Hack pointed out, Menger of 1871 saw no difference between the relation of economic actions, which is originally a mental one, and the causal relations of the phenomena such as in the natural sciences, and regarded the influential factors of the economic action only in the physical conditions outside the sphere of the free will, in particular, the scarcity of the available goods in relation to the quantities needed for want satisfaction. What I called his "easy understanding" before is that Menger of 1871 made no distinction among the following three relations, namely; a) the causal relation in the physical (external world) process and the physiological (mind and body of man) process, b) the recognition of the causal relation in a), and c) the teleological relation in the action on the basis of a) and b). Presumably, Menger of 1871 might have thought that the ends-means relation in human action should be nothing but the objective cause-effect relation reversed in the recognition (mind) of the actor.[26]

However, from the point of view of methodology, this naive position has two difficulties. First, the recognition of the empirical regularity is not in itself to be seen as that of causal relation (rule) as dealt with in the theoretical science. Second, the teleological relation that emerges in the mind of the actor has a wide diversity that cannot be reduced to the scientific knowledge of causal relation of the external world - human mind and body. Such weakness is related to the second point raised by Hack. As for Knies' conclusion that denied the existence of law in social sciences as the result of the recognition of the free will, Menger of 1871 tried to think that economic theory does not deal with economic action itself (especially not with its purpose i. e., needs) but deals only with the influence of objective conditions (scarcity of the goods) on the direction of economic action. However, actions of real individuals, even if they could be regarded as economic actions, namely as oriented to the attainment of the want satisfaction, might alter their appearance under the influence of social norms, consideration of other persons, ignorance and misunderstanding, lacking of capacities and so on. Therefore, Menger cannot avoid the problem of free will in the construction of his economic theory. In

---

25 *Zusätze*, p. 25.
26 Cf. D/H, p. 70f. (*GWI*, p. 24f.)

other words, the weakness of the methodological view of 1871 can be found in the lack of distinction between real economic actions and the so-called "ideal type" of actions requested for the construction of the law in theory.

III. Themes of the Menger-Schmoller Duel of 1883/84

The interpretation of Menger's reaction to the reviews has led us to the conclusion that problems which made Menger to start his methodological investigation resemble very much to those of Max Weber's shown in his "Roscher und Knies"(1903-06). Apart from the question how conscious Menger had been at the stage of the *Grundsätze* in this respect, the assumption of the dominance of the self interest in economics is according to Menger not the approval of the materialistic view but a procedure of the isolation of that aspect of the human being out of his various dispositions. In case that another disposition should be observed in isolation, it should serve as the starting point for another species of social theory (ethics, aesthetics, etc.). If Menger should reply to Hack and Schmoller as follows, it is precisely Menger's view of economics stated in the *Untersuchungen* of 1883, in which he did not regard the real economy as the object of the "exact" orientation of the theoretical research but the "analytically or abstractly conceived economic world".[27] And this was also the view of economics that M. Weber twenty years later accepted and developed under the name of "Idealtypus":

> [1] The theory of economics investigates the relation of goods and actions in the teleological consciousness of actors whose actions are aimed at the attainment of the satisfaction of their wants by goods.
> [2] The action postulated in the economic theory is not the representation of a real economic action in our usual life, but an ideal economic

---

27 This is Nock's translation of "Gesetze der Wirtschaftlichkeit". See p. 72n of CARL MENGER: *Problems of Economics and Sociology*, ed. by L. Schneider and trans. by F.J. Knock, Urbana, Ill. (University of Illinois Press) 1963 (hereafter S/N). (*Untersuchungen über die Methode der Socialwissenschaften, und der Politischen Ökonomie insbesondere*, Leipzig, 1983, in: *Gesammelte Werke*, Hrsg. von F. A. Hayek, Bd. 2, Mohr (Siebeck), Tübingen, 1969 (hereafter *GW*II), S. 59).

action freed of other non-economic factors and also freed of the influence of misunderstandings and errors.

[3] The man in economic theory is surely "egoistic", but it is the representation of at least one of the most important dispositions of man and is an inevitable abstraction for the theoretical analysis of the economic aspect of human relations.

Menger's Diary tells us that he first embarked on writing a methodological work as early as December 1874[28]. This was interrupted in the spring of the next year by the preparation of the course of public finance. In the following year the teaching of the Crown Prince Rudolf prevented him from continuing his research. The book that was stumbling in the starting period of its gestation appeared at last in 1883 as *Untersuchungen über die Methode der Sozialwissenschaften, und der Politischen Ökononie insbesondere* (Investigations into the Method of Social Sciences, and of Political Economy in particular).

Menger was surely aware of the barrenness of methodological investigations, as he knew well from his own experience that "positive research talent has often enough created a science or changed it in an epoch-making fashion without developed methodology. But the methodology without talent never has done this."[29] Further, the problems he had taken in the *Untersuchungen* were not substantial issues in the improved research in economics by which researchers could be guided. In his words, "theoretical investigations in the field of political economy, particularly in Germany, have by no means progressed as yet to a true methodology of this science." "This work, too, in conformity with the present-day standpoint of theoretical investigations, is primarily concerned with determining the nature of political economy, of its subdivisions, of its truths, in brief, with the goals of research in the field of our science. Methodology in the narrower sense of the word is chiefly to be reserved for future investigations."[30]

The ground by which Menger justified the publication of a book in methodology is the danger that a methodological misconception of powerful schools might block any progress of a science. According to Menger, it was

---

28 In the p. 18 of his Diary (Tagebuch: Box 21, Carl Menger Papers) Menger noted: "Ich fasse Plan zur Methodologie." Further, "1875 März-April Ich unterbreche meine Arbeit an der Methodik, die ich seit December 1874 unter der Feder habe und arbeite an Collegienheften für Finanzw."

29 S/N, p. 27. (*GWII*, p. XII)

30 S/N, pp. 23, 25f. (*GWII*, pp. V, X)

precisely the situation of German economics under the dominance of the Historical School. In 1870s Menger noted in the author copy of the *Grundsätze* a fundamental question to this school: "There is a historical way of presentation; further the history can be the object for the research of laws; but is there really a historical method of the research?"[31] However, Menger was not blind to the value of historical or statistical research as it had been suggested by his reviewer. He just separated historical research in which the phenomena were viewed in their individuality from the field of theoretical research in which they were viewed in their generality. Further he differentiated the "realistic-empirical orientation" of theoretical research from its "exact orientation". This differentiation corresponded to that distinction between "empirical laws" and "exact laws". In economics, the former represents only "the regularities in the succession and coexistence of the real phenomena" with many deviations and exceptions, whereas the latter are abstract but universal laws that reveal the relations of economic phenomena in their purest form. If we should imagine the empirical validity of "exact laws", they would demand several preconditions:

> Those presuppositions that automatically result from any orderly presentation of theoretical economics are: (1) that all the economic subjects considered here strive to protect their economic interests fully; (2) that in the price struggle they are not in error about the economic goal to be pursued nor about the pertinent measures forreaching it; (3) that the economic situation, as far as it is on influence on price formation, is not unknown to them; (4) that no external force impairing their economic freedom (the pursuit of their economic interests) is exerted on them."[32]

However, Menger did not confine himself in defense. Through careful examination of the literature of the Historical School, Menger found that a peculiar organic view of the "national economy" lay behind their argument. In spite of the variations in their research style, "historical-philosophical" or "statistical-theoretical", the common fallacy to the historical economists is that they consider the "national economy" which is in itself "a complex of individual economies" as "a large individual economy in which the "nation"

---

31 "Es giebt eine Methode der Darstellung, es kann ferner die Geschichte das Object der Erforschung von Gesetzen sein; giebt es aber eine historische Methode der Forschung?" (*Zusätze*, p. 26).
32 S/N, p. 71. (*GW*II, p. 56)

is to represent the needing, economic, and consuming subject."[33] Though Menger did not think that the "national economy" is only the ensemble of isolated individual economies, they really are "closely tied together by traffic with one another"[34], it is, to Menger, never an independent unity on which the "exact" theory could be applied. However, the idea of the "laws of national economy" among historical economists had, according to Menger, had a very fragile basis when it was considered seriously.

Schmoller not only repeated his criticism on the arbitrary abstraction[35], but also expressed his attachment to the concept of "national economy". Admitting Menger's concession about the usefulness of the analysis on the level of national economy, Schmoller blamed Menger that Menger had given no theory of the "general essence of national economy". To Schmoller, "national economy" was a real collectivity to which no individualistic reasoning could effectively approach.

It is, of course, impossible for Menger to recognize the essential grounds and necessity of the Historical School. For he has no organ for it. The Historical School represents the return to the real scientific recognition from those vague and abstract images without any reality. Menger could not understand that every important phenomenon of na-

---

33 S/N, p. 194n. (*GWII*, p. 234n)
34 S/N, p. 194. (*GWII*, p. 233)
35 "It could be seen as useful to explain basic phenomena on the markets, when one would make a departure from the self-love as an apparently constant number for the reseaarch of prices at his time. However, establishing this way as a single rule for every future research, particularly for research of the complex process of national economies is erroneous. We must know that, by doing so, one is only acquiring hypothetical results out of hypotheses. It should be avoided to give such reasoning an appearance of the strict scientificity by using such a confusing term as "exact"." (Yagi's tr.) "Wenn man für die Preisuntersuchungen seiner Zeit vorläufig vom Eigennutz als einer scheinbar festen Größe ausging, so war das heilsam, um die einfachsten Vorgänge des Marktes zu erklären; aber es ist verfehlt, dies zu einer Regel für alle künftige Forschung, für die Untersuchung aller komplizierteren volkswirtschaftlichen Vorgänge aufzubauschen. Und jedenfalls muß man, soweit man so verfährt, sich immer klar sein, daß man nicht durch das mißverständliche Wort "exact" den Schein der strengsten wissenschaftlichkeit verleihen sollte." (GUSTAV SCHMOLLER: "Zur Methodologie der Staats- und Sozialwissenschaften", *Jahrbuch für die Gesetzgebung, Verwaltung und Volkswirtschaft im Deutschen Reich*, N. F. Jg. 7, 1883, p. 979)

tional economy extend so widely in time and space that only a collectivistic observation such as performed in history and statistics can approach to them. This is closed to him. For he always begins with a single observation of individual economy and remains in theorizing only exchange, value, and money etc. and never dares to reflect on the institutions and structures on the national economy level of which the body of a national economy is composed.[36]

Didn't Menger deal with history and institutions, really? In this context it is noteworthy that Menger's *Untersuchungen* had another theme in its latter sections that could properly be interpreted as his alternative to the collectivist view of the Historical School in this area. It is, in Menger's own words, "the exact understanding of the origin of "organically" created social structures."[37] This is the way of viewing historical development of institutions as the unintentional result out of the behavior of numbers of individuals whose efforts are solely directed to their own interest. The collectivistic conception of national economy would be so severely damaged, in as much as this challenge of Menger in his foes' own battlefield should win. It was, to Menger, even more, as he described it as the solution of "the most noteworthy problem of the social sciences." The problem is: "How can it be that institutions that serve the common welfare and are extremely significant for its development come into being without a common will directed toward establishing them?"[38]

After one century from the publication of the *Untersuchungen*, this view of the historical development was revived by F. A. Hayek and has become

---

36 "Die wesentliche Ursache und Notwendigkeit der historischen Schule freilich kann Menger gar nicht verstehen, weil ihm dazu das Organ fehlt: sie repräsentiert die Rückkehr zur wissenschaftlichen Erfassung der Wirklichkeit an Stelle einer Anzahl abstrakter Nebelbilder, denen jeder Realität mangelt. Menger sieht auch nicht, daß alle wichtigeren volkswirtschaftlichen Erscheinungen räumlich und zeitlich so umfassend sind, daß sie nur einer kollektivistischen Betrachtung, wie sie die Geschichte und die Statistik anstellen, zugänglich sind. Das ist ihm verschlossen, weil er ausschließlich von der singularen Betrachtung der Einzelwirtschaft ausgeht, immer nur an Tausch, Wert, Geld etc. denkt, nicht an die Volkswirtschaftlichen Organen und Institutionen, die das Knochengerüste des Volkswirtschaftlichen Körpers ausmachen." (SCHMOLLER: "Zur Methodologie", p. 983).

37 S/N, p. 151. (*GW*II, p. 161)

38 S/N, p. 146. (*GW*II, p. 163)

one of the most salient arguments for the neo-liberalism under the new naming of the "spontaneous order". Why, however, this was so neglected in the late nineteenth century is an interesting question with which I would like to deal later. Before that I have to explain Menger's assertion in this theme in more details.

According to Menger, two ways of interpretations are discerned in viewing the historical development process of institutions. One is the "pragmatic approach" in which they are explained by the agreement or positive legislation, or generally speaking by intentions of those who established them.[39] Another is the "organic" understanding in which no such explicit intention is supposed in the emergence of institutions. Both are necessary in the historical analysis since both of the intentional establishment and the spontaneous development, often in combined way, exist in the real process. To Menger, it was the finding of this "organic origin" first among jurists that gave birth to the Historicism in German social sciences. Rejecting the positivistic idea of law, G. v. Savigny envisaged the origin of laws in the "spirit of nation" (Volksseele, Volksgeist). In reality, this is his recognition of the common law that has its basis in the customs of the people. According to Menger, the historical economists misunderstood the true Historicism in their sympathy with the pragmatic legislation in the area of economic policy.

Menger maintained that "the acknowledgment of a number of social phenomena as 'organism' is in no way in contradiction to the aspiration for exact (atomistic!) understanding of them."[40] Menger took the example of the origin of the money. Without money exchange of goods can occur only when both sides want the goods in the hands of their counterparts. So, the institution of money brings benefit to every person in its service as general means of exchange. However, if one takes the act of exchange of a good with money in isolation, it is difficult to explain why one would give his good in exchange with another on whose utility he is not at all attracted. By such an argument Savigny considered it impossible to explain the existence of money from the individual interest of men.

Menger's reasoning starts with the difficulty of direct exchange. But Menger assumes that some community members find the merit of exchanging their goods with some more salable goods in order to attain their final goal of exchange. Sooner or later other members of the community join in the ring

---

39 S/N, p. 145, 148. (*GW*II, p. 162, 166)
40 S/N, p. 141. (*GW*II, p. 155)

of indirect exchange by observing their success. Through this diffusion process a certain good become the customary exchange media in the community, de facto money. According to Menger, this spontaneous process of emergence and diffusion of indirect exchange is solely driven by the progress in the recognition of economic interest of individuals:

> The economic interest of the economic individuals, therefore, with increased knowledge of their individual interests, without any agreement, without legislative compulsion, even without any consideration of public interests, leads them to turn over their wares for more marketable ones, even if they do not need the latter for their immediate consumer needs.[41]

This is the spontaneous basis for the market economy on which legislation or intervention of the government operates. Menger mentioned other institutions such as market and village, even the state as appropriate for this way of exact understanding of the "organic" origin. If one imagines that Menger took it granted that law and language, the favorites of romanticist as the product of mystical "spirit of nation", are included in the group of phenomena of "organic" origin, this way of interpretation will appear as a fundamental theory of the development of institutions.

The superiority of this view of the origin of institutions lies in that it assumes no concept of collective entity such as "nation" to explain the unintentional outcome of the interactions of the individuals. The rationality of the behavior of individuals lies in the accurate recognition of their own needs and conditions in external world from which the most efficient selection of the ends-means relation emerges. To Menger, it is the same "exact" way of abstraction and reconstruction applied in the theoretical construction of price formation. The difference lies only that the social conditions for the rational behavior changes gradually with the diffusion of certain type of behavior.

> The methods for the exact understanding of the origin of the "organically" created social structures and those for the solution of the main problems of exact economics are by nature identical.[42]

Schmoller seemed to have had no strong impression from Menger's solution of "organic" process as he judged it 'exact' explanation, which is not dis-

---

41 S/N, p. 154. (*GW*II, p. 176)
42 S/N, p. 159. (*GW*II, p. 183)

tinguished by surprising novelty."[43] Not only to the problem of "organic" origin, but also to the romantic ancestors of German Historicism, Schmoller kept distance. Schmoller laughed at "Menger's strong sympathy to the mysticism of spirit of a nation in the way of Savigny" and proudly declared: "It was really a progress, compared to Savigny, that Roscher did not start with such a mystical idea of romanticism."[44] Schmoller further attributed Menger's sympathy to Savigny to his "antipathy in the way of Manchesterian" against every offense of the principle of laissez faire.

Obviously Schmoller overlooked the significance of Menger's destruction of the mystical entity of romanticism. The charge of "Manchesterian" was also wrong. Menger did not deny the necessity of the conscious legislative works for the welfare of the people from the pragmatic view point. On the other side, it is true that Menger added a high tone of sympathy to the confidence in the spontaneous formation of institutions contrasted with pragmatic interventions of governments. Menger was counted by Schmoller in the ranks of enemies to the social reform on the ground of Menger's criticism to the one-sided "pragmatic" orientation of Historical School in Economics. In the late of the nineteenth century, European nations were busy in working out various institutions by legislative activity. The negligence to Menger's solution of "organic" process could be partly explained in such intellectual context then.

Opposing to the "exact" understanding of the institutions, Schmoller presented his own view:

> Menger is right in his assertion that every social structure can be in the end traced back to the mental process of the individuals. However, the mental process of individuals is not composed of the opposing pair of cooperation and egoism but also of infinite numbers of egoistic sentiments and efforts as well as sympathetic ones. Both by conscious cooperation or unconscious cooperation, or by merely emo-

---

43 "... diese keineswegs durch überraschende Neuheit sich auszeichnende "exacte" Erklärung", in: "Zur Methodologie", p. 249.

44 "Diese lebhafte Sympathie für den Mystizismus des Savigny'schen Volksgeistes entspringt offenbar der manchesterlichen Abneigung gegen jede bewußte Thätigkeit kollektiver Gesellschaftsorgan." "Es war Fortschritt gegen Savigny, daß Roscher diese mystischen Vorstellungen der romantischen Schule nicht zu seinem Ausgangpunkt machte." In: "Zur Methodologie", p. 250.

tional conformist encouraged the development of economic and social life up to the definite result.[45]

This is rather a sound statement of an empiricist position that most of the historical economists then shared. It is reflected in their assertion of the integration of ethical elements in economics.[46] It seems that Menger's criticism against Historicism proved fruitless.

IV. Max Weber's Reception of Menger

Menger made his rejoinder by publishing *Die Irrthümer des Historismus in der deutschen Nationalökonomie* (The Errors of Historismus in German Economics). To this polemical book, in which Menger's journalistic talent was impressively shown, rejected Schmoller the answer. As Schmoller succeeded in showing his leading position of the mighty Historical School, so Menger could establish the "living space" (Lebensraum) to the new school he was going to found.

Perhaps, the most exciting scene in the aftermath was that of the inaugural lecture of Lujo Brentano at the Vienna University (1888). In this lecture whose original title was "The Classical Economics", Brentano argued, "the description of economic phenomena, even that of the most trifle one, has more value to empirical economists, so long as it is accurate, than the

---

45 "Darin hat er [Menger ... YAGI] freilich recht, daß alle Sozialgebilde zuletzt auf individuelle psychische Vorgänge zurückzuführen sind. aber das individuelle Seelenleben erschöpft sich nicht in dem Gegensatz: Verabredung und egoistische Bestrebung, es setzt sich aus einer unendlichen Menge von selbstischen und sympatischen Gefühlen und Strebungen zusammen, die beide teils durch bewußte Verabredung, teils durch unbewußte oder nur gefühlte Übereinstimmung zu weiteren Ergebnißen, zu festeren Gestaltungen des wirtschaftlichen und sozialen Lebens führen." ("Zur Methodologie", p. 249).

46 In spite of his stress on the positivistic research style penetrated peculiar ethical elements still everywhere of Schmoller's works. B. PRIDDAT's *Der ethische Ton der Allokation*, Baden-Baden (Nomos) 1991 maintained its Aristotelian origin and regarded Menger as the break-through for this tradition.

sharpest deduction from the economical egoism. Results of such deduction are, admitted that they are formally correct, are incompatible with reality."[47] In the next year, Böhm-Bawerk, Menger's pupil and co-founder of the Austrian School, rebutted Brentano that the Classic School should be blamed not by the charge of their "egoism" but their theoretical failure of the labor value theory. In other words, Böhm argued the "clear economic man" as the indispensable assumption for any economic theorizing.[48]

Brentano stayed in Vienna only one year. After his move to Leipzig a geographical division of the two schools seemed to have been established. The true cross-over of both schools was first performed by a young historical economist, Max Weber, around the turn of the century.[49] Max Weber is nowadays known as a sociologist, but by a look of his career before his leave

---

47 "Die Beschreibung selbst der bescheidensten wirtschaftlichen Erscheinungen, die genau ist, muß für den empirischen Nationalökonomen einen größeren wissenschaftlichen Wert haben als die scharfsinnigste Deduktion aus dem wirtschaftlichen Egoismus, deren Ergebnisse trotz aller formalen Folgerichtigkeit mit den Tatsachen im Widerspruch stehen." (LUJO BRENTANO: "Die klassische Nationalökonomie", in: BRENTANO: *Der wirtschaftende Mensch in der Geschichte*, Leipzig (Meiner) 1923, p. 31f.).

48 EUGEN VON BÖHM-BAWERK: "Die klassische Nationalökonomie", in: *Gesammelte Schriften*, ed. by F. X. Weiß, Bd. 1, Leipzig (Hölder-Pichler-Tempsky) 1924, S. 149-156.

49 In the preparation period of this paper I read KEITH TRIBE's *Strategies of Economic Order*, Cambridge (Cambridge University Press) 1995, whose chap. 4, "Historical Economics, the Methodenstreit, and the economics of Max Weber" covered similar themes with this paper. Tribe's view of the nineteenth century German economics that it developed through this century without sharp disjunction is valuable. However, his denial of the Austrian orientation of Max Weber seems to me rather one-sided, because it was the transplantation of Menger's individualism in different soil that turned to be very fruitful. On the theme of Max Weber and economics see also, YUZO DEGUCHI: "The economic theory conceived by Max Weber", *The Kyoto University Economic Review*, 27 (1), April 1957, WILHELM HENNIS: "'A Science of Man'. Max Weber and the Political Economy of the German Historical School", MANFRED SCHÖN: "Gustav Schmoller and Max Weber", both in: W. J. MOMMSEN, J. OSTERHAMMEL (Eds.): *Max Weber and his Contemporaries*, London (Allen and Unwin) 1987, W. HENNIS: "The pitiless, sobrity of Judgement: Max Weber between Carl Menger and Gustav von Schmoller in the academic politics of value freedom", *History of the Human Sciences*, 4, 1991.

from lecture halls due to illness, we find in him an enthusiastic reformer of research and teaching of economics in the two universities he had belonged. It was confined not only to the institutional structure of the economics in the university teaching, but also to the contents of teachings. The editor of the Max Weber's *Collected Works* provided us with an observation from a student of some socialistic tendency:

> ... the mentioned professor Weber, who might be known to you from the national-social party, was invited in the last term from Freiburg to occupy the chair of Knies, the primus of the Historical School. Fairly great expectation was set on him by some groups for the young power he had concealed in gray. What kind of spirit this child kept was shown from the first lecture. After saying some radical words he presented himself out of the chrysalis now as the fighter of the Austrian school who wished to import the system of Böhm-Bawerk and Menger to Germany. Regrettably our professor was not content with this moderate role of the supporter. He wanted to be also a Marx-critic. ...[50]

This report corresponds to Weber's syllabus of the course of "General (theoretical) Economics" of 1898. According to this syllabus[51], Weber first talked on the tasks and methods of theoretical economics ("Einleitung: 1. Aufgabe und Methoden der theoretischen Nationalökonomie") referring the literature which included those of the 1883/84 dispute and entered the theoretical presentation of basic concepts of economics. This part of the course is composed as following:

---

50 "Der erwähnte Professor Weber, der Ihnen wohl von der nationalsozialen Partei her bekannt sein dürfte, wurde im vergangenen Semester aus Freiburg hierher berufen, um den Platz von Knies, einer der Koryphären der historischen Schule, einzunehmen. Von gewisser Seite wurden große Erwartungen auf ihn, als auf eine jüngere Kraft gesetzt, die er indessen grausam getäuscht hat. Schon die ersten Vorlesungen zeigten, wes Geistes Kind er sei. Nach einigem radikalen Wortklingel entpuppte er sich gar bald als Vorfechter der österreichischen Schule, der es unternommen, die Systeme einer Lehrmeister Böhm-Bawerk und Menger nach Deutschland zu importieren. Leider begnügt sich unser Professor nicht mit dieser seiner bescheidenen Vorfechterrolle. Er will auch Marx-Kritiker sein. ..." (Aus: *Der Sozialistische Student*, 2. Jg. 1898 Nr. 9, vom 21. Jan.). MAX WEBER: *Gesamt Ausgabe*, Bd. I/4, hrg. v. Wolfgang J. Mommsen, 1993, p. 45n.

51 MAX WEBER: *Grundriß zu den Vorlesungen über allgemeine ("theoretische") Nationalökonomie: (1898)*, Tübingen (Mohr) 1990.

CARL MENGER AND THE HISTORICISM IN ECONOMICS

I. Book. Basic concepts of the Political Economy
  § 2. Economy and its elementary phenomena
    1. Concept of economy
    2. So-called "economicity" principle and theoretical construction
       of economy
    3. Economic needs
    4. Economic goods
    5. Classification of goods
    6. Economic value
    7. Scale of value and imputation of value
    8. Elements of economy
      a) production and factors of production
      b) economic exchange
  § 3. National economy and its elementary phenomena
    1. Concept of national economy (Exchange economy)
    2. Problems of scientific recognition of national economy
    3. Elementary phenomena of national economy
      1) Autonomy of the possession and exchange of goods
        (freedom and property)
      2) Value in national economy
        a) Determination of price
        b) Money and monetary price
        c) Exchange value
      Appendix: Criticism of the value theory of classical school
        and socialism
      3) Production in national economy
        a) Regulating principle
        b) Division of labor
        c) Means of production: α Material goods - β Labor
        d) Enterprise
      4) Wealth and income
      5) Credit[52]

---

52 "I. Buch. Die begrifflichen Grundlagen der Volkswirtschaftslehre
    § 2. Die Wirtschaft und ihre elementaren Erscheinungen.
      1. Begriff der Wirtschaft;
      2. Das sogennante "wirtschaftliche" Prinzip und die theoretische
        Konstruktion der Wirtschaft
      3. Die wirtschaftlichen Bedürfnisse
      4. Die "Güter"
      5. Die wirtschaftlichen Güter

Judging from the modern eyes, of course, this lecture retains still the traditional style of German economics that begins with the discussion of the concepts of needs and goods. It is also conspicuous that Weber used such terms as "economic action" (wirtschaften), "provision in advance" (Vorsorge), "services of use" (Nutzleistungen), "marginal utility" (Grenznutz), "imputation" (Zurechnung), etc., which easily reminds us of Menger, Böhm-Bawerk and Wieser. Surely, Weber was enormously influenced by Austrians in this part, although it seems that he had to work out the theory of production and the credit based on some literature.

What is more interesting in this lecture is that Weber's several conclusions from the "debate on the methods" are incorporated in it.

The first is the limitation of the "abstract theory" which he called attention in his reception of the Austrian theory. This limitation is twofold, on one side historical and on the other side logical:

6. Güterkategorien
7. Der wirtschaftliche Wert
8. Das Wertmaß und die Wertzurechnung
9. Die Elemente der Wirtschaft:
   a) die Produktion und die Produktionsfaktoren
   b) der ökonomische Tausch.
§ 3. Die Volkswirtschaft und ihre elementaren Erscheinungen.
  1. Begriff der Volkswirtschaft (Verkehrswirtschaft)
  2. Probleme der wissenschaftliche Betrachtung der Volkswirtschaft
  3. Elementare Erscheinungen der Volkswirtschaft:
    1) Die Autonomie des Güterbesitzes und Güterverkehrs (Freiheit und Eigentum)
    2) Der Wert in der Volkswirtschaft:
     a) Preisbildung
     b) Geld und Geldpreis
     c) der Verkehrswert Anhang: Kritik der Wert-Theorien der klassischen Schule und des Sozialismus
    3) Die Produktion in der Volkswirtschaft
     a) das regulierende Prinzip
     b) die Arbeitsteilung
     c) die Produktionsmittel: α. Die Sachgüter, - β. die Arbeit
     d) die Unternehmung
    4) Vermögen und Einkommen
    5) Der Kredit" (*Grundriß*, pp. 7-8.)

CARL MENGER AND THE HISTORICISM IN ECONOMICS

Historical limitation:

> Economic behavior has been imposed on men and women through a thousands-years-long adjustment process. The degree of the planned economic behavior in its modern meaning was and is historically, according to the difference in race and - also in the modern western culture - according to the difference in vocation, education, intelligence, and character of individuals very different. It is developed totally or incompletely. The motivation that determines the behavior of individualsshould be grasped correspondingly. The abstract theory begins with the modern western type of men. It at first endeavors to know the most elementary phenomena in the life of economically civilized men.[53]

Logical limitation:

> For this purpose the abstract theory presupposes a constructed "economic subject", in respect of which, by contrast to empirical men it
> a. ignores all those motives not specifically economic in nature; considers, that is among all those motives that influence empirical men, only those arising from the satisfaction of material needs and treats the remainder as not present;
> b. fabricates the presence of specific qualities in empirical men, when they are in fact either absent or only partially present, to wit
>   α. complete insight into the prevailing situation - perfect economic knowledge;
>   β. unfaltering selection of the most appropriate means for a given end - absolute "economic rationality";
>   γ. exclusive devotion of one's own powers to the attainment of economic goods - unwearing economic endeavor.

---

53 "Das wirtschaften ist dem Menschen durch einen jahrtausendlangen Anpassungsprozeß anerzogen. Das Maß des planvollen Wirtschaftens im modernen Sinn war und ist historisch, nach Rasse und - auch innerhalb der modernen occidentalen Culture - nach Beruf, Erziehung, Intellekt und Charakter der Individuen sehr verschieden, durchweg aber unvollkommen entwickelt; demgemäß ist auch der das Handeln des Einzelnen bestimmenden Triebfedern einnehmen; ein historisch und individuell höchst wandelbar. Die abstrakte Theorie geht von dem modernen occidentalen Typus des Menschen und seines Wirtschaftens aus. Sie sucht zunächst die elementarsten Lebensphänomene ders wirtschaftlich voll erzogenen Menschen zu ermitteln." (*Grundriß*, p. 29)

It therefore argues on the basis of unrealistic men, analogous to a mathematical ideal.[54]

It is noteworthy that in making a logical limitation Weber actually repeated Menger's position in the *Untersuchungen* and Weber's originality lay in his identification of this theory with modern occidental "economic man". The second is his rejection of the holistic concept of national economy. Here, too, Weber presented an "ideal type" of the market economy as the concept of the national economy and added its logical and historical limitations.

The economic community in which these individual economies maintain in mutual interdependency owns now the name of "national economy." It is characterized: a) negatively, by the lack of the planned organization for mutual provision of needs of individual economies, b) positively, by that the exchange of goods as mass phenomena - circulation of goods functions as the substitute of such planned organization and one leading will in regulating production, house-keeping, distribution and consumption of goods automatically.[55] Neither the

---

54 This is the translation by K. Tribe on p. 91 of his article mentioned in note 49. The original follows: "Zu diesem Zweck legt sie [abstrakte Theorie ... YA-GI] ein constituiertes 'Wirtschaftssubjekt' zu Grunde bezüglich dessen sie im Gegensatz zum empirischen Menschen

   a. alle nicht spezifisch wirtschaftlichen, d.h. der Vorsorge für die materiellen Bedürfnisse entspringender Motive, welche auf den empirischen Menschen Einfluß üben, als nicht vorhanden behandelt, - ignoriert;

   b. bestimmte, dem empirischen Menschen nicht oder unvollkommen anhaftende Qualitäten als vorhanden fingiert, nämlich:

      α) vollkommene Einsicht in die jeweilige Situation - wirtschaftliche Allwissenheit;

      β) ausnahmlose Ergreifung des für den jeweiligen Zweck geeignetsten Mittels - absolute "Wirtschaftlichkeit";

      γ) vollkommene Verwendung der eignen Kräfte im Dienste der wirtschaftlichen Güterversorgung - 'trägheitslosen Erwerbsbetrieb'.

Sis [Sie...YAGI] argumentiert also an einen unrealistischen Menschen, analog einer mathematischen Idealfigur." (*Grundriß*, p. 30)

55 "Die Wirtschaftsgemeinschaft, in welcher diese aufeinander angewiesenen Einzelwirtschaften demgemäß stehen, trägt heute den Namen "Volkswirtschaft". Charakterisch ist ihr: a) negativ das Fehlen einer planvollen Organisation der gegenseitigen Bedarfsversorgung der Einzelwirtschaften, b) positiv, daß als Ersatz dieser planvollen Organisation und eines leitenden Willens der Gütertausch als Massenerscheinung - Güterverkehr - fungiert, welcher Pro-

principle of private property nor that of economic freedom is totally
and unexceptionaly introduced. However, its dominant position is the
specific distinction of modern (not always every) exchange economy, -
the "national economy".[56]

In his methodological reflection on Roscher and Knies, Weber's orientation to the "dispute on Method" is salient. As Weber himself declared, Weber
in this uncompleted article endeavored to show "how the elementary logico-
methodological problems which were discussed in recent period in historical
science and in our discipline [economics ... Yagi] in the beginning of the
Historical School their validity had"[57] Weber maintained that Roscher's historical method was by itself an amalgam of the contradictory elements of
empiricism and the "emanation theory" of the organic whole. This is just
Menger's charge on the Historical School that Schmoller had proudly rejected.

The problem of the "irrationality" in Knies was also the problem that an-
noyed Menger and led him to the methodological reflections on his own theory. Knies maintained that it was the existence of "free human will" that
gave to the society and history the uniqueness that could not be fully explained by objective laws. The outcome of the freedom in action is the "un-
accountability", which is, to Knies, namely the "human dignity". From this
view Knies concluded that not exact "laws" but some sorts of resemblance or
"analogies" only are compatible with the uniqueness of historical phenomena.

Weber's answer was the opposite to Knies. To Weber the dignity of the
"personality" (Persönlichkeit) of men lay not in the "irrationality" or "unac-

---

duktion, Haushalt, Verteilung und Verbrauch der Güter automatisch reguliert."
(*Grundriß*, p. 42)

56 "Weder das Prinzip des Privateigentums noch dasjenige der wirtschaftlichen
Freiheit sind voll und restlos durchgeführt, aber ihre beherrschende Stellung
ist das spezifische Merkmal der modernen (nicht notwendig jeder) Verkehrswirtschaft, - der "Volkswirtschaft"." (*Grundriß*, p. 44)

57 "Wie gewisse elementare logisch-methodische Probleme, welche im letzten
Menschenalter in der Geschichtswissenschaft und in unserer Fachdisziplin zur
Erörterung standen, in den Anfängen der historischen Nationalökonomie sich
geltend machten". (MAX WEBER: "Roscher und Knies und die logischen Prob-
lemen der historischen Nationalökonomie", in: WEBER: *Gesammelte Aufsätze
zur Wissenschaftslehre*, 2. Al., 1951, Tübingen (Mohr) 1951 (hereafter
GAzWL), S. 1.

countability" but in the active transformation of some ultimate "value" and the "significance" of life into purposeful and rational deed.[58] This is the switch that the recognition of the "human free will" turned out to be the foundation of the rational economic theory:

> The 'freer', i.e., the more the decision of the actor is based on their own ground and guided by the examination which is not disturbed by the 'coercion' from outside or by irresistible 'affection', the more completely would the motivation, ceteris paribus, be orderly put in the categories of 'means' and 'ends'; the more completely would the rational analysis of action or, where appropriate, its arrangement in the scheme of rational action succeed; the larger would therefore the role that the lawful knowledge - on the side of actors as well as on that of analyzing researchers - plays; the more ›determined‹ would be the actors in relation to the 'means'.[59]

We have already seen that Menger changed the interpretation of his theory from that of causal relations to that of teleological relations. Though Max Weber did not know that Menger was willing to change the related passages in the Grundsätze along this direction and complained often over the psychological bias of Menger's description, Weber's interpretation of the economic theory as the "explanation by the teleological scheme of rational action"[60] fit just Menger's revised interpretation. We can further argue that Max Weber later coined his concept of the "instrumental rationality" (Zweckrationalität) by the guide of the marginal utility theory. Because the attainment of the maximization of the utility by so allocating the scarce resources to various needs as to equalize their marginal utility has just the same structure of the higher level of rational behavior in which not only the selection of the means

---

58 *GAzWL*, S. 132.
59 "Je 'freier', d.h. je mehr auf Grund 'eigener', durch 'äußeren' Zwang oder unwiderstehliche 'Affekte' nicht getrübter 'Erwägungen', der 'Entschluß' des Handelnden einsetzt, desto restloser ordnet sich die Motivation ceteris paribus den Kategorien 'Zweck' und 'Mittel' ein, desto vollkommener vermag also ihre rationale Analyse und gegebenfalls ihre Einordnung in ein Schema rationalen Handelns zu gelingen, desto größer aber ist infolgedessen auch die Rolle, welche - beim Handelnden einerseits, beim analysierenden Forscher anderseits - das nomologische Wissen spielt, desto 'determinierter' ist ersterer in bezug auf die 'Mittel'." (*GAzWL*, p. 132)
60 "ein teleologisches Schema rationalen Handelns" (*GAzWL*, p. 131).

but also the selection of ends in each time is dealt of.[61] If the action concerned should be freed from the limitation of the "economic" nature, namely the relatedness to the satisfaction of human needs by material goods, Menger's economic theory would turn to be a sociological theory. Of course, also in this case, still, the rational explanation is the construction of the "ideal type".

Thus, Weber's methodological reflection around the turn of the century is to be considered as the extension of Menger's efforts after some interval. However, there is one assertion in Menger's *Untersuchungen* that Weber would not adopt. That is the Mengerian view of the "exact understanding of the 'organic' origin of social structures."[62] To answer this question we must first take notice that the "organic" process contains the real time dimension that is not necessarily equipped in the value-price theory. Indeed it could be interpreted, as Menger maintained, in the same style of individualism. But in the time dimension the premise of perfect information and perfect ability does not hold and some hypothetical diffusion process must be introduced. This is the problem whether the exact direction of economics can keep the same exactness if it assimilates the evolutionary process.

This question is related to Weber's concept of "social economics" which is an empirical science of concrete reality and not purely theoretical science. In Weber's view, the two German founders of "social economics" were Marx and Roscher. Both men were not "exact" theoreticians in Menger's sense but promoted the "investigation of the general cultural significance of the social-economic structures of the human community and its historical forms of organization."[63] Weber's vision of the economic development was different from Menger's in that Weber would not consider economic aspect not in iso-

---

61 My old paper, "Economic Theory and home oeconomicus in C. Menger and M. Weber" (Japanese), *Okayama Daigaku Keizai Gakkai Zassi*, 11 (1,4), 1979-80, argued that Weber's theory of action is the generalization of Menger's theory of economic rationality. Weber's obligation to Menger was even higher than his respect to L. Brentano. See Weber's defense of Menger in his letter to L. Brentano, 29. May and 30. Oct, 1908 (MAX WEBER: *Gesamt Ausgabe*, II/5, 1990, pp. 578f, 688f.).

62 This is the translation of "Wirklichkeitswissenschaft" by E. A. Shils and H. A. Finch. MAX WEBER: *The Methodology of Social Sciences*, trans. by E. A. Shils and H. A. Finch, Glencoe, Ill (The Free Press) 1949, p. 72. (*GAzWL*, p. 170).

63 WEBER: *Methodology*, p.67. (*GAzWL*, p. 165)

lation but under the mutual interaction with political and cultural elements of the society. I'll quote from the famous "Objectivity" article (1904):

> All the activities and situations constituting a historically given culture affect the formation of the material wants, the mode of their satisfaction, the integration of interest-groups and the types of power which they exercise. They thereby affect the course of "economic development" and are accordingly "economically relevant." To the fact that our science imputes particular causes - be they economic or noneconomic - to economic cultural phenomena, it seeks "historical" knowledge.[64]

So, despite his full reception of Menger's criticism against the Historicism, Weber could still name himself as an heir of this school. Max Weber placed the abstract rational theory once more in the real world for heuristic purposes and discovered the problematic of the "rationalization" as the real historical process. This became the fundamental theme of Weber's later investigations.

> Because the categories of 'ends' and 'means' condition the rationalization in their application to the empirical reality. Only from this ground such a [rational, Y.] construction becomes possible.[65]

---

64 WEBER: *Methodology*, p.66. (*GAzWL*, p. 163)
65 "Weil die Kategorien 'Zweck' und 'Mittel' bei ihrer Anwendung auf die empirische Wirklichkeit deren Rationalisierung, bedingen, deshalb und nur deshalb ist die Konstruktion solcher Schemata möglich." (*GAzWL*, p. 131)

Chapter 11

The 'Irrelevance' of Ethics for the Austrian School

RAIMONDO CUBEDDU

I. The Problem
II. Menger
III. Considerations on the Problem
Raised by Menger

I. The Problem

In order to address the issue of the 'irrelevance' of ethics for the exponents of the Austrian School, I will base my arguments on the following contentions: only a subset of the participants' initial expectations are fulfilled through the temporary results of the process of catallactics, and since such results are not determined by their initial motivations, ethical assessment of the latter is irrelevant for the purposes of understanding and explaining how this occurs.

The theme of the position and specific ranking of ethics within the field of practical and theoretical social sciences is undoubtedly one of the major issues in the philosophy of social science to have raised attention in recent years, and indeed in earlier times as well. It is no coincidence that some political philosophers, e.g. Leo Strauss, have seen the freeing of politics and economy from the shackles of ethics –and more generally the process of autonomization of science– as leading to the birth of 'modernity'. Over the last decade or so, the theme of the relationship between ethics and the market has been taken up again by many authors, of divers political slant, and – partly due to the success of John Rawls' theories perhaps, but thoroughly mistakenly, in my opinion– it has become one of the crucial themes of debate concerning the foundations of liberalism[1].

The debate centering on this matter reflects the belief that the market system is an excellent tool for the production of wealth, but highly unsatisfactory for its distribution. According to one commonly held school of thought, since this disparity of distribution is regarded as despicable, the need arises to set up measures to ensure fair distribution of wealth, on the assumption that this represents a sort of moral obligation for political and economic activities. In contrast, 'Austrian' liberalism considers the market not as an instrument exploited by politics in the attempt to achieve fair distribution of resources and individual opportunities, but rather as a system for the transmission of information by means of prices, whereby the latter are held to reflect the degree of consumer enjoyment of goods and services. In such a perspective, the market will not produce any injustice to be corrected, but only information that is available to individuals, who are free –inasmuch as they are different by nature and knowledge– to make whichever use of it they wish, possibly even a mistaken use.

In the eyes of the exponents of the Austrian School, therefore, any intervention on the market that aims to accomplish exogenous goals will be transformed into the insertion of false information into the system of catallactics. Such information is likely to affect the functioning of the market and eventually provoke its failure. In effect, the market is nothing other than the way in which a set of subjective demands and expectations of sundry inspiration are combined by means of the price-driven information system. Such demands and expectations produce an order which, in turn, acts as a reference point for the other individuals who, *through the market*, aim to satisfy further subjective demands and expectations. Market activity is therefore a conceptual framework of reference undergoing perpetual change, having the func-

---

1   Just to give one example, since the positions are complex and literature on this subject is virtually never-ending, N. P. BARRY: in *On Classical Liberalism and Libertarianism*, London (Macmillan) 1986, p. 7 (this work, among other things, gives a remarkably clear description of the theses of its main exponents), wonders whether the economic success of liberal systems in terms of prosperity "is said to be paid for in terms of a loss in morality precisely because the mechanisms [...] that drive the economic system are successful to the extent that they violate western moral orthodoxy", hence "a necessary contrast [...] between 'commerce' and 'virtue'" characterizing the history of western political thought.

tion of providing information as to whether subjective demands and expectations can be fulfilled: that is to say, it is a system of criticism and impersonal evaluation whose outcome is that of retaining those demands and expectations that are feasible without entailing any negative consequence for others, as well as those whose consequences seem to be compatible and exchangeable with the other expectations.

As such, market activities provide information that can be used at will and for whatever purposes desired by the individuals who participate in the market. To assert that the market is a tool designed for achieving goals different from this would mean endowing it with exogenous ends. However, by so doing, its main function, i.e. that of implementing a process of free discussion and impersonal criticism of the goals, would be lost. But it is precisely this process that results in the survival of only those goals that lead to the least number of negative consequences for the participants, and tends to reward the goals that have the greatest number of positive consequences for the participants. Therefore, it is a process of selection, which evaluates subjective expectations not in relation to the position or the intentions of those who formulated them, but in relation to the extent to which they can favour the accomplishment of other subjective expectations.

The problem of the ethical justification of social institutions is thus connected to the problem of the ethical justification of the state. In the tradition of classical liberalism there was no need for this type of justification, since the state was essentially a tool for guaranteeing individual rights. The shift to an interventionist and finalist conception of the state renders it necessary to search for a justification of such goals. However, there can be no exclusively political justification, for this would be tantamount to an attempt at justifying power. Hence the search, by the theorists of interventionism, for an ethical justification of political and social institutions, and chiefly of the market, which substantially coincides with the search for an ethical justification of the extension of the authority of the state. This perspective is radically different from the traditional wariness of liberalism *vis-à-vis* the state. No longer is the state conceived as a tool for guaranteeing inalienable natural rights: rather it is seen as a tool for the accomplishment of ends that are non-natural, and, as such, need to be ethically justified. From the point of view of *methodological individualism* and of the theory of human action and political institutions on which methodological individualism rests, it is undoubtedly a paradox that the state –an abstract construct, or ideal type– can be conceived as having an ethical character and as the bearer and accomplisher of a 'public ethics' that is superior to that of individuals.

Thus, in the opinion of the Austrian School exponents, the attempt to favour the ethical point of view in the analysis and evaluation of social institutions seems to be linked to a finalist vision of such institutions. More generally, it seems to be connected to a concept of the state not as the guarantor of the universality of the rules and results of catallactics, but as the promoter of the 'common welfare'. This implies state interventionism requiring a justification which is clearly different from and superior to that of the real outcomes of catallactics.

In order to understand the origins of the 'Austrian' critique of the type of interventionism that is a blend of politics, economics and ethics, it is interesting to recall the approach adopted by Carl Menger in his *Methodenstreit*. Even the most inattentive reader of the works by the exponents of the Austrian School cannot fail to have been struck by the scanty importance they attributed to ethics. This contrasts starkly with other traditions of social sciences, which are even defined as *moral sciences*.[2] This is, in my opinion, one of the more striking illustrations of the difference between the Austrian School and other tendencies in the philosophy of social sciences.

It has to be stated, at this point, that Menger's criticism of the 'so-called ethical approach to political economics' (*Appendix IX*) has not attracted a great deal of attention among scholars. Nevertheless, perhaps due to the fact that this Appendix marks the end of the *Untersuchungen*, Menger's critical stance reveals his intention to make radical innovations in the study of the phenomena of theoretical social sciences. Thus, it is worth noting that the peculiarity of the position he took up in the *Methodenstreit* (characterized by the contrast between *Naturwissenschaften* and *Geisteswissenschaften*) resided not so much in the distinction between the *realistic-empirical orientation* and the *exact orientation* (a distinction that remains within the debate on inductivism[3]), or in the classification and tripartition of science into *historical*,

---

2   Except for F.A. VON HAYEK: *The Fatal Conceit. The Error of Socialism, The Collected Works of F.A. von Hayek*, vol. I, London (Routledge), 1988.

3   See: K. MILFORD: *Introduzione* to C. MENGER: *Sul metodo delle scienze sociali*, Macerata (Liberilibri) 1996, pp. xxx-xxxvii; Italian trans. of C. MENGER: *Untersuchungen über die Methode der Socialwissenschaften, und der Politische Oekonomie insbesondere*, Leipzig (Duncker & Humblot) 1883; reprinted in *Gesammelte Werke*, edited by F. A. von Hayek, Tübingen (J.C.B. Mohr [Paul Siebeck]) 1968-70, Bd. II.

theoretical and *practical* sciences, but more importantly in the fact that he criticized the widespread feeling of an assumed privileged role of ethics in the evaluation of human action and social institutions.

Furthermore, Menger did not only place some other kind of knowledge on the pedestal from which he had implicitly dislodged ethics, but he also held that ethical phenomena should be understood and evaluated on a scientific basis, in just the same way as other phenomena that form the object of theoretical social sciences are understood and evaluated. In other words, he maintained that ethics does not occupy a privileged position among theoretical and practical social sciences. As a consequence, it is not possible, he argued, to place the evaluations that ethics can legitimately express concerning events, actions and social institutions at the tip of a hypothetical and universally shared hierarchy of tools of judgement: for the results of catallactics may have nothing to do with the fact that the intentions or initial expectations –to which such results can be traced back following the method of causal attribution, typical of methodological individualism– are either good or bad. Good intentions, as the old adage goes, do not always produce good results.

Yet, in these reflections, Menger was far from suggesting that ethical motivations of human action are irrelevant to an understanding of the birth of social institutions[4]. On the contrary, he held that the peculiar procedure through which institutions take shape –a sort of blend of 'genetic elements', 'rigorous laws regulating the sequence of phenomena', subjective knowledge (limited and fallible) of such laws ('natural-exact') by the agents, and subjective judgement of the results of the process (based on the knowledge possessed at that specific moment)– ends up by making any possible ethical motivation to human action causally irrelevant. Based on such conditions and dynamics, the result of catallactics is then likely to be very different from the

---

4   C. MENGER: in *Die Irrthümer des Historismus in der Deutschen Nationalökonomie*, Wien (Alfred Hölder) 1884; reprinted in: *Gesammelte Werke*, edited by F.A. von Hayek, Tübingen (J.C.B. Mohr [Paul Siebeck]) 1968-70, Bd. III, p. 43, confirms that "together with history, the common experience of life (the knowledge of motives, goals, circumstances determining success and the successful results of individual economic activity) is likewise a necessary foundation of theoretical economics" ["da? neben der Geschichte auch die gemeine Lebenserfahrung (die Kenntniss der Motive, der Ziele, der den Erfolg bestimmenden Umstände und der Erfolge individualwirthschaftlicher Thätigkeit) eine nothwendige Grundlage der theoretischen Volkswirthschaftslehre sei"].

outcome expected according to the agent's motivations and initial expectations – except when specific conditions occur, as we will examine later on.

The relationship between ethics, economics and politics will then have to be conceived and solved by viewing the task of theoretical social sciences as an attempt "*to trace the unintended social repercussions of intentional human actions*"[5]. And from this standpoint, discussion as to an ethical evaluation of economic or political processes does not seem to be of particular importance for the purposes of understanding those phenomena. Neither is it therefore of any greater relevance in endeavouring to change them should they entail a number of unexpected consequences greater than, or structurally different from, the number of expected consequences. Indeed, for Menger, *order* consists in progressively approaching the *essence* of social phenomena and the laws that regulate them; and the characteristic of such '*exact natural laws*' –as we will see– is that no exception is admitted. Thus the task of the science of economics is not to teach how to distinguish between needs and goods according to their goodness or ethicalness, but according to their naturalness and rationality. Order will then consist of progressive adaptation of one's behaviour to those exact natural laws which regulate phenomena and their reciprocal relations, whose characteristic is precisely that of admitting no exceptions, that is to say no unexpected events. This is well described in the *Grundsätze*, where Menger does not connect the distinction between *true goods* and *imaginary goods*, or the hierarchy of the satisfaction of needs, to ethical considerations, asserting that:

> more deeply into the true constitution of things and of their own as a people attains higher levels of civilization, and as men penetrate nature, the number of true goods becomes constantly larger, and as can easily understood, the number of imaginary goods becomes progressively smaller[6].

---

5   K. R. POPPER: *Conjectures and Refutations*, London (Routledge & Kegan Paul) 1963, reprinted in 1976, p. 342. As is well known, the theme of the unintentional consequences of intentional human actions has been the classical theme of the liberal individualist tradition since Mandeville, Ferguson, Hume, Smith and Menger.

6   C. MENGER: *Grundsätze der Volkswirthschaftslehre*, Vienna (Wilhelm Bruamüller) 1871; reprinted in *Gesammelte Werke*, ed. by F. A. von Hayek, Tübingen (J.C.B. Mohr [Paul Siebeck]) 1968-70, Bd. I, p. 4 (Engl. trans. *Prin-*

From another complementary point of view, if the process of catallactics is based on the market taken as a system of price-driven transmission of information (which individuals may use as they wish[7]), then it would be possible to attribute priority to the ethical evaluation of this process and its results only if the kind of ethical knowledge involved were superior to that of catallactics. This would occur if ethical knowledge were capable of leading the process towards the expected results without producing unexpected outcomes. This, in its turn, would also mean that ethical rules are distinguished in their origin and mode of formation from other kinds of rules; furthermore, it would in any case mean grounding ethical knowledge on something other than human knowledge, with all the hermeneutical problems that this entails.

II. Menger

In the *Untersuchungen*, by criticizing the theory of an organicistic origin and the thesis of a pragmatic origin of social institutions, Menger focused on the fact that the most important among these –language, religion, law, the State, markets, competition, money, prices, etc., which still *"serve the common welfare and are of utmost importance for its development"*– have arisen *"without a* common will *directed towards their foundation"*[8]. In this context, Menger did not mention ethics –even though the reference to religion is

---

ciples of Economics*, Glencoe [Free Press] 1950; reprinted New York, London [New York University Press] 1976, p. 53).

7   Here we can say we are dealing with an application of the assumption made by Hayek's philosophy of social science, according to which *"an order arising from the separate decisions of many individuals on the basis of different information cannot be determined by a common scale of the relative importance of different ends.* This brings us close to the issue of marginal utility [...] Freedom involves freedom to be different"*, see F. A. VON HAYEK: *The Fatal Conceit, loc. cit.,* p. 79.

8   C. MENGER: *Untersuchungen, loc. cit.,* pp. 163-65 (English transl., *Problems of Economics and Sociology,* Urbana (University of Illinois Press) 1963; reprinted as *Investigations into the Method of the Social Sciences with Special reference to Economics,* New York - London (New York University Press) 1985, pp. 146-48).

rather important and significant–, but he did broach the question of *ethical phenomena* in the fourth chapter of the first book, where he wrote that their comprehension cannot be distinguished from that of the other phenomena constituting the field of the problems of *theoretical social sciences*

> the nature of this exact orientation of *theoretical* research in the realm of ethical phenomena, however, consists in the fact that we reduce [*zurückführen*] human phenomena to their most original and simplest constitutive factors. We join to the latter the measure corresponding to their nature, and finally try to investigate the laws by which *more complicated* human phenomena are formed from those simplest elements, thought of in their isolation[9]

The last and final *Appendix* to the *Untersuchungen* is dedicated –as we have already said– to a critique of the 'so-called ethical approach to political economy'. Menger's position on this matter is clearly expressed by his assertion that an ethical approach to theoretical economics is

> a vague postulate of research devoid of any deeper content. A similar vagueness underlies the so-called 'ethic orientation' in respect to the *practical* economic sciences[10].

Certainly, it is unthinkable that this is to be taken as an implicit denial of the possibility of pronouncing value judgements on individual ends and social institutions. Menger, distancing himself from the Historical School of Law and alluding to the famous work by Friedrich Carl von Savigny[11], stated:

> but never, and this is the essential point in the matter under review, may science dispense with testing for their suitability those institutions which have come about 'organically'. It must, when careful investigation so requires, change and better them according to the measure of scientific insight and the practical experience at hand. No era may renounce this 'calling'[12].

Taking into account the fact that, according to Menger, the goal of 'theoretical-exact science' is the elaboration of 'rigorous laws' –that is to say, the

---

9   *Ibid.*, p. 43 (Engl. trans. p. 62).

10 *Ibid.*, p. 290 (Engl. trans. p. 236).

11 F. C. VON SAVIGNY: *Vom Beruf unserer Zeit für Gesetzgebung und Rechtswissenschaft*, Heidelberg (Mohr und Zimmer) 1814.

12 C. MENGER: *Untersuchungen, loc. cit.*, p. 287 (Engl. trans. p. 234).

elaboration of "laws of phenomena which are not only absolute, but according to our laws of thinking simply cannot be thought of in any other way but as absolute"–, the task of theoretical science is identified as the attempt at attaining the discovery of "exact laws, the so-called 'laws of nature' of phenomena"[13]. It should therefore be clear that the assumption that social institutions are the unintended result of the naturally limited knowledge of 'exact laws' by individuals –that is to say, a largely unexpected consequence of the results of individual actions aiming at satisfaction of subjective needs, and thus a consequence of the subjective value that individuals attribute to goods– does not imply that it is impossible to express an evaluation of how these needs are satisfied and the social outcomes of such modes of satisfaction. It only means that evaluation of intentions cannot be separated from the evaluation of results, and that both intentions and results should be evaluated in the light of a knowledge of 'exact natural laws' and their unintended and unwelcome consequences.

The ascertainment that the main institutions of associative life ("language, religion, law, even the State itself, [...] money, markets, [...] the prices of goods, interest rates, ground rents, wages, and a thousand other phenomena of social life in general and of economy in particular exhibit exactly the same peculiarity") are "to no small extent the unintended result of social development" leads Menger to claim that:

> the solution of the most important problems of the theoretical social sciences in general and of theoretical economics in particular is thus closely connected with the question of theoretically understanding the origin and change of 'organically' created social structures[14].

---

13 *Ibid.*, p. 42 (Engl. trans. p. 61).

14 *Ibid.*, pp. 163-65 (Engl. trans. pp. 146-47). Menger often uses the expression 'common welfare' [*Gemeinwohl*], but he is referring to the birth of institutions (law, language, money, religion, etc.: "in the case of money, we are met with a social structure which in the most outstanding sense benefits the common welfare [*Gemeinwohl*]. Indeed, it really conditions it and yet does not appear as the result of a will of society directed toward this", see *ibid.*, p. 270 [Engl. trans. p. 223]); such a concept does not therefore refer to a common welfare, but rather to common instruments. It is then used in a meaning that is not unlike the one used by Oakeshott. The above mentioned example has been taken from *Appendix* VIII, where is treated the 'organic' origin of law and the exact understanding thereof.

267

And consequently, that

> every theory, of whatever kind it may be and whatever degree of strict-
> ness of knowledge it may strive for, has primarily the task of teaching
> us to understand the concrete phenomena of the real world as exempli-
> fication of a certain regularity in the succession of phenomena; i.e.,
> genetically [...] *This genetic element is inseparable from the idea of
> theoretical sciences*[15].

After rejecting the thesis by Bruno Hildebrand, C.W. Ch. Schütz, K. Dietzel, J. Kautz and by the "majority of the historical economists of Germany", according to which the tasks of economics can be associated to the tasks of ethics, Menger observed that "we cannot rationally speak of an ethical orientation of theoretical economics". He also held that this would mean confusing two kinds of investigations of the real world that are legitimate but different. Therefore, by attributing to 'exact economics' the task of studying "the *economic aspect* of national life", he not only rejected the idea of an 'ethical approach' in theoretical economic science, but also maintained that such an approach cannot even be countenanced among *practical* economic sciences. Discarding the trivial observation that all economic activity is subject to moral as well as juridical and customary rules, he argued that this approach would have to be viewed as an assertion of the necessity of submitting economics to ethical considerations: effectively a moral treatment of economic activity or "to unite the tasks of ethics and economics". Consequently,

> the requirement of an ethical orientation of exact economics could
> only mean that this science must render to us exact understanding not
> only simply of economic phenomena but of those influenced by ethi-
> cal tendencies or even of those conformable to the demands of ethics.

And this, to his eyes, "contradicts the nature of the exact orientation of theoretical research"[16], and is just as unacceptable as the position held by those who believe an ethical approach to theoretical economics consists "in considering the phenomena of national economy from the point of view of morality", that is to say expressing "a *moral* judgement on single phenomena of national economy"[17].

---

15 *Ibid.*, p. 88 (Engl. trans. p. 94).

16 *Ibid.*, pp. 288-89 (Engl. trans. pp. 235-36).

17 *Ibid.*, p. 289n. (Engl. trans. p. 236n.).

Menger did not exclude the possibility of imagining a "justified orientation of the desire for knowledge which establishes the *relationship* between law, morals, etc., on the one hand and economy on the other, or between ethich and economics. But the notion of an *ethical orientation of economics* has no greater justification than, for istance, that of an economic orientation of ethics"[18]. Moreover, he did not exclude the possibility that many economic phenomena (real prices of goods, real land rents, real interest on capital) "are in any case not only the result of specifically economic propensities, but also of ethical ones"[19]. Nor did he exclude that all kinds of practical activity (politics, pedagogy, therapy, technology and war) and "human endeavors" are "under the moral code". Yet, he maintained that the supporters of *an ethical approach to economics* did not intend to make such a statement, but to assert the superiority of an ethical judgement over economic phenomena. By so doing, however, this would result

> on the one hand in a failure to recognize the nature and peculiar problems of the theoretical and the practical sciences of national economy. On the other hand, it is rooted in the underestimation of the economic aspects of national life in realtion to other more highly esteemed aspects [...] As if the worth of a science were dependent on its object [...] The desire for an ethical orientation of our science is in part a residue of a philosophy that comes from antiquity, and, in a different sense, of medieval-ascetic philosophy. In good part, however, it is a lamentable crutch for scientific insufficiency [...] of those who show insufficient ability for the solution of the problems of their science to want to get satisfactory solutions in their own field of research by briging in the results of other sciences and utilizing them mechanically[20].

Menger thus broke with the tradition that had subjected economics to ethics and, since he did not distinguish the process of formation of ethical rules from that of the other social institutions, he implicitly stated that the rules of ethics are themselves also the involuntary product of human action. In other words, as Hayek was to specify later, it is a group of rules that have formed as the unintended consequence of a process of cultural selection and imitation of types of behaviour that have prevailed on account of the reduced

---

18 *Ibid.*, p. 291 (Engl. trans. p. 237).
19 *Ibid.*, p. 69 (Engl. trans. p. 80).
20 *Ibid.*, pp. 290-91 (Engl. trans. p. 237).

number of unexpected consequences. Thus, the re-iteration of the importance that ethical motivations have as regards human action becomes linked to rejection of the thesis stating that ethics is a privileged point of view for an evaluation and judgement of human actions and social institutions. For even if an ethical evaluation were expressed on goods,

> an ever so 'untrue' or 'immoral' item of goods is subject to the economic laws of value, of price, etc., and is thus from the economic standpoint an 'item of goods' whose value, price, etc., must be interpreted theoretically just as well as the value or price of goods serving the highest purposes. Or should an 'etical' theory of national economy perhaps reject in principle the interpretation of *economic* phenomena to be observed in connection with goods which serve immoral purposes? Is it to limit itself to the theoretical interpretation of that part of economic phenomena which are in harmony with the principles of ethics or a certain ethical orientation? What science, then, would have the task of giving us theoretical understanding of the laws of 'not true' goods, or of the 'not ethical' phenomena of national economy?[21] .

When he stated that social institutions and religion itself did not derive from a collective will directed towards their creation, Menger laid the basis for the subsequent positions of the exponents of the Austrian School in this scientific field[22]. Ludwig von Mises and Hayek, for instance, sometimes even from different positions, insisted that ethics could not be considered as a privileged point of view for the evaluation of individual actions and social policy[23]. For in order to evaluate either of the latter, one cannot avoid taking their results into consideration.

It seems to be possible, therefore, to express an evaluation of 'organically' derived social institutions on the basis of a 'scientific vision' (knowledge of 'exact natural laws') and the available practical experience (unintended consequences). Social institutions are in fact the unintended result of the way in-

---

21 *Ibid.*, p. 289n. (Engl. trans. p. 236n.).

22 For instance, this sentence of Menger's "*how can it be that institutions which serve the common welfare and are extremely significant for its development come into being without a* common will *directed towards establishing them?*" is quoted as a *motto* in: F.A. von HAYEK: *The Fatal Conceit*, cit.

23 Many of their works are imbued with such a conviction, even though not always explicitly. The most evident case is F. A. VON HAYEK: *The Mirage of Social Justice*, II vol. of *Law, Legislation and Liberty*, London (Routledge & Kegan Paul) 1976, rev. edited in 1982.

dividuals interpret 'exact laws' with a view to the satisfaction of their subjective results and the realization of subjective goals.

It could thus be stated that the task of scientific knowledge (*exact research*) in the field of theoretical social sciences is that of ensuring that social institutions conform to the "typical relationships, the *laws* of phenomena": efforts must be directed towards "the determination of regularities in the relationships of phenomena which are guaranteed to be absolute and as such to be complete", but there must be total awareness that they will never be fully known by the human mind. Further, the object of scientific knowledge is the relationship among these laws concerning "strict types and typical relationships (exact laws) of phenomena [...], not only in respect to their nature, but also to their measure". In other words, scientific knowledge is concerned with tailoring to such 'absolute regularities', "how more complicated phenomena develop from the simplest, in part even unempirical elements of the real world in their (likewise unempirical) isolation from all other influences, with constant consideration of exact (likewise ideal!) measure"[24]. This occurs when concrete phenomena are compared to the "typical relationships of phenomena". Consequently,

> without the knowledge of empirical forms we would not be able to comprend the myriads of phenomena surrounding us, nor to classify them in our minds; it is the presupposition for a more comprehensive cognition of the real world. Without cognition of the typical relationships we would be deprived not only of a deeper understanding of the real world [...], but also, as may be easly seen, of all cognition extending beyond immediate observation, i.e., of any *prediction* and *control* of things. All human prediction and, indirectly, all arbitrary shaping of things is conditioned by that knowledge [...][25].

Any attempt to predict the results of an action and to dominate them therefore seems to be connected to the degree of knowledge of the 'genetic' connection of the "typical relationships of phenomena". The more restricted the knowledge, the greater the number of unintended consequences that will ensue. Menger eventually ended up characterizing theoretical activity in the field of social sciences as a continuous work of elimination of those solutions to problems that will bring with them a higher number of unintended consequences. The quantity of unintended consequences is therefore indirectly

---

24 C. MENGER: *Untersuchungen, loc. cit.*, pp. 41-42 (Engl. trans. pp. 61-62).
25 *Ibid.*, p. 5 (Engl. trans. p. 36).

proportional to the exactness of the knowledge of the 'exact laws' which regulate that succession of phenomena. It could thus be said that 'exact laws' are those that, if fully applied, do not produce unintended consequences.

In effect the ethical approach to economics provides no help for an understanding of phenomena and social institutions that have arisen in a 'unintended' manner. There would be no point, in fact, in awarding the ethical evaluation of goods and needs, and therefore individual actions and social institutions, a privileged position as compared to other types of scientific knowledge. Moreover, even within the field of the institutions that have arisen in a 'pragmatic' manner (that is to say, in the case of institutions specifically directed towards achievement of a goal), evaluation takes on the connotation of an adaptation of the means to the goal:

> we interpret these phenomena pragmatically by investigating the aims which in the concrete case have guided the social unions, or their rulers, in the estabilishment and advancement of the social phenomena under discussion here. We investigate the aids which have been at their disposal in this case, the obstacles which have worked against the creation and development of those social structures, the way and manner in which the available aids were used for establishing them. We fulfill this task so much the more perfectly the more we examine the *ultimate* real aims of the active subjects on the one hand, and the most original means which they had at their command on the other, and the more we come to understand the social phenomena referring back to a pragmatic origin as links in a chain of regulations for the realization of the above aims.

Hence, there follows what Menger defined as "the historical-pragmatic criticism" of social phenomena, which consists in verifying in each concrete case

> the real aims of the social unions or of their rulers by the needs of the social unions in question, when we test the application of the aids to social action, on the other hand, by the limitations of success (the fullest satisfaction possible of the social needs)[26].

It is important to point out that in the case of this kind of institutions and their goals Menger did not even mention a criterion for an ethical evaluation: instead he took the discussion back to the theme of the naturalness of

---

26 *Ibid.*, pp. 162-63 (Engl. trans. pp. 145-46).

needs without expressing any ethical evaluation, as in the theory of goods and needs.

If we then were to try to look for a possible ranking of ethics within the framework of the distinction between *historical, theoretical and practical sciences*, we would be disappointed once again. Here, in fact, when he treated *"practical sciences* or *arts"*, Menger only wrote that they teach how

> to determine the basic principles by which, according to the diversity of conditions, efforts of a definite kind can be most suitably pursued. They teach us what the conditions are supposed to be for definite human aims to be achieved[27].

Yet, Menger did not mention –either here or in *Appendixes* III and IV, where he again took up the distinction– the possibility of an ethical evaluation of goals. However, this should not be taken as the impossibility of performing such an evaluation, but rather as an assertion of the fact that, even in the field of practical sciences, the imputation criteria are not different.

What has been said up to this point seems to be an exemplification in the wider context of social sciences of the origins of the position of the Austrian School, according to which the most important element for a thorough comprehension of the phenomena of theoretical social sciences does not consist in an evaluation of the results of individual and collective actions in the light of their original intentions, but rather their evaluation in the light of their social consequences. The so-called unintended consequences are such that, from the point of view of social science, it is not very meaningful to evaluate a result by starting from the intentions. At the base of the Austrian the-

---

27 *Ibid.*, pp. 7-8 (Engl. trans. p. 38). On pages 8-9 (Engl. trans. pp. 38-39) Menger distinguishes sciences into: "the *historical* sciences (history) and statistics of economy, which have the task of investigating and describing the individual nature and the individual connection of economic phenomena; second, *theoretical* economics, with the task of investigating and describing their general nature and general connection (their laws); finally, third, the *practical* sciences of national economy, with the task of investigating and describing the basic principles for suitable action (adapted to the variety of conditions) in the field of national economy (economic policy and the science of finance)". On the theme of the classification of sciences, see also C. MENGER (1889) "Grundzüge einer Klassifikation der Wirtschaftswissenschaften", *Jahrbücher für Nationalökonomie und Statistik*, 19 (1889); reprinted in: *Gesammelte Werke*, edited by F. A. von Hayek, Tübingen (J.C.B. Mohr [Paul Siebeck]) 1968-70, Bd. III, pp. 199ff.

ory there lies the assumption that a variety of voluntary motivations and casual circumstances contribute to the production of a social event. Therefore, it would be impossible *to reduce* and evaluate this process in the light of only one of the possible initial motivations. For such a process could be dramatically distorted by the occurrence of other concomitant circumstances and by the fact that the evaluation of outcomes –whether expected or unexpected– largely depends on the subjects who are, even involuntarily, subjected to the consequences and the new situations produced.

These involuntary results of human actions, which for the most disparate reasons strive to achieve subjective goals, do *not necessarily* give rise, in their turn, to an *order*, that is to say, a reference point the individuals consider as a yardstick in their attempts at achieving subjective goals. Consequently, the problem is not that the motivations to action (as well as the order) are either good or despicable, but that the result may constitute an effective reference point allowing agents to foresee the feasibility and the possible outcomes of individual and collective actions. An ethical evaluation of the intentions and results of an action can undoubtedly be expressed, but this does not mean that there is a causal natural-deterministic or mechanicistic relation between good intentions and good results. And this is so because there is a moment between intention and result when other individuals express an evaluation of that particular intention based on their own subjective values, interests and knowledge; moreover, in so doing, they base their evaluation on the assessment of the possible consequences of that action in relation to their own values, interests, etc. In other words, a social outcome is not the result of a single will, but the result of a number of wills and of their acting concurrently (*catallactics*). In the formation of an order, the casual elements cannot be excluded. Yet, this does not mean that the whole process is casual.

The process of formation of an order in ethical rules is therefore not different from the formation of social institutions. Moreover, beyond a consideration of ethics as the practical or secular side of a religious system (that is to say, of a system considering ethics as the worldly side of revelation), the formation of a system of ethical rules cannot be separated from considerations regarding its effectiveness.

III. Considerations on the Problem Raised by Menger

Menger's position thus appears as an extension to social science as a whole of the basic assumption that value is not so much determined by the will of the producer of a given good, or by the set of material circumstances concurring to bring about its production, but rather by the judgement consumers express on the good itself.

But the fact that a socially good result does not derive from the goodness of initial motivations does not mean that ethics has lost its traditional role as a guide for human behaviour. Like the other social institutions discussed earlier, ethics itself can be interpreted as a set of behavioural rules aiming at a reduction of the number of unwelcome or unintended consequences which ensue from intentional action due to the limitations and fallibility of human knowledge. From this point of view, ethics retains its importance within social science, even if it is not the only criterion, or even the most important one, for an evaluation of action and its results. What becomes really important are not individual motivations, but rather social outcomes. The parallel with the *theory of subjective values* is evident. While in classical economics the value of a good depends on work and production factors, here it depends on the consumers' judgement. The Austrians placed little emphasis on the problem of ethics not only because they rejected the theory of the value-labour, but also because they were not utilitarians.

From another point of view, ethical rules do not differ from the rules of law, as they both aim at reducing those consequences that are unexpected, and usually unpleasant, for other individuals. In fact, they both constitute an organic set of rules that individuals cannot ignore if they wish to obtain certain results. Such rules are the product of a selection of behaviours tending to achieve predictability of the results of actions carried out by individuals who possess the freedom to choose among the various possibilities that can improve their condition. Each individual, on the basis of his own knowledge, chooses that which, in his opinion, allows him to accomplish his goal with the smallest foreseeable number of unexpected consequences.

Each individual action aiming at the accomplishment of a goal must therefore take into consideration the way that particular goal will affect others. The individual will tend to avoid those types of behaviour which he thinks are likely to jeopardize accomplishment of his goals. This is true in the field of ethics, just as in the fields of language, law, economics, etc.

By the light of these considerations, it may be useful to divide the problem of the relationship between ethics and economics into three distinct parts. The first regards the possibility of subjecting the economic sphere to the ethical sphere, or the ethical sphere to a logic of economic efficiency. The second regards the theoretical and practical relations between the ethical and the economic sphere. The third regards the problem of the relevance of ethical motivations in economic choices[28].

I will try to defend the thesis that, in the first case, what we are dealing with is a mistaken approach to the problem and, in the third case, we are dealing with an assertion that is easy to share inasmuch it is totally trivial[29]. Therefore, it is perhaps useful to start from the second, that is to say from the statement –again trivial, one might say– that every human action has a number of unintended consequences which, regardless of the initial motivations of each action, can be perceived and evaluated in different ways by those who are subjected to its consequences. To give an example, an action performed on the basis of widespread and commonly shared ethical motivations can nevertheless have consequences that may be considered as unfair by those who suffer them.

Taking Menger's thesis as a starting point, one may wonder whether the contraposition between the market and ethics is not actually a false opposition, due to the fact that it presupposes that the market –taken as the impor-

---

28 The terms of this problem have been clearly explained by P. KOSLOWSKI in: *Prinzipien der Ethischen Ökonomie. Grundlegung der Wirtschaftsethik*, Tübingen (J.C.B. Mohr [Paul Siebeck]) 1988; and in *Ethical Economy as Synthesis of Economic and Ethical Theory*, in: P. Koslowski (Ed.), *Ethics in Economics, Business, and Economic Policy*, Berlin, Heidelberg, New York (Springer-Verlag) 1992. A recent attempt to show how understanding moral philosophy can improve economic analysis has been made by D. M. HAUSMAN and M.S. MCPHERSON in: *Economic analysis and moral philosophy*, Cambridge (Cambridge University Press), 1996.

29 However, attention has rightly been focused on this thesis by A. SEN, in: *On Ethics & Economics*, Oxford (Basil Blackwell) 1987, p. 7, where he observes that the 'engineering-like approach to economics' that is typical of 'positive economics' "[it] has also had the effect of ignoring a variety of complex ethical considerations which affect actual human behaviour", and where he maintains that taking the complexity of motivations for human action into consideration cannot but be mutually advantageous as regards both economics and ethics.

tance of useful[30], or as an instrument for the accomplishment of ethical goals– clashes with ethics. In such a perspective, the market would be evaluated in the light of its contribution to the accomplishment of ethical or political goals, and it would in any case be desirable for it to possess no independent life of its own, because in such a case society would be transformed into the bloody battlefield of irreconcilable egoisms. But at the basis of such a conception there lies a conception of the market that the 'Austrians' discredited and replaced with the conception of the market as a 'discovery process' and of the competition as a "process in which people acquire and communicate knowledge"[31].

If, as Hayek wrote quoting Hume: "the rules of morality are not the conclusions of our reason"[32], then ethics is the product of a cultural evolution that includes social institutions, as well as theories[33], to the point that it can

---

30 Menger, Böhm-Bawerk and Hayek were not utilitarians, whereas Mises was, even in Hayek's opinion (see F.A. VON HAYEK: *Law, Legislation and Liberty, loc. cit.,* vol. III, p. 205n). On the differences among the main exponents of the Austrian School, see R. CUBEDDU: *The Philosophy of the Austrian School,* London-New York (Routledge) 1993.

31 The first definition is a paraphrase of the title of the volume by I. M. KIRZNER: *Discovery and the Capitalist Process,* Chicago (The University of Chicago Press), 1985; by the same author, see also *The Meaning of Market Process. Essays in the Development of Modern Austrian Economics,* London-New York (Routledge) 1992; and see the title of a paragraph ("Competition as a discovery procedure") of the volume by F. A. VON HAYEK: *Law, Legislation and Liberty, loc. cit.,* III, p. 67; the second is the well-known Hayekian definition; see, in the same work, pp. 68, 71-73, but also, in volume II, pp. 107-32. On the connection between ethics and the market, see also M. N. ROTHBARD, *Power & Market. Government and the Economy,* Kansas City (S. Andrews and McMeel) 1970, and *The Ethics of Liberty,* Atlantic Highlands, N.J. (Humanities Press) 1982; on the market process: L. M. LACHMANN: *The Market as an Economic Process,* Oxford (Basil Blackwell) 1986. On this theme, see J. M. BUCHANAN, V. J. VANBERG: "The Market as a Creative Process", *Economics and Philosophy,* 7 (1991), n. 2, pp. 167-86.

32 See *The Fatal Conceit, loc. cit.,* p. 66.

33 F. A. VON HAYEK: *Law, Legislation and Liberty, loc. cit.,* III, p. 163. He writes: "the basic tools of civilization –language, morals, law and money– are all the result of spontaneous growth and not of design". Such an assertion, clearly stemming from Menger's ideas, is repeated, with some variants, in: F. A. VON HAYEK: *The Origins and Effect of Our Morals: A Problem for*

even be claimed that "as moral views create institutions, so institutions create moral views"[34]. These rules –morals, law, language, etc.– are, in his opinion, "the only common values of an open and free society". They are not

> concrete objects to be achieved, but only those common abstract rules of conduct that secured the constant maintenance of an equally abstract order which merely assured to the individual better prospects of achieving his individual ends[35].

In fact, Hayek maintained that "no argument about morals –or science, or law, or language– can legitimately turn on the issue of justification". In his view, therefore, the process of the birth and evolution of ethics is analogous to that of the other institutions which give rise to "extended order"[36]: that is to say, that ethics itself is also the result of a process of "group selection" which, just like "all the paradigms of culturally evolved institutions, morals, exchange, and money, refers to such practices whose benefits transcend the individuals who practice them in the particular instances"[37]. Rules, and moral rules in particular, are then "a self-ordering process of adaptation to the unknown"[38].

From this standpoint, it can readily be understood why classical liberalism is characterized by a process of reduction of religion and morals from the public sphere to the individual sphere. Yet this is not resolved by repudiating the role and importance of morals and religion in social life[39], but by reasserting individual responsibility. Thus the "extended order" of the liberal

---

Science, in *The Essence of Hayek*, edited by C. Nishiyama, K. R. Leube, Stanford (Hoover Institution Press) 1984, p. 319 and in: *The Fatal Conceit, loc. cit.*, p. 68.

34 F.A . VON HAYEK: *Law, Legislation and Liberty, loc. cit.*, III, p. 170.

35 *Ibid.*, p. 164.

36 F.A. VON HAYEK: *The Fatal Conceit, loc. cit.*, pp. 68-70.

37 F.A. VON HAYEK: *The Origins and Effect of Our Morals: A Problem for Science, loc. cit.*, p. 319.

38 F.A. VON HAYEK: *The Fatal Conceit, loc. cit.*, p. 76.

39 *Ibid.*, pp. 136-37. Here, Hayek writes that religion too is born from a 'group selection' and that there is an "undoubted *historical* connection between religion and the values that have shaped and furthered our civilization, such as the family and several property". Even if this "does not of course mean that there is any intrinsic connection between religion as such and such values [...] *the only religions that have survived are those which support property and family*".

state does not set itself the goal of achieving ethical ends or "natural good-ness", but aims, by means of an "evolutionary selection of rules of conduct", *"to adapt, through [...] partial and fragmentary signals, to conditions foreseen by and known to no individual,* even if this adaptation is never perfect"[40]. Consequently, it will not be founded on a 'public ethics', but only on the ne-cessity of certain types of individual behaviour, regarded as absolutely neces-sary for the existence of an *"extended order"*. At this point, rather than won-dering if behaviour that takes place in the market is, or should be, also moral behaviour, one should ask whether such behaviour is subject to rules, and what are the origin and nature of such rules. Or, to restate the question slightly, should moral, economic, and political behaviour be subjected to the same *Law,* as is implicitly stated in one of the main principles of liberalism: that is to say, in the *Rule of Law*?

Obviously, market choices can also be devoid of moral motivations, but this does not mean that if the market is the place where mutual subjective expectations can be achieved by means of free exchange, the range of be-haviour through which these ends are pursued is not subjected to rules. Nor does it imply that those who violate them are not expelled. These individuals suffer a cost for their behaviour, just as those who violate those moral rules which affect others are subjected, in this world or in the other, to reproach or punishment. Therefore, similarly to the situation observed in the market, moral rules have negative connotations, in that they concern types of be-haviour that must not be carried out if the known or unknown consequences are to be avoided. Obviously, these consequences are of a different nature, but what they have in common is their uncertainty; that is to say, they are un-welcome and unexpected consequences that can derive from having behaved in a certain manner.

Yet I think that when we are dealing with the relationship between ethics and the market, this is not what we have in mind. Rather, it is a question of whether the so-called market laws are of a different nature from ethical rules, whether a different ethics regulates the market, or whether the market is a means to achieve ethical ends. Personally, I do not think this is possible; I am wary of 'special' ethics or 'public ethics'; moreover, I do not believe that

---

40 *Ibid.,* p. 76.

these are compatible with a liberal order which is a *nomocratic* and not a *teleocratic* order.[41]

In this connection, it is very interesting to see how Kant's considerations on the relationship between politics and morals, and between the *moral politician* and the *political moralist*[42], are still useful today for an analysis of the relationship between ethics and the market. This question can, obviously, be broached only summarily, but within the confines of the relationship between freedom and law, and therefore in the sphere of the *a priori* requisites for a 'republic', one should recall Kant's assertion that the republic is the best political regime even for "a nation of devils (so long as they possess understanding)". This is because the law is what allows "a group of rational beings" to calculate the consequences of their actions, whatever "their private attitudes"[43]. Indeed, in my opinion, both in the field of politics and in that of economics, the problem of the motivation of an action must be distinguished from the problem of the consequences of such action. What is needed, therefore, are not good intentions, but good rules. In other words, any mode of behaviour that has consequences upon others, and whatever its motivations, must be subject to universalizable and, in some way, foreseeable rules. In effect, such rules are but attempts at calculating the consequences of actions. In this respect, one could also recall the *formal principle* of Kant's practical reason: "'act in such a way that you can wish your maxim to become a universal law (irrespective of what the end in view may be)'"[44]. If this principle is universally applicable, is it still meaningful to speak of a contrast between ethics and the market? Or rather, are we not facing two aspects of action which are both characterized by having the same rules in force? The problem, if anything, concerns the origin of the law. Kant still thought in terms of

---

41 I am using these two terms as F. A. VON HAYEK took them in *Law, Legislation and Liberty*, loc. cit., II, pp. 15, 29, 38-42; and as M. OAKESHOTT used them in *On Human Conduct*, Oxford (Oxford University Press) 1975, pp. 185ff.

42 I. KANT: *Zum ewigen Frieden. Ein philosophischer Entwurf*, Köngisberg (Friedrich Nicolovius) 1795, in: I. KANT: *Werkausgabe*, Bd. XI (*Schriften zur Anthropologie, Geschichtsphilosophie, Politik und Pädagogik* 1), Hrsg. W. Weischedel, Frankfurt (Suhrkamp) 1977, p. 239 (Engl. trans. *Perpetual Peace: A Philosophical Sketchp.*, in *Political Writings*; ed. by H. Reiss, translated by H.B. Nisbet, Cambridge (Cambridge University Press) 1991, p. 122).

43 *Ibid.*, pp. 223-24 (Engl. trans. pp. 112-13).

44 *Ibid.*, p. 239 (Engl. trans. p. 122).

natural law and did not conceive of legislation as an activity independent from the latter; we unfortunately live in the era of legislative production of law by politicians who no longer consider the problem of the relationship between positive law and natural law. That is to say, we live in an era where the state is no longer content merely to establish universal laws for the guarantee of individual rights, but is concerned instead with achieving specific ends by means of a finalistic or goal-oriented legislation. Forcing Kant's thought slightly, it might well be said that we are living in what Kant would have defined not as a 'republic', but rather as a 'despotism'[45]; and the subordination of the market to ethics would be typical of such a form of government, while, on the contrary, in a 'republic', they would both be subject to the very same law.

What has been said so far does not mean that we are exonerated from asking ourselves whether the individual should not be called upon to shoulder the consequences of his actions[46]. Hegel had already highlighted that "the maxim [*Grundsatz*] which enjoins us to disregard the consequences of our actions, and the other which enjoins us to judge actions by their consequences and make the latter yardstick of what is right and good, are in equal measure [products of] abstract understanding", and that in real action the two positions are unified. The problem consists, if anything, in answering the question as to whether a social science can rest content with the contraposition between ethics, morals and politics, which would divest it of any practical dimension.

---

45 *Ibid.*, pp. 206-07 (Engl. trans. pp. 100-01).

46 G.W.F. HEGEL: in: *Grundlinien der Philosophie des Rechts*, Berlin (Nicolaischen) 1821, § 118 (Engl. trans. *Elements of the Philosophy of Right*; ed. by A. W. Wood, translated by H.B. Nisbet, Cambridge (Cambridge University Press) 1991, § 118), had already observed that "action has multiple consequences" and that "the will thus has the right *to accept responsibility* only for the [...] set of consequences, since they alone were part of his *purpose*" since "the distinction between contingent and *necessary* consequences is indeterminate inasmuch as inner necessity comes into existence in the finite realm as external necessity, as a relationship between individual things [*Dingen*] which, as self-sufficient entities, come together in mutual indifference and in an external manner. The maxim [*Grundsatz*] which enjoins us to disregard the consequences of our actions, and the other which enjoins us to judge actions by their consequences and make the latter yardstick of what is right and good, are in equal measure [products of] abstract understanding [...] From this point of view, to act therefore means to submit oneself to this law".

In other words, dutiful calculation of the consequences that every action can have (which is in itself a moral imperative) should not be confused with the other moral imperative according to which the individual, in pursuing his own subjective ends, should observe universalizable behavioural rules.

From this point of view, Weber's perspective could be seen as an attempt – carried out with some degree of awareness – at avoiding the fundamental problem of the philosophy of social sciences and political philosophy. If actions inspired by an 'ethics of responsibility' had the same legitimacy as actions inspired by an 'ethics of intention', it would not only be impossible to propose the problem of the best political order, but *civil society* itself would be impossible. But since man –like any organism– "is continually concerned with the solution of problems; and problems originate from the evaluation of his own conditions and environment, which he tries to improve"[47], such problems cannot be separated from the problem of the unwelcome consequences of his own actions and from compliance with universalizable behavioural rules that can guarantee the achievement of legitimate subjective expectations, which is the assumption upon which an order is based.

In fact, if we start from the trivial assertion that all human knowledge is limited and fallible (therefore, even ethical knowledge) and that every living creature tries to improve its condition by using the knowledge possessed as a tool (analyzing, possibly even erroneously, its own situation and trying to improve the latter by the light of its own ideas concerning both the external environment where such attempt will be enacted and also the laws that regulate the environment in the agent's opinion), then both the achievement of the goal and the unexpected consequences (in which the agent may take no further interest) will derive from the greater or lesser exactness of the way the agent pictured his goal and the external situation.

The moral problem to which theoretical and practical social science must provide an answer could thus be formulated as follows: *is it right, in aiming to improve one's situation, to engage in action while ignoring the negative consequences such action could have upon other individuals?* Obviously, one could answer that it would be unfair, and that it would be equally unfair to carry out an action based on noble ethical values while ignoring its foresee-

---

47 K. R. POPPER: *Auf der Suche nach einer besseren Welt. Vorträge und Aufsätze aus dreissig Jahren*, München-Zürich (Piper) 1984, p. i. ["ist dauernd damit beschäftigt, Probleme zu lösen. Und die Probleme entstehen aus Bewertungen seines Zustandes und seiner Umwelt, die er zu verbessern sucht"].

able negative economic effects. It would be difficult indeed to define such action as a 'good' action.

In actual fact, it is difficult to deny that economic science has greater knowledge of economic phenomena (and therefore of the economic consequences of economic actions) than does ethics. Moreover, just as there exist economic, juridical and political effects of ethical decisions, so also there are juridical, political and ethical effects of economic decisions. Is there any reason to believe that facing economic problems from an ethical point of view would lead to a better knowledge of such problems and better results as regards economic effectiveness?

It is therefore extremely difficult to keep the various points separate; and it would be equally difficult to imagine social dynamics as an abstract struggle among them. In an order resulting from one of the possible balances among the various aspects into which human action can be *abstractly* distinguished, each change in any one of them produces consequences, both in the given aspect itself and in the relation among the various aspects. The case of a decision producing consequences only within its own confines is highly controversial, and in any case it does not concern the relationship between ethics and the market. The case is more commonly found of changes within one aspect which have consequences upon the others. For instance, if any kind 'public ethics' were to become predominant that strongly opposed so-called conspicuous consumption, this would obviously lead to a decrease in production, in exchanges and even in employment.

Quoting the famous conclusion of *The Fable of the Bees* by Mandeville: "Bare Virtue can't make Nations live / In Splendor; they, that would revive / A Golden Age, must be as free, / For Acorns, as for Honesty"[48], we could conclude by saying that even the pursuit of virtue has an economic cost. The same distinction between economic activity and simple consumption was made by Menger: it was a distinction based upon the fact that over time the economy tends to ensure "the necessary means for the satisfaction of our needs"[49]. This fixes very strict limits on consumption and has undeniable ethical and political consequences linked to the distinction between 'true

---

48 See B. DE MANDEVILLE: *The Fable of the Bees, or Private Vices, Public Benefits* (1714-29), F. B. Kaye (Ed.), Oxford (Clarendon Press) 1924; quotation from the ed. Indianapolis (Liberty Classics) 1988, I, page 37 [24].
49 See MENGER: *Grundsätze der Volkswirtschaftslehre*, Zweite Auflage, Hrsg. von Karl Menger, Wien (Hölder-Pichler-Tempsky A.G.) 1923, pp. 61-62. ["die Mittel zur Befriedigung unserer Bedürfnisse"].

needs' and 'imaginary needs'. Precisely this distinction can be taken as an example of the way in which an economic choice is important for ethics or politics. On the other hand, to consume only what can be reproduced can be seen both as a moral obligation and as a cautionary criterion (because, otherwise, what will happen cannot be foreseen), or even as a utilitarian-hedonostic criterion (to extend enjoyment).

What I am arguing, in other words, is that the two spheres of *ethics* and *economics* interact in such a manner that it is not possible to subordinate the one to the other without distorting their nature. If this were to happen, the choice for one or the other would be made upon no theoretical foundation and, moreover, with significant consequences both of a political and practical nature. The fact that it is extremely hard to reach a balanced position in this field is due to the circumstance that each human action is set in an environment characterized by the existence of individuals endowed with partial and fallible knowledge; precisely for this reason, such individuals may evaluate action directed towards the elevation of their general level of well-being in a different manner compared to those who set the action in motion. Furthermore, such individuals might also fail to realize that the action in question is truly capable of leading to the achievement of that goal.

Discussion Summary

ANNETTE KLEINFELD

Paper discussed:
KIICHIRO YAGI: Carl Menger and the Historicism in Economics
RAIMONDO CUBEDDU: The 'Irrelevance' of Ethics for the Austrian School

The first part of the discussion dealt with Carl Menger's theory of social development. It was questioned if Menger himself had assumed organic origins of socialist institutions, as it was said in the paper, instead of simply pragmatic ones. Starting from the necessary differenciation between a teleological and a genetical aspect of developmental theory, it was stated that Menger is in favor of the latter, though not in an evolutionistic sense (CUBEDDU). His genetical approach may not be taken in a literal sense. According to Menger, the real origin of social development is in fact the individual human action. The term "genetic" here is not connected to the process of evolution but refering to a logical process. With regards to this point, Weber disagreed with Menger (YAGI).

However, Menger may not be assigned to the pragmatic tradition: According to him, institutions cannot be traced back to individual goals. This illuminates from Menger's discussion with Savigny about this issue. Menger regards Savigny - unlike himself - as a representative of a naturalistic organism theory with regard to the development of social institutions, which has to be differentiated from a theory refering to natural law. Menger himself can be considered as a kind of "essentialistic realist", which means that he is in search for the approximation of a knowledge of the exact natural law in an Aristotelian sense (CUBEDDU).

This led to a discussion about the relationship between law and ethics. Are unintended results of human action the results of ethics? In what consists the difference between law and ethics (KABELE)? First of all, we have to differentiate between law and right. A coexistence of different religious beliefs and law is possible (CUBEDDU). As we can learn also from Plato, who considers ethics as the preface to the law, ethics and law are not to be understood as forming a contradiction (KOSLOWSKI).

Another line of the discussion dealt with the relationship of Menger to the Austrian and to the Historical School. The question was raised, how the Austrian School could have had the conviction that the market works by the unintended results of human action only. Why did it ignore the question of responsibility for side-effects, i.e. for the unintended outcomes of action, as it was discussed within the scholastic tradition, for instance by the School of Salamanca? Here, the reflection of side-effects was included in the process of rational decision making (KOSLOWSKI).

Unlike the Historical School, Menger was convinced that there are only two relevant factors for the evolution of the rules of the market: the mechanism of the market itself and politics. Ethical reflections or socio-cultural factors are according to him of no influence to the rules of the market. That the problem of side-effects was not reflected like in the School of Salamanca can be explained in the case of Menger by the lack of a catholic background, and thus of an influence by the Aristotelian-Thomistic tradition. As a result of the tendency to reduce ethics to law, the problem of responsibility is either transmitted completely to politics, or it is left to the individual as it is generally the case in liberalism. However, none of the two alternatives alone is able to solve the problem adequately (CUBEDDU).

The irrelevance of ethics for the older Austrian School is quite obvious. What is the position of the representatives of the new Austrian School, like Hayek and von Mises, with regards to this question (AVTONOMOV)? There is a significant difference to the older Austrian School due to a new orientation on liberal values. Individual ethics plays a central role, but is not understood in the Aristotelian sense any more (CUBEDDU).

Concerning the problem of side-effects, it was pointed out that under the conditions of modernity due to organizational and technological developments, the effects of economic activity often are the results of chains of action, which cannot be clearly identified any more as the effects of certain actions, i.e. they cannot be ascribed to certain persons or institutions. This problem of imputation has lead to a new dimension of the question of moral responsibility for side-effects (NOPPENEY). Another problem connected with this is the question of the predictability of the effects of an action carried out on the basis of a certain technology, for instance. Against this background it is often hard to decide whether the outcome of an action or its side-effects could have been foreseen or not. Sometimes, they may be declared as unintended since unpredictable, but had in fact been intended (YAGI).

Defining the side-effects of economic activity in terms of social costs, for instance, presupposes a moral perspective. The question was raised, which person or institution within the economic decision making process defines what social costs are (ACHAM). Besides, is the moral perspective alone sufficient to prevent unintended effects of economic activity, or does this problem not rather require governmental measures and laws? How helpful are the two criteria of moral evaluation mentioned by Cubeddu - generalizability of rules and plausibility - with regards to the problem of side-effects (FURUBOTN)?

Part Five

The Historical School and American and British Economists: John R. Commons, Frank Knight, Alfred Marshall

Chapter 12

The Historicism of John R. Commons's
Legal Foundations of Capitalism

JEFF BIDDLE and WARREN J. SAMUELS

It is widely appreciated that American institutional economics (of the now "old" type) bears a family resemblance to the German, and even the English, historical schools. They share emphases on a broad conception of the economic system, an empirical rather than strictly deductive apriorist approach to knowledge, the importance of institutions, the conduct of case studies, and a deep sense of the historicity of the economic system and of economics as discipline. It is also widely appreciated that, although one can make strong exclusivist cases for rationalism and for empiricism, and for pure deduction and for pure induction, in practice these approaches to knowledge are not mutually exclusive; they are always used in some combination. Facts are always theory-laden and theory is always tied to some perception of facts/phenomena. All this applies to historicism.

The objective of this article is to examine John R. Commons's *Legal Foundations of Capitalism* (all page numbers are to this book) with a view to showing not only its emphases on a broad conception of the economic system, the importance of institutions, and its combination of history and empiricism in a particular case study, but also its particular combination of theory and historical empiricism. In particular we identify both the nature of Commons's combination of historicism and empiricism and the substantive content of his combination of theory and historical empiricism. The latter is important: Too often scholars have limited their cognizance of the work of historical economists to broad themes regarding their historicism and have neglected the substantive content of what the historical economists found and on what basis. This we intend to remedy in the case of Commons's *Legal Foundations of Capitalism*. We start, not conclude, with the recounting of characteristics, as in the second sentence of this article, but then examine the details of the product of Commons's historicism, his analysis of the origins of the modern, capitalist economic system and the processes through which they operated. Part I examines the characteristics of Commons's historicism. Part II examines selected aspects of his substantive historical analysis, his theory of the legal foundations of capitalism.

I. Commons's Historicism

Historicism. Commons was unequivocally historicist if by historicism is meant a focus on both the reality of change and the ongoing processs of *becoming*. For Commons the historicist the meaning of anything resides in its history, its process of becoming what it is at any point in time, and not solely either a generalized ahistorical, ideal type, conception of it or what it is (hypothesized to be) at a point in time. On the one hand, history is seen to be characterized by substantive change; on the other, the status quo is transient. Moreover, for Commons the historicist, the story of anything -- for example, capitalism -- is in the details, especially the continually transformed details, and not in broad, ideological generalizations which both beg the question of details and/or make selective antecedent assumptions as to what they are and/or use generalizations (for example, "capitalism") derived from experience to explain that experience, often as part of the very nature of the object of study.

Finally, for Commons the historicist history was a record of gradual change. Selective perception and ideological valuation could emphasize either the gradualness or the change but both were present. Commons found the gradualness of change of law to be so great and subtle that people, even those most directly affected by it, failed to appreciate how legal terms of long standing were given significantly changed definitions and thereby functioned as both cause and consequence, in a system of cumulative causation, of legal-economic change.

Case-study Approach. Glenn Johnson, the agricultural economist, maintains that there are three kinds of economic research: disciplinary (for example, pure theory), subject-matter, and problem-solving. Most of Commons's work, although it involved theory, was of the subject-matter and problem-solving kind. He typically was interested in particular subjects which were related to particular problems, for example, industrial conditions. worker interests, consumer interests, economic insecurity, public utility prices, and so on. In all these instances Commons's principal mode of research was the case study.

A fundamental element in his conduct of case-study research was historicism. Commons's "method" as he called it was that of "look and see," and what he looked for were the details of a subject and/or problem, and among the details which were important to him were the historical details. For the present state of a topic -- subject or problem -- for him was but a stage or point in an ongoing process of becoming. Case-study work for Commons thus included historical research to determine how we got where we are, as that would reveal both the foundations and details of the present and the mode of change operative in both the past and arguably the present. So it was with his study of the legal foundations of capitalism, a system which emerged through a continuous process of change and was continuing to undergo change in more or less in the same manner. Historical and other empiricism was a hallmark of Commons's case-study approach.

Legal-economic History. In the *Legal Foundations* Commons provides a theory of the origins and foundations -- the emergence and evolution -- of capitalism. It is, as its title informs, a theory which emphasizes the *legal* foundations of capitalism. The analysis is in part historical in character and relies on empirical legal history for its materials. The legal history is combined with theories of social control, social change, and conflict resolution; theories of systemic and institutional organization; a theory of markets, especially of the institutions which form and operate through them; a particular legal-economic model of interpersonal relationships; and a theory of behavior. Altogether Commons presents a theory of the legal-economic nexus as the venue in which all the foregoing meet and which is both a theory of the legal foundations of capitalism and a theory of the economic foundations of law. It cannot be overemphasized that Commons's theory of history focuses on the legal-economic nexus as the arena or process of social change, that is, of history; legal history is given a critical place in total social or socioeconomic history. The law is both influenced by practice and channels economic organization and practice, accomplishing the latter by effectively choosing between alternative customs or modes of organization and practice. The keys for Commons are judicial determinations of public purpose in choosing between parties to litigation, as a mode of transforming property and liberty and forming the legal bases of transactions and going concerns through adopting and changing the working rules.

Critical and Inexorable Importance of Government. Commons makes two overriding points with regard to government, points which he considers historically empirically demonstrated, given that they must be comprehended within the larger model of the legal-economic nexus. One point is the fundamental and inexorable role of government in the creation of the economic system through its generation of institutional details, notably the working rules. That this directly contradicts the dominant individualist and noninterventionist ideology of Western civilization, and appears as statism to some, is understood by Commons. To this Commons basically replies that the ideology misrepresents both the legal history of capitalism and the role of law in apportioning economic relationships. Commons argues that it is not possible meaningfully to comprehend the economy in non- or apolitical terms. The economy is fundamentally what it is because of the uses to which the modern state is put, and those uses are the result of conflict resolution among actors and groups which are largely economic in character. Government is both fundamental and important to the economic system. Commons makes at least two further arguments: first, that law is important in determining which individuals' interest will be protected by government as rights; and second, that individuals operate only within larger social structures and processes in which government and other social control forces operate. Commons also argues that there is no escape from some conception of social or public purpose in choosing between conflicting interests and claims. If one accepts Commons's theory, then most conventional arguments about the economic role of government are either naive or disingenuous, in either case functioning to channel the use of government even when government is explicitly denigrated and minimized. It is no conclusive objection to this that Commons himself had an agenda (discussed below); he attempts both to make his premises explicit and to ground his arguments historically.

The second point is that, given the fundamental systemic role of government, the critical question of policy is decidedly not government versus no government, or minimal government, but legal change of law, which is to say, legal change of the interests protected by law. Commons insists that there is (or if there is not yet, there will be) a law(s) pertaining to all economic relationships and phenomena, such that proposals for policy overwhelmingly represent legal change of law and not the introduction of law into a situation or system in which it hitherto has been absent. These emphases on the critical and inexorable importance of government (law) and legal change are aspects of both Commons's approach to history and his substantive theory of the legal foundations of capitalism.

Value Theory. Given the presence and importance of the working rules which apportion opportunity and regulate interpersonal relationships -- for example, access to and exercise of power --, Commons argues that the most fundamental values and value decisions are not those with regard to the prices of commodities. They are the valuations ensconced within working rules which represent choices between alternative interests and between alternative organizational and power structures. The *Legal Foundations* contains an enormous amount of material illustrating how government, the courts in particular, have made decisions about interests, relations and organizational structures, often through the reformulation of the concepts of property and liberty. He subsequently devoted a great deal of effort to produce a theory of "reasonable value" to a significant extent using the same materials. Of present importance is his identification of the valuation process undertaken by government in general and by the judiciary in particular by which changing values are newly embodied in the working rules as part of the central process of the legal foundations capitalism, an historical process of social construction.

Social Constructionism. Commons argues here one principal and four correlative points. The principal point is that both the polity and the economy as neither given nor transcendental but are worked out through human action. That is to say, both the polity and the economy are artifacts and therefore the product of human social construction. The first correlative point is that the social construction has been a continuous process; it is an historical process of continual reconstruction. The second point comprises a rejection of given undifferentiated transcendent metaphysical absolutes, such as property, freedom, the economy, capitalism, and so on. The third point is his emphasis on the story being in the details. Capitalism as it exists exists in the form generated by the details of human individual and collective action, especially the cumulative product of court decisions and legislation. Apropos of the second and third points, Commons rejects the existence, for example, of property as a generalized category with preexisting content in favor of an understanding that property is the name given to bundles of legal definitions and protections known as rights. In each respect property is not protected by law because it is property but it is property because it -- and not some other interest -- is given legal protection. The fourth point is that, contrary to the retrospective judicial emphasis on past cases, especially on precedent, the fundamental meaning of law is its role in creating the future, its futurity. Central to the exercise of legal discretion is not reliance on precedent, jurisprudential ideology notwithstanding, but judicial selection among alternative lines of precedent.

These views of Commons's are all evident in a famous statement in the *Legal Foundations* in which he refers to certain neglect of the role of the common law in choosing between and standardizing the customs of people that he considered so central to the genesis and evolution of capitalism:

> This oversight of the Physiocrats, of Adam Smith and the classical economists, is explicable in the fact that what they mistook for the order of nature or divine providence was merely the common law silently growing up around them in the decisions of judges who were quietly selecting and standardizing the good customs of the neighborhood and rejecting the bad practices that did not conform to the accepted rules of reason. Legislatures and monarches are dramatic, arbitrary and artificial; courts are commonplace and natural. (pp. 241-242)

Earlier in the book Commons had given, in a different context, an explanation for this:

> Perhaps one of the reasons why judges do not like to discuss questions of policy, or to put a decision in terms upon their views as law-makers, is that the moment you leave the path of merely logical deduction you lose the illusion of certainty which makes legal reasoning seem like mathematics. But the certainty is only an illusion, nevertheless. Views of policy are taught by experience of the interests of life. Those interests are the field of battle. Whatever decisions are made must be

296

against the wishes and opinions of one party, and the distinctions on which they go will be distinctions of degree. (p. 73)

Commons's social constructivism is most directly evident in his interpretations of language, law, and the legal-economic nexus. All three will be discussed in Part II. Apropos of language, for example, Commons rejects any idea of the representational nature of words, considering them matters of signs and symbols as parts of modes of human discourse and communication. The meaning of words is that given by authoritative persons. In the cases of law and the legal-economic nexus, this is particularly and very importantly evident in the alterations made by courts in the meaning of property.

So far as we can see, Commons is silent on the question of the self-referentiability of his ideas. But he seems well aware that he, too, is engaging in constructionism. For example, the model of legal correlatives and opposites produced by W. N. Hohfeld and adopted by Commons, is itself not necessarily representational of reality. On the other hand, he quite obviously believes that, using language, he has in fact identified the critical elements and processes involved in the legal foundations of capitalism. At any rate, the issue seems to be not as practically critical with regard to Commons as it seems to have been in the case of Thorstein Veblen (Samuels 1990). That Commons would have accepted the self-referentiability of his ideas to his own ideas is also suggested by the agenda which he does not hesitate to make explicit.

Commons's social constructivism has two elements in it. One comprises the nondeliberative elements of habit and custom, such that components of the legal foundations of capitalism are reinforced by use. The other is the exercise of deliberative judgment by individual economic actors, including, and analytically most critically, government in the form of legislatures, courts, and administrative agencies. The social construction and reconstruction of the economy is the continuing result of both types of behavior.

It is therefore the case that for Commons the economic system has been transformed in a manner consistent with the principle of unintended and unforeseen consequences, though in a complex and nonideological manner. Individual buyers and sellers and individual litigators were presumably seeking only their own interests (as they have come to know their interests) throughout the centuries during which capitalism was formed and evolved. But actions and decisions were taken which cumulatively resulted in the transformation of late feudalism into capitalism and eventually in the transformation of capitalism itself. Part of this complex process undoubtedly included the behavior and decisions of various actors, especially legislators and judges, motivated by conceptions of the kind of economic system they wanted, at least insofar as the matter arose in connection with the legislation or case presently under consideration. Images of the economic system entered into their decisions both consciously and unconsciously, deliberatively and nondeliberatively. Expressed differently, the forces of social construction generated an "order" through both "spontaneous" or organic modes and deliberative assessment of existing arrangements by legislatures and courts.

Commons's Agenda. Commons was interested in government and in the interrelations between nominally legal and economic processes and activities, that is, in the legal-economic nexus, as a problem in its own right. He early on came to appreciate the driving force, and therefore historically explanatory power, of the legal-economic nexus explicit in the *Legal Foundations*. But if Commons was interested in knowledge of the legal foundations of government as a matter of subject-matter research, he also had a normative objective. That objective was to make an intellectual case for the recognition of labor interests alongside interests historically designated "property." Commons believed that capitalism, in succeeding feudalism, represented not just a transformation of the economic system but an extension of the range of interests given significant legal protection. Protection of the interests of workers -- for example, through protective labor legislation and labor relations legislation enabling them to form and join unions and engage in collective bargaining and peaceable strikes -- were seen by Commons as a continuation of this process of extending the range of interests given legal status and protection.

Commons was motivated by the desire to show that just as land and commodity markets have undergone enormous transformation in their legal foundations, so too have labor markets and, moreover, that it is legitimate to consider contemporary developments as part of that process. The emergence of the labor market was due to the recognition by law of the right of the worker to his own labor. But labor is bought and sold in the market under conditions importantly established by law, that is, the legal foundations of the labor market. And here Commons points to the differential treatment by the courts in the late nineteenth century of corporations and unions. Each represents collective action, but one is abetted and the other hindered by the courts. This is all a matter of legal choice, says Commons, just as it was in the evolution of the corporation itself. The courts have simply chosen the customs of business over those of workers, at least to that date. Law, therefore, is presented as the result of a choice of customs.

Commons juxtaposes the regime of ostensibly "free contract" to that of "industrial government," in which empowered labor, through unions, can participate in the making of decisions in matters of material concern to them. The judiciary must respond to labor claims in terms of liberty and property just as the courts did in the earlier stages of capitalism. Commons thus applauds the adoption of the legal foundations of industrial government. One aspect of this is the restriction on the use of the labor injunction, which did in fact transpire within the next decade.

II. Commons's Historical Analysis of the Legal Foundations of Capitalism

Commons's historical analysis of the legal foundations of capitalism has several elements, comprising the dynamics of legal language: the continuing but declining role of myth and mystification; a general model of legal-economic relationships; accounts of systemic and structural political and economic change; an account of the transformation of private property (already present in the dynamics of legal language) and of legal-economic change in terms of certain "great bargains." These will be considered in turn.

Dynamics of Legal Language. Words embody the meanings which human beings attribute to them. Notwithstanding the static conflict between prescriptive and permissive attitudes toward definitional and other usage, as an empirical matter definitions of words have evolved over the centuries. Words have taken on, that is, been given, new meanings as social organization and practice has changed. Linguistic change has come to be recognized as an important facet of historical analysis.

John R. Commons's *Legal Foundations of Capitalism* contains important analysis of legal, or legal-economic, discourse. Here is found early and remarkably sophisticated attention to considerations of language and of how words, as artifacts, encapsulate changing interpretations of experience and of values -- and have done so as part of the transformation from feudal to capitalist society.

299

Commons adopted a social constructivist and not a representational conception of language. "Words, prices and numbers," he wrote, "are nominal and not real. They are signs and symbols needed for the operation of the working rules. Yet each is the only effective means by which human beings can deal with each other securely and accurately with regard to the things that are real. But each may be insecure and inaccurate" (p. 9). Certain words embody and give effect to theories -- for example, of property, liberty and value -- which are sometimes erected into metaphysical and ontological absolutes, but however held serve as the basis for the formulation and reformulation of rights, duties, etc. And it is out of these processes that both the economic system known as capitalism emerged and evolved and the words given ascriptive meaning.

Commons focuses on the reinterpretation of legal and constitutional terms by the courts, especially the Supreme Court, as a result of which concepts such as property and liberty have been redefined, giving effect to new theories thereof, often inadvertently. Changes in legal semantics thus incorporate more or less subtle but typically important changes in law and therefore in relative rights, opportunities, exposures and immunities. Commons also indicates the privileging of certain specifications of concepts like private property as natural and therefore antecedent to and independent of government, in contrast to the actual process of the human social construction of property as an institution, although those selective privilegings function as part of that process.

Commons, and also Veblen, had a social constructivist (or rhetorical), and not a representational, conception of language. Moreover, the language he uses to discuss language could have been employed today, for it is remarkably close to present-day usage.

Near the end of the book Commons writes, "Ideals are ideas projected into the future by means of symbols" (p. 349). The symbols are for the most part linguistic.

Commons devotes enormous attention to the critical role of legal terms and to the important consequences of changes in their meanings and definitions. He principally emphasizes the growth of the legal definition of property to include incorporeal and intangible property, the transformation of the meaning of property from use-value and exchange-value (and the correlative change from an emphasis on one's own use to others' potential use and the role of withholding). Changes in the legal definition of property were a function of changes in judicial theories of property and liberty, all involving words with socioeconomic consequences. He writes that "when property began to yield exchange-value as well as use-value, the term 'uses' was simply enlarged by the courts to include it" (p. 113). "[M]odern business is conducted and ... American legislatures, executives and inferior courts are held in conformity to the Constitution of the United States ... as latterly interpreted by the Supreme Court ..." (p. 7). Commons indicates the process and results of selectively privileging certain specifications of property and other terms (such as the police power, pp. 35-36) as natural and therefore antecedent to and independent of government, in contrast to the actual process of the human social construction of property utilizing language.

Commons is thus a social constructivist with regard to jurisprudence as well as language, that is, the language and meanings of law. Changes in definition are in part the means whereby both legislature and, especially, the courts can legislate; such changes in definition, Commons writes, "are of course not arbitrary. They spring from new conditions. Yet they are discretionary" (p. 356). Legal change for Commons is more than a matter of changing conditions; it is also a matter of changed perceptions and evaluations of experience, for example, changes in which/whose customs the courts will embody in law and enforce on others, and so on. Changing definitions can arise from new conditions but conditions can be variably experienced and evaluated, depending upon purposes and values, so that even new conditions can be variably interpreted and lead to different changes in language or no change. All this is central to the social reconstruction of reality.

As seen above, Commons rejects the "illusion of certainty" -- given. for example, by natural law and natural rights doctrines -- which "gives rise to metaphysical 'entities' and 'substances' conceived as existing apart from and independent of the behavior of officials and citizens ... . These illusions naturally arise," he says, "from the hopes and fears of mankind which substitute wishes for behavior. We conceive that what we wish is the reality, the real thing. Thus rights and duties also, like the state, are given the illusion of a reality existing apart from the conduct of officials" (pp. 124, 125). Commons's point is that "The state is what its officials do" (p. 122). "Legal rights and duties are none other than the probability that officials will act in a certain way respecting the claims that citizens make against each other" (p. 125).

This is all empirical rather than metaphysical or mythic, though Commons is obviously aware of the use of such ideas for legitimation and psychic balm. He emphasizes that preconceived absolutes have been revised through the device of changing the definitions of terms. These changing definitions revised the mode of discourse, and therefore perception, and permit both (1) adjustment to and revision of the socially constructed reality and (2) psychic balm, a sense of the predetermined to accompany the reality of change:

> A change in definitions is such a simple and natural way of changing the constitution from what it is to what it ought to be, and the method is so universal and usually so gradual in all walks of life, that the will of God, or the will of the People, or the Corporate will, scarcely realizes what has happened. The method is, indeed, that common sense device whereby man can go on believing in unchanging entities, and yet be practical. (p. 373)

Commons's total model of legal-economic change is vast and complex. Part of it amounts to the dualism that generalized perceptions of legal-economic reality (for present purposes, Thomas Kuhn's "paradigm") influence behavior and policy and thereby the social construction of reality, through language, and, also through language, are the result of changes in the social construction of reality.

Commons's historicism thus includes, as a central theme, the evolution of the subjective and variable but ostensibly representational language in terms of which people have approached and changed the law and thereby the foundations of the economic system.

The Continuing but Declining Role of Myth and Mystification. The converse of Commons's social constructionism is his identification and substantive rejection of mystification and myth making. Commons is aware of such roles of mythology as absolutist legitimation and psychic balm. He understands that the processes of mystification and myth making do exist within the larger array of total social processes. But he is unwilling to accept the myths on their own terms as either descriptive or explanatory of legal-economic phenomena; moreover, he believes that their historical significance is diminishing. This is a development which he considers to be laudatory, inasmuch as he both recognizes and accepts the substitution of rationalism for irrationalism, deliberative for nondeliberative decision making, Enlightenment for feudal values, and open democratic for narrow/closed feudal decision making.

Commons emphasizes that the concept of good or bad economy, meaning good or bad proportioning of opportunities, is so self-evident and so continually present that it "has often been either taken for granted or erected as an entity existing outside or above the parts" (p. 2). Rejecting the erection of the habitual and customary into something transcendental, metaphysical and mythical, Commons stresses, as did (for example) secularism, utilitarianism and pragmatism before him, that

> a mark of the progress that has occurred in economic theory, from the time of Quesnay and Adam Smith, has been the emergence of the concept of good or bad political economy out of mythical entities such as nature's harmony, natural law, natural order, natural rights, divine providence, over-soul, invisible hand, social will, social-labor power, social value, tendency towards equilibrium of forces, and the like, into its proper place as the good or bad, right or wrong, wise or unwise proportioning by man himself of those human faculties and natural resources which are limited in supply and complementary to each other. (p. 2)

Commons thus calls attention to and rejects the privileging of certain specifications of private property as natural and therefore antecedent and independent of government -- in contrast to the actual process of the human social construction of property.

This position undergirds, as has been indicated above, one of Commons's central points regarding the legal foundations of capitalism and their ongoing revision, the "illusion of certainty."

Commons often returns to his theme distinguishing mechanical transcendental explanations from those involving the exercise of human choice. While of historical origin, the working rules of going concerns have

> been ascribed to many different sources, such as gods, ancestors, conquerors, "nature," "will of the people," etc., the general idea being to clothe them with a certain sanctity or authority above that of the particular [conflict resolver, e.g., priest, chieftain, judge]. (p. 68)

> We have noticed [he says] the interesting contrast [he says] that while the economists, since the latter half of the eighteenth century, have been constructing theories of value out of man's relation to nature in the form of commodities and feelings, the courts have been constructing theories of value out of the approved and disapproved transactions of man with man in the form of goodwill and privilege. These processes of valuation are inseparable, but they belong to different orders of thought. (p. 203)

303

The nub of the matter has to do with legal change of law, especially changing the working rules:

> A working rule, in other words, is a social process and not a metaphysical entity, a more or less flexible process of acts, transactions and attitudes; yet with a discernible trend; and it is this trend that may be abstracted in thought and formulated in words as a statement of the rule in question. (p. 141)

One aspect of the use of mythology is to create arguably false or presumptuous disjunctions between determinism and free will; between legislature, executive and judiciary in the exercise of governance; and between normative and positive, or between subjective and objective. In an interesting and important example of how majority and minority opinions in a court decision approached the question of reasonable rates for a railroad, both positions attempting to constrain administrative discretion but differing in recognizing the range of discretion (pp. 357-359), Commons says that

> Probably these metaphysical and mechanistic conclusions are required in order to conform to the Eighteenth Century attempt both to separate government into legislative, judicial and executive branches and to separate the human will into will, intellect and action. They tend to preserve the primitive notions of a complete dualism of the objective and subjective world. The objective world is the world of facts, the subjective is the world of feelings, emotions, caprice. (p. 359)

Commons establishes his position by quoting a law-review author concerning delusion through the illusion that, in such matters, "there is a fact which can be discovered if we are only persistent enough in our search for it, and which, once it is found, will provide a mathematical solution of all rate-making problems" (p. 359). In "reality," says Commons, "facts are facts as our habits, investigations and purposes deem them to be facts" (p. 359).

The basic argument is reiterated in his rejection of the existence of transcendental rights. Commons both rejects and explains

> the metaphysical notion that there exists somewhere an objective world of rights and duties superior to the actual rights and duties, ... [which] goes along with the metaphysical notion that there is somewhere an entity "the state" apart from the officials who determine and execute the will of that state. These metaphysical notions have, indeed, a powerful influence on men's minds, simply because man lives in the future but acts in the present. Thus constituted, he projects

outward into a world of ideas his hopes and fears, and gives to his expectations a local habitation and a name.

Yet these ideas are but ideals -- they exist, but they exist in the mind. They exist because man craves security for his expectations, and could not act at all as a rational being without the feeling of security .... When his rational expectations are gone the savage in him takes possession. No wonder he fills the sky with deities and entities -- they are his hopes.

But the real world of rights and duties about him is the collective will expressed in working rules necessitated by the scarcity of resources. His "freedom" is his power to command the officials according to those rules, who are both the instruments of that will and the actors who determine what that will shall be when it acts. They, too, like him, move toward their habits and ideals, and respond, according to those habits and ideals, to his call for help, if needed. To that extent he enjoys "freedom" as well as liberty, for he has the aid of collective power to give effect to his will. (p. 364)

But Commons is wary about reifying the idea of a collective will -- which he himself uses to refer to processes of collective decision making, not a transcendent operating entity or force. With regard to two modes of discourse which tend, in his view, to be more aprioristic and mythological than empirical, Commons calls attention to

certain ontological mysteries which attend notions of a collective will, springing from that twofold weakness of the human mind which creates abstract images endowed with souls and identifies what *ought* to be with what *is* ... .

Generally, it will be found that what is intended is that sovereignty *ought* to be the Will of God or the Will of the People, and this idea is expressed as an entity living apart from the actual state which evidently does not meet that ideal; or that the corporate will *ought* to be a human soul but is a bloodless entity different from the human beings who act in its name. (p. 371).

Evidently Commons was motivated to make these remarks, and comparable remarks found elsewhere in the book, by two things: first, his adoption of an objective (non-normative) and non-teleological model of legal-economic organization and evolution; and second, by his perception that most other people are operating within the three standpoints in subjective and normative, indeed typically highly charged, terms. Commons's quite different approach is evident in his historical and empirical analyses of the legal foundations of the economic system and its (the system's) problematic ontological and epistemological status.

Commons acknowledges the social role of "these ontological mysteries," in a manner reminiscent of Vilfredo Pareto's principle of the social utility of falsity. Commons writes:

> the mystery is so far removed from the actual that it can accommodate all kinds of wishes without being discovered. In this way these mysteries have a certain pragmatic value, for, in the name of God, or the People, or the Corporate will, the particular official or agent can do many things which he would not do in his own name. He can always say that he has no discretion in the matter, and that, while as an individual he would do differently, yet etc., etc. (p. 372)

This perception by participants "undoubtedly has a degree of accuracy," says Commons. But changes occur, often with great difficulty in overcoming the mysteries, after "the ontological mystery is partly dissolved, and it is seen that the will of the concern is what the concern does, and what the concern does is what its functionaries do" (p. 372). Commons takes such an empirical and secular approach not only with regard to going concerns but in his treatment of the formation and operation of the working rules and in other respects as well.

Commons also examines the practice of these ontological mysteries in the face of new varieties of facts. These predetermined absolutes have been revised through the device of changing the definitions of such terms as property and liberty by a court which "enjoyed a degree of immunity, ... no superior authority that could prevent the change in definitions, or give to that change a different slant." These changing definitions revise the mode of discourse and both permit both (1) adjustment to and revision of the socially constructed reality and (2) psychic balm, a sense of the predetermined to accompany the reality of change. One pertinent statement, quoted above, is worth repeating:

> A change in definitions is such a simple and natural way of changing the constitution from what it is to what it ought to be, and the method is so universal and usually so gradual in all walks of life, that the will of God, or the will of the People, or the Corporate will, scarcely realizes what has happened. The method is, indeed, that com-

mon-sense device whereby man can go on believing in unchanging entities, and yet be practical. (p. 373)

General Model of Legal-Economic Relationships. From the foregoing discussions of language and myth, presented largely in Commons's own words, one can readily sense the gradualness, the complexity and the indirection of historical change. The play of the principle of unintended and unforeseen consequences is evident, though not in a Whiggish manner; history is the history of gradual change, with the emphasis equally on both its gradualness and the fact of change. Part of the story is the evolution of the substantive content adduced to words and the predication of action, belief and policy on one myth or another, on one socially constructed conception or another. These are important parts of Commons's historical analysis of the legal foundations of capitalism, centering on the ideological, metaphysical and discursive (rhetorical) elements incorporated in legal theory and legal (judicial and legislative) decision making and their systemic and structural consequences -- in all facets of which are evident gradualness, complexity and indirection, not least in his general model of legal-economic relationships.

Commons's general model has several elements, which may be identified and summarized as follows:

1. a legal-economic nexus in which nominally economic and nominally legal (political, governmental) activities are not only mutually determinative and interactive but, especially, co-evolve from a common set of sources

2. a model of economic relationships grounded in legal relationships, ultimately in terms of rights, powers, duties, opportunities, liabilities, exposures, and immunities

3. these relationships are the foundation, the changing foundation, of transactions and of going concerns, the former being for Commons the fundamental unit of analysis and the latter the embodiment of organizational, structural and change variables

4. conflicts between claims of relative rights and of power and immunity, etc., historically have involved an inexorable necessity of choice, typically by courts, of which/whose custom will prevail

5. also inexorably involved are determinations of public purpose, on the basis of which effective choices between conflicting claims of right, etc. are made

6. determinations of public purpose are embodied in the working rules of law, which, among other things, govern the distribution, access to, and use of power among economic actors
7. the working rules apportion power within the nominally private sphere, within the nominally public or governmental sphere, and between the two spheres
8. other forms of working rules exist, including those formulated within organizations, such as businesses, albeit always within the zone of authorized discretion permitted by the external working rules, especially those of law
9. combining recognition of both the variety of forms of working rules and the diffusion of power within the economy, the economy is seen as a system of power and therefore of combined private and public governance, each selectively perceived and each given its selective discursive and symbolic (mythic) expression and rationalization, but together constituting the total legal-economic nexus
10. historical change within this system is brought about or driven by changing practices, changing beliefs, changing values, and so on, especially as ensconced within changing theories of law, property and liberty
11. the crux of historical change is the legal change of law, that is, the legal change of the interests given legal definition and protection, epitomized in the historical transformation of property

In summary, Commons's treatment of history involves the identification of the legal-economic nexus, from which emanates the polity and the economy, as the core set of institutions and activities which are the agents of systemic and structural change. This history has taken some four hundred and more years and has encompassed the transformations of the political system from monarchy to representative government and of the economic system from feudal to commercial, industrial and financial activity, but especially, for Commons, the establishment of new types of property.

Systemic Political and Economic Change. A central thread of historical change for Commons was the transformations and inversions of legal/political organization and concepts. What had originally been monarchical prerogative became transformed and constrained during the rise of republican, or representative, government; from autocratic monarchy came the modern state. What had initially been legal privileges of the aristocracy under Magna

Carta were later reinterpreted, selectively, into common rights. Correlative with the transformation of government from feudal to modern was the transformation of the economy from feudal to commercial/capitalist.

Government and economy became decreasingly the domain of the landed aristocracy; the middle class, the business man, came to share in the power of government and it was the customs and power of business which came to dominate both law and economy. The new state embodied a new set of working rules, the new always a compromise with the old. Government increasingly became both in fact and in contemplation a collective bargaining process, a representative rather than a participatory parliament, a mixture of legislative, executive and judicial law making, a system of delegation of state authority to officials, and the performance of official responsibilities.

What had been the combination of "property" and sovereignty that constituted feudalism -- lords and their subjects -- now became free citizens and their government. Commons recounts the initial predominance of more or less absolute monarchs with their royal prerogatives; the emergence of royal courts and courts at the levels of the lower aristocracy; conflicts between monarch and lesser nobility, between monarch and courts, and between monarchical and other courts; and the growth of the common law of free men arising from the use of their customs and beliefs in the resolution of local inter-party conflicts.

This historical story can be understood as several stages of the Anglo-American economic system represented by different systems of law and government. But both economy and polity coevolve: The changing system and structure of government led to systemic and structural economic change, and changing economic change led to changing political change.

The Transformation of Private Property: The "Great Bargains." Commons portrays a broad, complex and deep series of transformations of English society and does so in terms of the transformation of property through the emergence of several bargains. One was the rent bargain, the origin of modern private property in land, with an enormous social and economic diminution of the rights of feudal landlords (the name "landlord" *is* significant) correlative with the growth of fee simple property ownership of land. Here the landlords kept their physical land but with greatly reduced social and economic power, or rights.

Another was the price bargain, with the monarchy and feudal lords retaining their physical landed property (diminished as just described) but now, along with the gilds, having relatively negligible control over private economic activity in an economy of free people and not subjects and serfs, etc. In a correlative bargain, the landed aristocracy, including the monarch, would retain their physical land but lose much of their control over government and its policy. Governments were increasingly in the hands of both a parliament (representative government), in whose operation the business or middle class predominated, and courts whose judges were increasingly amenable to recognizing and protecting the interests of the middle class.

Eventually the interests of the landed and nonlanded (capitalist) property owners were challenged by the working class, and another bargain was worked out: the owners of property retained their physical property and many of the rights associated therewith but now had, through the extension of the franchise and the resulting greater responsiveness of elected politicians to worker interests, to increasingly share the goals of government policy with a wider range of interests. One result was the formation of what has been called the Welfare State, meaning thereby the passage of legislation and programs promotive of the interests of workers and others in a manner comparable in substance though not in name to the promotion through property rights of the interests of those who came to own property. Another result was the growth of a system of industrial governance, centering on the rise and increasing legal recognition of labor unions. All of this took centuries, the negotiation, as it were, over the Welfare State and labor unions continuing to the present day.

No wonder that Commons believed that modern government was a "collective bargaining state." Government was the arena in which these bargains (solutions) were worked out.

In the feudal rent bargain "no distinction was made between ownership and government. The King was both landlord and sovereign. So with the barons and subbarons. Each was both landlord and a combined legislature, executive and chief justice of his baronial estate." The rent-bargain, therefore, "was two-fold, economic and governmental. One was rent, the other was taxes" (p. 219; the use of the term "taxes" in somewhat anachronistic -- he notes that the two were "[a]s yet undifferentiated" -- but it clearly points to the umbilical relation between private, in contrast with feudal, property).

Commons traces a 450-year evolution of private property in land, through a revised rent bargain. This evolution involves several strands, together constitutive of the complex transformation from feudalism to capitalism. The strands included: changing the foundations of society "from bargains in terms of use-values to bargains in terms of exchange values" (p. 224); the elimination of private baronial courts and armies; the monetization of feudal obligations; escape from unilateral monarchical setting of rents and related obligations in various forms; and the creation of "an agricultural commonwealth" in replacement of baronial fiefdoms (p. 224). The details of the story vary as between different hitherto subordinate groups.

The monetization of feudal obligations was deeply significant, a critical part of the formation of modern private property. Taxes became relatively definite, established collectively by the monarch and representatives of the tax payers, rather than an indefinite duty to pay rent in commodities and services determined at the whim of the monarch. The commutation of physical rents into money-rents in the form of taxes meant that they "are not something taken from private property by the sovereign, but property is sovereignty taken collectively from the King by his tenants. The result was that pecuniary taxes became the governmental rent of land, and landed property became assimilated to the law of business freedom and security, so that, eventually, like movables, it could be bought and sold in expectation of its money values" (p. 221). In this interpretation, land taxation represents, therefore, not an exaction by the monarch but the payment of funds by owners of private property in amounts and for purposes collectively determined through representative government. The alternative historically was not the absence of taxes but feudal dues.

Capitalism represented a new system of transactions and a new system of opportunities, a new way of living; all this is included in what Commons refers to as the price bargain. Commons traces the decline of the monopolistic and governmental features of franchises granted as privileges by monarches seeking gain and advantages from their recipients. Just as baronial control of land was replaced by private property in land, the collective control of economic activity enjoyed by the gilds was replaced by relatively free and open markets.

Commons insists that the gilds, for all their collective control and practice of what he calls Defensive Capitalism, represented the origins of capitalism. The reason is that the gilds had been given power relative to and immune from the power of the feudal landlords.

> The gilds ... grew in wealth and power. Their defensive privileges became exclusive privileges in proportion as markets and commerce advanced over militarism and agriculture and increasing numbers of peo-

ple depended on buying and selling for a living, where formerly they depended on command and obedience. (p. 226)

When the gilds were dispossessed of their controls over economic activity, the immunity from feudal superiors (who were already being weakened in other respects) continued but was now enjoyed by individual economic agents. Thus the creation of free economic actors took two step: immunity from the feudal lords, then abolition of the gild power which had been juxtaposed to the feudal lords. A similar process occurred in the cities with regard to both political and economic rights.

Commons articulates the "basic principle of the commonwealth," created by a combination of practice, judicial decision, and governmental reforms, as follows:

> Let any person get rich in so far as he enriches the commonwealth, but not in so far as he merely extracts private wealth from the commonwealth. (p. 227)

Later, economic theory and judicial temperament would demonstrate to any objective observer how complex and subjective is the distinction between enrichment and extraction and the conditions under which legislatures *cum* courts could/would "intervene." At the extreme the idea of Pareto optimality would assert that any trade was *ipso facto* beneficial to both parties and *therefore* to the commonwealth (society). But the principle stated by Commons was a manifestation of a great transformation of socio-legal philosophy, one both reflecting and reinforcing the practices and mind-set of a growing capitalism.

The businessman was now in a more legally secure and opportune position:

> The business man now, like the Yeoman and copyholders, could have his customs inquired into by the King's justices, and his rights and privileges asserted against private jurisdiction of both gilds and barons. (p. 228)

Eventually, equally important both historically and analytically,

> Capitalism entered upon its offensive stage, intent on controlling the government whose aid it had petitioned during its defensive period. Eventually its petitions became its rights. (pp. 228-229)

There emerged, then, the common law courts "willing and able to convert their [the businessmen's] customary bargains into a common law of property and liberty" (p. 229).

Apropos of the wage bargain, Commons traces the conceptual origins and certain nuances of the right of a worker in his own labor and to choose a calling. He examines U.S. cases dealing with efforts to protect labor interests, especially protective labor legislation (wages, hours and working conditions) and legislation protecting the right to unionize and strike.

Commons critiques the majority opinions in these cases using his model of liberty, duty, etc. Commons had used this model to affirm the sensibleness of the reasoning used by courts in working out the legal foundations of capitalism in a manner consonant with business interests relative to those of monarches. Now he uses that model to show how labor and business interests are treated quite differently, even though the model suggests they are analytically equivalent. The difference, says Commons, is that "the preference is given by the court to that association of persons deemed to be of the greater public importance" (p. 298). Apropos of such premises of courts, he also writes that such reasoning is not a matter of logic but "a matter of beliefs and this belief is none other than the habitual wish of the judge who decides and who … can always find precedents and logic to back up what he wishes. It is the judge who believes in the law and custom of business and not the judge who believes in the law and custom of labor, that decides" (p. 298). Thus, the corporation, which as he explains was the "child of privilege [,] has now become a privileged association of men" (p. 293)

Of interest also is Commons's statement regarding legal selectivity in a cognate matter:

> The meaning of a corporation, like the meaning of property and liberty, has been changing during decades and centuries, and when a corporation appears in court it takes on a variety of shapes derived from different parts of its history. It is not a citizen within the meaning of the Federal Constitution but is a "person" within the meaning of the Fourteenth Amendment. At one time it appears to be an *association* of persons, at another time *a person*; at one time it is an independent existence separate from its members, at another a dummy concealing the acts of its stockholders. At one time it is a fiction existing only in contemplation of law and limited strictly to the powers granted in the act that created it; at another it is a set of transactions giving rise to obligations not authorized expressly by the charter but read into it by operation of law. (p. 291)

Judicial participation in the social construction of the economy does not need to, perhaps cannot, treat all interests equally in all matters. Where interests conflict, the courts must make a choice. A bourgeois economy will be supported by bourgeois law produced by bourgeois judges unless and until judges come to have different preconceptions and preferences (which does not mean that there cannot be different versions of bourgeois law, but that is not the present point). There will be one or another set of the legal foundations of capitalism. As Commons sees it, the law will absorb one set of customs or another; in these cases, either the customs of business or those of labor. (Commons is aware that each set of customs is itself an artifact and has changed over time. But the conflicts between the two sets of customs were conflicts over power, with government inexorably being used to support one interest or the other when in conflict.) The important underlying theme is that courts have chosen the customs of business over those of labor.

Commons contrasts two theories of law, one maintaining that law is *made* by the command of a superior, the other holding that law is *found* in the customs of the people. Commons's analysis effectively rejects the conventional juxtaposition. He argues that courts make law by choosing between the customs of different groups of people and in that way "reconstruct society" (p. 299). Commons writes that

> Customs are, indeed, the raw material out of which justice is constructed. But customs differ, customs change, customs are good and bad, and customs conflict. They are uncertain, complex, contradictory, and confusing. A choice must be made. Somebody must choose which customs to authorize and which to condemn or let alone .... Somebody must choose between customs. Whoever chooses is the lawgiver. (pp. 299-300)

The choices are continually being made and the law is continually changed, sometimes by fiction, sometimes "by new meanings for old words" (p. 301). There is the "conflict, choice and survival of customs, according to the changing political, economic and cultural conditions and governments" (p. 302).

As for business and labor, "The customs of labor and of labor organizations are as different from the customs of business, as the customs of business were different from the customs of feudal agriculture" (p. 301). The courts have viewed labor contracts in much the same theoretical way that they have viewed commodity and other contracts but, says Commons, the relevant practices are different (pp. 302-303). This is particularly the case

314

when it comes to collective action by workers in the form of unions. The point is that "the courts do not comprehend and sanction" the customs of unions, any more than do the capitalists" (p. 305). This is particularly the case with regard to

> what may be distinguished as the common law of labor springing from the customs of wage earners, as distinguished from that historic common law springing from the customs of merchants and manufacturers, [the former of which] consists in those practices by which laborers endeavor to achieve their ideas through protection against the economic power of employers. (p. 304)

Law is a choice between customs, ergo a choice between different psychologies and between different interests.

Commons juxtaposes the business conception of free contract -- which for businessmen permits the exercise of superior economic coercion, taken to be the natural state of things -- to the system of "industrial government" in which labor interests are given protection against their "traditional" exposures.

In Commons's view, history repeats itself in a new context. The conservative courts have responded to "the demand for new definitions of liberty and power on the part of the aggressive laborers," thereby taking "over the protection of the liberty and power of business, just as the prerogative courts protected the privileges of the monarch and his party ... . The prerogative today is the prerogative of business, and the common law of today seeking recognition is the customs of propertyless laborers developing in their own assemblies and industrial courts" (p. 307).

Commons identifies both the process and the results of the continued evolution of law, with which he deeply concurs:

> A common law of labor is constructed by selecting the reasonable practices and rejecting the bad practices of labor, and by depriving both unions and management of arbitrary power over the job. An amendment is gradually worked into the constitution of industrial government: "No employer shall deprive any employee of his job without due process of industrial law, nor deny to any employee within his jurisdiction the equal protection of the common law of labor." ... Out of the wage-bargain a constitution for industrial government is being constructed by removing cases from the prerogative of management and the arbitrary power of unions and subjecting the foremen, the su-

perintendents and the business agents to the same due process of law as that which governs the laborers. (p. 312)

As an example, Commons examines the labor injunction and the correlative problem of whether policy is to be made by the legislature or the courts, in both regards the questions of legal recognition of relative coercive power and of which interest is to prevail inevitably arise.

Subsequent legislation and court decisions within the next dozen or so years after 1924 were to further the promotion of labor interests, and the reconstruction of industrial government which Commons identified and applauded. Apropos of the wage bargain, as in the case of the rent and price bargains, Commons has both identified some of the legal foundations of an evolving capitalism as it came to exist and provided an intellectual legal-economic foundation for its further revision.

Reviewing the foregoing, it is understandable that Commons could at different junctures of his analysis emphasize, implicitly or explicitly, different factors as historically critical. Certainly the co-evolution of rent, price and wage bargains constitutes such an emphasis. So too does the legal-economic nexus of capitalism. At one point Commons focuses on the

> reproportioning [that] has kept on according to the purposes of those who controlled the governments. Not Adam Smith but William the Conqueror was the founder of Anglo-American political economy. Adam Smith started the theory, but William started the economy. Nor did Smith start the whole of the theory." (p. 324)

-- here Commons points to the work of legal theorists and judges, and again emphasizes the evolving separation of public purpose from the private purposes of the sovereign, which is to say, the evolution of the fields of property and sovereignty.

Also, at many points Commons stresses as critical the transformation of the substantive content of the legal definition of property, especially the enlargement of property beyond use-value to exchange value, which encompasses the addtion of incorporeal and intangible property, so that "the meaning of property and liberty spreads out from the expected uses of production and consumption to expected transactions on the markets where one's assets and liabilities are determined by the ups and downs of prices" (p. 21).

Thus Commons refers to the Act of Settlement which significantly revised the relationship of King to all other citizens (see pp. 50, 104), saying that

> This situation, consummated by the Act of Settlement in 1700, is the culmination of the business revolution and the origin of modern capitalism. (p. 106)

The reason for this is that "property was finally separated from sovereignty; not only for the King, but also for all other citizens" (p. 104).

Along a different line, Commons refers to certain "substantive powers and remedial powers" to which

> modern capitalism owes its powers of expansion, for it is they that enable the business man who is citizen of a great enduring nation to extend his sway ...; that endow him with power to breathe into his going business the immortality of a corporation. (p. 121)

Along a still different line, it has been noticed above that Commons found the gild, as the initial form of capitalism, to have constituted the origins of capitalism. Commons's treatment of bank credit and negotiable instruments and therefore of money and capital markets constitutes another emphasis thereon as the source of capitalism as we know it.

That Commons could effectively stress so many different sources of capitalism is due to both the complexity of capitalism as an historical phenomenon and his use of a certain discursive or rhetorical mode of emphasis.

But equally significant is Commons's emphasis on *process*. Thus he writes that

> A working rule ... is a social process and not a metaphysical entity, a more or less flexible process of acts, transactions and attitudes; yet with a discernible trend; and it is this trend that may be abstracted in thought and formulated in words as a statement of the rule in question. (p. 141)

Similarly, he writes that "[t]he government is not a thing, it is a process according to definite rules" which are subject to change; it is a "going business" (p. 150). Both examples of his identification of process underscore Commons's sense and stress on historicity.

III. Conclusion

For John R. Commons, people are living, breathing and acting agents; not merely passive responders to stimuli, whether they be prices or anything else. For him, too, the economy is a process of life, and neither a given nor a passive mechanism. Systemic, structural, processual, and other change is the result of both nondeliberative and deliberative forces and processes. History does not merely evolve; it is made in a process of social construction and re-construction of society though the interaction and aggregation of acts both nominally private and public and both nominally legal/governmental and economic. The heart of that process in one respect are the actions of people in the ordinary business of life, making a living (in the terminology of Alfred Marshall). Another, and for Commons the most critical respect, is the legal-economic nexus. This nexus represents the arena in which the polity and the economy are worked and reworked out. Therein are the multiplicity of actions and interpersonal relations and conflicts which give rise to the need for deliberative working rules and which lead to their production by litigation and by lobbying/legislation. All of this constitutes the substance of Commons's analysis of the economy as a set of phenomena that are not just *is* (*being*) at a point in time but is *becoming*. The legal-economic nexus is the critical domain of this process of transformation. It is the centerpiece of Commons's historicism.

References

COMMONS, JOHN R.: *Legal Foundations of Capitalism*, New York (Macmillan) 1924.

SAMUELS, WARREN J.: "The Self-Referentiability of Thorstein Veblen's Theory of the Preconceptions of Economic Science", *Journal of Economic Issues*, 24 (September 1990), pp. 695-718.

Chapter 13

Frank Knight and the Historical School[*]

CLAUS NOPPENEY

I. Introduction and Summary

The present paper is concerned with Frank H. Knight (1885-1972) and his attitude towards the historical school of economics[1]. It is argued that Knight paid attention to the historical school during his whole life and struggled to develop his own historical framework. The paper falls into five sections. Following this overview the second section recalls the conventional view that there is no real relation between Knight and the historical school; Knight is introduced as a stranger to the historical school. In contrast to this textbook

* Special thanks to Ross B. Emmett and Stephen A. Marglin for extensive discussions of and comments on earlier drafts. Thanks also to Klaus Rathe, the participants at the Political Economy Seminar at Harvard University and the Kress Seminar on the History of Economic Thought. This article is based upon work supported by the Schweizerischer Nationalfonds.

1   The term "historical school" refers to the German historical school. Using the term "historism", I refer to the broader phenomenon in intellectual history including among others American institutionalism.

version the following passages analyze Knight's way of thinking in three steps. His extensive commentaries on the historical school and their protagonists are discussed in the third section. Focusing on Knight as a promoter of Max Weber, the fourth section examines Knight's role in the dissemination of German social thought into the Anglo-American context. Moreover, Weber is identified as a crucial influence on Knight. Comparing his notion of ideal competition with Weberian ideas it is shown how close his critical stand on the ethical consequences of ideal competition is to the dominant figure of the younger historical school. The fifth section aims at a reconstruction of a historical dimension in Knight's economic methodology. The final conclusion reflects on the gap between Knight as a stranger to the historical school and his efforts to develop a historical framework of his own. It tries to understand the obvious tensions in Knight's work from different angles and considers why Knight finally remained reluctant to convert to the historical school.

II. Frank Knight as a Stranger to the Historical School

To a historian of economics, the pursuit of this paper might seem rather obscure since Knight was never affiliated with the development of the historical school. Rather, the stories ascribed to Knight in the textbooks, dictionaries and encyclopedias might even suggest that he was an outspoken, or at least tacit, opponent of the historical school.

Knight pursued his education through a series of schools and small colleges in the Midwest and Tennessee. In 1913 he finally began graduate work at Cornell University in philosophy, and then, a year later transferred to the economics department. Thus, Knight belongs to the first generation of American economists who were trained in American universities, but whose teachers were mostly trained in Germany. Among Knight's teachers were Allyn Young, Alvin Johnson and A.P. Usher. His dissertation, which later became the classic *Risk, Uncertainty and Profit* (1921), is regarded as the "definitive statement of the emerging neoclassical concept of perfect competition".[2] Fol-

---

2   STIGLER (1956), p. 270.

lowing academic appointments at Cornell, the University of Chicago and the University of Iowa Knight finally succeeded John Maurice Clark at Chicago in 1927, where he taught until 1958 and remained for the rest of his life. Scholars as varied as Gary S. Becker, Kenneth E. Boulding, James M. Buchanan, Edward Chamberlin, Milton Friedman, Donald Patinkin, Paul A. Samuelson, Henry Simons, George J. Stigler were at some time students of Knight, and it is generally agreed that Knight was a dominant intellectual influence upon economics students at Chicago in the 1930s and 40s. Together with Jacob Viner and Henry Simons, Knight is often regarded as one of leading figures in the foundation of the Chicago school of economics.

When Carl Menger's *Grundsätze* appeared in an English translation in 1950, Knight wrote the introduction and presents this ardent opponent of the younger historical school as someone "known to every student of economics" and as "one of the pioneers of the modern theory of 'utility'".[3] As Knight remarks, the "everlasting credit and renown of Menger" comprises the extension of the utility principle in two directions: "in the field of *complementary* goods and in that of *indirect* goods".[4] Contributing to the dissemination of Carl Menger's thought, Knight gains a strong reputation as a non-adherent to the historical school.

Finally, also the archives provide only very few hints at exchange or interaction between Knight and followers of the historical school.[5] Therefore it is no wonder that the relationship between Knight and the historical school has been widely neglected in the literature. While we might thus be inclined to cease further consideration and assume a mutual disinterest between the two poles, the present paper focuses on a more subtle relationship between Knight and the historical school.

---

3 KNIGHT (1950), p. 10.
4 KNIGHT (1950), p. 15.
5 The only exception is a little correpondence with Carl Brinkmann, a former student of Gustav Schmoller. In 1936 Brinkmann offered Knight a honorary doctorate of the University of Heidelberg. Referring to the "present state of political opinion" Knight declined this offer.

CLAUS NOPPENEY

III. Frank Knight as a Commentator on the Historical School

After almost ten years at Chicago, Knight recalls in a letter to Talcott Parsons the reasons for having originally moved to this particular university: "I came to Chicago expecting this 'institutionalism' to be my main field of work. But Viner went to Geneva two different years, leaving me the main course in theory."[6] This autobiographical remark shows that Knight (at least in his own retrospect) started out with a strong interest in institutional and historical issues, but had to concentrate far more on narrow economic theory due to his colleague's leaving unexpectedly for a post in Geneva. That is the reason why Knight had to abandon his initial goals.

Given this restriction and the above stated non-existent connection between Knight and the historical school, one would therefore not expect what a closer reading of Knight's work reveals. For instance, in his Britannica article on economics, Knight reports quite extensively on the critical schools, which he cites as having had a "wholesome influence on the progress of economic science". Knight openly agrees with the critical insight that economic life is a historical category and "therefore only to be understood through a study of that past". Thus, wisdom of particular economic policies is relative to conditions of place and time. Moreover, the supposedly universal laws of abstract economics need to be supplemented by, or even subordinated to, the study of concrete facts of the national situation. Knight's sympathy for the historical approach becomes obvious when he speculates that "the historicists

---

6   Knight in a letter to Parsons on May 1st (Harvard University Archives HUG (FP) 42.8.2 Talcott Parsons, Correspondence and Related Papers 1923-1940, Box 2, Folder "Personal Correspondence 1935-1936"). Courtesy of the Harvard University Archives (This and the following quotations from the Harvard University Archives).
Since Knight's attitude towards the outstanding leaders of the three main currents of institutionalism has already been extensively examined, institutionalism is generally omitted; for Knight's opinion on Veblen: TILMAN (1992), pp. 47-60; the interaction between Clarence E. Ayres and Knight is discussed by BUCHANAN (1976), DEGREGORI (1977) and SAMUELS (1977); a comparison between John R. Commons and Knight is provided by SCHWEIKHARDT (1988).

would have found many to agree with them"[7], if they had limited their approach to this. Going beyond relativizing abstract economic principles was just too far removed from scientific method.

Reflecting on the economic interpretation of history, Knight diagnoses a convergent development. On the one side, historians tend to explain history as a process driven by efficiency and economic motives, while economists from the historical school advocate a historical interpretation of economics. Knight himself recommends a dialectical method. It is the combination of the seemingly contradictory approaches that "makes a good starting point for a real discussion of the general subject of social and historical interpretation".[8] Knight's discussion of the economic interpretation of history may serve as an example of the continuity in his work. In his *Ethics and Economic Interpretation* (1922), Knight considers for the first time the economic interpretation of history. On this occasion he refers to the doctrine of scientific socialism, according to which history is determined by materialistic considerations. A closer examination however, reveals that the foundations for a science of conduct based on economic motives are weak. In a methodological and highly critical context the motif of the economic interpretation of history is used to conclude that "the treatment of conduct in the concrete takes the form of history rather than science".[9] Moreover, the scientific treatment of conduct is restricted to its abstract form and its "concrete content can only be explained 'historically'".[10] When writing a new preface to the re-issue of his *Risk, Uncertainty and Profit* (1921/1933) Knight addresses our theme in the context of the capital controversy with Hayek. After stating the Marxist view that economic motivation explains historical change, he focuses on the conditions affecting economic life such as wants, resources and technology. Insofar as they are the result of rational abstinence and investment, these conditions can themselves be explained in economic terms. Thus, in an intertemporal perspective uncertainty is introduced as a new limitation on the economic view of motivation.[11] Finally, in 1942 he once again takes up the *Economic Interpretation of History* in an interdisciplinary context (humanities, cultural history, social sciences). The economic interpretation of history is described as "one of the intellectual vices of the [...] excessive 'rationalization' of human

---

7   KNIGHT (1951a), p. 930.
8   KNIGHT (1942), p. 228.
9   KNIGHT (1922), p. 37.
10   KNIGHT (1922), p. 39.
11   KNIGHT (1933), p. xxxii.

behavior and human nature" resulting from the European Enlightenment, utilitarianism and classical economics.[12] As stated above, the historical school is characterized as a necessary counter-movement pointing at the excessive use of an economic interpretation.

While conventional wisdom regarding Knight's position vis-à-vis the historical school would assume absolute opposition, it becomes clear from a closer consideration of Knight's reaction to key historical figures of the time that his opinion of the school is a far more differentiated and cognitively complex one. For instance in one of Knight's more general attacks on the historical school he mentions Karl Knies as the only valuable and notable exception. In his view Knies refrains from the broad pattern of making the "historical method something arbitrary and doctrinaire".[13]

Another example of Knight's defense of the historical tradition concerns his treatment of Gustav Schmoller. Knight defends Schmoller and the historical school against Lionel Robbins, who made them responsible for the "intrusion of all sorts of sociological and ethical elements which cannot, by the widest extension of the meaning of word" be included in economic analysis.[14] Referring to Schmoller, the British economist speaks of the "degrading mystique of historicism".[15] This attack seems to awake Knight's historical temperament: "I must say that there is a vast amount of truth in historicism, and also that it affords a sorely needed corrective to the naive utilitarian individualism of the English classical economists. Like the latter, it must be generously interpreted and freed from extremism - and confronted with its opposite. Both schools, more or less equally, were propagandists, with honorable objectives, and were alike seekers and promoters of important truth."[16]

In contrast to Knies and Schmoller, Karl Bücher and his method is for Knight just a "conspicuous example" for economic generalizations.[17] Implicitly characterizing the approach taken by Bücher, Knight blames the historical school for ambitious extremism: "Not content with looking to history for the causes of these concrete differences of economic structure in which they were interested, they proposed to derive from history itself universal and binding laws akin to those of the physical sciences. They were fond of schemes

---

12 KNIGHT (1942), p. 217.
13 KNIGHT (1951a), p. 930.
14 ROBBINS (1932), p. 40.
15 ROBBINS (1952), p. 40.
16 KNIGHT (1953), p. 280.
17 KNIGHT (1941), p. 256.

of stages of economic development through which they thought every nation must pass. In these speculations they were really elaborating suggestions found not in historical research, but in Greek speculative historians. They regarded the forms taken by economic life, past and present, as inevitable products of historical forces; and at the same time, unconscious of the inconsistency, they advocated a rather heavy-handed control of economic activities by the state."[18] For Knight this approach is beyond any reason: "But surely no serious student needs to be warned against the implication that human development has proceeded by a uniform linear serial sequence, with exact uniformity over the whole earth at a particular date in evolution or history".[19] Knight objects to the alleged mechanical character of Bücher's approach. Economic history is to be studied viewing its content as opinion, principles and interpretive ideas rather than acts in any literary sense.

Let us come back to Carl Menger's *Grundsätze*, because a more detailed examination mirrors how remarkably close to Schmoller and the historical school Knight argues in this context. His above mentioned introduction to Menger's "Grundsätze" goes well beyond a mere appraisal of the Austrian framework. In addition to his criticism on narrow theoretical grounds, Knight finds fault with Menger's notion of the "economizing man". The Chicago economist doubts whether Menger was aware of "the many other 'men' who walk about and variously perform 'in the same skin' as the creature who merely uses means to satisfy 'needs'".[20] Not mentioning the "conventional man, the playful, humorous, contentious, prejudiced, capricious, perverse, obdurate, destructive, benevolent man, the idealist, the esthete, the malicious man, etc, etc.". Menger is blamed for a "naive economism in an extreme form".[21] As an illustration of Knight's ambivalence and his idiosyncratic position, Knight's comment on Menger can be sharply contrasted with the following justification and defense of the economic man: "The concept of eco-

18 KNIGHT (1951a), p. 930. A juxtaposition with Knight's conception of economics might enhance the understanding of his objection against Bücher: "Economic theory is not a descriptive, or an explanatory, science of reality. Within wide limits, it can be said that historical changes do not affect economic theory at all. It deals with ideal concepts which are probably as universal for rational thought as those of ordinary geometry", KNIGHT (1935), p. 277.
19 KNIGHT (1941), p. 257.
20 KNIGHT (1950), p. 16.
21 KNIGHT (1950), p. 16.

nomic man has indeed been attacked and generally rejected, verbally. This was intellectually a step backward, since the notion is essential to scientific analysis, and the only hope was to use it while making its limitations clear. In essentials it has been revived in the concept of the indifference function of the mathematical economists. But while certain so-called economists, notably the 'historical schools' of Germany and England, were repudiating the idea without understanding it, much of its content in the bad, absolutistic sense was being preached with even less understanding by social philosophers and politicians; among the former were especially Spencer; under the latter head come the Manchester Liberals"[22]. For Knight, the economic man functions as an analytical tool methodologically analogous to the frictionless machine of theoretical mechanics. For analytical economics, this concept is essential in the same way.[23]

In the same context Knight points at Schmoller and Sombart as an alternative to Menger. While the Austrian economist always speaks of "need" not of want, desire or craving, these categories are in the eyes of the latter two "characteristic of medieval life, in *contrast* with that of the modern age, devoted to endless profit-seek".[24] Knight maintains that the satisfaction of needs, which according to Menger originates in human drives, only accounts for a negligibly tiny fraction of ordinary economic activity. Menger's conceptualization "is just not true of any particular good that is either offered in the market, or wanted". In this respect Knight once again hints at one of his fundamental objections to the free-market economy, namely the fact "that it takes the 'units,' individuals, families, etc. as 'given,' which is entirely unrealistic. In the economic aspect specifically, it 'assumes' given 'wants, resources, and technique,' in possession of each and all".[25]

Summarizing, one can state that Knight's treatment of the protagonists of the historical school is far from being consistent and unambiguous. Despite faithfulness to his own approach of abstract economic principles no fundamental objections to the way of the historical school can be noticed. In dealing with opponents of the historical school Knight himself then takes a stand very similar to their arguments.

---

22 KNIGHT (1935), p. 286-87.
23 KNIGHT (1941a), p. 134.
24 KNIGHT (1950), p. 16.
25 KNIGHT (1951), p. 271.

IV. Frank Knight as a Promoter of Max Weber

In his treatment of Max Weber as an economist, G. Eisermann has argued that the historical school dialectically reaches its final completion in Weber.[26] Frank Knight played a crucial role in the spread of Weberian ideas in the American social sciences. Since this is widely unknown, the following section is concerned with Knight's role in the dissemination of Weberian ideas in America and Weber's influence on Knight.

Knight's translation of Max Weber's *Allgemeine Wirtschaftsgeschichte* in 1927 was the first work of the German social scientist to be published in English.[27] Knight begins the translator's preface by introducing Max Weber to the American audience: "Max Weber is probably the most outstanding name in German social thought since Schmoller".[28] Arguing for the necessity of this translation, Knight continues: "At a time when the main emphasis in English, and particularly American, economic thought has shifted from general deductive theory to the other two corners of the methodological triangle, namely, psychological and historical interpretation on the one hand and statistical study on the other, there is abundant reason for making available to English readers this last product of Weber's thought, his economic history". It was not before the mid 1930s that Weber was widely known among American social scientists.[29] Thus, Knight was almost a decade ahead and he can truly be regarded as one of the American discoverers of Max Weber. However, it remains an open question how Knight, who had not studied in Germany, came to know Weber.[30]

Common interest in Max Weber initiated a lifelong friendship between Frank Knight and Talcott Parsons. During his academic year at the University of Heidelberg (1925/26) the latter was exposed to Weber's work. Parsons encountered the surviving members of the Weber circle and was finally captivated by *Die protestantische Ethik und der Geist des Kapitalismus*. Upon his

---

26 EISERMANN (1993), p. 12.
27 Talcott Parsons, who is usually given credit for promoting Weber in America, published his translation of *Die Protestantische Ethik und der Geist des Kapitalismus* in 1930.
28 KNIGHT (1927), p. xv.
29 ERDELYI (1992), pp. 99-126.
30 It seems plausible that his former teacher, the economic historian A. P. Usher might have introduced him to the works of Weber.

return, Parsons contacted and suggested to Knight a joint translation project consisting of the *Religionssoziologie*, the *Protestantische Ethik* and the *Wirtschaftsgeschichte*. Parsons did not want to endanger the success of the undertaking by competition between Knight and himself.[31] Contacting Knight for the first time in late 1927 Parsons was too late. The *General Economic History* was published separately. Nevertheless, 1927 marks the beginning of an ongoing interaction between Knight and Parsons, sparking off their mutual interest in the translation of Weber.

Although Knight never mentioned sociology or sociologists in his teaching, he devoted some attention to Max Weber. In an autobiographical paper Edward Shils tells us that Knight offered a seminar on Weber in 1935 or 1936. The procedure was a line-by-line reading of the first three chapters of Weber's *Wirtschaft und Gesellschaft*.[32]

Despite this experience and interest in the work of Weber, Knight nevertheless makes few explicit references to Weber in his work. Knight and his second wife, Ethel Verry, went to Europe in 1930 and spent six months on a Guggenheim Foundation fellowship especially in Heidelberg and Vienna. His paper "Das Wertproblem in der Nationalökonomie" (1932) was primarily a lecture delivered then at Vienna. Even in this paper, which can surely be regarded as a reflection on Weber's *Wissenschaftslehre*, the German social scientist is not mentioned once.[33]

In one of the very few comments on Weber, his American translator praises the Puritanism theory for being the only one that really deals with "the problem of causes".[34] Knight speaks with approval of Weber for being a "leader in the emphasis on non-technological factors, political, psychological, intellectual and religious, underlying economic change".[35] It is probably Knight's fascination for ideas, their evolution and consequences that refrains him from accepting a more empirical approach such as Bücher's stage theory. Furthermore, Weber towers above all other writers, because he approached the

---

31 Talcott Parsons in a letter to Paul H. Douglas on November 13th 1927. In this letter Parsons asks Douglas, who was also a Professor at Chicago, to help as an intermediary between Knight and himself (Harvard University Archives HUG (FP) 42.8.2 Talcott Parsons, Correspondence and Related Papers 1923-1940, Box 2 of 3, Folder "Misc. Correspondence 1925-1929").

32 SHILS (1980), p. 184.

33 KNIGHT (1932).

34 KNIGHT (1928), p. 101.

35 KNIGHT (1928), p. 96.

material from the angle of comparative history in the broad sense and raised the question why capitalism did not develop in other times and spaces. Knight's unequivocally positive attitude towards Weber is unique. One can hardly think of any other social scientist, philosopher or economist Knight reviews in a similar way. Taking into account how severe and harsh Knight often passes his judgement, one might even speak of an admiration and enthusiasm for Weber and his thought. For this reason, it is not surprising that Knight once made the autobiographical remark: "There has been the work of one man whom I have greatly admired. If I were to start out again, I would build upon his ideas. I am referring of course to Max Weber".[36]

In spite of this admiration it is a common view that "Knight's theories [appear] far removed from Weber's ideas".[37] While it is beyond the scope of this paper to analyze the full influence of Weber on Knight, a sharp analysis of Knight's concept of ideal competition reveals a strong connection to Weber's notion of capitalism. For the latter, the evolution of capitalism leads to the transformation of human relationships (including the most intimate) into impersonal and bare market relationships: "Where the market is allowed to follow its own autonomous tendencies, its participants do not look toward the persons of each other but only toward the commodity".[38] Capitalism becomes an objective and automatic system to which the individual must conform, a dead system in which there is no room left for creative forces. While the Puritan wanted to lead this rational ascetic life, we are forced to do it.[39] As the "partner to a transaction is expected to behave according to rational legality and, quite particularly, to respect the formal inviolability"[40], individual action is replaced by a mere mechanistic response or execution. "The capitalistic economy of the present day is an immense cosmos into which the individual is born, and which presents itself to him, at least as an individual, as an unalterable order of things in which he must live. It forces the individual, in so far as he is involved in the system of market relationships, to conform

---

36 SCHWEITZER (1975), p. 279.
37 SCHWEITZER (1975), p. 279. This impression is disputed by Raines/Jung who plainly assert that Knight was "profoundly influenced by Weber". Unfortunately they do not present a single argument or example in their treatment, RAINES/JUNG (1992), p. 110. Apart from these short hints at Weber his influence on Knight has not been examined.
38 WEBER (1922), p. 636.
39 WEBER (1904-05), p. 181.
40 WEBER (1922), p. 636.

to capitalistic rules of action. The manufacturer who, in the long run, acts counter to these norms, will just as inevitably be eliminated from the economic scene as the worker who cannot or will not adapt himself to them will be thrown into the streets without a job".[41]

Knight's characterization of competition points at the same phenomenon. His description is more vivid as well as provocative. In his view, competition brings about "an essentially impersonal, quasi-mechanical control of economic relationships". Even the entrepreneur in his control of production is relatively helpless. "Under perfect competition he would of course be completely helpless, a mere registrar of the choices of consumers".[42] Furthermore, Knight connects the power of the competitive forces to his common metaphor of competition as a voluntary game. In contrast to the fundamental assumption of contemporary game theory, the players are not primarily interested in the pay-off matrix, but in enjoying the game. "In a social order where all values are reduced to the money measure in the degree that this is true of modern industrial nations, a considerable fraction of the most noble and sensitive characters will lead unhappy und futile lives. Everyone is compelled to play the economic game and be judged by his success in playing it, whatever his field of activity or type of interest, and has to squeeze in as a side-line any other competition, or non-competitive activity, which may have for him a greater intrinsic appeal."[43]

In his discussion of Sombart's revised edition of *Der Moderne Kapitalismus*, Knight goes on by correcting the common assumption that the spirit of capitalism is that of bargaining between individuals. All parameters are determined by the system. Thus, "nothing could be farther from the truth".[44] Stating that there is "no implication of a universal harmony of interests"[45], Knight deviates from the well-established "communist fiction" (G. Myrdal) of economic harmony. That is the reason why he is able to avoid any normative inference from the economic ideal. Accordingly, it is a fallacy to attribute ethical significance to distribution based on what the individual puts into the social total.[46] In his presidential address at the American Economic Association, which was essentially a statement of his credo, Knight returned

---

41 WEBER (1904-05), pp. 54-55.
42 KNIGHT (1928), p. 92.
43 KNIGHT (1923), p. 66.
44 KNIGHT (1928), p. 92.
45 KNIGHT (1953), p. 10.
46 KNIGHT (1928), p. 95.

to his criticism of the ideal competition: "Our economic ills are not due to the failure of competition; on the contrary, the result of perfect functioning of the system would be socially quite intolerable."[47] In contrast to prevalent economic doctrine, it is therefore not only or primarily the imperfect or incomplete market, which raises ethical concerns, but the perfect and ideal version too. Since for Knight the "actual performance of the economic order diverges surprisingly little from the theoretical"[48], this criticism of the ideal and perfect market system is more relevant than any evaluation of the real life. Therefore, the "main real issue is the ethical quality of the theoretical ideal".[49]

Up to this point our main focus has been on Knight's view and critique of the historical school. As Ross Emmett clearly indicates, "Knight stood at odds with the modes of methodological thinking in American social science [one might even say 'at odds with all modes', C.N.]: the objectivist, behavioristic approaches common to the other social sciences and to the American Institutionalist tradition; and the positivistic approach that emerged with the American neoclassical tradition between the wars".[50] For that reason, Knight can easily be characterized as an opponent of a particular view, but it is at the same time hardly possible to give a constructive and positive outline of Knight's position.

V. Traces of a Historical Approach in Knight's Work

From the very beginning of his academic career, Knight works on an integral conception of economics. Explaining the methodological foundations of his dissertation, Knight advocates an intimate relation between deduction and induction, because there is abundant use for both in economics as well as in other sciences. "In the present writer's view the correct 'middle way' between these extreme views, doing justice to both, is not hard to find. An abstract deductive system is only one small division of the great domain of economic

---

47 KNIGHT (1951), p. 270.
48 KNIGHT (1956), p. 52.
49 KNIGHT (1956), p. 53.
50 EMMETT (forthcoming).

science, but there is opportunity and the greatest necessity for cultivating that field".[51]

Beginning in 1930, over a period of 20 years Knight develops, particularly in exchange with Parsons, his approach to economic aspects of human action. He recognizes that the allocative-economic aspect cannot exhaustively state the problem which a human being is attempting to solve in any concrete economic situation. For that reason, he suggests a pluralistic methodology, according to which human behavior is susceptible to systematic study on four distinct layers[52]:

• The *mechanistic level* deals with human beings in the perspective of stimulus and response.

• Secondly, the *historical-institutional level* aims at interpreting behavior in terms of historical processes and historical laws. The first two layers have in common that "behavior is treated as caused in the sense of positive science". Thus, for Knight the first two approaches are below the level of problem solving.

• The lowest level of problem solving is that which is dealt with by the *economic* theorist. He works at a third general level of interpretation. His focus is on the correct allocation of the given means among the different interests.

• Since "ends also present problems", the fourth level is concerned with the choice between ends. It is the problem of *values* or evaluation of truth, beauty, and goodness.

This framework can by analyzed as a mirror reflecting Knight's fundamental categories in three dimensions. Firstly, it illustrates Knight's concept of variables and constants. Layer by layer one exogenous datum is transformed into a variable[53]. Secondly, the level of certainty decreases with every new layer. Consequently, the economic agent is more likely to make a mistake.[54] Thirdly, as far as the time-horizon is concerned, the static and mechanical view is replaced by a dynamic conception.

There seems to be, however, an inherent weakness, in so far as Knight tends to conceptualize his levels like close systems. Therefore, he might ignore the interplay between them. Furthermore, Knight develops over the

---

51 KNIGHT (1921), pp. 6-7.
52 KNIGHT (1932), KNIGHT (1941a).
53 KNIGHT (1922), p. 20.
54 KNIGHT (1932), p. 61.

years a variety of different terminologies and changes the number and sequence of the levels.

With respect to Knight's overall conception, Parsons provides us with an important insight. In the final letter to Knight on this topic, Parsons admits: "On the whole I do feel that in this exchange I have come nearer to understanding what has inhibited us from fruitful discussion over a considerable period. I might try to state it as follows: Your principal concern has been to attempt to place economic theory and the cognate phenomena in a philosophical setting, perhaps particularly in relation to its ethical significance and lack of it. I have, on the other hand, grown progressively away from such preoccupations and been devoting myself to the development of a theoretical system on the level of empirical science which, while touching on the peripheries of such questions has never really come to grips with the philosophical terms. Both, it seems to me are legitimate tasks, yours being much the bigger and ultimately the more important. I do, however, feel that my job not only needs to be done, but is in a sense a prior job, since it is important in defining the perspective in which the philosophical problems are to be arised."[55]

VI. Conclusion

Let us finally come back to the initial question, how is Knight related to the historical school? Obviously, Knight shows a sustained engagement with the problems posed by the historical school. Again and again Knight addresses the issue of the scope of economics and stresses the narrowness and abstractness of orthodox theory. However, at the same time, he also defends this heavily criticized economic theory against severe attacks by the historical school and other dissenters. The co-existence of the two traits lead us then to the question, of whether there is anything beyond this seemingly obvious contradiction. Assuming that Knight was aware of this tension, two possible ways of integrating the opposing views can be identified:

---

55 Letter to Frank Knight on July 9th 1950 (Harvard University Archives HUG (FP) 42.8.2 Talcott Parsons, Miscellaneous Correspondence and Other Papers, 1923-1940, Box 3, Folder "Misc. Correspondence Knight").

1. Firstly, Knight might not have seen the historical and theoretical way as mutually exclusive approaches in economics. In one of his last papers, an article entitled *Economic History*, Knight surveys the history of economic thought. The final passage is devoted to historism and institutionalism in economics as opponents to orthodox economics. Knight compares the evolution of the German branch with parallel developments in Britain. After that he deals with American institutionalism as an "offshoot of the German movement". Finally, Knight concludes his survey quite astonishingly: "What should be said about these opposition movements is that there is no conflict at all with orthodoxy. One can advocate a policy or write historical or sociological economics at will, distinguishing the result from history of sociology as far as possible. [...] One may contend that inductive treatment is superior, or even that no other economics should be written. But it remains true that price theory yields laws more useful for guiding action than any other comparably simple view of social phenomena (e.g. criminology)."[56] His concluding emphasis on the importance, legitimacy and validity of price theory is typical of Knight, who never lost his faith in economics as being merely abstraction and analysis. But he never advocated for the exclusivity of this approach. Either a co-existent or even cooperative and complementary approach constituted the core of his methodology. In a positive sense Knight could support the historical school as long as the existence of an analytical dimension was not questioned. Although Knight contributed and initiated a couple of debates, he also regrets the lack of consensus of economists. "The attack on deductive analysis begun and continued by successive historical schools is kept up by the institutional economists, and now the statisticians are making it a three-cornered fight. To one who sees, or at least believes, not merely that all these methods and perhaps others are useful and necessary, but that friendly intelligent co-operation among those who pursue them is equally so, it is disheartening to find them engaged so largely in reading each other out of the kingdom."[57]

2. As a second attempt to solve the apparent tension, one can focus on the contextuality of Knight's contributions. Then looking at Knight in the broader intellectual and economic setting, the Chicago economist was not so much concerned with what he was arguing for or against, but, instead,

---

56 KNIGHT (1973), p. 61.
57 KNIGHT (1928), p. 90.

was more concerned with the needs and historical challenges of a specific time and place. Consequently, Knight can only be understood in relation to the time and place he was addressing at a particular moment. Instead of primarily conceptualizing, modeling or stringently formulating, Knight appears as a reacting and responding critic. Taking into account how much Knight was devoted to reviewing, replying and discussing, the argument becomes plausible. In his reviews, Knight appears to be less concerned with describing and evaluating books in terms of their authors' objectives than with judging them by the proximity to his own (and often unclear) position. As far as the role of government is concerned, Knight once illustrated the importance he ascribed to responding to the needs of the Zeitgeist by outlining the different challenges: "There was a time, no doubt, when society needed to be awakened to the possibility of remedying evils and stirred to action, mostly negative action, in establishing freedom, but some positive action too. Now we have found not only that mere individual freedom is not enough, but that its excess can have disastrous consequences. And a reaction has set in, so that people have too much faith in positive action, of the nature of passing laws and employing policemen, and the opposite warning is needed."[58] Recalling Knight's treatment of Schmoller in his response to Robbins, the same argument can be revealed. It was not Schmoller himself Knight was defending. It was Schmoller attacked by Robbins as a representative of a marginalized tradition. That is the reason why, instead of inherently theoretical reasons, Knight refers to Schmoller as a "corrective to the naive utilitarian individualism".[59] The changing context of American social science and political discourse during the 1930s and early 1940s allows us then to understand why Knight moved away from his initial project.

Dealing with an almost lost tradition in intellectual history, one might ask why this particular approach was not widely accepted; why this alternative did not influence the further development of the discipline; and why it was even widely rejected. As far as the historical school is concerned, Eberhard K. Seiffert raised this question at the previous SEEP-Conference: "Why did the historical school have only an insignificant impact on non-German research?" According to the brief discussion summary three possible answers were mentioned: "first, the language problem should not be underestimated.

---

58 KNIGHT (1951), p. 281.
59 KNIGHT (1953), p. 280.

Secondly, pure ignorance might play a role. And thirdly, when you try to introduce a new approach, you do not want to swim against the mainstream".[60] In the case of Frank Knight, one can easily exclude the first two possibilities. Knight was familiar with the German literature, he reviewed and summarized quite a few works. Consequently one cannot consider this scholar either incapable of advanced scholarship in the German language or ignorant of the historical school. Thus discounting these two hypotheses, one must infer that the approach taken by the historical school has been more influential than is often assumed (at least in the question raised by E. K. Seiffert). However, whilst the influence of the historical school is undeniable, we must also conclude that Knight, despite his efforts, was not entirely convinced of the prospects for the historical approach in economics. Whether the reasons for Knight's not fully embracing the historical perspective lay in the inherent weaknesses of the arguments themselves or in the deep skepticism of Knight's personality is still an open question. At least in a letter to his friend Talcott Parsons, Knight explained why he adhered to the dominant orthodoxy and why he was afraid of converting to radicalism:

"'Up to a point,' I'm quite happy to be called a 'reactionary'; beyond, I'm as radical as they come, in the narrow sense of critical judgement of the market organization. But I don't like the idea of throwing away freedom and turning the country over to any brand of politicians without a betting chance of getting something in return. [...] I incline to 'be careful'—a reactionary again."[61]

---

60 EIDENMÜLLER (1995), p. 105.
61 Letter to Talcott Parsons on March 2nd 1950 (Harvard University Archives HUG (FP) 42.8.4 Talcott Parsons, Correspondence and Other Papers, 1935-1955, Box 13, Folder "Knight, Frank H.").

References

BUCHANAN, J. M.: "Methods and Morals in Economics: The Ayres-Knight Discussion", in: W. BREIT, W. P. CULBERTSON (Eds.): *Science and Ceremony: The Institutional Economics of C. E. Ayres*, Austin (University of Texas Press) 1976, pp. 164-174.

DEGREGORI, T. R.: "Ethics and Economic Inquiry: The Ayres-Knight Debate and the Problem of Economic Order", *American Journal of Economics and Sociology*, 36 (1977), pp. 41-50.

EIDENMÜLLER, I.: "Discussion Summary", in: P. KOSLOWSKI (Ed.): *The Theory of Ethical Economy in the Historical School*, Berlin, Heidelberg, New York (Springer) 1995, pp. 104-105.

EISERMANN, G.: *Max Weber und die Nationalökonomie*, Marburg (Metropolis) 1993.

EMMETT, R. B.: "Frank H. Knight", in: J. DAVIS, W. HANDS and U. MÄKI: *Handbook of Economic Methodology*, Aldershot (E. Elgar) (forthcoming).

ERDELYI, A.: *Max Weber in Amerika: Wirkungsgeschichte und Rezeptionsgeschichte Webers in der anglo-amerikanischen Philosophie und Sozialwissenschaft*, Wien (Edition Passagen) 1992.

KNIGHT, F. H.: *Risk, Uncertainty and Profit*, Reprints of Economic Classics, New York (A. M. Kelley) 1964. Original: Boston and New York (Houghton Mifflin) 1921. (Quoted as Knight [1921] and Knight [1933]).

KNIGHT, F. H.: "Ethics and the Economic Interpretation", in: F. H. KNIGHT: *The Ethics of Competition and Other Essays*, Essays selected by Milton Friedman, Homer Jones, George Stigler, and Allen Wallis, New York, London (Harper & Brothers) 1935, pp. 19-40. Quoted as (Knight [1922]).

KNIGHT, F. H.: "The Ethics of Competition", in: F. H. KNIGHT: *The Ethics of Competition and Other Essays*, Essays selected by Milton Friedman, Homer Jones, George Stigler, and Allen Wallis, New York, London (Harper & Brothers) 1935, pp. 41-75. Quoted as (Knight [1923]).

KNIGHT, F. H., "Translator's Preface", in: M. WEBER: *General Economic History*, translated by Frank H. Knight, London (George Allen & Unwin) 1927, pp. xv-xvi.

KNIGHT, F. H.: "Historical and Theoretical Issues in the Problem of Modern Capitalism", in: F. H. KNIGHT: *On the History and Method of Economics: Selected Essays*, Essays selected by William L. Letwin and Alexander J. Morin, Chicago (University of Chicago Press) 1956, pp. 89-103. Quoted as (Knight [1928]).

KNIGHT, F. H.: "Das Wertproblem in der Wirtschaftstheorie", in: H. MAYER (Ed.): *Die Wirtschaftstheorie der Gegenwart,* Zweiter Band: Wert, Preis, Produktion, Geld und Kredit, Wien (Julius Springer) 1932, pp. 52-72.

KNIGHT, F. H.: "Economic Theory and Nationalism", in: F. H. KNIGHT: *The Ethics of Competition and Other Essays,* Essays selected by Milton Friedman, Homer Jones, George Stigler, and Allen Wallis, New York, London (Harper & Brothers) 1935, pp. 277-359.

KNIGHT, F.H: "Anthropology and Economics", *Journal of Political Economy,* 49 (1941), pp. 247-268.

KNIGHT, F. H.: "Social Science", *Ethics* 51 (1941), pp. 127-143. (Quoted as (Knight [1941a]).

KNIGHT, F. H.: "Some Notes on the Economic Interpretation of History", in: AMERICAN COUNCIL OF LEARNED SOCIETIES (Ed.): *Studies in the History of Culture: The Disciplines of the Humanities,* Menasha (Wisconsin) (George Banta Publishing) 1942, pp. 217-231.

KNIGHT F. H.: "Introduction", in: C. MENGER: *Principles of Economics: First General Part,* translated and edited by James Dingwall and Bert F. Hoselitz, Glencoe (Illinois) (Free Press) 1950, pp. 9-35.

KNIGHT, F. H.: "Economics", in: W. YUST (Ed.): *Encyclopaedia Britannica,* Vol. 7, Chicago, London, Toronto (University of Chicago Press) 1959, pp. 925-934. (Quoted as (Knight [1951a]).

KNIGHT F. H.: "The Role of Principles in Economics and Politics", in: F. H. KNIGHT: *On the History and Method of Economics: Selected Essays,* Essays selected by William L. Letwin and Alexander J. Morin, Chicago (University of Chicago Press) 1956, pp. 251-281. (Quoted as (Knight [1951])

KNIGHT, F. H.: "Economic Freedom and Social Responsibility: An Essay in Economics and Ethics", *Studies in Business and Economics,* School of Business Administration, Emory University, No. 7, Atlanta (Georgia) 1952.

KNIGHT, F. H.: "Theory of Economic Policy and the History of Doctrine", *Ethics,* 63 (1953), pp. 276-292.

KNIGHT, F. H.: "Structure and Operation of the Economic Order", *University of Arizona Bulletin,* The Kennecott Lecture Series No. 27, April, Tuscon (University of Arizona Press) 1956, pp. 31-68.

KNIGHT, F. H.: "Economic History", in: P. P. WIENER (Ed.): *Dictionary of the History of Ideas,* Vol. II, New York (Scribner) 1973, pp. 44-61.

RAINES, J. P., JUNG, C. R.: "Schumpeter and Knight on Economic and Political Rationality: A Comparative Restatement", *Journal of Socio-Economics,* 21 (1992), pp. 109-124.

ROBBINS, L. C.: *An Essay on the Nature and Significance of Economic Science,* London (Macmillan) 1932.

ROBBINS, L. C.: *The Theory of Economic Policy in English Classical Political Economy,* London (Macmillan) 1952.

SAMUELS, W. J.: "The Knight-Ayres Correspondence: The Grounds of Knowledge and Social Action", *Journal of Economic Issues*, 11 (1977), pp. 485-525.

SCHWEIKHARDT, D. B.: "The Role of Values in Economic Theory and Policy: A Comparison of Frank Knight and John R. Commons", *Journal of Economic Issues*, 22 (1988), pp. 407-414.

SCHWEITZER, A.: "Frank Knight's Social Economics", *History of Political Economy*, 7 (1975), pp. 279-292.

SHILS, E.: "Some Academics, Mainly in Chicago", *American Scholar*, 50 (1981), pp. 179-196.

STIGLER, G. J.: "Industrial Organization and Economic Progress", in: L.D. WHITE (Ed.): *The State of the Social Science*, Chicago (University of Chicago Press) 1956, pp. 269-282.

TILMAN, R.: *Thorstein Veblen and His Critics*, Princeton (Princeton University Press) 1992.

WEBER, M.: *The Protestant Ethic and the Spirit of Capitalism*, translated by Talcott Parsons, New York (Scribner) 1930. Original: "Die Protestantische Ethik und der 'Geist' des Kapitalismus", *Archiv für Sozialwissenschaft und Sozialpolitik*, 20/21 (1904-05), pp. 1-54 and 1-110. Quoted as (Weber [1904-05]).

WEBER, M.: *Economy and Society*, edited by Guenther Roth and Claus Wittich, New York (Bedminster) 1968. Original: *Wirtschaft und Gesellschaft* Tübingen (J.C.B. Mohr) 1922. Quoted as (Weber [1922]).

Discussion Summary

NORBERT F. TOFALL

Paper discussed:
CLAUS NOPPENEY: Frank Knight and the Historical School

The discussion was opened by the contribution that, first, Frank Knight is a critic with the goal of making progress in sciences, that, secondly, Knight is a pessimist since his criticism is endless, and, thirdly, that Knight only looks at separate parts of the subjects and that he does not show the whole picture (CASSON). Concerning the influence of Weber and Knight's opinion about the Historical School, it is pointed out that the Historical School of economics only wanted to make clear that situations and people's values change in history (CASSON).

Because of the enormous changes in economics in the last 100 years it is necessary to ask if Knight did not analyse this changes and if Knight did not change himself (MOGGRIDGE).

About this it is said that Knight did not change his social philosophy over the years. Knight only analysed different subjects which were on vogue but ever from the same point of view (NOPPENEY).

It is asked for the thoughts of Knight about welfare theory and his contribution to the ethical implications of this theory (FURUBOTN). NOPPENEY points out that there is a contribution from Knight, especially Knight's criticism of Pigou. Knight thinks about a relation between price theory and welfare theory with regard to the discussion of the economic systems and in view of the dicussion "planned economy or free market economy".

But a mayor issue in welfare theory is also the distribution of ownership which leads to the distribution of income. It is not possible to understand a welfare function without ethics and therefore the results of welfare theory have a normative standard, not only a positive one (FURUBOTN).

Very important is Knight's notion to power, because the market can only work, if there is no power. A market without competition, however, builds up power (NOPPENEY). This is why the Anti-Trust-legislation is necessary (MOGGRIDGE).

DISCUSSION SUMMARY

KOSLOWSKI wonders, why Noppeney describes Knight as a reactionary man. That is a very American point of view. From this point of view, the German Historical School of economics cannot be judged properly, because in Germany and in Europe the position of Knight is not conservative, but liberal, and the Historical School is the conservative school. This is important because, from a liberal point of view, it is difficult to legitimate inheritance, whereas from a historical point of view, it is possible since history and historical continuity legitimizes (KOSLOWSKI).

In Knight's theory the social units are not the individuals, but the families, and in Knight's theory the logic of the market is not the logic of power. Both are topics which call in mind Schumpeter's thoughts. In his famous article *Die sozialen Klassen im ethnisch homogenen Milieu* Schumpeter insists that the social units are the families and in his famous paper on imperalism Schumpeter argues that the logic of the power system is not the logic of the market system. What does Knight think about Schumpeter? (ACHAM).

Knight seldom agrees with the authors he quotes, and Knight does not quote in an exact way, NOPPENEY answers and adds that he has not found Schumpeter in Knight's writings.

In Knight's view economic theory has always to be ethical theory. In general, and against Knight one can say that it is better for economics as well as for ethics to separate this different types of theories because only in this way it is possible to ensure clear explanations. Even if we take moral input to economics for getting moral output, the economic theory is not ethical itself (ACHAM).

From the relation between ehtics and economics we can not conclude that ethics determines economics. Knight is an outsider in regard to his ethical economics (NOPPENEY).

One can say that the economic system is one system in society and that there are other parallel systems which influence a lot of other things, especially individual preferences and attitudes. It is clear that if the preferences take a special coloration than the results of economic theory depend on this preferences. This is a very mechanical view, but it is consistent with the idea that we are influences by several degrees of ethical coloration (FURUBOTN).

Chapter 14

Method and Marshall

D. E. MOGGRIDGE

Economists, or rather some of the most gifted spirits among them, have continued in recent years to conduct a running debate on the more elemental, though by no means more elementary, topic of what sort of a study economics is, and what it is all about. This is a topic which, when I started to read economics at Cambridge in 1910, it was not, I think, fashionable among us to think much about -- less fashionable, I dare say, than it may have been a few years previously, when the separate course in economics had not yet been extracted like Eve from the rib of the Moral Sciences Tripos. To us, I think, it seemed a topic more suitable for discussion by Germans than by Englishmen. There was on our reading-list what I have since come to regard as a good, if dry, book about it, J.N. Keynes's *Scope and Method of Political Economy*, but to be quite honest I doubt if many of us read it. We thought we knew pretty well what sort of things we wanted to know about, and were glad enough to take the counsel given by Marshall himself near the beginning of the *Principles* (p. 27),[1] 'the

---

1   ALFRED MARSHALL: *Principles of Economics*, 9th (variorum), ed. by C. W. Guillebaud, London (Macmillan) 1961, p. 27. This material has been in place since the second edition. Marshall actually used the word 'trouble' rather than the word 'concern' quoted by Robertson.

less we concern ourselves with scholastic enquiries whether a certain consideration comes within the scope of economics the better'.[2]

This quotation, with its wonderful sense of Cambridge-centred insularity, is an accurate picture of the position in Cambridge in 1910.[3] By that stage, the Economics Tripos had been well-established and what David Collard has called 'The Production of Cambridge Economists by Means of Cambridge Economists'[4] was under way. The Tripos lists of the next three years would contain the names of Frederick Lavington, Gerald Shove, Hubert Henderson, Dennis Robertson, Claude Guillebaud and Philip Sargent Florence, all of who would later teach in Cambridge. By that stage, as well, almost all of the 'old guard' had gone -- Marshall had retired in 1908 and Foxwell, disgusted by the subsequent professorial election had withdrawn from most of the affairs of the Faculty -- only to attempt a return as a spoiler during World War I, when he tried, unsuccessfully, to prevent Pigou's exemption from military service by offering to cover his lectures.[5] By 1910, the main teaching for the Tripos was in the hands of A.C. Pigou, Maynard Keynes and Walter Layton, all 'students' of Marshall's, supported by such figures as W.E. Johnson (another student) and C.R. Fay. They would soon be joined by the other graduates of the Tripos mentioned above and their further products; so that if, for example, one were to look at 1925, all the teaching (with the exception of Leonard Alston, Udney Yule and Marjorie Tappan) was in the hands of Marshall students or Tripos graduates. And with significant exceptions (such as Piero Sraffa, Nicky Kaldor and Richard Goodwin as long-term appointments and John Hicks as a short-term one) the Faculty would remain the self-reproduc-

---

2   D. H. ROBERTSON: *Utility and All That*, London (Allen and Unwin) 1952, pp. 13-14.

3   It may not have been far from the views of some in the profession almost two decades earlier. When reviewing NEVILLE KEYNES's *Scope and Method of Political Economy*, Edgeworth remarked that 'we cannot conceal a certain impatience at the continual reopening of a question on which authorities appear to be substantially, if not in phrase, agreed' [*Economic Journal*, I (June 1891), p. 423].

4   DAVID COLLARD: "Cambridge After Marshall", in: J.K. WHITAKER (Ed.): *Centenary Essays on Alfred Marshall*, Cambridge (Cambridge University Press) 1990, p. 170.

5   Foxwell rejoined the Board of Studies for Economics in January 1912 and remained on it until 1920.

ing, insular institution of the 1950s wickedly, but accurately, described by Harry Johnson in his memoir.[6]

I. Introduction

But that is how the story ended. We should go back to the beginning and trace through how Cambridge got over the methodological hurdle, if there was one, and allowed its economics to take the shape it did. In tackling this subject I have the advantage of the large literature on Marshall and the professionalisation of British economics, supplemented by Peter Groenewegen's recent, massive biography of Marshall, *A Soaring Eagle* (1995), and John Whitaker's wonderful, three-volume, Royal Economic Society edition of Marshall's correspondence (1996).[7] In the course of this discussion, I will not concern myself with Marshall's views of ethics in relation to economics, not because he did not have them but because they did not affect his views on method.[8]

The outcome of the Cambridge -- and, given Cambridge's dominance resulting from its offering the most specialised and technically demanding degree course then available,[9] most of the British -- discussions was the resultant of several forces, in particular the nature of English economics before the

---

6   H. G. JOHNSON: "Cambridge in the 1950s: Memoirs of an Economist", *Encounter*, 42 (January 1974), pp. 28-39.

7   J. K. WHITAKER (Ed.): *The Correspondence of Alfred Marshall, Economist*, 3 vols., Cambridge (Cambridge University Press), 1996. In citing Whitaker's edition below, I use the form WHITAKER, volume number (roman numeral), letter number (arabic numeral), correspondent, date.

8   For a good discussion of ethics see A. W. COATS: 'Marshall and Ethics', in: R. McWILLIAMS-TULBERG (Ed.): *Alfred Marshall in Retrospect*, Aldershot (Edward Elgar) 1990, pp. 153-77 reprinted in: A. W. COATS: *On the History of Economic Thought: British and American Economic Essays*, vol. I, London (Routledge) 1992.

9   It would remain dominant until the development of the taught M.Sc. at LSE began to offer competition during the Robbins/Hayek renaissance of the 1930s.

historicist reaction, the English historicist agenda, institutional factors and, inevitably, personalities.

Before, say, about 1870, English political economy as relatively homogeneous. As Foxwell retrospectively put it in 1899,[10] 'after the appearance of Mill's *Principles*, English economists, for a whole generation, were men of one book'. Around 1870, although Mill remained the dominant text and the basis for simpler volumes, this consensus began to crumble. Assaults from a variety of sources resulted in the collapse of certain key doctrines such as the wages fund. Various streams of criticism cast doubt on the method and relevance of traditional theory -- historical economists' criticisms, marginalist criticisms, Comtist criticism. A changing, less laissez-faire, political agenda made older theories seem less relevant, although the later editions of Mill had allowed a very broad range of policies. One indication of the effects of criticism came in 1877 when Francis Galton headed a committee which recommended that Section F (Statistics and Economics) of the British Association for the Advancement of Science be excluded because its papers were not up to acceptable scientific standards. The committee's recommendation was not acted on, but the underlying difficulties did not disappear quickly.

Historicism in England was largely an indigenous growth.[11] This does not mean that the individuals involved did not take account of foreign trends in thought. However, they adapted these to their own domestically determined, ends and predilections. The work, for example, of the younger German historicists did not leave an imprint on English historical economics until after 1880 when it began to affect the younger generation of Ashley, Cunningham and Hewins, particularly the first.[12] Historicists generally undervalued the role of formal economic analysis: indeed their manifestos were often innocent of systematic theory. In emphasising the relativity of economics to circumstances, they tended to underestimate and misunderstand the general organising role of economic theory. Moreover, I think it can be fairly said that

---

10 ANTON MENGER: *The Right to the Whole Produce of Labour* (translated by M. E. Tanner with an introduction and bibliography by H.S. Foxwell), London (Macmillan) 1899, p. lxxviii.

11 A. W. COATS: 'The Historicist Reaction in English Political Economy', *Economica*, NS, XX (May 1954), pp. 143-53; GERARD KOOT: *English Historical Economics, 1870-1926*, Cambridge (Cambridge University Press) 1987, ch. 2.

12 For a discussion of German influences on Ashley see ANNE ASHLEY: *William James Ashley: A Life*, London (P.S. King) 1932, esp. pp. 22-3.

the historicist programme was largely negative: it did not really have a formal positive agenda around which one could organised a school -- even if, economic history, a sub-discipline within economics, was the ultimate result of English historicism.[13]

At the time these discussions were taking place, it was impossible to obtain a degree in political economy, much less one in economics, in any British university. At best, political economy was a part of something else -- Greats (Classics) or Modern History in Oxford; Moral Sciences or History in Cambridge. It was also normally only a small part of the relevant degree -- so small that the amount of knowledge required often did not necessitate specialist teaching. In London it was only part of a pass degree at University College and it was not a part of the University of London's examinations. Yet, when one thinks of it, this should not be surprising. University College had a one-person department until 1883, when the Newmarch Lectureship, with an obligation to deliver six lectures annually, was added to the Professorship. Initially, this made little difference, as H.S. Foxwell, already the Professor, filled both posts until 1891. At King's College, London, there was also a chair, but one whose incumbent gave no lectures for almost a generation before the College left the chair vacant for a further five years. Even when Thorold Rogers took over the successor professorship, named after Thomas Tooke, in 1862, the numbers enrolled remained small until the 1870s, when they expanded briefly before collapsing again in the next decade. With Rogers' resignation in 1890, F.Y. Edgeworth held the chair for a matter of months before leaving for Oxford and turning the chair over to William Cunningham, but Cunningham's régime was of a piece with those his predeces-

---

13 Here one might allow for one exception, Ashley's extremely influential model for a degree in commerce, which was not what one would now know as a degree in management. This model travelled very well within the Empire, but less well in Britain. And even when it did travel, it often acquired a larger component of economic theory than it had in Birmingham. For example, the Manchester programme was 'sharply distinguished from its Birmingham counterpart, where economics teaching was only weakly developed within the syllabus and the faculty'. KEITH TRIBE: 'Political Economy in the Northern Civic Universities' in: ALON KADISH & KEITH TRIBE (Eds.): *The Market for Political Economy*, London (Routledge) 1993, p. 208. See also IAN DRUMMOND: *Political Economy at the University of Toronto: A History of the Department, 1888-1982*, Toronto (Faculty of Arts and Science, University of Toronto) 1983, pp. 38-40.

sors in that he was much more interested in what was happening in Cambridge and he did nothing to make political economy a serious part of any London degree programme. It was only with the founding of LSE that economics came to London as a serious subject, and, given its size and the common University examination, LSE economics dominated London economics in the succeeding decades.[14]

Of course, the rise of LSE economics and the inauguration of the programmes in commerce at Birmingham roughly coincided with, and politically provided support for, the culmination of Marshall's campaigns for the autonomy of economics in Cambridge. By that stage, however, the dominance of Marshall's vision in Cambridge was virtually complete and he was in the process of ensuring that his chair would pass into the 'safe' hands of Pigou rather than the more eclectic Foxwell.[15] Thus we should return to the beginning.

II. Alfred Marshall

Alfred Marshall graduated from Cambridge as Second Wrangler in 1865. After a few months teaching at Clifton College in Bristol, he returned to Cambridge in October and became a Fellow of St. John's College from November 1865. Initially Marshall supplemented his Fellowship income by

---

14 JOHN MALONEY: "The Teaching of Political Economy in the University of London"; and ALON KADISH: "The City, The Fabians and the Foundation of the London School of Economics", both in: ALON KADISH & KEITH TRIBE (Eds.): *The Market in Political Economy*, London (Routledge) 1993; RALF DAHRENDORF: *LSE: A History of the London School of Economics and Political Science, 1895-1995*, Oxford (Oxford University Press) 1995.

15 R. H. COASE: "The Appointment of Pigou as Marshall's Successor: Comment", *Journal of Law and Economics*, XV (October 1972), pp. 473-85; A. W. COATS: "Political Economy and the Tariff Reform Campaign", *Journal of Law and Economics*, XI (April 1968), pp. 181-229; A. W. COATS: "The Appointment of Pigou as Marshall's Successor: Comment", *Journal of Law and Economics*, XV (October 1972), pp. 487-95; T. W. JONES: "The Appointment of Pigou as Marshall's Successor: The Other Side of the Coin", *Journal of Law and Economics*, XXI (April 1978), pp. 234-43.

coaching in mathematics but he abandoned this in 1867-8.[16] By this stage, he had decided that his future did not lie in mathematics and the natural sciences and his interests were in philosophy, psychology and, most recently (probably under the influence of Henry Sidgwick) political economy. He was appointed a College Lecturer in Moral Science in 1868.[17] There was one other College Lecturer in Moral Sciences in St. John's at the time, J.B. Pearson. Pearson took advantage of the appointment and the lecturer's interests to transfer his courses in political economy to Marshall, although Marshall also lectured on utilitarianism. Marshall's systematic and significant writings on economics date from 1870, by which time, at least from the evidence of his surviving papers, he had abandoned metaphysics and psychology.[18]

In coming to political economy, Marshall took advantage of his mathematical training to work through J.S. Mill's *Principles of Political Economy* and formalise it, more often than not geometrically. He also read Smith, Ricardo and Cournot, but probably not at this early stage von Thünen.[19] He also appears to have read some of the same German literature that influenced Menger -- Hermann, Roscher and Rau -- for its theoretical rather than its historical content. He also displayed considerable enthusiasm for a time, for the history of economics, although later he could not find it much use in his teaching (Whitaker, I, 51, H.S. Foxwell, 3 July 1878):

> I don't much recommend the history of economic science; though I most strongly recommend the history of economic phenomena. I spent a good part of a year on it, made voluminous notes, lectured on them twice, came to the conclusion that anything like an elaborate treatment was not profitable for me & most unprofitable for the class; & have seldom used my notes since.

---

16 PETER GROENEWEGEN: [*A Soaring Eagle: Alfred Marshall, 1842-1924*, Aldershot (Edward Elgar) 1995, p. 108] is ambiguous as to when he gave it up, saying both that he carried on coaching during the first two and a half years of his Fellowship and that he abandoned it in the course of 1867. MAYNARD KEYNES: ["Alfred Marshall, 1842-1924", *Economic Journal*, XXXIV (June 1924) pp. 311-72 reprinted in: J. C. WOOD (Ed): *Alfred Marshall: Critical Assessments*, London (Croom Helm) 1982, vol I, p. 10] did not attempt to be as precise.

17 St. John's had created 10 College lectureships in 1860 whose incumbents had the obligation to make their classes open to all.

18 PETER GROENEWEGEN: *A Soaring Eagle*, ch. 5.

19 *Ibid.*, p. 151.

Although Marshall may have had 'a full fresh enthusiasm for the historical study of economics' (Whitaker, II, 418, L.L. Price, 4 August 1892), his reading did not make him an economic historian. He obviously liked historical generalisations long before his *Principles* and he may, as he told readers of the *Economic Journal* have 'once proposed to write a treatise on economic history, and for many years collected materials for it',[20] but history was not his forte. 'Marshall may have been an empiricist but he was not an historian'.[21] Nor did he fully grasp the nature of the documentary research being pioneered by English historians.[22] Moreover, as with methodological speculations, as he grew older Marshall became more critical of the usefulness of history, especially in teaching undergraduate economists.[23] Nonetheless, historical facts, especially 'modern' ones, were important as source of illustrations for his economics, and *Industry and Trade* contained substantial case studies of modern industrial development in Britain, France, Germany and the USA.

But this has taken us too far forward. All we need recognise at this point is that in Marshall's education as an economist, there were substantial doses of history.

Immediately before Marshall returned to Cambridge, he spent four terms in Oxford, the centre of English historical economics. He noticed the difference, writing to Foxwell toward the end of his second term: 'I like Oxford very much: but I have not yet got hold of many people who are willing to go through much for the sake of econ. science.' (Whitaker, I, 137, 10 March 1884) Certainly at this stage he did not think much of W.J. Ashley.[24] His characterisation of Oxford to Neville Keynes (and he was trying to persuade him to take a post there!) was (Whitaker, I, 149, 28 December 1884):

> I have not ... the strength to carry through the work single handed at Oxford. You w^d. be alone there. There is no one else who has given

---

20 ALFRED MARSHALL: 'A Reply', *Economic Journal*, II, (September 1892), p. 507.

21 ALON KADISH: *Historians, Economists and Economic History*, London (Routledge) 1989, p. 131.

22 GERARD KOOT: *English Historical Economics*, p. 29.

23 PETER GROENEWEGEN: *A Soaring Eagle*, pp. 165, 471.

24 When thinking of him as a possible Toynbee lecturer, he remarked 'he wd. not do at all: he wd. have his heart in the work, but not much else' (WHITAKER, I, 138, H.S. Foxwell, 30 March 1884).

the best part of his life to mastering economic theory. On the other hand teachers of history abound there; there is a plethora of them.

By the time Marshall became Professor in Cambridge, he had made his mind up over method. His Inaugural Lecture, 'The Present Position of Economics' made this position clear. That inaugural is a vigorous defence of economic theory which 'supplies a machinery to aid us in reasoning about those motives of human action which are measurable'.[25] He defended economic theory, which was 'not a body of concrete truths but an engine for the discovery of concrete truth",[26] against both its Comtist and its historicist critics. To the Comtist, he simply remarked[27]

> It is vain to speak of the higher authority of a unified social science. No doubt if it existed Economics would gladly find shelter under its wing. But it does not exist; it shows no signs of coming into existence. There is no use in waiting idly for it, we must do what we can with our present resources.

To the 'real' or 'historic' school of economists, who proclaimed the paramount role of facts, he remarked[28]

> [F]acts by themselves are silent, Observation discovers nothing directly of the actions of causes, but only of sequences in time ... Experience in controversies ... brings out the impossibility of learning anything from facts till they are examined and interpreted by reason: and teaches that the most reckless and treacherous of all theorists is he who professes to let facts and figures speak for themselves, who keeps in the background the part he has played, perhaps unconsciously, in selecting and grouping them, and in suggesting the argument *post hoc ergo propter hoc.*

> In order to be able with any safety to interpret economic facts, whether of the past or present time, we must know what kind of effects to expect from each cause and how these effects are likely to combine with one another. This is the knowledge which is got by the study of eco-

---

25 ALFRED MARSHALL: "The Present Position of Economics" (1885), reprinted in: A. C. PIGOU (Ed.): *Memorials of Alfred Marshall*, London (Macmillan) 1925, p. 156.
26 *Ibid.*, p. 159.
27 *Ibid.*, p. 160.
28 *Ibid.*, pp. 166-8.

nomic science; while, on the other hand, the growth of the science is chiefly dependent on the careful study of the facts by the aid of this knowledge.

This did not mean that he did not see an important role for economic history, but it was history informed by economic theory. As he put it in a deliberately provocative way:[29]

> To say that any arrangement is due to custom, is really little more than to say that we do not know its cause. I believe that very many economic customs could be traced, if we only had knowledge enough, to the slow equilibration of measurable motives: that even in a country such as India no custom retains its hold long after the relative positions of the motives of demand and supply have so changed that the values, which would bring them into stable equilibrium, are far removed from those which the custom sanctions ...

> We are able to cross-examine the facts of modern India; and I believe that our science working on those facts will gradually produce a solvent which will explain much that is now unintelligible in mediaeval economic history.

He had by that stage also decided that in Cambridge economics should have more autonomy within the Moral Sciences Tripos -- an autonomy which would ultimately result in its exclusion from that Tripos.

Marshall's was an apposite inaugural: he set out his agenda for himself and his subject. In the his ensuing 23 years in the Chair he elaborated on the themes of that lecture. Let us look at two of those elaborations in his discussions with William Cunningham and Neville Keynes.

III. William Cunningham

The beginnings of Marshall's disagreements with Cunningham coincided with his return to Cambridge in 1885. A former student of Marshall's from the Moral Sciences Tripos, Cunningham, a University Lecturer in History, under the Fawcett régime more or less had things his own way and had de-

---

29 *Ibid.*, pp. 169-71.

voted all his lectures to economic history, leaving the political economy lectures required for the Historical Tripos to J.D. Thorneley (another University Lecturer in History, who was a graduate of the Law and History Triposes). Unhappy with this régime, Marshall, with the support of the Special Board for History and Archaeology, insisted that Cunningham spend at least one term a year teaching political economy to the historians. Cunningham did so until he resigned his University Lectureship in 1891, on becoming Tooke Professor in London.[30]

While Marshall was proceeding to re-arrange Cunningham's teaching, he was also preparing his inaugural lecture with its attack on historicism. Cunningham, who was far happier as a controversialist than the thin-skinned Marshall, was incensed by both, but he bided his time, waiting for an appropriate public occasion on which to reply. In 1888, he applied for the Drummond Professorship in Oxford, where he could use his inaugural lecture as the vehicle, but, unfortunately, he didn't get the chair. However, he soon found other occasions: a lecture to Section F of the British Association in 1889, a presidential address to Section F in 1891, an inaugural lecture as Tooke Professor at King's College, London, in 1891 and finally a lecture to the Royal Historical Society in March 1892,[31] as well as less important venues. Initially, Cunningham's target was Marshall's inaugural lecture. He dismissed Marshall's rejection of Comte as being an echo of Mill's, which he did not regard as conclusive. He was also unhappy with Marshall's notion of economic analysis as 'a solvent'. These attacks could be quite clever. For example in his 1891 address to Section F:[32]

> Professor Edgeworth has rightly pointed out that economists often blunder in treating something as constant that is really variable, and I should like to add that the most common illustration of this error may

---

30 However, he retained his other Cambridge posts such as Vicar of Great St. Mary's and College Lecturer at Trinity.

31 WILLIAM CUNNINGHAM: "The Comtist Criticism of Economic Science" (1889), reprinted in: R. L. SMYTH (Ed.): *Essays in Economic Method*, London (Duckworth), 1962, pp. 98-111; "Nationalism and Cosmopolitanism in Economics", *Journal of the Royal Statistical Society*, LIV (December 1891), pp. 644-62; "The Relativity of Economic Doctrine", *Economic Journal*, II (January 1892), pp. 1-16; "The Perversion of Economic History", *Economic Journal*, II (September 1892), pp. 491-506.

32 WILLIAM CUNNINGHAM: "Nationalism and Cosmopolitanism in Economics", p. 654.

be found in arguments which seem to assume that human nature is constant,[33] and that the variations, even in long periods, may be neglected. Such is the discussion of the applicability of Ricardo's law, with all it involves, to rents, several centuries ago; but perhaps this is meant as a sort of scientific witticism; it is not always easy to tell when a professor of the dismal science is making a joke.

However, in his lecture to the Royal Historical Society he turned his attention to the historical chapters of the first edition of Marshall's *Principles*: Chapters 2 and 3, 'The Growth of Free Industry and Enterprise'.

After Neville Keynes drew his attention to his 1889 British Association paper (Whitaker, I, 275, 11 October 1889), Marshall remonstrated with Cunningham in correspondence which has not survived. The upshot was that the printed version of the paper contained two footnotes explicitly attributed to Marshall: one providing a quotation in full and another suggesting that Cunningham had misinterpreted him.[34] In the second footnote, Cunningham used his editorial control to maintain that, despite Marshall's claim, his own view was nonetheless substantially vindicated. Marshall let the Presidential Address to Section F and the Tooke Inaugural pass by without comment. It was only when 'The Perversion of Economic History' was submitted to the *Economic Journal* that, with Edgeworth's co-operation,[35] Marshall came to approach Cunningham head on and attempted once and for all, as he thought, to confront his critic and, hopefully, to discredit him.

In many ways confrontation was easy, as some of Cunningham's points 'involved wilful -- and because so transparent, curiously pointless -- intellectual dishonesty'.[36] As usual, Marshall took the line that he had been misun-

---

33 A reference to Marshall's inaugural appeared here.

34 WILLIAM CUNNINGHAM: "The Comtist Criticism of Economic Science", pp. 99 n.3 & 109 n.2.

35 The correspondence has not survived, but as Marshall wrote his reply in Switzerland (ALFRED MARSHALL: "A Reply", p. 507, n. 2) and did not return to England until just before his reply appeared (WHITAKER, II, 420, F.Y. Edgeworth, 4 September 1892) there almost certainly was some.

36 JOHN MALONEY: *Marshall, Orthodoxy and the Professionalisation of Economics*, Cambridge (Cambridge University Press) 1985, p. 103. Maloney classifies the apparent disagreements as 'one genuine difference of judgement ..., one correction of a factual mistake, two misinterpretations of Marshall's meaning invited by the extreme compression of his account, one misinterpretation arising from a misprint, one manipulation of Marshall's meaning

derstood or misquoted. He summarised his case, after deploying the evidence:[37]

> On the whole, then, Dr. Cunningham has discovered one sentence in which there has been a slip, and which is not defensible, even if it is intelligible; and one wrong reference. Further, he and I disagree as to Roman business, and other matters. But, speaking broadly, his criticisms proceed on assumptions that I hold opinions which in fact I do not hold, and which I believe I have not expressed; while in several cases I think I have definitely expressed opposite opinions. The criticisms of his present papers are part of a series, all with the same general purport, which he has recently published. The first were in a paper read before the British Association in 1889, in which he represented my attitude towards the main body of the historical school of economists as one of antagonism. I think, indeed, that the most urgent need of our age is the investigation of contemporary economic conditions; but my position is, and has always been, one of respect and gratitude to those who, without contemning the good work that has already been done in scientific analysis, have given their lives to the study of economic history.

> Thus his endeavours to interpret me to other people are almost as conspicuous for their industry as for their incorrectness. Some of them may be read by foreign historical economists and others who do not know my views at first hand; and that facts that he is a colleague, and was formerly (as he has just indicated) a pupil of mine might reasonably suggest to such readers that he could not fail to have entered into my point of view, to speak on full information, and to report me accurately. For these reasons I have broken through my rule of not replying to criticism.

There matters ended as far as the *Journal* was concerned. Edgeworth told Cunningham that the controversy must end with Marshall's reply. Cunningham returned to the matter with a letter of 23 September 1892 that appeared in both *The Pall Mall Gazette* (29 September) and *The Academy* (2 October). When it appeared Marshall remarked, 'I shall rest patient under the imputation of "not being aware" of facts that are so well known that it is not necessary

---

by quoting his words out of context and one infiltration of a rogue word into a plausible generalisation so as to turn it into an absurd one' (*Ibid.*, p. 103, n.*).

37 ALFRED MARSHALL: "A Reply", pp. 517-18.

to state them: & shall not even suggest that Cunningham has read his history almost as hastily as he has Ricardo & my poor little self.' (Whitaker, II, 421, J.N. Keynes 10 October 1892). Inevitably, when it came to the debates on the desirability of a technically demanding, independent, Economics Tripos in Cambridge, Marshall and Cunningham were on opposite sides. However, one should also note that the offending chapters of the *Principles* were relegated to Appendix A from the third edition onwards.

IV. John Neville Keynes

As well as Marshall's *Principles*, 1890 also saw the completion (publication came early in 1891) of Neville Keynes's *Scope and Method of Political Economy*. Marshall and Keynes had been regularly reading proof for each other over the previous few years. Given Neville Keynes's diaries and his correspondence (along with Marshall's comments to a few others such as Foxwell), it is possible to use the creation of Keynes's book as another source of Marshall's views on method.[38]

Keynes's book had its origins in Marshall's move to the Cambridge chair from Oxford, for when Keynes stood in for Marshall in Oxford in the spring of 1885 his lectures were on method. He then slowly worked them up for publication. By the beginning of 1888, the first two chapters of Keynes's book were in proof for Marshall to read before writing a testimonial in support of Keynes's application for the Drummond Professorship.[39] Marshall's initial reaction was quite positive: he found the proofs 'excellent' and his only point of criticism concerned the presentation of 'references of a controversial nature to the opinions of individuals' where he allowed his own ideas were 'somewhat extreme' (Whitaker, I, 227, 7 February 1888). Later in February, he still thought the proof 'extremely good', but he warned Keynes he would 'venture to make one or two suggestions of a general character about it: espe-

---

38 The first person to use Keynes in this way was RONALD COASE: "Marshall on Method", *Journal of Law and Economics*, XVIII (April 1975), pp. 25-31.

39 Keynes also intended that the proofs circulate among the electors. He had, however, put the chapters into proof without his final revisions. Keynes eventually withdrew from the competition. Marshall's testimonial has not been traced.

cially as to your references to the Germans' (*Ibid.*, I, 232, 24 February 1888).
These suggestions did not come until a meeting or 21 April, supplemented
by a letter with enclosures from both himself and Mary Marshall (*Ibid.*, I,
240, 26 April 1888). Although he began by allowing for the difference in his
intellectual style from Keynes's,[40] Marshall's 'general remarks' captured his
worries:

> A new book on the subject ought to be very German & based more on
> 'new School' difficulties in Germany & in America & England. Too
> much prominence is given to the doctrines of writers who [are] sink-
> ing out of memory; too little in comparison is said in anticipation of
> the difficulties of the coming generation.

> On the German side too little said of the historical origin of a great
> part of the science, e.g. cameral wissenschaft.

> As regards general pitch of the book:-- I shd be inclined to separate a
> the didactic from the controversial, & ß that part wh is designed to
> help the beginner & clear away the prejudices of the vulgar (including
> the working man), from that wh is designed to remove the subtler
> mystifications from the minds of those who have already considered
> for themselves the philosophic problems of 'the many in the one &
> the one in the many' as applied to Social Science.

Those comments sent Keynes back to his reading chair and his desk and
during the ensuing fifteen months his diaries were full of his attempts, with
his wife Florence's linguistic assistance, to cover the relevant German literature. It was only in August 1889 that he began to put his revised text into
print. By mid-month the printer had five chapters and the end of the month
saw the beginnings of comments from Marshall and J.S. Nicholson. Marshall's comments were, in general,[41] more conciliatory and his distinctions
less sharp than those Keynes wished to make. Thus on the distinction be-

---

40 'Our minds are a little different. Yours is more orderly than mine: & when we
differ on a point of this kind, it is more likely that you are right than I. ...'
41 One of the exceptions was the following:
I have gradually become convinced that whatever the Irish man Cliffe Leslie
undertook to set right about the facts of English life, he was wrong in consequences of the paucity of facts at his disposal: though he made of show of
knowledge by putting all he knew in the shop window. (*Ibid.*, I, 268, August
1889)

tween German and English methods in economics he wrote (*Ibid.*, I, 269, August 1889):

> I object in toto to the distinction between German & English ....
>
> Suppose you were to compare the English chemists of 1800-40 with the German chemists of 1840-90 & call the methods of the former English & the latter German, you w^{d.} I think change what is fundamentally a difference of time into one of geography. Every one of your contrasts and oppositions is too sharp for me ...
>
> I think you are most harsh & unfair to your own countrymen. What German has ever had one half of the knowledge of the facts of life possessed by McCulloch the bête-noire of those who call the 'English' school abstract.
>
> What country has a mass of economic statistics to be compared to ours ...
>
> I think the picture you give is in general effect a libel on England. What country produced Arthur Young & Eden, Anderson, Porter, Tooke, McCulloch & McPherson? What country can show a series of statistical volumes to be compared with our Journal. what German investigations are nearly as realistic, statistical and ethical, as our Blue books especially our recent ones. What private German has done work as good as Booth's Life and Labour?
>
> Eh??
>
> Yours most frankly. But with great admiration on all points bar this

The same letter also had an enclosure from Mary Marshall also encouraged him to be conciliatory. For example:

> I think the account given of the English exposition of method is rather extreme. I think Mill w^d only have subscribed to it in his earlier days, & I fancy Bagehot w^d take some exception to 'the economic

man'. Mills longer title to his Principles[42] shows that he considered P.E. as having an applied side.

I think it should be brought out that the German school have devoted a much greater part of their energy to talking about method than the English; & that the trifling amount that has been said by the English doesnt represent the view of English Economists as a whole on the subject of method & it doesnt at all represent the methods w[h] have been adopted by English economists; the best work in England has been done by the best available methods without troubling to say what the method is. ...

The method pursued by the English School of P.E. is not at all represented by what has been written on method.

The discussion continued [43]-- and the differences narrowed with Keynes's extensive revisions. Marshall still complained of Keynes's tendency to make contrasts more sharply than he would. However, Marshall also introduced a change in language (Ibid., I, 321, 20 September 1890):

... [Y]ou continually use the word *theory* where I shd use *analysis*. This seems to me to cause confusion wh is increased by the fact that later on you exclude modern facts from history & yet you do not boldly say that they are a part of theory. If they are then I agree with you that a study of theory should come before a study of history. But I do not myself like to put the case this way. My own notion is

i Begin with analysis, which is an essential introduction to all study of facts whether of past or present time; with perhaps a very short historical introduction.

ii Go on to call to mind the students knowledge of the economic conditions in wh he lives. Show the relations in wh they severally stand to one another & carry analysis further making it more real & concrete.

---

42 *The Principles of Political Economy with some of their Applications to Social Philosophy.*
43 See WHITAKER, I, 271, 272, 278, 309, 321 and 322, J.N. Keynes, 27 August, September and 17 November 1889; 14 July, 20 September and 2 October 1890.

iii Build up a general theory or process of reasoning applicable to Value Money Foreign Trade &c, with special reference to the conditions in wh the student lives, & pointing out how far & in what ways it can be made to bear on the other conditions.

iv Give a general course in economic history.

v Qe. Return to economic theory & carry it further.

vi Consider economical conditions in relation to other aspects of social life.

vii Treat of the economic aspects of practical questions in general & social reform in particular

§V. May come almost any where; or, for some classes of students, may be omitted altogether.

Marshall later summarised his suggestions to Keynes (*Ibid*, II, p. 516, H. S. Foxwell, 30 January 1897);

> Most of the suggestions which I made on the proofs of Keynes' *Scope and Method* were aimed at bringing it more into harmony with the views of Schmoller. Some were accepted. But it still remains true that as regards method I regard myself as midway between Keynes + Sidgwick + Cairnes and Schmoller + Ashley.

After Keynes's book appeared, Marshall continued to reflect on the differences between German and British economic education and patterns of publication, generally making comparisons that favoured England, particularly Cambridge.[44]

---

44 See, for example, *ibid.*, II, 448, E. C. K. Gonner, 9 May 1994; II, 451, J. N. Keynes, 10 June 1894. The relevant paragraph of the second letter ran:
My own opinion is that the most astonishing feature of contemporary economic history is the fact that England, where not more [than] a tenth or a twentieth part as many special students of economics are found as in Germany, yet does nearly as much, that is really important. I believe the reason of this is that those very few students of economics whom we get in our English Universities are taught to use the inductive method in a scientific way. I believe that scarcely any of the great German Economists of the Historical School would endorse the suggestion that the 'empirical method' should be encouraged; but that nearly all of them hold that that method is suitable only for newspaper writers & should be left to them. It is however doubtless true that the zeal to produce something new & sensational does cause the young German student often to tackle questions for which he is inadequately

D. E. MOGGRIDGE

V. Foxwell and Cambridge

Thus far I have largely concentrated on Marshall on method and contrasted his views with what might be regarded as the two extremes in Cambridge, although it is hard to describe Cunningham's views concisely or coherently, for he took greater pleasure in controversy than consistency. I have not placed Marshall vis-a-vis Foxwell, who was even more eclectic and, over time, less enamoured with economic analysis.[45] Marshall knew this and, for example, at no stage did he give Foxwell his *Principles'* proofs for comment. The differences in view meant that there were regular disagreements between Marshall and Foxwell over book selections for the Tripos, although to call them 'altercations', as Groenewegen does,[46] is to go too far. Foxwell supported Marshall over the big issues, the formation of the Royal Economic Society and the founding of the Economics Tripos,[47] although here there were disagreements in detail. Nonetheless, from the turn of the century the tone of their relations became testier. Much of the testiness almost certainly resulted from Marshall's fondness for Pigou and the younger man's gradual replacement of Foxwell as Marshall's lieutenant in matters economic and eventual

---

equipped; not because his best teachers would advise him to, but because they have no means at their disposal of getting him to go through that training wh would be good for him. To this fact I attribute the very small output per head of really thorough work on the part of the young German writers who are so prolific of words.

45 Foxwell summed up the evolution of his own thought very nicely in his obituary of William Cunningham [*Economic Journal*, XXIX (September 1919), pp. 387-8]:
Perhaps what his Cambridge colleagues could least understand, and therefore most resented, was his general depreciation of economic theory or, as the phrase now goes, of analysis. I remember that in the early days I was in constant though friendly controversy with him on this point, and found his position unintelligible. It seemed to me that there was no necessary opposition between the theoretical and the realistic habit, as the example of Jevons so brilliantly showed. But on further consideration I have not only learned to understand Cunningham's mistrust of economic theory, but found myself more and more inclined to move in his direction.
46 PETER GROENEWEGEN: *A Soaring Eagle*, p. 674.
47 In this regard GERARD KOOT: *English Historical Economics*, p. 132 is incorrect in suggesting the opposite.

successor.[48] There were also new disagreements over policy, most notably free trade, and Foxwell's lectures, whose content seemed less and less appropriate for the new Tripos, before the two broke off relations completely in 1908.

This brings me to a final note. Marshall may have been methodologically more moderate than some of his contemporaries, less moderate than others. Yet, in the end at considerable personal cost to himself,[49] he left behind several monuments, one of which is the Tripos. It is not clear from his Inaugural Lecture that he envisaged that greater independence for economics would entail a separate Tripos, but the failure of attempts at greater autonomy within Moral Sciences led him to make the decisive move soon after Sidgwick's death in 1900. That this move succeeded owed a lot to Marshall's single-mindedness once he had decided on a course of action. But it also owed a considerable amount to the way economics had developed in Cambridge since before 1885.

Moreover, the institutional context in which all this occurred did matter, more so than I think that previous commentators such as Alon Kadish and Gerard Koot allow.[50] Indeed, I think it can be argued that the major differences between Oxford and Cambridge in the way they dealt with the position of economics in the curriculum depended heavily on institutional factors. Here, the difference is less one of whether the earlier or less comprehensive development of intercollegiate lectures in history at Oxford fatally shifted the balance of power against central control by disciplinary leaders.[51] Rather, I

---

48 One can see a similar resentment later in Dennis Robertson at being replaced by Richard Kahn as Maynard Keynes's lieutenant and confidant.

49 There was the financial cost, which in a few years after 1900 came to as much as £200. There was also a large personal cost, assuming that he regretted losing the friendships of Sidgwick, Foxwell and Neville Keynes. But as GROE-NEWEGEN again and again makes clear [*A Soaring Eagle*, esp. chs. 8, 18 & 21], Marshall was so self-centred that he may not have noticed or cared.

50 A. W. COATS: ['Sociological Aspects of British economic thought (ca. 1800-1930)', *Journal of Political Economy*, LXXV (October 1967, pp. 706-29 reprinted in: A. W. COATS: *The Sociology and Professionalization of Economics: British and American Essays*, vol. II, London (Routledge) 1993, esp. pp. 106-7] has started the line of thought touched on here.

51 At least ALON KADISH puts it as slower developing ["Marshall and the Cambridge Economics Tripos", in: ALON KADISH & KEITH TRIBE (Eds.): *The Market for Political Economy*, p. 58], In terms of beginnings, it is at best really

believe that is lies more in the way the Universities organised their academic affairs in general.

In both Universities, political economy (or economics) was embedded in two Schools or Triposes. However in Oxford in neither Greats nor Modern History was the subject sufficiently central, or sufficiently demanding, to justify separate College appointments, particularly given the numbers involved. The same *might* be said to be true of economics within Cambridge Historical Tripos, although other developments in Cambridge made this less likely. For what was said of political economy in Oxford could *not* be said to be true of the Cambridge Moral Sciences Tripos. Here there were the possibilities for a fair measure of specialisation in economics in Part II (3 of 10 papers) even *before* Marshall started his professorial campaigns. Moreover, even before Marshall took up his chair the Tripos has produced a good run of distinguished graduates who could lay claim to being economists: Foxwell, Cunynghame, J.N. Keynes and J.S. Nicholson -- a much more substantial output than from contemporary Oxford This difference also showed up in the personnel available: when Marshall returned to Cambridge in 1885 to succeed Henry Fawcett, Foxwell, Keynes, Sidgwick were already in place in Moral Sciences.[52] But then so were William Cunningham and Thomas Thornely in history. Moreover, of these named individuals, only Foxwell did not have a *University* post, for Keynes,[53] Thornely and Cunningham held new University Lectureships created under the recent university reforms and Sidgwick

---

only a matter of months, for both movements start in 1868 with history taking the lead in Oxford and Moral Sciences in Cambridge, while the details as to development do not suggest that there was any difference in speed [ALON KADISH: *Historians, Economists and Economic History*, p. 44; SHELDON ROATHBLATT: *The Revolution of the Dons*, London (Faber and Faber) 1968, p. 230]. There may have been differences in power, but that brings us back to the differences in the power of the central institutions in the two universities, a matter discussed below.

52 One should also note that as well as Marshall, Keynes and Sidgwick were mathematically trained. Foxwell was not, but one must remember that he had fallen under Jevons's spell, especially in his earlier years (see p. 27, note 1, above). Cunningham was also not mathematically trained.

53 Keynes may now be thought of more as a philosopher, but if one looks back at the Lecture List of the University in the academic year Marshall reappeared, he was responsible for the most technically advanced segment of the curriculum, advanced political economy using diagrammatic methods.

was Knightbridge Professor of Moral Philosophy, a post he took up in 1883, the same year as his *Principles of Political Economy* appeared. Of course, the existence of these new University Lectureships was also symbolic of the greater power that had gone to the University in Cambridge under the reforms of 1882. True, it was to turn out that the agricultural depression of the late nineteenth century meant that the system of College taxation for University purposes did not generate the revenues necessary to bring many of the reformers hopes to fruition -- that would only come after the next round of a Royal Commission and reform after 1919. However, it was still the case that *in principle* there was, and still is, more power -- and more resources -- at the centre in Cambridge.

Take, for example, the governance of the two Cambridge Triposes. That for Moral Sciences Tripos rested with a Special Board which consisted of the Professor of Political Economy, the Knightbridge Professor of Philosophy and, after 1897, the Professor of Mental Philosophy and Logic, plus 'such Readers, University Lecturers, Examiners and other persons as may be appointed from time to time by or under the authority of a Grace of the Senate'[54]. In 1885, if one goes by *The Cambridge University Reporter*, this rubric seems to have meant up to six examiners and four others in Moral Sciences. In the case of History, that rubric meant that the Special Board of Studies, in addition to six named professors (the Regius Professor of Modern History, the Disney Professor of Archaeology, the Dixie Professor of Ecclesiastical History, the Slade Professor of Fine Art, the Professor of Political Economy and the Whewell Professor of International Law) consisted of six examiners and five others. Thus, although the Professors were not in a majority, they had a strong presence, not to mention a direct interest in what was going on. As the initial contretemps between Sidgwick and Marshall and between Marshall and Cunningham indicated, either the Chair of the relevant Board of Studies or the Professor of the relevant discipline also had considerable power over what was taught by those with University appointments.

In Oxford in Modern History, the situation was only different in one respect, for there the Faculty Board consisted of six named professors (Chichele Professor of Modern History, Regius Professor of Modern History, Regius Professor of Ecclesiastical History, Chichele Professor of International Law and Diplomacy, Rawlinson Professor of Anglo Saxon and Drummond Professor of Political Economy), three co-opted members elected for two or more

---

54 Cambridge University, *Statutes 1882*, Ch. V (3).

years, plus the current examiners and all previous examiners for the last three years. The titles of the six named professors in Oxford were not that different from their Cambridge counterparts in history; so it does not really seem that the Oxford History Board was, any more than the Cambridge one, 'a refuge for the destitute, into which all the anomalous Professors, who had no other refuge, were indiscriminately shovelled'.[55] Perhaps it really had something to do with the way the two universities organised themselves.

Finally, the way matters eventually turned out in political economy or economics, both before, and even after, 1914, may also have had something to do with the another underlying difference between the two universities. Cunningham picked it up in one of the addresses critical of Marshall. He was discussing the differences between the two new economic journals -- Oxford's *The Economic Review* and *The Economic Journal* -- which appeared in the year before his Presidential Address to Section F:[56]

> The old contrast between these two universities comes out strongly and distinctly. The intense interest which Oxford has always shown in the study of man and of conduct has put her in practical touch with many sides of actual life and has caused her to be the mother of not a few great movements. But in Cambridge we are so engrossed in the study of things that we have no time to spare for trying to know ourselves. If we ever do give our thoughts to man, we like to think of him as if he were a kind of thing; so that we may apply the same methods which we are wont to use in the study of physical phenomena. If we turn our attention to history, we try to classify the various forms of constitution that have existed on the globe, and then we call the results political science. We may devote ourselves to ancient or modern literature, but they seem to interest us not as vehicles of thought or forms of art, but as the bases for philological or phonological science. If we investigate human industry, we like to treat the individual as if he were a mere mechanism, and busy ourselves in measuring the force of the motives that may be brought to bear upon him. It is when we deal with physical things that we can be precise; this we are determined to be at all hazards....

---

55 ALON KADISH: "Oxford Economics in the Late Nineteenth Century", in: ALON KADISH & KEITH TRIBE (Eds.): *The Market for Political Economy*, p. 59.

56 WILLIAM CUNNINGHAM: "Nationalism and Cosmopolitanism in Economics", pp. 644-5.

Perhaps some things never change.[57]

VI. Conclusion

Let me try and bring matters together. In terms of his views on method, Marshall was eclectic. As he told Neville Keynes in September 1889 (Whitaker, II, 272):

> I take an extreme position at to the *methods & scope* of economics. In my new book I say of *methods* simply that economics has to use every method known to science.

In other words, he was prepared to use any method that produced helpful and useful results. Moreover, except perhaps for his famous strictures on the use of mathematics,[58] his methodological views are resonant with those of his modern successors -- something that is not the case with his views on ethics. This does not mean that he did not have strong views about, say, the basic content of an undergraduate degree in economics, as his correspondence with Foxwell indicates. But it does mean that within that context he was fairly catholic in his attitudes. As he told Foxwell on 12 February 1906 (Whitaker, III, 836):

> Of course our ideals in economics are different. I have noticed that when a book or a pamphlet pleases you greatly you describe it as

---

57 See, for example, NOEL ANNAN: *Our Age: Portrait of a Generation*, London (Weidenfeld and Nicolson) 1990, pp. 4-5 and LORD JENKINS OF HILLHEAD: *An Oxford View of Cambridge*, Cambridge (Cambridge University Press) 1988, pp. 13-15.

58 Whitaker, III, 840, A. L. Bowley, 27 February 1906, also printed in: A.C. PIGOU (Ed.): *Memorials of Alfred Marshall*, pp. 427-8:
I have a growing feeling in the later years of my work at the subject that a good mathematical theorem dealing with economic hypotheses was very unlikely to be good economics: and I went more and more on the rules -- (1) Use mathematics as a shorthand language, rather than as an engine of inquiry. (2) Keep to them till you have done. (3) Translate into English. (4) Then illustrate by examples that are important to real life. (5) Burn the mathematics. (6) If you can't succeed in (4), burn (3). This last I did often.

'scholarly': whereas I am never roused to great enthusiasm about anything wh does not seem to me thoroughly 'Scientific'.

I have two or three times referred to this difference, when discussing our curriculum, and described it as an advantage. I think it is very important that there should be considerable diversities of temperament among the teachers of any subject, and especially of one of which the past and present are so meagre, and the future is so uncertain as economics.

References

ANNAN, NOEL: *Our Age: Portrait of a Generation*, London (Weidenfeld and Nicolson) 1990.

ASHLEY, ANNE: *William James Ashley: A Life*, London (P. S. King) 1932.

COLLARD, DAVID: "Cambridge After Marshall", in: J. K. WHITAKER (Ed.): *Centennial Essays on Alfred Marshall*, Cambridge (Cambridge University Press) 1990.

COASE, R. H.: "The Appointment of Pigou as Marshall's Successor: Comment", *Journal of Law and Economics*, XV (October 1972), pp. 473-85, reprinted in J. C. WOOD (Ed.): *Alfred Marshall: Critical Assessments*, London (Croom Helm) 1982, vol. IV.

COASE, R. H.: "Marshall on Method", *Journal of Law and Economics*, XVIII (April 1975), pp. 25-31, reprinted in: J. C. WOOD (Ed.): *Alfred Marshall: Critical Assessments*, London (Croom Helm) 1982, vol. I.

COATS, A. W.: "The Historicist Reaction in English Political Economy, 1870-1890", *Economica*, NS, XX (May 1954), pp. 143-53, reprinted in: A. W. COATS: *On the History of Economic Thought: British and American Economic Essays*, Vol I, London (Routledge) 1992.

COATS, A. W.: "Sociological Aspects of British Economic Thought (ca. 1800-1930)", *Journal of Political Economy*, LXXV (October 1967), pp. 706-29, reprinted in: A. W. COATS: *The Sociology and Professionalization of Economics: British and American Economic Essays*, vol II, London (Routledge) 1993.

METHOD AND MARSHALL

COATS, A. W.: "Political Economy and the Tariff Reform Campaign of 1903", *Journal of Law and Economics*, XI (April 1968), pp. 181-229, reprinted in: A. W. COATS: *On the History of Economic Thought: British and American Economic Essays*, vol. I, London (Routledge) 1992.

COATS, A. W.: "The Appointment of Pigou as Marshall's Successor: Comment", *Journal of Law and Economics*, XV (October 1972), pp. 487-95 reprinted in: J. C. WOOD (Ed.): *Alfred Marshall: Critical Assessments*, vol. IV, London (Croom Helm) 1982.

COATS, A. W.: "Marshall and Ethics", in: R. MC WILLIAMS-TULBERG (Ed.): *Alfred Marshall in Retrospect*, Aldershot (Edward Elgar) 1990, pp. 153-77, reprinted in: A. W. COATS: *On the History of Economic Thought: British and American Economic Essays*, vol. I, London (Routledge) 1992.

CUNNINGHAM, WILLIAM: "The Comtist Criticism of Economic Science" (1889), reprinted in: R. L. SMYTH (Ed.): *Essays in Economic Method: Selected papers Read to Section F of the British Association for the Advancement of Science, 1860-1913*, London: (Duckworth) 1962, pp. 98-111.

CUNNINGHAM, WILLIAM: "Nationalism and Cosmopolitanism in Economics", *Journal of the Royal Statistical Society*, LIV (December 1891), pp. 644-62.

CUNNINGHAM, WILLIAM: "The Relativity of Economic Doctrine", *Economic Journal*, II (March 1892), pp. 1-16.

CUNNINGHAM, WILLIAM: "The Perversion of Economic History", *Economic Journal*, II (September 1892), pp. 491-506.

DAHRENDORF, RALF: *LSE: A History of the London School of Economics and Political Science, 1895-1005*, Oxford (Oxford University Press) 1995.

DRUMMOND, IAN: *Political Economy at the University of Toronto: A History of the Department, 1888-1982*, Toronto (Faculty of Arts and Science, University of Toronto) 1983.

EDGEWORTH, F. Y.: "Review of J. N. Keynes, *Scope and Method of Political Economy*", *Economic Journal*, I (June 1891), pp. 420-3.

FOXWELL, H. S.: "Archdeacon Cunningham", *Economic Journal*, XXIX (September 1919), pp. 382-90.

GROENEWEGEN, PETER: *A Soaring Eagle: Alfred Marshall 1842-1924*, Aldershot (Edward Elgar) 1995.

JENKINS OF HILLHEAD, LORD: *An Oxford View of Cambridge (with some reflections on Oxford and other universities*, The Rede Lecture 1988, Cambridge (Cambridge University Press) 1988.

JOHNSON, H. G.: "Cambridge in the 1950s: Memoirs of an Economist", *Encounter*, 42 (January 1974), pp. 28-39.

JONES, T. W.: "The Appointment of Pigou as Marshall's Successor: The Other Side of the Coin", *Journal of Law and Economics*, XXI (April 1978), pp. 234-43, reprinted in: J. C. WOOD (Ed.): *Alfred Marshall: Critical Assessments*, London (Croom Helm) 1982, vol. IV.

D. E. MOGGRIDGE

KADISH, ALON: *Historians, Economists and Economic History*, London (Routledge) 1989.

KADISH, ALON: "Oxford Economics in the Late Nineteenth Century", in: ALON KADISH & KEITH TRIBE (Eds.): *The Market for Political Economy: The Advent of Economics in British University Culture, 1850-1905*, London (Routledge) 1993, pp. 42-77.

KADISH, ALON: "Marshall and the Cambridge Economics Tripos", in: ALON KADISH & KEITH TRIBE (Eds.): *The Market for Political Economy: The Advent of Economics in British University Culture, 1850-1905*, London (Routledge) 1993, pp. 137-61.

KADISH, ALON: "The City, the Fabians and the Foundation of the London School of Economics", in: ALON KADISH & KEITH TRIBE (Eds.): *The Market for Political Economy: The Advent of Economics in British University Culture, 1850-1905*, London (Routledge) 1993, pp. 227-50.

KEYNES, J. M.: "Alfred Marshall, 1842-1924", *Economic Journal*, XXXIV (September 1924), pp. 311-72 reprinted in J.C. WOOD (Ed.): *Alfred Marshall: Critical Assessments*, vol. I., London (Croom Helm) 1982.

KEYNES, J. N.: *The Scope and Method of Political Economy*, London (Macmillan) 1891[59].

KOOT, GERARD: *English Historical Economics, 1870-1926: The Rise of Economic History and Neomercantilism*, Cambridge (Cambridge University Press) 1987.

MALONEY, JOHN: *Marshall, Orthodoxy and the Professionalisation of Economics*, Cambridge (Cambridge University Press) 1985.

MALONEY, JOHN: "The Teaching of Political Economy in the University of London", in: ALON KADISH & KEITH TRIBE (Eds.): *The Market for Political Economy: The Advent of Economics in British University Culture, 1850-1905*, London (Routledge) 1993, pp. 20-77.

MARSHALL, ALFRED: "The Present Position of Economics" (1885), reprinted in: A. C. PIGOU (Ed): *Memorials of Alfred Marshall*, London (Macmillan) 1925, pp. 154-74.

MARSHALL, ALFRED: *Principles of Economics*, London (Macmillan) 1890.

MARSHALL, ALFRED: *Principles of Economics*, 9th (variorum) ed. by C. W. Guillebaud, London (Macmillan) 1961.

MARSHALL, ALFRED: "A Reply", *Economic Journal*, II (September 1892), pp. 507-19.

MENGER, ANTON: *The Right to the Whole Produce of Labour* (translated by M. E. Tanner with an introduction and bibliography by H. S. Foxwell), London (Macmillan) 1899.

ROBERTSON, D. H.: *Utility and All That*, London (George Allen and Unwin) 1952.

---

59 Although the title page says 1890, the preface was dated 12 December 1890 and the book actually appeared early in 1891.

ROTHBLATT, S.: *The Revolution of the Dons: Cambridge and Society in Victorian England*, London (Faber and Faber) 1968.

TRIBE, KEITH: "Political Economy in the Northern Civic Universities", in: ALON KADISH & KEITH TRIBE (Eds.): *The Market for Political Economy: The Advent of Economics in British University Culture, 1850-1905*, London (Routledge) 1993, pp. 184-226.

WHITAKER, J. K. (Ed): *The Correspondence of Alfred Marshall, Economist*, 3 vols., Cambridge (Cambridge University Press) 1996.

Discussion Summary

ANNETTE KLEINFELD

Paper discussed:
D. E. MOGGRIDGE: Method and Marshall

A first part of the discussion dealt with the question how far specific national or historical factors have influenced Alfred Marshall's method and theory of economics.

Regarding the situation of universitites in Scotland in comparison to the British universities at that time (FURUBOTN), it was pointed out that the university of Edinburgh was not equipped yet with a real chair of economics, but only with certain degree-courses for economists, for instance in commercial laws. Marshall himself considered teaching to be of great importance for the development of the new discipline of economics. The reasons for this view were not so much seen in the British background of Marshall than in the nature of the subject, i.e. in the practical relevance of economics in general (MOGGRIDGE). From the second half of the nineteenth century on, the leading universities of the world were German. And it was also here where the combination of research and teaching was developed and became common. This is the reason why most of the American economists of the years from 1870 to 1933 had been educated in Germany. In the United States an analogue model of the university was not established before the 1870ies and 1880ies (NOPPENEY). However, the American higher education has always been more oriented towards practice whereas in Germany civil service was the main background of the educational system, thus making the education of academics for being academics become a major task of the universities (MOGGRIDGE, RINGER).

Unlike the usual attitude of British academics, to look down on economic practicioners, Marshall had a great respect for businessmen, which also made up the background and motivation for his writings. The intention to secure usefulness is therefore the actual basis of his theory (AVTONOMOV, MOG-GRIDGE).

A second part of the discussion dealt with the influence of the Historical School on British economics.

According to Marshall, Keynes was overestimating the role and importance of the Historical School for the development of economics, and due to this, held an extreme position in the eyes of Marshall. Were there any other British economists who shared Keynes' opinion or gave their comments on this question (KOSLOWSKI)?

In Manchester, for instance, the influence of the Historical School could clearly be noticed. At the beginning of this century, a number of comparative studies about the development of industrialization appeared. Until the 1930ies Cambridge played an important role because of its research on the field of economic history. On the basis of the practically oriented approach of Marshall and Cunningham, however, Manchester as the main centre of industry also became the main centre of economics, while Oxford and Cambridge due to their mere emphasis on history lost importance in the field of economic theory (CASSON, MOGGRIDGE).

The question was raised if there are any reflections within Marshall or others about the relevance of the historical approach for industrially underdeveloped countries. Today this relevance is seen in the case of China and Russia, to which universalistic models cannot be simply applied. In order to establish the system of market economy in these countries, a historistic approach is required that takes into account the historical and cultural particularities of the respective nation. It was exactly for this kind of reasons and with regard to countries not yet being on the same level of industrialization as England that the German Historical School developed its specific non-universalistic approach (KOSLOWSKI). Marshall however, starting from the American case, where history plays a less important role than in other countries, did not recognize this relevance of historistic thought (MOGGRIDGE). After the process of industrialization had been accomplished, for others like Cunnigham, the main aim now was to conserve and protect the economic achievements (CASSON).

Part Six

The Historical School and the Development of Economics in Japan and Russia

Chapter 15

Two Developments of the Concept of *Anschauliche Theorie* (Concrete Theory) in Germany and Japan

TETSUSHI HARADA

I.   Emergence of the "Anschauliche Theorie" Concept
II. Development of the Concept in Germany
III. Development of the Concept in Japan
IV. Some Remarks

In the "method debate" (Methodenstreit) at the end of the 19th century, Gustav Schmoller, confronting Carl Menger, argued that there should be no hurrying of theoretical abstraction, but that priority should be given to extensive explanation and analysis of historical facts. But this standpoint of Schmoller, which included an extremely untheoretical tendency, aroused the dissatisfaction of some younger scholars who had grown up under the influence of the "historism" (Historismus). After Schmoller's death (1917), the concept of "anschauliche Theorie" emerged in the 1920s as an attempt to overcome this perceived weakness.[1] In the following, we explain the emergence of the concept, and then consider and compare two further branches of development in Germany and Japan in the years around 1940, taking the circumstances of the two countries at that time into account.

---

1   Cf. K. BRANDT: *Geschichte der deutschen Volkswirtschaftslehre*, Vol. 2, Freiburg (R. Haufe) 1993, pp. 251-9; J. A. SCHUMPETER: *History of Economic Analysis*, 8th pr., London (G. Allen & Unwin) 1972, pp. 815-8; T. RIHA: *German Political Economy*, Bradford (MCB University Press) 1985, pp. 112-4; E. VON BECKERATH, N. KLOTEN: "Wirtschaftswisssenschaft", *Handwörterbuch der Sozialwissenschaften*, Vol. 12, 1965, pp. 294-301.

TETSUSHI HARADA

I. Emergence of the "Anschauliche Theorie" Concept

Edgar Salin (1892-1974) at Heidelberg University refers to the "method debate" and incisively criticizes Schmoller in the first edition of his *Geschichte der Volkswirtschaftslehre* (1923). According to Salin, Schmoller, who lacked theoretical and philosophical talents, refused abstract theories in general in his controversy with Menger and consequently dissolved such bonding between history and theory as had been elaborated by Knies and the Older Historical School. In effect, therefore, Schmoller was making light of theory.[2] According to Salin, the fundamental task of the Historical School is not to explain particular historical phenomena, but to construct a theory which facilitates the understanding of the whole of a national economy including those phemonena; this task was clearly not accomplished by Schmoller, and therefore the assignment of carrying out "what the Schmoller School had neglected"[3] should now be faced squarely.

Although Salin does not accomplish the construction of such a theory either, he finds clues to its configuration in *Der moderne Kapitalismus* of Werner Sombart (1863-1941), especially vol. 3, *Das Wirtschaftsleben im Zeitalter des Hochkapitalismus* (1927). Already in the introduction to vol.1 of the first edition (1902), Sombart, while considering his own method "historical", criticized his "admired teacher Schmoller", on the grounds that history and theory were not things to be treated as mutually antagonistic, but rather to be reconciled through unification at a higher level. In Sombart's criticism of Schmoller, we find two points of important relevance to our later arguments. Firstly, according to Sombart, theorization in the field of social sciences requires "different theories for historically distinct economic periods", in contrast to the situation in the natural sciences, which have everlasting phenomena as their research objects. Secondly, Marxism does not contradict "historism".[4]

---

2 Cf. E. SALIN: *Geschichte der Volkswirtschaftslehre*, 1st ed., Berlin (Springer) 1923, p. 36.
3 *Ibid.*, p. 40.
4 W. SOMBART: *Der moderne Kapitalismus*, Vol.1, 1st ed., Berlin (Duncker & Humblot) 1902, pp. XXI, XXIX. cf. S. TAMURA: *Studies on Gustav Schmoller* (Jap. *Gustav Schmoller Kenkyu*), Tokyo (Ochanomizushobo) 1993, pp. 348-9.

Salin in his 1927 essay "Hochkapitalismus. Eine Studie über Werner Sombart, die deutsche Volkswirtschaftslehre und das Wirtschaftssystem der Gegenwart" makes the following assertions.

In the tentative search for a "new direction" after Schmoller, the attempts of Max Weber are well known, but Sombart tends to be treated too lightly in the academic world, as presenting ideas more "suitable to journalism".[5] However, Weber overemphasizes objectivity and value-neutrality, so that his various concepts, as ideal types, become mere "instruments of cognition" (Erkenntnismittel), he has theoretically no concern for the truthfulness of his concepts, and his social science is therefore "self- and spirit-voided" (entselbstet und entseelt). Sombart's concept of capitalism can be subjected to verification and reveals a path of complete cognition including theory and experience. This concept not only connects globally with cognitions of causal relationships among empirical historical facts and with theoretical representations of them, but additionally attempts to identify current problems and to suggest ways to overcome these. In other words, it follows in the tradition of List, Knies and Hildebrand and contains a combination of "historism and socialism"[6] viz. the criticism of capitalism by Marx. In this sense, Sombart's concept of capitalism is more comprehensive than Weber's.

Salin refers also to the tradition of German culture. Goethe created a feminine emblem of soul nobility (die Schöne-Gute) in his novel *Wilhelm Meisters Wanderjahre*, and used it to lament the spread of mechanical modes of production and to voice his skepticism about capitalism in general. This critical stance towards capitalism was taken up by such intellectuals as Hölderlin, Schopenhauer, the Romantics and Nietzsche. Hence, the true German intellectual heritage to be followed, according to Salin, is not a "self- and spirit-voided" one (as in Weber), but the critical spirit toward contemporary matters (as in Sombart). Here Salin's argument is an amplification of Sombart's combination of "historism and socialism" from Salin's German ideological viewpoint. The argument may perhaps be colored by a psychological impulse to guard his ideas, because he is a scholar of Jewish origin. However, his

---

5   E. SALIN: "Hochkapitalismus: Eine Studie über Werner Sombart, die deutsche Volkswirtschaftslehre und das Wirtschaftssystem der Gegenwart", *Weltwirtschaftliches Archiv*, 25 (1927), pp. 317-8.

6   *Ibid.*, pp. 318, 324.

statement of German nationalistic sentiment is not of a chauvinistic character, but remains within the humanistic ethos.[7]

According to Salin, Sombart's "path of complete cognition"[8] is not merely a history, but a theory for two reasons. Firstly, Sombart attempts to arrive at essences through the leaving out of accidental circumstances, when he aims to understand sequences of facts in the totality of their rational and irrational relations. Secondly, the view may be taken in German tradition that theory is found not only in cosmopolitanly abstract formalizations, but also in the understanding of fact relations in national historical contexts. Sombart's "path of complete cognition" is an example of this latter type.[9] Salin highly appreciates all the above-mentioned aspects of Sombart's theory, even though he faults it for such problems as a too easy acceptance of Marx's surplus value theory, a miscategorization of certain noneconomic facts as acccidental, and a failure to grasp the metaphysical and historico-philosophical significances of capitalism.[10] Salin adds some further original tones to Sombart's theory, and renames it the "anschauliche Theorie",[11] meaning a theory which views the whole of the national economy just as it exists, graphically (the adjective "anschaulich" comes from a verb "anschauen" which means "to view exactly"). This concept is not to be found in the previously referred to first edition of *Geschichte der Volkswirtschaftslehre* (1923).

Among adaptations made by Salin, the distinction and relation between the "anschauliche Theorie" and its counterconcept "rationale theorie" are notable. According to Salin, the "anschauliche Theorie" is essentially grounded in inductive reasoning and resists attempts at absolute rational deduction, but the relative significance of rational theory as a "heuristic instrument" (heuris-

---

7   Cf. *ibid.*, pp. 314-5; *Goethes Werke*, Vol. 25, Weimar 1895, photomechan. reprint, Tokyo (Sansyusya) 1975, pp. 246-52; B. SCHEFOLD: "Salin, Edgar", *The New Palgrave*, Vol. 4, 1987, p. 233; B. SCHEFOLD: "Nationalökonomie als Geisteswissenschaft - Edgar SALINS Konzept einer Anschaulichen Theorie", *List Forum für Wirtschafts- und Finanzpolitik*, 18 (1992), pp. 305-311; C. VON DIETZE: "Lieber Freund Salin!", in: E. VON BECKERATH, H. POPITZ et al. (Eds.): *Antidoron*, Tübingen (J.C.B. Mohr) 1962, pp. 6-7.

8   E. SALIN: "Hochkapitalismus", p. 325.

9   Cf. *ibid.*, pp. 326-7.

10 Cf. *ibid.*, pp. 336, 340-1, 343.

11 *Ibid.*, pp. 327ff. passim.

tisches Mittel)[12] is acknowledged. That is to say, rational theory is subsumed in the higher and more comprehensive "anschauliche Theorie". Salin notes that "For all classical and post-classical [Menger's - T.H.] 'theory', the abstracting reduction of the economy to some small number of rationally defined, logically solvable problems"[13] is characteristic. If this kind of rational theory is considered as absolute, peculiarities of any given national economy are overlooked and complete cognition is not achieved. Although rational theory can at most perceive "one part of economic phenomena", dogmatic rational theorists mistake it for "'the' economy".[14] However, provided the partial role of rational theory as a contributor toward the overall complete cognition achieved through "anschauliche Theorie" is correctly understood, then rational theories are acceptable. We can understand this argument of Salin's as a move to accommodate modern abstract theories within the inductive method of the Historical School, that is to say, as a solution of the conflict between the Historical School and the Austrians from the point of view of the former. However, because of his failure to confront the arguments of Schmoller and Menger in sufficient detail, his "anschauliche Theorie" is left with many points of obscurity.

Following this presentation of the concept "anschauliche Theorie" in the essay of 1927, Salin, professor at Basel University from the same year on (but after the publication of this essay)[15], followed up the same arguments in the revised and enlarged second edition of the *Geschichte der Volkswirtschaftslehre* (1929), in which he defines the concept "anschauliche Theorie" more clearly, and thoroughly analyzes many economic ideas of the past from the viewpoint of the concept.

The "anschauliche Theorie" is explained in the following way: whereas the cognition processes of rational theory are only or mainly rational and their end is a rational but partial cognition, the "anschauliche Theorie" provides not only rational cognition, but mainly "sense cognition, cognition of totality, unity, form and essence" (sinnliche Erkenntnis, Ganzheits-, Einheits-, Gestalt-, Wesenserkenntnis). When focusing primarily on "sense cog-

---

12　*Ibid.*, p. 332. Schmoller considers "Teleologie" as "heuristisches Hilfsmittel", in his article "Volkswirtschaft, Volkswirtschaftslehre und -methode", *Handwörterbuch der Staatswissenschaften*, 3rd ed., Vol. 8, 1911, p. 437. This point is not mentioned by Salin here.

13　E. Salin: "Hochkapitalismus", pp. 326-7.

14　*Ibid.*, p. 327.

15　Cf. B. Schefold: "Salin, Edgar", p. 233.

nition", "anschauliche Theorie" is a historical theory, because it takes historical and political elements of sense-accessible existent relations into account, as if the elements constituted a "supra-economic casing" (überwirtschaftliches Gehäuse). In contrast, rational theory abstracts these elements, and searches, by means of this abstraction, for inexistent "timeless" economies or economic laws. Salin further insists on the "logical and existential precedence" of "anschauliche Theorie" over "merely-rational" (nur-rational) theory for the reason that the "cognition of essence" includes "rational partial cognition" (rationale Teilerkenntnis)[16].

Salin identifies two types of theories in the history of economics. One is the "type of mercantilism - German national economy"[17], namely the "anschauliche" type, of which typical past theorists are Adam Müller and List, followed in modern times by Sombart, Spiethoff, Spann and Gottl-Ottlilienfeld (intermediate between the two periods is Knies). The other is the rational type of theories, to which belong Quesnay, Ricardo and Pareto. Among the "anschauliche" theorists, Müller was the first to express skepticism about individualism and cosmopolitanism pointedly. While not overlooking a certain exaggerated quality in this skepticism, Salin appreciates Müller highly for having presented society in its totality and its growth as an organism, for having linked the past to the present, and for his role in influencing the Historical School.[18] List's theory is appreciated as the hitherto best countertheory to Ricardo's rationalism.[19] Spiethoff shows a "full, lively reconciling"[20] of rational and historical theory in his description of economic crises. While having little to say about Gottl, Salin gives Spann positive credit for having adopted appropriate parts of rational theories within the universalistic view of his *Fundament der Volkswirtschaftslehre* (1. ed., 1918; 4. ed., 1929). However, he balances this with negative criticism of Spann's claim of an irreconcilable confrontation between universalism and individualism. This idea of

---

16 E. SALIN: *Geschichte der Volkswirtschaftslehre*, 2nd ed., Berlin (Springer) 1929, p. 55.

17 *Ibid.*, p. 53, cf. 102.

18 Cf. *ibid.*, pp. 77-8. In his article "Hochkapitalismus", p. 328, Salin sees Müller's work as "an example of 'anschauliche' theory without 'rationale' theory".

19 Cf. E. SALIN: *Geschichte der Volkswirtschaftslehre*, 2nd ed., p. 79.

20 *Ibid.*, p. 101; A. SPIETHOFF: "Krisen", *Handwörterbuch der Staatswissenschaften*, 4th ed., Vol. 6, 1925, pp. 8-91.

confrontation is rejected by Salin.[21] In contrast to Spann, Sombart asserts not a mere face-to-face opposition, but an internal reconcilement between theory and history, and provides economics with a new fertile basis. In this sense, Sombart excels Spann.[22] Thus, Salin's high appraisal of Sombart, which was noticeable in the essay of 1927, remains a feature of the second edition of his *Geschichte der Volkswirtschaftslehre*.

Some other significant theorists who are named here as not very typical of either type are discussed carefully and precisely by Salin. His account of the "method debate" is as follows. First, he cites from Schmoller's *Grundriß der Allgemeinen Volkswirtschaftslehre* (1st ed., 1900/04; 13. ed., 1923) "that it [the Younger Historical School - T.H.] is less rash in its wish to generalize, that it feels a much stronger desire to shift from the erudite accumulation of data to special studies of particular periods, nations and economic situations".[23] Salin finds it problematic that Schmoller had so little inclination for theory and was therefore all along engaged in historical detail-studies. In this connection, Salin judges in favor of Menger as far as the "method debate" is concerned, at least to the extent that Menger opposed this replacement of theories with historical enquiries as practiced by Schmoller, even though Menger, too, considered a utilization of historical findings important for economics. However, it is Salin's view that, in spite of his advantage in the debate, Menger had one serious failing in precisely the area in which Schmoller supplied significant hints for the economics of the future. Menger's failing is that he regarded rational theory, in its pure timeless form, as meaningful, even though it is on principle set apart from historical research. On the other hand, Schmoller's richest bequests to posterity are materials he left in the form of historical studies. These materials are lacking in unity and synthesization, and it is for this reason that Schmoller remains at the level of a provider of data. But these materials are potentially the basis for the new edifice of "anschauliche Theorie", and in this sense Schmoller is "a provider of materials for a new scientific building". "Humanly, he has been a path beater towards fertile fields for many of his disciples and friends, though he himself has never set foot in these fields."[24] In this way, while criticizing

---

21 Cf. E. SALIN: *Geschichte der Volkswirtschaftslehre*, 2nd ed., p. 53, 101.
22 Cf. *ibid.*, p. 100.
23 *Ibid.*, p. 88; G. SCHMOLLER: *Grundriß der Allgemeinen Volkswirtschaftslehre*, Part 1, 1st ed., Leipzig (Duncker & Humblot) 1900 (Facsim. ed., Düsseldorf 1989), p. 118.
24 E. SALIN: *Geschichte der Volkswirtschaftslehre*, 2nd ed., p. 94.

Schmoller's method, Salin asserts the prospect of possible developments from Schmoller's contribution to the "anschauliche Theorie".[25]

In order to connect with our following arguments, we must also survey Salin's estimation of Smith and Marx. According to him, Smith described a framework of classical theory centering on price mechanism, namely a "strange dream of commercial economy" in which social harmony is realized through free competition. Thus it was Smith who first showed the way to the pure theory of the 19th century. In this sense, his ideas belong to the type of rational theory. However, if later economic scientists appreciate Smith's work only in its aspect as a fount of "pure" theory, this is one-sided, because in fact his work displays a "multiplicity"[26] of aspects. *The Wealth of Nations* (1776) contains not only the theoretical First Book, but also the Third Book, which has many historical and sociological statements, as well as the Fourth and Fifth Books in which Smith appears as a commercial and fiscal authority. Smith also carried out analyses of social psychology in *The Theory of Moral Sentiments* (1759). In this way, Smith does display a kind of completeness of historical and empirical cognition, similar in range to what the "anschauliche Theorie" tries to cover.

Salin points out that Marx also exhibits a certain completeness of historical cognition. His economic analysis, as Salin sees it, is characterized by class "conflict and exploitation", which contribute to the destruction of the harmony illusion of the classical theory; in this respect, it displays "historically correct cognition", valid "for several decades of high capitalism". Salin regrets that there should be a lack of proper understanding of "the historical greatness of Marxism"[27] even in Germany. However, he also recognizes that Marx fell into socialistic illusions, and that in this aspect he remains an epigone of classical economics, incapable of entirely overcoming the established ideas. In this context, Salin refers to Nietzsche, who explained exploitation more accurately in terms of real-life humanity.[28]

As explained above, Salin presents his definition of the "anschauliche Theorie" and its relation to other theories more clearly in the second edition of *Geschichte der Volkswirtschaftslehre*. But the "anschauliche Theorie" itself is not yet systematically elaborated. Indeed he appeals to his readers in his fi-

---

25 Cf. *ibid.*, pp. 88-90, 94.
26 *Ibid.*, pp. 46-7.
27 *Ibid.*, pp. 70-71.
28 Cf. *ibid.*, p. 71.

nal section for aid in its further construction.[29] Thus, it is left to Salin's successors, Spiethoff and Takashima, to take up the challenge.

II. Development of the Concept in Germany

Arthur Spiethoff (1873-1957), professor at Bonn University after studies under Adolph Wagner and an assistantship under Schmoller,[30] treats the "anschauliche Theorie" in his 1932 essay "Die Allgemeine Volkswirtschaftslehre als geschichtliche Theorie. Die Wirtschaftsstile", in which he refers to Salin's "Hochkapitalismus" and the second edition of *Geschichte der Volkswirtschaftslehre* as well as to Sombart's *Der moderne Kapitalismus* and other works. This is an attempt by Spiethoff to apply and develop the "anschauliche Theorie", at the same time modifying some of the original categories, e.g. in his almost exclusive use of the term "pure theory" (reine Theorie)[31] in place of Salin's "rational theory".

Spiethoff's theoretical starting point is "the fundamental idea of the historical direction of national economics" beginning with List, and the key elements of this idea are "the rejection of absolute solutions which claim equal validity for all economic circumstances"[32] and the construction of a new type of theory limited to a particular time and region. For example, mercantilism is valid for territorial states in the 16th to 18th centuries, and classical economics is valid for England between 1760 and 1850. List was against any claim for the general validity of classical economics, and tried instead to work out an original theory for the Germany of his day.[33]

In accordance with "the fundamental idea of historical direction", Spiethoff calls each "economic coexistence" (wirtschaftliches Zusammenleben) bounded by a particular period and region a "style of economy" (Wirtschaftsstil), and

29 Cf. *ibid.*, p. 102.
30 Cf. E. SALIN: "Spiethoff", *Staatslexikon*, 6th ed., Vol. 7, Freiburg (Herder) 1962, p. 504.
31 A. SPIETHOFF: "Die Allgemeine Volkswirtschaftslehre als geschichtliche Theorie", *Schmollers Jahrbuch*, 56th annual issue, part II, 1932, pp. 55ff. passim.
32 *Ibid.*, p. 54.
33 Cf. *ibid.*, pp. 54-5.

he calls the theory which is valid for a single particular "style of economy" "General National Economics" (Allgemeine Volkswirtschaftslehre). "One General National Economics is possible for each such style". That is to say, from the viewpoint of the Historical School, theory in principle possesses validity only within bounds of region and especially (historical) time, so that even the "General" theory is in any particular case valid in only one historical setting. In this sense, Spiethoff claims that his "General National Economics" is a "historical theory".[34] The influence of Sombart's thesis of the need of "different theories for historically distinct economic periods" is clearly seen here.

Spiethoff considers "General National Economics" as a comprehensive theory, by means of which the "style of economy" with its various spiritual and social features is understood, and he refers to it as "anschauliche Theorie", borrowing both the name and the theoretical framework from Salin and developing the concept through his own analyses of Sombart and others.[35] Spiethoff says that this "anschauliche Theorie" is obtained through the analysis and consideration of as many different partial phenomena of "economic coexistence" as possible followed by the extraction of unifiable relations. Hence, the method is mainly inductive and the aim is to obtain a theoretical "transcribed picture of reality" (Abbild der Wirklichkeit).[36]

This stands in contrast to "timeless" pure theory, in which inexistent abstract logical relations are centered in the theory, and reality is explained with these relations as criteria. As examples of pure theory, Spiethoff mentions the ideal type concepts of Max Weber, and especially their theoretical economic application in the equilibrium theory of J. A. Schumpeter, who was a colleague of Spiethoff's at Bonn University (1925-32). Spiethoff sees Schumpeter as setting up an inexistent state of affairs, namely the equilibrium between entrepreneur and money creation, as a theoretically given condition, and then measuring business fluctuation through phases of boom and depression against the supposed standard of equilibrium. Through this method, some appropriate insights about, for example, the meanings of disequilibrium states can be obtained, but historical phenomena and anything else unrelated to this standard scarcely enter the field of view and are therefore very

---

34 *Ibid.*, pp. 52-5. On p. 52, n.1, Sombart's Introduction to *Der moderne Kapitalismus* (1st ed., Vol. 1.) is cited.
35 Cf. *ibid.*, pp. 55, 79-80. On p. 79, n.3, Salin's essay "Hochkapitalismus" is cited.
36 *Ibid.*, pp. 55, 59, 79, cf. p. 56.

difficult to perceive. As a result, business fluctuation as a whole cannot be adequately understood. Spiethoff demonstrates his own way of understanding business fluctuation. In this, theoretically given conditions are first derived from a comprehensive attempt to identify as many particular real phenomena as possible. Next, through consideration of these given conditions, he obtains the essential relations required to explain the whole of the business fluctuation, and then proceeds to construct the "transcribed picture of reality" grounded on those relations. According to Spiethoff, this "transcribed picture of reality" is, metaphorically speaking, not so much a photograph as a picture painted by an artist. The task of the economist, like that of the artist, is not simply to describe each particular phenomenon in precise detail, but to render his exact view of the totality of relations, omitting such details as he considers insignificant.[37]

By means of this method, Spiethoff had already composed a voluminous article on economic "Crises" (Krisen) in the *Handwörterbuch der Staatswissenschaften* (4th ed., 1925). As we saw above, this article is appreciated by Salin as an example of the beginning of an "anschauliche Theorie". It was equally highly estimated by Schumpeter, who wrote that "the real conflict in scientists' mentalities" between "fact collecting and theoretical analysis" now "seems for the first time to be overcome through the action"[38] i.e. the article (Schumpeter adds the qualification that both types of scientists have reasons to find fault with Spiethoff). Spiethoff draws attention to both of these appreciations,[39] which is an indication of his self-confidence in the article. In 1948 he refers again to the same two remarks, saying that the "anschauliche Theorie" is first briefly described by Schumpeter with reference to the article "Crises" and then named by Salin. But one may ask whether this claim is not exaggerated, because Spiethoff in his essay of 1932, far from presenting Schumpeter as an advocate of the "anschauliche Theorie", on the whole takes a rather critical stance toward Schumpeter, although conceding some points to him. In 1932, Spiethoff mainly draws upon Salin and Sombart. However, these statements are interesting for the hints they provide of links between

---

37 Cf. *ibid.*, pp. 59-60; A. SPIETHOFF: "Krisen", pp. 59, 70; J. A. SCHUMPETER: *Theorie der wirtschaftlichen Entwicklung*, 1st ed., Leipzig (Duncker & Humblot) 1912, (facsim. ed., Düsseldorf 1988), pp. 103ff., 414ff. (ch. 3 and 6), Spiethoff uses the 2nd ed.,1926.

38 J. A. SCHUMPETER: "Gustav v. Schmoller und die Probleme von heute", *Schmollers Jahrbuch*, 50th annual issue, part I, 1926, p. 41.

39 Cf. A. SPIETHOFF: "Die Allgemeine Volkswirtschaftslehre", p. 79

Spiethoff and Schumpeter, and of the latter's understanding of the Historical School.[40]

On the one hand, Spiethoff in 1932 writes that Schumpeter is not unconscious of the historically conditioned character of theory, and that his argument about static and especially dynamic states is significant for an understanding of changes in capitalistic economy through the activities of entrepreneurs.[41] But on the other, Spiethoff also stresses, precisely like Salin in 1927, that pure theory can contribute only as a "heuristic aid instrument" (heuristisches Hilfsmittel) for the elaboration of "anschauliche Theorie". The "mistake", according to Spiethoff, is that pure theory misunderstands its limitations and aspires to be timelessly valid. The "great danger" is that it may therefore forget its "heuristic" role and misrepresent itself as a "prescribed picture of reality". An approach to reality undertaken exclusively from a viewpoint of ideal types and pure theory can never achieve the same completeness of cognition that is obtained from "anschauliche Theorie". "In the treatments of Schumpeter and v. Wieser, pure theory with the priority of market processes preponderates too greatly."[42]

Spiethoff's view of Sombart is that Sombart allows insufficient room for theorization and systematization because of his excessive stress on "historically non-recurring"[43] phenomena. At the same time, however, Spiethoff highly appreciates Sombart's overall view of economic development and its bases, as we shall now see.

Spiethoff compares theories of economic development stages as proposed by various economists of the Historical School, namely List, Hildebrand, Schönberg, Schmoller, Bücher and Sombart. He analyzes each development theory, focusing on the viewpoint from which the type of economy is categorized and the economic stages, or historically changing "styles of econ-

---

40 Cf. A. SPIETHOFF: "Anschauliche und reine volkswirtschaftliche Theorie und ihr Verhältnis zueinander", in: E. SALIN (Ed.): *Synopsis*, Heidelberg (L. Schneider) 1948, p. 648. For elements from the Historical School in Schumpeter's system, cf. Y. SHIONOYA: *Schumpeter's Thought* (Jap. *Schumpeterteki Shiko*), Tokyo (Toyokeizaishinposha) 1995, esp. ch. 8.

41 Cf. A. SPIETHOFF: "Die Allgemeine Volkswirtschaftslehre" pp. 55,78-81; J. A. SCHUMPETER: *Theorie der wirtschaftlichen Entwicklung*, pp. 103ff. (ch. 2); J. A. SCHUMPETER: "Gustav v. Schmoller und die Probleme von heute", p. 36.

42 A. SPIETHOFF: "Die Allgemeine Volkswirtschaftslehre", pp. 55-6, 82.

43 *Ibid.*, p. 82.

omy" in Spiethoff's phrase, are differentiated. Among the above scholars, Hildebrand and Schmoller work with only one criterion in each case, i.e. the transition in exchange media for Hildebrand and the enlargement of the political organization on which economic life depends for Schmoller. For this reason, it is difficult for either Hildebrand or Schmoller to perceive and explain the totality of a "style of economy" taking all its many various elements into account.[44]

In contrast, Sombart analyzes a "style of economy" - a "system of economy" (Wirtschaftssystem) in his terminology - polyvalently in relation to three main viewpoints, "economic mentality" (Wirtschaftsgesinnung), "order and organization" (Ordnung und Organisation) and "technology" (Technik).[45] This enables him to understand more precisely the complicated relations involved in each national economy and its changes of stage, and makes his analysis much superior to the others. On the basis of this survey, Spiethoff enlarges on Sombart's three categories, and proposes five of his own: 1. "economic spirit" (Wirtschaftsgeist), 2. "natural and technological bases" (natürliche und technische Grundlagen), 3. "social constitution" (Gesellschaftsverfassung), 4. "economic constitution" (Wirtschaftsverfassung) and 5. "course of economy" (Wirtschaftslauf). It is explained that of these, for example, the fourth category includes the political organization of Schmoller, while the fifth category with its subcategories "constant economy" and "progressive economy"[46] includes the static and dynamic states of Schumpeter.

According to Spiethoff, Schmoller confined himself to a sort of straight-line development of the national economy, attending to only one element. Spiethoff calls this mode of historical description "longitudinal cuttings" (Längsschnitte). This method has its limitations for theoretical cognition of the various "styles of economy", so that its use is not sufficient to build up a "General National Economics" to be regarded as the "historical theory of the style of present-day economic life", i.e., the theory possessing validity for

---

44 Cf. *ibid.*, pp. 61-75; B. HILDEBRAND: "Naturalwirthschaft, Geldwirthschaft und Creditwirthschaft", *Jahrbücher für Nationalökonomie und Statistik*, Vol. 2, 1864; G. SCHMOLLER: "Das Merkantilsystem in seiner historischen Bedeutung", in: G. SCHMOLLER: *Umrisse und Untersuchungen zur Verfassungs-, Verwaltungs-, und Wirtschaftsgeschichte*, Leipzig (Duncker & Humblot) 1898.

45 *Ibid.*, p. 71. cf. W. SOMBART: *Die Ordnung des Wirtschaftslebens*, Berlin (Springer) 1925, esp. pp. 14-20.

46 A. SPIETHOFF: "Die Allgemeine Volkswirtschaftslehre", pp. 76-7.

the historical stage of the "present" day. Schmoller's *Grundriß* comprises a "comprehending synopsis" (verstehende Zusammenschau), which relates also to theoretical matters and is "an enormous undertaking". But this "synopsis" did not go so far as to provide "short, impressive and instrumentally usable formulas". On the other hand, Spiethoff calls Sombart's method "lateral cuttings" (Querschnitte),[47] a term taken from Schumpeter's critical assessment of Schmoller. In the case of "lateral cuttings", each historically conditioned "style of economy" is understood by explaining its relations from the three above-mentioned viewpoints, following which the period of transition from one "style of economy" to the next is scrutinized. In the course of this inquiry, the internal structure and development of the "style of economy" is described systematically, so that this method of Sombart's can also be more meaningfully applied to a theoretical and historical perception of the "style of present-day economic life" than other methods, such as Schmoller's, and therefore deserves to be integrated into the "anschauliche Theorie" concept.

At the end of his 1932 essay, therefore, Spiethoff adopts a critical stance with regard to Schmoller. Although Spiethoff, Schmoller's former assistant and now editor of *Schmollers Jahrbuch*, has nothing to say about Schmoller's lack of theoretical and philosophical talents, the criticisms of Salin, who is not Schmoller's direct disciple,[48] are in this way taken up by Spiethoff, and then elaborated and enlarged. With this, the discussion of "anschauliche Theorie" has entered its second stage, that is to say, it has developed into a self-criticism at the heart of the Schmoller School after his death.

Further, it should be remarked that Spiethoff, in spite of his acceptance of elements from Salin and Sombart, does not refer to the ideological aspect of Sombart's criticism of capitalism. This is the aspect stressed by Salin, and related by him to the German intellectual tradition since Goethe, which he connects with the unification of "historism and capitalism" in Sombart. Similary, Spiethoff's criticism of Max Weber remains confined to the problem of the ideal type not inductively derived from reality, without any deprecating reference to the problem of the "self- and spirit-voided" social science attacked by Salin. This also helps to explain Spiethoff's use of "pure" theory, instead of "rational" theory, as the counterconcept for "anschauliche Theorie". Spiethoff, it would seem, is intent to avoid discussions about ideology, criticism

---

47 *Ibid.*, pp. 83-4; J. A. SCHUMPETER: "Gustav v. Schmoller und die Probleme von heute", p. 51.

48 Cf. B SCHEFOLD: "Salin, Edgar", p. 233.

of capitalism and any other matters, such as the conflict of "rational" and "irrational", that lead to ideological controversy. The reason for this avoidance is never explained. One assumption we might make is that Spiethoff sides to a certain extent with Weber in the argument about "self- and spirit-voided" social science. Another is that there are external circumstances which prevent him from broaching such matters. The first assumption is not impossible, but if this were the true reason, Spiethoff would suggest some criticism of Salin, which we cannot see. So what of the second one?

Taking this question into account among others, we now survey his essay of 1938, "Gustav von Schmoller und die anschauliche Theorie der Volkswirtschaft".

This essay is published in *Gustav von Schmoller und die deutsche geschichtliche Volkswirtschaftslehre* edited by Spiethoff in commemoration of the 100th birthday of Schmoller. In the preface of this book, Spiethoff describes his position vis-à-vis Schmoller. The Historical School of German national economics which is characterized by historism, realism and ethics, has developed from List through Roscher, Hildebrand and Knies to Schmoller. But even Schmoller is "a milestone and not an end", because he died on his way toward tackling the tasks of the Historical School. Those left behind need to face him critically to perceive what he was unable to accomplish, and need to search for ways of developing the ideas further. "We criticize Schmoller not to reject him, but to obtain a free road for fruitful continued work and a new setting of objectives in his spirit."[49]

At the beginning of his 1938 essay, Spiethoff considers the charge that Schmoller is searching only for descriptions of economic phenomena, and never arrives at a cognition of economic laws. Schmoller himself, in the preface to the second part of the *Grundriß*, refers to this as "a false charge", and attempts to exhibit his arguments about theories. Spiethoff, therefore, examines Schmoller's positions concerning theories. Schmoller's view in this question is, according to Spiethoff, the same as the "starting view held by the founders of the German Historical School",[50] whose ultimate aim was to obtain theories from historical research. After making this point, Spiethoff

---

49 A. SPIETHOFF (Ed.): *Gustav von Schmoller und die deutsche geschichtliche Volkswirtschaftslehre*, special issue of *Schmollers Jahrbuch*, 62nd annual issue, part II, 1938, p. VI.

50 *Ibid.*, p. 16. cf. G. SCHMOLLER: *Grundriß der Allgemeinen Volkswirtschaftslehre*, part 2, Leipzig (Duncker & Humblot) 1904, (facsim. ed., Düsseldorf 1989), p. VI.

analyzes the *Grundriß*, with particular reference to its arguments about value and price theories in the second part.

Schmoller's concern there is "the approach [rapprochement - T.H.] of assumptions and simplifications of pure theory to reality".[51] In this case, the instances of pure theory in question are those of the "Manchester School" and the "Austrians". For the Manchester School, "with supply and demand as fixed quantities, a certain corresponding market price is constantly given, and calculated, as it were, through a simple arithmetical set-formula".[52] Complicated social and psychological relations are disregarded, in spite of their significance. Schmoller therefore rejects the method of the Manchester School, which recognizes "only the quantitative statements"[53] as meaningful.

In the case of the Austrians, intensity of demand for a certain sort of commodity is analyzed as a function of available reserves and consumers' aims, so that social relations are taken better account of. Therefore, Schmoller does not reject the Austrian theories outright. But, he argues, "demand in its totality, or its grading [of intensity - T.H.] according to various desires is, however, not explained this way". To solve this defect, scientists essentially need to survey "the manner of economic consumption in all nations and classes, as well as in all periods, in a unifying way", so as to perceive "all physiological and psychological causes" and to gain understanding of "the total history of the development of human sentiments, of customs, culture and luxury".[54] But these tasks are not accomplished by the Austrians. Although Schmoller admits that he himself is unable to complete all of them either, he does produce a vast wealth of materials and empirical studies designed to develop and sophisticate the total scheme more systematically.

However, says Spiethoff, "What is the result derived from the empirical materials supplied by Schmoller? He himself does not produce anything of this kind".[55] According to Spiethoff, whereas Schmoller rightly pointed out the defects of the Austrians and provided the voluminous materials needed to overcome them, he did not arrive at any theoretical conclusions based on the materials. Of course, it is impossible to accommodate all of the tasks enu-

---

51 A. SPIETHOFF: "Gustav von Schmoller und die anschauliche Theorie der Volkswirtschaftslehre, in: A. SPIETHOFF (Ed.): *Gustav von Schmoller und die deutsche geschichtliche Volkswirtschaftslehre*, p. 20.

52 G. SCHMOLLER: *Grundriß*, part 2, p. 114.

53 A. SPIETHOFF: "Gustav von Schmoller und die anschauliche Theorie", p. 23.

54 *Ibid.*, p. 23, from: G. SCHMOLLER: *Grundriß*, part 2, pp. 128-9.

55 A. SPIETHOFF: "Gustav von Schmoller und die anschauliche Theorie", p. 24.

merated by Schmoller within the theoretical framework of the Austrians. The required new theory, which would include the Austrian theories as valid partial systems, "must itself come from researched experience" (erforschte Erfahrung).[56] Schmoller, who had "preferred to describe only the facts" rather than construct "airy theories",[57] proceeded with his critical consideration of the old theories "up to its limits", but fundamentally speaking, "this road had to be pursued one day to the end",[58] that is, to the construction of the new theory. Spiethoff calls the new theory "fully developed historical, 'anschauliche', political national economics" [' '- T.H.], and says that the construction of this theory will require "generations" of effort from the present "starting point".[59] Such is the meaning of Spiethoff's statement in the editorial preface that Schmoller is "a milestone and not an end". For Spiethoff, the "new setting of objectives in his [Schmoller's - T.H.] spirit" means the need to develop the research into the materials amassed by Schmoller more systematically and, by this means, to build up the "anschauliche Theorie". The course to take toward this end will become naturally apparent from a careful and exact reading of the *Grundriß*. It will be wrong to search for some other way by "applying some alien standard to Schmoller".[60]

Spiethoff's essay of 1938 is also interesting for the relationship it suggests between him and Salin. Through his analysis of the *Grundriß*, Spiethoff reasserts precisely what Salin stated in the second edition of *Geschichte der Volkswirtschaftslehre*. Salin wrote, we remember, that, as a "provider of materials", Schmoller was the "path beater towards fertile fields for many of his disciples and friends, though he himself has never set foot in these fields". Spiethoff, too, proposes that the proper task for the disciples and friends left behind is to "set foot in these fields" in Schmoller's place, in other words, to construct the "anschauliche Theorie".

Although Spiethoff is obviously to be seen as Salin's successor with regard to the content of the essay, we never find the name Salin mentioned in it. The reason for this omission can be assumed to have to do with the taking over of government by the Nazis in 1933 and the Jewish origin of Salin. Salin had already transferred to Basel University in 1927. But relations with

---

56 *Ibid.*, p. 28.
57 G. SCHMOLLER: *Grundriß*, part 2, p. VI.
58 A. SPIETHOFF: "Gustav von Schmoller und die anschauliche Theorie", pp. 28-9.
59 *Ibid.*, p. 35.
60 *Ibid.*, p. 34.

him were dangerous under the Nazi regime,[61] so that there was a hesitation to cite him affirmatively. By not mentioning Salin's name, Spiethoff avoids trouble, but at the same time he assures the survival of Salin's arguments in the German scientific world by adopting their substance in his essay.

Spiethoff's assertion of the "anschauliche Theorie" inherited from Salin is also significant in relation to other contemporary currents of thought.

The greatest blow for the Historical School following 1933 was the dissolution of the Verein für Socialpolitik in 1936. The Nazi Party had demanded that the chairmanship of the Verein should go to Erwin Wiskemann, Professor at Berlin University (later Bräuer, because of Wiskemann's serious war injury). Rather than accede to this, the Verein chose self-dissolution.[62] Wiskemann, in his essay "Der Nationalsozialismus und die Volkswirtschaftslehre", in *Der Weg der deutschen Volkswirtschaftslehre* (1937) edited by him and H. Lütke, writes that National Socialism considers itself "heir of the best of the German past" and claims "an absolute precedence of state policy over the economy". Further, from his National-Socialist viewpoint, Wiskemann praises the achievement of Schmoller in advancing the cause of "Prussian socialism",[63] which allows the "totality" priority over individual destinies. In another essay in the same book, the state socialism of A. Wagner is mentioned as providing a valuable lesson for National Socialism, although Wagner's ideas, according to this essay, still display insufficiencies in biological and racial matters.[64]

For the Nazis, it seems to have been exasperating that Spiethoff, a former disciple of Wagner and Schmoller, one of the most influential scholars in the Historical School after Schmoller himself, did not take up the interpretation of Schmoller proposed by Wiskemann. Carl Brinkmann in Heidelberg was, in contrast to Spiethoff, inclined to express a view similar to that of Wiskemann. Firstly, in *Gustav Schmoller und die Volkswirtschaftslehre* (1937), Brinkmann argues that Schmoller's tendency to approve of state intervention in "Die Reform der Gewerbegesetzgebung" (1877) can be considered as "a preview of our 'states economy'" (ständische Wirtschaft). In reality, Schmol-

---

61 Cf. B. SCHEFOLD: "Salin, Edgar", p. 233; C. VON DIETZE: "Lieber Freund Salin!", pp. 6-10.

62 Cf. F. BOESE: *Geschichte des Vereins für Sozialpolitik 1872-1932*, Berlin (Duncker & Humblot) 1939, pp. 290-1.

63 E. WISKEMANN, H. LÜTKE (Eds.): *Der Weg der deutschen Volkswirtschaftslehre*, Berlin (Junker & Dünhaupt) 1937, pp. 8, 10, 13.

64 E. EGNER: "Adolph Wagner, der Staatssozialist", *ibid.*, pp. 135ff.

ler's proposed interventions were from the viewpoint of J.S. Mill, whereas Brinkmann takes these expectations regarding the actions of beaurocrats to extend as far as the "emergency decrees" (Notverordnungen)[65] after the First World War. Thus, Brinkmann tries to force a connection between Schmoller's general ideas and social-political changes of the more recent past. Secondly, in an essay entitled "Schmollers Gerechtigkeit", published in 1938 in the mentioned centenary volume edited by Spiethoff, Brinkmann argues that "Schmoller fought unremittingly for the dominion of the state"[66] ever since the 1874 conference of the Verein für Socialpolitik. Thoughts of this kind were already circulating in Spiethoff's vicinity by 1938. Furthermore, Sombart, too, writes in the preface of *Deutscher Sozialismus* (1934) that this work in its own way "can best serve my country" under "the Hitler government"[67], and it is from such a viewpoint that criticisms of modern society by past German intellectuals such as Goethe are there appreciated. Here, we can confirm that Sombart's criticism of capitalism, which was endorsed by Salin, has now merged with the National Socialist trend of thought. Of course Sombart does not mention the Jew Salin here.[68]

These are the circumstances in which Spiethoff stresses that the construction of the "anschauliche Theorie" concept, inherited from Salin, is the natural and proper direction for the further development of Schmoller's ideas. This assertion contains no open criticism of the Nazis, but at least an implied and moderate one, because it suggests, even if indirectly, that the National Socialist interpretation of Schmoller does not contribute to the appropriate de-

---

65 C. BRINKMANN: *Gustav Schmoller und die Volkswirtschaftslehre*, Stuttgart (Kohlhammer) 1937, pp. 93,152. cf. G. SCHMOLLER: "Die Reform der Gewerbegesetzgebung: Rede, gehalten in der Generalversammlung des Vereins für Socialpolitik am 10. Oktober 1877", in: G. SCHMOLLER: *Zur Social- und Gewerbepolitik der Gegenwart*, Berlin (Duncker & Humblot) 1890, p. 151; S. TAMURA: *Studies on Gustav Schmoller*, pp. 155-8, for the influence of J. S. MILL on Schmoller in "Die Reform der Gewerbegesetzgebung".

66 A. SPIETHOFF (Ed.): *Gustav von Schmoller und die deutsche geschichtliche Volkswirtschaftslehre*, p. 61.

67 W. SOMBART: *Deutscher Sozialismus*, Berlin (Buchholz & Weisswange) 1934, p. XII.

68 Cf. *ibid.*, pp. 2, 29-31. In: *Die drei Nationalökonomien*, Berlin (Duncker & Humblot) 1930, pp. 8ff., Sombart still praised Salin's *Geschichte der Volkswirtschaftslehre* (2nd ed.) in comparison with other authors' works on history of economics.

velopment of his achievement and is thus distorted. In his essay of 1938, Spiethoff argues against attempts to interprete Schmoller by means of "some alien standard", though without saying what that "standard" is. Taking all of the above considerations into account, we may assume that he means Nazism. As in the case of the essay of 1932, Spiethoff in 1938 again has nothing to say about the ideological aspect of Sombart praised by Salin, in spite of his acceptance of Salin's mode of thought. It may also be significant that even Sombart's "Querschnitte" approach is not mentioned in the essay of 1938. One assumes that Spiethoff wishes to avoid ideological controversies between his own and the Nazi line of Schmoller interpretation, in order to be able to make his appeal, without unnecessary confusions, for the construction of the "anschauliche Theorie".

III. Development of the Concept in Japan

The second edition of Salin's *Geschichte der Volkswirtschaftslehre* was translated into Japanese in 1935 by Zenya Takashima (1904-90), who was in the same year promoted to professor in the preparatory course at Tokyo Commercial College (later renamed Hitotsubashi University).

In his translator's preface, Takashima explained the whole of the book in outline, particularly the confrontation between "merely-rational" theory and "anschauliche Theorie", as well as the logical subsumption of "rationale Theorie" under "anschauliche Theorie". In Takashima's view, these arguments make this work superior to other treatments of the history of economics, e.g. those of Gide and Rist or of Schumpeter. Concerning Salin's estimation of Marx, Takashima emphasizes Salin's recognition of Marx's work as "one of the most distinguished examples of syntheses of this kind" [of socialist and historist approaches - T.H.]. Salin's "deep insight into Marx particularly", says Takashima, "is unlikely to be encountered among other German professors of the present day."[69] These statements of Takashima's are interesting in that they show that some relation of Salin to Marx already exists in his mind at the outset.

---

69 Z. TAKASHIMA's translation of: E. SALIN: *Geschichte der Volkswirtschafts-lehre*, 2nd ed., under the Jap. title *Kokuminkeizaigakushi*, 1st ed., Tokyo (Sanseido) 1935, pp. 4, 8, 9.

Takashima, who had previously treated Schumpeter in his graduation thesis, attempted to allot Marx's economics a higher position combining both the static and the dynamic states. He was also engaged in a Japanese translation (unpublished) of Marx's *Theorien über Mehrwert*. In the course of activities such as these in the years around 1930, he was extending his interest and insight regarding Marxism.[70] However, it was becoming increasingly difficult for him to express his arguments about Marx directly in the political situation of the mid 1930s, which would seem to explain his motives in drawing attention to Marxism indirectly, through stressing Salin's comparatively high estimation of Marx.

Takashima published *Fundamental Problems in Economic Sociology: Smith and List as Economic Sociologists* in 1941, the year in which he was named professor in the senior class at the same college. By this time, the political and social circumstances were becoming more stringently militarized. In this work, he proposes a more critical acceptance of Salin's "anschauliche Theorie".

Still, his interest in Marxism does not waste away. In the original manuscript draft of the book, his "readiness to deal with Marx's matters stands forth clearly";[71] but on the exhortation of his disciples, anxious for his safety, such passages were deleted prior to printing. Because of these deletions, as well as some obscure turns of description to hide his real intentions from the eyes of administration, the book has several portions which are far from easy to understand. To elucidate these, we need to take Takashima's post-war reminiscences into account. However, even here, while not denying the earlier rumor that his standpoint was "Marxism in disguise"[72], he still does not identify his "economic sociology" with Marxist economics.[73]

To assess Takashima's relations to Salin, two points in his preface are important. First, he expresses "suspicion" both of the "growing power of political economy" and of the "pure development of modern economics". Ac-

---

70   Cf. Z. TAKASHIMA et al.: "Speaking of my Economics" (Jap."Watashi no Keizaigaku o Kataru"), first publ. 1980, later in: Z. TAKASHIMA: *Man, Climatology and Social Science* (Jap. *Ningen, Fudo to Shakaikagaku*), Tokyo (Akiyamashobo) 1985, pp. 208-13.

71   Z. TAKASHIMA: "When my First Book was Published" (Jap. "Shojosaku no Koro"), first publ. 1971, here republ. in: Z. TAKASHIMA: *Man, Climatology and Social Science*, p. 66.

72   *Ibid.*, p. 67.

73   Cf. *ibid.*, pp. 64-7.

cording to Takashima, it is necessary to construct an "economic sociology" that unifies at a higher level the unrefined "anschauliche Theorie" of "political economy" and the rational comprehension of "modern economics". This task is to be accomplished by means of Salin's "logic of reflection, mediation and regulation" within "anschauliche Theorie" through rational theory, that is, by means of the logic which Takashima calls "logic of mediation". Second, while Takashima concedes that Salin's view of affairs certainly offers a significant incentive to his own research, the more closely Takashima has come to consider the relation between "anschauliche Theorie" and rational theory, the more important he has found it to investigate the essential relation between Smith and List. According to Takashima, therefore, the "process of self-enlargement of political economy" by means of the "logic of mediation" should proceed hand in hand with an investigation of the "transition from the human productive powers of Smith to the national productive powers of List". Thanks to the inclusion of this relation, Takashima concludes, "economic sociology" takes "one step forward beyond Professor Salin".[74]

Regarding the first point, we find Takashima's standpoint contrasting with the dominant trend of thought at the time. By "political economy" he means the economic ideas which originated from Germany and dominated academic economics in Japan from the 1930s to the end of the War, with the "support of circumstances".[75] Takashima considers "political economy" as his prime opponent, and strives to refute it.

The Anti-Comintern Pact of 1937 between Japan and Germany had developed by 1940 into a Three-Power Pact including Italy. Under the influence of these alliances, and of the politico-military climate, currents of German economics that supported - or seemed to be supporting - the Nazi regime were enthusiastically accepted into Japan. H. Kaneko, translator of the above-named *Der Weg der deutschen Volkswirtschaftslehre* (1937) edited by Wiskemann and Lütke, says in 1938 in the translator's preface that "the new German economics is National Socialist economics," and that this book, written from that viewpoint and theoretically grounded on Gottl, "gives us an opportunity for reflection from which we may profit, even though we have a differ-

---

74 Z. TAKASHIMA: *Fundamental Problems in Economic Sociology: Smith and List as Economic Sociologists* (Jap. *Keizaishakaigaku no Konponmondai: Keizaishakaigakusha toshiteno Smith to List*), Tokyo (Nihonhyoronsha) 1941 (photom. reprint,Tokyo 1991), pp. 1-3, cf.p. 27.

75 Z. TAKASHIMA: "When my First Book was Published", p. 64.

ent form of state and nation."[76] A translation of Spann's *Kämpfende Wissenschaft* (1934) was published in 1939 with a translator's comment that Spann's theory is "considered the most influential theoretical basis of National Socialism"[77] (although Spann was in fact arrested by the Nazis in 1938).[78] A translation of the same author's *Der wahre Staat* (1931) also appeared in 1939. Sombart's *Deutscher Sozialismus* (1934) had been translated and published in 1936.

Through Salin, Takashima criticized "political economy" in the first part of *Fundamental Problems*, "Tasks of Economic Sociology". In Spann and Gottl, Takashima argues, an intentional concern for total cognition, and elements of practice and creative synthesis can indeed be recognized. These are the features in which "the superiority of German economics in general to English economics in general" is descried. For example, Gottl rejects economic systems which merely treat material goods mechanically, and proposes instead the "theory of life" (Lebenslehre) which aims to build up community relations in such a way as to unite individuals and the whole, the level at which all the various individual judgements and intentions can be taken into account.[79] However, as Salin points out that the higher "anschauliche Theorie" also subsumes rational theory, even "the superiority of German economics in general" "should be established not on a mere denial of English economics or theoretical economics, but on a viewpoint embracing these within it".[80] Considered in this light, Spann and Gottl cannot be said to offer a higher "anschauliche theorie", because they assert their own theories, e.g.

---

76   H. KANEKO's translation of: E. WISKEMANN, H. LÜTKE (Eds.): *Der Weg der deutschen Volkswirtschaftslehre*, under the Jap. title *Doitsukeizaigaku no Michi*, 2nd ed., Tokyo (Nihonhyoronsha) 1943, pp. 2-3. In 1942, Kaneko also translated Gottl's *Der Mythus der Planwirtschaft* (1932) and *Volk, Staat, Wirtschaft und Recht*, Part 1 (1936).
77   S. AKISAWA's translation of: SPANN: *Kämpfende Wissenschaft*, under the Jap. title *Zentaishugi no Genri*, Tokyo (Hakuyosha) 1938, p. 3.
78   In T. TODA's translation of: SPANN: *Krisis in der Volkswirtschaftslehre* (1930), under the Jap. title *Gendaikeizaigaku no Kiki*, Tokyo (Mikasashobo) 1940, Toda notes briefly, in the translator's preface, p. 98, that Spann is in prison following the German army's march into Austria. Cf. W. HEINRICH (Ed.): *Othmar Spann, Leben und Werke*, Graz 1979, p. 65.
79   Cf. Z. TAKASHIMA: *Fundamental Problems*, pp. 19,74-6.
80   *Ibid.*, p. 19.

Spann's universalism, which Salin takes as his example, in a strongly hostile opposition to English individualism, refusing the latter.

According to Takashima, the "anschaulich"-theoretical tradition of German economics which extends "through Fichte, Müller, List, Roscher and Knies to the 20th century" consists in both relations together, "the opposition to and the dependence on English economics at the same time".[81] In this sense, the efforts of Spann and Gottl fail to ground themselves on this eminent heritage, even if they seem to have traditional elements. Exponents of "political economy" in Japan have simply accepted the theories of Spann, Gottl and others without any reflection on this problem.[82] From arguments like these put forward by Takashima, readers of insight might penetrate through to the real but concealed theoretical and political implication, that Spann, Gottl and Wiskemann have inherited the tradition of German economics in a biased way, which caters to the dictates of Nazi totalitarianism, and that Japanese scholars should be very cautious and skeptical about accepting this German "political economy" in such a form. Incidentally, we also confirm Takashima's estimation of Sombart here. On the one hand, he partially admires Sombart as a thinker, as does Salin, for the recognizing of rational theory. But on the other, Takashima adopts a negative critical stance toward him, on the whole, because of the "freqently unsettled state of mind which Sombart displays in response to the change of social circumstances",[83] i.e. the Nazis' rise to power.

In a later reminiscence, Takashima expresses awareness in those years of a problematic reality, namely the fact that the "pure development of modern economics" in Japan did not constitute an effective counterforce against the fascistoid "political economy".[84] Such a statement appears in the first part of his *Fundamental Problems*, as a criticism of "modern economics", which lacks the elements of practice. This "pure economics", which Takashima also calls "modern economics", attempts to search for a "systematic consistency" transcending history, through "abstraction of the historical social characteristics of human economies into more general relations of economic quantities".

---

81   *Ibid.*, pp. 5-6. Takashima sees a critical acceptance of Smith even in the most conservative thinker Adam Müller, cf. *ibid.*, pp. 439, 449, and T. HARADA: "Über 'romantische' Ausgleichsmechanismen bei Adam Müller", *Jahrbücher für Nationalökonomie und Statistik*, 213 (1994).

82   Cf. Z. TAKASHIMA: *Fundamental Problems*, pp. 5-6, 15-26, 112-3.

83   *Ibid*, pp. 72-3.

84   Cf. Z. TAKASHIMA: "When my First Book was Published", p. 64.

Moreover, it is a matter of some pride for "pure" economists to stay within the bounds of scientific "modesty" by the avoidance of stepping "from science into practice". But the situation at the time teaches: if scientists are armed with no "critical principles against policy makers who are a given fact of the outside world", the scientists fall into such peril that "even their basic right to exist in the here and now becomes threatened".[85]

According to Takashima, the lack of the aspect of practice in "modern economics" goes together with a lack of a view of history and totality. This whole complex of problems is inherent in the theoretical structure of "modern economics". He refers to K. Sugimura's attempt to identify economic "active subjects" in the field of "modern economics" (the term "active subjects" is translation of the Japanese term "shutai", meaning persons who actively assume the task or administration of practice within a given state of relations, or else work to construct or change it). Sugimura distinguishes the "active subjects" in the social economic relations described in the marginal utility theory of Menger. In this case, the "active subjects" are "the most ordinary"[86] ones, who as consumers carry out their economic activities while rationally calculating in favor of their own interests. Takashima points out that this model of "active subjects" is shortsighted, because they act only within the narrow fields of their own consumptions, making it impossible for them to reach up to a knowledge of the economic system as a whole or of its historical development, much less to the recognition of a mode of practice capable of changing the political and economic system. In a similar way, "modern" economists themselves tend to ignore the questions of total cognition and the aspects of practice required to change the system. This criticism applies especially to Japanese "modern" economists, says Takashima, but is also a serious problem in Menger himself.[87]

The relative significance of "modern", "pure" economics, including even that of Schumpeter and Keynes, argues Takashima grounded on Salin, can indeed be vitalized, in the sense that it constitutes a system of "technology"[88] which includes the marginal utility and the equilibrium theories. This eco-

---

85 Z. TAKASHIMA: *Fundamental Problems*, pp. 90, 96-7.
86 *Ibid.*, p. 101.
87 *Ibid.*, pp. 89-110. cf. K. SUGIMURA: *Fundamental Problems in Economic Philosophy* (Jap. *Keizaitetsugaku no Kihonmondai*), Tokyo (Iwanamishoten) 1935.
88 Z. TAKASHIMA: *Fundamental Problems*, p. 93.

nomics should therefore be considered as an "instrument"[89] toward the higher "anschauliche Theorie". With regard to totality, practice and historicity, the "political economy" of Gottl and others is superior to the "modern" economics, even though "political economy" lacks the unification of history, theory and policy as well as being biased in its traditionality.[90]

These arguments of Takashima's reveal that he is plainly in agreement with Salin's criticism of Weberian value-free objectivism.[91] This differentiates him from Spiethoff, who doggedly avoids mentioning the topic. On the other hand, Takashima resembles Spiethoff in his relatively high esteem for Schumpeter compared with other "modern" economists, acknowledging Schumpeter's detailed understanding of the internal mechanism of capitalism from his positivistic viewpoint, although Takashima does not here choose to investigate the static and dynamic states.[92]

Takashima's aim, then, is to construct the "anschauliche Theorie" so as to unify "political economy" and "modern economics" through the critical consideration of both. However, in parts 2 and 3 of his book, he does not proceed as far as the construction itself, but confines himself to investigations of Smith and List respectively.

In the second part, "Problems of Adam Smith and the Civil Society", Takashima states that Smith considered civil society in England in the second half of the 18th century as his subject and described it in his research. The civil society described by Smith "has historical concreteness, even though at first glance the account is characterized by abstract rationality, and Smith's view of it supports creative integrality in that period, even though at first glance the view is characterized by individualistic abstraction"[93]. Thus, Takashima explains the theories and social ideas of Smith while paying attention to the elements they contain of historicity and totality, namely what Salin calls the "multiplicity" of Smith.

With regard to historicity, the Fifth Book of *The Wealth of Nations* should be mentioned. In his explanation of historical change in expenses on

---

89   *Ibid.*, p. 17.
90   Cf. *ibid.*, pp. 73-6, 112-3.
91   Cf. Z. TAKASHIMA: "Structure of History of Economics" (Jap. "Keizaigakushi no Kozo"), in: 2nd ed. of his translation of: E. SALIN: *Geschichte der Volkswirtschaftslehre*, 2nd ed., under the Jap. title *Keizaigakushi no Kisoriron*, Tokyo (Sanseido) 1944, pp. 321, 331.
92   Cf. Z. TAKASHIMA: *Fundamental Problems*, p. 94.
93   *Ibid.*, p. 128.

defense, Smith asserts four stages of historical development: 1. "hunters", 2. "shepherds", 3. "husbandmen" and 4. "a more advanced state of society".[94] This fourth stage is also called "commercial society",[95] in which both manufacturing industry and commerce are already developed. So Smith classifies his historical stages according to grades of productive powers and, in relation to this, explains developments of defense, judicature, public institutions and such like. In this way, he already achieves a grasp of economic development similar to the picture which List will later describe in his development theory centering on the development of national productive powers. The "modern" economists with their "timeless" theories should return to their origin in Smith, and learn from his historicalness.[96]

Further, they should learn from his way of total cognition. Smith himself published not only *The Wealth of Nations* (economics) but also *The Theory of Moral Sentiments* (ethics). More strictly, his system as a whole consists not only of two, but of three subsystems. The third is the jurisprudential and political subsystem, his treatment of which can be seen in his students' notes on his *Lectures on Jurisprudence*, edited and published by E. Cannan in 1896. Takashima investigates the relations of these three spheres, also taking into account the recollections of J. Miller (one of Smith's students), as written up by D. Stewart, and a study by A. Oncken[97], in the following way.

For Smith, economics is "the most important and definitive, but still only one part" of jurisprudence. And jurisprudence is the "part of justice among virtues".[98] The three virtues of "benevolence", "justice" and "prudence" form the main subject matter in the ethics, so that jurisprudence is in fact just one part of ethics in general. Therefore, economics ultimately becomes subsumed into ethics through the intermediary of jurisprudence. In this connection, the concept of "self-love" or "private interest", which is of

---

94 A. SMITH: *An Inquiry into the Nature and Causes of the Wealth of Nations* (1776), ed. by R. H. Campbell, A. S. Skinner et al., Oxford, New York etc. (Oxford University Press) 1976, pp. 689ff.

95 *Ibid.*, pp. 37,784.

96 Cf. Z. TAKASHIMA: *Fundamental Problems*, pp. 116,131-135.

97 Cf. D. STEWART: "Account of the Life and Writings of Adam Smith, LL.D.", in: A. SMITH: *Essays on Philosophical Subjects*, ed. W.P.D. Wightman, J. C. Bryce et al., Oxford, New York etc. (Oxford University Press) 1980, pp. 274-5; A. ONCKEN: "Das 'Adam Smith-Problem'", *Zeitschrift für Sozialwissenschaft*, I (1898).

98 Cf. Z. TAKASHIMA: *Fundamental Problems*, p. 146.

special significance in economics, finds its place within ethics as a support for "prudence", one of the cardinal virtues, so that economic "self-love" stands in no contradiction to ethics itself in Smith's system as a whole. Each person who acts in his own interest has also a "self-command", by means of which he attempts to keep his own acts from becoming excessive; that is, he restrains them to such a moderate degree as would earn him "sympathy" from an imagined third-person "impartial spectator".[99] This point in his ethics corresponds with his argument in economics that one's pursuit of profits in one's private interest contributes to advancing the interests of others also, if the pursuit is moderated through the price mechanism based on free competition. If an act performed in private interest exceeds propriety and violates the freedom of another person, such an act is to be restrained by a legal or political force, ethically based on the virtue of "justice", to defend the other's freedom. The virtue of "benevolence" supported by the love for others, or "beneficence" as it materially shows itself, is indeed admirable as a motive for an act spontaneously performed in the interest of others, or as such an act itself. But "benevolence" or "beneficence" is merely an "ornament" for the "building" of civil society, the "main pillar" of which is "justice".[100] The fact is that Smith's starting assumption for his arguments is that individuals in civil society perform their free acts mainly from a motive of "self-love". Through his arguments about the relations of the ethical, political and economic subsystems, Smith explains how these individual acts serve to construct society.[101]

In this system of Smith's, the state has its raison d'être mainly in the obligation to protect the free acts of the citizens by the exercise of "justice". So the state, in principle, does not intervene in other affairs of the citizens, especially economic matters in general. In Smith's state, says Takashima, one finds no contradiction between the state and civil society, such as is often seen in German concepts of the state, e.g. Hegel's in his *Philosophie des Rechts* (1821)[102]. Nor is there to be found any battle of citizens against the state, such as seen e.g. in J. Locke. "The state in the case of Smith includes

99   A. SMITH: *The Theory of Moral Sentiments* (1759), ed. D. D. Raphael, A. L. Macfie, Oxford, New York etc. (Oxford University Press) 1976, pp. 24-6, 69-71, 78-9, cf. p. 9.
100   *Ibid.*, p. 86, cf. p. 79.
101   Cf. Z. TAKASHIMA: *Fundamental Problems*, pp. 143-87.
102   Cf. T. HARADA: *Politische Ökonomie des Idealismus und der Romantik*, Berlin (Duncker & Humblot) 1989, pp. 134-59.

civil society, but, on the other hand, is itself also absorbed into civil society. [...] The state is now digested entirely into the new society, and in place of it another new state is born." Here, Takashima confirms systematic complete- ness and stability within the system of the "consistent liberalist" Adam Smith, grounded on the England of the second half of the 18th century, a so- ciety made up of mature citizens after their "triumph"[103] over feudalism. From these remarks of Takashima, we may ascertain the following two points.

First, through his presentation of Smith's system as an example of how orders of state and economy can be constructed even when the free acts of in- dividuals are taken as the positive starting point of the construction, Taka- shima is indirectly criticizing Japanese scholars, for their "political economy" and their acceptance of the semifeudalistic system of Japanese militarism as a background.

In Japan, ever since the Meiji Restoration (1867-8), political freedoms had always been restrained. And in the ethical and moral field, the govern- ment was forcing the nation to constitute ethical orders conforming to the Emperor system ideology, which had been intentionally constructed by the governing class through a combination of Shintoism with Confucianism. These orders meant the absolute subordination of the people to the Emperor and the governing class around him. Even in their internal private thoughts, individuals were to suppress impulses of self-interest or independence, and subordinate themselves to principles of self-effacement and heteronomy. This ethical compulsion was strongest during the Second World War, when the values of selfless devotion to the state were enthusiastically taught in schools, and any soldier who had come back alive rather than fighting on till the death had to be ashamed of himself for falling short of the ideal of the "Kamikaze" warrior.[104]

---

103 Z. TAKASHIMA: *Fundamental Problems*, pp. 198-9.

104 Cf. S. FUJITA: *Ruling Principles of the Emperor State System* (Jap. *Tenno- seikokka no Shihaigenri*), 2.ed., Tokyo (Miraisha) 1982, pp. 20-7; Y. KUME: "Genealogy of the Moral Science of the Nation" (Jap. "Kokumindo- tokuron no Keifu"), in: *Commercial Science of Meijo University* (Jap. *Mei- joshogaku*), 44 (1995), pp. 10-11. Takashima's spirit of resintance was also apparent in his teaching. A former student recalls in his reminiscences how Takashima would see off called up students of their departing for the front, with the word: "You must come back alive, then you can begin with your [real - T. H.] tasks!". H. MIZUTA: "My Teacher Zenya Takashima: Three and a

In economic science at that time, research into Smith's ideas was tolerated as "old" economics. Accordingly, Takashima treated and explained the consistently liberalist system of Smith, including his ethics and politics, and offered a critical counterstance to militarism, even though direct criticism was out of the question.[105]

Second, according to Takashima, Smith's system, while characterized by its completeness and political and social stability, has one weak point, in its lack of the aspect of practice. For Smith, his research "object is already mature" because of the civilized state of England with its higher productive powers, so that the realization of his system does not on the whole mean the creation of a new system through a changing of the object, but rather means "leaving it to the working of nature". Smith provides analyses of the productive powers as they exist, but no theory of how to create them, in other words, no "theory for productive powers"[106] and no "logic for creation". Therefore, it is possible to learn the aspects of history and totality, but difficult to learn the aspect of practice from Smith. In this sense, Smith "does not answer the present needs"[107] of Japan. From this conclusion, Takashima now proceeds, in the third part of his book, to treat "Friedrich List and Problems of the National Productive Powers", since he considers that List, from whom the German Historical School traces its origins, reveals the role of practice more clearly.

For List, the "powers to create wealth are much more important than wealth itself"[108]. The concept of "productive powers", which he uses to mean the "powers to create wealth", includes various creative elements, "industriousness, thrift, morality and the intelligence of individuals", "natural resources and material capital", "social, political and civil institutions and laws", as well as the "guarantee of continuance, independence and the power of their nation state"[109]. Thus, it is a "synthetic concept"[110] which contains

Half Years after his Death" (Jap. "Takashima Zenya Sensei: Yukite Sannenhan"), *Asahi Shinbun* (News Paper), Nagoya ed., Aug. 27, 1993.

105 Cf. Z. TAKASHIMA et al.: "Speaking of my Economics", pp. 214-5.

106 Z. TAKASHIMA: *Fundamental Problems*, pp. 238-40.

107 *Ibid.*, p. 243.

108 *Ibid.*, p. 264; F. LIST: *Das nationale System der politischen Ökonomie* (1844), ed. A. Sommer (*List, Werke*, Vol. VI), Berlin (R. Hobbing) 1930, p. 173.

109 F. LIST: *Das nationale System*, p. 51.

110 Z. TAKASHIMA: *Fundamental Problems*, p. 265.

as its elements not only material productivities in the narrow sense, but also immaterial entities contributing to the creation of material powers indirectly. Whereas Smith considered the productive powers in an objective and quantitative way, thus opening the road to the later rational pure economics, List regards immaterial and qualitative, spiritual and institutional elements as no less important, so that, in List's view the concept of productive powers is "freed from a quantitative category",[111] a redirection which marks one of the most significant starting points for the synthetic development of German economics.

What kind of economic system is List aiming for? This is Takashima's next question. It is well known that List proposes an economic development concept consisting of five stages: 1. the "state of original barbarism", 2. the "state of herdsmen", or nomadism, 3. the "state of agriculture", 4. the "state of agriculture-manufacturing", 5. the "state of agriculture-manufacturing-commerce"; and that he proposes trade protectionism in the transitional periods from the third to the fifth stage as a measure for fostering industrialization. In this concept, it should be noticed that the goal to be reached is the fifth stage which List calls the state of the "normal nation". This is a concept of normality modeled on England, the economically most advanced country of List's time, of which it might be said that "agriculture, manufactures, commerce and navigation are developed in it equally, [...] Constitution, laws and institutions afford its people a high degree of security and liberty".[112] When List maintains that this "normal state" should be the ideal pursued by all developing countries (but limited to the temperate regions), e.g. Germany or the United States of America, his intention is evidently to propose a "transition to the English [stage of a - T.H.] nation". Therefore List's aim is to develop to the stage of the "nation which Smith considered as the object of his analysis".[113]

Takashima maintains that the relation linking List's goal and Smith's world is markedly more significant than the more often mentioned opposition between the protectionist List and the liberalist Smith. "For List, Smith was the model and outstanding prior example. When List fought against this

---

111 *Ibid.*, p. 271.
112 F. LIST: *Das nationale System*, pp. 210, 212.
113 Z. TAKASHIMA: *Fundamental Problems*, pp. 277, 291.

man, it was rather because he respected him"[114]. To regard List as the fore-runner of the "theory of controlled economy"[115] is out of the question. Taka-shima implicitly proposes a counter-interpretation of List opposing the inter-pretation presented by economists of "political economy". For example, Wiskemann appreciates List's theory of productive powers for its characteris-tic of "powers to create wealth" and, yet, considers his criticism of free trade a kernel of National Socialist economics.[116]

As mentioned above, Takashima inherits Salin's concept of an "anschau-liche Theorie" which simultaneously includes rational theory. However, like Spiethoff, he makes no attempt to construct the new theory itself but is con-tent to put theoretical materials in order, in preparation for its future con-struction. From his standpoint of resistance to pre-modernistic militarism in Japan, Takashima appreciates Smith's system of civil society as a historical and total social science, but he does not overlook its weak point, that is to say, the fact that it is so little oriented to practice. This is Smith's definitive limitation, and, to the extent that Smith can rightly be taken as an outstand-ing forerunner of rational theory, it is also the limitation of all succeeding "modern economics", especially in Japan. List considers Smith's civil society as the ideal, and his own theories are notable for their inclusion of creative practices for realization of this ideal. These practice-orientated elements in-volving institutional and spiritual entities are indispensable for theories of development in countries such as Germany at the time of List, and, even more particularly, Japan at the time of Takashima, as a prerequisite for the creation of higher productive powers and the realization, through this, of the kind of civil society described by Smith.

For Takashima, the concept of "anschauliche Theorie", originally pro-posed by Salin, should be constructed in a very sophisticated - Spiethoff would have said "biased" - form, modeled on relations in the practice-oriented economics of List, which attempts to realize the economic society described by Smith. List's economics, which both the later Historical School and the "political economy" appreciate, has a firm respect for Smith's social science

114 *Ibid.*, p. 283, cf. p. 477. cf. also F. LIST: *Outlines of American Political Economy* (1827), in: *List, Werke*, Vol. II, ed. W. Notz, Berlin (R. Hobbing) 1931, p. 102.

115 Z. TAKASHIMA: *Fundamental Problems*, p. 283.

116 Cf. E. WISKEMANN: "Friedrich List", in: E. WISKEMANN, H. LÜTKE (Eds.): *Der Weg der deutschen Volkswirtschaftslehre*, pp. 74 ff; E. WISKEMANN: "Der Nationalsozialismus und die Volkswirtschaftslehre", *ibid*, p. 14.

as a sort of - yet not merely a - rational theory. This connection supplies the ideal model relation for the higher-level unification of "political economy" and "modern economics". Takashima refers to this higher-level unified "anschauliche Thoerie" as "economic sociology".

Takashima says: "The understanding of List through Smith suggests itself not merely from a scientific interest in the history of economics, but indeed from the pressing claim of the present day to transcend List through the internal analysis of his ideas." Thus, the task for Takashima is to pave the "way from Smith to the List of the present day".[117] The expression "claim of the present day to transcend List" is matched by other remarks, for example, that List's limitation lies in his self-understanding as a follower of Smith, that is, his "inability to view Smith from a forward position", and that Takashima's contemporaries "need to take a more forward view of Smith "from a standpoint of how to transcend civil society".[118] In such comments as these, we see suggestions of Takashima's concealed Marxist aim of overcoming capitalism, while we have already confirmed his economically, politically and ethically liberalist standpoint with respect to his analysis of Smith. Since this latter point is one of the most important features of the *Fundamental Problems*, we cannot simply summarize the whole of his standpoint as "Marxism in disguise". If we must find a name for it, his standpoint as a whole is a highly liberalist Marxism. This can also be confirmed from arguments in the book which seem to criticize orthodox Marxism, or from his preface to the new edition after the War.[119] Whereas the "modern" economists had no "critical principles", and the orthodox Marxists had no voice because of ruthless oppression, it was highly liberalist Marxism that was left to play the most important role in the criticism of militarism within the Japanese academic world of economics during the Second World War.

---

117 Z. TAKASHIMA: *Fundamental Problems*, p. 306.

118 *Ibid.*, p. 340.

119 Cf. *ibid.*, p. 30; Z. TAKASHIMA: *Smith and List as Economic Sociologists* (Jap. *Keizaishakaigakusha toshiteno Smith to List*), Tokyo (Josuishobo) 1953 (new revised ed. of *Fundamental Problems*), pp. 5-8.

IV. Some Remarks

Spiethoff and Takashima are both inheritors of Salin's concept of "anschauliche Theorie", each in a form revised and developed according to his own arguments. Although their arguments differ greatly, each of them takes a critical stance to fascism in the country concerned.

Spiethoff, in his argument about "styles of economy" accepts the proposal of Sombart in *Der moderne Kapitalismus* (1st ed.) that different economic theories ought to be constructed for different economic stages, or "economic systems" (Sombart's term). Spiethoff's own theoretical scheme is constructed on the framework of the "anschauliche Theorie" as corresponding with his description procedure in the article "Krisen". As the "anschauliche Theorie" is capable of including pure theory, Spiethoff, an eminent leader of the Historical School after Schmoller's death, extends an hand to Schumpeter, and stresses that Schmoller's criticism of the Austrian School, having been taken to its logical limits, is now due to be raised one stage higher. In other words, a new model of "anschauliche Theorie", this time including the marginal theories, is now to be constructed on the basis of the materials provided by Schmoller. However, Spiethoff remains discreetly silent about the ideological nationalistic unification of "historism and socialism" proposed by Sombart and praised by Salin, which, in the situation of the time, tends to merge with Nazism.

Takashima, for his part, accepts Salin's affirmative endorsement of ideological value judgements, as an indispensable practice-oriented element of economics. But the value scale is, as Takashima sees it, to be grounded on the criticism of militarism, not cooperation with it. From this point of view, the acceptance of "anschauliche Theorie" in a form also including rational theory means nothing less than the construction of a new "economic sociology", of which the external frame is to be the unification of the practice-oriented "political economy" and the rational "modern economics"; but this "economic sociology" means in effect a new and total social science modeled on List's national economics, which aspires to development into a "normal nation", i.e. the ideal civil society of Smith.

Both Salin and Spiethoff essentially maintain the inductive method of Schmoller, in spite of their own proposals to adopt some rational-theoretical approaches[120]. On the other hand, scarcely any traces of the inductive method are to be found in Takashima, who is much more an heir to the ideological tendencies of Salin, to which Takashima gives a new function. In Takashima's arguments, the relation of List to Smith, as he interprets it, and the concept of Smith's civil society itself are used exactly as if they were the kind of teleological model which Schmoller criticised as a "heuristic aid instrument" (heuristisches Hilfsmittel).[121] However, it would be unfair merely to fault Takashima for his distance from Schmoller, even though his work lacks some of the benefits of the inductive method. To discuss this question justly, we need to consider the following four points:

First, Spiethoff's way of encountering Nazi-like patterns of thought is mainly through avoidance of ideological discussions. Takashima criticizes Japanese militarism through the liberalist counterview of Smith. Even though he argues almost only by implications, his stance of confrontation goes one stage deeper than Spiethoff's in the ideological field, and is thus more effective, at least to the extent of alerting readers against fascism.

The second point relates to Schmoller's method itself. Schmoller stressed the necessity of empirical detail research, and criticized the "teleological thinking" which makes use of "liberty or justice or equality".[122] In reality, however, he seems to be inclined to a kind of Prussian nationalism, in which the role of Prussia in German unification is highly extolled, and to the kinds of sentiments and functions of community, which appear tacitly in his work as presupposed ideals.[123] Indeed, even in Schmoller's own work, the significance of these tacit ideals needs investigating.

Third, the inductive method was originally intended as a way of perceiving the social individualities of various nations from their historical roots. For a similar purpose, Takashima later develops his socio-cultural "climatology".[124]

---

120 After the War, Spiethoff inclines more to acceptance of pure rational theories. In: *Die wirtschaftlichen Wechsellagen* (1955), he treats business cycles again and uses mainly mathematical models for his theoretical explanations. cf. E. SALIN: "Spiethoff", p. 505.

121 Cf. G. SCHMOLLER: "Volkswirtschaft, Volkswirtschaftslehre und -methode", p. 437.

122 *Ibid.*, pp. 437,439.

123 Cf. S. TAMURA: *Studies on Gustav Schmoller*, pp. 344-5.

124 Cf. Z. TAKASHIMA: *Man, Climatology and Social Science*, pp. 140-98.

The fourth point relates to the new approach of "Economics as Ethical Economy" based on the Historical School, especially Schmoller. One of the most influential Japanese expounders of this approach suggests that perhaps this new economics has no other choice but to remain silent about "pre-modern oppressive situations"[125] existing in non-Western countries. If this is so, how does the theory of "Ethical Economy" confront this point ?

---

125 N. YAMAWAKI: *Toward a New Philosophical Foundation of Social Science* (Jap. *Hokatsuteki Shakaitetsugaku*), Tokyo (Tokyo University Press) 1993, p. 38. Cf. P. KOSLOWSKI: "Economics as Ethical Economy in the Tradition of the Historical School: Introduction", in: P. KOSLOWSKI (Ed.): *The Theory of Ethical Economy in the Historical School*, Berlin, Heidelberg etc. (Springer) 1995.

Discussion Summary

NORBERT F. TOFALL

Paper discussed:
TETSUSHI HARADA: Two Developments of the Concept of *Anschauliche Theorie* (Concrete Theory) in Germany and Japan

Edgar Salin criticizes Schmoller for being not theoretical enough. Spiethoff is more theoretical. Then Eucken criticizes Spiethoff as being not theoretical enough. And in the next generation someone criticizes Eucken and so on. Is it possible that this process is a typical natural process? How can the concept of *Anschauliche Theorie* (Concrete Theory) used or rejected nowadays? (AVTONOMOW).

Spiethoff's *Anschauliche Theorie* does not conflict with the rational theory. With rational theory we can only win parts of knowledge, because the cognitive capacity of rational theory is not integral. In contrast to the concept of rational theory, Spiethoff's *Anschauliche Theorie* is directed at entirety. Spiethoff wants to win concreteness by the inductive method which means that the concrete theory starts with the regarding of the facts. Therefore Spiethoff wants to retain the baselines of the younger Historical School. But after World War II, Eucken did not want to keep anything from the tradition of the Historical School for the economics (HARADA).

Today, the possibilities of *Anschauliche Theorie* are the same as the possibilities of ethical economics. But our situation is quite different from the historical situation of Salin who wanted to include rationality into historical theory in a period when the historical theory was the dominant method. Nowadays the rational and mathematical theory is dominant so we have to take historical and empirical elements more and more into account (HARADA).

For a historian this point of view could be allright, but for an economist the question has to be whether this kind of theory is sound or unsound (RINGER). HARADA points out that he thinks in the same way as Salin. Pure rationality can not be an acceptable type of theory because it is too selective.

DISCUSSION SUMMARY

The Weberian ideal types allow different abstractions. Therefore the *Anschauliche Theorie* must not be inconsistent with the concept of ideal types (SHIONOYA).

For giving a sound opinion of this topic it is necessary to differenciate between Salin and Spiethoff. Salin criticizes Weber in mainly three points: Firstly, Salin thinks that the scientist should have value judgements. Secondly, in the view of Salin, Weber deals with an unsound method. Salin thinks that Weber's concept of ideal types is false. Thirdly, Salin points out that it is necessary to collect material and facts at the beginning of theoretical work. Salin approves the inductive method. Spiethoff criticizes Weber only in the point that Weber's ideal types have an a-priori-character (HARADA).

Chapter 16

Some Reflections on Ethics and Economics Concerning the German Historical School and Its Reception in Russia

VLADIMIR S. AVTONOMOV

I. Homo oeconomicus and His German Adversaries

It is widely known that the emergence of economic theory as a separate science was connected with /caused by/ its emancipation from moral philosophy. The discovery of Homo oeconomicus, nothing but economic man motivated by self-interest played the major role in that process. But it certainly meant that something like homo oeconomicus could be found in real life. Market economy, turning into a relatively autonomous subsystem of society, provided a mechanism of social coordination alternative not only to orders and traditions, but also to moral norms. This morally neutral way to reconcile private and public interests - the economic way - was emphasized in Mandeville's "Fable of bees". Private passions and even vices could be turned into public benefits in case they are given the harmless form of economic interests.[1] Detesting Mandeville's cynicism, Adam Smith was still impressed

---

1   A. HIRSCHMAN: *The Passions and the Interests: Political Arguments for Capitalism before its Triumph*, Princeton (Princeton Univ.Press) 1977.

by his paradox.[2] Smith became the first moral philosopher who had two separate images of man for ethics and political economy - and this made him the founder of economics as a separate social science.[3]

The English classical political economy and the model of man proper to it met the strongest opposition from the German Historical School. The constellation of historical conditions producing this opposition are especially important for us because they resemble the Russian situation we'll be later.

First, we must mention the relative backwardness of capitalist development in German states, strong guild traditions, nondeveloped competitive mechanisms in the internal market and weak national industry,- all this contributed to the rejection of free-trade ideology and the underlying individualistic model of "economic man".

Secondly, the German ideology was much more state- and policy-oriented than the English one. In the politically split Germany state legislations, customs, policy measures had more immediate relation to everyday life, than in England. For English classics the state existed for the individuals, for German scholars the relation typically was just the opposite (for instance, in Adam Müller's opinion the state was the highest human need). This doesn't mean that governments in Germany were more absolutist and penetrating than elsewere: in fact, just the opposite seems to be the case. But the mere quantity of independent states on the German territory was so big that the quantity of civil servants and other people dealing with governnental activities was relatively high. Preoccupation with state contributed to the more practical, policy-oriented character of German economic theorizing while in England, beginning with Ricardo, the pure, abstract economic theory gained the ground. The simple homo-oeconomicus concept was no doubt more appropriate for the abstract economic analysis than more complex models of man including moral motivation.

Thirdly, the difference in ethical traditions was substantial. English utilitarian ethics, especially represented by J. Bentham, was associated with the

---

2   Cf. P. KOSLOWSKI: *Prinzipien der Ethischen Ökonomie*, Tübingen (J.C.B. Mohr) 1988, pp. 22-24

3   Of course the interrelationships between Smith's two major works, *Theory of Moral Sentiments* and *The Wealth of Nations* and the interplay between self-interest and sympathy are not that simple but it needn't delay us here. See: A. MEYER-FAYE, P. ULRICH (Eds.): *Der andere Adam Smith: Beiträge zur Neubestimmung von Ökonomie als Politischer Ökonomie*, Bern/Stuttgart (Haupt) 1991 (= St. Galler Beitrage zur Wirtschaftsethik, Band 5).

development of economic theory through classical and marginalist periods. Regarding the happiness of mankind as the sum total of measures of individual happiness, Bentham concentrated mostly on the latter variable - growth of *individual* happiness. Individual action had to be judged by its consequences, and the best consequence possible was that which maximized happiness of the greatest number of people. Sofar as the concept of society was "additive" and homogenous this ethics didn't contradict the economic point of view of the classical school. On the other hand, German (Kantian) tradition of deontological ethics, judging the actions by their design and not by consequences was remarkably "uneconomical" from the same point of view. The German Historical school used ethics in two aspects: descriptive and normative (as a guide to social policy). The descriptive aspect involved the strong opposition to the concept of "homo oeconomicus" as the rudimentary psychology and the pleading for the recognition of altruistic moral motives by economic theory: the sense of belonging to the social whole (Gemeinsinn) and the sense of equity (Gerechtigkeitsinn) as Karl Knies put it.[4] In his opinion this imperative reflected the moral progress of society since the XVIII century when the model of economic man was legitimate (at least in England). So the incorporation of moral motives was considered as an attribute not of economic backwardness (which was materialistic-marxian point of view) but as a sign of moral advancement.

The normative component was added by the new generation of German Historicists headed by Gustav Schmoller who advocated social and economic reforms promoting social peace and security. The German Historical school occupies a very specific place in the history of economics. It was the greatest rebellion against the mainstream, the most important attempt to represent the other side of the famous dilemma "truth versus precision", where the Post-Ricardian and of course marginalist economics stood for precision. It can be argued that the acknowledgement of moral motives besides self-interest deprived the economic theory of the great deal of its analytical power. But in course of its further development the mainstream economic theory and governsent policy making inevitably came across numerous ethical problems which were first raised by the German Historicists.

---

4   K. KNIES: *Die politische Okonomie vom geschichtlichen Standpunkte*, Braunscweig 1880, pp. 234-235, 241.

VLADIMIR S. AVTONOMOV

II. Germany and Russia: Parallel Developments and Differences

The German Historical School influenced the development of economic thought in many countries during the last quarter of the XIX century. But in Russia it probably encountered the most enthusiastic reception. The parallel development of social sciences including economic theory based on ethical foundation in both countries is a remarkable phenomenon which was caused by two main factors. The first of them was of course the direct influence of German professors on their Russian students - future prominent Russian scholars - who used to study at German Universities. But much more important was the economic, social and cultural background in Russia after the Great Reforms of 1860-es that made it ready to absorb the influence of German philosophy and social sciences.

Speaking about the economic situation in the post-reform Russia we can easily find parallels to the German situation in the first half of the XIX century. Important elements of feudal economic order were still in action, especially in agriculture where the majority of Russians were employed and where the village communities retained their redistributive role securing the rough equality of peasant families and letting noone get rich. The influence of competition was not sufficient to make the Russian people behave like "economic men".

The role of the state was still more pronounced in Russia with the long tradition of absolute monarchy, than in Germany. The government sector was the most important one in the economy and a lot of private enterprise existed because of government purchases of goods and services. At the same time national industry was not strong enough to withstand foreign competition. One needn't be surprised to find that Friedrich List was one of the most popular economists among Russian economists and policy-makers.[5] Obviously there wasn't any good ground for preaching the principles of laissez faire in Russia. In these circusctances the economic theory had to be mostly occupied with the problems of government economic policy.

---

5   Count Sergej Witte who later became one of the most efficient Russian Finance Ministers wrote a special monograph on the subject. See: S. YU. WIT-TE: *Nazionalnaya ekonomiya i Friedrich List* (National Economy and Friedrich List), Kiev 1889.

GERMAN HISTORICAL SCHOOL AND ITS RECEPTION IN RUSSIA

In the tense political-ideological atmosphere of the post-reform Russia German Historicists were accepted as natural allies in the struggle against the emerging capitalism. The resulting Russian variant of "Socialism of the Chair" (Katheder-Sozialismus) was greatly influenced by marxism, (though the German variant was proposed as an alternative to marxist socialism), and by the specific Russian ideological and political movement called "narodniki" stressing the uniqueness of Russian economic and social development and alleged advantages of traditional collective forms of economic activity.[6] At the same time the radical wing of this movement were professional terrorists who assassinated the czar Alexander II. Russian followers of the German Historical School and Katheder-Sozialismus proved to be radical and even revolutionary unlike their teachers. From the political point of view our historicists were mostly in opposition to the government. They were not politically conservative.

At last the ethical aspect which is of particular interest for our conference. The economic problems in Russia were frequently considered as part and parcel of a wider package including moral, religious, esthetic values. The social sciences at the moment in question had not yet gained the status of specialised disciplines being only fragments of general knowledge about what was morally right and what had to be done to achieve the social (non-utilitarian) ideal in real life.[7] Paradoxically this gave the Russian social thought *practical* und *utopian* character at once. It is possible to see here some parallels with the Kantian transcedental practical philosophy interpreted by Schmoller and his disciples. Though of course there were also remarkable differences between Russian and German intellectual scenery. The aspired ideal of society in Russia was conceived more in religious-esthetic terms than in ethical and law terms. Reflecting about the relevant causes we can mention the fact that, on the one hand, genuine (in the sense of unimported) Russian moral philosophy was either profoundly religious (orthodox) or embodied in the works of classical Russian literature (Gogol, Dostoyevski, Tolstoy and others). On the other hand Russian philosophy of law, as far as it altogether

---

6   See: P. B. STRUWE: *Istoricheskoye vvedeniye v politicheskuyu ekonomiyu* (The Historical Introduotion to The Political Economy), Petrograd 1916, pp. 5-7.

7   See: N. MAKASHEVA: *Eticheskiye osnovy ekonomicheskoy teorii* (Ethical Foundations of Economic Theory), Moscow (INIONInstitute), 1993, p. 107.

existed (Vladimir Solovyov being probably it's first representative[8]) was founded on simple moral norms without invoking any *norms of law*. It could even be asserted, that this "moral absolutism" was considered at that time a special benefit of Russian culture in comparison with Western civilization based on "limited", "bourgeois" norms of law.[9] Quite to the contrary, practical activity of the Younger German Historical School concentrated on legislation designed to settle "the social question".

All the parallels taken into account, it cannot be very surprising that Russian social and economic thought of the period in question evolved in close and conscious connection with the development of the German Historical school. Numerous examples can be drawn illustrating this argument. Like the German Historians some influential Russian thinkers including economists rejected methodological individualism and the self-interested "homo oeconomicus". (Vladimir Solovyov was also a fervent opponent of the invisible hand principle, depriving individuals of their conscious choice). They supported the methodolocical approach, regarding an individual and the society as a parts of harmonic whole (this point was especially stressed by the orthodox philosopher and economist S. Bulgakov, arguing that only the whole mankind can be the "transcedental subject of the economy"[10]). Vladimir Solovyov emphasized that it was amoral and wrong to regard a human being only as an economic subject.[11]

We can also state that Russian economists of all directions prefered to be practical and reform-oriented and were not attracted by abstract descriptive theory. But an economist himself had to develop a fair position among vested interests and political currents. An interesting example is M. Tugan-Baranovski's[12] approach from Kantian ethical perspective. He argued that in the realm of economics where group interests are omnipresent the researcher has to base on the ethical princinciple of the supreme value of a human personality and

---

8 V. SOLOVJEV: *Opravdaniye dobra* (The Justification of the Good), Moscow (Respublika) 1996.

9 See: E. SOLOVJEV: "Defitsit pravoponimaniya v russkoy moralnoy filosofii (Lack of understanding of law in Russian moral philosophy)", *Voprosy filosofii*, N 9 (1988), pp. 137-140.

10 S. N. BULGAKOV: Filosofia hosyajstva (Philosophy of the Economy), Moscow (Nauka) 1990, pp. 90-127.

11 V. SOLOVYOV, *Op.cit.*, p. 296.

12 Well-known Russian economist contributing among other things to the theory of business cycle and the analysis of the cooperative movement.

the equal value of each human being which must be not a means to any given end, but the end in itself.[13] The same author considered it *ethically* founded to adopt both labour theory of value and marginal utility theory, stressing the value of different aspects of a human being (labor and wants) and invented an original synthetic theory. In Bulgakov's orthodox conception ethics even supplanted economics, the latter turning into the "applied ethics of economic life".[14]

III. Some Implications for the Present Situation in Russia

The questions concerning economic ethics and the reception of the ideas of the German Historical school in Russia aren't the issues of pure historical interest in contemporary Russia. The posttotalitarian Russia in many respects resembles the postreform country of the XIX century. Relative economic backwardness, the initial phase of building a civic society, religious and nationalist revival, social protest against harsh realities of economic transition and the mighty anticapitalist political movement can be mentioned. In the economy more active government interference and more protectionism are advocated both by government and the oposition as a reaction to rapid liberalization of recent years. To my mind incorporation of some ethics into economic research is badly needed in a country like Russia. First: we need the descriptive side of economic ethics. The specific economic ethos of Russian population formed both by national character and by communist ideology has greatly shaped the economic problems of transition in our country. A lot of major institutions of Western market economies so far as the legal basis is concerned were imitated in Russia but since these laws had not the moral legitimation they actually failed to operate. It would be false to assert that Russian economic mentality is amoral though stealing and cheating are tradition-

---

13 M. TUGAN-BARANOVSKI: *Osnovy politicheskoy economii* (The Principles of political economy), St. Petersburg 1911, p. 26.

14 S. N. BULGAKOV: "Ob ekonomicheskom ideale (On economic ideal)", in: S. N. BULGAKOV: *Geroism i podvizhnichestvo*, Moscow (Russkaya kniga) 1992, p. 339.

ally tolerated by public opinion when the victim is impersonal (the state, a plant, a collective farm etc). But it could be argued that Russian economic ethos is informal, it does not contain respect for formal laws and written contracts, preferring informal agreements based on personal relations.[15] Therefore it is considered moral to prefer not paying wages to laying off employees (promising to pay some time in the future). This specific feature of Russian economic ethos provided a kind of buffer which dampened the immediate social effects of the structural crisis in Russian economy. Under a system of effective law and contract enforcement the majority of our enterprise would have been already closed and their employees laid off. Instead we have got the so called crisis of payments - the situation of everybody being in everyones debt including the federal budget. The participation of government in the chains of indebtedness serves as a certain moral multiplier legitimizing the indebtedness of others. In principle this omnipresent payments crisis leaves enterprise and workers time to look for a new niche in emerging market economy though a lot of them doesn't use this possibility relying instead upon paternalistic attitudes of state authorities and enterprise directors. Besides the so called non-payments give the producers a sort of commercial credit which can't be obtained otherwise (The interest rates being very high). Certainly this ethical buffer could be regarded only as a temporary compromise solution because it is slowing down the structural adjustment process. And much more important, employees who don't get wages for 3 and more months break the informal contract of "paying as soon as possible" and begin strikes and other forms of protest. All this means that not much can be understood in Russian economy of today without taking into account the ethical factors.

On the other hand, the normative use of ethics in choosing the appropriate direction of economic policy is also demanded in contemporary Russia. The ethical ideal of opposition now represented by a strange mixture of nationalist phantasies and some official communist values like equality, collectivism, the responsibility of state for its citizens still has appeal to many Russians. These values which were not practiced by those who preached them were taken by the majority of population seriously. On the contrary the process of transition to market economy has not got any moral backing. New

---

15 These features of Russian national character were discussed long before the Bolshevik revolution of 1917. See: I. YANZHUL: *Ekonomicheskoye znacheniye chestnosti* (The Economic Significance of Honesty), Moscow 1912.

Russian reformers have not proposed any alternative to the traditional Russian and partly communist values constituting the economic ethos of the country except market economy, political democracy and individual rights and liberties which do not seem to be attractive to our population as such. And without any ideals one can hardly accomplish anything significant in a country like Russia. So it is very important to stress the economic significance of honesty and moral norms which underly every stable market economy.

Taking all this into consideration the German tradition of economic ethics coming from the Historical School has right now considerable chances to assert itself in Russian intellectual debate. Libertarians and neoliberals like von Hayek and von Mises and American consultants like Jeffry Sachs have fallen out of favour. On the other hand the interest to the German economic thought and German post World war II economic reforms is growing, though it has been complicated by the inability of the majority of our scholars to read German. Now a series of translations mostly of Walther Eucken and other representatives of Ordo-liberalism are being published which will improve the situation. At any rate concepts like "social market economy" or "economic order" are used approvingly by all sides of the debates. But up to now in my opinion we borrow from German theoretical and practical experience mostly some wrongly understood fragments. It is very seldom realised that the moral of social market economy is the moral of individual responsibility, not of paternalism; that economic order is the order of competition, not of state-owned or state- supported monopolies. So we may adopt a distorted image of these concepts. A lot of efforts are needed to improve the situation.

The conclusion I want to draw is that somehow Russia seems to be constantly prone to adopt the ideas close to those of the German Historical school. They are always more attractive in this country than the ideology of liberalism. However, due to the lagging economic and social development and some national traits of Russian people we always tend not only to adopt but also to adapt them in a radical and mystical way.

Discussion Summary

ANNETTE KLEINFELD

Paper discussed:
VLADIMIR S. AVTONOMOV: Some Reflections on Ethics and Economics
Concerning the German Historical School
and Its Reception in Russia

A first line of the discussion dealt with the economic ethos in Russia before the October Revolution and today.

From the beginning on, the communist propaganda had drawn a picture of the economic ethos in Russia before the revolution, that later on allowed them to trace back the economic disaster under the communist regime to the specific Russian mentality. In their propaganda they simply ignored the fact that this specificly Russian economic ethos has been suppressed and thus more or less destroyed by the consequences of the revolution (KOSLOWSKI). In their description of the Russian mentality the communists could refer to Dostojewski who criticized the Russian people for its passivity and contemplative outlook on life. And in fact, it was exactly this attitude that smoothed the path for the revolution. Thus, on the one hand, it is true that the revolution had a certain influence on the ethos of the Russian people, on the other hand, the communists, especially Lenin, took advantage from this ethos. It is also true, that the communist propaganda blamed the Russian mentality for the economic disaster, but nowadays it is just the other way around: everybody blames the revolution and the communist regime for the present economic situation in Russia (AVTONOMOV).

As another example illustrating the Russian mentality, the hostile reactions of the Russian people concerning the attempts of Peter the Great to modernize Russia were mentioned: He was considered as a raider, his reformatory efforts refused. The problems of today's Russian economy have their main roots in a lack of morality leading to economic criminalism. Thus, instead of using the financial support of the West to build up the economic system, the money is going into the wrong channels. Another causal factor for these abuses was seen in the Libertarian tradition in Russia and the narrow mindedness connected with it, which allows neither to establish a solid political system nor to mobilize the public against this kind of politics (CHMIELEWSKI).

A second part of the discussion was dedicated to the reflection of possible solutions for the problems of Eastern Europe today.

The belief in fiscal mechanisms alone was considered to be the wrong basis with reference to the situation in the East. The promise of Geoffrey Sachs for instance, to remedy the abuses in Polen within a few months by a sort of "Marshall-plan", could not be kept (CHMIELEWSKI). It was also doubted that pivate ethics which are still in the centre of the present reform will be able to solve these problems in an adequate manner. This model of ethics might have been sufficient within the paternalistic structures of the former Eastern societies, with regards to the transformation process, however, it has to be supplemented by an ethics of the market economy as well as by laws and institutional measures (KABELE, RINGER). In how far can the theory of the Historical School be helpful here? Reducing human costs by social protection and a buffering network for instance, primarily is a political problem, not an academic one. The connections between the Historical School and real live were considered to be much too abstract (RINGER).

The question was raised, whether the model of "homo oeconomicus" would be able to support the transformation process, or if it did suffer from a lack of practical relevance as well (MAGUN). The differenciation between models and reality was considered to be inadequate since they are mutually influencing each other. The behaviour of a society or nation is not only shaped by its specific mentality and cultural ethos but also by the theoretical framework it adopts for politicial or economic reasons although the underlying theory might not originate from its own culture. In this sense, a certain normative function has to be ascribed to the "homo oeconomicus" indeed (NOP-PENEY). Against this, an empirical study about the problem of "free riders" was mentioned which had the puzzling result that only university professors behaved according to the model of "homo oeconomicus" (AVTONOMOV).

A practicable way with regards to the transformation process was seen in the theory of New Institutional Economics on the basis of principles like the reduction of transaction costs or investment decisions that do not presuppose a certain societal framework or method for its application (FURUBOTN).

The third part of the discussion focused on the question of the present relevance of the Historical School both, for the process of economic transformation in Eastern Europa as well as for the process of economic globalization in general.

Even though there might not be an immediate relevance of the theory of the Historical School for practical problems, there do exist certain parallels between the practical developments of the Historical School and today's Russia. Both, policy makers and scientists, thus can and should learn from the German Historical School in order to counterweigh the present tendencies towards a radical form of capitalism (AVTONOMOV).

According to Müller-Armack, the Social Market Economy is a form of capitalism. Today, there are two legitimate versions of capitalism: the Anglo-American form and this more moderate form of the Social Market Economy. That there is a certain preference for the capitalist system of the United States, may be connected with the fact that it is felt to be more exciting than Social Market Economy as Michel Albert assumes. The crucial question facing the process of economic globalization, however, is, which version should and can be implemented world wide. Right now, this process of globalization is lead by an irrational economic optimism only that tends to completely neglect the conditions of the national market. Against this tendeny, the authors of the Historical School, such as Friedrich List for instance, have always emphasized the need to equilibrate the development of the national economy with the global market before striving for a world wide free trade (KOSLOWSKI).

As far as Russia is concerned, it is mainly Suganov who stands up for a social market economy instead of a free trade market economy. What does he mean by this, and in how far could he relate to arguments of the Historical School for defending his position (TOFALL). Suganov actually aims at a socialist market economy. But only one quarter of the Russian population is communist now. The private owners existing so far do not have any responsibility yet, since everything is still controlled by the enterprise directors. Therefore, the greater part of the Russian society does not want any kind of centralized or governmentally controlled economic system any more, and rather tends to a free trade market economy (AVTONOMOV).

DISCUSSION SUMMARY

As an argument for the relevance of the Historical School with regards to the transformation process the case of Geoffrey Sachs was mentioned again. The failure of his project can clearly be traced back to two shortcomings, to a lack of insight into the specificly Russian respectively Polish circumstances, namely in the kolkhose system, as well as to a lack of interest in the cultural tradition of the two countries at stake. Taking into account these national particularities and frameworkal conditions will lead in the case of Russia and Poland to the insight that within their special historical context a mercantilistic system might be more adequate than a liberal form of the market economy (ACHAM).

Part Seven

The Historical School of Economics and Today's Economics

Chapter 17

The Old and the New Institutionalism in Economics

EIRIK G. FURUBOTN

I. Introduction: Institutionalism as Extended Neoclassical Theory

As the limitations of mainstream neoclassical theory became increasingly evident during the post-war period, there occurred a remarkable expansion of research activity in modern institutional economics. Not only did the quantity of institutionally oriented research and writing grow over time but, in addition, modern institutional economics began to secure recognition as a distinct and significant area of study.[1] Nevertheless, it is important to realize that neoinstitutionalist scholars do not speak with one voice, and that the boundaries of the field have not been established with great precision. This is so, in

---

[1] It can be noted, for example, that in recent years, Nobel prizes have gone to economists such as COASE, BUCHANAN and NORTH who have written in the general area of modern institutionalism.

part, because modern institutionalism was not developed in systematic fashion by individuals sharing a common vision, or by those who saw themselves as engaging in a bold new movement designed to bring about a revolutionary approach to economic theory. Rather, theoretical advance took place largely through innovative work in particular sub-fields such as: transaction-cost economics, property-rights analysis, law and economics, constitutional economics, etc. Indeed, during the formative years of what we now call the New Institutional Economics, the writings produced in the various specialized areas tended to be rather diverse in style and methodology as well as in content. And, even today, there are real divisions among scholars about how best to treat institutional and organizational questions in economics. Of course, shared intellectual ground does exist. At a fundamental level, the core element that binds different groups of neoinstitutionalist researchers together is the conviction that orthodox neoclassical analysis is overly abstract and incapable, without some modification, of dealing effectively with many problems of interest to theorists and policy makers.

With the development of the New Institutional Economics, it was inevitable that questions would be raised about how the new approach compares with the older institutionalism of the German Historical School or with the work of the American institutionalist movement. The issue clearly has interest. At first blush, one might expect that since both the new and the old institutionalism proceed from a criticism of conventional neoclassical theorizing, exponents of the NIE would show some interest in, and respect for, the earlier writings. But this is not really the case. The characteristic view of NIE contributors concerning the value of the old institutionalism tends to parallel the one Ronald Coase has expressed so forcefully:

>...I know little about the German Historical School but I gather from Hutchison that their position was essentially the same as that of the American institutionalists. .... Stigler in a recent issue of the *Journal of Law and Economics* said that American institutionalism failed because it had no positive doctrines. All it had was a stance of hostility to the standard economic theory. It certainly led to nothing. ... The American institutionalists were not theoretical but anti-theoretical, particularly where classical economic theory was concerned. Without a theory they had nothing to pass on except a mass of descriptive material waiting for a theory, or a fire. So if the modern institutional economists have antecedents, it is not what went immediately before (Coase 1984, pp. 230-31).

This statement has importance because it seems to reflect quite accurately the position of most of the early NIE writers who were at pains to disassociate themselves from the approach followed by the old institutionalists.

What gave the NIE group such confidence that they could disregard the older work on institutions was the belief that standard neoclassical analysis could be readily generalized or "extended" to treat institutional problems. Fundamentally, the thought was that, although neoinstitutionalists felt dissatisfaction with what mainstream economists were doing, the dissatisfaction was not so much with the theory being used as with the *manner* in which it was used. Thus, it could be argued that:

> ...What distinguishes the modern institutional economists is not that they speak about institutions, the American institutionalists after all did this, nor that they have introduced a new economic theory, although they may have modified the existing theory in various ways, but that they use standard economic theory to analyze the working of these institutions and to discover the part they play in the operation of the economy (*ibid.*, p. 230).

It should be observed here that if Coase was able to make this assessment of the situation, other economists, such as those more committed to formal, mathematically based, methods, were predisposed to be even more enthusiastic about the "generalization" approach to institutional analysis.

For those trained in the traditional microeconomic doctrine that was dominant at most universities in the English-speaking countries from the thirties onward, there was, of course, something very satisfying about the notion that a straightforward transition could be made to a more flexible, institutionally oriented theory by simply modifying certain neoclassical assumptions while holding others unchanged. The procedure seemed to promise the best of all outcomes. The "neoinstitutional" approach could, presumably, expand understanding of institutional questions while preserving the rigor of the deductive neoclassical model, and permitting continued use of the standard technical tools that were part of the neoclassical legacy. In short, research could be conducted more or less as usual. There was no necessity to engage in the kind of massive historical-descriptive studies that were associated with the old institutionalism, but empirical work could still be undertaken. Indeed, as Williamson has pointed out, the new type of empirical and theoretical analysis in such specialties as industrial organization, labor economics, economic history, and comparative systems strongly influenced the renaissance of "institutionalism" (Williamson 1975, p. 1).

To speak of a renaissance of institutionalism is not mere rhetoric. Despite the methodological problems inherent in the early neoinstitutional writings, there can be no doubt that they served to clarify the role of institutional arrangements in an economy. At a minimum, institutions were now seen to count. The specific patterns of transaction costs and property rights in existence could be shown to have predictable effects on incentives and, hence, on economic behavior. Moreover, the strong emphasis on methodological individualism that underlay this kind of analysis made it apparent that the individual decision maker, rather than the organization or collectivity, had to be the focus of attention. Thus, in the case of the theory of the firm, there occurred a significant shift to utility as the maximand in constrained optimization problems. This change, simple as it was technically, opened up new possibilities for studying business operations in various socio-economic environments, and permitted deeper understanding of different forms of managerial behavior. In general, then, it seems fair to say that considerable knowledge was gained through these initial attempts to explain institutions within the basic framework of neoclassical theory.

II. The Initial Model Reconsidered

The systematic consideration of transaction costs and property-rights structures by neoinstitutional writers represented a crucial development in modern institutional thought because, once having moved in this direction, microeconomic theory could no longer return to a position that suggested institutional arrangements were *neutral* elements having no independent effect on economic behavior. Nevertheless, the approach initially taken by the New Institutional Economics, with its heavy reliance on neoclassical theory, had the effect of oversimplifying problems and moving discussion in less productive directions. The crux of the difficulty lay in the way in which the "extended neoclassical model" was specified. It was true, of course, that since positive transaction costs and bounded rationality were assumed to exist, there was recognition that the neoinstitutional approach had to be somewhat different from the one used in the frictionless neoclassical model. Thus, for example, constraints not found in the orthodox case were introduced and accepted as important, e.g., (Eggertsson 1990, p. 6). But what did not seem to be fully appreciated was the fact that the new assumptions had very far-reaching consequences, and that the changed view of the world they represented led inevitably to a significantly different interpretation of neoclassical analysis.

In an economy in which decision makers do not have the ability to acquire and process information instantly and costlessly, the elements traditionally taken as data in the neoclassical model can no longer by accepted as simply given. Thus, in the theory of the firm, the hypothetical entrepreneur has to do more than find the profit-maximizing point on the boundary of a clearly delineated production set. When operations are conducted in a world of frictions and cognitive limitations, the extent of the technological knowledge possessed by the firm's entrepreneur or manager is a *variable* to be determined as part of a more extended and complex optimization process than the one considered under pure neoclassical assumptions. Similarly, the levels of information possessed about factor quality, commodity and input prices, etc. are also variables to be determined. Questions arise, therefore, about where, by whom, and at what cost information search should be pursued. In other words, far from representing simple and innocuous changes, the new assumptions about transaction costs and bounded rationality have the effect of revolutionizing the orthodox neoclassical model. The older conceptions of what constitute data do not hold, and there is need for a general respecification of the structure of the model.

Inter alia, it is necessary to establish precisely what information is potentially available to decision makers, and what is not. The focus has to be on potentially attainable information - with due regard to the effective cost of acquiring and processing that information. This is so because it is wrong to assume that information about certain critical elements (such as the firm's production function) comes to the decision maker as a *free good*, or that the act of assessing alternatives and deciding on a particular policy is without cost. The idea that activities in the real world involve opportunity costs would seem to be straightforward enough but, unfortunately, this understanding has not been effectuated in a *consistent* way by the NIE literature. Thoroughgoing reconstruction has been avoided. Rather, the approach has been to formulate "neoinstitutional" models that combine *some* new analytic concepts (such as transaction costs) with traditional neoclassical assumptions. The objective here is modest. It is to "extend" neoclassical analysis by making only a few limited changes in the orthodox neoclassical framework.

Given this procedure, the constructs that emerge are best conceived as "hybrid" models (Furubotn 1994). Such models are composite in the sense that they are based on assumptions drawn from two *disparate* universes - the neoinstitutional and the neoclassical. And, as a consequence, serious problems exist with the approach. There are good reasons to believe that a satisfactory theory cannot be "half" neoclassical and "half" neoinstitutional. For example, in the case of the firm touched on above, it is inconsistent to suggest that a decision maker who is boundedly rational can have *complete and accurate* knowledge of the set of efficient technological options available for producing a given commodity, and wrong to say that he can employ *rational-choice* decision methods to arrive at a true profit-maximizing equilibrium. This general issue will be taken up in greater detail below. However, it is easy to understand that in an economic situation where significant limitations of time and cognitive capacity exist, and where the cost of optimization processes must be *fully accounted for*, the solution reached for the firm will not closely approximate that found in neoclassical theory. The addition of a few new constraints to the standard neoclassical model does not create a structure that can explain behavior in an environment characterized by positive transaction costs and bounded rationality. Unfortunately, the solutions attained by hybrid models are fundamentally flawed because they are derived from data and decision methods that are well beyond the reach of individuals operating in a world of frictions and uncertainty.

III. The Question of a New Paradigm

Granting the logic of the preceding discussion, it follows that neoinstitutionalism, properly understood, is *not* extended neoclassical theory. But if this conclusion is correct, we may ask why the economics profession has not placed greater emphasis on the task of finding a superior approach to institutional analysis. There is certainly broad recognition that neoclassical theory has limitations. Indeed, some would argue that the theory has disabling limitations:

> The economists of the twentieth century, by pushing the neoclassical model to its logical conclusion, and thereby illuminating the absurdities of the world which they had created, have made an invaluable contribution to the economics of the coming century: they have set the agenda, work on which has already begun (Stiglitz 1991, p. 136).

434

Nevertheless, while the orthodox assumptions concerning perfect information, complete rationality, perfect markets, etc. may be rejected, there is still great reluctance to make a real break from mainstream microtheory. And it is this predisposition that goes a long way toward explaining why neoinstitutional models of the hybrid type continue to appear so prominently in the current literature.

It is, of course, understandable that economists are hesitant about moving to a fundamentally different form of analysis. There is fear that complete abandonment of the neoclassical model would leave the profession without a clear analytical focus, and open the door to a flood of dubious, non-rigorous theorizing. Moreover, the record seems to show that conventional methods have some potency. The early development of transaction-cost/property-rights analysis was accomplished through the incorporation of new themes into the standard model and, as noted in section I, some useful results were achieved. Finally, it can be noted that, despite the contributions to economic understanding that have been made so far by evolutionary economics, the NIE, and other non-standard approaches, there is as yet no well articulated and generally accepted alternative theory that appears to produce the same range and richness of results as neoclassical theory.

It is perhaps debatable whether an outright shift to a new paradigm is required to deal adequately with institutional questions, or whether movement to a more imaginative revision of the neoclassical model will suffice. What does seem to be clear, though, is that theoretical efforts to date have been less than satisfactory. A continuing issue here concerns the degree of emphasis that should be placed on *formal theorizing*. As Nelson and Winter have noted:

> If the contemporary critics of orthodox theory can be accused of not appreciating the importance of a coherent theoretical structure and of underestimating the resiliency and absorptive capacity of prevailing orthodox theory, the defenders of orthodoxy can be accused of trying to deny the importance of phenomena with which orthodox theory deals inadequately and at the same time overestimating the potential ability of models within the orthodox framework somehow to encompass these phenomena. Perhaps economists should be less pessimistic about the prospects of developing a broad-gauge economic theory that encompasses much of what contemporary orthodoxy does but is not subject to its basic difficulties (Nelson and Winter 1982, p. 48).

This assessment is relatively upbeat and seems to suggest that, with the use of some ingenuity, neoclassical theory can be modified appropriately.

Given what we know today, however, it is arguable that a more basic change in approach is necessary. Even though its outlines can now be seen only dimly, there are certainly reasons to believe that a shift in paradigm cannot be avoided. It does not seem possible to relax the highly specialized assumptions of neoclassical theory without altering the whole nature of the analysis. What is at issue is not just a matter of adding complications from the real world and then securing results that are "less than perfect" and that only approximate those promised in pure theory. Rather, in models where transaction costs and bounded rationality play key roles, the very process by which economic solutions are generated is quite different from that envisaged in the neoclassical case. In particular, it can be shown that, under the assumptions just noted, the basic neoclassical concepts of rational choice and maximizing behavior cannot be justified.

When it is recognized that decision makers have limited cognitive ability and must use time and other scarce resources to acquire and process information, an optimal decision (insofar as one exists in these circumstances) can be determined only after the *full cost* of reaching the decision has been taken into account.[2] Moreover, once the matter of optimization cost is broached, a question arises about what *mode* of decision-making behavior should be used in undertaking optimization and choosing among options. Although the point is normally ignored in neoclassical discussion, the fact is that , quite apart from rational choice, various other choice or decision methods exist - as, e.g., random choice, imitation, obeying an authority and habit (Pingle 1992, p. 8). It follows, therefore, that some decision methods may be preferable to others because some are cheaper than others. The basic objective, of

---

2   A significant difficulty with the standard neoclassical formulation of optimization problems has been described by GOTTINGER as follows:
     The calculation of the optial decision by the agent is generally assumed to be costless in this methodological approach. However, certain results in the theory of computation indicate that a useful requirement for a function to be 'computable' is that it can be realized by a step-by-step procedure that can be implemented mechanically (MINSKY [1967]). Since implementation of each step in the procedure requires the services of some human or mechanical agent, any computation requires the use of scarce resources; and agents may not perform the computation required for the continuous optimization of their criterion functions. Therefore, the optimal decisions of agents in an economy are determined after the cost of reaching the decision is taken into consideration (GOTTINGER [1982], pp. 223-224).

course, must be to select the particular method that serves best to economize on optimization costs. In other words, given such cost considerations, there can be no presumption that the (costly) rational decision-making approach associated with orthodox neoclassical theory either will be, or should be, adopted by individuals seeking to adjust to the conditions of the neoinstitutional environment.[3]

In light of what has just been said, it would seem that if future improvement in neoinstitutional theory is to take place, it will have to occur within an essentially new paradigm. This is a somewhat depressing conclusion, however, because it means, inter alia, that familiar mathematical techniques that have played an important part in neoclassical analysis will become less valuable, and that conventional welfare economics (which is also tied to orthodox neoclassical reasoning) will no longer find useful application as a benchmark for policy assessments. There is also a certain irony in the situation. For many neoinstitutionalist writers, a major advantage of the approach that maintained close contact with mainstream neoclassical theory lay in its (supposed) capacity to preserve logical rigor and mathematical tractability (Posner 1993, pp. 74-75). It was on this basis that the old institutionalism, with its perceived anti-theoretical bias, could be rejected so forcefully. But, even from a purely formal point of view, neoinstitutional constructs are far from impeccable. Models that are based on inconsistent assumptions and that suffer from the methodological problem of infinite regress cannot be regarded as rigorous products. Moreover, unless very generous standards are used, the predictive value of these models is not impressive.[4] Thus, while the old institutionalism was seen as having methodological deficiencies, it is not clear that any superiority found in neoinstitutional writings derives from the fact that these writings reflect high levels of formalism and rigor (DeAlessi 1990).

If the criticism of the NIE presented above is correct and movement must be made into a new paradigm, the problem of comparing the new and the old institutionalism becomes more complicated. That is, with variant formulations possible, a question can arise as to what body of doctrine truly consti-

---

3   Rational-choice decision making is also plagued by the serious methodological problem of infinite regress. This difficulty will be discussed below in section VI.

4   To say that, e.g., market demand curves slope downward does not represent a triumph of prediction for neoclassical analysis. See: (BECKER [1962]), (STIGLITZ, [1994], chaps. 3 and 4).

tutes the "new institutionalism."[5] The fact that modern institutional theory is in flux and still evolving adds to the basic difficulty of comparing theories (the old and the new) that, in actuality, have quite different objectives. What has to be understood is that:

> ...the German Historical School analyzed a different segment of the real world than classical or neoclassical economics. They analyzed the institutional framework while traditional economics dealt with the economic process. It may be that Schmoller did not argue in this manner because he was convinced (as Coase is today) that his style of research was "economics as it ought to be." Instead Schmoller got involved in the "deductive vs. inductive" debate which lead nowhere (Richter 1995, p. 21).

By undertaking descriptive studies of institutional structure, the old institutionalists were able to consider matters that were given only limited attention in neoclassical theory. Such work had value, but since the older approach lacked concern with an underlying base of formal theory, it has to be regarded as distinct from modern institutionalism. As Richter has put it:

> Both the old German Historical School and the New Institutional Economics are similar insofar as they stress the first point-determining the relevant segment of the real world for study. They differ in that the Historical School, more or less, avoided rational choice arguments, whereas the representatives of the New Institutional Economics, in spite of their criticism of the concept of *homo oeconomicus*, use classical analysis in the property-rights approach, and the "mixed" concept of bounded rationality in the transaction-cost approach. In this respect, they differ also from Old American Institutionalism (*ibid.*, p. 22).

The new institutionalism's attachment to mainstream theory sets it apart from the old institutionalism but, as the present paper has argued, the way in which neoinstitutional models have been formulated leaves much to be desired. Hybrid models, whatever insights they may have offered us, are unsatisfactory from a technical standpoint. Thus, it would seem that if modern institutionalism is to develop in a scientifically appropriate manner, something beyond neoclassical theory is required. In what follows, an attempt will be made to explain more fully the case that can be made against the current NIE

---

5   Even today, a distinction is drawn by some writers between neoinstitutionalism and the New Institutional Economics. See, e.g., (EGGERTSON [1990], p. 6).

position, and to give some indication of the general type of institutional theory that may emerge in the future.

IV. The Introduction of Additional Constraints

Given certain simplifying assumptions, neoclassical theory asserts that a competitive capitalist economy will reach an equilibrium that is also a first-best Pareto-optimal configuration of the economy. In this conception, markets are interpreted as the institutional means through which the marginal equivalencies for the general equilibrium of production and exchange are met. Although institutions play only a passive role in this pure neoclassical formulation, they are at least understood to exist. Thus, when theorists began to take some interest in generating a more empirically robust model, and it was recognized that differences in transaction costs and property-rights structures led to differences in economic behavior, it was an easy step to the representation of institutions as special constraints that had to be given serious consideration within the standard neoclassical framework.

> We may say that institutions consist of a set of constraints on behavior in the form of rules and regulations; a set of procedures to detect deviations from the rules and regulations; and, finally, a set of moral, ethical behavioral norms which define the contours that constrain the way in which the rules and regulations are specified and enforcement is carried out. This framework rests on three fundamental assumptions which we must explore. First, an individualistic behavioral assumption; second, an assumption that specifying and enforcing the rules that underlie contracts is costly; and third, an assumption that ideology modifies maximizing behavior (North 1984, p. 8).

The ideas expressed in this passage are fully consonant with the view that the basic structure of neoclassical theory can be preserved when attention is turned to institutional questions. While it is suggested that individual maximizing behavior may be affected somewhat by ideological factors, rational choice is still seen as dominant. Rational choice will operate to shape economic behavior in a more complex system that now reflects positive transaction costs and various institutional constraints.

439

EIRIK G. FURUBOTN

Essentially the same interpretation of the neoinstitutional approach was provided by DeAlessi:

> Neoclassical theory...can be generalized to eliminate some of these limitations. A major step is to end the dichotomy between the theory of consumer choice and the theory of the firm by extending the utility-maximization hypothesis to all individual choices, including those made by business managers, and government employees. Another step is to broaden the concept of the limits on individual choices to include institutional constraints (the system of property rights) as well as more of the constraints (for example, including transaction and adjustment costs) imposed by nature and the state of the arts (DeAlessi 1983, p. 66).

From a technical standpoint, the modifications suggested here have straightforward application. Thus, for example, in the theory of the firm, the usual procedure is to define the particular utility function that reflects the decision maker's preferences, and to determine the actual set of options (penalties-rewards) that is attainable by the decision maker. Then, the formal problem emerges as one of maximizing the utility function subject to the constraint pattern imposed by the opportunity set (Furubotn and Pejovich 1972, p. 1138). It is clear from this treatment that marginalism is not rejected. The standard techniques are simply extended to new applications.

Generalization of the neoclassical model seemed to be the natural and logical way to proceed even though objections had been raised in the profession from time to time about the lack of realism in mainstream theory, and about the legitimacy of assuming maximizing behavior. Such criticisms tended to be waved off, however, because it was argued strongly by Friedman (1953, p. 30) and others that the *predictive value* of a theory, not the realism of its assumptions, was the prime consideration for evaluating the theory. Specific examples were used to bring home the correctness of this position. Thus it was noted that , in a biological model, one could assume that each leaf of a plant deliberately sought to maximize its exposure to the sun's rays. And then, even though the notion of such volitional action on the part of a leaf is *unrealistic*, good predictive results about plant behavior could still be obtained. However persuasive this kind of example may be, there should be no confusion over the fact that an acceptable theory must be structured so that it

440

contains no *contradictory* assumptions.[6] If, in addition to the optimizing leaf assumption, it was also assumed that the physical characteristics of a leaf were such that it could not make any change in its orientation, the model would be fundamentally flawed. But this is the general "conflict" situation that obtains with hybrid neoinstitutional models. Characteristically, these constructs presuppose the simultaneous existence of: (i) bounded rationality, (ii) positive transaction costs, (iii) complete knowledge of essential data, and (iv) rational-choice decision making. Models of this type have to be rejected because, under conditions where all decisions are *costly* (as they must be when bounded rationality and positive transaction costs hold), decision makers simply cannot operate in the way implied by the models. The solutions reached by hybrid models are defective because they are based on structures of inconsistent assumptions; in effect, solutions are derived from data that cannot be in the possession of the relevant actors, and from decision methods that are too costly to be of practical use.

The difficulties just alluded to could be overcome if the neoinstitutional assumptions concerning bounded rationality and transaction costs were dispensed with. But, then, models would obviously revert to the traditional neoclassical (frictionless) form, and there would be no neoinstitutional theory to discuss. From an analytical standpoint, the whole point of modern institutionalism is to take systematic account of certain constraints on economic activity that have previously been neglected. Insofar as we wish to understand economic behavior as it occurs in the real world, we cannot abstract from *fundamental features* of economic reality, and bounded rationality and transaction costs represent such fundamental features. We know from everyday experience that decision makers have only limited cognitive ability and limited time per period to devote to choice problems. Thus, economization is necessary. Similarly, we appreciate that the acquisition of information requires the use of scarce resources, and that the initiation and completion of transactions involves a variety of contracting costs. Arguably, the special costs associated with bounded rationality can be conceived as a particular class of transaction costs (or "frictions"). Whatever the classification system used, though, it is

---

6 Hausmann suggests the need to be cautious when attempting to determine the role that particular scientific methodology plays in generating "good" theory (HAUSMAN [1989]). However, it would seem difficult to argue that a theory based on contradictory assumptions can be regarded as satisfactory.

true that, together, bounded-rationality costs and the more conventional transaction costs exercise a profound effect on economic outcomes.

Neoinstitutional theory is open to some criticism on grounds that it fails to give clear and unambiguous definition either to the concept of "transaction costs" or to that of "bounded rationality." For example, it has been pointed out that the distinction between transaction costs and production costs can be particularly hard to make, and that, in certain circumstances, transaction costs cannot be determined in advance of the actual unfolding of contractual negotiations (Furubotn and Richter 1991, pp. 25-26). Moreover, in the case of bounded rationality, we know that economists differ considerably in their understanding of the term. Scott has noted that:

> As I listened to the various presentations and discussions, it seemed to me that the concept of bounded rationality was being employed in at least three reasonably distinct ways. (1) Some authors were referring to the consequences of the fact that there can be significant costs to acquiring and processing information. (2) Some were referring to capacity constraints - to the limits of the present stock of scientific knowledge or of the unaided information storage and reasoning capacity of the human mine. (3) Some were referring to the asserted existence of systematic distortions in human perception or thinking (Scott 1994, p. 315).

The questions raised about both transaction costs and bounded rationality are important, and suggest that the formulation of a comprehensive neoinstitutional model will not come about easily. Nevertheless, what is clear is that, regardless of which view of these concepts is held, it is apparent that as long as individuals have to use scarce resources (human and non-human) in order to acquire and process information, certain things follow. First, costs must exist wherever people make decisions - i.e., *wherever economic activity takes place*. Second, the decisions made tend to be *quite different* from those made in a frictionless system by "completely rational" individuals.[7] The latter condition holds because of the cognitive peculiarities of humans, and because resource limitations force decision makers to use imperfect data and to

---

7   Note that an individual is viewed as "completely rational" if his capabilities can be characterized as follows: ". . . A completely rational individual has the ability to foresee everything that might happen and to evaluate and optimally choose among available courses of action, all in the blink of an eye and at no cost" (KREPS [1990], p. 745).

adopt decision methods that do not consider and compare all alternatives extant (Day and Pingle 1991).

The analysis so far points to the fact that the hybrid models put forward in much of the neoinstitutional literature are based on inconsistent assumptions and are, by their inherent nature, incapable of yielding accurate predictions of events in the real world. Despite this criticism, however, it is often suggested by the defenders of hybrid models that, although these constructs embody certain "simplifications," they are still able to generate useful results, and do indeed have empirical support for their predictions. The question arises, then, as to how such claims can be made. And, interestingly, one reason for the confusion would seem to be that the standards used to assess "predictive accuracy" are extremely loose. Traditional analysis, carried on in formal terms and at high levels of abstraction, tends to produce solutions which, while plausible technically, carry very little real content. Thus, in respect to the standard neoclassical model of demand, Thaler has observed:

> Economists rarely draw the distinction between normative models of consumer choice and descriptive or positive models. Although the theory is normatively based (it describes what rational consumers *should* do), economists argue that it also serves well as a descriptive theory (it predicts what consumers in fact do). This paper argues that exclusive reliance on the normative theory leads economists to make systematic, predictable errors in describing or forecasting consumer choices.
>
> In some situations the normative and positive theories coincide. If a consumer must add two (small) numbers together as part of a decision process then one would hope that the normative answer would be a good predictor. So if a problem is sufficiently simple the normative theory will be acceptable. Furthermore, the sign of the substitution effect, the most important prediction in economics, has been shown to be negative even if consumers choose at random (Becker 1962). Recent research has demonstrated that even rats obey the law of demand (Kagel and Battalio 1975; Thaler 1994, pp. 3-4).

If the existence of downward sloping demand schedules in the economy can be taken as evidence of the predictive accuracy of a hybrid model of demand, it seems clear that the empirical testing process is not very rigorous. But such a relaxed approach is the norm. Various detailed questions about consumption are routinely ignored by purely formal analysis. For example, in an n commodity system, it would be interesting to know what the theory's predictions are with respect to such matters as: (I) How many distinct types of goods are consumed at equilibrium? and (ii) Which particular types of the n goods available are actually taken? We know the theory is flexible, but is it reasonable to believe that the consumer may specialize deliberately in the consumption of a single good, or that he may decide to consume simultaneously each type of consumer good produced in the system, or that he will show an infinite demand for any good that carries a zero price? Regardless of what even casual empiricism suggests, a hybrid model tied to orthodox utility analysis is consistent with the realization of any of the solutions just noted (Furubotn 1974).

Actually, the problem with hybrid models goes deeper, and there is no reason to believe that such constructs can ever make accurate predictions, given their premises. Consider an example from the area of production economics. While the typical hybrid model may recognize that the firm's entrepreneur must incur costs in order to learn about input prices and input quality, the model assumes (implicitly) that the entrepreneur is able to use a *fully defined* production function in his optimizing adjustments. The latter information about technology, despite its extent and complexity, is assumed to be freely available. But this position is in conflict with other assumptions of the model that accept positive transaction costs and bounded rationality. Of course, if the fully defined production function is employed in the mathematical formulation of the problem, the solution is *inevitably biased*. This is so because the model makes it appear that search for the firm's ideal operating position can extend over a far greater range of technical alternatives than when the production alternatives have to be discovered by the entrepreneur though a costly discovery program. When discovery is necessary, the production function is attenuated and appears merely in *partial form*. Quite possibly, the partial (discontinuous) function, as established through the imperfect perception and limited cognitive capabilities of the human entrepreneur, can be so attenuated that what are, in theory, the most advantageous technical options available in society will not even be represented in the production set being reviewed by the entrepreneur. In short, the solution generated by the hybrid model of our discussion will not reflect empirical reality closely, and the model cannot be regarded as a device for achieving accurate predictions of real-world behavior.

This pessimistic conclusion is reinforced when it is realized that hybrid models also presuppose that optimization involves the use of rational choice and maximization procedures based on the calculus. Such an approach implies costs which are not accounted for within the hybrid framework, but which have an important effect on what can actually be chosen by decision makers operating in a real-life system. The analysis of optimization costs will be the topic of the next section.

V. The Role of Optimization Costs

At various points in the preceding sections, references have been made to the fact that optimization costs exert a major influence on economic behavior in the real world. Unfortunately, however, these costs are totally neglected in neoclassical theory, and play no fundamental role in the hybrid neoinstitutional models that are derived from neoclassical theory. This area clearly requires more study; in particular, it is essential to demonstrate precisely why the operation of optimization costs can be said to have such great significance for neoinstitutional analysis. Thus, in what follows, an attempt will be made to explain more fully the nature of optimization costs, and to show how they affect the way in which decisions are reached in an economy characterized by "frictions." To simplify exposition (without loss of generality), it will be useful to conduct discussion in terms of the elementary theory of the firm.

According to neoclassical doctrine, when decisions concerning the firm are made by "completely rational" individuals functioning within a world of costless transactions, the process of optimization is straightforward and takes place instantly (and costlessly). The institutional arrangements envisioned are rudimentary. The entrepreneur or owner-manager is assumed to possess unattenuated property rights in the "classical" firm, and to make all decisions on enterprise policy (Alchian and Demsetz 1972). Then, in the special environment postulated, decisions are costless and each owner-manager can count on having comprehensive and accurate information about the firm's production function, about prevailing market prices, about factor qualities, etc. Then, since this is so, he is able to compare *all* of the operating alternatives open and select the best, or profit-maximizing, option. However, things change radically when a shift is made to a world of frictions. When entrepreneurs have limited cognitive abilities and are forced to use time and other

445

scarce resources to acquire and process information, the whole nature of the firm's optimization problem is altered. What occurs is not simply a transition to a moderately changed environment where only a few variables have been affected. Rather, the new environment is one in which many crucial elements have changed simultaneously. The so-called hybrid models are unacceptable precisely because they take account of only some informational needs of the firm (such as data on current input prices) while ignoring others (such as information on the set of technical production alternatives).

Given frictions, it is appropriate to assume that the entrepreneur controlling the firm has less than complete knowledge of the economic environment in which he is to function. This situation implies that when the structure of the firm is first established, it will be based on the entrepreneur's imperfect initial knowledge endowment, and influenced by his need to economize on the cost of decision making. Depending on how well the initially chosen structure is adapted to actually existing technological and market conditions, the firm's profits will be greater or lesser. Of course, at any time period (including the initial one) the entrepreneur is aware that his understanding of economic alternatives is restricted, and that he may conceivably be able to increase his welfare level by *allocating greater resources to securing and processing information*. The urgency of the entrepreneur's desire for improved enterprise performance is likely to be related closely to the organization's level of profitability. Low profits imply modest reward for the entrepreneur who is the residual claimant, and may signal difficulties that can imperil the firm's survival. Obviously, other factors than profit can affect the decision in question. Individual owner-managers differ in respect to their willingness to assume risk, the aggressiveness with which they seek profits, their capacity to make good decisions, etc. But, regardless of the details here, the very nature of the real-world environment postulated ensures that firm adjustment will tend to take place over time.

We assume, then, that optimization is an ongoing process involving period by period adjustments as resources are made available at various dates for search, and as learning by doing takes place. Insofar as the firm's activities lead to progressively greater knowledge of production options and improved economic arrangements, there will be successive reformulations of the firm's profit function, and a series of new operating solutions will be established over time. It is true, of course, that at any period (including the initial one), the cognitive and financial resources that can be devoted to maintaining or enhancing the firm's profit position are necessarily limited. Despite the constraints in existence, however, there should be continuing movement and structural adjustment as long as the entrepreneur believes that the prospective gains from corrective action are greater than the costs of such action.

This interpretation of enterprise behavior indicates that the optimization process (and the costs of such optimization) will tend to be spread out over time. There are still questions, of course, about precisely how the entrepreneur is likely to carry out the optimization process. What should be clear too is that optimization costs, which are completely disregarded by neoclassical analysis, have central importance for the neoinstitutional firm. That is, in order to make a normal profit and remain in the industry in the long run, a firm must receive sufficient revenue from commodity sales each period to cover its per period outlays on the factors of production that are actually employed in the act of production itself, the array of standard transaction costs, plus (all) current costs attributable to the process of decision making and optimization.[8]

Insofar as a fully defined production function is not known to the firm automatically, the entrepreneur must make deliberate efforts to gather at least some information on technical production alternatives. He must, therefore, select a particular *decision method*, from among various possible decision methods extant, to guide his accumulation of data. Understandably, it is costly, in terms of the entrepreneur's time and resources, to select a decision method. The task is important, however, because the method actually chosen will determine: (I) how intensively and in what manner the subsequent search for technical information will be conducted, and (ii) the costs that will be incurred in applying the decision method to the search process. Precisely how much in the way of resources the entrepreneur will be willing to commit at any time period to the process of selecting a decision method (or search plan) is a subjective matter. What has to be noted, though, is that the pool of relevant technical knowledge in the economy is very large relative to the capacity of any one (small) firm to discover and utilize new information. Thus, if the entrepreneur is to economize on the overall use of his valuable time (and other resources), he must give enough attention to the choice of a decision method to avoid the mistake of using a method (such as rational choice) that attempts systematic and close consideration of the system's total knowledge

---

8   Note, however, that rational-choice decision making cannot be used exclusively in the optimization process if all of the costs of decision making are to be established. See section VI below.

stock. It would seem that any search plan chosen and employed would have to be quite selective, and would be designed to do no more than sample certain areas of technological information that the entrepreneur views as likely to be promising.

What has been described so far are certain preliminary steps in the total optimization process. We find that the firm's entrepreneur, who is always operating with imperfect information, may seek to add to his stock of knowledge at any period. To do this, he must first incur what can be called *decision-method costs*. These costs are those associated with the process of selecting a particular decision rule. Whatever the decision rule or search plan chosen, additional costs will be incurred when the rule is actually *applied* to secure technological information. The costs in question may be termed *data costs*. The entrepreneur is free to determine how much total investment he is willing to make at each period in order to expand his perception of available production techniques. Nevertheless, he will not possess, either at the outset of operations or subsequently, anything like a comprehensive production function. In practice, information on technology is so extensive and complex that the total stock possessed by society will never be assembled by any single individual facing finite transaction costs.[9] The collection of data, like any other economic activity, is subject to the discipline imposed by cost-benefit calculus. and, beyond some point, the cost of additional information will outweigh the perceived benefits of that information.

Depending on the judgment exercised by the entrepreneur, the firm will have established, at any period, a certain set of alternative production techniques. This highly attenuated "production function" will then represent a key datum facing the entrepreneur. It is from among the possibilities in this set of technological options that he must choose the particular production arrangement that he believes will conduce to the greatest net profit for the enterprise. But choice among options is not a costless process. Consequently, the entrepreneur must use some care in selecting another *decision method* (from among contending possibilities) that will be able to deal with the technological choice problem efficiently. It can be re-emphasized here that while

---

9 According to the standard definition, a production function "presupposes technical efficiency and states the maximum output obtainable from *every possible input combination*" (HENDERSON and QUANDT [1980], p. 66), italics added. It does not have to be emphasized that the consideration of every possible input combination represents a tall order. See also (NELSON and WINTER [1982], pp. 59-65).

the rational choice method (which underlies neoclassical optimization) will necessarily lead to the best solution theoretically attainable from the attenuated production set, the method is *likely to be costly* in terms of decision time (and other resources) because it implies that *all* of the alternative options being surveyed will be considered and compared (Day and Pingle 1991; Gottinger 1982). In other words, the rational choice method is undeniably best in a zero-transaction-cost, unboundedly rational world where optimization costs are nil. In the real world, however, the situation is quite different. On balance, a decision method that is less systematic and exacting in pursuing the search for the "ideal" production arrangement (as, e.g., random choice or imitation) can be superior to the maximizing behavior of rational choice.

What we may call *selection costs* emerge at the final stage of the firm's optimization process in any period. These costs, which can be taken as essentially one-period flow costs, appear after the firm's set of technical production options is in place as a datum, and when the entrepreneur must apply his chosen decision method to select what he believes to be the best solution from among the known options. The arrangement in question is the one that promises to yield the greatest net profit for the firm when followed, given the existence of the various costs of optimization, standard transaction costs, and the other significant limitations under which the entrepreneur must operate.

In summary, then, we can say that the firm in our simple illustration faces optimization costs that fall into the following categories: (i) decision-method costs, (ii) data costs, and (iii) selection costs. Note however that, in the case of decision-method costs, two entries must appear. Specifically, time and resources must be employed by the entrepreneur to determine: (a) the search plan to be adopted for deciding what technological information to secure, and (b) the decision method to be used for deciding which particular production option should be selected for the firm's operations. It follows, of course, that the larger the optimization costs (i) - (iii), the greater is the departure of the (pure) neoinstitutional model from the orthodox neoclassical model , which assumes that optimization costs are zero.

VI. The Problem of Infinite Regress

There is good reason why neoclassical theory, and the *hybrid* neoinstitutional models that are derived from it, choose to abstract from optimization costs. Once the existence of optimization costs is recognized, it is no longer possible to defend the assumption that purposive individuals reach their decisions on the basis of orthodox maximizing behavior. Rational choice as a universally used decision method has to be rejected because, when bounded rationality holds and all decisions made by human agents are costly, it leads to a logical dilemma (Winter 1975; Gottinger 1982; Conlisk 1988). Pingle has explained the essence of the situation as follows:

> ...This difficulty with strict optimization theory has become known as the "circularity problem" - there does not exist an optimization problem which can be solved that fully incorporates the cost of decision making (Pingle 1992, p. 10).

Relative to the discussion presented earlier in section V, the problem arises because of the ambiguities connected with what we have termed "decision-method costs." It was noted that the entrepreneur had to incur cost (especially time cost) in deciding on the particular decision method (say A) to use in, e.g., selecting the optimal production option for the firm from the known set of alternative technical options. What is apparent, however, is that no attention was given to the question of how the entrepreneur happened to choose the method (say B) that was used to choose among the array of possible decision methods (of which A was one element), or of the cost of selecting method B. A *higher order* problem was totally ignored. That is, some method (say C) must have been employed (at some cost) to choose B from among the different possible methods for selecting decision methods (of which B was one option). But, then, a further question emerges: How was C decided on? The general situation here indicates that the methodological problem of *infinite regress* obtains and, thus, certain costs associated with rational-choice decision making cannot be accounted for. Indeed, we know that:

> ...the decision-cost associated with solving the higher order problem is necessarily larger than that associated with the lower order problem. It follows that decision-costs act to limit the extent to which rationality can be displaced to higher levels. There must come a point where ... the "rational thing to do is to be irrational" and simply choose a choice method without reason. Otherwise, all resources would be used in decision-making (*ibid.*, p. 11).

In effect, the conclusion here is that a viable model of choice behavior has to include more than one mode of decision making behavior. Actually, given the high costs of the rational choice method in terms of decision time and other resources, we would expect that, in practice, the entrepreneur will normally shun rational choice and economize by using alternative decision methods. Contrary to the neoclassical model and hybrid neoinstitutional models that are linked to rational choice, the general rule would seem to be that the entrepreneur, the consumer and other decision makers will act according to rules-of-thumb or similar "short-cut" devices when seeking solutions that are, on balance, the best attainable.

If, as suggested, there is a general tendency for decision makers to follow "optimizing" behavior different from that presupposed by rational choice, it is clear that first-best Pareto efficiency will not be realized in the system. It is equally true, however, that second-best Pareto optimality, or constrained Pareto optimality, will not be realized either.[10] This point has some interest because the literature that sees modern institutionalism as extended neoclassical theory is based on the idea that adding constraints to the orthodox model can lead to outcomes that reflect "constrained efficiency" (Demsetz 1969, p. 11). From this perspective (of comparative institutional analysis), a correctly formulated equilibrium model must reach beyond the over-simplified neoclassical structure and include all of the real-life constraints that decision makers actually face when seeking to maximize profit or utility. But the approach has only superficial plausibility. In the context of a neoinstitutional environment where transaction costs and bounded rationality exist, *optimization costs also exist*, and it is easy to show that second-best Pareto optimality is an illusion. Specifically, we know that if limited cognitive capacity is a universal condition of humankind, individuals must find it costly to make decisions. Under such conditions, though, there will surely be attempts to reduce decision costs by adopting other modes of decision making behavior than rational-choice optimization. And, of course, when other decision methods are used, the characteristic, constrained-Pareto efficient solution cannot appear.

It would be convenient if a gradual transition could be made to a new, more flexible economic theory by simply modifying some neoclassical assumptions while holding others unchanged. Such procedure, however, does not work. The so-called hybrid models that appear so prominently in the literature reveal the logical difficulties that are inherent in any attempt to push

---

10 See: (STIGLITZ [1994], chapts. 3, 4) for a useful summary of the problems that arise in welfare economics when the orthodox assumptions about perfect information and complete markets are dropped.

the neoclassical model into areas beyond its competence. Ultimately, the case against hybrid models can be reduced to these basic considerations:

(i) The models are unsatisfactory because they are constructed on the basis of contradictory assumptions. Specifically, the assumptions made about the information possessed by decision makers are inconsistent with the assumptions concerning bounded rationality and positive transaction costs, assumptions that are crucial to neoinstitutional analysis.

(ii) As a result of the information structure assumed in hybrid models, the characteristic decision problem presupposes the availability of data (e.g., a comprehensively defined production function or utility function) that cannot be known to individuals operating in a neoinstitutional environment.

(iii) Only one mode of decision-making behavior is admitted (i.e., rational choice) even though other decision methods could lead to preferable solutions by reducing decision costs, and even though rational choice implies a logical dilemma (infinite regress) in a system where bounded rationality holds and all decisions are recognized as costly.

(iv) The solution reached by a hybrid model (which, by definition, involves both neoclassical and neoinstitutional elements) may appear plausible in purely technical terms, but is fundamentally misleading because it is derived from data and decision procedures that are effectively beyond the power of real-life individuals to achieve.

The behavior that the New Institutional Economics seeks to explore takes place within a world that is significantly different from the universe considered by orthodox neoclassical theory. And, because this is so, there seems to be no way to escape the conclusion that if neoinstitutional problems are to be dealt with successfully, something beyond hybrid models is required.

VII. In Search of the New Institutional Economics

Arguably, the New Institutional Economics has reached a watershed in its development. Although there are still writers who seek to deal with institutional questions through the use of extended neoclassical theory, this approach is coming under increasing criticism and would seem to be unsustainable in the long run. At the same time, it is difficult, as yet, to point to any well articulated alternative theory that can replace existing NIE practice and dominate thinking. Indeed, if the objective is to create a "grand design" for neoinstitutional analysis that is comparable in scope and detail to the general equilibrium models we are familiar with from neoclassical theory, a formidable task lies before us. Such a construct may not ever emerge, and certainly cannot be expected to appear in the near future. However, to say that we are unlikely to achieve this very ambitious objective in a short span of time should not be too disheartening. A substantial foundation exists for future research, and other, less demanding, approaches to institutional analysis are currently being explored. Thus, for example, important insights can be gained when the field of industrial organization is viewed from the standpoint of transaction-cost economics. As Masten has noted:

> ...Rather than stress strategic pricing and output decisions, these studies emphasize transactors' efforts to discover and adopt organizational arrangements that constrain strategic behavior and facilitate mutually beneficial transactions, efforts whose success depends in important ways on the content, operation, and limitations of the legal system. But the feature that most distinguishes this literature from the mainstream is its empirical content and, especially, the progress researchers have made identifying and collecting detailed transaction-level information on organizational practices and the nature and attributes of transactions (Masten 1996, p. vii).

Empirically based studies of the type just described do not seek to establish a comprehensive model that will supplant neoclassical theory, although their findings must inevitably modify, or call into question, certain aspects of that doctrine. In general, it seems likely that the NIE will continue its development as a somewhat fragmented field, and we can anticipate that different lines of research, involving different methodologies, will be pursued. What is interesting, though, is the growing belief in some quarters that research should move away from models of a highly mechanistic type that presuppose the possibility of precise optimizing solutions engineered by rational actors. Thus, relative to the problem of organizational control, it has been suggested that the central issue is quite different from the one put forward in principal-agent theory.[11] That is, the function of the manager in a hierarchical firm is

---

11 Formal models in the area of principal-agent theory make far-reaching assumptions in order to justify the idea that rational actors can reach favorable solutions by manipulating incentives and disincentives in establishing contracts. The basic situation envisioned is one in which the principal is "blind"

not to shape the behavior of subordinates by designing an optimal system of incentives and sanctions but, rather, to provide "leadership." This new approach is seen as superior to principal-agent theory (which lies much closer to neoclassical precepts) because, as political scientists and behaviorists have noted, organizational economics is based on an extremely narrow view of the possibilities of leadership and is politically naive. Along these lines, Miller says that the literature on principal-agent theory contrasts sharply with:

> ...the more organic view of organizations, which is centered primarily in political science and organizational psychology. From this perspective, resource allocation results from the decisions of individual leaders. The literature regards the manager's primary job to be one of leadership - that is, inspiring a willingness to cooperate, to take risks, to innovate, to go beyond the level of effort that a narrow, self-interested analysis of the incentives would summon (Miller 1992, p. 2).

Whatever we may think of the leadership hypothesis, it is generally consistent with the idea that rational-choice maximization becomes less and less appropriate for model building as information about economic variables becomes more and more uncertain and difficult to obtain, and as human motivations are recognized as complex and beyond simple categorization. The argument of the present paper has been that the earlier NIE literature, in maintaining close contact with neoclassical theory, has achieved neither analytical rigor nor satisfactory explanations of economic behavior in a world of bounded rationality and costly transactions. In effect, *the orthodox neoclassical model has proved to be an essentially misleading guide for modern institutional economics.* An approach that produces precise deterministic solutions is out of step with the requirements of institutional theory that deals, characteristically, with fuzzy outcomes. Preceding sections of the paper have discussed the problems that plague hybrid models. We saw that, if nothing else, their failure to consider as obvious a phenomenon as optimization costs is sufficient to cast serious doubt on their usefulness. But difficulties do not

---

as a direct monitor of his agent, but otherwise has full knowledge of his agent's characteristics (i.e., the agent's preference function), as well as precise knowledge of the distribution function of the external disturbances in the system that affect economic performance. In short, the presumption here seems to be that infinite and zero transaction costs can coexist. Such a conclusion, however, denies the possibility of bounded rationality (FURUBOTN [1994], pp. 14-15), (RICHTER and FURUBOTN [1996]).

end there. It should also be emphasized that when strict neoclassical assumptions are relaxed so that a neoinstitutional environment can be considered, even the concept of *economic efficiency* becomes impossible to define meaningfully. And since "efficiency" plays so large a role in economic discussion, this condition represents an absolutely crucial deficiency. The problem here illustrates, quite clearly, the specialized nature of the neoclassical model, and suggests why any attempt to extend the model to treat institutional questions must lead to unreliable conclusions.

At an early stage, some neoinstitutionalist writers questioned the legitimacy of the orthodox neoclassical definition of efficiency. The argument was that a definition based on the operation of a highly idealized, frictionless system could not serve as an adequate foundation for deciding allocation and distribution policies in the real world. It was pointed out that, for the purposes of positive economics, the only outcomes that are meaningful are those that are potentially attainable in a real-life economy. Thus, Demsetz observed that:

> The view that now pervades much public policy economics implicitly presents the relevant choice as between an ideal norm and an existing "imperfect" institutional arrangement. This *nirvana* approach differs considerably from a *comparative institution* approach in which the relevant choice is between alternative real institutional arrangements. In practice, those who adopt the nirvana viewpoint seek to discover discrepancies between the ideal and the real and, if discrepancies are found, they deduce that the real is inefficient. Users of the comparative institution approach attempt to assess which alternative real institutional arrangement seems best able to cope with the economic problem (Demsetz 1969, p. 1).

It follows from this interpretation of the problem that if each decision maker is rational and behaves consistently with the maximization postulate, the best *attainable* option will always be sought and reached. Thus, it can be argued that:

> ...efficiency is being defined as constrained maximization. Efficiency conditions are seen as the properties of a determinate (equilibrium) solution implied by a given theoretical construct. On this view, a system's solutions are always efficient if they meet the constraints that characterize it (DeAlessi 1983, p. 69).

In essence, the constrained-maximization theory of efficiency accepts the basic neoclassical definition and, then, extends it to cover situations in which a system operates with constraints that are additional to those considered in the orthodox case. The approach asserts that the effective opportunity set (which is established on the basis of all actually existing constraints) always lies *inside* the hypothetical efficiency frontier of neoclassical theory. Consequently, the most a decision maker can do is to reach the boundary of the effective set. In the absence of saturation, an individual is assumed to have motivation to exploit all of his (known) options to the fullest extent so as to maximize his welfare. If his perceived opportunity set is A, he will maximize and reach an equilibrium point on the boundary of this set. At the same time, any failure to reach the boundary of A can be interpreted to mean that the original opportunity set A was specified incorrectly. The idea is that some constraint must exist that was not recognized in the original determination. However, when this neglected element is accounted for properly, a different opportunity set B will be generated. And, given B, an optimum position on the boundary of B will, presumably, be attained by the decision maker. In short, any solution can be rationalized as efficient.

Understandably, opposition developed to the provocative view that behavior is always efficient and choice is always optimal in properly specified models. Thus, writers such as Leibenstein argued that the constrained-maximization definition was tautological and contradicted common-sense interpretation. The point made was that:

> Any decision procedure that does not permit nonoptimal choices denies the essential meaning of the word optimization, that is, the necessarily comparative element involved (Leibenstein 1985, p. 11).

While it is true, as Leibenstein indicates, that understanding is not improved very much when any observed outcome can be rationalized as "efficient," his criticism tends to underestimate the importance of unavoidable, real-world constraints. Fundamentally, he accepts the traditional view that efficiency exists only when the idealized Pareto conditions for the optimum are met. Thus, an inefficient choice is defined as one that deviates from the frontier of the idealized opportunity set. This conclusion is troubling, however, because deviation from the idealized set (which is derived from a frictionless economic system) must occur inevitably in the real world of positive transaction costs and bounded rationality.

To question the position taken by Leibenstein is not to accept the logic of the constrained-maximization approach. At first view, the latter explanation has a claim to reasonableness because it is hard to say that transaction costs and other constraints that set limits to human action in practice are the *causes* of inefficiency. Insofar as certain obstacles encountered in economic life are *unavoidable*, they must be represented as constraints in the maximization problem or the nirvana fallacy will obtain. Problems appear, however, because, apart from the matter of tautology, it seems clear that constraints cannot always be separated neatly on a priori grounds into the avoidable and the unavoidable. Some constraints, especially those relating to the personal qualities, tastes and capabilities of individuals, do not lend themselves to straightforward classification. Further, insofar as there is interest in determining the potential capacity of the system to produce desired output (Furubotn 1986), it would be useful to know something about the cost, time, and conditions required to change any constraint from the status "unavoidable" to "avoidable."[12] Finally, it should be recognized that, in a neoinstitutional environment, there can be no presumption that rational-choice decision making will prevail. Thus, literal maximization (constrained or otherwise) need not occur.

What emerges from the preceding efficiency discussion is this. Depending on which of the two explanations one accepts, all solutions are *efficient* or all are *inefficient*. This outcome has to be regarded as disconcerting. If economists cannot agree on what the concept of efficiency represents, mainstream economic theory is seriously undermined. The neoclassical tradition has always placed great emphasis on the possibility of arranging things so that the greatest benefits could be wrung from given resources. The central idea is that rational individuals, starting from specified ownership conditions and operating in a competitive system, can reach a unique, Pareto-optimal solution for production and distribution. We have seen, however, that when neoinstitutional themes are introduced into the basic neoclassical model, the results change dramatically and ambiguities appear. Even taken on its own terms, questions can be raised about the internal logic of the standard competitive model (Furubotn 1991), but what seems abundantly clear is that the model does not have the flexibility to be able to accommodate to new assumptions

---

12 In an economy characterized by asymmetrical information and other barriers to action, all moves that are potentially beneficial need not be taken even though their effective costs may be modest.

that depart very far from the original set. Thus, attempts to introduce such concepts as bounded rationality or Knightian uncertainty (Wiseman 1991) can only lead to confusion. In short, the neoclassical model represents a poor vehicle for promoting the development of institutional economics.

The paper has undertaken an extended discussion of the efficiency question in order to suggest why the NIE must loosen its connections with neoclassicism. If we are to achieve a more balanced understanding of economic efficiency (and other areas), a less rigid and mechanistic approach is needed than the one provided by neoclassical doctrine. This would appear to be the lesson learned from the neoinstitutional research of the last few decades. But, unfortunately, to the extent that movement is made toward a less confining analytical framework, results are likely to become less definite and precise. Given a neoinstitutional environment in which information is incomplete and asymmetrical, preferences are in flux (Furubotn [1994], pp. 27-35), extensive forward markets are missing, etc., it is possible to define allocative efficiency only in loose, qualitative terms. At best it can be claimed that such a system may display a capacity to eliminate high-cost producers, force the allocation of resources in directions desired by consumers, and promote the innovation of new products and technologies. However, favorable outcomes are not assured - as the work on rent-seeking behavior, the political assignment of property rights, path dependency, etc. have shown.[13] Behavior in a world of frictions can be quite varied because different individuals will see both the present and the future differently. It is also true that other mechanisms than the market may have to be used to permit responses to changed economic conditions to proceed in an orderly and coordinated manner (Nelson 1981).

Neoinstitutional writers, of course, are now becoming aware that an efficiency standard different from the traditional one must be considered.

> ...current concepts of efficiency are firmly rooted in the mathematics of constrained optimization that characterize neoclassical economics and focus on the comparison of alternative equilibrium conditions. To compare institutions on the basis of equilibrium conditions that will never be attained in a world of change and uncertainty, however, ig-

---

13 In a neoinstitutional context, competitive pressures will not necessarily force economic actors to make rational decisions or be progressively reduced in economic power over time. Thus, Alchian's suggestion that trial-and-error operations will lead to "perfect actions" need not be vindicated (ALCHIAN [1950]).

nores all information about the process of change itself (DeAlessi 1992, p. 340).

While there is as yet no general agreement on precisely how a new, more reasonable standard should be defined, there is recognition that its basic nature is likely to be quite distinct from that of the neoclassical variant. A definition that implies sharp optimality properties seems inappropriate. Presumably, the level of efficiency in any given situation will not be gauged relative to some ultimate criterion representing a hypothetical ideal outcome (such as a point on the neoclassical welfare frontier). Rather, the focus will be on a comparison of known alternatives. Option A may be seen as preferable to option B but there will be nothing to indicate that A represents the best of all hypothetically possible choices. And even this type of modest assessment may not be feasible if a dynamic system is contemplated and individual preferences are either not fully defined or are in a continual state of flux.

Just as there is movement toward a less mechanistic conception of efficiency so there seems to be a growing tendency on the part of modern institutionalism generally to adopt a broader approach in analyzing social questions. In particular, more concern is being shown with the interrelations between economics and other phenomena. Thus, for example, North, as an economic historian interested in institutions, wishes to study the numerous factors that influence the performance of economies through time. He notes:

> A theory of economic dynamics is also crucial for the field of economic development. There is no mystery why the field of development has failed to develop during the five decades since the end of World War II. Neoclassical theory is simply an inappropriate tool to analyze and prescribe policies that will induce development. It is concerned with the operation of markets, not with how markets develop. How can one prescribe policies when one doesn't understand how economies develop? The very methods employed by neoclassical economists have dictated the subject matter and militated against such a development. That theory in the pristine form that gave it mathematical precision and elegance modeled a frictionless and static world. When applied to economic history and development it focused on technological development and more recently human-capital investment but ignored the incentive structure embodied in institutions that determined the extent of social investment in those factors. In the analysis of economic performance through time it contained two erroneous assumptions: (i) that institutions do not matter and (ii) that time does not matter (North 1994, p. 359).

The research plan suggested by North to deal with institutions and time certainly involves information from a variety of social scientific areas but, interestingly, does retain the idea that neoclassical theory can somehow be reworked to serve as the analytical framework for the venture. This willingness to maintain contact with neoclassicism may be more apparent than real, however, since North emphasizes the need to modify the rationality assumption, and seems to equate neoclassical theory with the concepts of scarcity and competition.

Another Nobel prize winner, Kenneth Arrow, takes a more critical position with respect to the orthodox doctrine while echoing at least one of the themes touched on by North. That is, Arrow argues that to explain economic outcomes one must go beyond the set of individual decisions in the search for explanatory variables and consider the roles of social knowledge and societal learning.

> It is a touchstone of accepted economics that all explanations must run in terms of the actions and reactions of individuals. Our behavior in judging economic research in peer review of papers and research, and in promotions, includes the criterion that in principle the behavior we explain the policies we propose are explicable in terms of individuals, not of other social categories. I want to argue today that a close examination of even the most standard economic analysis shows that social categories are in fact used in economic analysis all the time and that they appear to be absolute necessities of the analysis, not just figures of speech that can be eliminated if need be. I further argue that the importance of technical information in the economy is an especially significant case of an irreducibly social category in the explanatory apparatus of economics (Arrow 1994, p. 1).

Sampling the work of a few leading economists does not, of itself, tell us very much about the way in which the NIE is likely to unfold in the future. Indeed, future research in the area may show considerably more diversity of approach than was observable in the era when major attention was given to hybrid models and the modification and extension of neoclassical theory. Nevertheless, regardless of diversity, it does seem true that there is a general movement toward broader, empirically richer economic models. The nonseparability of economics from other phenomena is being recognized increasingly, and heed is being paid to the significance of such "esoteric" factors as the moral rules of behavior, fairness, trust, human learning, legal evolution, etc. In this sense, at least, the NIE is drawing closer to the older institutionalism. To make such a statement, though, does not mean that modern institutional economists are now intent on discovering nothing less than the laws of socioeconomic development, or that the historico-inductive method of the German school will soon be widely adopted. But what is happening is still important; we see the slow retreat of the neoclassical paradigm from its position of dominance.

References

ALCHIAN, A.A.: "Uncertainty, Evolution, and Economic Theory," *Journal of Political Economy*, 58 (1950), pp. 211-221.

ALCHIAN, A.A., DEMSETZ, H.: "Production, Information Costs, and Economic Organization," *American Economic Review*, 62 (1972), pp. 777-95.

ARROW, K.: "Methodological Individualism and Social Knowledge," *American Economic Review*, 84 (1994), pp. 1-9.

BECKER, G.S.: "Irrational Behavior and Economic Theory," *Journal of Political Economy*, 70 (1962), pp. 1-13.

COASE, R.H.: "The New Institutional Economics," *Zeitschrift fur die gesamte Staatswissenschaft*, 140 (1984), pp. 229-231.

CONLISK, J.: "Optimization Cost," *Journal of Economic Behavior and Organization*, 9 (1988), pp. 213-228.

DAY, R., PINGLE, M.: "Economizing Economizing," *Handbook of Behavioral Economics* 2B (J.A. I. Press) 1991, pp. 511-524.

DEALESSI, L.: "Property Rights, Transaction Costs, and X-Efficiency: An Essay in Economic Theory," *American Economic Review*, 73 (1983), pp. 64-81.

DEALESSI, L: "Form, Substance, and Welfare Comparisons in the Analysis of Institutions," *Journal of Institutional and Theoretical Economics*, 146 (1990), pp. 5-23.

DEALESSI, L: "Efficiency Criteria for Optimal Laws: Objective Standards or Value Judgments?," *Constitutional Political Economy*, 3 (1992), pp. 321-342.

DEMSETZ, H.: "Information and Efficiency: Another Viewpoint," *Journal of Law and Economics*, 12 (1969), pp. 1-22.

EGGERTSSON, T.: *Economic Behavior and Institutions*, Cambridge, New York (Cambridge University Press) 1990.

EIRIK G. FURUBOTN

FRIEDMAN, M.: *Essays in Positive Economics*, Chicago, London (University of Chicago Press) 1953.

FURUBOTN, E.G.: "The Quasi-Concave Utility Function and the Number of Distinct Commodities Chosen at Equilibrium," *Weltwirtschaftliches Archiv*, 110 (1974), pp. 228-307.

FURUBOTN, E.G: "Efficiency and the Maximization Postulate: Another Interpretation," *Journal of Behavioral Economics*, 15 (1986), pp. 41-48.

FURUBOTN, E.G: "General Equilibrium Models, Transaction Costs, and the Concept of Efficient Allocation in a Capitalist Economy," *Journal of Institutional and Theoretical Economics*, 147 (1991), pp. 662-86.

FURUBOTN, E.G: "Future Development of the New Institutional Economics: Extension of the Neoclassical Model or New Construct?", *Lectiones Jenenses*, 1 (1994), pp. 3-42.

FURUBOTN, E.G., PEJOVICH, S.: "Property Rights and Economic Theory: A Survey of Recent Literature," *Journal of Economic Literature*, 10 (1972), pp. 84-107.

FURUBOTN, E.G., RICHTER, R.: *The New Institutional Economics*, Tübingen (J.C.B. Mohr (Paul Siebeck)) 1991.

GOTTINGER, H.: "Computational Costs and Bounded Rationality," in: W. STEGMULLER, W. BALZER, W. SPOHN (Eds.): *Studies in Contemporary Economics*, Vol. 2, Berlin (Springer Verlag) 1982, pp. 223-238.

HAUSMAN, D.M.: "Economic Methodology in a Nutshell," *Journal of Economic Perspectives*, 3 (1989), pp. 115-127.

HENDERSON, J., QUANDT, R.: *Microeconomic Theory*, New York (McGraw-Hill) 1980.

KAGEL, J., BATTALIO, R.: "Experimental Studies of Consumer Behavior Using Laboratory Animals," *Economic Inquiry*, (1975), pp. 22-38.

KREPS, D.: *A Course in Microeconomic Theory*, Princeton (Princeton University Press) 1990.

LEIBENSTEIN, H.: "On Relaxing the Maximization Postulate," *Journal of Behavioral Economics*, 14 (1985), 3-16.

MASTEN, S. (Ed.): *Case Studies in Contracting and Organization*, New York, Oxford (Oxford University Press) 1996.

MILLER, G.J.: *Managerial Dilemmas*, Cambridge, New York (Cambridge University Press) 1992.

MINSKY, M.: *Computation: Finite and Infinite Machines*, Englewood Cliffs (Prentice Hall) 1967.

NELSON, R.: "Assessing Private Enterprise: An Exegesis of Tangled Doctrine," *Bell Journal of Economics*, 12 (1981), pp. 93-111.

NELSON, R., WINTER, S.: *An Evolutionary Theory of Economic Change*, Cambridge (Harvard University Press) 1982.

NORTH, D.C.: "Transaction Costs, Institutions, and Economic History," *Zeitschrift fur die gesamte Staatswissenschaft*, 140 (1984), pp. 7-17.

NORTH, D.C: "Economic Performance Through Time," *American Economic Review*, 84 (1994), pp. 359-368.

PINGLE, M.: "Costly Optimization: An Experiment," *Journal of Economic Behavior and Organization*, 17 (1992), pp. 3-30.

POSNER, R.A.: "The New Institutional Economics Meets Law and Economics," *Journal of Institutional and Theoretical Economics*, 149 (1993), pp. 73-87.

RICHTER, R.: "Bridging Old and New Institutional Economics: Gustav Schmoller, the Leader of the Younger German Historical School, Seen with Neoinstitutionalists' Eyes," Working Paper, Department of Economics, University of the Saarland, 1995, pp. 1-26.

RICHTER, R., FURUBOTN, E.G.: *Neue Institutionenökonomik: Einführung und Kritische Würdigung*, Tübingen (J.C.B. Mohr (Paul Siebeck)) 1996.

SCOTT, K.: "Bounded Rationality and Social Norms," *Journal of Institutional and Theoretical Economics*, 150 (1994), pp. 315-319.

STIGLITZ, J.: "Another Century of Economic Science," *Economic Journal*, 101 (1991), pp. 134-141.

STIGLITZ, J: *Whither Socialism*, Cambridge (MIT Press) 1994.

THALER, R.H.: *Quasi Rational Economics*, New York (Russell Sage Foundation) 1994.

WILLIAMSON, O.E.: *Markets and Hierarchies: Analysis and Antitrust Implications. A Study in the Economics of Internal Organization*, New York (Free Press) 1975.

WINTER, S.: "Optimization and Evolution in the Theory of the Firm," in: R. DAY, T. GRAVES (Eds.): *Adaptive Economic Models*, New York (Academic Press) 1975, pp. 73-118.

WISEMAN, J.: "The Black Box," *Economic Journal*, 101 (1991), pp. 149-155.

Discussion Summary

BETTINA LÖHNERT

Paper discussed:
EIRIK G. FURUBOTN: The Old and the New Institutionalism in Economics

The discussion focussed on the question of how to define the limits of rational choice theory, how to integrate additional, non-rationalistic decision-making factors within the models of the New Institutional Economics (NIE) and thus arriving at a new articulate, alternative paradigm to neoclassical economics.

It was discussed whether the allocation of information within a firm can be solely analysed according to rational choice theory. Generally people have choices about what information to collect. So every decision about the allocation of resources takes place in two stages: the first stage is the question about what information we want to collect and in the second stage we have to decide what to do with it. The principle of rationality applies to both stages. Analysing these information search procedures according to rational choice theory thus provides insight into organisational structures because they are a routinization of these optimal information search procedures (CASSON).

On the other hand rational choice theory results into endless choice-taking and thus a loss of rationality. This does not mean that we should rely on irrational criteria. There are, nevertheless, certain rules of thumb, i.e. pragmatic decision-making criteria that seem to work and have limited costs. Deciding which method to choose depends of the context respectively of the complexities of the problem. If you have a rather simple problem, than, indeed, you can consider all alternatives and use rational choice methods, but beyond that it is difficult to define the limits of this process. Within NIE new models have yet to be found, that would be as comprehensive and attractive as the general equilibrium model and yet reflect these new difficulties (FURUBOTN).

The question was raised whether the speaker's obvious dissatisfaction with the current state of the art in NIE theory is due to the internal, theortical inconsistency of the principles or due to a certain unfuitfulness in respect to some practical problems. Could a retreat to neoclassical theory be a possible solution? (AVTONOMOV).

Although neoclassical economics is still relevant, it is self-contradictory in respect of transaction cost analysis. It is often argued in neoclassical theory, that one of the major advantages of capitalism is its ability to optimize the flow of information, but at the same time the neoclassical model of general equilibrium assumes that all economic agents constantly have access to all relevant information. Therefore in this model there is no need to economize in transaction costs.

The speaker is more concerned with the theoretical structure of NIE than with its immeadiate practical applicability. In order to introduce a new paradigm in economics NIE has still to devolop an articulated theory. So far NIE has only come up with hybrid models that do give insights and are useful in the intermediate sense. Nevertheless they leave inconsistencies that have to be solved (FURUBOTN).

The concept of methodological individualism is one fundamental premise of neoclassical economics. As the dominance of the neoclassical model slowly retreats in economic theory also the idea of methodological individualism might become dubious (KABELE).

Although the new models of NIE want to deminish the pervasive dominance of the concept of methodological individualism, it will not be replaced. As Arrows suggests individual motives may not be the only influence on economic agents, and we thus should add to it and recognize that there are other effective mechnisms (FURUBOTN).

In the general search for a new paradigm in economics, parallels between the models Furubotn asked for in his paper and Etzioni's critique of neoclassical economics and his program of socio-economics seem to be obvious. Also Etzioni criticizes the excessive use of methodological individualism and wants to add the consideration of non-rational factors in economic models (LÖHNERT).

The new comprehensive models requested by the speaker should in fact have a very broad applicability and thereby include also the kind of considerations, like e.g. fairness, Etzioni wants to integrate. These models would result in a broader view of economics the Historical School was also interested in (FURUBOTN).

DISCUSSION SUMMARY

The objection was raised that if this requested theory tries to be very broadly applicable it has to be rather simplistic and for instance assume some uniformity of economic agents (CASSON).

According to the speaker this simplicity is avoidable by using a series of alternative models that we can adjust to the actual problems. This kind of context-bound theory does not yet exist, but nevertheless we should rather try to find new modelling strategies than keep relying on neoclassical or hybrid models and their internal contradictions. In general, other paths should not be too easily disposed (FURUBOTN).

Despite the uncertainty whether these requested new models will ever be realized, it is already today obvious that the theories of the NIE offer a greater potential for solution in the struggle for rebuilding institutional economic frameworks in Eastern Europe than traditional hard-nosed neoclassical concepts (MLCOCH).

Chapter 18

Moral Leadership in Ethical Economics*

MARK CASSON

I. Introduction

This paper considers the relationship between ethics and economic performance. It is argued that culture has an important intermediating role in this relationship. Cultural intermediation is personified by the social or political leader, who promotes ethical values and is one of the principal beneficiaries of the improved economic performance that results from them.

Not all ethical systems improve economic performance, of course. An ethical system must have instrumental value in order to achieve this. This instrumental value is the prerogative of functionally useful moral values which reduce transactions costs within the economic system. The clearest example

---

*   I am grateful to Peter Koslowski for providing the stimulus to write this paper, and to the participants at the Fourth Annual SEEP Conference for their comments on it. I am particularly grateful to Fritz Ringer for interesting discussions on the subject.

of this instrumental value is the way that an ethic of honesty engineers a climate of trust and so reduces the cost of trade.

The concept of ethical economics that is appropriate for this analysis is a distinctive one. It is a concept that embraces not only the pursuit of ethical policies by governments and others in power, but the behaviour of an economy composed of ethical agents too. Ethical behaviour by government alone may have a limited impact on economic performance if private agents merely seek to take advantage of government policy - for example, by accepting subsidies but offering nothing in return. Conversely, ethical behaviour by economic agents may be difficult to sustain when a corrupt government taxes away the gains from private trade and generally sets a poor example to the rest of society. Economic success generally requires both a government that is honest and a private sector that follows the example of the government and is honest as well. It is by establishing this link between the behaviour of the powerful and the behaviour of the ordinary citizen that culture acquires such an important economic role.

The main problem confronting any study of the relation of culture to economic behaviour is the unsatisfactory nature of the intellectual division of labour in the social sciences. Specialisation in academic research has created different disciplines. The performance of an economy in meeting material needs is studied by economics. Culture, on the other hand, is studied pre-eminently by anthropology. But any attempt to synthesise insights from these two disciplines runs into the problem that their dominant research methodologies are different. Economics tends to be quantitative and positivist, whilst anthropology tends to be qualitative and anti-positivist. Thus there is no unified methodology of social science in which the two disciplines are embedded.

Similar problems have been encountered before - for example in synthesising economics with political science and with law. The response by economists in these cases has been to extend the domain of their methods of analysis by creating the new subject fields of public choice and the economics of law respectively. A similar form of 'economic imperialism' is advocated here (Buckley and Casson 1993). It is proposed that the practical insights of anthropology should be restated using economic discourse. By standardising the discourse on economics, and applying the methods of economic analysis, the two subjects can be synthesised in a logically consistent way. The qualitative factors emphasised by anthropology are handled by introducing categorical variables (for example, zero-one variables) into the economic theory. Unobservable factors are handled either by relating them causally to observable factors, or by treating them as random variables which give the predictions of the theory a probabilistic nature. The result is an integrated theory fully equipped to examine the connection between ethics, culture and economic performance in a rigorous way.

Previous attempts to synthesise economics with other disciplines have achieved only limited success because many of the simplifying assumptions of economics have been transferred to the new subject area without proper critical scrutiny. Assumptions that are plausible in the context of markets are carried over to non-market environments where they may create unnecessary difficulties. It is particularly important to adapt assumptions when applying economic analysis to anthropology because of the very great differences in the relative weights that the two disciplines attach to the study of market and non market institutions.

The principal change advocated here is to replace the concept of 'economic man', as commonly understood, with 'ethical man' (Casson 1995). The main effect is that the instrumental rationality of economic man, which links ends and means, is supplemented by another rationality - value rationality - which explains the formation of ends. This concept of value rationality is inspired by the work of Weber (1947) and Knight (1935), although it is not claimed that the particular interpretation of value rationality offered here is directly implied by their work. Because the instrumental rationality of economic man is retained intact, the conventional techniques of economic analysis can be retained. However, the policy implications of the economic models are radically changed. This is because the welfare analysis which is conventionally applied to economic models assumes given individual ends, and its results are subverted once the influence of value rationality upon these ends is recognised. The models cease to function as apologies for *laissez faire*. It is possible that they could become instead a vehicle for articulating rigorously the benefits of communitarian policies. They certainly demonstrate the improved economic performance that can result when government fosters a high-trust culture. This culture inculcates a special form of social solidarity which is compatible with flexibility in resource allocation. This is not a justification for protectionism, nor for a proactive industrial policy. Rather it is an argument for integrating economic policy, social policy and the cultural life of the nation more coherently than has been usual in the West.

II. Economics and Anthropology Compared

Two objections to this approach will now be considered. The first is that economics is too rigid and dogmatic to fulfil the role ascribed to it here. But in fact economics has proved itself to be very versatile. The 'lesson of history' is that economics has evolved in response to criticism (the lags have often been quite long, however). For example, the criticism of the American institutionalists that economics was committed to an assumption of perfect competition was overcome thirty years later by the development of the theory of monopoly. What has remained constant whilst other things have changed is the mainstream economist's commitment to methodological individualism. There are two technically important features of this:

rational action (in sense of Menger); and

equilibrium (in sense of Hayek and others)

Within the constraint of its commitment to these two principles, there are a range of possible forms that economics can take. Economics does not have to be as it now is. It can be different. It may be suggested that because of its increased ethical content, its policy implications will be so different that it should be given a different name. Ethical economics is one possibility, for instance. But there is a risk here. A new name may suggest that the new economics is unorthodox and deviant. Economics as a technical discipline can become ethical without a major confrontation with the mainstream (see, for example, Frank, 1987). On balance, it seems better to allow economics to evolve naturally into a more ethical discipline than to suggest a radical break with the past through a change of name.

The second objection is that anthropology as a discipline is perfectly alright as it is because its methods are well adapted to its field of study. This objection is also false. The disciplines of economics and anthropology were born at different times. While economics was born at an extremely fortuitous time in intellectual terms, anthropology was born at an extremely unfortunate one. Economics emerged as a separate discipline at the time of the Scottish Enlightenment, and was developed by a group of scholars who were committed to the rigorous analysis of human nature as it really is. Living as they did in a commercial society that was beginning to industrialise, they had a bias towards a rather selfish and materialistic view of human motivation. But this bias is not crucial to the theory - only to the *laissez faire* policy conclusions that were sometimes drawn from it. Thus while Adam Smith's criticisms of state regulation of trade were important for the rhetorical impact of the *Wealth of Nations* they are not crucial to the logical structure of his market analysis.

Anthropology, by contrast, developed about a century later. The intellectual climate was dominated by Darwin and Marx, and later by Freud as well. Primitive societies encountered in the course of European colonisation were to be subjected to scientific analysis. But the science was infused with value judgements. Some anthropologists argued that primitive peoples were racially inferior, thereby justifying their political subjugation. Others saw the primitive peoples as romantic. Looking at the emotional traumas of late-nineteenth century European society, they detected the psychology of the primitive beneath the veneer of respectability. The primitive person was happy because he was in harmony with nature and had not been alienated by industrialisation. His spontaneous behaviour showed that he was true to his own emotions; he had not been repressed by the social customs which sustained the illusion of 'civilisation'.

Sociology emerged as a spin-off from this approach. Purportedly a science of society, in reality it was little more than a critique of industrialisation and modernity which used anthropological studies as a reference point. The radical Biblical critiicism prompted by Darwin's account of human origins turned Christianity from a theological framework for study into the subject matter for study instead. It allowed sociologists and anthropologists to analyse religion as a survivor of primitive pre-scientific systems of belief. Rejecting the Old Testament as an historical work opened up the way for writing a fully secular history of humanity - an enormous task which anthropologists promptly took on. But in taking the whole field of human social development for study, they overreached themselves. Their techniques were certainly not adequate for the purpose (Casson 1996). But the romanticism of the age was tolerant of their metaphysical speculations which masqueraded as scientific theory. Detached scientific study of complex issues was partially driven out by emotive diagnoses of contemporary social problems. Since then anthropology has been almost continuously under the sway of every passing fad and fashion in romantic philosophical thought, culminating in its current flirtation with Post-modernism. Under these conditions, an alliance with economics would seem to offer anthropologists the best immediate prospect for the restitution of their scientific aims.

III. Economic Modelling of Cultural Change

It must be emphasised that the proposed synthesis of economics and anthropology is not itself a purely speculative and utopian one. Models of ethical man already exist (see for example Casson 1991). The main problem confronting the modeller is one of complexity. Economic modelling is guided by the principle of parsimony, and it is vital to apply this principle in the present context. One recommended strategy is as follows. There are four main steps.

(1) *Introduce legitimacy into the utility function.*

(a) The utility function is a formal mathematical representation of preferences. In economic theory the utility function implies a consistent ranking of alternatives - no more. The Benthamite view of people as mechanisms driven by the pursuit of pleasure and the avoidance of pain is quite misleading in respect of modern utility theory.

(b) The utility function contains some observable variables - for example, consumption and the supply of work, which describe the behaviour of the individual. If ethics matter, they must change the levels at which these variables are set. Thus ethical variables are introduced in such a way that they affect the marginal utilities of the other variables. The ethical variables do not need to be directly observable themselves, for reasons explained below, although the theory is easier to apply if they are.

(c) One of the simplest ways to introduce the ethical dimension is to postulate a need for legitimacy. The perceived legitimacy of an act increases the utility that can be derived from it. Conversely an act that is perceived as illegitimate incurs a utility penalty. A neutral act confers no utility besides the normal material satisfaction involved. If all legitimate acts confer the same moral utility gain, all illegitimate acts incur the same moral utility loss, and all acts are either legitimate or illegitimate, then the ethical variables impact on utility simply by defining the boundary of the set of legitimate actions.

(d) The situation can be explained intuitively as follows. Each act by an individual is followed by a period of reflection. At this time of reflection the action is evaluated. A good feeling is engendered by having performed a legitimate (good) act and a bad feeling by having performed an illegitimate (bad) act. It is the anticipation of these feelings that influences decision-making. If the emotional gain from performing a good act instead of a bad act exceeds the material loss involved then the good act will be performed.

472

(e) In purely formal terms, a set of additional variables has been introduced into the utility function, but so far no explanation has been given of the way these variables are set. If the variables remain free then almost any kind of behaviour can be rationalised by choosing appropriate values for these variables. What is needed is a theory which explains how the values of the ethical variables are set.

(2) *Legitimacy is determined by a moral authority.*

(a) It is important to explain why different individuals from the same social group conform in their view of what is legitimate, whilst members of different social groups often disagree on this. The simplest explanation is that each group has a single source of moral authority, which disseminates information about legitimacy as a 'public good' within the group. It may be spread either by broadcasting or by word of mouth.

(b) The person who acts as a moral authority may be called the leader. Most groups exhibit an internal division of labour between leaders and followers. This allows leaders to specialise on the difficult task of forming moral judgements. In some cases a leader may claim to be simply a representative of another (sometimes impersonal) moral authority - the ultimate moral authority (see Table 1).

(c) What exactly is the nature of the moral message? From the standpoint of an economic model, the formalism does not require that this be specified. What matters is simply the cost of sending the message and the effect that it has on the recipients' utility function. Given the utilitarian formulation, though, it is fairly clear that the nub of the message is

"Your leader approves/disapproves of this action and so if you perform it you will obtain, on reflection, an emotional reward/penalty."

The leader may back this up with reasons for his disapproval. This could merely amplify the utilitarian content:

"God approves/disapproves of this action and so if you perform it you are likely to go to heaven/hell and enjoy eternal bliss/damnation."

Alternatively he may construct a philosophical argument; for example,

"If everyone performed this action then the result would be harmony/chaos and that is why it is legitimate/illegitimate."

(d) Not everyone can be a moral authority. There are a number of qualifications for doing the job successfully. Consistency and clarity are the two main requirements. Consistency manifests itself in three possible ways.

473

Table 1
Examples of group organisation

Type of group	Leader	Ultimate authority
Nuclear family	Parent	-
Extended family/ tribe/clan	Head of tribe	Ancestors, spirits
Church	Priest	God
Nation	Political leader	National spirit or will

Charisma. If the leader is in touch with an ultimate authority he should behave in a manner which suggests this.

Cogency. If he advances a philosophical argument it should be plausible even though it may not be immune to sceptical criticism.

Commitment. If legitimacy is related to realising a vision or furthering a social goal then the leader should be willing to make a personal commitment of his own to the goal in which he claims to believe.

Taken together, therefore, this shows that the message, the supporting evidence and the actions of the leader must all cohere with each other. In addition to consistency, clarity is also required. It must be easy for the followers to understand what is being said. Clarity is facilitated by

- simple attention-grabbing rhetoric
- ritual acts that symbolise the message; and
- conspicuous behaviour that it is easy for followers to imitate.

(3) *The supply of leaders.*

(a) Leadership generates economic rents from improved coordination (see below). Not all of these rents may be readily appropriable though. If the moral leader also has political power, or works for those who have it, then the rents can be appropriated through taxation. Otherwise the leader may have to rely on voluntary contributions.

(b) The costs of leadership include the expenses of communication and the opportunity costs of the leaders' time. Since it is important that the leader is a talented person, preferably the person best equipped to meet the qualifications described above, his opportunity earnings may be quite high. The payment must equal or exceed these earnings to attract the right person to the job.

(c) If the leader enunciates principles of social justice, however, then his own payments may have to be constrained in the interests of consistency, as described above. In this case the leader may be "paid" indirectly, by an expense account, or by being accorded social deference on account of his high status.

(d) The supply of potential leaders is also a function of demography (the number of people of suitable age) genetics (the intelligence of the population) and training. In the context of education and training it is, of course, the moral dimension as well as the technical dimension that is important. The more abundant the supply of trained and talented people, the lower the scarcity premium that a leader can command.

(e) Generally, it can be said that there is a market for leaders, but that this market is bedevilled by substantial problems of quality control.

IV. Functional Values

(a) To maximise the rents that the leader generates, it is important that the leader chooses functionally useful values. The simplest way to analyse the functional value of an ethic is to postulate an economy populated by pairs of transactors, or teams of workers, each of whom has a material incentive to cheat. The transactors, for example, may bluff in negotiations over price, causing the negotiations to fail. If the negotiations succeed, they may then attempt to cheat by not paying for the goods they receive. In the context of team production, workers may shirk in the hope that they will not be discovered doing so. These classic problems are associated with the Prisoner's Dilemma in game theory, and with asymmetric information in the theory of the firm. In an economy bedevilled by incentive problems of this kind, the role of an ethic is simply to prevent cheating. Individuals who know they will feel guilty if they cheat decide to be honest instead, and this allows the gains from coordination to be generated to the full.

(b) While honesty is the pre-eminent value that is endorsed in this way, there are many other values that are important in various circumstances. These include

loyalty   -   important in creating a high-trust culture to support partner-specific investments;

persistence - important in realising long-term goals such as economic development;

solidarity - important in a primitive society with limited opportunities for division of labour and trade, and vulnerable to external aggression; and

self-sacrifice - important under war conditions.

(c) The role of the leader is to examine the environment of the group and then optimise the ethic by choosing the set of followers' actions on which he confers legitimacy. In this respect the leader remains autonomous in the traditional way; the model does not therefore dispense with autonomy altogether, but focuses autonomy on the leader. Everyone is rational - both leaders and followers - but only the leader is autonomously so.

V. Some Extensions of the Basic Model

The basic model is very simple, but because of its transparent logical structure it is readily extended in various ways. There are three developments of the model which are particularly relevant to the main theme of this paper.

(i) *Moral pluralism and competition between groups.*

(a) So far the analysis has focused on a single social group. Many people (particularly Western liberals) may feel uneasy about the prominent role of the leader within this group. From the standpoint of personal freedom, however, the crucial thing is not whether groups have leaders, but whether people are free to join whatever group they want to. Indeed, extreme individualism can be accommodated within this theory by allowing each individual to form their own group to which they alone belong. In this case they behave as a leader, and not a follower, within their own group. They are morally autonomous, but have no-one they can trust because everyone else is autonomous too.

(b) An individual could, indeed, belong to no group at all. This would mean that he had no moral system. All his actions would be neutral in terms of legitimacy. In terms of reflection, all of his acts would be meaningless. Such an individual is likely to have a low level of utility relative to others, unless there are a lot of really enjoyable material outcomes which are ruled out by all moral codes. The morally committed person can ensure that he only gets emotional benefits from his morality by the simple strategy of always doing what is right and never doing anything that is wrong. Provided that the material costs are not too great, this is likely to be better than living in an emotional vacuum.

(c) The advantages of belonging to a group are likely to be even greater when people can choose to which group they belong. There is, however, a problem of inter-group relations where moralities are very different. This is particularly so if the moralities are conspicuously different - affecting public behaviour, for example, as in the case of dress - and if the groups share public space together. In this case mutual affiliation to some higher-order group will normally be necessary to avoid physical conflict between the members of different groups. Mutual respect and tolerance are likely to be important functional values in the ethos of the higher-level group.

(ii) *Comparison with a legal system.*

(a) But what of the role of law? Ethics and law are both normally universal. They both legitimate *classes of actions* for *all* individuals. The law is normally given an ethical justification. But there is a crucial difference. The legal system relies on external monitoring, both by fellow citizens and by specialists such as the police. It also relies on formal methods of adjudication in which witnesses present evidence against the accused. The ethical mechanism dispenses with external monitoring; it is based on people being *self-monitoring*, through the *power of reflection*. If this system works it effects a major economy in information costs, since no other party is involved in the process.

(b) Another difference between ethics and law is that the law relies on material penalties whilst the ethical mechanism relies on emotional ones. Emotional penalties are usually much cheaper in material terms. There is no destruction or confiscation of the offender's property, and no cost of administering this either. It is, however, sometimes difficult to fine-tune ethical penalties. Some individuals who are insensitive to moral argument may experience little guilt from a given crime, whilst very sensitive individuals may suffer guilt for the rest of their lives. Societies relying on emotional penalties need to have not only an effective way of sensitising people to moral values, but also a mechanism for forgiving people after they have made a suitable admission of their guilt.

(c) Ethics and the law are, in fact, at two extremes of a broader spectrum. While ethics associates self-monitoring with emotional penalties, the two do have to be linked in this way. In some primitive societies, for example, guilty individuals punish themselves materially - for example, by making sacrifices to the gods. Conversely, it is possible to have emotional penalties based on external monitoring, such as the penalties of shame or 'loss of face' when an offence is discovered by other people. This latter mechanism of 'peer group pressure' works reasonably well in small compact and stable groups where everyone knows each other well, but is less suitable in larger groups whose membership is more mobile and dispersed. Ethical mechanisms have the power to extend the scope of the emotional mechanism by encouraging the individual to adopt the group point of view when making judgements on himself. A strong ethical mechanism may, however, require fairly frequent communication between the leader and his members. The ethical system may therefore have a comparative advantage in groups of medium size, leaving the relatively impersonal legal system as the system most appropriate to large, dispersed and highly mobile groups.

(iii) *Language, communication and leadership.*

Note how the moral mechanism economises on information. Making difficult moral judgements of functional value is specialised with the leader. The leader broadcasts a simple message expressed vividly. It covers classes of actions and applies to everyone. Individuals then apply this information to themselves. They do not, for example, report their actions to the leader for individual approval/disapproval.

Not only does the leader not have to monitor individuals, but individuals do not have to refer their proposed actions to the leader for advice or judgement.

One way of looking at this is to say that the leader coordinates the society by taking an intermediating role. Other examples of intermediation involve entrepreneurs creating markets in new goods and services. All intermediation, of whatever kind, depends on communication, and communication in turn requires language. But language is costly - it requires a considerable investment for individuals to learn a vocabulary and acquire the rules of grammar.

There is a significant difference between moral leadership and entrepreneurial market-making in the amount of such investment that is required. Markets economise on language because they rely on highly quantified communication. In its limiting case a market simply requires three numbers to be communicated: a code number to identify the product, the quantity demanded or supplied, and the price. But moral rhetoric requires much more than this. It requires a language capable of describing emotions such as guilt and shame, social concepts such as peace and harmony, and their opposites war and con-

478

flict, and so on. It requires a grasp of grammar sufficient to understand a complicated argument explaining why it is plausible to require people to enter into certain obligations to one another. Thus if a society is to benefit fully from the reduction in monitoring costs afforded by a system of moral obligation it must invest in educating its citizens in the language necessary to communicate and assimilate moral reasoning.

An effective moral leader will therefore wish to ensure that he is supported by a suitable educational system. Leadership is not a simple activity based solely on the display of personal charisma in a public setting, but a sophisticated activity involving a complex of related activities. Just as leadership itself emerges from a fundamental division of labour between leaders and followers in a society, so leadership itself requires a division of labour between the members of the elite who assist in leadership activities. This division of labour creates professions such as the religious priesthood, an incorruptible judiciary, and, above all, the teaching profession which imparts linguistic skills and provides the population as a whole with the cultural and historical context in which the leader's rhetoric can be understood.

VI. Objections to the Model

Finally, some possible objections to this research agenda are noted. Six objections are considered.

(1) *"It undermines the autonomy of the individual"*.

The force of this objection is weakened by the fact, already noted, that individualism is just a special case of the general leadership model in which each individual belongs to their own group. But a more vigorous defence can be mounted for the approach adopted here. The developmental view of human nature found in the social psychology literature - and especially works on educational psychology - emphasises that in many respects adults are just children grown older. 'The child is the father of the man,' in other words. Children need parents and as they grow older and prepare to leave home they find role-models elsewhere. This search for moral authority continues throughout adult life. For some the search takes a religious dimension; for academics it may become a search for abstract truth. But usually there is a human intermediary who plays a leadership role - the saintly priest, the eminent professor, and so on.

From this perspective, the essence of human rationality lies not in freedom from emotion but in our ability to anticipate our emotions and to control them. The exercise of control is directed towards regulating the display of emotions, rather than to repressing them altogether. Indeed, persistent repression of the emotions is one of the causes of psychological illness. Civilised people may conceal their emotions, sometimes out of politeness, and sometimes out of duplicity, but they will still give vent to them in the security of the home. Given that people have to control their emotions, they are always seeking guidance on how to do so, and this is a service that leaders can provide.

(2) *"Groups don't need leaders. Spontaneous order will emerge in a group because it is in everyone's interests for it to do so".* This view is closely identified with the later writings of Hayek (for example, Hayek 1963). It is often asserted to be a method of addressing the problem of unintended consequences of human action, particularly in the provision of public goods where conventional market processes may be difficult to use. Unfortunately there is no formal model that has shown exactly how the emergence of spontaneous order occurs, or set out the conditions under which the mechanism will work and under which it will not. There are models that have a bearing on the problem, such as those of repeated games, or theories of focal points. Those who hold the faith that suitable models of this kind will be forthcoming may still like to give a provisional endorsement to the leadership approach, however. In critical situations leaders do indeed tend to emerge, and so to this extent the emergence of the leader may be identified with the emergence of spontaneous order.

(3) *"It exalts the leader. In practice, leaders tend to be (or to become) corrupt".* The model only exalts *good* leaders, though. It provides a criterion by which the effectiveness of leaders can be judged in economic terms. It relates these to the qualifications that leaders require. It emphasises the need for the moral training of the leader. It also emphasises the role of status as a reward to encourage good leaders to come forward. In this context it may actually suggest a solution to the problems of finding high-quality leaders in contemporary Western countries in which leaders are typically offered difficult jobs, little training and limited rewards.

(4) *"It does anthropology out of a job. It is not politically correct to subordinate one discipline to another in the manner proposed."* Unfortunately,

though, political correctness is a feature of anthropology and not of economics. While it is quite valid for anthropologists who use political correctness as one of their main criteria of good theory to protest about, it is equally valid for economists, on their criteria, to ignore the objection. Moreover, there is still room for anthropological inquiry of the speculative and romantic kind, in the sense of imagining what it might feel like to belong to a different society - particularly a strange or exotic one. Economists are not concerned with this kind of speculation, except as a source of intuitive ideas for extending their formal models. Economics, according to its positivist methodology, is concerned purely with the systematic relations between observable variables. It shows how followers respond to their leaders, and how these leaders respond to their environment. The question of imaginative empathy with the leader and the followers is simply ignored. This leaves untouched a quite distinct programme of inquiry, which is to speculate on what it may feel like to 'be in someone else's shoes'. This is an activity to which anthropologists have traditionally been quite attached, and which can be carried on in parallel with economic modelling. Anthropologists who do not wish to convert to economic modelling can therefore still find plenty to do.

(5) *"It demeans ethics by reducing it to a utilitarian form. It inverts ends and means by turning ethics into a means of engineering improved economic performance."*

This is not so. It has already been noted that the utilitarian framework is purely formal - 'utility' is simply short-hand for 'that which people maximise', whatever that happens to be. The philosophical status of the messages disseminated by the leader is not itself a part of the model. The model is essentially an exercise in positive economics. The only connection between the philosophical status of the leader's ethical argument and the behaviour explained by the model lies in the fact that a naive or absurd ethical argument would fail to convince the followers. All the model does is to draw attention to the obvious fact that moral arguments are widely used to influence other people's behaviour, and to this extent are regularly employed as means, even though the arguments themselves clearly refer to ends.

(6) *"There must be a better way than this of integrating anthropological insights with economics".* Other authors have certainly carried out research on related lines. The flexibility of economics means that there are a number of different paths along which this type of theory can evolve. There is not an unlimited number of such paths, however, because the need to confront complexity means that one of a small number of simplifying strategies must be

employed. The use of the leader-follower distinction is arguably the strategy which comes closest to explaining a wide range of anthropological phenomena in simple terms.

VII. Relevance to the German Historical School

What has all of this to do with the German Historical School?

(1) The theory has an intellectual pedigree which includes at least one prominent member of the school, namely Max Weber (1947). It also draws on insights of Weber which were subsequently developed by Frank Knight (1935). Indeed, it is possible to conceive of a tradition of economic thought, whose culmination is ethical modelling, which begins with Menger and progresses through Weber and Knight, and then by way of Coase (1937), Richardson (1960) and Marschak (1972), to recent work by Akerlof (1982), Etzioni (1988), and others.

(2) The dependence of the leader's optimal strategy on the environment of the social group suggests a possible formulation of a theory of cultural change. The resulting theory makes it possible to reconsider some of the central issues addressed by writers of the German Historical School in a rigorous and modern way. As exogenous shocks alter the group's environment, culture adjusts as a result of the leader's rational response to these shocks. This idea can be applied in various ways. As transport costs fall, new opportunities for the division of labour increase, and this encourages a shift from "primitive" values such as solidarity towards more universalistic values such as telling the truth. Falling communication costs also provide an opportunity for disseminating moral rhetoric over a wider population, facilitating the spatial dispersion of social groups. They also encourage investment in a wider vocabulary, which encourages more sophisticated moral justifications. These abstract justifications replace the simple rituals which are only practical in a compact face-to-face society.

The questions asked by historical economists about the long term evolution of commercial and industrial society continue to be relevant, even though their answers have become hard to understand because of the spirit of romantic idealism with which they are expressed. By attempting to answer these questions in terms of the rational action approach, which is more widely favoured today, insights can be obtained which may assist the interpretation of what these earlier writers had to say. The links between cultural change and economic growth are deep and profound. It is difficult for any generation of scholars to give a definitive answer to these questions, but it is certainly desirable that each generation should reach as good an understanding as possible of what previous generations had to say.

References

AKERLOF, G. A.: "Labour Contracts as Partial Gift Exchange", *Quarterly Journal of Economics*, 97 (1982), pp. 543-569.

BUCKLEY, P. J. and M.C. CASSON: "Economics as an Imperialist Social Science", *Human Relations*, 46 (1993), pp. 1035-1052.

CASSON, M. C.: *Economics of Business Culture: Game Theory, Transactions Costs and Economic Performance*, Oxford (Clarendon Press) 1991.

CASSON, M. C.: *Entrepreneurship and Business Culture*, Aldershot (Edward Elgar) 1995.

CASSON, M. C.: "Economics and Anthropology: Reluctant Partners", *Human Relations* (forthcoming) 1996.

COASE, R. H.: "The Nature of the Firm", *Economica* (New Series) 4 (1937), pp. 386-405.

ETZIONI, A.: *The Moral Dimension: Towards a New Economics*, New York (Free Press) 1988.

FRANK, R. H.: "If *Homo Economicus* could choose his Own Utility Function, would he want one with a Conscience?", *American Economic Review*, 77 (1987), pp. 593-604.

HAYEK, F. A. VON: "The Theory of Complex Phenomena", in: M. BUNGE (Ed): *The Critical Approach to Science and Philosophy: Essays in Honour of Karl Popper*, New York 1963.

KNIGHT, F. H.: *The Ethics of Competition*, London (George Allen and Unwin) 1935.

MARSCHAK, J.: "Economics of Inquiring, Communicating, Deciding", *American Economic Review*, 58 (1968), pp. 1-18.

MENGER, C. (1871): *Principles of Economics* (trans. J. Dingwall and B. Hoselitz) Glencoe, Ill (Free Press) 1950.

RICHARDSON, G. B.: *Information and Investment*, London (Oxford University Press) 1960.

WEBER, M.: *The Theory of Social and Economic Organisation* (trans. A.M. Henderson and T. Parsons; ed. by T. Parsons) New York (Oxford University Press) 1947.

Discussion Summary

BETTINA LÖHNERT

Paper discussed:

MARK CASSON: Moral Leadership in Ethical Economics

The main interest of the discussion lay in the model of leadership Casson had presented in his paper. It was criticized as being too optimistic and having a tendency to be autocratic.

It was objected that in this model of leadership the problem of free-riding was insufficiently addressed. The notion that for most people the reflexion on the overall negative effects of free-riding would lead to serious changes in their behavior was doubted (FURUBOTN).

The speaker agreed that the picture he gives is a rather optimistic picture that only occationally manifests itself. But nevertheless it is historically important because periods of high-trust cultures and effective leadership can substantially transform the forms of an economy.

In these models a certain amount of free-riding is tolerable, without without giving rise to cheating as a response to cheating. If I am going to be cheated only 2% of the time, I will be honest. But if I am going to be cheated 50% of the time, I will cheat first. We have to recognize that leaders must contain deviance and make it very clear while there is deviance, that it is only a very small minority of people that are involved.

Leaders who are successful in this, do create a process of wealth growth, because a well-functioning high-trust economy will work. When, however, either this dynamic fades, consumption growth standards are not realized, or a new leader comes to power who has not got the same skills. Then the system goes to pieces and it requires another leader to come along and turn the situation around again (CASSON).

It was expressed that the model of leadership presented tends to trigger feelings of egalitarian resentment against authoritarian systems.

DISCUSSION SUMMARY

Furthermore the theory implies a kind of moral leadership that is similar to that of preachers. The leader presents and communicates moral options. The problem is that his behavior modes can be contradictory to this communication. The question was raised what the real mechnism could be that protects the moral guidance function of leadership in modern cultures. In today's world not the rainmaker or schamane but an extraordinary complex and pluralistic structure is responsible for moral orientation. This complex web does only indirectly destill into a kind of guidance function. Can we have a sociologically realistic account of leadership in a modern, not a primitive society ? Have the anthropological accounts of leadership translated in a way that it begins to resemble structures that might function in modern society?

In addition, it was suspected that this model of leadership might result into a kind of extended utilitarianism or functional rhethoric. The moral leader enhances the efficiency of the economy and yet she or he has to have that kind of exemplary role that persumably does not ask for consequences. He is the Durkheimian functinionist leader who thinks of himself as a Weberian "*Gesinnungsethiker*" (deontologist) (RINGER).

The speaker agreed that the egalitarian sentiment against his model is valid. But he explained that the validity of these fears depend on whether you have an elitist leadership class who thinks demeaningly about their followers or elected leaders whose followers recognize that the leader's function is to perpetuate traditions of the group. In the last case fears about an authoritarian leadership could be weakened.

On the question about the contemporary relevance in advanced societies no simple answer can be given. It should be clear, though, that postmodern values promulgated through media that say that "everything goes" and there is nothing to root yourself in, are not only emotionally and psychologically disturbing, but actually are bad for the economy.

Since the paper has also to convince economists, who are generally utilitarians, the argumentation of the paper might appear to be guilty of extended utilitarianism. The model concentrates on consequences in economic terms because they are more readily measurable, but it is obvious that the consequences of the model are not only materialistic (CASSON).

It was asked to clarify the relationship of the moral leader and the political leader. To be charismatic does not mean to be ethical. In a pack of wolves the leader will be the strongest or the most aggressive one, but not the most ethical wolf. Also among robbers the cruelest will be the leader. Even in democracy the market for leadership is a cynical market. But still people who become political leaders gain also undeserved ethical leadership (AVTONOMOV).

The model examend cannot solve these problems but it provides at least criteria by which one can distinguish between good and bad leadership and make observations about improving the supply of leaders. For reasons of simplicity leadership has been treated as a lively function but, in fact, leadership is an activity performed by an elite, in which there is a division of labour among e.g. intellectuals, military, politicians, priests, businessmen, intellectuals and priests. Since we acquire our most fundamental values when we are young there is hope that it will be the priests and intellectuals have the power to influence the values of the next generation (CASSON).

Part Eight

Theories of History and of Education, and a Philosophy of the Historical School

Chapter 19

Theories of History and of Education in Germany and France During the 19th Century

FRITZ RINGER

I. Bildung in the German Tradition
II. The Crisis of German Academic Culture
III. German Theories of History
IV. The Educational Revolution in France
V. French Theories of Education
VI. French Theories of History

I normally resist separating intellectual history from the social and institutional history of intellectual life.[1] For this brief presentation, however, I must reduce my comments on social and intellectual history to one broad thesis: Just as the industrial revolution took place at different times and rates in the major European countries - with significant historical consequences, so too there was something like an *educational revolution* with a time scale of its own. Unlike the industrial revolution, the educational revolution took place much earlier in the German states than it did in England and certainly in France, and this too had notable consequences. Moreover, the radical trans-

---

1 This essay summarizes key arguments more fully developed in: FRITZ RINGER: *Fields of Knowledge: French Academic Culture in Comparative Perspective, 1890-1920*, Cambridge (Cambridge University Press) 1992. Portions on Germany draw upon FRITZ RINGER: *The Decline of the German Mandarin*, Cambridge, Ma. (Harvard University Press) 1969, (reissued 1990 by University Press of New England); see also the revised German translation, *Die Gelehrten: Der Niedergang der deutschen Mandarine*, Stuttgart (Klett) 1983, which of course contains German originals of quotations.

formation of secondary and higher education in the German states during the decades around 1800, much like the English industrial revolution, set patterns that subsequently recurred, with certain variations, in other European countries, including in France from the 1870s on. One important element in this educational revolution was the emergence of the so-called research imperative, the institutionalized expectation that university faculty must do original research, while also introducing their students to an increasingly codified set of research practices. The other crucial component in the educational revolution was the establishment of research-based professional qualifications for future secondary teachers, as well as for civil servants and clergymen, and the ultimate extension of educational prerequisites and entitlements to a whole range of other learned professions.

The importance of this pattern for European social and intellectual history should not be underestimated. For in several major countries of the 19th century, and especially in Germany, advanced education was almost as important a source of middle-class social standing as wealth and economic power, and this was even more plainly true of middle-class self-images and ideologies. In illustration, I now turn to the theories of secondary and higher education that emerged in European countries, and especially in Germany and France, during the 19th century. As might be expected, these theories resembled each other to some degree, as did the pedagogical practices they reflected. Yet the earliest and philosophically most ambitious of these theories emerged in Germany, where the educational revolution first occurred during the decades around 1800, and where the educated middle class soonest attained and longest retained a position of social prominence and cultural leadership.

I. Bildung in the German Tradition

The 19th-century German theory of *Bildung* or of 'cultivation' was neither univocal nor stable over time. Nevertheless, I want to begin by portraying it in an ideal-typically simplified and static form, drawing for this purpose upon a key dictionary definition, upon the writings of German university professors, and especially upon the work of such outstanding cultural theorists as

Georg Simmel, all sources that date from the late nineteenth and early twentieth centuries.[2]

First, *Bildung* in these sources refers to the cultivation or self-development of a unique individual. Second, the process of *Bildung* takes place by way of an interpretive relationship between a learner and a set of venerated texts, typically those of classical antiquity, that are held to embody moral and cultural *values*. In the simplest and ideologically most loaded account of *Bildung*, the relationship of the student to the revered text was conceived as a total *identification*. The reader became one with the author of the text; he was thus in a position to *reproduce* and to internalize the values embodied in the text. Learning became a transfer of grace, which morally *and socially* 'elevated' the reader, conferring upon him the essential quality *and status* of the cultivated man.

In a more sophisticated version of the theory, the interpretive relationship was conceived as an *interaction*, not as a subjective identification. The student was imagined actively involved in the interpretive process; perhaps he began by positing *possible readings*, which he then tested empirically, to see whether they helped to make sense of the text. In this more complex and interesting version of the theory, learning was less a transfer than an awakening of grace within the reader, the fulfillment of a *potential* for cultivation. But however it was imagined in detail, learning necessarily meant interpretation, and the notion of some kind of empathetic involvement with the text was so typical that I like to call this element in the theory of *Bildung* the *principle of empathy*.

The other crucial component in the theory that seems deeply significant can be called the *principle of individuality*. For there was virtually universal agreement that the self-cultivating learner was absolutely *unique*, imbued with an utterly distinctive, purely individual potential for *Bildung*. The German theory of advanced education thus radically diverged from a recurrent French view of education as the 'socialization' of the younger generation in the light of pre-established socio-cultural norms. Nor was *Bildung* merely the enhancement of a universal capacity for rationality. It was the cultivation of a total personality, a theoretically incomparable individuality. Obviously, this vision had certain strengths, along with potential problems. On the one hand,

---

2   *Ibid.*, pp. 95-97. The dictionary is *Der grosse Brockhaus* (1928-35); see also GEORG SIMMEL: "Der Begriff und die Tragödie der Kultur", in his *Philosophische Kultur: Gesammelte Essais*, Leipzig 1911, esp. p. 248.

it could take on a utopian thrust, suggesting that human beings are infinitely diverse, and that they can and should transcend their present limitations. On the other hand, the idea of self-perfection through *Bildung* , at least in some of its variants, took little account of the social realm, and of human perfection as at least partly a collective enterprise.

Listening to all this, a traditional historian of ideas might want to raise questions about the doctrines that *influenced* the German theory of *Bildung*: What about the 'impact' of neo-humanism, of Romanticism, and/or of post-Kantian philosophical Idealism? - But I must say that this sort of question about intellectual 'influences' does not strike me as particularly fruitful. I am tempted to turn the question around, and ask whether the German theory of *Bildung*, as it emerged during those vital decades around 1800, actually shaped German Romantic and Idealist doctrines, for example. Or, more cautiously and following the French sociologist Pierre Bourdieu, I want suggest that the attitudes and aspirations that came to expression in the theory of *Bildung* were *simultaneously* or even *secondarily* elaborated in various ways by writers we have come to call Romantics or Idealists, typically without being able to specify exactly where Romanticism ends and Idealism begins. After all, explicit intellectual doctrines may be grounded in shared assumptions that are implicit, less than fully conscious, and sustained by changing social relations and cultural practices.

In any case, even a cursory sketch of the theory of *Bildung* allows us to understand salient aspects of 19th-century German academic culture, including the metaphysical depth of the commitment to *Bildung*. In the language of post-Kantian Idealism, the world exists so that, in coming to know it, the human mind may realize its potential. Such crucial human institutions as the state, too, exist less to pursue the interests of its citizens than to sustain the pursuit of individual cultivation and of national culture. This was the vision of the *Kulturstaat*, the cultural state.

Equally significant was the way in which the *principle of individuality* affected habits of thought in subject areas well beyond its context of origin in the theory of *Bildung*. The commitment to uniqueness and individuality is bound to favor what are usually considered Romantic accounts of change as the teleological unfolding of preexistent potentialities, rather than the rearrangement of essentially similar elements, as in physical mechanics. Let me quote from a 1923 essay by Ernst Troeltsch, another unusually perceptive analyst of the German tradition. Troeltsch placed the "concept of individuality" at the heart of the German Romantic critique of the "mathematical-mechanical West European scientific spirit".

> The basic constituents of reality are not similar material and social atoms and universal laws...but differing unique personalities and individualizing formative forces... The state and society are not created from the individual by way of contract and utilitarian rationality, but from suprapersonal spiritual forces which emanate from the most important and creative individuals, the spirit of the people or the religious idea.[3]

One begins to see how such views could affect conceptions of history. One also begins to grasp why the dominant paradigms of original research or *Wissenschaft* in the German universities from the late 18th century on were not shaped by the natural sciences, but by the interpretive disciplines, broadly speaking. Hermeneutic models inherited from theology were transmitted to philology, and ultimately to history, and the source-critical methods that marked German history as a rigorous inquiry owed much to the classical philologists. The *Altertumswissenschaft* of Friedrich August Wolf, as Anthony LaVopa has reminded us, was an almost incongruous combination of exact philological scholarship with an ideological commitment to Greek culture as an antidote to narrow occupationalism and specialization.[4] Wolf's neo-humanism aimed at an interpretive understanding of Greek texts *and of their cultural context*, not at a study of imperial Rome or of the Latin language alone.

---

3   ERNST TROELTSCH: "Naturrecht und Humanität in der Weltpolitik" Berlin 1923, pp. 13-14, cited in: RINGER: *Die Gelehrten*, p. 95: "gegen den ganzen westeuropäischen mathematisch-mechanischen Wissenschaftsgeist." "Nicht materielle und sozial gleichartige Atome und universale Naturgesetze, sondern jeweils verschieden-eigenartige Persönlichkeiten und individualisierende plastische Kräfte liegen der Wirklichkeit zugrunde... Nicht Vertrag oder zweckrationale Konstruktion schaffen von den Individuen her den Staat und die Gesellschaft, sondern die von grundlegenden Individuen ausstrahlenden überpersönlichen geistigen Kräfte, der Volksgeist oder die religiös ästhetische Idee."

4   ANTHONY J. LAVOPA: "Specialists against Specialization: Hellenism as Professional Ideology in German Classical Studies", in: GEOFFREY COCKS: KONRAD H. JARAUSCH (Eds.): *German Professions, 1800-1950*, New York (Oxford University Press) 1990, pp. 27-45.

Of course it was a long way from the neo-humanist ideals of Wolf and others around 1800 to the routinization of predominantly Latin learning in the classical *Gymnasien* of the late 19th century. In Mannheim's terms, indeed, there was a long-term shift from utopia to ideology. In principle if not quite in fact, *Bildung* around 1800 was universally accessible; it could thus signify a utopian alternative to social distinctions based upon birth. But a century later, higher education had itself become a socially distinguishing privilege, and the cultivated elite was closing ranks against less advantaged groups in quest of social mobility through education.

II. The Crisis of German Academic Culture

From about 1890 on, moreover, a large majority of German academics expressed a sense of crisis and even of pessimism about the future of the educational and cultural traditions they had come to represent. The more numerous and conventional among them, those I have called 'orthodox mandarins', feared a range of modern developments that posed a threat to their cultural leadership, among them political democracy, mass culture, the role of technology, and the advent of the high capitalist class society.[5] Within the educational system itself, pressures for increased rates of access per age group could be perceived as serious dangers, and so could the arrival of non-classical forms of secondary schooling. Interestingly enough, while a majority of German academic humanists and social scientists opposed the opening of the universities to graduates of non-classical secondary schools around 1900, a dominant group among their contemporary French colleagues took the opposite position.

Even more interesting in the present context, however, were the misgivings widely expressed in German academic circles after 1890 about the prospects for *Bildung* itself. Many were deeply troubled by the inroads of specialization and of so-called 'positivism' upon the more comprehensive aspirations initially associated with *Bildung* . This concern was sometimes expressed in

---

5   RINGER: *Fields of Knowledge*, pp. 102-108 is based in part upon RINGER: *Decline of the German Mandarins*; see esp. pp. 23-32, 48-51, 67-79, 109-117, 126-127, 274-293, for this and what follows.

the claim that *Wissenschaft* no longer engendered *Weltanschauung*, a total and partly evaluative orientation toward the world. A chasm had apparently opened between merely specialized or 'technical' knowledge on the one hand, and personal knowledge or wisdom on the other.[6]

I can touch upon these matters only briefly; but I do have to mention them, because they provoked divergent reactions. The orthodox majority of German academics, as might be expected, strenuously repudiated any concession to the disruptive forces of the day. Instead, they sought an escape from the 'materialism' of the age, and especially of 'the masses', to a new, vaguely defined 'idealism'. Some of them ultimately encouraged irrationalist reactions against the apparently impoverished norms of science and reason.

In the meantime, a creative minority I have loosely termed 'modernists' undertook a deliberately critical review of their traditions, including that of *Bildung*, in the hope of selectively 'translating' the most vital among them into an idiom suited to the changing times. Their labor of 'translation' was of course immensely fruitful, though it also provoked much intellectual conflict. Its results in the work of such men as Georg Simmel, Ernst Troeltsch and Max Weber have retained their exemplary force into our own day. I need only mention the neo-idealist revival of the *Geisteswissenschaften* that began with the work of Wilhelm Dilthey in the 1880s. The term *Geisteswissenschaften* did not come into common use until the later 19th century; it referred to the interpretive study of the human mind in its creations or 'objectifications'. The discussions that took place about it can be understood as attempts to codify both German theories of education and German theories of history.

III. German Theories of History

I cannot, of course, develop a systematic account of German theories of history in a few paragraphs; but I can try to point up a few connections between the vision of *Bildung* , and key characteristics of the German historical

---

6 RINGER: *Fields of Knowledge*, pp. 196-206, which draws partly on RINGER: *Decline of the German Mandarins*, pp. 128-134, 144-149, 203-227, 234-282, 295-309.

tradition. There was a time when some American students detected scientistic implications in Leopold von Ranke's much-cited injunction to find out 'how it actually was' in the past. Even today, Ranke is pictured exclusively interested in politics, and especially in international relations. Yet his theoretical essays do not fully sustain this claim. What he mainly recommended there, apart from rigorous source-critical methods, was a kind of past-mindedness, a moderate variation upon the principle of empathy. He wrote of "placing oneself back into (a given) time, into the mind of a contemporary."[7] This attitude may be called historicist, and it becomes problematic only when it is taken too literally.

In line with the concept of the *Kulturstaat*, moreover, Ranke saw states as the outward embodiments of "intellectual forces", "moral energies" that could be understood only by means of "empathy".[8] That is why his history of inter-state relations took its significance from the cultural conflicts it presumably expressed. Thus Friedrich Meinecke was a legitimate heir of the Rankean tradition. It was only the history of society and of 'civilization' in Voltaire's sense that failed to attract Ranke's attention.

At the same time, Ranke persistently championed the principle of individuality. He not only believed that great statesmen and great thinkers truly *stood for*, and thus legitimately guided, their nations; he also saw states themselves as "individualities" with their own distinctive "tendencies".[9] Indeed, he repeatedly insisted upon the discontinuity between "the general" and "the particular". "From the particular", he wrote, "you may ascend to the general; but from general theory there is no way back to the intuitive understanding of the particular".[10] What the historian must start from, therefore, is "the

---

7 LEOPOLD VON RANKE: *Die grossen Mächte*, ed. by F. Meinecke, Leipzig 1916, p. 22: Versetzt man sich in jene Zeit, in den Sinn eines Mitlebenden zurück...

8 *Ibid.*, p. 60: Es sind Kräfte, und zwar geistige ... schöpferische Kräfte .... moralische Energien ... Zu definieren, unter Abstraktion zu bringen sind sie nicht; aber anschauen, wahrnehmen kann man sie; ein Mitgefühl ihres Daseins kann man sich erzeugen.

9 LEOPOLD VON RANKE: *Das politische Gespräch und andere Schriften zur Wissenschaftslehre*, Halle 1925, p. 25: Individualitäten (mit) ihnen eigenen Tendenzen.

10 *Ibid.*, p. 22: Ohne Sprung...kann man aus dem Allgemeinen garnicht in das Besondere gelangen. Das Real-Geistige, welches in ungeahnter Originalität dir plötzlich vor den Augen steht, läßt sich von keinem höheren Prinzip ableiten. Aus dem Besonderen kannst du wohl ... zu dem Allgemeinen aufstei-

unique intellectual and spiritual character of the individual state, its principle".[11]

Among 19th-century German theorists of history, only Johann Gustav Droysen equaled Ranke in authority. Long available to students in lectures and manuscript outlines, Droysen's reflections on history reached their final printed form in 1882.[12] They first explicitly elaborated the contrast between explanation and interpretive understanding (*Verstehen*). Droysen associated the latter with intuitive insight, but also with the recovery of past human actions and beliefs from the "traces" they have left in the historian's own time. Like Dilthey after him, Droysen distinguished between processes "internal" to the human agent from their outward "expressions".[13] The point of historical inquiry, as he conceived it, is our need to orient ourselves in the human, "moral world", our finding a meaningful link between past and future. Droysen also related individual to transcendental purposes, drawing upon a Hegelian terminology to make the point. Much like Hegel, he insisted that "the state is not the sum of the individuals it encompasses; nor does it arise out of their wills or exist for the sake of their wills". In line with the neo-idealist theory of *Bildung* , he described history as "humanity's coming to consciousness".[14]

---

gen; aus der allgemeinen Theorie gibt es keinen Weg zur Anschauung des Besonderen.

11 *Ibid.*, p. 19: Als ursprünglich setzest du das eigentümliche geistige Dasein des individuellen Staates, sein Prinzip.

12 JOHANN GUSTAV DROYSEN: *Grundriß der Historik*, Leipzig ³1882, ed. by Peter Leyh, Stuttgart (Frommann) 1977, pp. 415-488, esp. pp. 423-424, 464.

13 *Ibid.*, p. 422: Nur was Menschengeist gestaltet ... hat, die Menschenspur leuchtet uns wieder auf.... In jeder Äußerung gibt der Mensch Ausdruck seines individuellen Wesens ... Was von solchen Ausdrücken ... uns noch ... vorhanden ist ... ist uns verständlich; p. 423: Die einzelne Äußerung wird verstanden als eine Äußerung des Innern im Rückschluß auf dies Innere; p. 424: Von dem logischen Mechanismus des Verstehens unterscheidet sich der Akt des Verständnisses. Dieser erfolgt...als unmittelbare Intuition, als tauche sich Seele in Seele.

14 *Ibid.*, pp. 435-336, 441-444. See pp. 435, 442-443 for "sittliche Welt", "Zweck", "Zweck der Zwecke", and Hegel; p. 44: Der Staat ist nicht die Summe der Individuen, die er umfaßt, noch entsteht er aus deren Willen, noch ist er um deren Willen da; p. 444: Die Geschichte ist das Bewußtwerden und Bewußtsein der Menschheit über sich selbst.

Some of Droysen's views were developed in opposition to H. T. Buckle's two-volume *History of Civilization in England* (1858-61), which sought to transform history in the image of the natural sciences.[15] Droysen sharply criticized this project, partly because it left no room for human agency and free will. He believed that history alone could overcome the growing estrangement between the exact and the "speculative" disciplines. But his main argument had to do with the divide between the scientist's search for regularities and the historian's predominant concern with the interpretive understanding of the unique and particular.

> The natural sciences... see only the same and the unchanging in the transformations they observe... In the individual being, they see and seek no more than either a class concept or a mediator of chemical change.... They have neither room nor a term for the concept of purpose.[16]

These formulations begin to suggest how the issue of 'positivism' posed itself to German historians during the late 19th century.

There is little evidence that rigorously positivist theories played much of a role in 19th-century German academic thought, at least outside the natural sciences. Followers of Auguste Comte and *self-confessed* positivists were rare indeed, and they were more likely to be found at the margins than at the center of the academic system. Between about 1840 and 1880, to be sure, the decline of philosophical Idealism and the routinization of specialized research may have encouraged an *unreflected* scientism. Perhaps too, the successes of experimental psychology and psycho-physics suggested reductionist strategies of a certain type, which apparently affected physical anthropology as well.[17]

---

15 *Ibid.*, pp. 451-469, esp. pp. 461-466, 468.

16 *Ibid.*, p. 467: Die naturwissenschaftliche Betrachtungsweise ... sieht in den Veränderungen, die sie beobachtet...nur das im Wechsel Gleiche und Bleibende ... In dem individuellen Sein sieht und sucht sie nur entweder den Gattungsbegriff oder den Vermittler des Stoffwechsels.

17 WOODRUFF D. SMITH: *Politics and the Sciences of Culture in Germany, 1840-1920,* Oxford (Oxford University Press) 1991 is useful on its particular subject. Unfortunately, Smith makes a tiny fragment of the German intellectual community stand for the whole. Among the handful of individuals he covers are Riehl (a positivist?), Virchow (a scientist, and an unusual one), the geographer Ratzel, the physical anthropologist Bastian, such scientistic popularizers as Haeckel and Ostwald, and the psychologist Wundt, whose position was at least ambivalent.

Still, for the vast majority of German academic humanists, and certainly for the historians, 'positivism' was a vaguely defined heresy, not a methodological option one might seriously consider.

Against this background, we can begin to understand the virulent debate that arose over Karl Lamprecht's "cultural history" during the 1890s.[18] In fact, that debate in turn has caused contemporary historians to wonder whether German historians of the late 19th century were significantly more reluctant than their French colleagues to move from political and intellectual to social history. Christian Simon has recently raised this question, along with related issues, in interesting new ways. He has observed that both French and German historians of that era *practiced* a monographic history with a mainly political emphasis, while voluntarily helping to legitimate the regimes they looked to for material and moral support. But after all, the two political regimes involved were far from similar. Most German historians after 1871 considered the bureaucratic monarchy a legitimate embodiment of the cultural state; they distrusted the Socialists, and even parliamentary democracy itself. French historians were more divided among themselves; but those who became dominant at the Ecole Normale and the "New Sorbonne" from the late 1870s on were committed republicans, and capable of sympathy with moderate Socialism. Above all, they believed in the 'principles of 1789', considered France a nation of citizens, and could therefore see the social interests of ordinary Frenchmen driving the history of politics. Georg Iggers has cited a wealth of new works in social history that appeared in France during the decades around the turn of the century. In Germany, the traditions of the cameralist *Staatswissenschaften* and of the historical school of economics might enable a Gustav Schmoller or an Otto Hintze to perceive economic and social conditions as pertinent to politics, but more as *conditions of statecraft* than as sources of historical change in their own right.[19]

---

18 New and detailed on Lamprecht and the controversy is ROGER CHICKERING: *Karl Lamprecht: A German Academic Life, 1856-1915*, Atlantic Highlands, NJ (Humanities Press) 1993. See also RINGER: *Decline of the Mandarins*, pp. 142-151, 302-304, 316-334.

19 See initially: GERHARD OESTREICH: "Die Fachhistorie und die Anfänge der sozialgeschichtlichen Forschung in Deutschland", *Historische Zeitschrift*, 208 (1969), pp. 320-363. More recently, comparatively and comprehensively: CHRISTIAN SIMON: *Staat und Geschichtswissenschaft in Deutschland und Frankreich 1871-1914*, Bern (Lang) 1988, and my review of the book in *History and Theory*, XX (1990), pp. 95-106; GEORG IGGERS: "Geschichtswis-

Above all, it is hard to imagine French historians reacting to Lamprecht with anything like the passionate hostility he aroused among his German colleagues. The fiercest attacks upon him typically raised the specter of 'materialism'. Nevertheless, the main objections he provoked were in fact methodological or theoretical. Startlingly careless in his handling of sources, Lamprecht also espoused a simplistic scheme of socio-psychological 'laws' and stages of development. He thus drew fire not only as a dilettante, but as a 'positivist' as well. He gave insufficient attention to the interpretive models that helped to define the German historical tradition, and especially to the principle of individuality. In 1894 and 1902, that principle was forcefully restated and more fully developed by Wilhelm Windelband and Heinrich Rickert in the antithesis between the "nomothetic" abstractions of the natural sciences and the "idiographic" representation of the particular in the historical and cultural studies.[20] Unfortunately, I cannot here analyse this extraordinary and yet deeply characteristic product of the German educational and historical tradition.

IV. The Educational Revolution in France

Turning to France, I again have to start from the briefly stated thesis that an educational revolution of the type I have described took place there only late in the 19th century. The main changes occurred between the late 1870s and the turn of the century. Chiefly affected by the introduction of regular research requirements were the faculties of letters, including what came to be called the New Sorbonne. Along with the transformation of higher education, the newly confirmed Republic carried out a substantial reorganization of the public secondary schools. It ultimately chose to admit the graduates of nonclassical secondary programs to the university faculties, while also reducing

---

senschaft in Deutschland und Frankreich 1830 bis 1918 und die Rolle der Sozialgeschichte", in: JÜRGEN KOCKA, UTE FREVERT (Eds.): *Bürgertum im 19. Jahrhundert: Deutschland im europäischen Vergleich*, vol. 3, Munich (dtv) 1988, pp. 175-199. See also RINGER: *Fields of Knowledge*, pp. 258-264.

20 WILHELM WINDELBAND: "Geschichte und Naturwissenschaft", *Präludien*, Tübingen 1924, vol. II, pp. 136-160; HEINRICH RICKERT: *Die Grenzen der naturwissenschaftlichen Begriffsbildung*, Tübingen 1902.

the curricular barriers between the several branches of the secondary system. The simultaneous reforms of the secondary schools and university faculties were widely perceived as related elements in a socially progressive initiative that would cement an alliance between 'science', 'democracy', and an emphatically 'laic' Republic.[21]

During the public debates that led up to the reform of the secondary curriculum, a parliamentary commission chaired by Alexandre Ribot asked French academics and experts to testify publicly on the alternatives confronting the French educational system. Treating the witnesses before this commission as a 'sample' of French academic opinion on educational reform, I divided them into two groups. A cluster of traditionalists proposed to restrict university access to graduates of the classical secondary stream; a group of reformists took the opposite position. The traditionalists, I found, were almost all members of the French Academy or 'Institute'; a good number of them also taught at the institutionally conservative professional faculties or at certain elite *grandes écoles*. The reformists were typically younger than the traditionalists; they came predominantly from the faculties of letters and of sciences, including the Sorbonne, and they consistently favored the institutionalization of research in higher education, along with the reform of the secondary curriculum.[22]

V. French Theories of Education

The traditionalists before the Ribot Commission referred a great deal to the ideal of *culture générale*, the opposite of specialized training and the nearest French equivalent to the German *Bildung*. They claimed that only the classical languages, mainly Latin, offered a truly general education; but their conception of *culture générale* was largely instrumental in character. As if to recall the original agricultural connotation of *culture* as the cultivation of the soil, they wrote in muscular terms of *'une forte culture de l'esprit'*, a rigorous

21 RINGER: *Fields of Knowledge*, pp. 114-127.
22 France, Chambre des Députés, Session de 1899, Commission de l'Enseignement (pres. Ribot), *Enquête sur l'enseignement secondaire: Procès verbaux des dépoitions*, vols I-II, Paris 1899; RINGER: *Fields of Knowledge*, pp. 141, 160.

training of the mind, or of Latin as 'intellectual gymnastics'. They also put much emphasis upon the *formal* perfections of the classical texts, their exemplary clarity, literary beauty and rhetorical force. When they addressed the *contents* of the ancient Roman literary works at all, they stressed their pedagogical uses. Such primordial human virtues as love of family and fatherland, they argued, were presented by the Roman authors in ways that were both *timeless* and particularly accessible to young Frenchmen. After all, Rome was the mother of France's characteristically Latin civilization.[23]

It would be hard to overstate the difference between this late 19th-century French version of classical pedagogy and the thought of a Friedrich August Wolf. To begin with, the German neo-humanists of the early 19th century identified almost polemically with Greece, not with Rome. Moreover, they idealized a whole culture, not just a language. That is how they came to practice *Altertumswissenschaft*, not Greek classical philology alone, and certainly not just a species of literary or rhetorical emulation. Above all, they sought an interpretive understanding of the classical sources that necessarily implied an awareness of the *distance* between the ancient authors and the contemporary readers. Even the identificationist model of interpretation at its most mysterious and problematic did not as radically suppress that distance as the French traditionalists' simultaneous recourse to the myth of timelessness and the ideology of 'Latinity'. How could a tradition of rigorous philological and historical scholarship possibly have grown from such weak roots?

In any case, the French educational reformists found it easy to demolish the case made by their opponents. They insisted that minds could only be trained in the serious study of a *subject matter*. They were merciless in their attacks upon the 'formalism' of the traditional pedagogy, its 'merely literary' or 'rhetorical' character. Again and again, they called for a new emphasis upon 'positive knowledge' (*connaissances positives*). Not that many of them were followers or even careful readers of Auguste Comte; Comte's influence was neither as great nor as clear in its implications, even in France, as some historians seem to believe. To our French educational reformists, at any rate, *connaissances positives* were defined primarily in opposition to 'formal' or apriori reasoning on the one hand, and to merely 'literary' or 'rhetorical' habits of thought on the other.[24]

---

23 *Ibid.*, pp. 141-160.
24 *Ibid.*, pp. 160-176, 225-237 for this and what follows.

Of course the prestige of the natural sciences had grown considerably during the interval between the German and the French educational revolution. The most determined French reformists liked to associate the traditional literary education with the courtly or gentlemanly tradition of the *honnête homme*, with the Old Regime, and of course with the Jesuits. To a moralist of Emile Durkheim's convictions, the whole idea of the cultivated individual as a work of art was downright shocking in any case. In the eyes of the reformists, the new society was not only democratic; it also depended upon a complex division of labor. Like scientific progress itself, it required specialization, cooperation, and a sense of obligation to the group. Specialized research was much celebrated at the New Sorbonne precisely at a time when it aroused profound misgivings in the German academic community. In any case, Durkheim and others were able to detect an interdependence between science, democracy and civic solidarity. And an education in 'positive knowledge' struck them as better suited to the new symbiosis than the literary formalism of the old *culture générale*.[25]

VI. French Theories of History

Among the most determined critics of the inherited literary education and the firmest champions of the new research ethos were a cluster of historians, some of them already well known and others on the way to distinguished reputations. The historians included Alphonse Aulard, Ernest Lavisse and Charles Seignobos, and they had strong support from the famous literary historian Gustave Lanson and the young Germanist Charles Andler. Together, this group perfectly exemplified what came to be called the 'spirit of the New Sorbonne'. One of their contributions to the reformist argument was the historicist tactic of associating the traditional education with outdated social and political conditions. Perhaps they knew, too, that if the classicists lost their hold upon the secondary curriculum, the historians would figure prominently among their heirs. But they were also singularly well equipped to expose the weaknesses in the traditionalists' case.

---

25 For Durkheim on education, see *Ibid.*, pp. 282-299; for Gustave Lanson on science, democracy and solidarity, pp. 183-186.

Here, for example, is a particularly effective passage by Ernest Lavisse.

> Why (during my secondary schooling) was I never told that the spirit of a people is expressed by (its language)...and that its manner of thinking determines its way of acting... A misuse was made to our detriment of the superficial and incomplete truth that man is the same in all times and places. We were not helped...to imagine the persons and things of former times... Even less...were the civilizations explained to us, of which the works of art are representative monuments.

In history courses, Lavisse complained, "assorted facts" were presented; but there was no sense of "the transformation in the way of life, nor of the stages in the march of humanity toward us".[26]

Lavisse's critical standard, obviously, was that of the contextual historicist; yet he felt no unease about the relativist conundrum of *Historismus* that so greatly concerned German historians of the early 20th century. Perhaps the Germans suffered from an overly literal sense of having to 'put themselves in the place of' other persons and times. Lavisse's cheerful remark about humanity's "march toward us" may seem naive and presumptuous by comparison. But perhaps it merely signals the inescapable need to *begin* a historical interpretation in the language - and from the standpoint - of the present.

Even more interesting, in the context of our discussion, is Lavisse's firm sense of the *distance* that separates us from the classical sources; this was the salient point of his attack upon the traditionalists' recourse to 'timelessness', 'primordial' sentiments, and the genetic identity of 'Latin civilization'. Lavisse simply insisted upon the difference between the world of antiquity and that of modern France; but he did not construe this difference as a hermeneutic or purely philological one. For his emphasis was not upon the distance between the classical author and the modern reader *as individuals*, nor upon the dissimilarity between their languages alone. Instead, he moved immediately to the two divergent ways of thinking *and of acting*, and to the historical transformations that have altered whole "civilizations". He asserted not only that texts must be rescued from the false immediacy of the 'eternal', but also that they become truly interesting only as "representative monuments" of a "way of life". He wanted students to imagine the "words *and things*" of

---

26 *Ibid.*, pp. 177-189, esp. pp. 177-178, 187-188 for the historians' arguments. The passage from Lavisse, cited on pp. 177-178, is taken from ERNEST LAVISSE: "Souvenirs d'une éducation manquée", in: E. LAVISSE ET AL.: *L'Education de la démocratie,* Paris 1903, pp. 3-4, 10, and esp. pp. 5-8.

the past; his emphasis was on patterns of practice, and on something like mentalities, rather than on the psychological individual.

A brief paragraph by the literary historian Gustave Lanson makes the same general point.

> No longer concerned to transmit the 'immutable precepts of good taste', we shall (offer) our pupils an understanding of the life of antiquity; there they will surely (learn to) love the...art that...the civilizations of the Greeks and Romans created in order to express themselves. In the moral, political and social ideas of the ancients too, we can only show our pupils ideas relative to certain states of mind and to certain conditions of existence.[27]

Again, there is the move from the literary text to the "life of antiquity", the arts as "expressions" of "civilizations", and "ideas" rooted not only in "states of mind", but also in "conditions of existence". More could be said about how the concept of 'civilization' became as dominant in France from the 18th century on as the term 'culture' did in Germany. Certainly 'civilization' in France always encompassed institutions and practices, along with values and ideas. Even before Ranke looked to politics and to culture, one could say, Montesquieu and Voltaire looked to society and to 'civilization'. Tocqueville might be called a social or structural historian of politics, and Hippolyte Taine a scientistic environmentalist as well as social historian. But I do not want to make too much of long-term 'antecedents'. Instead, I intend an essentially synchronic analysis of French *academic* theories of history as of the educational revolution of the late 19th century.

One way to complete that project is briefly to consider the most famous French handbook of historical method written at that time, which can also be compared with Droysen's somewhat earlier reflections on the same subject. In 1898, Charles-Victor Langlois and Charles Seignobos published their *Introduction to Historical Studies*.[28] While Langlois concentrated on the auxiliary sciences, Seignobos dealt with the internal criticism of the sources and the construction of historical accounts. Seignobos has often been called a 'posi-

---

27 RINGER: *Fields of Knowledge*, p. 188 cites GUSTAVE LANSON: *L'Université et la société moderne*, Paris 1902, pp. 118-120.

28 CHARLES-VICTOR LANGLOIS, CHARLES SEIGNOBOS: *Introduction aux études historiques*, Paris 1898; CHARLES SEIGNOBOS: *La méthode historique appliquée aux sciences sociales*, Paris 1901; RINGER: *Fields of Knowledge*, pp. 265-276 for this and what follows.

tivist'; but this label is open to question. While trying to distinguish history from Durkheimian sociology, for example, Seignobos insisted that historical change is not produced by "abstract laws", but by causes that are necessary (not sufficient) conditions, and that immediately precede their effects. Indeed, according to Seignobos, these causes can be "chance" concurrences, "accidents", and even such "small facts" as the shape of Cleopatra's nose. These adventurous suggestions provoked a fiercely dismissive response from Francois Simiand, a Durkheimian reader of John Stuart Mill, and a truly systematic positivist.[29]

In another context, Seignobos clearly acknowledged that historians are interested only in those among the "facts" that have had significant consequences; it is therefore mainly a certain indifference to the problems of *interpretation*, an indifference he shared with Durkheim, that may legitimate his being termed a 'positivist'. The historian's task, he argued, is the recovery of historical "facts" from what traces they have left in the documents. While he certainly recommended a rigorously critical approach to the surviving reports of former actions and events, he apparently saw reports about beliefs as more immediately accessible - and thus unproblematic - than reports about other kinds of "facts". Here the absence of an interpretive tradition in France certainly set Seignobos apart from Droysen.

In compensation, Seignobos benefitted in important ways from the French educational reformists' commitment to the integral study of 'civilizations'. Some of the founders and disciples of the so-called *Annales* school in 20th-century French historiography have tended to portray Seignobos as an incurably old-fashioned narrative historian of 'kings and battles'. Perhaps his *practice* partly or wholly justifies this characterization. But if one actually reads his handbook of 1898, one can find things in it that could have been put there by a 20th-century social historian, perhaps even an *Annaliste*. Thus to help historians draw together their findings in a general model of a society, he sketched the following scheme.

I. Material conditions

1. Population: (physical) anthropology, demography;
2. General material environment: natural environment (geography), artificial environment (agriculture, buildings, means of transport, etc.)

---

29 *Ibid.*, pp. 278-282, including on FRANCOIS SIMIAND: "Méthode historique et science sociale," *Revue de synthèse historique*, 6 (1903), pp. 1-22, 129-157.

II. <u>Intellectual conditions</u>

(subheadings omitted by FR)

III. <u>Voluntary material customs</u>

1. Practices of material life (food, clothing, finery, hygiene);
2. Practices of private life (daily schedules, ceremonies, entertainments, travel);
3. Economic practices, production (agriculture, mining, industry), transportation, exchange, appropriation, transfers and contracts.

IV. <u>Social institutions</u>

1. Property arrangements and inheritance;
2. The family;
3. Education;
4. Social classes.

V. <u>Public institutions</u>

1. Recruitment and organization of government personnel ... official regulations of government, actual procedure of government operations;
2. (As in the preceding, except for church government);
3. Organization, recruitment, regulations and practices of local authorities.

VI. <u>Relations among sovereign social groups</u>

1. Organization of the personnel in charge of international relations;
2. Conventions, regulations, and common customs making up international law, officially and in reality.[30]

Under the heading of geography, I should explain, Seignobos included the climate and soil conditions, and he was influenced by the 'human geography' of Vidal de la Blanche as well. Beyond that, he came back again and again to "typical" or repeated patterns of behavior, to customs, common practices, and "habits", including "intellectual habits". Thus he could really be considered a precursor of a French conception of history that is still with us, and so could some of his colleagues among the French reformist historians of 'civilization'.

---

30 LANGLOIS, SEIGNOBOS: *Introduction*, pp. 138-140.

Chapter 20

A Philosophy of the Historical School: Erich Rothacker's Theory of the *Geisteswissenschaften* (Human Sciences)

PETER KOSLOWSKI

I. What Is the Historical School?
II. Particularism Versus Universalism
III. What Are the *Geisteswissenschaften* (Human Sciences)?
IV. Rothacker's Historism and Present Postmodernism
V. Critique and Conclusion

Erich Rothacker has developed, at the end of the Historical School of the Social Sciences and the Human Sciences (*Geisteswissenschaften*), the philosophy of the Historical School. In his theory of the human sciences as well as in his philosophy of history he tries to give an answer to the question what the essence of the Historical School is and how its philosophy and basic presuppositions distinguish it from other approaches to the social and human sciences.

Erich Rothacker was born in 1888. He recieved his doctorate at the University of Tübingen in 1912 and his habilitation at the University of Heidelberg in 1920 where he became Associate Professor in 1924. From 1928 to 1954 he was Professor of Philosophy at the University of Bonn. Rothacker died in 1965.

In his work Rothacker was strongly influenced by Wilhelm Dilthey. Following Dilthey's programme of a „critique of the historical and social sciences", Rothacker tried to further clarify the philosophical presuppositions of the Historical School. In some sense, Rothacker's work forms the end and fulfilment of the Historical School.[1]

I. What Is the Historical School?

Rothacker gave the following definition of what the Historical School is: „The Historical School is a homogeneous although very differentiated mass of thought that developed from Herder to Dilthey through different stages, stands in certain, however not yet explained, relationships with the early and late Romantics with which also Goethe in some of the essential and seldom noticed aspects of his individuality associates himself and by which in many respects even Nietzsche is influenced."[2]

---

1 Rothacker's major works are *Logik und Systematik der Geisteswissenschaften* (Logic and Systematics of the Human Sciences), 1926, 2nd ed. 1970; *Einleitung in die Geisteswissenschaften* (Introduction to the Human Sciences), 2nd ed. 1930; *Geschichtsphilosophie* (Philosophy of History), 1934; *Geschichte der Persönlichkeit* (The History of Personality), 1938, 4th ed. 1965; *Probleme der Kulturanthropologie* (Problems of Cultural Anthropology), 1942, 2nd ed. 1948; *Philosophische Anthropologie* (Philosophical Anthropology), 1964, 2nd ed. 1960.
For the literature on Rothacker cf. H.-W. NAU: *Die systematische Struktur von Erich Rothackers Kulturbegriff*, Bonn (Bouvier) 1968. - W. PERPEET: *Erich Rothacker. Philosophie des Geistes aus dem Geist der Deutschen Historischen Schule*, Bonn (Bouvier) 1968. - O. PÖGGELER: „Rothackers Begriff der Geisteswissenschaften", in: H. LÜTZELER (Ed.): *Kulturwissenschaften. Festgabe für W. Perpeet zum 65. Geburtstag*, Bonn (Bouvier) 1980, pp. 306-353.
2 E. ROTHACKER: *Einleitung in die Geisteswissenschaften* (Introduction to the Human Sciences), Tübingen (J.C.B. Mohr [Paul Siebeck]) 2nd ed. 1930, p. VI: „(Die) Historische Schule (ist) eine einheitliche, wenn auch vielfach differenzierte Gedankenmasse, die sich von Herder bis Dilthey in verschiedenen Stufen entfaltet, die nicht allein in bestimmten übrigens ungeklärten Beziehungen zu Früh- und Spätromantik steht, der auch Goethe mit wesentlichen und selten beachteten Seiten seines Wesens sich eingliedert, von der in vielen Beziehungen noch Nietzsche gespeist ist." (All translations from Rothacker in this paper are by P.K.)

For Rothacker, the Historical School is the body of thought in philosophy, literature, and the social sciences in Germany that arose about 1750 and forms the dominant cultural achievement of Germany.

„The flourishing of our *Geisteswissenschaften* (human sciences) has to be understood as an element of equal worth and of own standing in the triumvirat besides our classical and romantic literature and besides the idealist philosophy, as third element of the ‚German movement'."[3]

Thus it is the Historical School of the Social and Human Sciences, the classical and romantic German literature and the idealist philosophy, particularly Hegel, that form, according to Rothacker, the German contribution to the European culture. The *Geisteswissenschaften* to which also the social sciences and economics belong form the third part besides the classical literature and the idealist philosophy in a coherent whole of German culture. Although Rothacker admits that the Historical School is not the only school of the *Geisteswissenschaften* in Germany he maintains that it is its main stream. Rothacker sees an intensive interchange between the human sciences and the idealist philosophy of the spirit.

It is the task of the human sciences, of the *Geisteswissenschaften*, to „develop explicitly the implicit and hidden philosophy of the spirit of the Historical School and to further by its own intellectual power the theoretical philosophy of the spirit."[4] Rothacker makes clear that this interchange goes both ways, from the human sciences to the theoretical philosophy of the spirit and from the idealist philosophy of the spirit to the differentiated disciplines of the human sciences. He makes also clear that, for him, the human sciences are not only specialized disciplines but aim at the same time at a unified theory of the spirit. Thus, the human sciences are not only scientific disciplines defined by a certain material object, but they are also determined by a shared philosophical conception of „the spirit", of *Geist*, and they have and ought to have repercussions on the philosophy of the spirit. Rothacker sets himself the task to clarify the foundations of this philosophy and of the

---

3 *Ibid.*: „Die Blüte unserer Geisteswissenschaften (wäre) als selbständiges ebenbürtiges Glied eines Triumvirats neben unserer klassischen und romantischen Dichtung und der idealistischen Philosophie der ‚Deutschen Bewegung' einzuordnen."

4 *Ibid.*, p. XVI: „Explicite die implicite und heimliche Geistphilosophie der Historischen Schule zu entwickeln und aus ihrer Kraft heraus die theoretische Philosophie des Geistes zu befruchten."

differentiated human sciences. He aims at developing that shape of the philosophy of the spirit that is required by a scientific age.

For the tradition of the Historical School from Dilthey to Rothacker and others like Eduard Spranger, it is not the material object only that defines the human sciences. It is also their relationship to and their impact for the philosophy of the spirit in the Hegelian sense.

What is therefore the characteristic trait of the relationship of the human sciences to the spirit and what is the character of the spirit in the Hegelian philosophical tradition? The common trait of both is the fact of historicity, the fact that the spirit in its absolute form, even the absolute spirit or God, is historical and has a fate, is not unalterable and constant:

„The Historical School alone has made clear, in competition and in interaction with the idealist systems and in insurmountable deepness, that the spirit as such has a fate and what that implies for humankind and the shaping of its life and actions."[5]

The Historical School is founded on the assumption of a metaphysical historicity of being or on the metaphysics of historicity. It is this particular trait that distinguishes it from other philosophies and concepts of the human sciences like those of scholasticism or positivism. These other metaphysical systems do not deny history but they maintain - and that marks their difference from historism - that the categories of thinking and the laws of reality as well as the last principles of reality are not historical and changing but constant. In contrast, the Historical School and its philosophy of spirit assumes that even the absolute has a history and that all being is subject to historicity and therefore subjected to historical change. This metaphysical historicity of being assumed by the Historical School is what it shares with the Hegelian philosophy in which also the absolute is thought to have a history of fate, or, as the Hegelian Rosenkranz stated it, even the absolute or God has a „curriculum vitae".

The Historical School diverges from Hegel, however, in its emphasis on the particular. The human sciences in the tradition of the Historical School put far more emphasis on the particular and raise the particular to a much higher ontological status than the particular is thought to have in Hegel's philosophy. The Historical School defends a relativism and particularism of

---

5   *Ibid.*, p. 18: „Die Historische Schule allein (hat) im Wettbewerb und in Wechselwirkung mit den idealistischen Systemen aber in unübertrefflicher Tiefe erkannt, daß der Geist als solcher ein Schicksal hat und was das für den Menschen und die Gestaltung seines Lebens und Tuns bedeutet".

cultures, institutions and styles that is not only derived from their historicity but also from the fact that they are individuations of equal worth, individuations of the spirit of the time and of the space in which they develop, of the *Zeitgeist* and *genius loci*, and of the spirit of a people that realizes them, of the *Volksgeist*.

Hegel although being the father of the *Geistphilosophie*, the philosophy of spirit of the Historical School, has not affirmed a metaphysical value to the particular, to the particular in the historical development of small cultures. He rather assumes that the development of world history passes over the particular and the particularities of small cultures and peoples. For Hegel, the particularist forms of cultures are just a means to be overcome in the development of the absolute spirit. It is therefore important to note that the human sciences or *Geisteswissenschaften* do not only explicate Hegel's philosophy of spirit but develop it further and transcend it in an important respect. They transcend it by the new and specific value they give to the particular.

II. Particularism Versus Universalism

The historicist attitude and the frame of mind of historism means concrete and not abstract reason, concrete substantiality and not general substance for Rothacker. The binomial concepts characteristic for the historicist ontology are not historism-naturalism, but historism-universalism.[6] The historicist ontology which lies at the foundations of the Historical School emphasizes the particular and the historically unique. The relativism linked to it is, by its nature and origin, not a sceptical, but a pluralistic one.[7] Historism has an affect for the particular, and the result of this affect for the particular is a pluralism of concrete substantialities, not the monism of the universal and universally valid. Its pluralism follows Leopold Ranke's postulate that not that society yields the greatest pleasure and development of the individuals where

---

6 E. ROTHACKER: *Logik und Systematik der Geisteswissenschaften* (Logic and Systematics of the Human Sciences), Bonn (Bouvier) 2nd ed. 1947 (1st ed. 1926), p. 164.
7 *Ibid.*, p. 148.

only one speaks up and dominates the discourse („*wo nur einer das große Wort führt*").

The pluralism of historism does not deny the criteria of correctness and valuableness but affirms them. Its relativism is not a nihilistic relativism that denies that there are criteria of correctness and valuableness. It has, by no means, a destroying tendency. Its pluralism rather stems from the acknowledgment of the fact that all conceptual synthesis is codetermined by the will and, therefore, dogmatic. The main forms of culture and the departments of culture like the economy, law, religion, and art are dogmatic inasmuch that they select one out of many possibilities by the will. They are also dogmatic since the provinces of cultures in them follow a common style. Since these provinces follow the same premises and a shared weltanschauung this common style of a culture can be found in all their provinces.[8] Rothacker emphasizes that by the fact that the unity of a culture is intended by the will and therefore influenced by the will to unity, it is always shaped by an element of a dogmatic form or a form founded in the will to cultural validity and dogmatic definition.

It is this dogmatic form originating in a will to the unifying form that unites the provinces of a culture and subjects them at the same to the spirit of a historical epoch: „The Historical School has first of all made a very simple statement: It has recognized that the specific cultural actions of human beings are intertwined with each other, but also with a consistent characteristic of the people and the spirit of the time".[9] Rothacker writes this in his contribution to the Schmoller-Festschrift at the occasion of Schmoller's one hundred's birthday in 1938. Historicity, therefore, does not only imply sub-

---

8   Cf. E. ROTHACKER: *Die dogmatische Denkform in den Geisteswissenschaften und das Problem des Historismus* (The Dogmatic Form of Thinking in the Human Sciences and the Problem of Historism), Wiesbaden (F. Steiner) 1954 (= Abhandlungen der Geistes- und Sozialwissenschaftlichen Klasse der Mainzer Akademie der Wissenschaften und der Literatur, Nr. 6).

9   E. ROTHACKER: „Historismus", in: A. SPIETHOFF (Ed.): *Gustav von Schmoller und die deutsche geschichtliche Volkswirtschaftslehre. Dem Andenken an Gustav von Schmoller, Festgabe zur hundertsten Wiederkehr seines Geburtstages 24. Juni 1938*, Berlin (Duncker & Humblot) 1938, p. 5: „Die historische Schule hat zunächst einmal eine sehr schlichte Feststellung gemacht: Sie erkannte, daß die besonderen Kulturtätigkeiten des Menschen jeweils untereinander, dann aber im ganzen jeweils mit der relativ bleibenden Eigenart des Volksgeistes oder Zeitgeistes ihres Trägers verflochten werden können."

jection to time but also subjection of a culture to the common spirit of a time and of a people. Historicity means that individuation is not only derived from the singular position of a culture in space and time but also from its singular relationship to the spirit of a time and a people.

„The Historical School is a ‚historical' school and has a relationship to history for philosophical purposes since the idea of individuation became the highest problem for it."[10] Since individuation is not only caused by singularity in space and time, but also by the singular relationship to the spirit of a time and space, the idea of individuation is for historism not only a matter of fact but also a normative task that has to be realized: the individual relationship of a culture to the spirit of the time and people in which it is individuated is a telos to be realized, not a fact that is automatically realized by historical time. Not only the individuation of human individuals, but also the individuation of the „intermediate powers", of the *Volksgeist* (the spirit of the different peoples), and of the different historical periods, the *Zeitgeist*, ought to happen. Between the realm of the universally valid and the individuality of the human individuals, historism assumes an individuality of the spirit in the different peoples and in the spirit of the different periods of history, of Volksgeist and Zeitgeist. Their individual realization *ought* to take place since humankind has „not the slightest hope, to become anyone else than an always again historically concrete, historically bounded, a temporal and finite being ... Such it is not only, but such it ought to be since only in this way humankind can reach its fruitful development."[11]

The development of the particular is postulated and demanded by the nature of humankind since reason idealistically understood is metaphysically divided in history and by history into the different spirits of the peoples (*Volksgeister*). Ideal humanity is divided into different kinds of spirits, although the zoological kind of the human is uniform. The historical individuations of truth are not departures from truth but the legitimate offspring from

---

10 E. ROTHACKER: *Logik der Geisteswissenschaften,* loc. cit., p. 17: „Die Historische Schule ist eine ‚historische' und hat in philosophischer Absicht ein Verhältnis zur Geschichte, weil für sie die Idee in ihrer Individuation zum höchsten Problem geworden ist."

11 E. ROTHACKER: „Historismus", p. 5: Der Mensch ist ein Wesen „das ... nicht die geringsten Aussichten hat, jemals etwas anderes zu werden als ein immer wieder historisch konkretes, historisch gebundenes, zeitliches und endliches Wesen ... so sei es nicht nur, sondern so solle es auch sein, denn nur so komme die Menschheit, wie sie ist, zu ihrer fruchtbaren Entfaltung."

the one truth. Against the reproach that this implies the dangers of relativism, Rothacker contends that „not the individuation of truth in circles of cultures, peoples, epochs is the deadly poison of which the truth as such is dying but it is the naturalization of these individuations, namely the replacement of the tree of the life of truth full of meaning by the simple givenness of nature that causes the most radical relativization."[12] He continues:

„Only when the cultural forms are interpreted as the mere function of something else that has no ideal content and no claim to truth, only if the cultures are naturalized and thought of as being expressions of something not cultural and valuable at all, the truth value of the different cultures is annihilated."[13] Thus, it is not relativism and historism but naturalism that kills the truth and meaning of cultures and cultural artefacts. It is the naturalist reductionism with its idea that cultures are only the veal that is thrown over the real causal factors of the Darwinian struggle for survival or of the sociobiological maximization of inclusive fitness that destroys the intrinsic values of the particular cultures.

Individuation and particularization are the means by which the spirit realizes itself, and since the individual and the particular can only be realized in history, and not in an unchanging, static medium, history becomes the medium in and by which the spirit realizes itself in individuation and particularization. „,Life' and ,history' have therefore something in common: Both affirm not general ideals, but particular ideals: ideals that are related to time, that are related to concrete living totalities ... The deepest root of historism is not to be found in his will to practice history *only*, but in his insight that particularly the creative realizations of human practice ought to be ,individu-

---

12 *Ibid.*, pp. 5ff.: „Entscheidend ist es jedenfalls, daß für ihn (den Historismus) die historischen Besonderungen der Wahrheit noch immer Abkömmlinge ,der' Wahrheit sind und daß weiter überhaupt nicht die Individuation dieser Wahrheit nach Kulturkreisen, Völkern, Epochen das tödliche Gift ist, an dem die Wahrheit als solche stirbt, sondern daß erst die Naturalisierung dieser Individuationen, das heißt die Ersetzung des sinnhaltigen Lebensbaumes der Wahrheit durch bloße Naturgegebenheiten die radikale Relativierung herbeiführt. Erst wenn die angebliche Wahrheit eines Kulturgebildes umgedeutet wird zu einer abhängigen Funktion von etwas, was an sich gar keinen ideellen Gehalt und gar keinen Wahrheitsanspruch mehr besitzt, sondern bloß naturgesetzlich abläuft, wie es seiner Artung nach ablaufen muß, erst dann ist der Wahrheitsanspruch vernichtet."

13 *Ibid.*

al', that is, that they should always and necessarily be related to the concrete tasks of concrete communities."[14]

The individuation of a culture can not be only particularist, however. Every culture must also assimilate the universal powers. It is, according to Rothacker, the contribution of Savigny's historical and cultural school of legal science to have demonstrated that the spirit of a people, the *Volksgeist*, can only realize itself if it assimilates the universally valid powers and principles, and that a particular culture cannot restrict itself to its individuality only. Savigny demonstrated that „the Historical School does not work with the scheme ,each spirit of a people must realize that which is appropriate to its physiognomy!' Rather it has also used the scheme of the historical assimilation of the universal powers."[15] „Every historical life is constitutively influenced by the tension between the universal and the particular forces."[16]

The criterium of truth for historism can only be the historical idea of fruitfulness. „The achievement of historism is that it has been the first attempt to capture the experience, gained in the years around 1750 for the first time in history, of the historical and creative consciousness and to work it into the consciousness of the world."[17]

In his contribution to the Schmoller-Festschrift to 1938, Rothacker does not interpret historism as a specifically German experience, but as the first expression of the experience of modernity, of the experience of the historical and creative character of humankind. It is also this discovery that the character

---

14 E. ROTHACKER: „Historismus", *loc. cit.*, p. 8: „Das ,Leben' und die ,Historie' haben also etwas gemeinsam: beide bejahen nicht allgemeine Ideale, sondern besondere Ideale: zeitbezogene, auf konkrete lebendige Ganzheiten bezogene ... Die tiefste Wurzel des Historismus liegt nicht in seinem Willen, bloß Historie zu treiben, sondern in seiner Einsicht, daß gerade die schöpferischen Eingriffe in die Praxis ,individuell' sein müßten, das heißt immer und notwendig auf konkrete Aufgaben konkreter Gemeinschaften zu beziehen seien.".

15 *Ibid.*, p. 11: Savigny beweist deutlich genug, „daß die Historische Schule nicht allein mit dem Schema arbeitet: ,jedem Volksgeist das ihm physiognomisch Gemäße!', sondern daß sie auch das Schema einer historischen Assimilation universaler Mächte handhabe."

16 *Ibid.*: „Alles geschichtliche Leben ist konstitutiv durchwirkt von einer Spannung universaler und partikularer Kräfte."

17 *Ibid.*, p. 15: „Gewürdigt kann auch dieser Universalismus nur werden aus dem Sinn des schlechthin lebensnäheren Historismus. Seine Leistung war der erste Versuch, den seit 1750 neugewonnenen Erfahrungsgehalt des historischen und schöpferischen Bewußtseins in das Weltbewußtsein einzuarbeiten."

of humankind is historical and creative that links historism with romanticism and separates it from classicism. The historicity of the mind and the creativity of reason are human universals and, at the same time, express themselves in the particular. Historism is the consciousness of the dialectical nature of universalism and particularism, of their belonging together. It is the universal task of reason and the universal trait of all cultures and peoples of humanity that they, reason and culture, realize themselves in the particular.

That there has been a particularly strong emphasis on historism in the German culture is due to the fact, according to Rothacker, that Germany is the late comer amongst the national cultures of Western Europe. By historism, the late comer claimed, at the same time, to realize its right to develop its own culture and to be on equal footing with those European cultures that developed their individual culture earlier in European history, like the national cultures of Italy, Spain, France, and England.

By the coincidence that Germany has given a particularly intense expression of the new experience of modernity in Historism and that she has claimed by it to develop a culture of its own, German historism has gained its strength and its particular impact in European culture. It is the result of the historical experience of modernity to discover that the claim to the development of a national culture is not the result of a human weakness and relativity but the postulate of the specific characer of humanity and of its need to develop the individuality of particular cultures: „One cannot complain about the relativity of human truth when just this relativity is demanded. The German specific character beside the French one does not result from any human weakness which ought to be overcome but is postulated and demanded."[18]

It should be added that by the influence of Herder the Historical School also gave theoretical support to the rise of the national cultures of the smaller East European nations. Herder as the first thinker of historism discovered the rights of the particular popular cultures of the smaller nations and gave the first intellectual support for the national cultures of Eastern Europe.

For Rothacker, the relativism of cultures is not an unwanted side-effect but a very positive postulate derived from the intrinsic value of the Volksgeist and Zeitgeist. This intrinsic value of the realization of the historical and

---

18 E. ROTHACKER: *Logik und Systematik der Geisteswissenschaften*, loc. cit., p. 168f.: „Man kann sich aber über die Relativität der menschlichen Wahrheiten nicht beklagen, wenn dieselbe gefordert ist. Die deutsche Eigenart neben der französischen folgt aus keiner menschlichen Schwäche, die überwunden werden müßte, sondern ist postuliert."

particular in the human cultures is expressed in Ranke's dictum that all periods are equally immediate to God.

The Historical School is, therefore, critical of the idea of metaphysical progress which implies that one epoch is closer than the others to the realization of the absolute. This is also the point where the Historical School departs from Hegel's philosophy of history and his idea of a continuous progress in the realization of the absolute. „The relativism is a completely positive postulate. One cannot complain at the same time about relativism and at the same time admit that the epochs are equally immediate to God. They ‚are' not at all immediate to God - where should we know this from? - but they ought to be immediate to God. They ought to be immediate to God due to the fact that they deserve it according to the judgment of our value consciousness that examines the values anew again and again. This would, however, not be the case if these epochs would not develop in their particularity a productivity which - in the consciousness of the Historical School has more weight than the advantages of a ‚grey Internationale'. ... In contrast with this experience of value, the universalism is not only a matter of course the realization of which is only failing due to the blunt resistance of the matter void of all ideas. Rather the universalism demands the decision of a will of an extreme biasedness and of extreme consequences: It demands the sacrifice of the total plurality of culture. ... It demands of each singular individual his or her substantial positivity."[19]

---

19 E. ROTHACKER: *Logik und Systematik der Geisteswissenschaften*, loc. cit., p. 169: „Der Relativismus ist eine ganz positive Forderung. Man kann nicht in einem Atem über Relativismus klagen und zugleich zugeben, daß die Epochen unmittelbar zu Gott sind. Sie ‚sind' nämlich gar nicht unmittelbar zu Gott - woher wissen wir das? -, sondern sie sollen es sein. Allerdings aufgrund der Tatsache, daß sie es vor dem Richterstuhl unseres immer erneut die Werte prüfenden Wertbewußtseins verdienen. Das aber wäre nicht der Fall, wenn diese Epochen nicht in ihrer Eigenart eine Produktivität entfaltet hätten, welche - vor dem Bewußtsein der Historischen Schule schwerer wiegt als die Vorzüge der ‚grauen Internationale' ... Diesem Werterlebnis gegenüber stellt der Universalismus nichts weniger als eine Selbstverständlichkeit dar, deren Durchführung bloß am stumpfen Widerstande der ideenlosen Materie scheiterte, sondern er verlangt eine Willensentscheidung von äußerster Einseitigkeit und äußerster Tragweite: Er verlangt zum Opfer die ganze Mannigfaltigkeit der Kultur ... Er verlangt von jedem einzelnen seine substantiale Positivität."

Universalism claims that the manifold humankind so rich in different forms of cultures ought to impose upon itself the duty: Become one! Rothacker admits that the idea of this duty is a lofty and awe inspiring idea. He objects however: „There is not only the obstacle of multilingualism to it, but also the fact of the eminent fruitfulness of the many languages".[20]

The criterium for the debate between universalism and particularism is the fruitfulness or productiveness of both positions. It is, therefore, not surprising that in history there has been a mutual assimilation of particular forces by universalist ones and vice versa. Rothacker points to the fact that the universal powers of Christianity, of the Roman law, and of modern science and technology that took up the science of antiquity as well as the classical art have, for a long time, created the common historical and cultural background of European culture from which the particularities of the national cultures took their leave only ex post. He points also to the fact that the universal powers contain many particular traits. They are at the same particular powers which follow the imperialist tendency immanent to all powers.[21]

III. What Are the *Geisteswissenschaften* (Human Sciences)?

The German term *Geisteswissenschaften* seems to have appeared first,[22] according to Rothacker,[23] in the German translation of an English book, in

---

20 *Ibid.*, p. 169: Der Universalismus „spricht das Soll aus, daß die gestaltenreiche Menschheit sich die Pflicht aufzuerlegen habe: Eins zu werden." Es steht ihr „nicht nur die Tatsache der Mehrsprachigkeit, sondern die Tatsache ihrer eminenten Fruchtbarkeit entgegen."

21 *Ibid.*, p. 170.

22 This guess of Rothacker has in the mean time been corrected by research into the history of ideas. The first appearance of the term *Geisteswissenschaft* is in an anonymous publication of 1787 *Wer sind die Aufklärer?* (Who are the People who Enlighten?) although here *Geisteswissenschaft* means more pneumatology and the science of the angels and is therefore quite far away from its later meaning. Cf. A. DIEMER: Article „Geisteswisenschaften", in: J. RITTER (Ed.): *Historisches Wörterbuch der Philosophie*, Basel (Schwabe) 1974, Vol. 3, col. 211.

23 E. ROTHACKER: *Einleitung in die Geisteswissenschaften*, loc. cit., p. 6.

Schiel's[24] translation of the sixth book of John Stuart Mill's *System of Logic, Ratiocinative and Inductive* of 1843 titled „The Logic of the Moral Sciences". It is, indeed, remarkable that the German term *Geisteswissenschaften* is first used in its present meaning in a translation of the concept of the moral or mental sciences applied by Mill. The notion, if not the term, „Geisteswissenschaft", however, has been introduced by the disciples of Hegel although not by Hegel himself. Friedrich Theodor Vischer, a member of the Hegelian school, first speaks about a „science of the spirit" (*Wissenschaft des Geistes*).

In Hegel's system, the philosophy of the spirit forms the equivalent to the philosophy and science of nature in the realm of the social and covers all the moral, mental, political, and social sciences. Rothacker demonstrates that Dilthey, in his paper „Über das Studium der Geschichte der Wissenschaften vom Menschen, der Gesellschaft und dem Staate" (About the Study of the History of the Sciences of Man, of Society and of the State) of 1875, discussed Mill's „Logic of the Mental Sciences" under the title „Logik der Geisteswissenschaften".[25] Dilthey does, however, not yet accept the term *Geisteswissenschaften* for the sciences that Mill includes under the title „mental sciences". Dilthey calls these sciences „moral-political sciences". Only from the year 1883 on, from the publication of his *Einleitung in die Geisteswissenschaften. Versuch einer Grundlegung für das Studium der Gesellschaft und Geschichte* (Introduction to the Human Studies. An Essay for a Groundwork for the Study of Society and History) of 1883, Dilthey uses the term *Geisteswissenschaften* for the „whole of those sciences that have as their object the historical-societal reality".[26] It is with this work of Dilthey that the term „Geisteswissenschaften" becomes classical.[27]

---

24 J. ST. MILL: *Die induktive Logik. Eine Darlegung der philosophischen Principien wissenschaftlicher Forschung*, übersetzt von J. Schiel, Braunschweig (Vieweg) 1849.

25 W. DILTHEY: „Über das Studium der Geschichte der Wissenschaften vom Menschen, der Gesellschaft und dem Staate", in: W. DILTHEY: *Die geistige Welt. Einleitung in die Philosophie des Lebens. Erste Hälfte: Abhandlungen zur Grundlegung der Geisteswissenschaften, Gesammelte Schriften*, V. Band, Stuttgart (Teubner), Göttingen (Vandenhoeck & Ruprecht) 7th ed. 1982, pp. 31-73, here p. 56.

26 W. DILTHEY: *Einleitung in die Geisteswissenschaften. Versuch einer Grundlegung für das Studium der Gesellschaft und Geschichte, Gesammelte Schriften*, I. Band, Stuttgart (Teubner), Göttingen (Vandenhoeck & Ruprecht) 8th ed.

ROTHACKER'S THEORY OF THE *GEISTESWISSENSCHAFTEN*

The human sciences of the historical school do not aim at the analysis and normative guidance of moral and social action as it is the intention of the tradition of the moral sciences to which Mill still belongs. Rather they aim at the discovery, analysis, and positive, not yet normative understanding of the realm of the objective spirit in the Hegelian sense, of that realm of reality that is formed by history and society, by the culture and the institutions of a time and of a people, and by the spirit and style these peoples have developed in a certain historical epoch. The human sciences in the tradition of the *Geisteswissenschaften* do not aim at the mere history of facts and at historiography but at the understanding of the unifying spirit of an epoch and people.

Rothacker can therefore contend that truly historical thinking aims more at the unifying historical understanding of certain fields or systems of culture than at the knowledge of historical facts or at what traditionally is called history. „Truly historical thinking is more at home in the field of philological studies and studies of the history of art, of the history of law, and the history of religion than in those fields that are traditionally called ‚historical‘. ... What one calls ‚historical thinking‘, in the emphatic and dramatic use of these words does not aim primarily at the description of facts, but at the most congenial understanding of the appearances as being the result from an eminent logos, of styles, under which these facts can be classified."[28]

Nations and epochs develop a concrete style the norms of which are formulated in a dogmatic. These cultural dogmatics expound the cultural and aesthetic conventions and rules of an epoch and a nation that has adopted a

---

1979, p. 4: „Das Ganze der Wissenschaften, welche die geschichtlich-gesellschaftliche Wirklichkeit zu ihrem Gegenstande haben, wird in diesem Werke unter dem Namen der Geisteswissenschaften zusammengefaßt."

27 Cf. E. ROTHACKER: *Einleitung in die Geisteswissenschaften*, loc. cit., p. 9

28 E. ROTHACKER: *Die dogmatische Denkform in den Geisteswissenschaften und das Problem des Historismus*, loc. cit., p. 42: „Wahrhaft historisches Denken ist also mehr im philologischen und dementsprechend kunst-, rechts-, religionsgeschichtlichen Bereich zuhause als in dem, der traditionell ‚historisch‘ genannt wird ... Was man ‚Historisches Denken‘ in dem emphatischen und pathetischen Gebrauch dieser Worte nennt, zielt ja nicht primär auf Feststellung von Fakten, sondern auf die tunlichst kongeniale Erfassung von Erscheinungen des immanenten Logos, von Stilen, denen diese Fakten sich einordnen."

concrete culture. These styles, in the plural, of epochs and cultures are what the Historical School aims to understand by its *Geisteswissenschaften*.

Since historism acclaims the fact that different cultures develop different individual dogmatic styles it must face the problem of the possible clash or competition of these styles or the clash of civilizations. Rothacker admits this possibility or danger. Every cultural dogmatics start from a basic decision, a *Grund-* or *Vorentscheidung*, which is not deducable or explainable by causal factors, but is the result of decisions by intention and will. Only these basic decisions can be relativized, not the dogmatics that follow from them. The dogmatics are as they are and are in their own right for different cultures.

The irreducibility of the dogmatic element in the weltanschauung and style of a culture and of the acknowledgement of their equal worth and value when they prove to be equally fruitful and creative presents the greatest problem and challenge to historism: „The most difficult problem and the real crux of historism will remain for ever that a plurality of directions of creation (that can be formulated in different dogmatics) come up and stand up with the same claim to truth that transcends the mere correctness of the facts and theories expounded in them, that these many approaches to the creation of a culture compete with each other, and that they cannot be refuted for the time being."[29]

The final reason for the irreducible conflict between the different cultural dogmatics and cultures and for the relative instability of the human and social sciences is to be found in the instability of their object, the human life and the human institutions. The human and social sciences are instable because their object is instable whereas the natural sciences are more stable since their object, the laws of nature, is more stable. „The relative instability of the human sciences is caused by the instability of life."[30] By using the concept of science as being a field of culture, a concept assumed by the Historical School, the stability of the natural sciences can be interpreted as a particularly successful dogmatics, the dogmatics of the science of nature. It is particularly successful since it is particularly stable. Its stability, in turn, is founded in its objectivity. The claim of the natural sciences to „general valid-

---

29 *Ibid.*: „Das schwierigste Problem und die eigentliche Crux des Historismus bleibt allerdings dies, daß eine Mehrzahl von Schöpfungsrichtungen (formulierbar als Dogmatiken) über die Richtigkeit der in sie aufgenommenen Fakten und Theorien hinaus mit demselben Wahrheitsanspruch auftreten, miteinander konkurrieren und sich bis auf weiteres nicht widerlegen lassen."

30 *Ibid.*, p. 51.

ity" however is also caused by the fact that possible other directions of inquiry and therefore „research dogmatics" have reached massive general acceptance only in very rare cases.[31]

IV. Rothacker's Historism and Present Postmodernism

Rothacker's work is close to present postmodernist thought. It is furthermore interesting for today's human and social sciences for the following reasons:

First, Rothacker shares the emphasis on cultural pluralism with postmodernism.

Second, he shares the postmodern affect against the universal.

Third, he agrees with postmodernism, and particularly with Jean-François Lyotard, about the need to defend „the different" or the differences between the various cultures. Rothacker would probably have found very little difficulty in acclaiming Lyotard's „le différend" as the principle of individuation of cultures.

Fourth, Rothacker's insistence on the dogmatic character of different cultures equals Lyotard's emphasis of the irreducibility of the dogmatic claims of systems of laws and cultures, of the fact that the claims of cultural systems and of systems of law are irreducibly dogmatic, and of the fact that there exists no higher principle of law that could decide and reconcile the different dogmatic claims of systems of law and culture.

Lyotard is perhaps more radical than Rothacker in saying that the different systems of law just cannot understand each other and cannot reach a common frame of reference whereas Rothacker might contend that it is very difficult but not impossible to reconcile their claims to define the right.

Rothacker's historism and present postmodernism[32] diverge, however, in one crucial point: Rothacker shares with other historicists the belief that the

---

31 *Ibid.*, p. 49.

32 Cf. P. KOSLOWSKI: „Is Postmodernism a Neohistorism? On the Absoluteness and the Historicity of History", in: P. KOSLOWSKI (Ed.): *The Theory of Ethical Economy in the Historical School. Wilhelm Roscher, Lorenz von Stein, Gustav Schmoller, Wilhelm Dilthey and Contemporary Theory*, Berlin, Heidel-

human sciences are a means to understand other styles and cultures. They are not only means to understand one's own culture but also to understand alien cultures. The methodology of the human sciences is a tool for understanding intercultural differences. As this instrument, the hermeneutics of the Historical School are also a means for the conflict resolution between different cultures, and they can serve as such just because they do not deny the differences - in contrast to certain dogmatic forms of universalism.

On the other hand, they do not try to marginalize cultural differences and conflicts as it is the case in approaches of multi-culturalism which seem to assume that cultural differences just do not matter, must be kept up, and can simply be affirmed in a dogmatic pluralism.

Since economics is a cultural and human science which includes the analysis of the cultural determinants of the economy - that economics is a human science or *Geisteswissenschaft* is the conviction of all the authors of the Historical School from Schmoller and Dilthey to Rothacker and Spranger - it cannot be modeled according to the natural sciences. Rather economics must include the theory and method of understanding, the method of hermeneutics, in its methodology and tools of analysis. As an analysis of economic systems, economic cultures, and economic styles, the economics of the Historical Schools is a kind of economic theory that is *geisteswissenschaftlich* oder based on the methodology of the human sciences. In Rothacker's and the Historical School's point of view, economic theory must start from the humanities and must be founded on the analogy of the human sciences, not upon the analogy of the natural sciences. As the protagonist of a methodology, logics and systematics of the human sciences, Rothacker contributes to the logics and systematics of economic science as well.

V. Critique and Conclusion

Where lie the limits of Rothacker's theory of the human sciences? It seems that the critical feature of Rothacker's approach to the human sciences is to be found in its basic decision to look for the unifying spirit of a people and an epoch. Although this endeavour can be very fruitful and produce most

berg, New York, Tokyo (Springer) 1995, pp. 286-309 (= Studies in Economic Ethics and Philosophy, Vol. 7).

interesting studies on the spirit of a period of art or of literature, of law and of religion, there seems to be the tendency in Rothacker's work to overemphasize the unity of the spirit of a people and a period. One can rightfully ask the question whether the spirit of an epoch is the same in all of its fields of culture, the same in the visual art, in music, literature, law, religion, and philosophy. Is there e.g. one single and unified „spirit of romanticism" and of the period of Romanticism in all these fields of culture?

One can further ask whether the spirit of a people and period is unified in the sense that all creative authors of a people or period in question follow the same „objective spirit". Even if the existence of a certain dogmatic spirit of a period is admitted there remains the fact that there exist diverging and heterodox schools of thought and culture at the same time and in the same people. The whole problem of orthodoxy and heterodoxy is not mentioned in Rothacker's work.

This „over-unifying" tendency of Rothacker's thought can be demonstrated by his powerful synthesis of the results of German culture between 1750 and 1930 as „the German movement". Looking back from the 1990ies it seems that this is an over-unification of the different strands of German culture in the 180 years in question.

Despite its over-unifying tendencies, Rothacker's philosophy of the Historical School and his attempt to synthesize the endeavours of the particular disciplines of the human sciences with the endeavours of German Classical and Romantic literature as well as with those of the philosophy of German idealism is an impressive achievement of the theory of the human sciences and of the history of ideas.

Furtheron Rothacker's attempt to describe the common convictions shared between German Idealism and the human sciences of the Historical School is convincing. Although Rothacker's metaphysics and affirmative position towards the total historization of metaphysics in the Hegelian tradition is unacceptable from the point of view of speculative philosophy and theology, it is, nevertheless, correct to find in the principle of total historization the unifying principle between the Historical School and German Idealism.

Many thinkers of the Historical School and of its subdisciplines might, however, not have agreed with Rothackers synthesis. Particularly Leopold von Ranke would have pointed to the fact that the Historical School started as a critique of the over-historization of the absolute in Hegel and of his metaphysical historicism. There is no doubt, however, that there is a close

527

„metaphysical" relationship between German idealism and the *Geisteswis-senschaften* of the Historical School.

The over-historization of metaphysics and culture can be interpreted as the characteristic feature of the German culture between 1750 and 1930 in spite of the fact that other schools like positivism and the Nietzschean critique co-existed. Judging from the historical experience of our age, it can be said that this complete historization of being hindered historicism to recognize the limits of historization and the limits of relativizing the ethical and cultural standards. Even if one follows Rothacker's emphasis on the creativeness and legitimacy of different cultures and accepts his critique of a shallow universalism, one must maintain that there are meta-historical principles of right and wrong that must be upheld as the possible criteria for judging between those cultures that further humankind and those that make people ill or destroy the good life of a society.

Discussion Summary

ANNETTE KLEINFELD

Paper discussed:
PETER KOSLOWSKI: A Philosophy of the Historical School: Erich
                    Rothacker's Theory of the *Geisteswissenschaften*
                    (Human Sciences)

A first part of the discussion dealt with the two different traditions within the Historical School: the Hegelian stream on the one hand and the tradition to which Rothacker belongs on the other hand. Popper, for instance, subsummed Marx under the Historical School (RINGER). Certain similarities can be noticed between the English communist perspective towards economics and the position of Rothacker. Both of them are emphasizing the necessity to understand the dynamics of cultural change and the laws of economic culture (CASSON). Especially the value-aspect within the Historical School has its roots in the Hegelian position (CUBEDDU). However, the Hegelian tradition is more radical, considering everything as a form of "Entäußerung des Geistes", an exteriorisating realization of the spirit. Rothacker also criticizes this radical position, mainly because it neglects the particular. His intention is not to explain but to understand the taste, the style of a culture and its unifying spirit. According to him, all expressions of a culture, like its religion, language, art etc. are expressing the common spirit underlying this culture. This spirit shows itself, for instance, in a feeling of national unity or in a specific national mentality. Such a nationalistic or contemporary spirit was considererd as an important category. Although it is difficult to grasp in what it precisely consists, it is a fact that there are certain common styles in each country which play an important role for finding both, a national and an individual identity (KOSLOWSKI). The specific trait of Rothacker's understanding of the humanities (*Geistwissenschaften*) is the insistence on interpretation. This stress on an intuitive notion of the spirit was criticized by Max Weber, who objected against it that it was not able to replace abstract insight. The particular is not identical with the concrete (RINGER). Weber too was against the so called "iron cage" and saw the necessity to compensate the technical character of the modern world. However, the interpretation of ideographic thinking only as a form of compensation for technological modernisation is too harmless (KOSLOWSKI).

The differenciation between the term "historism" and "historicism" (ACHAM) corresponds to the two different streams mentioned above, i.e. the former is refering to the Historical School in the sense of Rothacker, the latter to the Hegelian position (KOSLOWSKI).

A second part of the discussion refered to the relationship between the Historism of Rothacker and the position of Habermas respectively a postmodern position like the one of McIntyre. Does historism provide the superior solution in order to reconcile tradition with the presence (CHMIELEWSKI)? In the respect of understanding different cultures the hermeneutical position may claim to be superior indeed both to universalistic theories and to postmodernism. This might be the reason why Habermas to a certain degree turned to hermeneutics, however using it mainly in an ethical sense (KOSLOWSKI, RINGER). Lyotard´s position on the other hand, though not being universalistic, lacks of a theory of empathy. Dilthey played the major role for the development of hermeneutics, in spite of the fact that his system stayed incomplete (KOSLOWSKI). The difference between Rothacker's understanding of historism and postmodernism for which KABELE asked lies mainly in a specific philosophy of the mind (*Geistphilosophie*) that does not exist in the works of Lyotard, Bataille or other representatives of postmodernism. There is however also a parallel consisting in the emphasis on the will: Rothacker's irrational will that he considers as the basis of all action corresponds to the creative will (*Gestaltungswille*) functioning as an aesthetical category within the postmodern discussion (KOSLOWSKI).

Besides, Historism and Postmodernism have in common a cultural approach in the field of economics. According to this view, the economic system is a form of culture itself that cannot be considered separately from the specific culture in which it is embedded. Today's economic culture however is in fact a universalistic culture as phenomena like the woldwide implementation of fast food and Coca Cola have demonstrated during the last years and which is now shown by the process of economic globalization. Are the moments of particularity and of cultural specificity still of any impact for this development (NOPPENEY)?

DISCUSSION SUMMARY

The relevance of the method of hermeneutics for economics in general which has been stressed by the representatives of the older Historical School like Schmoller, or by Eduard von Spranger, gains an additional importance with regards to the process of economic globalization today. So far, little work has been done in order to develop a cultural philosophy of the economy. Rothacker himself did not apply his insights to the economy (KOSLOWSKI).

A third part of the discussion concentrated on the comparison of Rothacker's position with actual tendencies of the social sciences. Today, there are two completely different perspectives: the perspective of the social sciences and the perspective of the humanities or *Geisteswissenschaften* (CUBEDDU). Originally, the perspective of the humanities in the sense of a hermeneutical culture-oriented scientific approach was a major insight with regards to all the social sciences. Especially the theory of Eduard von Spranger had a great influence here. As a conseqence of the radical break with this tradition these insights were forgotten too, and have not been taken into account within the social sciences anymore (KOSLOWSKI).

Conclusion

Chapter 21

Germany, Japan and National Economics: An Alternative Paradigm of Modernity?

DAVID WILLIAMS

Scripture tells us that the truth will set us free. But we moderns hold that only freedom permits the discovery of that liberating truth. This search assumes the existence of an inexhaustible empirical terrain which awaits exploration. But there is another enabling assumption, one equally important but often denied, at work here: intellectual pluralism or the belief that there is more than one method of doing sound social science. The goal of this essay is to show, in a concise and reasoned way, why Friedrich List and the German Historical School stand at the heart of the contemporary defence of such pluralism, of this social scientific freedom to choose.

The European tradition of thought is a mansion with many rooms. While the sunshine of scientific scrutiny may now powerfully illuminate one room or another of this tradition, other chambers remain shrouded in darkness, sometimes for centuries. But these obscured chambers, and the ideas that shelter in them, lie in wait, like souls, poised and patient, for the age which will, either from curiosity or necessity, resurrect them. This essay is a call for such a rebirth.

DAVID WILLIAMS

I. Friedrich List: Modern Master

Time for dissent

Nietzsche insisted that the life of the mind is a zone of unceasing struggle between alternative visions of existence and truth. This struggle sets text against text. Contemporary preferences for pulp fiction over romantic poetry or Roland Barthes over Racine or Nietzsche himself over Scripture are crucial indices of textual wars won or lost.

This battle of the books has been radically redefined by the postmodern condition. The mental torpor fostered by television and other popular media increasingly conspires with our high-tech obsessions to preclude generous reading in the old manner. One consequence of this revolution in how we spend the hours we set aside for reflection and cultivation is a new ignorance, less of the great names of the past than of the eccentric dissenters and proponents of minority or unorthodox ideas, interpretations and insights.

The fast pace of modern life contrasts disturbingly with the luxuries of past generations who have had both the leisure and the inclination to explore the neglected corners of the Western mind. To say as much is not to defend dilettantism or a pedantic weakness for minutiae. Quite the contrary, the goal of the contributors to books as recent as *Rediscoveries: Some Neglected Modern European Political Thinkers*, edited by John A. Hall, is to re-assay the ore of the European tradition lest some marvellous intellectual gem be lost through haste or oversight.[1]

Such alertness defines the whole programme of inspired contrariness and oppositional thinking that has driven the labours of Sir Isaiah Berlin. To argue 'against the current' is to insist on the centrality of the canonic tradition in order to have something tough and lasting to tilt against.[2] The psychology of Berlin's project could not, in this sense, be more different from the urge to debunk tradition, to 'de-throne it', that animates the recent revival of the study

---

1   JOHN A. HALL (Ed.): *Rediscoveries: Some Neglected Modern European Political Thinkers*, Oxford (Claredon Press) 1986.

2   In discussing Berlin's oeuvre, writers as different as Mark Lilla and John Gray stress Berlin's critical posture towards liberalism. But in the present climate of political correctness, it is equally important to recognize how much the role of canonicity, as a tradition to dissent from, matters to Berlin's enterprise.

536

of the history of political thought in Europe.[3] When Berlin urges us to return to Herder or Herzen or Hamann, he stands at far remove from the empirical anarchy and academic nihilism which threaten the viability and relevance of the history of ideas today.[4] It is with Berlin's canonic contrariness in mind that I seek here to quicken the pace of the rediscovery of Friedrich List (1778-1846), perhaps the most consequential neglected thinker of our times.

Rediscovering Friedrich List

Intellectual life, like national politics, is a daily plebiscite. Each day, whom we read or quote or think about contributes in ways large and small to the survival and continuing relevance of this or that thinker. Economic thought is as vulnerable to this plebiscite as any other vocation of the mind. When I was in secondary school, in the 1960s, it was still possible to find, in the bookshops of suburban Los Angeles, the name 'Friedrich List' mentioned even in brief introductions of economic thought for the general public. Eighteenth- and nineteenth-century theories of mercantilism were still regarded as a body of *respectable* ideas. Later, in my first course in economics at UCLA, the lecturer raged against the theoretical pretensions of Marxist economics and what he saw as the absurdities of the economic policies of Soviet communism, but it was mercantilism, particularly the notion of 'infant industries', which gave him pause.

Since the 1960s, economic theory, both academic and popular, has been shaken by a series of revolutions. The change in what constitutes sound economic policy associated with Hayek and Friedman, with Thatcher and Reagan, has redrawn the cosmos of economic argument. The stature of mercantilism has not escaped the pressure of this revolution. Despite the recent campaign in *The Atlantic*, the American intellectual monthly, for a List revival and the publication of books such as James Fallows' *Looking at the Sun: The Rise of the New East Asian Economic and Political System*, it appears

---

3   IAIN HAMPSHER-MONK: *A History of Modern Political Thought*, Oxford (Blackwell) 1992, p. ix.
4   My dissatisfactions with the thrust of much of the recent scholarship produced by historians of political thought forms a *leitmotif* of D. WILLIAMS: *Japan and the Enemies of Open Political Science*, London (Routledge) 1996; particularly in chapters 4 and 11.

that national economics may be gradually receding into hibernation.[5] Or so I might have been led to believe had I never gone to Japan.

In a series of lectures delivered by Otsuka Hisao, one of the most influential Japanese historians of the post-war period, at International Christian University in Tokyo during the early 1970s, I encountered a version of List's system and a recognition of the importance of the German Historical School, particularly Gustav von Schmoller, which was all but unthinkable in the United States at the time. This was ironic because, as Otsuka made clear, a precise genealogy of ideas links the seventeenth-century English mercantilists and Alexander Hamilton, the American founding father, with List's own reflections on protectionism.[6]

In this short essay, I would like to nominate List as a modern master. To support this nomination, I offer an unorthodox interpretation of the modern rise of Germany and Japan which stresses the impact of the Historical School on both countries. It is the potent blend of the facts of the German and Japanese economic experience with the ideas of the Historical School which allows one to ask whether national economics offers an alternative paradigm of modernization and modernity. Second, it is crucial to understand that List borrowed, adapted and developed a series of policy ideas that worked. But such inspired practicality, and the national ethos which underpinned it, was not exhausted by nineteenth-century protectionism. To illustrate the point, I propose a Listian gloss of the recent troubles of Mazda, the Japanese auto maker. Then I review some of the objections raised about List's relevance at the 1994 Studies in Economic Ethics and Philosophy conference.

Finally, I would like to comment on the methodological and moral issues implicit in the claim which I issued in *Japan: Beyond the End of History* that

---

5   JAMES FALLOWS: *Looking at the Sun: The Rise of the New East Asian Economic and Political System*, New York (Pantheon Books) 1994. While economic historians such as Eric Roll continue to include summaries of List's views on economic theory, it remains to be seen whether Roll's presentation of List's ideas under the rubric of "German Romanticism" is best understood as a way of fending off List's detractors rather than as a failure on Roll's part to appreciate List's true importance. See ERIC ROLL: *A History of Economic Thought*, revised edition, London, Boston (Faber & Faber) 1992 (fifth edition), pp. 204-207.

6   See, in particular, OTSUKA HISAO: *Otsuka Hisao Chosakushu, Dai-roku-kan, Kokumin Keizai* (The Collected Works of Otsuka Hisao, Volume 6: National Economics), Tokyo (Iwanami Shoten) 1969.

List has been one of the 'secret kings' and intellectual prophets of the twentieth century.[7] If the last half of the present century appears to have convinced many people that 'Europe is nothing but a grave yard' (Dostoyevsky), then the only way to correct the present intellectual imbalance between the Old World and the New is 'to resurrect our dead'.

II. Germany, Japan and National Economics: An Alternative Paradigm of Modernity?

Turning points and revelations

Hegel taught the world to understand itself historically. He took the long view. But the doctrine of 'the cunning of reason' also encourages one to suspect that history may travel underground, like a river, for great distances. The often-misunderstood doctrine of 'the end of history' merely urges us to pay special attention when this underground river bursts into view. The death of European feudalism that Hegel heard in the canon fire at the Battle of Jena of 1806 is an example of such a moment. The French Revolution is another.

The importance of 1945 as the decisive turning point of the twentieth century remains an issue of intense debate. But that violent year serves as a benchmark of extraordinary, of the hidden strength which rescued the Germans and the Japanese from national catastrophe. The ashes of Berlin and Tokyo, Dresden and Hiroshima, obscured the potential of these two nations, despite horrific losses, both human and material, for almost instanteous national reconstruction. Beneath the rubble something still gleamed. It was the economic machine, archored in light or heavy manufacturing, that had been carefully fostered since the middle of the nineteenth century.

In other words, there may be moral reasons for arguing that 'the German economic miracle is ironically but exactly proportionate to the extent of ruin

---

7   In English, see Friedrich List: *The National System of Political Economy*, trans. by Sampson S. Lloyd, London (Longmans, Green and Co) 1922; DAVID WILLIAMS: *Japan: Beyond the End of History*, London (Routledge) 1994. Hannah Arendt applied the expression "secret king of thought" to Heidegger, but it may be also be applied, albeit in a different sense, to List.

in the Reich'.[8] It is nevertheless equally vital, in any discussion of List's ideas, to understand that the extraordinary post-war prosperity of Germany and Japan is unthinkable without the foundations laid under Bismarck and the Meiji oligarchy for what the Japanese call *'kokuryoku'* or national strength or power.

The road from List to Erhard

What the Japanese and the Germans accomplished between the 1860s and 1933 permanently modified world history. Not even the destructive force of the great European civil war of 1914-1945 could bury this achievement. This truth does not contradict the claim that '(West) Germany's economic success after World War Two was not based on nationalist economic policies', but it should temper the liberal urge to relegate the contribution of List's theories to Germany's *'kokuryoku'* to the remoteness of the mid-nineteenth century.[9] The impulse to banish List from contemporary concern is the stuff of liberal mythology, and must be combatted.

The ways in which the recent recession have again exposed the tramlines of world history explains why. It is a commonplace of economic analysis of the troubled 1990s to contend that the German and Japanese models have exhausted their usefulness. Both the 1995-96 crisis of Japan's banking system and the hollowing-out of German manufacturing are cited as evidence of the limits of the post-war models. More telling, the Japanese commitment to the labour-market rigidities of the 'salary-man' ideal, no less than the deep involvement of labour unions in German corporate decision-making, suggests that capitalist 'down-sizing' (if that indeed is what is required to cut German and Japanese wage costs to make both economies more competitive in global markets) will be hard to achieve for the foreseeable future. Hence, the conclusion which is being so widely drawn: that the Germans and the Japanese are caught not in web of temporary cyclical difficulties but in a crisis of economic system.

These are not the only lessons that the 1990s teach. Despite the financial burdens involved, German unification and the collapse of the Soviet empire in Central and Eastern Europe have opened the way for Germany to reclaim

---

8 GEORGE STEINER: *In Bluebeard's Castle: Some Notes towards the Redefinition of Culture*, New Haven, Connecticut (Yale University Press) 1971, p. 59.

9 Franz Waldernberger, Cologne University, private correspondence.

her natural spheres of economic influence. The circulatory system of German investment, and other forms of economic organization and penetration first created before 1914, is already pumping with its old vigour. When Keynes observed in 1919 that before the Great War 'The whole of Europe east of the Rhine thus fell into the German industrial orbit, and its economic life adjusted accordingly', he was describing a phenomenon which has now outlived not only the most destructive war in human history but almost a half-century of communist economic abuse as well.[10] Imperial Germany created permanent changes in the economic of life of Central and Eastern Europe which outlasted war, fascism and communism. Such durability has a precise parallel in the Japanese recovery of their old markets denied to them by the ideological divisions imposed on East Asian business and commerce by the iron disciplines of the cold war.

The permanent restructuring of the main patterns of global trade and investment achieved by imperial Germany and Meiji Japan challenge any purely liberal reading of the economic history of these two nations. So does the second lesson, the 1990s recesssion. This insight is best formulated as a question: if Germany, even more than Japan, is so economically liberal, then why is it so threatened by the growth of global markets for capital and labour? That the Soviet Union was inevitably crushed by the 'end of history' and the triumph of liberal capitalism was predictable from Fukuyama's premises.[11] That Japan is now under assault from the same forces is less surprising if one acknowledges that the Japanese have never regarded their economic system as particularly liberal. But the West Germany of Ludwig Erhard and Helmut Kohl? How could it be that this Germany is not, as it were, liberal enough?

The answer to this question should force economic liberals to return to List and the 'pre-history' of the Federal Republic of Germany. This pre-history provides the indispensable context for one of the most important debates of the 1990s: why the American and British models of economic policy remain vital while the German, French and Japanese versions of the 'mixed

---

10 JOHN MAYNARD KEYNES: *The Economic Consequences of the Peace*, The Collected Writings of John Maynard Keynes, Volume II, London (Macmillan/ Cambridge University Press) 1971, p. 10.

11 FRANCIS FUKUYAMA: "The End of History?", *The National Interest*, Summer 1989 issue, pp. 3-18.

economy' are under unprecedented challenge.[12] It is my argument that pace the historical amnesia of German economic liberals, the German and Japanese versions of the mixed economy bear the stamp of the statist, nationalist and collectivist philosophies of economic organization and statecraft which defined German and Japanese public and private practice before 1945.

Anti-Enlightenment

This continental inheritance--anti-Smith, anti-Ricardo and anti-Mill--secured the freedom to develop a 'liberal' economic system that departed at numerous points from the individualistic, market-driven ideals that have triumphed in the English-speaking world during the past three decades. Which stands closer to the Catholic social democratic ideals which helped to underwrite the creation of the post-war German welfare state: the social insurance programme of Bismarck or the Anglo-American libertarian insistence that 'society does not exist'?

In *Japan: Beyond the End of History*, I argued that modern Germany and Japan illustrate, with unique force, an alternative tradition in modern public policy, one quite different in important ways from the Anglo-American approach.[13] Bismarck's Germany was heir to a triple legacy. First, there was the nationalist ideology of Herder and Fichte (both ornaments of Japanese nationalist thought). Their ideas consciously blurred the distinction between 'state' and 'nation', between *Staat* and *Volk* (In Japanese, *kokka-shugi* may mean either nationalism or statism). The second legacy was the tradition of effective state administration inherited from Brandenburg and Prussia, a tradition nourished from late medieval times to the reforms of Stein after Napoleon's defeat. This tradition underwrote Weber's conclusion that the efficiencies of the modern bureaucracy and the modern corporation arise from the same source, an idea so incomprehensible to the English mind that not even the formidable Mill could grasp it.[14] Third, there was the influential body of

---

12 One is mindful of the pressure the current climate exerts on the arguments contained, for example, in: ANDREW SHONFIELD: *In Defence of the Mixed Economy*, Oxford, New York (Oxford University Press) 1984.

13 DAVID WILLIAMS, *op. cit.* Particularly the chapter titled "Japan, Germany and the Alternative Tradition in Modern Public Policy", pp. 117-132.

14 Contrast the comments on bureaucracy in MILL's *Principles of Political Economy* (1848) with those of MAX WEBER in the posthumously published *Econo-*

mercantilist policy insight cultivated under the star of what List called 'national economy'.

War and national emergency decisively coloured this Prusso-German approach to the cultivation of bureaucratic effectiveness and national strength. Mindful of the threat posed by Western colonization, the leaders of the Japanese state were instinctively drawn to the German model. The findings of the Iwakura Mission, dispatched by the Meiji government between 1871-73 to report on conditions in America and Europe, leave no room for doubt on this point. The practical wisdom of this Japanese elective affinity for things German was confirmed when Prussia crushed Napoleon III in 1870. The impact of German law, administrative practice, constitutional philosophy and, perhaps most important of all, German mercantilist thought, on the Meiji elite is beyond dispute.

Hence the suspicion that German and Japanese economic and political practice forms the core of an alternative paradigm of modernity. List cannot be responsibly confined to a dusty corner of economic history called 'the protection of infant industries'. Quite the contrary, List sketched a programme for late-developing nations to catch up with the British and the Americans who have successively dominated the world economy. In this way, List's ideas helped to transform the history of the modern world.

III. Listian Logic in Germany and Japan Today

Ideas that work

The assumption that List's place in the history of economic thought is limited to his theory of 'infant industries' is indefensible. This approach to List's ideas is designed to belittle his significance. Such feeble analysis should be contrasted with this Japanese assessment of mercantilism during the key period in the key country at issue: Germany between the 1830s and 1870s:

> Drawing on the experience of the 1818 Prussian tariff law, the German Customs Union was brought into effect in 1834. The impact of

---

my and Society (1922). The issue figures prominently in: DAVID WILLIAMS: *Japan and the Enemies of Open Political Science*, London (Routledge) 1996.

this legislation was promptly felt, and from the latter half of the 1830s German industrialization proceeded at a rapid pace. By the early 1860s, the customs union covered a wide territory (all of Germany outside the old free towns of the Hansa). The result was that by the beginning of the 1870s Germany had managed to transform herself from a net importer of heavy manufactures to a net exporter, and this revolution was achieved despite the continuing domination by the British of the international division of economic labour that prevailed in the middle of the nineteenth century.[15]

A century later, these same ideas were put to work in order to create transform Japan, South Korea and Taiwan into globally competitive manufacturing powers. The rise of these industrial economies signalled the renewal of Asian energies after centuries of decay, dependence and defeat. It also marked the end of the era of Western global hegemony. On both counts, the impact of national economics on the making of the twentieth century may properly be described as revolutionary. It allows one to conclude that Friedrich List was the intellectual godfather of Asia's modern economic miracle.

Mazda and National Economics

These are strong claims for the contemporary relevance of national economics. Here, some of these claims will be tested against assessments of List's thought aired recently in Germany. But before doing so, I would like to offer an interpretation of one of the Japanese dramas of the 1990s recession which highlights List's usefulness as a guide to understanding the pyschology of Japanese economic nationalism.

In the spring of 1996, Henry Wallace, an Scots-born executive of the Ford Motor Company became president of Mazda, Japan's fifth largest car manufacturer. Wallace's appointment marked the effective takeover of Mazda by Ford. This was the first time foreign capital had won control of a significant share of Japanese domestic car production since the expulsion of General Motors and Ford from Japan in the late 1930s.

---

15 TSURADA TOSHIMASA: *Sengo Nihon no Sangyo Seisaku* (Industrial policy in post-war Japan), Tokyo (Nihon Keizai Shinbun-sha) 1982, p. 9. The translation is from DAVID WILLIAMS: *Japan: Beyond the End of History*, op. cit, p. 131.

AN ALTERNATIVE PARADIGM OF MODERNITY?

Mazda is the largest economic enterprise in Hiroshima, a city with about one million inhabitants. It is estimated that, directly or indirectly, the car maker accounts for one quarter of all economic activity in city. If Ford decides to move Mazda's production facilities abroad to exploit cheaper wages, this may, over the short-term and perhaps the long-term as well, generate high levels of local unemployment. Such concerns matter because the destiny of this company town is now, to a degree almost unprecedented in modern Japanese history, in the hands of a foreigner who has an infamous reputation as a specialist in corporate restructuring or 'down-sizing'. Whether Mr. Wallace's assiduous pursuit of his private economic interest will rebound to the benefit of the citizens of Hiroshima is now the question of the hour. This is the gamble which they have been condemned to take.

Market forces and private sector failure have reduced Hiroshima to an experiment in Smithian economics. The whole thrust of List's ideal of national economic sovereignty seeks to preclude the need for such experiments. Many Japanese have concluded that nothing could have been done to prevent Mazda's takeover, given their country's reluctant acceptance of the liberal rules of the globalizing world order. But such acquiescence is frequently qualified by the hope that someday soon Japanese economic strength will allow Hiroshima to slip Ford's leash.

To regard Ford's takeover of Mazda as a national defeat--and this is the way it is viewed in Japan--is entirely consistent with the fundamental nationalist impulse which animates List's thought. This contrasts powerfully with the singular inability of classical economic thinking, even in its modern reformed guise, to deal satisfactorily either with the claims of national identity or with the developmental role of the nation as an economic actor. As a result, the vigilant defence of economic sovereignty through national strength has defined corporate strategies and public policymaking in modern Japan, South Korea, Taiwan, Singapore and Malaysia in ways that neo-classical economists are able neither to explain nor to accept. To repeat, List's *The National System of Political Economy* offers more than a theory of how to promote infant industries. It is a guidebook on how to defend national autonomy amidst the shifting currents of global market forces. List can be dismissed only if one rejects that the importance of *national* economic well-being and self-government.

List in Germany today

In 1994 the Hannover Conference of the Studies in Economic Ethics and Philosophy (SEEP) met to discuss the contemporary relevance of Friedrich List and the Older Historical School. Before reviewing the views on Friedrich List aired at this meeting, it might be useful to restate the four key assumptions of the Historical School:

(1) Politics has priority over economics.

(2) Positive economics, after Smith, is too narrowly focused on 'price-quantity-relations'.

(3) Community, not the monadic individual, is the lynch-pin of economic reflection, properly conceived.

(4) Economics must be theoretical enough to be true, but practical enough to be effective in the real world.

In treating the 'Older Historical School', Birger P. Priddat spoke at the SEEP conference on the 'Intention and Failure of W. Roscher's Historical Method of National Economics', and this presentation, together with an unpublished paper on List himself, provided an opportunity for a discussion of the work and relevance of List, summarized by Bettina Löhnert.[16]

The opinions offered about national economics suggest that the influence of political and economic liberalism makes it very difficult to paint a just portrait of List's stature today. He may be best known for his advocacy of protective tariffs, but his reasons for doing so outflank the pedestrian objections repeated so tirelessly in conventional textbooks of positivist economics where the role of aggressive protectionism in fostering industrial power of the front rank, first in Britain, then Germany, the United States and Japan, is consistently denied.

To describe Listian theory as a justification for 'state interference in the economy' is to surrender to a persuasive definition of List's project, that is to describe national economics in the hostile and distorting language of neo-classical economics. To bring positivist ideas, such as 'efficient allocation', for example, into play when attempting to introduce List's ideas is inherently biased and unscientific. Contrary to the claims of rational choice theorists,

---

16 See PETER KOSLOWSKI (Ed.): *The Theory of Ethical Economy in the Historical School: Wilhelm Roscher, Lorenz von Stein, Gustav Schmoller, Wilhelm Dilthey and Contemporary Theory*, Berlin (Springer-Verlag) 1995, pp. 15-38.

the mere existence of pressure groups does not preclude an effective industrial policy, it just means that the institutions of state power and collective public-sector will must find ways to finesse them. As for the proposal that East Europeans should ignore the teachings of Listian national economics because they have hardly any products which can be successfully marketed abroad, one is inevitably reminded that positivist economists believed that post-war Japan should have confined itself to light manufacturing and the export of cheap toys. It was thinkers such as List, not the advocate of neo-classical economics, who encouraged the Japanese to dream that they, too, could one day become formidable exporters of steel, cars and semi-conductors.

In a German context, there is also an inevitable and wholly understandable temptation to resist Listian ideas on the grounds that nationalism may be dangerous. But the contribution of mercantilism to the rise of Japan and East Asia will never be grasped if one evokes the doctrine of individualistic ethics *before* a fair and balanced understanding of national economics has been achieved.

IV. German Renaissance: The Historical School and the Renewal of the Mind of Europe

Methods and morals

The systematic denial of this East Asian achievement continues to this day, most scandalously in the writings of Paul Krugman, the American economist and controversialist[17]. This denial is a stain on Western social science. It provides ample grounds for seeking an end to the monopoly exerted by positivism on the way economics is taught in so many of the world's universities today. In methodological terms, the rediscovery of List points to the need for the uncompromising defence of empiricism against the procrustean dogmatism of economic positivism. In this battle, the empiricist is the defender of open social science and methodological pluralism.[18] Those in

---

17 See, for example, PAUL KRUGMAN: "The Myth of Asia's Miracle", *Foreign Affairs*, November-December 1994, pp. 62-78.

18 This is the main argument developed in: DAVID WILLIAMS: *Japan and the Enemies of Open Political Science*, op. cit.

search of still more reasons for reviving the Historical School need look no further than its instinctive defence of empiricism against the nomological impulse which perpetually tempts both the metaphysician and the positivist.

More is involved in this plea than methodology. For much of the past half century, too much of the burden of sustaining the adventure of the Western mind has fallen on the shoulders of the New World. The intellectual condition of Europe still suffers from formidable losses, both human and material. The contrast between the mental vitality of the United States and the impression of enervation that has until very recently characterized the European intellect is the case in point. Only the extraordinary flowering of French thought since the war offers powerful evidence of the greatness which might have been achieved had the rest of Europe escaped, to a like degree, the massive slaughter which unfolded between 1933 and 1945.

From catastrophe to renaissance

Nowhere, outside Eastern Europe, has the weight of this cataclysm been felt more strongly than in Germany, in so many ways the intellectual powerhouse of continental Europe since the age of Kant, Goethe and Gauss. When we mourn the loss, it is almost inevitable to ask, yet again, how this tragedy was allowed to happen and how can it be prevented from happening again. Any deliberation over the fate and future of the German Historical School must touch on this controversy. This is because Listian mercantilism represents a powerful counter-Enlightenment vision of modernity laced with a set of explosive, even dangerous, ideas. Jacob Viner, no mercantilist, sets out what he believed to be the main tenets of the mercantilist school, ancient or modern:

> I believe that practically all mercantilists, whatever the period, country, or status of the particular individual, would have subscribed to all of the following propositions: (1) wealth is an absolutely essential means to power, whether for security or for aggression; (2) power is essential or valuable as a means to the acquisition and retention of wealth; (3) wealth and power are each proper ultimate ends of national policy; (4) there is long-run harmony between these ends, although in particular circumstances it may be necessary for a time to make eco-

nomic sacrifices in the interest of military security and therefore of longrun prosperity.[19]

Although Viner fails to grasp the central spirit of mercantilism-patriotism and solidarity with one's fellow countrymen as part of a moral community with a historic destiny, his recapitulation does demonstrate the range and realism of mercantilist reflection. But it also underscores the fact that nineteen-century mercantilism flourished in an intellectual climate in which moral callousness, muscular Christianity and social Darwinism defined the spirit of the age. These ideas did not necessarily cause the horrors of 1914-1945, but they did little to inhibit them.

In re-examining the legacy of the Historical School, there has been an understandable desire to turn away from the rhetoric of 'realpolitik' and the *Volkgeist* which defined so much of the intellectual horizon of pre-Hitlerite Europe. One consequence has been a new stress on the essential but ambiguous term 'ethical economy' in the drive to revive the Historical School. Such ambiguities have their uses. They point to the body of objective insights and theories produced by the Historical School which remain untainted. But Peter Koslowski is certainly correct to conclude that:

> Compared to the social, economic and humane sciences (*Geisteswissenschaften*) of the other Western countries, the German social and economic sciences are characterized by a rather significant lost of tradition which, in the long run, must have damaging effects.[20]

One of these damning effects has been the failure of European thinkers to resist the intellectual bullying and hubris of, to cite a prime example, the Chicago school of positivist economics. It is inconceivable that List, Schmoller or Weber would not have risen to the challenge of routing this school's exaggerated claims to scientific pre-eminence. Germany's loss of tradition is not Germany's loss alone.

There is, of course, a moral dimension to this loss. George Steiner has lamented the 'dissolution' of the language of Goethe, Heine and Kleist which began not long after List's ideas started to be exploited to lay the economic

---

19 JACOB VINER: *The Long View and the Short: Studies in Economic Theory and Policy*, New York (Free Press) 1958, p. 286.

20 PETER KOSLOWSKI: "Economics as Ethical Economy in the Tradition of the Historical School", in: PETER KOSLOWSKI (Ed.), *op. cit.*, p. 11.

foundations for what would become the new Prussian-German empire.[21] *Das Nazionale System der politischen Ökonomie* reads, certainly in translation, as if it might have been written by Mill or Tocqueville, but it must be asked just how much Droysen, Schmoller or even Weber contributed not only to 'the academicism and ponderousness of German as it was written by the pillars of learning and society between 1870 and the First World War' but also to 'the pomp and mystification' of the 'Potsdam style'.[22] In the face of such criticism, and the German catastrophe which gives it force, it is perfectly understandable that many scholars might prefer to turn away from the past and pay the price of a lost tradition.

There are Japanese analogies to this dissent and loss of tradition. In his *Gendai Seiji no Shiso to Kodo* (Thought and Behaviour in Modern Japanese Politics), Maruyama Masao, perhaps Japan's most influential political thinker, attempts to trace the twisted path which transformed the Japanese, another nation of great modernizers, into the victims of ultra-nationalism.[23] Read closely, Maruyama's treatise is also an essay on language, on the Japanese gift not only for obscuring the true locus of power and responsibility but also for slippery vagueness and self-serving ambiguity when confronted with unspeakable behaviour.

Yet it is revealing that Maruyama works in the idiom of German idealism. He describes how the Japanese critical spirit, the spirit that broke the grip of feudalism, weakened and succumbed to militarism and authoritarianism as the loss of *shutaisei (Subjektivität)*.[24] The scarred story of the modernization of Japan and Germany does yield to Hegelian gloss. But any moral critique remains vulnerable to the fallacy of moralism (the belief that the correct ethical stance guarantees the correct scientific judgment) as long as it does not address the other half of the equation: how two peoples, two latecomers to modernity, managed to re-channel the global river of commerce, manufacturing, finance and, yes, *power*, in ways that have altered the course of modern world history. This double-barrelled question looms large in any

---

21 GEORGE STEINER: "The Hollow Miracle", *Language and Silence*, London (Faber & Faber) 1985, p. 119.

22 *Ibid.*

23 MARUYAMA MASAO: *Gendai Seiji no Shiso to Kodo*, Tokyo (Mirai-sha) 1964. In English, see: *Thought and Behaviour in Modern Japanese Politics*, ed. by Ivan Morris, London (Oxford University Press) 1969.

24 See, for example, MARUYAMA MASAO: *Chusei to Hangyaku* (Loyalty and betrayal), Tokyo (Chikuma-shobo) 1992.

reconsideration of the Historical School and its contemporary relevance. Today we have the moral reserves to tackle it. This is crucial because there can be no revival of what T.S. Eliot proudly called 'the mind of Europe' without a German renaissance.

List of Authors and Discussants

KARL ACHAM is Professor of Sociology at the University of Graz, Graz, Austria.

VLADIMIR S. AVTONOMOV is Professor of Economics at the Institute of World Economy and International Relations, Moscow, Russia.

JEFF BIDDLE is Professor of Economics at Michigan State University, East Lansing, Michigan, USA.

RAYMOND BOUDON is Professor of Sociology at the University of Paris-Sorbonne, Paris, France.

MARK CASSON is Professor of Economics at the University of Reading, Reading, England.

ADAM J. CHMIELEWSKI is Assistant Professor of Philosophy at the University of Wroclaw, Wroclaw, Poland.

RICARDO FERNANDO CRESPO is Professor of Philosophy at the University of Mendoza, Mendoza, Argentina.

RAIMONDO CUBEDDU is Professor of Political Philosophy at the University of Pisa, Pisa, Italy.

RAIMUND DIETZ is Senior Researcher at the Vienna Institute for Comparative Economic Studies (WIIW), Vienna, Austria.

EIRIK G. FURUBOTN is Research Associate, Private Enterprise Research Center, Texas A&M University, College Station, Texas, USA.

VITANTONIO GIOIA is Professor of History of Economic Thought at the University of Macerata, Macerata, Italy.

TETSUSHI HARADA is Professor of History of Social Thought at Yokkaichi University, Yokkaichi, Japan.

JIRI KABELE is Professor of Sociology at Charles University Prague, Prague, Czech Republic.

ANNETTE KLEINFELD, Forschungsinstitut für Philosophie Hannover - Hannover Institute of Philosophical Research, Germany.

PETER KOSLOWSKI is director of the Forschungsinstitut für Philosophie Hannover and its Centre for Ethical Economy and Business Culture, and

Professor of Philosophy and Political Economy at the University of Witten/Herdecke, Germany.

VOLKER KRUSE is lecturer in Sociology at the University of Bielefeld, Bielefeld, Germany.

FRIEDRICH LENGER is Professor of History at the University of Erlangen, Erlangen, Germany.

BETTINA LÖHNERT, Forschungsinstitut für Philosophie Hannover - Hannover Institute of Philosophical Research, Germany.

VLADIMIR MAGUN is Professor of Sociology at the Russian Academy of Sciences, Moscow, Russia.

LUBOMÍR MLČOCH is Professor of Economics at the Institute of Economic Studies, Charles University Prague, Prague, Czech Republic.

D. E. MOGGRIDGE is Professor of Economics at the University of Toronto, Toronto, Canada.

UDO NEUGEBAUER is research assistent at the Institute of Vocational Education (Berufs-, Wirtschafts- und Technikpädagogik) at the University of Stuttgart, Stuttgart, Germany.

CLAUS NOPPENEY is writing his PhD thesis at the University of St. Gallen, St. Gallen, Switzerland.

GUY OAKES is Professor of Philosophy at Monmouth University, West Long Branch, New Jersey, USA.

FRITZ RINGER is Mellon Professor of History at the University of Pittsburgh, Pittsburgh, Pennsylvania, USA.

WARREN J. SAMUELS is Professor of Economics at Michigan State University, East Lansing, Michigan, USA.

YUICHI SHIONOYA is Professor emeritus of Economics at Hitotsubashi University at Tokyo, Tokyo, and President of the Social Development Research Institute, Tokyo, Japan.

NORBERT F. TOFALL, Forschungsinstitut für Philosophie Hannover - Hannover Institute of Philosophical Research, Germany.

DAVID WILLIAMS is Senior Research Fellow in Japanese Politics at the School of East Asian Studies, University of Sheffield, Sheffield, England.

KIICHIRO YAGI is Professor of Economics at the Kyoto University, Kyoto, Japan.

Index of Names

Page numbers in italics refer to quotations in footnotes or references

Peter Koslowski (Editor)

The Theory of Ethical Economy in the Historical School. Wilhelm Roscher, Lorenz von Stein, Gustav Schmoller, Wilhelm Dilthey and Contemporary Theory

Contributions from B. P. PRIDDAT, E. PANKOKE, Y. SHIONOYA, H. K. BETZ, H. J. HELLE, P. SCHIERA, N. YAMAWAKI, D. SCHNEIDER, H. J. L. VAN LUIJK, B. SCHEFOLD, I. G. KIM, H. JOAS, P. KOSLOWSKI, L. A. SCAFF, 1995, 343 pp. (Studies in Economic Ethics and Philosophy)

The Historical School of Economics develops a historical theory of the economy and of business ethics. It investigates the ethical and cultural determinants of economic behaviour and economic institutions and forms an ethical and cultural theory of economics and business ethics as well as the origin of what, in the present, is called "institutional economics". Being one of the first comprehensive studies of the German "Historical and Ethical School of Economics" in the English language, the book presents the theory of ethical economy from Wilhelm Roscher to Gustav Schmoller, the foundations of historism and the humanities in Wilhelm Dilthey and their present relevance. It also makes visible which impact the Historical School has for the foundations of contemporary business ethics and the cultural theory of the economy.

Peter Koslowski (Editor)

The Theory of Ethical Economy in the Historical School. Wilhelm Roscher, Lorenz von Stein, Gustav Schmoller, Wilhelm Dilthey and Contemporary Theory

Contributions from B. P. PRIDDAT, E. PANKOKE, Y. SHIONOYA, H. K. BETZ, H. J. HELLE, P. SCHIERA, N. YAMAWAKI, D. SCHNEIDER, H. J. L. VAN LUIJK, B. SCHEFOLD, I. G. KIM, H. JOAS, P. KOSLOWSKI, L. A. SCAFF, 1995, 343 pp. (Studies in Economic Ethics and Philosophy)

The Historical School of Economics develops a historical theory of the economy and of business ethics. It investigates the ethical and cultural determinants of economic behaviour and economic institutions and forms an ethical and cultural theory of economics and business ethics as well as the origin of what, in the present, is called "institutional economics". Being one of the first comprehensive studies of the German "Historical and Ethical School of Economics" in the English language, the book presents the theory of ethical economy from Wilhelm Roscher to Gustav Schmoller, the foundations of historism and the humanities in Wilhelm Dilthey and their present relevance. It also makes visible which impact the Historical School has for the foundations of contemporary business ethics and the cultural theory of the economy.

Druck: Strauss Offsetdruck, Mörlenbach
Verarbeitung: Schäffer, Grünstadt